Destinies

CANADIAN HISTORY SINCE CONFEDERATION

SIXTH EDITION

R. DOUGLAS FRANCIS
University of Calgary

RICHARD JONES

DONALD B. SMITH
University of Calgary

NELSON / EDUCATION

NELSON / EDUCATION

Destinies: Canadian History Since Confederation, Sixth Edition
by R. Douglas Francis, Richard Jones, and Donald B. Smith

Associate Vice President, Editorial Director:
Evelyn Veitch

Editor-in-Chief, Higher Education:
Anne Williams

Executive Editor:
Laura Macleod

Marketing Manager:
Heather Leach

Senior Developmental Editor:
Linda Sparks

Photo Researcher/Permissions Coordinator:
Cindy Howard

Content Production Manager:
Imoinda Romain

Production Service:
GEX Publishing Services

Copy Editor:
Rodney Rawlings

Proofreader:
GEX Publishing Services

Indexer:
GEX Publishing Services

Production Coordinator:
Ferial Suleman

Design Director:
Ken Phipps

Managing Designer:
Katherine Strain

Interior Design:
Dianna Little

Cover Design:
Rocket Design

Cover Image:
Hulton Archive/Getty Images

Compositor:
GEX Publishing Services

Printer:
Courier

Library and Archives Canada Cataloguing in Publication

Francis, R. D. (R. Douglas), 1944–

Destinies : Canadian history since Confederation / R. Douglas Francis, Richard Jones, Donald B. Smith. — 6th ed.

Includes bibliographical references and index.
ISBN 978-0-17-644242-2

1. Canada—History—1867–. I. Jones, Richard, 1943– II. Smith, Donald B., 1946– III. Title.

FC164.F73 2007   971.05
C2007-904061-6

ISBN-13: 978-0-17-644242-2
ISBN-10: 0-17-644242-1

Brief Contents

PART ONE: Building the New Dominion, 1867–1914

PART TWO: Urban and Industrial Canada, 1867–1914

PART THREE: The Impact of Two World Wars and the Great Depression, 1914–45

PART FOUR: Modern Canada, 1945 to the Present

Contents

PART THREE: The Impact of Two World Wars and the Great Depression, 1914–45

List of Maps

The Nature of History

The word "history" refers to both the events of the past and the historian's study of them. While many naturally assume that what the historian tells us about past events is definitive, students of history realize that no conclusive or final study of any event in the past is possible. Historians constantly search for a deeper and richer understanding of, and new perspectives on, past events. As a result, our understanding of history is always being revised and history is always being rewritten.

The rewriting of history occurs for many reasons. New evidence, for example, constantly emerges through the discovery of new sources or documents. The work of scholars in other humanities and social science disciplines — such as archaeology and anthropology for Aboriginal history, or demography, sociology, and geography for social history — leads to new insights. As well, new perspectives result from historians asking new questions. When, for example, historians were preoccupied with the study of political figures and events, this perspective dictated the sources they consulted and the questions they asked of those sources. When a new generation of historians desired to learn more about the lives of "ordinary people" or of social events, they located different sources, and asked new questions of traditional ones. Today, the study of history has expanded significantly to include a host of sub-disciplines, such as women's, ethnic, Aboriginal, working-class, intellectual, military, and cultural history. Such a multiplicity of approaches enriches our understanding of the past.

Besides the unearthing of new sources and the emergence of varied types of history, new theoretical approaches add complexity to the study of history today. Theories of relativism, Marxism, feminism, and, more recently, postmodernism, force historians to question the nature of history, the role of the historian, and, in some cases, even the ability to write history if it is seen as some kind of objective study of the past. Still, historians continue to study the past in the belief that it provides knowledge essential for understanding the present, and for providing a perspective on the future. The current debates over the nature of history have influenced the writing of history within Canada and elsewhere.

The Nature of This Text

Origins and *Destinies*, our companion volumes of Canadian history, cover the study of Canada's past from the beginnings to the present. The texts reflect and incorporate the new trends in historical writing. First, we include the most recent and up-to-date research by Canadian historians. In a format and style that is clear and engaging for students interested in studying Canada's history, we present as comprehensive and rich a study of Canada's past as possible in a two-volume text. Second, we introduce students to the types of history broadly defined as the "new social history" and the "new cultural history," while also providing them with the more traditional political and economic accounts. Third, we include the historical development and contribution of the Aboriginal people, French-speaking and English-speaking Canadians, recent immigrants, women, and minority groups, realizing that together they make up Canada's rich past. As well, we include the history of each of the country's regions, while keeping Canada as the focal point. Fourth and finally, up-to-date annotated bibliographies appear at the end of each chapter to identify the major historical writings on the events covered in the chapter.

To review Canadian historians' lively debate on important events, issues, or trends in historical writing, *Origins* and *Destinies* provide a series of boxed inserts entitled "Where Historians Disagree" and "Where Social Scientists Disagree," highlighting differing views. These debate boxes remind students that the writing of Canadian history is an ongoing process. To show that history is the action of individuals, we include "Historical Portraits" that highlight the life of well-known, and not-so-well-known, persons who have made their mark. Individuals seldom act alone, however; they are part of a community. To demonstrate the contribution of selected communities to Canada's history, "Community Portraits" appear in *Origins* and *Destinies*.

In terms of format, *Origins* and *Destinies* are divided into thematic sections, each introduced by a brief overview of themes highlighted in the chapters within the section. Each chapter treats a major topic or period, and begins with a "Time Line" listing the key events discussed. *Origins* and *Destinies* follow a chronological approach to help students understand how events developed through time. As well, headings and subheadings throughout the chapters assist in organizing the material. At the end of each chapter is a section entitled "Beyond the Book," which directs students to additional information for selected topics on the World Wide Web and in films and novels. As well, a section entitled "Related Readings" identifies useful articles in the 7th edition of R. Douglas Francis and Donald B. Smith, eds., *Readings in Canadian History*, volume 1, *Pre-Confederation*, and volume 2, *Post-Confederation*.

In terms of content, *Origins*, the first volume, tells the story of pre-Confederation Canada — of the Indigenous peoples and of the coming of the Norse, the Portuguese, the Spanish, the Basques, and particularly the French and the British who eventually established permanent European settlements. Anyone seeking to understand our diversity must first examine the era when our present regional personalities first formed in Atlantic Canada, the St. Lawrence River valley, the Great Lakes region, the Red River area, and the Pacific coast.

Destinies, the second volume, takes Canada's story from 1867 to the present day. Unlike the United States, Canada did not experience a uniform wave of expansion westward from the Atlantic seaboard. In many cases, the European communities in Canada began as pockets of settlement, independent of one another, founded at different times, and with people of various European backgrounds. In *Destinies*, we show how Canada came to take the transcontinental form it did, and how the various groups within its boundaries came together. We focus on various regional, ethnic, and social tensions as well as including references to more harmonious events.

We hope that *Origins* and *Destinies* will provide students of Canadian history with a knowledge of Canada's past, a desire to explore that past in greater depth in more specialized courses in Canadian history, and an appreciation of the multilayered, vibrant, and exciting nature of the writing of Canadian history in keeping with the discipline of history as a whole.

Students seeking more extensive bibliographical information are directed to the following works. Important annotated bibliographical guides to the study of Canadian history include M. Brook Taylor, ed., *Canadian History: A Reader's Guide*, vol. 1, *Beginnings to Confederation* (Toronto: University of Toronto Press, 1994); Doug Owram, ed., *Canadian History: A Reader's Guide*, vol. 2, *Confederation to the Present* (Toronto: University of Toronto Press, 1994); Carl Berger, ed., *Contemporary Approaches to Canadian History* (Toronto: Copp Clark Pitman, 1987); and John Schultz, ed., *Writing about Canada: A Handbook for Modern Canadian History* (Scarborough, ON: Prentice-Hall, 1990). An invaluable bibliography (without annotation) is Paul Aubin and Louis-Marie Côté's *Bibliographie de l'histoire du Québec et du Canada/Bibliography of the History of Quebec and Canada*, published (in several volumes) by the Institut québécois de recherche sur la culture in Quebec City. Easy to use, it contains more than 100 000 titles, all published between 1946 and 1985. Current bibliographies of the most recent publications appear in every issue of the *Canadian Historical Review* and the *Revue d'histoire de l'Amérique française*.

Acknowledgments

In preparing six editions of *Origins* and *Destinies*, we have benefited enormously from the advice and suggestions of a large number of Canadian historians. They have read chapters and often the entire manuscript, providing us with useful criticism within their respective research areas. In particular, we wish to thank the following teachers and researchers: William Acheson; Gratien Allaire; Douglas Baldwin; Jean Barman; John Belshaw; Phillip Buckner; Anne Buffam; Robert Burkinshaw; Robert A. Campbell; Sarah Carter; Joseph Cherwinski; Gail Cuthbert-Brandt; Jean Daigle; George A. Davison; A.A. den Otter; Olive Dickason; Mark Dickerson; John English; A. Ernest Epp; Robin Fisher; Rae Fleming; Gerald Friesen; Donald Fyson; Michael Granger; Roger Hall; John David Hamilton; James Helmer; James Hiller; Raymond Huel; Bonnie Huskins; Helen Towser Jones; Jeffrey Keshen; Douglas Leighton; Ernest LeVos; Ingeborg Marshall; Marcel Martel; Bea Medicine; James Miller; Dale Miquelon; William Morrison; Suzanne Morton; Ken Munro; the late Howard Palmer; Martin Pâquet; Margaret Prang; Colin Read; Keith Regular; Daniel Richter; Patricia Roome; R.H. Roy; Eric Sager; Phyllis Senese; Thomas Socknat; Donald Swainson; M. Brook Taylor; John Herd Thompson; Jill Wade; Keith Walden; and William Westfall.

At Nelson, we benefited enormously from a dedicated and enthusiastic editorial team. In particular, we wish to thank Laura Macleod, Executive Editor; Linda Sparks, Senior Developmental Editor; Imoinda Romain, Content Production Manager; and Rodney Rawlings, Copy Editor. It was our pleasure to work with each of them. We also wish to thank our wives Barbara Grant, Lilianne Plamondon, and Nancy Townshend for their constant support throughout this project, begun nearly a quarter-of-a-century ago.

We wish to dedicate this 6th edition to our students over the years who have taught us so much.

Destinies

CANADIAN HISTORY SINCE CONFEDERATION

SIXTH EDITION

Chapter One

CONFEDERATION

TIME LINE	
1841	Union of the Canadas
1846	Britain adopts free trade and ends colonial timber and wheat preferences
1848	Winning of responsible government
1854	British North America enters into reciprocity agreement with the United States
1857	Queen Victoria chooses Ottawa as the future capital of Canada Economic recession
1861	Outbreak of the American Civil War
1864	Confederate raid on St. Alban's, Vermont from British North American territory Formation of the "Great Coalition" to work toward British North American federation Canadian and Maritime delegates discuss union at the Charlottetown and Quebec Conferences
1865	Canadian legislature approves the Quebec Resolutions, but only a narrow majority of French-Canadian members endorse them
1866	The United States government terminates the Reciprocity Treaty of 1854 Leonard Tilley's pro-Confederation party wins the election in New Brunswick Westminster Conference in London, England, prepares the passage of the British North America Act through the British Parliament
1867	The British North America Act is passed, creating the Dominion of Canada; it consisted of the colonies of Nova Scotia, New Brunswick, Canada East (Quebec), and Canada West (Ontario) John A. Macdonald becomes Canada's first prime minister

Proposals for the union of the British North American colonies had been considered well before the 1860s, but they never became reality. By the 1860s, however, threats of an American takeover as a result of the Civil War, pressure from Britain for unification of the British North American colonies, internal problems in the colonies, such as heavy public debt from extensive railway building and, in the case of the Canadas, political deadlock (and the desire to acquire the North West), led politicians from both the Canadas and the Maritime colonies to consider union. These immediate circumstances, more than a spirit of nationalism, prepared the way for Confederation. There was no assurance in 1867 that this new experiment in nation building would succeed. In this respect, Confederation can be seen as but the first step in an ongoing process of nation building that would continue well into the twentieth century. As well, Confederation set in place a new state with a bureaucratic structure that would grow over time to provide support and guidance for, but also regulate and control, the population under its jurisdiction. Meanwhile, the new nation had a number of immediate issues to work out: Dominion–provincial relations, English–French relations, association with Britain and the United States, and how to keep the new nation united.

The Impact of the American Civil War

The Alabama and the Trent Affairs

Fear of an American takeover during the Civil War contributed to British North American unification. Although Britain was officially neutral during the American Civil War, many Britons backed the Confederacy because of their dependence on Southern cotton for the textile industry. The international rules of neutrality prevented the legal construction of Confederate warships in British shipyards, but the South secretly had the C.S.S. *Alabama*, a swift and powerful cruiser, built in a shipyard near Liverpool. During its 22-month rampage on three oceans, the *Alabama* burned or captured 64 Northern merchant vessels and a Union warship before it was sunk in June 1864. The North held Britain responsible for the destruction by the *Alabama* and other British-built Confederate vessels, since, Northern leaders argued, Britain knew the uses to which the South put these ships. As compensation, one Northern proposal included the takeover of all of British North America.

Adding to Anglo–American antagonism was the *Trent* affair. In November 1861, an American warship stopped the British steamer *Trent* and forcibly removed two Confederate envoys on their way to England to secure assistance for the Southern cause. Tempers flared on both sides, with Britain threatening retaliation if the North did not free these Confederate agents, seized in neutral waters, and the North denouncing Britain for aiding the Southern cause. In the end, President Abraham Lincoln released the prisoners on Christmas Day, 1861, to avoid war with Britain.

The St. Alban's Raids

Meanwhile, by 1864, the Southern Confederacy planned attacks on the North via Canada. The largest of these attacks occurred at St. Alban's, Vermont, on October 19, 1864, during which 26 Confederate sympathizers terrorized the town, robbed three banks of $200 000, set several fires, wounded two men and killed another, and then fled to Canada. The government of the Canadas arrested them, but a Montreal magistrate released them on a legal technicality. This act of leniency infuriated Northerners. The Canadian government condemned the judge's decision. As well, the Canadian Assembly passed legislation to deport aliens involved in acts against a friendly foreign state. Nevertheless, Canada still remained suspect in American eyes.

The ensuing tension led Britain to send 14 000 soldiers to British North America to protect her colonies. Many of the troops had to reach their destination by sled since no rail link existed into the interior of British North America. Britain therefore saw a union of the British North American colonies as a means both to get the colonies to assume responsibility for their own defence, and to achieve a railway link to the Atlantic, by providing a larger financial base for railway construction.

Negotiating Confederation

The Great Coalition

In this tense atmosphere, the politicians in the United Canadas, formed in 1841, addressed the problem of political deadlock in their Assembly. Neither the Conservatives nor the Reformers could form a stable government. Between 1861 and 1864, for example, the Canadas experienced two elections and three changes of administration. On June 14, 1864, the most recent administration, the Macdonald–Taché coalition, went down to defeat. Governor General Monck urged John A. Macdonald, leader of the coalition, to negotiate with George Brown, leader of the Reform party, with the possibility of forming a larger coalition. Despite Brown and Macdonald's hostilities toward each other, the two men agreed to work together to resolve the deadlock. On June 30, a jubilant Assembly heard Brown announce that he and two other Reformers would enter a coalition cabinet to work for federation. Thus was born the "Great Coalition of 1864."

Brown made three demands in return for his support: a federation of all the British North American colonies; representation by population, or "rep by pop," as it became popularly known; and the incorporation of Rupert's Land, the vast territory to the west of the Canadas owned by the Hudson's Bay Company, into Confederation. Brown's interest in the North West lay in its benefits for the development of Canada West. On January 22, 1863, for example, the Toronto newspaper editor outlined his imperial vision:

> If Canada acquires this territory it will rise in a few years from a position of a small and weak province to be the greatest colony any country has ever possessed, able to take its place among the empires of the earth. The wealth of 400,000 square miles of territory will flow through our waters and be gathered by our merchants, manufacturers and agriculturists. Our sons will occupy the chief places of this vast territory, we will form its institutions, supply its rulers, teach its schools, fill its stores, run its mills, navigate its streams.

The Charlottetown Conference

In the early 1860s, the Maritime colonies of Nova Scotia, New Brunswick, and Prince Edward Island considered union among themselves. Despite reservations, the premiers of the three colonies agreed to meet. But before a date or place had been decided, the government of the Canadas asked permission to attend such a meeting so as to present a proposal for a wider British North American federal union. The Maritimers agreed. The meeting was set for September 1, 1864, in Charlottetown.

At the Charlottetown conference, the Canadian delegation presented an impressive *tour de force*. John A. Macdonald, along with George-Étienne Cartier, the main leader from Canada East (Quebec), set out the general terms of the Canadian proposal, particularly those aspects dealing with the division of powers between the central and provincial governments. Alexander Tilloch Galt, the minister of finance in the Canadas, dealt with economic issues, while George Brown handled constitutional concerns. The main features of their proposal included: continued loyalty to the British Crown through membership in the British empire; a strong central government within a federal union in which the provinces retained control over their own local affairs; and

John A. Macdonald appears seated in the centre of this photo, taken on the first day of the Charlottetown Conference, September 1, 1864. Immediately to the left of Macdonald stands his old political enemy George Brown, with D'Arcy McGee, the great orator in favour of British North American federation, standing directly behind Brown. A national tragedy was McGee's assassination on April 7, 1868, before the Dominion was but one year old.

Source: Library and Archives Canada/C-733.

representation in a lower house based on population and an upper house based on regional representation. Thomas D'Arcy McGee, the gifted poet-politician who had cultivated his oratorical skills as a young Ireland activist, spoke eloquently in terms of the need for a common British North American vision. Within seven days, the delegates agreed to meet again on October 10 at Quebec City to explore in greater detail the nature of a British North American federation.

The Quebec Conference

At Quebec, the Canadian delegates presented the broad general principles set out at Charlottetown in the form of Seventy-Two Resolutions. Within a two-week period, these Resolutions were debated and slightly altered to become the British North America (BNA) Act, the political framework for a union of the British North American colonies.

At the conference Macdonald clearly favoured a legislative union, or a strong central government, believing that the Civil War in the United States was the result of overly powerful state governments. The Maritime delegates feared a loss of their identity in a legislative union and favoured instead a federal union with powerful local governments. George-Étienne Cartier also favoured a federal union, with a local government in Quebec strong enough to protect French Canadians' language, civil law, and customs. As one Colonial Office official astutely noted of the challenge facing the Fathers of Confederation: "The great difficulty is to arrange for a real union of the five provinces … on terms which shall make the central or federal legislation really dominant, so as to make one body politic of the whole, and yet to provide security to French Canadians that this dominancy would not be used to swamp their religion and habits."

The delegates reached a compromise. They granted powers to the provincial governments, but gave the central government residual powers (powers not specifically assigned to the provinces). As well, they gave the central government the power "to make laws for the peace, order and good government of Canada." The federal government also gained the right to disallow provincial laws if they went against the national interest.

The delegates agreed on a federal lower house based on representation by population and an upper house based on regional representation, but disagreed on the number of representatives from each region in the upper house—the Senate. The smaller Maritime Provinces saw the Senate as a means of strengthening their regional representation to offset their numerical weakness in the lower house. In the end, the delegates agreed that the Maritimes would have 24 seats, the same number given to each of Ontario and Quebec.

The delegates also agreed, after much debate, that the new federal government would assume the public debts—up to a specified maximum amount—of each of the four provinces that joined. In addition, the federal government would finance the Intercolonial Railway, linking the Maritimes to the Canadas.

To cover these costs, the federal government was given unlimited taxing powers, including the collection of both direct taxes and indirect taxes, such as customs and excise duties, one of the main sources of revenue at the time. In contrast, the provinces could levy only direct taxes. To compensate the provinces for the cost of education, roads, and other local obligations, it was agreed that the federal government pay annual subsidies to the provinces based on 80 cents per head of their population.

The Debate on the Confederation Proposals in the Canadas

After the Quebec Conference, the delegates returned to their respective provinces to secure approval for the resolutions. The Fathers of Confederation had considered submitting the draft constitution for popular approval but later decided to follow the British procedure of ratification by the politicians only. As a result, the Confederation agreement did not at the time (or since) form the basis of a political community with a clear sense of itself and its political rights and constitutional freedoms.

In the Legislature of the United Canadas, considerable debate ensued. George Brown and his Reformers had some concerns about specific proposals but accepted the agreement reached at Quebec since it was based on "rep by pop." In general, Upper Canadian politicians favoured Confederation, realizing that they had the most to gain from the union.

In Canada East (Quebec), members of the radical Parti rouge, under the leadership of Antoine-Aimé Dorion, had serious reservations. Dorion argued: "It is not at all a confederation that is proposed to us, but quite simply a Legislative Union disguised under the name of a confederation. How could one accept as a federation a scheme … that provided for disallowance of local legislation?" Furthermore, he pointed out that in the new House of Commons the English-Canadian representation from Canada West and the Maritimes would greatly outnumber the French-Canadian representation. As well, he denounced the Fathers of Confederation for refusing to put the issue to the people.

George-Étienne Cartier countered Dorion's criticisms. He emphasized that in the new federal union, French Canadians would control their own provincial government and legislature, have their own local administration, and retain the Civil Code. Furthermore, the French language would be official in the province of Quebec as well as in the federal administration, and the rights of religious minorities for separate schools would be recognized in all the provinces. On the question of English-Canadian dominance, Cartier pointed out that the "new nationality" would be a "political nationality" only, not a "cultural nationality," and therefore did not require French Canadians to suppress their cultural differences for the sake of some common pan-Canadian nationalism. He also reminded his French-Canadian compatriots of the importance of the British connection to offset the threat of American annexation and the loss of identity that would ensue.

Cartier also presented Confederation to French Canadians as their best hope for cultural survival in a world of limited possibilities. The existing union, crippled by deadlock, could not go on; for French Canadians, union with the United States would be the worst possible fate. The independence of Lower Canada was not feasible. Only a larger federation of British North American colonies offered French Canadians possibilities beyond their own provincial boundaries at the same time as it protected their affairs within their own province.

Cartier turned to the clergy for support for Confederation, despite his personal concerns about mixing politics and religion. Bishop Ignace Bourget of Montreal, the most powerful French-Canadian bishop, feared for the future of the church in the new political union with other English-speaking colonies with large Protestant populations. He kept silent about his misgivings, however, since the other Quebec bishops were more favourably disposed, at least in principle. They realized that the alternative to Confederation was support of their arch-enemies, the *rouges*, who were strongly anticlerical.

In the final vote on Confederation in the Legislature of the United Canadas, 91 were in favour and 33 opposed. In the breakdown of votes in the two sections, 54 of the 62 members from Canada West favoured the proposal, as did 37 of the 62 members from Canada East. Of the 48 French-Canadian members present, 27 voted for and 21 against. Overall, Confederation won overwhelmingly, but among French Canadians the victory was narrow, indicating serious reservations on their part.

Opposition to Confederation in Atlantic Canada

In New Brunswick, Samuel Leonard Tilley, who had been premier since 1857 and who had represented the province at both the Charlottetown and the Quebec conference, argued the advantages of Confederation for New Brunswickers: Saint John would be a year-round, ice-free port for the export of Canadian goods, and a lucrative market would exist in central Canada for Maritime coal and manufactured goods. The promised Intercolonial Railway would make such trade possible.

But strong opposition to Confederation continued in New Brunswick. A.J. Smith, the opposition leader, headed the anti-Confederate forces. He argued that no guarantee existed that the Intercolonial Railway would be constructed and, if it were built, where it would run and thus which area of the province, the north shore or the southern Saint John River valley, would benefit from it. He also pointed out that New Brunswick's economic trade pattern, especially since the Reciprocity Treaty of 1854, had been north–south rather than east–west. Commercial interests in the province had no economic ties with the Canadas. Furthermore, union with Canada could lead to a flooding of the New Brunswick market by Canadian imports, and a high tariff structure. In addition, New Brunswickers would be forced to assume a portion of the heavy Canadian debt from canal and railway building. Finally, Smith argued that Confederation would diminish New Brunswick's political power by giving the province representation of only 15 members of Parliament in a House of Commons with 194 members. The Roman Catholic clergy also opposed Confederation, believing that a Canada dominated by Protestant "extremists" in Upper Canada could threaten Roman Catholic schools and the church itself throughout the proposed union.

These arguments were debated in the election campaign of early 1865, an election fought chiefly on the issue of Confederation. New Brunswickers responded clearly and decisively—the Tilley pro-Confederation government lost heavily.

In Nova Scotia, Charles Tupper, the pro-Confederation premier, faced a serious challenge from Joseph Howe, "Father of Responsible Government." Although he was no longer a member of the Assembly, Howe was still the most powerful political figure in Nova Scotia. He argued that in Confederation Nova Scotia would lose its identity and cease to be an important colony in the great British Empire. Furthermore, Howe pointed out that Nova Scotia looked eastward to the Atlantic Ocean and Britain, rather than westward to the continent and the Canadas. As he vividly expressed it: "Take a Nova Scotian to Ottawa, away above tide-water, freeze him up for five months, where he cannot view the Atlantic, smell salt water, or see the sail of a ship, and the man will pine and die." He favoured continuing colonial ties to Britain. In the winter of 1866–67, Howe went to England to present his case for Nova Scotia staying out of Confederation.

In Prince Edward Island, support for Confederation went from modest to none. At the Charlottetown and the Quebec conference, the island's representatives had driven a hard bargain, pressing for better terms on representation in the Senate and in the House of Commons, and for better economic terms. But when they returned home, their enthusiasm and interest waned when they realized that the islanders themselves opposed Confederation for a number of reasons. One was the problem of absentee landlordism. For over a century, absentee British landlords had controlled the island, much to the resentment of the local population. In 1860, a British commission appointed to investigate the question issued a report favourable to the islanders, only to have it rejected by the proprietors and the Colonial Office. Thus, when the Colonial Office pressured Prince Edward Islanders to adopt Confederation, they resisted. Also, many islanders saw Confederation as simply replacing one set of distant landlords in Britain with another in Ottawa. In addition, islanders believed that Confederation would give them very little. Union would mean higher taxes to support the enormous costs of the Intercolonial Railway, and higher tariffs to create interprovincial trade—neither of which would greatly benefit Prince Edward Island. They also disliked the proposed form of representation in the Senate and House of Commons, which would deny them a major voice in distant Ottawa.

Newfoundland failed to support Confederation out of apathy, not opposition. The island had not participated in the Charlottetown Conference, although it did send two representatives to the Quebec Conference, both of whom endorsed Confederation. They returned to a colony that was initially mildly interested as a result of Newfoundland's declining fishing industry, agriculture, and the timber trade. But if Newfoundlanders initially hoped that joining Confederation might solve their economic ills, they soon believed that Canada was simply too far away to be of benefit to them. R.J. Pinsent, a member of the Legislative Council, summed up the prevailing opinion as follows: "There is little community of interest between Newfoundland and the Canadas. This is not a Continental Colony." Essentially, the island continued to look eastward to Britain rather than westward to Canada.

External Pressures

By the end of 1865, public support for British North American Confederation had waned, except in Canada West. All four of the Atlantic colonies opposed it, while Canada East had serious reservations. Two external developments, however, altered the situation: British intervention and the American threat.

British Support for Confederation

By the mid-1860s Britain wanted to rid itself of the expense of defending British North America, and to ease tension in its relations with the United States. Thus, when in the autumn of 1865 a pro-Confederation delegation from the Canadas arrived in London, it was warmly welcomed; a counter-delegation from Nova Scotia under Joseph Howe was not. Instead, the British government replaced the anti-Confederation governor of Nova Scotia with one more supportive. The Colonial Office also ordered New Brunswick Governor Arthur Gordon to intervene in his province's politics to ensure the success of Confederation. Finally, Britain guaranteed the loan interest for the proposed Intercolonial Railway on the assumption that the Maritimes would join Confederation.

The American Contribution to Confederation

While Britain applied direct pressure, the United States did so indirectly. When the Civil War ended in 1865, Northern extremists advocated using the Northern army to annex the British North American colonies. Also, influential politicians in the American Midwest advocated taking possession of the British North West, as part of the United States' manifest destiny. Other American politicians, including Hamilton Fish, the secretary of state in Ulysses S. Grant's administration, urged possession of all the British territory in North America.

Amid such annexationist appeals, the American government announced that the Reciprocity Treaty of 1854 would terminate in 1866. American annexationists reasoned that the treaty's abrogation would cause such economic hardships for the British North American colonies as to force them to join the United States. Instead, the announced abrogation of reciprocity encouraged the colonies to consider an alternative commercial union among themselves.

Fenian raids also furthered the cause of Confederation. Fenians were fanatical republican Irishmen in the United States committed to fighting for the independence of Ireland. One scheme they devised was to capture the British North American colonies and use them as ransom to liberate Ireland from British rule. Their marching song explicitly set out their goals:

> We are the Fenian Brotherhood, skilled in the art of war,
> And we're going to fight for Ireland, the land that we adore.
> Many battles we have won, along with the boys in blue,
> And we'll go and capture Canada for we've nothing else to do

The Fenians expected the support of Irish Catholics in the British colonies, but few supported them. Some prominent Irish individuals, such as Thomas D'Arcy McGee, spoke out strongly against the Fenians.

The Fenians posed little threat until the end of the American Civil War when thousands of Irish-American soldiers, trained, receptive to mobilizing in defence of their native country, and now idle, became available. Furthermore, the Fenians had the support of the American government that sympathized with their anti-British sentiments. Many American politicians also feared that if they failed to support the Fenians, they then would alienate the large number of American Irish Catholic voters.

The Fenian threat tended to be more psychological than physical. The actual military skirmishes were few and restricted to border areas. The two most important took place in New Brunswick and in the Niagara Peninsula. In New Brunswick in April 1866, a small band of

Fenians crossed into New Brunswick, where they stole the flag from a customs house before the local militia and British regulars forced them back across the border. Although the raid was insignificant in military terms, it helped to turn the tide in favour of Confederation in the New Brunswick election that was taking place at the time. Then in May, 1500 Fenians crossed the Niagara River into Canada West. At Ridgeway on June 2, the Fenians defeated the Canadian militia, but then withdrew, never to return, although they continued to pose a threat to Canada until 1870.

Turning the Tide in New Brunswick

Finding it difficult to rule with a minority government, the Smith government resigned in April 1866. In the ensuing election campaign, Samuel Leonard Tilley resurrected his earlier arguments for Confederation and added new ones. He pointed out to the people of New Brunswick that in Confederation they could expect lower taxes, the Intercolonial Railway, a fair share in the running of the nation, and a market for their raw materials and manufactured goods—in other words, material progress and modernization.

During the campaign, both parties benefited from external funds. The anti-Confederates received money from Nova Scotia and possibly, it has been asserted, the United States, while the pro-Confederates obtained financial support from the government of the Canadas. "Give us funds," a desperate Tilley cabled John A. Macdonald. "It will require some $40,000 or $50,000 to do the work in all our counties." Macdonald agreed. He did not want Confederation to go down to defeat in New Brunswick simply for lack of money. Direct British intervention and threatened Fenian raids also assisted Tilley's cause. After his resounding electoral victory, Tilley had the New Brunswick legislature quickly endorse Confederation.

Final Negotiations

In the autumn and winter of 1866, delegates from Nova Scotia, New Brunswick, and the United Canadas met in London to prepare the passage of the British North America Act through the British Parliament. Although the Maritime delegates pressed for modifications of those aspects of the Seventy-Two Resolutions that provided for a strong central government, in the end the Resolutions were accepted with only a few minor, but significant, changes. Subsidies to the provinces would be increased beyond the agreed 80 cents a head by a fixed grant from the federal government. The contentious issue of separate schools was settled by applying the Quebec clause on education, which safeguarded the Protestant separate schools in Quebec, to all other provinces in the union, or to new provinces that had separate schools "by law" at the time they joined Confederation. Furthermore, provisions were included for religious minorities to appeal to the federal government if a provincial government threatened their school systems, as they existed before Confederation.

While the delegates were meeting in London to finalize the terms of Confederation, Joseph Howe continued his opposition to Nova Scotia joining Confederation. He urged British officials to reject union. But the British government refused to retract its support. When the British North America Act was signed on March 29, 1867, Howe returned to Nova Scotia cured "of a good deal of loyal enthusiasm" and embittered against the Canadians. He was not alone. Many Nova Scotians saw Confederation as the end not the beginning of a vibrant Nova Scotia. Elsewhere, Confederation was accepted, although not with enthusiasm, except in Ontario.

Naming the New Nation

John A. Macdonald wanted to call "the new nation" the "Kingdom of Canada," but the British government objected because it feared that the term would further offend the Americans, implying as it did a more autonomous country. Leonard Tilley had chanced upon an alternative title, as well as an appropriate motto, for the new country—*A Mari Usque Ad Mare* (From Sea Even Unto Sea)—while reading Psalm 72:

> *He shall have dominion also from sea to sea, and from the river unto the ends of the earth.*

On July 1, 1867, the Dominion of Canada was born. It consisted of the four provinces of Nova Scotia, New Brunswick, Quebec, and Ontario.

Politics

Confederation meant a new beginning in politics. The various political factions and parties that existed before Confederation—the Tories and the Clear Grits (or Reformers) in Canada West, the *parti bleu* and the *parti rouge* in Canada East, the conservative and reform factions in New Brunswick and Nova Scotia—coalesced into two major parties: the Conservatives and the Liberals (Reformers) with representation, and eventually a federal party machinery throughout the Dominion. Initially, these two national parties had genuine ideological differences. For the first thirty years after Confederation, the Conservatives generally favoured the establishment of a strong central government, a policy of tariff protection, and close association with Britain. In contrast, the Liberals championed provincial autonomy, free trade, and closer association with the United States.

The Conservative party won the first federal election in November, 1867. John A. Macdonald became Canada's first prime minister. A man with warm personal charm and a sense of humour, he preferred practical politics to philosophical debate. A masterful politician, he remained in the prime minister's office, with the exception of a five-year Liberal interlude in the mid-1870s, from 1867 until his death in 1891. Thus the late nineteenth century is often referred to politically as the Macdonald era.

To win support in Quebec, Macdonald relied on George-Étienne Cartier, particularly as he himself did not speak French. Macdonald once referred to Cartier as "my second self," and indeed he was. From 1867 until his death in 1873, Cartier came second only to Macdonald in the Conservative party.

Up until 1874, voting in federal elections was restricted to males who owned property, approximately only 20 percent of the Canadian population. As well, there was no secret ballot; voters had to declare their party preference openly. This system of open voting led to abuse. Street brawls often occurred at election time. Candidates openly bribed voters. Employers sometimes coerced their employees to vote "the right way." Elections were also held at different times in different areas of the country, greatly influencing electoral results. It would be the Liberal party under Alexander Mackenzie who would reform the electoral system.

Establishing Political Conventions

Macdonald and Cartier began a political convention that has often been effectively used in Canadian politics: the cooperation within the governing party of an English-speaking prime minister and a politically powerful French-speaking lieutenant, or vice versa. Such an alliance has ensured the French-Canadian minority an influential voice in federal politics.

Macdonald also established a second political convention. For his first cabinet, he chose individuals from various regions and interest groups—Maritimers, Quebeckers, and Ontarians; Protestants and Roman Catholics; Irish, Scottish, English, and French Canadians; business-people, farmers, fishers, and, occasionally, even working people. The Conservatives also created the first federal bureaucracy. This meant jobs, or rather rewards, for the party faithful. Most of the approximately 500 civil-service positions went to former bureaucrats from the United Canadas, with only a few token positions going to Maritimers.

The Nature of Confederation

Unity in diversity became the goal of the Fathers of Confederation. They sought to establish domestic peace between English- and French-speaking Canadians, and between Protestants and Roman Catholics, through the creation of a political rather than a cultural nationality. As Cartier noted during the Confederation debates in the United Canadas in 1865: "Now, when we were united together, if union were attained, we would form a political nationality with which neither the national origin, nor the religion of any individual, would interfere."

Despite their laudable intentions, Canada's founders built disunity into the political structure. The new Canadian system, by combining aspects of the American federal and the British parliamentary forms of government, resembled a carriage pulled by two horses moving in different directions.

Sir John A. Macdonald addressing a meeting in Toronto. From the Canadian Illustrated News, *April 31, 1878. "One thinks of those audiences, dead and gone now, the noise, the whisky, the laughter, the tobacco, the smell of unwashed humanity: political meetings were entertainment, the translation of newspapers into life" (P.B. Waite, "Reflections on an Un-Victorian Society," in D. Swainson, ed.,* Oliver Mowat's Ontario *[Toronto: Macmillan, 1972], p. 26). Note all those in attendance are male; women would have to wait over a third of a century until they gained the federal franchise.*

Source: Library and Archives Canada/C-68193.

The Meaning of the BNA Act

Since the passage of the British North America Act in 1867, historians have disagreed as to its meaning. Some commentators view it as an act of the British Parliament; others, as a political contract among four British North American colonies to establish a new country. Still other observers see Confederation as a cultural compact between English- and French-speaking Canadians.

A.R.M. Lower, writing in the nation-building tradition of the 1940s, saw the BNA Act as an act of the British Parliament, imposed from above and with authority emanating from the Crown. "What happened in 1867," he writes, "was that the Crown, in the fullness of its wisdom, decided to rearrange its administrative areas in British North America.... All were cast into the crucible of Imperial omnicompetence and came out remelted, shining, new, and fused."[1] This interpretation implies that the central government—the new Canadian equivalent of the old imperial authority—alone inherited the wide-sweeping powers of the central authority, including the sole right to change the Constitution. Historian Donald Creighton supported this view.[2]

Those who oppose this interpretation question the centralizing nature of the BNA Act. They claim that the Constitution was the end result of a pact. But these historians disagree among themselves as to the nature of that pact. Some claim it was an agreement among the provinces; others, a compact between the two founding cultural groups—English-speaking and French-speaking Canadians.

Historians who support the idea of a pact of the provinces point out that the colonies (provinces after 1867) had decided on the nature of the new nation and on the powers that they would relinquish to the central government. They also argue that in all four colonies that made up Confederation in 1867, strong support for local control existed. Historical perspective is presented in the Tremblay Report of 1956.[3] The Report states that "the Union of 1867 met the common needs of the provinces," implying that what powers the provinces had given away could be taken back if they felt the federal government was using its delegated powers unwisely or unconstitutionally. More recently, historian Paul Romney reinforces this perspective.[4] He argues that Upper Canadians (Ontarians) fought for strong local control at the time of Confederation and provincial rights after Confederation as much as Quebeckers and Maritimers even though Ontario had the most to gain from a strong central government in Ottawa, since it had the largest representation.

A few historians argue that the BNA Act constituted a compact between the two founding linguistic groups—English- and French-speaking Canadians. This compact was not a legal or even a political commitment so much as it was a moral one, an unwritten understanding that underlay the negotiations of the BNA Act and indeed grew out of the historical circumstances of the time. Historian George F.G. Stanley claims that "the idea of a compact between races was not a new one in 1865; it had already become a vital thing in our history. It influenced both the political thinking and the political vocabulary of the day; and it was already on the way to becoming a tradition and a convention of our constitution."[5] The implication was that the compact remained only so long as it served the needs of both linguistic groups involved.

Since our current understanding of the nature of Canada rests to such a great extent on our view of the BNA Act, the debate over the nature of the BNA, now the Canada, Act remains central to our understanding of the nature of modern Canada.

1 A.R.M. Lower, *Colony to Nation* (Toronto: Longmans, Green, 1946), p. 328.

2 Donald Creighton, *Dominion of the North* (Toronto: Macmillan, 1957).

3 Province of Quebec, *Report of the Royal Commission of Inquiry on Constitutional Problems*, vol. I, 1956, p. 22.

4 Paul Romney, *Getting It Wrong: How Canadians Forgot Their Past and Imperilled Confederation* (Toronto: University of Toronto Press, 1999).

5 George F.G. Stanley, "Act or Pact: Another Look at Confederation," *Canadian Historical Association Report*, 1956, p. 13.

The third quarter of the nineteenth century marked the high point of Maritime-built sailing ships, to be replaced by iron and steel vessels. The image shows sailing ships in Courtenay Bay, New Brunswick about 1860.

Source: PANB P5–360: Sailing Ships, Courtenay Bay, 1860.

Debating Dominion–Provincial Relations

For more than a century, historians, political scientists, and legal experts have debated the Fathers of Confederation's true intentions. Those who believe they sought to build a strong central government point out that the BNA Act delegated only precise and very circumscribed powers to the provincial governments. In contrast, the federal government gained the important economic and taxation powers, including the right to grant subsidies to the individual provinces. Ottawa also received the right to make laws for the "peace, order and good government of Canada" in relation to all matters not exclusively assigned to the provincial legislatures. Centralists also contend that the phrase "peace, order and good government of Canada" and the phrase "regulation of trade and commerce" incorporated all powers not exclusively given to the provinces; hence the residuum of powers lay with the federal government. Furthermore, they point out that the lieutenant governors of the provinces, appointees of the Dominion government, could reserve and disallow provincial legislation.

In contrast, provincial-rights advocates argue that since the colonies established the union, Confederation constituted a compact made among them: a provincial compact. Furthermore, they point to the general phrase "property and civil rights in the province" in section 92 of the BNA Act, which deals with the constitutional rights of the provinces, as proof of the provinces' broad powers. They also note that the provinces received a structure of government parallel to that of the federal government, implying that the provinces' association with the Crown was similar, not subordinate, to the Dominion's. Finally, they direct attention to legal tradition: in the late nineteenth and early twentieth centuries, the Judicial Committee of the Privy Council, the highest court of appeal in the British Empire, consistently interpreted the BNA Act in favour of the provinces.

Canadian–British–American Relations

Nationhood did not mean independence. By law and by desire, Canada in 1867 remained a British colony, with the British Parliament controlling Canada's external affairs. In 1867, Canadians, particularly English-speaking Canadians, considered the imperial connection as the best means for Canada to fulfill its destiny. The alternatives were possible annexation by the United States, or existence as an insignificant and isolated nation on the northern half of the North American continent, both of which Canadians considered undesirable choices.

The Economy

More than 80 percent of the Canadian labour force in 1867 worked in the primary industries—farming, fishing, and lumbering—to produce the staple products of trade: wheat, fish, and timber. The Maritimes were the centre of the shipbuilding industry. In 1865 alone, for example, the region built more than 600 vessels. The ports of Saint John, Halifax, and Yarmouth were the major shipbuilding centres in the Maritimes, along with Quebec and Montreal in the Canadas. But as steel ships replaced wooden ones, and as steam replaced sails as the source of energy, the era of wood, wind, and sails would soon decline. Some Maritimers equated the decline of their "golden age" with Confederation, and they resented union.

The vast majority of Canadians in 1867 lived on farms. Agriculture was important in Nova Scotia, especially in the Annapolis valley, while in New Brunswick, farmers made up more than half the labour force. In southern Quebec, dairy farming predominated. Some Quebec farmers, with the encouragement of the Roman Catholic Church and the Quebec government, colonized further north in the Saguenay–Lake St. Jean region, in the Laurentians, or in Témiscamingue in the upper

Ottawa valley. These "colonist farmers" had to clear the land of forests before breaking ground. Even then, farming in these northern reaches was marginal because of poor soil, short frost-free periods, and long distances from market centres. As the joke went, northern farmers raised two crops: one stone, the other snow. Probably for every Quebecker who went north to farm, ten went south into the New England states, a movement known as "the Great Hemorrhage," in search of work.

Wheat farming served as "the engine of economic growth"[1] in Ontario, according to the economic historian John McCallum. At the time of Confederation the best agricultural land lay in the province, where 60 percent of the working population farmed. Coarse grain or flour made up half of all exports at mid-century. By the time of Confederation, the peak of wheat production had been reached, with most of the good farmland occupied and some of the older districts becoming exhausted. Fortunately for Ontarians, just as they faced an agricultural crisis, the Canadian government acquired the vast prairie land to the west, which served as an outlet for aspiring young Ontario farmers.

The Canadian economy was based on the exporting of raw materials to either Britain or the United States in return for manufactured goods: textiles, textile fibres, agricultural products, consumer goods, and iron products. But Confederation coincided with the rudimentary beginnings of the production of manufactured goods within Canada itself. Economic historian O.J. Firestone notes that in the decade of the 1860s, over 20 percent of Canada's gross national product (GNP) came from manufacturing—a dramatic increase from the preceding decade. Manufacturing employed nearly 200 000 Canadians in roughly 40 000 establishments. Most of these were small family businesses attached to the owner's residence and employing only a few people doing jobs by hand.

Mechanization, however, had occurred in some areas. In the agricultural-implements industry, Daniel Massey, a farmer at Newcastle, east of Toronto, manufactured ploughs, harrows, reapers, and other simple-horse-drawn implements in machine-based factories. Canadian shops and factories in the large urban centres of Montreal, Quebec City, Toronto, Hamilton, Saint John, and Halifax, had begun to specialize, and to break down tasks into smaller components of the production process. Already there was evidence that manufacturing would be concentrated predominantly in the Montreal area, in the vicinity of Toronto, and in the western end of Lake Ontario, from Hamilton westward to Brantford.

Urbanization

In 1867, only one in five Canadians lived in urban centres, communities with a population over 1000. Canada had only three large cities: Montreal with 105 000 people; Quebec City with 60 000; and Toronto with 50 000. Six other cities had populations greater than 10 000: Saint John and Halifax in the Maritimes, and Hamilton, Ottawa, Kingston, and London in Ontario. A host of smaller towns in the range of 1000–5000 dotted the Canadian landscape. The larger metropolitan centres serviced a hinterland region that went beyond the adjacent rural area, thanks to their extensive rail connections. Montreal's hinterland, for example, included the rural areas of southwestern Quebec as well as eastern Ontario.

The Maritime cities of Saint John and Halifax grew slowly, compared with cities in central Canada. Many of the manufacturers in these two port cities faced hard times because they lacked a large local market and faced competition from wealthier entrepreneurs in central Canada. In 1867, industrialists in the Maritimes looked forward to the completion of the Intercolonial Railway, which would, they hoped, make Ontario and Quebec economic hinterlands of Halifax and Saint John.

Canadian cities in 1867 were, with the exception of Montreal, pre-industrial. This meant that rich and poor lived in close proximity, with social distinctions marked by the size of one's house, its location on the street, or by the location of a particular street in a district. In Montreal,

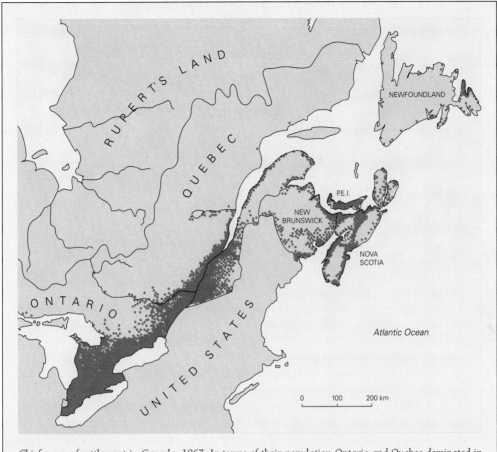

Chief areas of settlement in Canada, 1867. In terms of their population Ontario and Quebec dominated in the new Dominion.

Source: Based on John Warkentin, *Canada: A Geographical Interpretation* (Toronto: Methuen, 1968), p. 45.

however, there already existed predominantly working-class districts in the city core and along the St. Lawrence River and Lachine Canal. Well-to-do families were leaving the inner city to live in the spacious, clean, and airy suburban districts of the west end, with its numerous parks and good public services. Thus, in the case of Montreal, the modern industrial segregated city had made an appearance in 1867. By 1914, such segregated cities would be commonplace throughout the country.

Population

In 1867, the total population of the new Dominion of Canada was 3.5 million. The First Nations numbered approximately 30 000, or roughly 1 percent. The three largest groups were: the Ojibwa (Anishinabeg), in Ontario; the Iroquois, in Ontario and Quebec; and the Mi'kmaq (Micmac), in Nova Scotia and New Brunswick. They were "wards of the state"; section 91 (subsection 24) of the British North America Act assigned responsibility for "Indians and lands reserved for Indians" to the new federal government. They did not participate in shaping the new political community of Canada. As political scientist Peter H. Russell notes: "For the Europeans who fashioned the Canadian Confederation, the Aboriginal peoples were subjects on whom sovereignty could be imposed, not people with whom one formed a political community."[2]

First Nations Lacrosse players from the Kahnawake community near Montreal. The First Nations soon adapted the non-Aboriginals' tradition of team photographs, posed, with two players resting on their elbows on the ground at the front, others are seated behind, and two standing at the back.

Source: Lee Pritzker Collection/Library and Archives Canada/C-1959.

Those of French descent made up roughly a third of the total population. More than 85 percent resided in Quebec and had roots in North America extending back two centuries. The Acadians in New Brunswick and Nova Scotia numbered nearly 10 percent of the French-speaking population. Only 3 percent of Canada's francophones lived in Ontario, mainly in the area adjacent to Quebec.

People of British descent accounted for 60 percent of Canada's population in 1867. Some were descendants of Loyalists who had settled on British territory after the American Revolution. Most, however, were British immigrants and their descendants who had arrived in British North America between 1815 and 1860, some 1.3 million in total. In 1867, the Irish made up 25 percent of the total Canadian population, the Scots 16 percent, the English 15 percent, and the Welsh 5 percent.

English-speaking and French-speaking Canadians lived in two separate worlds in 1867. P.-J.-O. Chauveau, the first premier of Quebec after Confederation, compared Canada to the famous staircase of the Château de Chambord in France, built to allow two persons to ascend it without meeting, and even without seeing each other except at intervals. "English and French, we climb by a double flight of stairs toward the destinies reserved for us on this continent, without knowing each other, without meeting each other, except on the landing of politics."

The remaining 8 percent of the Dominion's population consisted of non-British and non-French immigrants and their descendants from Europe and the United States. The majority was from German-speaking states and was welcomed because of the close links between the British monarchy and German principalities. There were, as well, about 65 000 African Canadians. While some were of American Loyalist descent, many had arrived in the mid-1800s, either as freed African Americans, now facing increased discrimination in racially torn America, or as fugitive slaves on the eve of the American Civil War via the Underground Railroad, a loose network of African Americans (sometimes ex-slaves) and white abolitionists who aided slaves. Although slavery had not existed in British North America since the early nineteenth century, racial prejudice existed. Blacks faced discrimination in land grants, schooling, employment, and voting rights.

Ontario and Quebec had nearly four-fifths of the new Dominion's population, with more than 1.5 million in Ontario and about one million in Quebec. The other fifth of Canada's population resided in the Maritime provinces: roughly 400 000 in Nova Scotia and 300 000 in New Brunswick.

Social Life

In 1867, most Canadians lived and worked on their own farms, as close to neighbours, kin, and

An evening with friends in Quebec in days gone by. Family and friends provided social cohesion in rural Canada in the nineteenth century. Note the cross on the wall in the centre, indicating the influence of the Roman Catholic Church in late nineteenth century Quebec.

Source: Library and Archives Canada/C-1125.

their own ethnic group as possible. In Quebec, the seigneurial system had been abolished only thirteen years earlier, which meant individual farmers had acquired title to their lands. Limited financial means made consumer goods a luxury. The village elite generally consisted of the curé, the doctor, the notary, and the local merchants. In Quebec City and Montreal, French Canadians lived amid a substantial English-speaking population.

Next door in Ontario, most of the population consisted of recent British immigrants or children of immigrants. The majority were freehold farmers who had acquired their land within the last generation. In general, Ontario farmers were better off economically than their Quebec counterparts. They owned larger farms that were newly cultivated and subsequently more productive. People lived farther apart, however, and were divided by their different Christian denominational ties.

A HISTORICAL PORTRAIT

Josiah Henson

Josiah Henson was born into slavery on a Maryland plantation in 1789. His earliest recollection at the age of three or four was the day he saw his father return from a terrible beating. As Henson later recalled, "His right ear had been cut off close to his head and he had received a hundred lashes on his back." His "crime"? He struck a white man, the farm overseer, for brutally assaulting Josiah's mother.

Soon afterwards, the Hensons' master split the family up. He sold Josiah's father to a plantation in Alabama and auctioned off Josiah's mother, brothers, sisters, and Josiah himself to separate owners. Fortunately, Josiah was later reunited with his mother.

As slaves, Josiah and his mother lived in appalling conditions, eating corn meal and salted herring. "Our lodging," he recalled, "was in log huts, of a single small room, with no other floor than the trodden earth, in which ten or a dozen persons—men, women, and children—might sleep." By his twenties, the conscientious, hard-working man had so gained his master's respect that he appointed him farm superintendent. When it became clear, however, that his owner had no intention of granting him his freedom, Henson, who had married fifteen or so years earlier and now had a family, escaped with his wife and four children to Canada.

The Hensons spent six difficult weeks following the Underground Railway to Upper Canada. On October 28, 1830, they crossed the Niagara River. Immediately, Henson fell on his knees and gave thanks. In their new home, the Hensons founded an African community named Dawn, near present-day Dresden, Ontario. With the financial assistance of a group of Boston Unitarians, they began the British American Institute for Fugitive Slaves, a school to educate ex-slaves and to teach them a trade.

In the late 1840s, Henson dictated his life story. It was published in Boston as *The Life of Josiah Henson Formerly a Slave Now an Inhabitant of*

Queen Victoria receives Josiah Henson at Windsor Castle, March 5, 1877. In that same year the Canadian government signed Treaty Seven with the First Nations of Southern Alberta, in the Queen's name.

Source: The American Museum in Britain, Claverton Manor, Bath, England.

Canada in 1849. Three years later Harriet Beecher Stowe's novel *Uncle Tom's Cabin* appeared. It proved a sensation, the most popular anti-slavery book published before the outbreak of the American Civil War. The fact that many people identified Josiah Henson as the prototype for the fictional "Uncle Tom" made him famous. Stowe, however, never categorically stated this; people just inferred that it was true. As a result of his fame, Henson made several lecture tours of Britain to raise money for the Dawn settlement.

When the American Civil War ended, many African Americans in Upper Canada returned to the United States, and the community of Dawn died out. In his late eighties, Henson made his final visit to Britain to meet Queen Victoria at Windsor Castle. He died in Dresden in 1883.

In the 1860s, Ontarians were on the move. A study of several townships along Lake Ontario near Port Hope revealed that within a five-year span more than half the people were recent occupants or had moved from one place to another within the region. David Gagan's study of Peel County at mid-century confirms this, as does Michael Katz's study of mid-century Hamilton.[3] An increasing number were leaving the country for the cities and towns. Physical mobility, however, did not necessarily mean social mobility, even though the incentive for moving was often to better one's life.

In the Maritimes, people lived predominantly in rural areas or in small towns. Given the sparse populations, poor roads, and a topography that encouraged settlement along the coast, communities were often isolated. In 1867, no major railways yet existed to link communities. In addition, the region's diversified economy of fishing, lumbering, mining, and farming segregated people according to interests and livelihood. As a result, Maritimers in 1867 identified with their particular locale and lacked a provincial and regional consciousness.

Women

Women made up almost half of the population in 1867, yet they lacked basic rights: the right to vote, the right to higher education or professional training, and legal rights. They were not defined as individuals but by their role in the "domestic sphere," as wives and mothers at the service of husbands and children.

Montreal mourns Thomas D'Arcy McGee. The funeral cortege, April 13, 1868, of the victim of Canada's first political assassination, believed to be the work of Irish revolutionaries. McGee strongly opposed the Fenians, the Irish Americans who wanted to end English rule in Ireland. He was assassinated in Ottawa on April 7, 1868.

Source: Library and Archives Canada/ C-83423, photographer James Inglis.

Women relinquished their personal property and any wages earned upon marriage. Under British common law, in effect everywhere except Quebec, husband and wife were legally one. A wife could not sign a contract, be sued in her own name, take her husband to court, or initiate divorce proceedings. Despite such restrictions, over 95 percent of women married. They also bore large families, 7.8 children on average by mid-century. By the end of the century, that number would decline to an average of only four children.

Marriage was more a communal than private affair. Courting occurred in supervised settings, and marriage was a public event. But the few surviving women's diaries of this period speak little of love and romance in marriage, and instead emphasize economic security.

In the days before modern conveniences, women's duties lay in the arduous work of keeping a good home. Their daily tasks would consist of cleaning house, cooking, sewing, weaving, and making butter, the rhythm being broken only by church services on Sundays. The change of seasons varied the pattern only slightly, and added garden and field work at harvest time. (A satirical cartoon in *L'Opinion Publique*, an illustrated journal of the day, reveals what many working-class women's sentiments must have been. See the cartoon reproduced here.)

Children were the forgotten group in society, without any legal rights. Those from poorer families usually had to leave school early to help support their families. Most working-class children had little hope of rising above their parents' level and social status.

Trade Unions

The federal government only legally recognized unions in 1872. In the 1860s, the unions that did exist represented skilled workers in a particular locale or a special trade, such as typesetting, shoemaking, and moulding. The first unions for nonskilled workers appeared in shops that introduced modern technology, a development that was beginning to undermine skilled jobs. Increasingly, employers saw workers as employees rather than as apprentices. They brought workers under one roof and paid them according to the quantity, rather than quality, of their work.

LE TRAVAIL.

"Tu te plains, mon pauvre mari, de tes dix heures d'ouvrage ; voici quatorze heures que je travaille, moi, et je n'ai pas encore fini ma journée."

"Work," a drawing that appeared in the journal L'Opinion Publique, November 2, 1871. In the late nineteenth century, gender inequality was as common as class inequality. The woman states; "You complain my dear husband, of your ten hours of labour, I have already worked fourteen hours, and my day is still not finished yet."

Source: Library and Archives Canada/C-108134.

Some workers responded to these changed conditions in the workplace by rioting. By 1867, however, strikes and parades were replacing riots as more acceptable forms of protest, and as a means to demand better wages and working conditions. On June 10, 1867, for example, 10 000 workers paraded in the streets of Montreal as a show of worker solidarity and as an appeal for improved wages and working conditions.

Religion and Education

Religious Denominations

In 1867, almost all Canadians belonged to one of the major denominations. The Roman Catholic Church, the largest in Canada, claimed as members 40 percent of the country's population (in Quebec, 85 percent). In Quebec the Roman Catholic Church controlled the Catholic education system, supplying both its teachers and its curriculum.

Most of the teachers came from the female religious orders. The female orders also administered the hospitals and cared for the sick, the abandoned, and the poor. These female religious communities gave many of their members the opportunity to obtain an excellent education, to occupy responsible administrative positions, and to serve as teachers, nurses, and social-assistance workers. They also provided a strong sense of community.

In Protestant Canada, Anglicans slightly outnumbered Presbyterians, who outnumbered Methodists. These Protestant religious groups favoured voluntarism, the legal separation of church and state. They believed that religious instruction should be provided by the church only, in Sunday schools. The Roman Catholic Church, in contrast, maintained that the school system should provide religious, as well as regular, instruction. It therefore opposed the abolition of denominational schools.

Schooling

Schooling had little priority in Canada in the 1860s, although most provinces moved to a form of taxation on property holders to finance state-operated schools. Children fortunate enough to receive formal education might have their classes in the corners of warehouses, blacksmith shops, stores, tanneries, or private homes. Their schooling rarely went beyond the basic "3 Rs"—"reading, 'riting, and 'rithmetic." Very often teachers had little more education than their students. The most important requisite to teach was simply a willingness to work for low pay and to enforce discipline.

In Ontario, the middle and upper classes paid fees for their children to attend grammar schools (renamed "high schools" in 1871 by the superintendent of education, Egerton Ryerson) and collegiate institutes. In high school, the students learned English, commercial subjects, and natural science, especially agriculture; and in collegiate institutes they also studied the classics in preparation for university. In Quebec, the Roman Catholic Church operated classical colleges, which trained the province's future lawyers, doctors, and priests. Most of the seventeen universities in existence in 1867 were affiliated with a religious denomination, but four non-denominational universities already existed: the University of Toronto, McGill in Montreal, Dalhousie College in Halifax, and the University of New Brunswick in Fredericton. Universities served an elite of only 1500 students in total, mostly sons of the well-to-do (women were not admitted) or a few aspiring members of the upper middle class. Within the university curriculum, the faculties of arts and theology dominated, as teaching and the clergy were the favoured career options after graduation. The arts course was traditional, with an emphasis on classical languages, mathematics, and philosophy. Natural science was assuming greater importance. Engineering courses had not yet been introduced, but law and medicine were taught at some of the larger universities.

COMMUNITY PORTRAIT

The Community of the Sisters of the Congregation of Notre Dame

Founded in 1653 by Marguerite Bourgeoys as a religious community of uncloistered women to live and work among the ordinary people, and as a teaching order to provide schooling for the young women of New France, the Congregation of Notre Dame became, by the late nineteenth and early twentieth centuries, the largest and most prestigious religious community of women teachers in Quebec. By 1920, it had over 1600 members and over 150 Roman Catholic schools throughout Quebec, Nova Scotia, New Brunswick, and Ontario.

The teachers of Mont Ste-Marie Convent School, 1889.

Source : Congrégation de Notre Dame, 2330 ouest, rue Sherbrooke, Montreal, QC H3E 1G8, (514) 931-5891.

The Congregation of Notre Dame, like other women's religious orders, provided women with a community in which they could find meaningful work which, in the case of the Congregation, meant teaching. Many women who entered the Congregation of Notre Dame convents did so on the advice of family members who, in many cases, had preceded them. Thus a strong bond existed between members of the Congregation and their families. Even the terms "sisters" and "mothers" to identify members of women's religious communities, and, in the case of the Congregation of Notre Dame, the epithet of "Les Filles de Marguerite Bourgeoys" (Daughters of Marguerite Bourgeoys) reinforced the familial link. Members of the order prayed to Marguerite Bourgeoys, their founder. Within the community, the Golden Rule applied: sisters were expected to be charitable and compassionate to fellow members. The young and healthy, for example, took care of the sick and elderly nuns. At the same time, the community also allowed for a relaxation of the order's rules and regulations to foster camaraderie. At the mother house of the Congregation, for example, sisters were permitted on special occasions to "let loose" by engaging in such communal fun as playing harmless pranks, wearing costumes, or performing imitations of their superiors.

As the Congregation grew, it also became more affluent. Its members enjoyed improved diets of fresh fruits, vegetables, butter, and pastries. The sisters had lighter manual workloads, and thus more time for leisure activities together and for communal prayers. But prosperity also caused strains in the Congregation's communal life. In the 1880s, *les soeurs converses*, or domestic servants, were brought into the community to do the manual work previously done by the sisters themselves. Thus a two-tiered social order emerged, evident in the separation of recreation, clothing habits, and assigned work of the two groups. Furthermore, the Congregation's growth resulted in a more bureaucratic structure that mitigated against its earlier sense of a community of equals. Now a General Superior ruled and administered affairs at the centre, while local and provincial superiors in the Congregation's six "provinces," each corresponding to the regional district of the schools owned by the community, carried out the rulings of the central council and regulated the everyday activities of the sisters. A constitution dictated the rights and responsibilities of each office and outlined the procedure for the appointment of superiors. Nominally, sisters who had been with the community for at least ten years could cast a vote for their leaders, but in reality each chapter selected delegates who made the final decision. And within the community, nuns from upper- and middle-class households wielded greater power than those nuns from working-class or farming backgrounds.

Still, the community of the Congregation of Notre Dame provided its members with a communal and supportive setting in which women lived a religious life while also acquiring a profession and the skills to play a meaningful role in society. In 1908, the Congregation supported the establishment of the first French-language women's college in Quebec; the École d'enseignment supérieur (renamed the Collège Marguerite Bourgeoys in 1926). In this way, the Congregation of Notre Dame assisted French-Canadian females to obtain an education equal to their male counterparts.

In 1984, for the first time, the *Constitution and Rules* of the Congregation included some of the inspirational statements of Marguerite Bourgeoys, including the following: "Our Foundress invites us to imitate 'the life led by the Blessed Virgin throughout her time on earth.' Therefore, especially the mystery of the Visitation and in Mary's life among the apostles in the first Christian community, we find spiritual and apostolic inspiration."

Today, the Congregation of Notre Dame has a world-wide community of approximately 1700 sisters in Canada, the United States, Japan, Central and South America, and Africa.

FURTHER READING

Patricia Simpson, *Marguerite Bourgeoys and the Congregation of Notre Dame, 1665–1700* (Montreal/Kingston: McGill-Queen's University Press, 2005).

Marta Danylewycz, *Taking the Veil: An Alternative to Marriage, Motherhood and Spinsterhood in Quebec, 1840–1920* (Toronto: McClelland and Stewart, 1987).

Danielle Juteau and Nicole Laurin, *Un métier et une vocation: Le travail des religieuses au Québec de 1901 à 1971* (Montreal: Presses de l'Université de Montréal, 1997).

Nadia Famy-Eid and Micheline Dumont, *Les couventines: l'éducation des filles au Québec dans les congrégations religieuses enseignantes, 1840–1960* (Montreal: Boréal, 1986).

Congrégation de Notre-Dame website, www.cnd-m.com, accessed July 8, 2007.

This was the Canada of 1867 as the country embarked on its new experiment in nation building. It was a rural, predominantly farming, society. Social distinctions divided the rural population, and great physical distances isolated communities. In the few towns and cities, social distinctions existed, but segregation by social districts was only beginning. The Canadian economy remained largely preindustrial, but manufacturing had started in a few large urban centres. Exports included mainly wheat, timber, and fish. Politically, the new nation was about to experiment with a new two-party system and with a new Constitution that left relationships between the new federal government and the provincial governments to be resolved. The new Dominion also lacked a sense of nationalism. As Prime Minister John A. Macdonald put it: Confederation, "now in the gristle," needed to "harden into bone."

NOTES

1. John McCallum, *Unequal Beginnings: Agriculture and Economic Development in Quebec and Ontario Until 1870* (Toronto: University of Toronto Press, 1980), p. 5.

2. Peter H. Russell, *Constitutional Odyssey: Can Canadians Become a Sovereign People?*, 2nd ed. (Toronto: University of Toronto Press, 1993), p. 4.

3. David Gagan, *Hopeful Travellers: Families, Land, and Social Change in Mid-Victorian Peel County, Canada West* (Toronto: University of Toronto Press, 1981); and Michael Katz, *The People of Hamilton, Canada West: Family and Class in a Mid-Nineteenth Century City* (Cambridge, MA: Harvard University Press, 1975).

BEYOND THE BOOK

Weblinks

Territorial Evolution of Canada
http://atlas.nrcan.gc.ca/site/english/maps/historical#territorialevolution
Maps of the territorial evolution of Canada, beginning at 1867.

Canadian Confederation
http://www.collectionscanada.ca/confederation/index-e.html
Historical documents and images regarding the confederation of Canada. Biographies of the Fathers of Confederation.

Who Killed William Robinson?
http://www.canadianmysteries.ca/sites/robinson/home/indexen.html
William Robinson was an American of African descent living in British Columbia who was murdered in 1868. Using court documents of the time, revisit this murder trial which found an Aboriginal man hanged for Robinson's death.

Victoria, BC: November 28, 1867
http://www.ourroots.ca/e/toc.aspx?id=914
Experience life in Victoria, British Columbia in 1867 through this digitized account of a public meeting overseen by the city's mayor.

Photographs of Life in 1867
http://www.mccord-museum.qc.ca/scripts/search_results .php?Lang=1&keywords=1867
Explore the culture of Canada in 1867 through this vast database of photographs taken of individuals and objects in that year.

Immigration Handbook
http://ist.uwaterloo.ca/~marj/genealogy/papers/emguide1864.html
An 1864 handbook for immigrants to Canada.

Films & Novels

Glengarry School Days: A Story of Early Days in Glengarry. By Ralph Connor. 2005.

RELATED READINGS

The following article in R. Douglas Francis and Donald B. Smith, eds., *Readings in Canadian History: Post-Confederation*, 7th ed. (Toronto: Thomson Nelson, 2006) is relevant to this chapter: John A. Rohr, "Current Canadian Constitutionalism and the 1865 Confederation Debates," pp. 5–23.

BIBLIOGRAPHY

The three best general texts on Confederation, all written in the 1960s, are Donald Creighton, *The Road to Confederation: The Emergence of Canada, 1863–1867* (Toronto: Macmillan, 1964); W.L. Morton, *The Critical Years: The Union of British North America, 1857–1873* (Toronto: McClelland & Stewart, 1964); and P.B. Waite, *The Life and Times of Confederation, 1864–1867: Politics, Newspapers, and the Union of British North America* (Toronto: University of Toronto Press, 1962). The Canadian Historical Association has published a number of pamphlets on aspects of Confederation by leading scholars in their fields: J.M. Beck, *Joseph Howe: Anti-Confederate* (Ottawa, 1966); J.-C. Bonenfant, *The French Canadians and the Birth of Confederation* (Ottawa, 1966); P.G. Cornell, *The Great Coalition* (Ottawa, 1966); W.L. Morton, *The West and Confederation, 1857–1871* (Ottawa, 1962); P.B. Waite, *The Charlottetown Conference* (Ottawa, 1963); and W.M. Whitelaw, *The Quebec Conference* (Ottawa, 1966). Christopher Moore takes a more recent look at the topic in *1867: How the Fathers Made a Deal* (Toronto: McClelland & Stewart, 1997). A good primary source is P.B. Waite, ed., *The Confederation Debates in the Province of Canada, 1865* (Toronto: McClelland & Stewart, 1963).

On the Maritime provinces and Confederation in 1867, see Phillip A. Buckner, "The 1860s: An End and a Beginning," in Phillip A. Buckner and John G. Reid, eds., *The Atlantic Region to Confederation: A History* (Toronto: University of Toronto Press, 1994), pp. 360–86.

On the American influence on Confederation consult Robin Winks, *Canada and the United States: The Civil War Years* (Montreal: Harvest House, 1971 [1960]; Greg Marquis, *In Armageddon's Shadow: The Civil War and Canada's Maritime Provinces* (Montreal/Kingston: McGill-Queen's University Press, 1998); Adam Mayers, *Dixie and the Dominion: Canada, the Confederacy and the War for the Union* (Toronto: Dundurn Press, 2003), and Claire Hoy, *Canadians in the Civil War* (Toronto: McClelland and Stewart, 2004). Studies of Britain's influence include C.P. Stacey, *Canada and the British Army, 1841–1871*, rev. ed. (Toronto: University of Toronto Press, 1963 [1936]) and Ged Martin, *Britain and the Origins of Canadian Federation, 1837–67* (Vancouver: University of British Columbia Press, 1995).

Portraits of Canada's first prime minister are available in Donald G. Creighton, *John A. Macdonald: The Old Chieftain* (Toronto: Macmillan, 1955); and P.B. Waite, *Macdonald: His Life and World* (Toronto: McGraw-Hill Ryerson, 1975). For studies of George-Étienne Cartier see Brian Young, *George-Étienne Cartier: Montreal Bourgeois* (Montreal/Kingston: McGill-Queen's University Press, 1981). Gordon T. Stewart discusses the formation of political parties in *The Origins of Canadian Politics: A Comparative Approach* (Vancouver: University of British Columbia Press, 1986).

For a review of the Canadian economy at the time of Confederation consult Michael Bliss, *Northern Enterprise: Five Centuries of Canadian Business* (Toronto: McClelland & Stewart, 1987); Kenneth Norrie and Douglas Owram, *A History of the Canadian Economy*, 3rd ed. (Toronto: Nelson, 2002): and in the case of Quebec, P.-A. Linteau, R. Durocher, and J.-C. Robert, *Quebec: A History, 1867–1929* (Toronto: James Lorimer, 1983).

For a study of social life in Montreal, see Bettina Bradbury, *Working Families: Age, Gender, and Daily Survival in Industrializing Montreal* (Toronto: McClelland & Stewart, 1993). Sandra Gwyn provides a glimpse of governing society in Ottawa from 1867 to 1914 in *The Private Capital: Ambition and Love in the Age of Macdonald and Laurier* (Toronto: McClelland & Stewart, 1984). For the story of the Native peoples see E.S. Rogers and Donald B. Smith, eds., *Aboriginal Ontario* (Toronto: Dundurn Press, 1994). The best overview of African Canadians remains Robin Winks, *The Blacks in Canada: A History*, 2nd ed. (Montreal/Kingston: McGill-Queen's University Press, 1997).

On women at the time of Confederation, see the relevant sections of Alison Prentice et al., *Canadian Women: A History*, 2nd ed. (Toronto: Harcourt Brace, 1996). For Quebec, see Marta Danylewycz, *Taking the Veil: An Alternative to Marriage, Motherhood, and Spinsterhood in Quebec, 1840–1920* (Toronto: McClelland & Stewart, 1987); for the Maritimes see Janet Guildford and Suzanne Morton, *Separate Spheres: Women's Worlds in the 19th-Century Maritimes* (Fredericton: Acadiensis Press, 1994).

Craig Heron's *The Canadian Labour Movement: A Short History*, 2nd ed. (Toronto: Lorimer, 1996) surveys Canadian labour history. See, as well, Bryan D. Palmer, *Working-Class Experience: Rethinking the History of Canadian Labour, 1800–1991* (Toronto: McClelland & Stewart, 1992).

For further discussion of religion see John S. Moir, "Religion," in *The Canadians: 1867–1967* (cited earlier), pp. 586–605; and John W. Grant, *A Profusion of Spires: Religion in Nineteenth-Century Ontario* (Toronto: University of Toronto Press, 1988). On education consult Susan E. Houston and Alison Prentice, *Schooling and Scholars in Nineteenth-Century Ontario* (Toronto: University of Toronto Press, 1988); Bruce Curtis, *Building the Educational State: Canada West, 1836–1871* (London: Althouse Press, 1988); and J. Donald Wilson, Robert M. Stamp, and Louis-Philippe Audet, eds., *Canadian Education: A History* (Toronto: Prentice-Hall, 1970).

INTRODUCTION

The mid- to late-nineteenth century saw the formation of European nation states, including Germany in 1866 and Italy in 1871; national consolidation, as occurred in the United States after the Civil War; and imperial expansion, as in the case of Britain, France, Germany, and the United States. Canada witnessed all three developments in a phenomenally short period of time: the three British North American colonies of Nova Scotia, New Brunswick, and the United Canadas came together in 1867 to create the new nation state of Canada; within ten years, the country had expanded to include all of the existing British North American colonies with the exception of Newfoundland. The new nation had also undertaken expansion to the Pacific and the Arctic Oceans. In the 1870s, Canada made seven treaties with the First Nations in Western Canada. The country also became involved in two conflicts with the Aboriginal peoples, first in 1869–70 in the Red River colony, and then in 1885 in the North-West Territories to make the Prairie West "Canada's Empire."

Creating the physical boundaries of a new nation state proved easier than fostering a sense of nationalism. Since the traditional components of cultural nationalism—a common language, a common cultural tradition, or a common religion—were absent, national enthusiasts looked to geography and especially to an economic policy of railway building, protective tariffs, and large-scale immigration to promote a feeling of nationalism.

This so-called national policy, as well as the decision of the Fathers of Confederation to create a federal union with political power divided between Ottawa and provincial governments, necessitated the working out of Dominion–provincial relations. This proved acrimonious. Also to be resolved were relations between French-speaking and English-speaking Canadians. A century of bitterness and suspicion between these two dominant ethnic groups preceded Confederation, yet a *modus vivendi* had existed in the union itself. Tension and compromise prevailed from 1867 to 1914. Finally, the new country needed to work out relations with Britain and the United States. Most Canadians favoured continued affiliation with the British empire. Union of the colonies of the United Canadas, New Brunswick and Nova Scotia and the granting of Dominion status to the new nation did not mean independence from the British Empire. Equally, Canadians sought trade with the United States, while clearly rejecting any form of political union with their southern neighbour.

For most Canadians, Confederation left their daily lives unaltered. They continued to identify more with their colonial (now provincial) and local area than with the country as a whole, and they pursued their livelihood as they had prior to Confederation. The year 1867 and the event of Confederation were not momentous. Still, the very act of union of the three British North American colonies put into place a new structure and a new dynamic for economic, political, and social change. Part of that new structure was a federal bureaucracy that was small and insignificant in 1867, but that would grow to regulate all aspects of the public and to a large degree the private life of all Canadians and especially the First Nations people who became "wards of the state."

Chapter Two

THREE OCEANS, ONE COUNTRY: 1867–1880

TIME LINE

1867	Nova Scotia, New Brunswick, Quebec, and Ontario join Confederation
1868	Nova Scotia attempts to secede from Confederation
1869	Canada purchases Rupert's Land from the Hudson's Bay Company Act for the Temporary Government of Rupert's Land and the North-West Territory Outbreak of Métis resistance under Louis Riel Newfoundland rejects union with Canada
1870	Manitoba becomes a province Wolseley expedition sent to the Red River Colony
1871	British Columbia joins Confederation The first of seven treaties signed with the Canadian government covering the territory over present-day northern Ontario
1873	Prince Edward Island joins Confederation
1876	Treaty Six signed with the Canadian government covering the territory of present-day central and northern Saskatchewan and Alberta Indian Act passed
1877	Treaty Seven signed with the Canadian government covering the territory of present-day southern Alberta
1880	Britain transfers jurisdiction over the Arctic Islands to Canada

In his first administration, John A. Macdonald worked to keep the fragile creation called Canada together against the desire of Nova Scotia to secede. He also rounded out the country by purchasing Rupert's Land from the Hudson's Bay Company. From 1867 to 1872, he brought in Manitoba and British Columbia as provinces and prepared for Prince Edward Island's entry in 1873. Newfoundland, wanting better terms, refused to join. By 1880, Canada would acquire the Arctic region from Britain. Other challenges for the new Canadian government included putting down the resistance of the Métis in the North West, who resented Canadian takeover of the territory without consulting them, and then negotiating a settlement. As well, the government needed to sign treaties with the First Nations in the Prairie West to secure control over their land, and then bring them under federal government control through the Indian Act. These activities showed the extent to which the Canadian government would go to secure control over the region and its populace and to prevent an American takeover of the area.

The Nova Scotia Repeal Movement

Nova Scotia opposed union with the Canadas from the beginning. Charles Tupper, the province's pro-Confederation premier since 1863 and the leader responsible for bringing the colony into Confederation, had refused to hold a referendum or even to debate the question in the legislative assembly. He knew his government would lose on the issue. A report in the anti-Confederation newspaper, the *Novascotian*, made no secret of Tupper's unpopularity for supporting union: "Dr. Tupper was burned in effigy here on Monday night last. We are only sorry it was not in person." The Halifax *Morning Chronicle* included an obituary notice for the province of Nova Scotia in its issue of July 1, 1867.

When Nova Scotians had a chance to vote, in September 1867, they elected anti-confederates to 18 of the 19 federal seats. Tupper was the only confederate to win his seat, and then by less than a hundred votes. In a provincial election the same year, Nova Scotians elected 36 anti-confederates and only 2 pro-confederates. In the first meeting of the provincial legislature, the anti-confederates presented repeal resolutions to end the "bondage" of Confederation.

The Anti-Confederation League, later patriotically renamed the Nova Scotia Party, was formed in 1866 and led by Joseph Howe. The popular and seasoned politician, the "Father of Responsible Government in Nova Scotia" and premier from 1860 to 1863, represented a generation of Nova Scotians who remembered Nova Scotia's once-flourishing triangular trade with Britain and the West Indies. A dedicated British imperialist, he wanted to strengthen the colony's ties with Britain, not weaken them through British North American union. After the repealers' stunning victories over the Unionists in the elections of 1867, Howe headed a committee to London in early 1868 to obtain the Colonial Office's sanction for Nova Scotia's release from Confederation. The colonial secretary, however, refused to meet Howe. Britain wanted to lessen, not increase, its obligations to its British North American colonies through greater colonial autonomy.

Other anti-confederates, particularly the business interests in the province, favoured annexation to the United States. After Britain adopted free trade in the 1840s, Nova Scotians developed a lucrative trade with the United States through the Reciprocity Treaty of 1854, until a protectionist American Senate rescinded it in 1866. In 1867, many Nova Scotians preferred a renewal of reciprocity, even annexation to the United States, to union with Canada.

John A. Macdonald saw Canada's opportunity. He knew Howe opposed union with the United States. The prime minister promised Howe a cabinet position. He also offered him control over provincial patronage. Finally Macdonald offered better financial terms for Nova Scotia—an increased debt allowance and a 25 percent increase in the federal subsidy to the province. Although his opponents accused him of betraying Nova Scotia, Howe ran for federal office in a by-election. Assisted by a very generous campaign donation, supplied jointly by the federal Conservative government and central Canadian business interests, Howe won and subsequently joined the federal cabinet.

Howe's "conversion" to Canadian federalism weakened the repeal movement. Only the annexationists remained. In June 1869, the Anti-Confederation League formally changed its name to the Annexation League. The timing could not have been worse for them: their manifesto, advocating closer relations with the United States, coincided with a brief period of prosperity that undermined their economic grievances. Furthermore, the United States did not appear particularly interested at this time in annexing Nova Scotia.

The final offer of better terms for Nova Scotia won over the moderate anti-confederates. But Confederation would remain the central issue facing the province for generations to come. In order to weaken opposition to Confederation, Tupper, Howe, and New Brunswick's Charles Tilley successfully pressured Macdonald to give utmost priority to the construction of the Intercolonial Railway. The 800 km publicly funded railway line was completed in 1876 and ran from Rivière-du-Loup in Quebec, along New Brunswick's north shore, to link up with existing lines to Halifax and Saint John.

The Canadian Acquisition of Rupert's Land

Macdonald's Conservative government also faced serious trouble in the Northwest. American senators and congressmen talked openly of annexing the region. In 1864, the United States Congress granted a charter for the construction of the Northern Pacific Railway from St. Paul, Minnesota to Seattle, Washington. It was to be built close to the international border with the intention of capturing more of the trade of the British territory through the building of spur lines.

In 1868, the Canadian government began negotiations in London with the British government and representatives of the Hudson's Bay Company (HBC) to acquire Rupert's Land, roughly defined as all territory whose rivers flowed into Hudson Bay. Thus, unlike the American West which was won by military conquest, the Canadian West was bought by a government. The agreement reached in 1869–70 constituted one of the largest real-estate deals in history. For an area ten times the size of what was then Canada, the Dominion government agreed to pay the HBC a cash sum of £300 000 (approximately $1.5 million) and to allow the company to retain one-twentieth (roughly 2.8 million ha) of the land of the "fertile belt" (the area along the North Saskatchewan River), as well as the land immediately surrounding its trading posts. (Over time, the company would receive over $120 million from the sale of its land.) The company agreed to transfer the land to the British government, which then turned the territory over to Canada. Historian Chester Martin maintained that the land deal "transformed the original Dominion from a federation of equal provinces … into a veritable empire in its own right."[1] The Canadian government would rule the region as a colonial possession, suppressing any challenge to its authority, demanding conformity, and dictating to a significant degree the political, economic, and social life of the region's inhabitants.

Administering the Northwest

While the negotiations were under way, the Canadian government made preparations to administer the new territory. In June 1869, Parliament passed the "Act for the Temporary Government of Rupert's Land and the North-West Territory." It provided for a colonial system of government with an appointed governor and council only—a political structure similar to the ones that had existed in the British North American colonies prior to the granting of elected assemblies. Representative and responsible government, and provincehood, would await a larger population.

The Canadian government made immediate plans to build a road from the Lake of the Woods to Fort Garry in the Red River colony and dispatched a survey crew to the Red River for an eventual railway to link the Northwest to the rest of Canada. As well, it appointed William McDougall from Ontario as the first lieutenant governor. McDougall set off by way of St. Paul, Minnesota to take up his administrative duties in the Red River colony. But he never reached his destination. A group of Métis in the Red River colony, led by Louis Riel, a 25-year-old Métis from a well-established Red River family who had been educated in Montreal, forbade McDougall and his entourage to enter Rupert's Land. The Métis also drove out the survey crew. Since in 1869 the HBC had not yet officially transferred Rupert's Land to Canada, Ottawa had no legal authority to deal with the Red River uprising.

The mixed-blood population in the Red River area consisted of three groups. About half were French Métis, offspring of the intermarriage of French fur traders and First Nations women. About another third were the "country born," descendants of Scottish and First Nations parents. The remainder were the descendants of Selkirk's original Scottish settlers and newly arrived immigrants from the Canadas, who together numbered only about 1000 people, less than 10 percent of the total Red River colony's population in 1869.

The Métis Resistance of 1869–1870

The French Métis resented that they had not been consulted over the sale of their homeland. They also disliked the aggressive action and haughty attitude of the small group of Canadian expansionists in the Red River colony working to bring the region into Confederation. In their local newspaper, *The Nor'Wester*, these Canadians ridiculed the Métis and proclaimed Canada's right to take control of the Northwest as part of the country's "manifest destiny." The Métis reacted by occupying Upper Fort Garry, the seat of government, on November 2, establishing their own provisional government, thus gaining effective control of the Red River colony.

A family of Métis traders in camp, early 1870s. The Red River cart, built without any metal, allowed the Métis to harvest the buffalo herds, which at this point had been greatly depleted on the Canadian side of the border.

Source: Archives of Manitoba: Boundary Commission (1872–1874) 164 (N14100).

Without waiting for the announcement of the official transfer of the Red River colony to Canada on December 1, William McDougall forged his own royal proclamation, to which he attached Queen Victoria's name. On the night of November 30, he crossed the border to proclaim Canada's sovereignty over the Red River colony. He did so without knowing that the Canadian government had decided to delay taking over the territory until the dispute was resolved.

Fearing that the United States, which only two years earlier had purchased Alaska from the Russians and had clearly expressed interest in taking over the North West, might annex the area, prime minister Macdonald now acted. He dismissed William McDougall and asked the influential Bishop Alexandre Taché of the Red River colony to return from Rome, where he had been attending the Vatican Council, to assist in reaching a settlement. He also appointed Donald A. Smith of the Hudson's Bay Company to negotiate with the Métis on behalf of the Canadian government.

Riel's provisional government drew up a bill of rights in November 1869, outlining its grievances and demands. That bill became the basis for negotiations. At two very well-attended public meetings in the Red River colony held in mid-January, Smith promised the Red River colony a better deal, to be decided by a committee of Métis and the Canadian government.

Meanwhile, the Canadian expansionist party in the Red River colony took matters into its own hands, and prepared to oppose Riel's provisional government. The general store owned by John Schultz, a sometime medical doctor and merchant and the leader of the Canada party, became its headquarters. The Métis raided the store and imprisoned the Canadians. The Métis agreed to release those prisoners who promised either to leave the colony or to obey the provisional government. A few, like Schultz, refused to comply. He managed to escape from his Métis prison, by using a knife, hidden in a pudding by his wife, to cut the ropes on the windows and to lower himself out. He then gathered together supporters for an ill-fated attack on Upper

Louis Riel (seated directly in the centre) with his council, 1870. Riel and his council's resistance to Canada's attempted seizure of the Red River led to the Manitoba Act of 1870, which brought Manitoba into Confederation as the first new province.

Source: Library and Archives Canada/PA-12854; Manitoba Museum of Man and Nature/3661.

Fort Garry. The Métis captured members of the raiding party, including Thomas Scott, a virulent 28-year-old Protestant Irishman and member of the Orange Lodge.

Scott proved a difficult prisoner. He insulted and provoked his Métis guards. Riel decided to hold a Métis court to try Scott for contempt of the Métis provisional government. The court voted to execute the trouble-maker. Riel agreed, in order, he claimed, "to make Canada respect us." (Some historians have since argued that Riel complied with the court order so as to maintain his control of the Métis.) On March 4, 1870, a firing squad executed Scott.

Scott's execution turned the Métis resistance from a distant western struggle into a national crisis. Protestant Ontario now had its martyr. When a group of Scott's Red River associates arrived in Toronto to enlist support for their cause, a huge crowd assembled to hear their version of the uprising in the West:

> It would be a gross injustice to the loyal inhabitants of Red River, humiliating to our national honour, and contrary to all British traditions for our Government to receive, negotiate or meet with the emissaries of those who have robbed, imprisoned and murdered loyal Canadians, whose only fault was zeal for British institutions, whose only crime was devotion to the old flag.

Thomas Scott, executed March 4, 1870. The Scott Memorial Hall in Winnipeg was erected in his memory in Winnipeg between 1900 and 1902, by the provincial Grand Lodge of the Orange Order. See "Great Day for the Orangemen," Manitoba Free Press, July 13, 1900.

Source: Glenbow Archives/NA 576-1.

A different perception prevailed in Roman Catholic Quebec. French Canadians viewed Riel as the protector of the French-speaking Métis against an aggressive group of Canadianists from Ontario, backed by the Orange Order.

John A. Macdonald proposed a compromise. To appease the Métis and the French Canadians of Quebec, his government passed the Manitoba Act in May 1870, based on the negotiations between the Red River's three-person delegation and the Canadian government. The Red River colony could enter Confederation as a province. To satisfy Ontarians, the prime minister agreed to send immediately an armed force to the Red River colony to secure the Northwest and ensure that it did not fall into American hands.

The Manitoba Act

The Manitoba Act created the new province of Manitoba that included geographically only the 35 000 km^2 around the Red River settlement and Portage la Prairie to the west. The rest of the area became the North-West Territories. Manitoba received its own legislative assembly, four federal members of Parliament, and two senators. But, unlike the other provinces in Confederation, Ottawa denied Manitoba control over its own public lands and natural resources. The same was true of the North-West Territories. The land and resources remained under the federal government's control, to be used "for the purposes of the Dominion."

The Manitoba Act addressed the issue of linguistic and educational rights of the French-speaking population. In 1867 the Fathers of Confederation had not discussed the rights of

French Canadians outside the province of Quebec. They preferred to address the issue on an ad hoc basis when new provinces joined Confederation. Manitoba became the first new province to join, forcing Macdonald's Conservative government to address the issues of language rights and separate schools. Should French be recognized as an official language? Should separate schools be permitted in provinces with a sizable Roman Catholic population at the time of union with Canada? The Manitoba Act recognized both French and English as official languages. It also established a confessional school system on the Quebec model, with separate Protestant and Catholic divisions that would receive government funding.

Basing their opinion on the Manitoba Act, some historians have argued that the Fathers of Confederation intended to create a bilingual and bicultural country in which French-speaking Canadians would have the same linguistic and educational rights as English-speaking Canadians. Other historians disagree. Donald Creighton, for example, has held that no evidence exists that the Fathers of Confederation, particularly Macdonald, intended to create a bilingual and bicultural nation. According to Creighton, Macdonald agreed to French-language rights and separate schools only because he was being pressured by a "dictatorial Riel"[2] to act quickly; otherwise Canada might lose the Northwest to American expansionists. Creighton maintains that the "Act for the Temporary Government of Rupert's Land and the North-West Territory," drawn up in the spring of 1869, rather than the Manitoba Act, more accurately reflected Macdonald's and the Canadian government's views. This earlier act, he points out, contained no reference to separate schools.

In a rebuttal to Creighton, historian Ralph Heintzman points out that this earlier act was only temporary and therefore not expected to spell out in detail the nature of the new province.[3] Heintzman considers the Manitoba Act to be more representative of the Canadian government's views. He also goes on to argue that in its agreement on language and educational rights for French-speaking Manitobans, the Manitoba Act reflected an ongoing "spirit of Confederation" that was evident between English-speaking and French-speaking Canadians at the time of Confederation.

The Wolseley Expedition

After Manitoba's entry into Confederation tension continued in the region. In the spring of 1870, Macdonald sent out the promised military force under Lieutenant Colonel Garnet Wolseley. As the troops approached, Riel got word of their arrival and fled. Upon finding Fort Garry abandoned, Wolseley reported in his diary: "Personally, I was glad that Riel did not come out and surrender, as he at one time said he would, for I could not then have hanged him as I might have done had I taken him prisoner when in arms against his sovereign." Riel had left, convinced that he had achieved a great victory for his Métis people. He had won them provincial status, as well as land and cultural rights. Among those land rights was the agreement in the Manitoba Act to set aside a reserve of 600 000 ha for the Métis and their children.

Riel's victory proved transitory, however. Migrants from the rest of Canada, particularly Ontario, quickly moved into Manitoba and took over land once occupied by the Métis. One group of Ontarians seized Métis land on the Rivière aux Ilets de Bois and, in a symbolic gesture of defiance, renamed the river "the Boyne," after William of Orange's decisive victory over the Roman Catholics in Ireland on July 12, 1690. Ontarians soon dominated the political, economic, and social life of the new province. They worked to eliminate the land and cultural rights of the Métis population, by introducing amendments to the Manitoba Act that made it difficult for the Métis to prove that they owned the land. Discouraged, many Métis left the province and went farther west into either the North-West Territories or to the Dakotas and Montana to live.

Treaties with the First Nations

Having acquired the North West, the federal government took control of Indian affairs in the territory. First it undertook treaty negotiations with the First Nations in the region. The government adhered to the Royal Proclamation of 1763, which prohibited settlers from occupying territory that the First Nations had not first surrendered to the Crown. The Canadian government also made treaties to avoid the "Indian wars" that had occurred in the United States. Between 1871 and 1875, the government negotiated Treaties Number One to Five, affecting the Native peoples in what is now northwestern Ontario, Manitoba, and southern Saskatchewan. In 1876, Treaty Number Six was signed with the Cree of present-day central Saskatchewan and Alberta. The last of the treaties on the plains, Treaty Number Seven, followed in 1877 with the Blackfoot-speaking nations and the Sarcee (T'suu Tina) and Stoneys.

   According to the government's interpretation of the treaties, the First Nations agreed to "cede, release, surrender, and yield up to the Government … all their rights, titles, and privileges whatsoever" to the lands in question forever in return for certain reserve lands, amenities, and

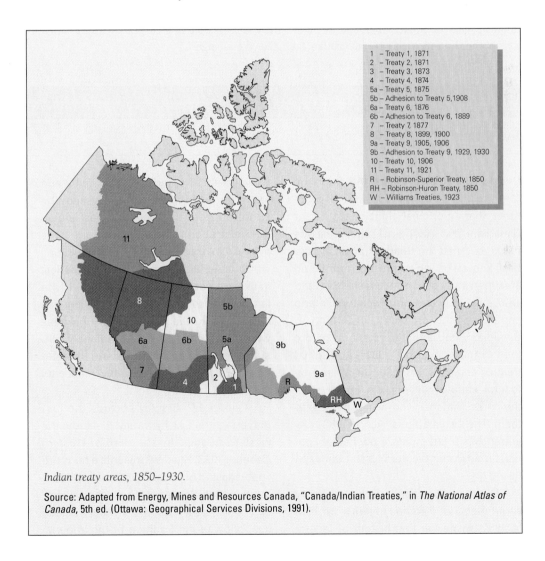

1 – Treaty 1, 1871
2 – Treaty 2, 1871
3 – Treaty 3, 1873
4 – Treaty 4, 1874
5a – Treaty 5, 1875
5b – Adhesion to Treaty 5, 1908
6a – Treaty 6, 1876
6b – Adhesion to Treaty 6, 1889
7 – Treaty 7, 1877
8 – Treaty 8, 1899, 1900
9a – Treaty 9, 1905, 1906
9b – Adhesion to Treaty 9, 1929, 1930
10 – Treaty 10, 1906
11 – Treaty 11, 1921
R – Robinson-Superior Treaty, 1850
RH – Robinson-Huron Treaty, 1850
W – Williams Treaties, 1923

Indian treaty areas, 1850–1930.

Source: Adapted from Energy, Mines and Resources Canada, "Canada/Indian Treaties," in *The National Atlas of Canada*, 5th ed. (Ottawa: Geographical Services Divisions, 1991).

the right to fish and hunt on Crown lands. In the case of Treaty Six, the federal government also promised assistance in the event of "any pestilence" or "general famine," along with a "medicine chest" to be kept by every Indian agent. The Cree insisted on these additional clauses, as already they felt the effects of disease and declining buffalo herds. The Blackfoot in the Treaty Seven area envisioned the treaty as a pact of friendship, peace, and mutual support between the two parties. They did not intend on giving up their sovereignty. Some of the Cree in Treaty Six believed the agreements allowed the newcomers only the use, not the ownership, of their land. First Nations people in general saw the treaties as their only hope of survival against the rapid encroachment and takeover by white settlers. Canadian officials, on the other hand, saw the treaties and the establishment of Indian reserves as the first step toward the assimilation and ultimate extinction of the First Nations people.

Having acquired Native land, the government next established the Indian Act in 1876, amended in 1880, which regulated all aspects of First Nations peoples' lives. It legally viewed the First Nations peoples as minors or special wards of the Crown, without citizenship privileges. Government officials saw the reserves as training grounds for entrance into the larger society. As John A. Macdonald, its first minister, pointed out, "The great aim of our legislature has been to do away with the tribal system and assimilate the Indian people in all aspects with the inhabitants of the Dominion, as speedily as they are fit for the change."

WHERE HISTORIANS DISAGREE

Interpreting Treaties One to Seven in Western Canada

Over the past thirty years the Supreme Court of Canada has upheld the argument that Aboriginal rights exist under Canadian law. Aboriginal rights include those outlined in treaties, possibly the best known of which are the numbered Treaties 1 to 7, signed between 1871 and 1877 in what is now northwestern Ontario and the prairie provinces. According to Canadian judicial interpretation—before the Constitution of 1982—Aboriginal treaties could be amended or altered by federal statute, without the approval of the First Nations who were parties to them. The Constitutional Act of 1982 now entrenches treaty rights. How have historians interpreted the numbered treaties of the 1870s?

Duncan Campbell Scott, deputy superintendent of Indian affairs from 1913 to 1932, wrote the first history of federal Indian administration in 1914. The federal civil servant stressed the honourable and just nature of Indian policy: "As may be surmised from the record of past Indian administration, the government was always anxious to fulfil the obligations which were laid upon it by these treaties. In every point, and adhering closely to the letter of the compact, the government has discharged to the present every promise which was made to the Indians."[1] No subtleties of interpretation here; the treaties were fair and honourably respected by Ottawa.

George F.C. Stanley became the first university-trained historian to study the western treaties. In *The Birth of Western Canada* (1936) Stanley presents a far more sophisticated and rigorous analysis of the treaties than Scott, yet he reached a similar conclusion: "On the whole, Canada has followed the tradition of the Imperial Government in its relations with native tribes, and has endeavoured to deal fairly with her aboriginal wards."[2] For the next thirty-five years or so, historians essentially accepted the "honourable and just" interpretation of the treaties—or ignored the agreements altogether; in fact no real historical debate about the western treaties emerged until the 1970s.

Much of the new criticism came from First Nations people frustrated that their side of the story had not received attention. In 1969, Harold Cardinal, a young Cree politician and author, published *The Unjust Society*, a fiery indictment of Canadian Indian policy: "The truth of the matter is that Canadian Indians simply got swindled. Our forefathers got taken by slick-talking, fork-tongued cheats."[3] First Nation oral traditions of the treaties also appeared, such as the interviews in the timely book edited by Richard Price, *The Spirit of the Alberta Indian Treaties.*[4] More recently the Treaty Seven Elders and Tribal Council have made available First Nation accounts of Treaty Seven in what is now southern Alberta, *The True Spirit and Original Intent of Treaty 7.*[5]

Other historians have joined in the debate.[6] Basically they argue that the First Nations were active agents in the treaty process. The First Nations recognized that it was in their interest to secure the best terms possible in the treaty, that schools and a helping hand to adjust to farming would assist them. Problems arose, however, when the federal government did not fulfill the First Nations' oral understandings of the treaties.

In 1983 George F.G. Stanley reentered the debate. He still dismissed the thought that there were deliberate attempts to deceive the First Nations during the treaty negotiations. Instead he saw the problems as arising from the misunderstandings of treaty terms. "The probability that promises were made to the Indians, which they remember and the Whites have forgotten, seems strong."[7] In short, a historical question that seemed in the early twentieth century to be well understood is now strongly debated. A new reading of the old documentary evidence and the availability of Aboriginal oral testimony, as well as a new postcolonial context for discussion, have contributed to this debate.

---

1   Duncan Campbell Scott, "Indian Affairs, 1867–1912," in Adam Short and Arthur G. Doughty, eds., *Canada and Its Provinces* (Toronto: Glasgow, Brook and Co., 1914), p. 600.

2   George F.G. Stanley, *The Birth of Western Canada* (London: Longmans, Green, 1936; Toronto: University of Toronto Press, 1960), p. 214.

3   Harold Cardinal, *The Unjust Society* (Edmonton: Hurtig, 1969), p. 39.

4   Richard Price, ed. *The Spirit of the Alberta Indian Treaties* (Montreal: Institute for Research on Public Policy, 1979; 3rd ed., Edmonton: University of Alberta Press, 1999).

5   Treaty Seven Elders and Tribal Council, *The True Spirit and Original Intent of Treaty 7* (Montreal/Kingston: McGill-Queen's University Press, 1996).

6   To list several of them: John Leonard Taylor, in his essays, "Canada's Northwest Indian Policy in the 1870s: Traditional Premises and Necessary Interventions"; and "Two Views of Treaties Six and Seven," in Price, ed., *Spirit*, pp. 3–46; John L. Tobias, "Canada's Subjugation of the Plains Cree, 1879–1885," *Canadian Historical Review*, 64(4) (1983): 519–48; David Hall, "'A Serene Atmosphere'? Treaty 1 Revisited," *Canadian Journal of Native Studies*, 4(2) (1984): 321–58; Jean Friesen, "Grant Me Wherewith to Make My Living," in Kerry Avel and Jean Friesen, eds., *Aboriginal Resource Use in Canada: Historical and Legal Aspects* (Winnipeg: University of Manitoba Press, 1991), pp. 141–56.

7   George F.G. Stanley, "As Long as the Sun Shines and Water Flows: An Historical Comment," in Ian A.L. Getty and Antoine S. Lussier, eds., *As Long as the Sun Shines and Water Flows* (Vancouver: University of British Columbia Press, 1983), p. 16.

Future Prime Minister W.L. Mackenzie King with two Plains First Nations people, taken on his western trip of 1905. King later served as leader of the federal Liberal party for 30 years, and prime minister for 21. As Liberal leader and prime minister he showed little interest in Aboriginal issues.

Source: Library and Archives Canada/C14157.

Both Conservative and Liberal governments endorsed the goal of "enfranchisement," or the relinquishment of Indian status by granting full citizenship privileges. Adult First Nations males, deemed of good character, free of debt, and fluent in English or French were eligible. They could, after a probationary period of three years, apply to relinquish their treaty and statutory rights under the Indian Act, as well as their right to live in the reserve community. In return, they gained British citizenship with all legal privileges including the right to vote, as well as private ownership of their share of band reserve lands and funds. Initially, the First Nations peoples of western Canada were excluded from this procedure because the government considered them still too "uncivilized."

Few of Canada's First Nations people agreed to enfranchisement, because it meant abandoning their reserves and relinquishing their traditional culture. In fact, only 102 First Nations people applied and were enfranchised between Confederation and the end of World War I. Status Indian women who married non-Indians (whites, Métis, or Native people not governed by the Indian Act) had no choice in the matter. Under the Indian Act, they lost their Indian status automatically when they married.

The federal government also attempted to assimilate the Native people by outlawing cultural practices. Particularly offensive from the government's perspective was the potlatch, the giving away of gifts in ceremonies, because it reinforced traditional Native beliefs and practices. The government used various tactics, including making it an offence in the amended Indian Act of 1884 "to encourage or participate in the potlatch." It instructed Indian agents to collect evidence to use in court cases, played off Christian Native converts who opposed the potlatch against traditionalists, and used extortion to pry ceremonial regalia from West Coast Native people. In spite of these efforts to end it, the potlatch survived and, in some areas, continued to flourish. The same held true for the Sun (Thirst) dances. While some bands altered certain practices to prevent a total ban on the dances, they prevented the government from eliminating such customs.

Schools became the third, and most draconian, of the assimilation schemes. Ottawa gave Christian missionaries control of the reserves and residential schools. Among residential schools

Before and after: Propaganda photos used to promote the benefits of Native residential schools. From Thompson Ferrier, Indian Education in the North West *(Toronto: Department of Missionary Literature of the Methodist Church, 1906), pp. 4–5.]*

Source: Library and Archives Canada/C-104585 and C-104586.

were industrial schools that taught skills in agriculture and trades for boys and household skills for girls between the ages of 14 and 18. The first three were established in western Canada in 1883–84, at Qu'Appelle, Dunbow (just east of High River), and Battleford. By the turn of the century, 20 such schools operated in the West.

Historian J.R. Miller has characterized these schools as "ineffective, harsh, unsafe."[4] Church workers taught the Native children in English or, in many parts of southern Quebec, in French, to become Christians, to denounce their own cultural traditions, and to assimilate into "white" society, especially to become farmers. A small number, particularly in Eastern Canada, adjusted; most did not. In Western Canada First Nations farms consisted of a small parcel of land, not always of good quality, and a few rudimentary implements—what historian Sarah Carter has described as "two acres and a cow."[5]

British Columbia Enters Confederation

With the Northwest secured, the Canadian government began negotiating with the colony of British Columbia to join Confederation. (Although First Nations constituted the majority of the population in this Pacific coast colony, no one thought to consult them about Confederation.) Over the years, two separate colonies had evolved, one on Vancouver Island and the other on the mainland. In 1866, the two united into the single colony of British Columbia. The united colony now had three options as to their future destiny: remain a separate British colony, join the United States, or unite with Canada.

Economically, British Columbia was tied closely to the United States. Many of the colony's business firms were branches of American establishments. Much of its trade of raw materials was to the south. In addition, the colony communicated with the outside world via the United States. American vessels, for example, provided the only regular steamship service. Mail required both local and American stamps on letters abroad, since it went via San Francisco. When railways made transcontinental travel feasible, it was an American line, the Union Pacific, completed in 1869, that provided British Columbia with connections to the Atlantic seaboard.

British loyalties, however, remained firm. According to historian Hugh Johnston, the non-Native population saw British Columbia as "a British outpost on the edge of an American frontier."[6] The Royal Navy provided protection. The colonial government followed British parliamentary tradition. The colony also had a predominance of British politicians, from the governor to the majority of representatives in the legislative council. By contrast the Americans, although large in numbers, had relatively few supporters in government.

While British Columbia had strong economic ties with the United States, and even stronger political and cultural ones with Britain, it had little contact at all with Canada. Few Canadians resided in the colony. Nor did any overland route exist to link this West Coast colony to the rest of British North America. Nevertheless, the small Canadian community that did reside in the colony constituted an influential and vocal minority: Amor de Cosmos ("Lover of the Universe," alias William Smith) became premier in 1872, while John Robson headed the Confederation movement in the colonial assembly. Prime Minister Macdonald corresponded with these pro-Confederation politicians. As well, Macdonald had the British government appoint Anthony Musgrave, the governor of Newfoundland and a known supporter of Canadian Confederation, as the new governor of British Columbia when Governor Seymour, who had opposed union, died in 1869. The Colonial Office agreed, since the British government wanted to lessen its commitment to its West Coast colony without losing it to the United States.

Britain valued British Columbia as an important link in its "all red route to the Orient"—an imperial trading network tying Britain to India and China through British territory. By convincing British Columbia to join Confederation, Britain could achieve both objectives. William Gladstone, Britain's prime minister at the time, argued that Victoria, as "the San Francisco of British North America," could achieve greater commercial and political power as part of Canada than as "the capital of the isolated colony of British Columbia."

British Columbia's settler population was very small in the 1870s. This photo, taken outside the legislative buildings in Victoria, shows the entire British Columbia civil service in 1878.

Source: British Columbia Archives/HP-17826.

The Canadian Government Negotiates

Soon after taking office, Governor Musgrave appointed a three-member delegation to open up negotiations with the Canadian government. The committee drew up its list of demands. British Columbia would consider joining Confederation if the Canadian government agreed to: assume the colony's $1 million debt; grant responsible government to the province; undertake a public works program; and complete a road to link British Columbia with the rest of the country.

The British Columbia delegation found a receptive audience in Ottawa. A committee headed by George-Étienne Cartier agreed to all the demands. Ottawa would assume the provincial debt and request Britain to implement responsible government. It would undertake a public works program to include underwriting a loan to build a dry dock and maintain a naval station at Esquimalt. In addition, the Canadian government promised not just a road but a railway, to be begun within two years of British Columbia's entry into Confederation and completed within ten years—a most ambitious promise. The United States, with ten times Canada's population, had only recently, and with great difficulty, built its first transcontinental railway.

On July 20, 1871, British Columbia joined Confederation. Canada now stretched from the Atlantic Ocean to the Pacific Ocean. In the same year, by the Treaty of Washington, Britain and the United States confirmed the borders between Canada and the United States, ending the threat of an American seizure of lands above the 49th parallel.

The agreement with British Columbia left one important issue unresolved, that of Aboriginal lands. At the time of British Columbia's entry into Confederation, land treaties had been concluded for only a tiny portion of Vancouver Island. In 1873, the federal government requested British Columbia to acknowledge Aboriginal land title and to increase the allotment of reserve land for a family of five from 10 to 80 acres (4 to 32 ha). Premier George Walkem objected, claiming that the Native peoples already had enough land. His government reflected the prevailing attitude of the time that the Native peoples never owned the land, that land ownership was a right reserved for non-Native settlers only.

An Unwilling Newfoundland and a Reluctant Prince Edward Island

Only the British colonies of Newfoundland and Prince Edward Island remained as potential new provinces. Of the two, Newfoundland seemed more likely to join. Although the colony had not sent representatives to the Charlottetown Conference in September 1864, it did send two representatives—Frederick B.T. Carter, leader of the opposition, and Ambrose Shea, Speaker of the House of Assembly—to the Quebec Conference a month later. Both men became converts to Confederation, especially after hearing the generous financial terms that Macdonald and the other representatives from the Canadas promised Newfoundland in Confederation. But neither they nor the governor of Newfoundland, H.W. Hoyes, could persuade a dubious public, especially the merchants in St. John's, and the Roman Catholic population, about the benefits of Confederation.

Opposition to Confederation in Newfoundland

In the 1860s, Newfoundland had little association with the other British North American colonies. Many Newfoundlanders believed that their island's destiny lay to the east—the Atlantic Ocean and Britain—rather than to the west in a transcontinental nation. Their economy was based on cod fishing and sealing. Eighty percent of the island's working population earned its

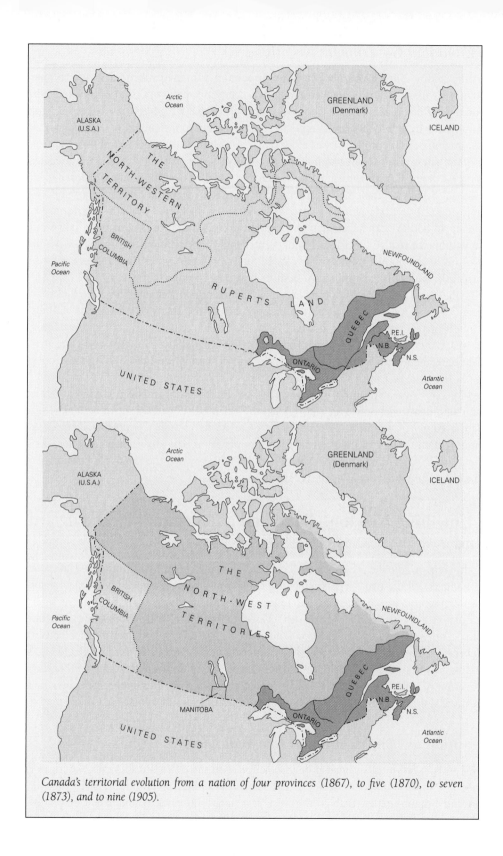

Canada's territorial evolution from a nation of four provinces (1867), to five (1870), to seven (1873), and to nine (1905).

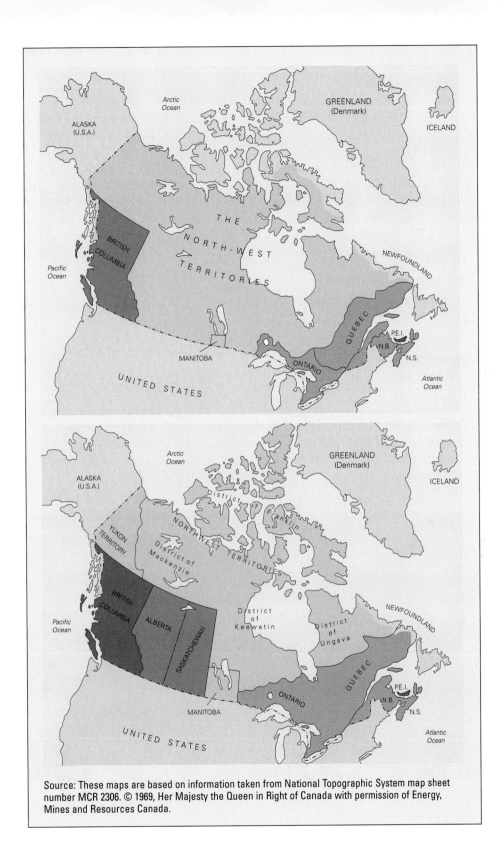

Source: These maps are based on information taken from National Topographic System map sheet number MCR 2306. © 1969, Her Majesty the Queen in Right of Canada with permission of Energy, Mines and Resources Canada.

living from the sea. Newfoundlanders traded with Britain and the West Indies, not with British North America.

Newfoundland Roman Catholics opposed joining Confederation because they feared that a wider union would offset their favourable position in the colony. They had their own government-funded schools, which many believed a union with "Protestant Ontario" might threaten. Also, Irish Catholics saw Confederation as comparable to the reviled union of Ireland and England.

Union with Canada became the chief campaign issue in the election of 1869. Charles Fox Bennett, a St. John's merchant, headed the anti-Confederation faction. He pointed out that Confederation would result in the imposition of Canadian taxes on boats and fishing gear, and in exploitive competition from the mainland. He reminded Newfoundlanders of Nova Scotia's opposition to Confederation, while injecting his own strong dose of local Newfoundland nationalism. As one contemporary folk song ran:

> *Would you barter the rights that your fathers have won?*
> *No! Let them descend from father to son,*
> *For a few thousand dollars Canadian gold,*
> *Don't let it be said that our birthright was sold.*
> *Newfoundland's face turns to Britain*
> *Her back to the Gulf.*
> *Come near at your peril*
> *Canadian wolf!*

Pro-Confederationists appeared on the defensive. They could only present union with Canada as an uncertain alternative to the current depressed economy of Newfoundland rather than as a bold positive move. Furthermore, an improved sealing and fishing season in 1869 worked against cause.

St. John's, around 1890. Its harbour and the heavily settled part of the island faced the Atlantic Ocean and Britain, not the North American continent and Canada.

Source: Provincial Archives of Newfoundland and Labrador/B4-25.

In the end, Newfoundlanders rejected Confederation, with 19 seats in the colonial assembly going to anti-confederates and only eight to confederates. According to one account, as soon as the election results became known,

> the fishermen and mechanics of St. John's ... put together a large coffin labelled "Confederation," which was placed on a vehicle draped in black, and this was drawn by scores of willing hands through the town, headed by a band playing the Dead March, and escorted by an immense crowd, to the head of the harbour, where a grave was dug below highwater mark and the coffin solemnly interred.

That defeat effectively ended the Confederation debate in Newfoundland for the next 25 years.

Opposition to Confederation in Prince Edward Island

Initially, Prince Edward Island opposed Confederation more strongly than did Newfoundland. Its representatives at the Charlottetown and Quebec conferences had pressed the Canadian delegates the furthest on the possible negative effects of Confederation for the Maritime region. Furthermore, only recently had some islanders succeeded in freeing themselves from absentee landlords who had extracted onerous rents from them. They had no desire to substitute a new set of landlords—Canadian proprietors—for the ones they had just lost. Even pressure through the Colonial Office failed to persuade the islanders to join Confederation. If anything, economic union with the United States had more appeal to many islanders, who saw it as a possible return to the prosperity the island had enjoyed during the period of the Reciprocity Treaty (1854–66). In 1868, American congressman Benjamin Butler visited Charlottetown to negotiate a reciprocal trade agreement.

Fear of American annexation of Prince Edward Island led Prime Minister Macdonald to reopen negotiations. Late in 1869 he extended another invitation to the islanders to join Confederation. He agreed to more generous financial terms than in 1864; guaranteed communication and transportation links with the mainland; and promised islanders assistance in buying off the remaining British absentee landlords who still owned large tracts. At the same time, the Canadian prime minister convinced Britain to block a reciprocal trade agreement between Prince Edward Island and the United States. Still the islanders resisted.

By the early 1870s, however, financial problems on Prince Edward Island made Confederation more appealing. A coalition government headed by J.C. Pope had embarked in 1871 on an ambitious railway-building scheme that threatened to push the island into bankruptcy. In 1872, work on the railway ceased for lack of funds. The Union Bank of Prince Edward Island, which held large numbers of the railway debentures, feared a financial collapse and appealed to Britain for assistance. London financiers replied that the island would be in a better negotiating position if it joined Canada.

This time Charlottetown approached Ottawa. In early 1873, the Canadian government renewed its earlier offer: to assume the island's debt; to pay the annual interest on an $800 000 imperial loan; to provide a special subsidy of $45 000 to buy out the absentee landowners and thus bring all land under provincial control; and to take over the railway guarantee. As well, it promised to establish and maintain an efficient all-year steamer service between the island and the mainland.

In the election of April 1873, the choice became Confederation or the imposition of increased taxes to pay off the debt. In the end, provincial debt and railways were the real "Fathers of Confederation" in Prince Edward Island. On July 1, 1873, Prince Edward Island joined the

Dominion of Canada as its seventh province. The Charlottetown newspaper the *Patriot* recorded the public's response:

> On Tuesday, July 1st, whether for weal or woe, Prince Edward Island became a province of the Dominion of Canada. At 12 o'clock noon, the Dominion flag was run up on the flag staffs at Government House and the Colonial Building, and a salute of 21 guns was fired from St. George's battery and from HMS Spartan now in port. The church and city bells rang out a lively peal, and the volunteers under review at the city park fired a feu de joie. So far as powder and metal could do it, there was for a short time a terrible din. But among the people who thronged the streets there was no enthusiasm.

With the exception of Newfoundland and the Arctic Archipelago, Macdonald's Conservative government had now completed the consolidation of British North America.

Initially, Canada had no interest in the Arctic Archipelago, seeing it only as a frozen wasteland. Britain had secured a prior claim to the region as a result of the sixteenth- and seventeenth-century journeys of Martin Frobisher, John Davis, and William Baffin, as well as the mid-nineteenth-century British naval expeditions in search of Sir John Franklin, whose party of more than 100 had disappeared in the mid-1840s in an attempt to find the Northwest Passage. In July 1880, the British government transferred title of its Arctic "possessions" to Canada, once again without bothering to consult the First Nations peoples in the region.

The Alert, *a ship in the British expedition led by Captain George Nares, by an ice floe, Dobbin Bay, 1875–1876. The* Alert *was the first vessel to land on the shores of northern Ellesmere Island.*

Source: Library and Archives Canada/C52521.

Three oceans, one country—in just thirteen years, Canada had become Britain's largest colony. In the first decade after Confederation, the Dominion of Canada acquired three new provinces and an enormous geographical area. Fear of American encroachment was a factor in its rapid expansion, but internal economic pressures such as the need for more land for agricultural development, the necessity of east–west trade, and a growing railway-building program also contributed. By 1880, Canada had become a transcontinental nation. Now came the challenge of working out new Dominion–provincial relations, reconciling regional differences, and creating a Dominion-wide economic policy.

NOTES

1. Chester Martin, *Dominion Lands Policy* (Toronto: McClelland & Stewart, 1973), p. 9.

2. Donald G. Creighton, "Macdonald, Confederation, and the West," in *Towards the Discovery of Canada: Selected Essays* (Toronto: Macmillan, 1972), p. 234.

3. Ralph Heintzman, "The Spirit of Confederation: Professor Creighton, Biculturalism, and the Use of History," *Canadian Historical Review* 52 (1971): 267–68.

4. J.R. Miller, *Skyscrapers Hide the Heavens: A History of Indian–White Relations in Canada* (Toronto: University of Toronto Press, 1989), p. 198.

5. Sarah Carter, "Two Acres and a Cow: 'Peasant' Farming for the Indians of the Northwest, 1889–97," *Canadian Historical Review* 70(1) (March 1989): 27.

6. Hugh Johnston, "Native People, Settlers and Sojourners, 1871–1916," in H.J.M. Johnston, ed., *The Pacific Province: A History of British Columbia* (Vancouver: Douglas & McIntyre, 1996), p. 177.

BEYOND THE BOOK

Weblinks

Newfoundland: The Confederation Debate
http://www.heritage.nf.ca/law/debate.html
An account with digitized newspaper images and photographs of Newfoundland's initial rejection of Confederation.

Canadian Illustrated News and the Red River Resistance
http://www.lac-bac.gc.ca/cin/026019-202-e.html
Articles from 1869 and 1870 in the *Canadian Illustrated News* regarding the Red River resistance.

Numbered Treaties Overview
http://www.canadiana.org/citm/specifique/numtreatyoverview_e.html
Contains digitized texts of all numbered treaties with First Nations.

1870 Wolseley Expedition Route and Google Earth
http://www.mhs.mb.ca/data/maps/huyshe/index.shtml
View the path of the 1870 Wolseley Expedition using Google Earth software. Visit http://www.mhs.mb.ca/data/maps/huyshe/index.shtml for help if necessary.

British Columbia Terms of Union
http://www.solon.org/Constitutions/Canada/English/bctu.html
Text of the original document detailing the terms of union under which British Columbia was admitted into Confederation.

The Manitoba Act, 1870
http://www.canadiana.org/ECO/mtq?display=9_03428+0669
The full text of the Manitoba Act of 1870. A compromise between the Canadian government and the Métis on Rupert's Land, this Act brought Manitoba into Confederation as the first new province.

Films & Novels

Canada: A People's History—Episode 9: From Sea to Sea. Directed by Jim Williamson. 2001.

BIBLIOGRAPHY

Students interested in the Atlantic region's resistance to Confederation should consult Ged Martin, *Britain and the Origins of Canadian Confederation, 1837–67* (London: Macmillan, 1995); and his edited collection, *The Causes of Canadian Confederation* (Fredericton: Acadiensis, 1990). For Nova Scotia also see R.H. Campbell, "The Repeal Agitation in Nova Scotia, 1867–1869," *Nova Scotia Historical Society Collections* 25 (1942): 95–130; George Rawlyk, ed., *The Atlantic Provinces and the Problems of Confederation* (St. John's: Breakwater, 1979); and Colin D. Howell, "Nova Scotia's Protest Tradition and the Search for a Meaningful Federalism," in David J. Bercuson, ed., *Canada and the Burden of Unity* (Toronto: Macmillan, 1977), pp. 169–91. Joseph Howe's views are presented in J. Murray Beck, *Joseph Howe*, vol. 2, *The Briton Becomes Canadian, 1848–1873* (Montreal/Kingston: McGill-Queen's University Press, 1983), and in Beck's booklet *Joseph Howe: Anti-Confederate* (Ottawa: Canadian Historical Association, 1965). A very good summary of historical developments in the Atlantic region since 1867 is E.R. Forbes and D.A. Muise, eds., *The Atlantic Provinces in Confederation* (Toronto: University of Toronto Press, 1993). On Newfoundland's resistance to Confederation see James Hiller, "Confederation Defeated: The Newfoundland Election of 1869," in *Newfoundland in the Nineteenth and Twentieth Centuries: Essays in Interpretation* (Toronto: University of Toronto Press, 1980), pp. 67–94; and the relevant section in Frederick W. Rowe, *A History of Newfoundland and Labrador* (Toronto: McGraw-Hill Ryerson, 1980). Francis Bolger reviews Prince Edward Island's decision to join Canada in *Prince Edward Island and Confederation* (Charlottetown: St. Dunstan's University Press, 1964). Popular studies include Donald Weale and Harry Baglole, *The Island and Confederation: The End of an Era* (Charlottetown: Williams & Crue, 1973); and the chapter entitled "Confederation" in D.O. Baldwin, *Land of the Red Soil: A Popular History of Prince Edward Island*, rev. ed. (Charlottetown: Ragweed Press, 1998). Ronald Tallman, "Annexation in the Maritimes? The Butler Mission to Charlottetown," *Dalhousie Review* 53 (1973): 97–112, shows the American influence, which almost caused Prince Edward Island to reject Confederation.

Alvin C. Gluek, *Minnesota and the Manifest Destiny of the Canadian Northwest: A Study in Canadian–American Relations* (Toronto: University of Toronto Press, 1965), examines American annexationist sentiments toward the Canadian Northwest. On the Riel resistance, see W.L. Morton's introduction to *Alexander Begg's Red River Journal* (Toronto: Champlain Society, 1956); see also George F.G. Stanley, *The Birth of Western Canada* (London: Longmans, Green, 1936; rep. Toronto: University of Toronto Press, 1960), and Stanley's *Louis Riel* (Toronto: Ryerson Press, 1963); and J.M. Bumsted, *The Red River Rebellion* (Winnipeg: Watson & Dwyer, 1996). On the military expedition see George F.G. Stanley, *Toil and Trouble: Military Expeditions to Red River* (Toronto: Dundurn Press, 1989). Hartwell Bowsfield's *Louis Riel: The Rebel and the Hero* (Toronto: Oxford University Press, 1971) is a short popular biography. Bowsfield has also edited a collection of articles on Riel entitled *Louis Riel: Selected Readings* (Toronto: Copp Clark Pitman, 1988). All of Riel's writings have been edited by George F.G. Stanley et al., *The Collected Writings of Louis Riel*, 5 vols. (Edmonton: University of Alberta Press, 1985). On Manitoba's entry into Confederation see W.L. Morton, *Manitoba: A History* (Toronto: University of Toronto Press, 1957); Donald G. Creighton, "John A. Macdonald, Confederation and the Canadian West," *Historical and Scientific Society of Manitoba*, 3rd series, no. 23 (1966–67), reprinted in Donald G. Creighton, *Towards the Discovery of Canada: Selected Essays* (Toronto: Macmillan, 1972), pp. 229–37; and Ralph Heintzman, "The Spirit of Confederation: Professor Creighton, Biculturalism, and the Use of History," *Canadian Historical Review* 52 (1971): 245–75. Three studies on the Métis in the Red River and Manitoba in the late nineteenth century are Thomas Flanagan, *Métis Lands in Manitoba* (Calgary: University of Calgary Press, 1991); Frits Pannekoek, *A Snug Little Flock: The Social Origins of the Riel Resistance 1869–70* (Winnipeg: Watson & Dwyer, 1991); and Gerhard Ens, *Homeland to Hinterland: The Changing Worlds of the Red River Métis in the Nineteenth Century* (Toronto: University of Toronto Press, 1996). Sarah Carter's *Aboriginal People and Colonizers of Western Canada to 1800* (Toronto: University of Toronto Press, 1999) is a useful summary of developments in the Red River and on the Prairies.

Useful surveys of First Nations relations with Canada that cover this period are J.R. Miller, *Skyscrapers Hide the Heavens: A History of Indian–White Relations in Canada*, 3rd ed. (Toronto: University of Toronto Press, 2000); Olive P. Dickason, *Canada's First Nations: A History of Founding Peoples from Earliest Times* (Don Mills, Ont.: Oxford, 2002); A.J. Ray, *I Have Lived Here Since the World Began* (Toronto: Key Porter, 1996); and his *The Canadian Fur Trade in the Industrial Age* (Toronto: University of Toronto Press, 1990). See as well J.R. Miller, *Canada and the Aboriginal Peoples 1867–1927*, CHA Historical Booklet No. 57 (Ottawa, 1997).

On the last numbered treaties on the Plains, see Richard Price, ed., *The Spirit of the Alberta Indian Treaties*, 3rd ed. (Edmonton: University of Alberta Press, 1999), which contains valuable essays and transcripts of interviews made in the mid-1970s with Native elders. Jean Friesen provides a modern view of the treaties in "Magnificent Gifts: The Treaties of the Indians of the Northwest, 1869–70," *Transactions of the Royal Society of Canada*, series 5, vol. 1 (1986): 41–51.

Arthur J. Ray, Jim Miller, and Frank Tough have written a recent study, *Bounty and Benevolence: A History of Saskatchewan Treaties* (Montreal/Kingston: McGill-Queen's University Press, 2000). In *Indian Treaty-Making Policy in the United States and Canada, 1867–1877* (Toronto: University of Toronto Press, 2001), Jill St. Germain reviews American and Canadian experiences. An examination of the white settlers' perspective on land settlement through the use of law can be found in Sherene H. Razack, *Race, Space and the Law: Unmapping a White Settler Society* (Toronto: Between the Lines, 2002).

Several good biographies of prairie chiefs have been published by Hugh A. Dempsey: *Crowfoot* (Edmonton: Hurtig, 1972), *Red Crow* (Saskatoon: Western Producer Prairie Books, 1980), and *Big Bear* (Vancouver: Douglas & McIntyre, 1984). Dempsey established the troubled context of the early 1870s on the northern plains in *Firewater: The Impact of the Whisky Trade on the Blackfoot Nation* (Calgary: Fifth House, 2002). For Big Bear see as well J.R. Miller, *Big Bear (Mistahimusqua)* (Toronto: ECW Press, 1996). Edward Ahenakew's *Voice of the Plains Cree* (Toronto: McClelland & Stewart, 1973) provides a valuable Native assessment of conditions for the First Nations of the Canadian prairies in the early twentieth century. Shorter treatments of these and other First Nations leaders appear in the *Dictionary of Canadian Biography*, vols. 11, *1881 to 1890* (1982), 12, *1891 to 1900* (1990), 13, *1901 to 1910* (1994), and 14, *1911 to 1920* (1998) (Toronto: University of Toronto Press).

Indian policy is reviewed by Brian Titley in the early chapters of his *A Narrow Vision: Duncan Campbell Scott and the Administration of Indian Affairs in Canada* (Vancouver: University of British Columbia Press, 1987). The government's farming policy for the Native peoples is outlined in Sarah Carter, *Lost Harvests: Prairie Indian Reserve Farmers and Government Policy* (Montreal/Kingston: McGill-Queen's University Press, 1990). A good case study of an eastern Canadian Indian reserve in the late nineteenth century is Hélène Bédard's *Les Montagnais et la réserve de Betsiamites: 1850–1900* (Quebec: Institut québécois de recherche sur la culture, 1988). Two historical studies of Indian residential schools are: J.R. Miller, *Shingwauk's Vision: A History of Native Residential Schools* (Toronto: University of Toronto Press, 1996); and John S. Milloy, *A National Crime: The Canadian Government and the Residential School System 1879–1986* (Winnipeg: University of Manitoba Press, 1999).

On British Columbia and Confederation see Margaret Ormsby, *British Columbia: A History* (Toronto: Macmillan, 1958), and Ormsby's "Canada and the New British Columbia," *Canadian Historical Association Report* (1948): 74–85. W. George Shelton's *British Columbia and Confederation* (Victoria: Morriss Printing [for the University of Victoria], 1967) is a worthwhile collection of essays. See also Jean Barman, *The West Beyond the West: A History of British Columbia*, rev. ed. (Toronto: University of Toronto Press, 1996) and Hugh J.M. Johnston, ed., *The Pacific Province: A History of British Columbia* (Vancouver: Douglas & McIntyre, 1996).

For maps and charts see L.R. Gentilcore et al., eds., *Historical Atlas of Canada*, vol. 2, *The Land Transformed, 1800–1891* (Toronto: University of Toronto Press, 1993).

A "NATIONAL POLICY"?

TIME LINE

1868	Founding of the Canada First Movement
1871	Joseph Guibord affair continues
1872	Dominion Lands Act passed
1873	North-West Mounted Police (NWMP) established Pacific Scandal Liberal party comes to power under Alexander Mackenzie
1875	Supreme Court of Canada established
1876	Alexander Graham Bell invents the telephone in Brantford, Ontario
1878	Conservatives re-elected under John A. Macdonald
1879	National Policy of high tariff established
1880	Canadian Pacific Railway Company formed
1885	Completion of the Canadian Pacific Railway Head tax imposed on Chinese immigrants
1896	Liberal party comes to power under Wilfrid Laurier Beginning of major wave of immigration
1897	British preferential tariff established as part of the Liberals' national policy
1901	First transatlantic wireless signal received by Marconi at Signal Hill, St. John's, Newfoundland

In 1874, Edward Blake, the premier of Ontario and future leader of the Liberal party, identified the challenge facing Canada: "The future of Canada depends very much upon the cultivation of a national spirit." Over a century and a half later, the challenge of creating a national spirit in such a large and diverse country remains the one constant in Canadian life.

In the late nineteenth century no agreement even existed on the definition of a Canadian. When French-speakers referred to "les Canadiens," they spoke of themselves alone. They called English-speakers *les Anglais*. British Canadians, in turn, considered themselves the only Canadians and termed those speaking French "French Canadians." The Native peoples did not use the term "Canadians" to describe themselves because they had their own designations for their own nations, such as Dene, Anishinabeg (Ojibwa), or Innu (Montagnais), names that meant "people" or "human beings" in their languages. Clearly the normal basis of national unity—common language, religion, or ethnic origin—did not apply to Canada. Nor did geography or history, both of which tended to divide rather than unite Canadians.

Could common economic goals and interests unite Canadians? John A. Macdonald's Conservative government believed so. In 1879, his party proposed a Dominion-wide economic policy of nation building based on a "National Policy" or national tariff to protect Canada's infant industries. Once in place, the Conservatives believed, the tariff would provide the capital to pay the expenses of building the transcontinental railway. The railway, in turn, would link an industrialized East with the soon-to-be-developed agricultural West. The growth of central Canadian industry, the settlement of the West, and the building of the transcontinental railway would create a nation. After 1896, the Liberals under Wilfrid Laurier implemented their own version of the Conservative's national policy. The shaping of this national policy for the benefit of the business interests of central Canada created discontent in western and eastern Canada and among the working class in all regions of the country. As well, the conformist attitude of the dominant British-Canadian elite created resentment among the new ethnic Canadians. These trends brought into question whether the national policy was indeed "national" in the sense of uniting the country.

Emerging English-Canadian and French-Canadian Expressions of Nationalism

In the spring of 1868, five young English-speaking Canadian nationalists met in Ottawa to launch the Canada First Movement. Concerned about the lack of myths, symbols, and national spirit surrounding Confederation, they sought to identify and promote a nationalism for the new Dominion of Canada. They believed that Canada's greatness lay in its northern climate and rugged landscape, which combined to create a superior Anglo-Saxon race. They saw English-speaking Canadians as the "Northmen of the New World."

French Canadians and the Native peoples rejected the Canada First Movement's vision of the new Dominion. In reality, "Canada First" meant "English Canada First." The members showed their true colours through their support of Dr. John Schultz's group of Canadian expansionists in the North West. Their divisive brand of nationalism or Canadian-ness placed French Canadians against English Canadians, and the Native peoples against non-Natives.

While Canada First sought a British and Protestant Canada, many French Canadians envisioned a French-speaking, Roman Catholic nation. In the late nineteenth century, Quebec became more French and Catholic than it had been since before the Conquest. The provincial government cultivated closer ties with France under Napoleon III, especially after the French helped to protect the papal lands in central Italy against Giuseppe Garibaldi's army, then fighting for the unification of Italy. Five hundred volunteer soldiers, the *Zouaves*, or "mercenaries of the Lord," left Quebec between 1868 and 1870 to serve in the papal army.

Ignace Bourget, the influential bishop of Montreal, and his disciple, Louis-François Laflèche, later named bishop of Trois-Rivières, led the ultramontane movement within the Roman Catholic Church. Laflèche set down the basic principles of ultramontane nationalism in 1866:

> A nation is constituted by unity of speech, unity of faith, uniformity of morals, customs, and institutions. The French Canadians possess all these, and constitute a true nation. Each nation has received from Providence a mission to fulfill. The mission of the French Canadian people is to constitute a centre of Catholicism in the New World.

Ultramontanes believed in the subordination of the state to the church. In their view, the Pope constituted the supreme authority over religious and civil matters. Bourget reminded his followers in a circular in 1876: "Let us each say in his heart, 'I hear my *curé*, my *curé* hears the bishop, and the bishop hears the Pope, and the Pope hears our Lord Jesus Christ.'"

The ultramontanes began a political movement in 1871. They issued a *Programme catholique*, which proclaimed the church's right to advise Roman Catholics on how to vote. Catholics were expected to vote for the *bleus* (Conservatives), blessed with the colour of heaven, and not for the *rouges* (Liberals), damned by the colour of the fires of hell. In all cases, the ultramontanes favoured candidates who endorsed the church's views on marriage, education, and social order. A number of French-Canadian politicians, including such Conservatives as George-Étienne Cartier and Joseph-Adolphe Chapleau, opposed this mixing of religion and politics.

Resistance to the ultramontanes arose among a small group of liberal French-Canadian men in the Institut canadien, begun in 1844 in Montreal. Later, other centres founded branches of the Institut canadien throughout Lower Canada. Initially organized as literary societies and debating clubs, branches of the Institut canadien encouraged free thought and sponsored their own libraries free of church censorship. Many of the Institut's members had been influenced by the writings of such French liberal thinkers as Voltaire, Rousseau, and Montesquieu, as well as by British liberal writers such as Bentham and Mill. They believed in the separation of church and state. Many members of the Institut canadien supported the Parti rouge in the 1850s and, after the demise of the Parti rouge, became Liberals.

Recruits for the Zouaves needed a letter of recommendation from their parish priest. They had to be unmarried, or widowers without young children, and between the ages of 15 and 40. The photo shows nine Quebec papal Zouaves in Italy in 1868. A former Zouave, Ephrem Brisebois, Inspector of the NWMP, founded what later became known as Calgary in 1875. Initially Fort Calgary was known as Fort Brisebois.

Source: Archives de la chancellerie de l'Archevêché de Montréal/ACAM-FP-Zouaves pontificaux.

The Guibord Affair

Bishop Bourget attempted to silence the opposition. He denied the sacraments to members of the Institut, including the right of burial in consecrated ground. When Joseph Guibord, a former vice-president of Montreal's Institut canadien, died in November 1869, the Roman Catholic Church refused to give him a Christian burial. Since the case addressed the larger issue of civil versus ecclesiastical supremacy, the Institut supported Henriette Brown Guibord, his widow, when she took her local *curé* to court. As the case proceeded through the various appeal courts, Guibord's coffin rested for six years in a vault in Montreal's Mount Royal cemetery. Finally the Judicial Committee of the Privy Council, the supreme law court in the British empire, ruled in 1874 that burial was a civil right.

Madame Guibord died shortly after this judgment. She was peacefully buried in the family plot in the Catholic cemetery. Friends of her late husband now demanded that he join her in their final resting place. This time, with an escort of more than 1200 militiamen and regular soldiers, they succeeded. They placed Guibord's coffin on top of his wife's grave in poured cement to prevent vandalism. Immediately, Bourget deconsecrated Guibord's plot, although he left the wife's, only centimetres beneath the husband's body, in a state of grace. Guibord's body still lies in unconsecrated soil in Montreal's Côte des Neiges cemetery, near today's Université de Montréal.

Thus, by 1870, extreme and conflicting nationalisms had surfaced in both English- and French-speaking Canada. These movements reflected an attempt on the part of extremists in both linguistic groups to define a nation in cultural, rather than strictly political, terms. They reinforced the realization that in Canada nationalism had to be based on an identity other than a common religion or language.

Liberal Rule: 1873–78

The Conservatives won the federal election of 1872, but just one year later a political scandal broke. It was revealed that Macdonald and Cartier had accepted more than $300 000 in campaign funds from Sir Hugh Allan, president of a large shipping concern, whose newly created Canada Pacific Company was a major contender for the government charter to build the transcontinental railway promised to British Columbia. The major financial backing for Allan's group came from the United States.

An American railway tycoon, angry at his exclusion from the consortium, supplied the Liberal opposition with the incriminating evidence of a financial kickback to the Conservatives from Allan and his American backers. While donations of this sort were part of the political customs of the day, one of this magnitude was not. The Liberals accused the Conservatives of immorality and corruption. Macdonald denied involvement: "These hands are clean," he assured the House of Commons. But fearing a want-of-confidence vote, he announced his cabinet's resignation on November 5. The governor general asked the Liberals to form a government, which they did without an election being held. Two months later, in January 1874, the new prime minister, Alexander Mackenzie, dissolved Parliament and called an election, which the Liberals won.

Liberal Leadership

Alexander Mackenzie, a poor farmer's son, was born not far from Macdonald's birthplace in Glasgow. He came to Canada from Scotland at the age of 20 and worked as a stonemason. The acerbic political critic Goldwin Smith once remarked that if Mackenzie's strong point as prime minister consisted in his having been a stonemason, his weak point consisted in his remaining one: cold, hard, and colourless.

Mackenzie inherited numerous political problems. For one thing, the Liberal party had little internal unity. It was a freewheeling coalition of factions—*rouges*, Clear Grits, and Liberal Reformers—that had come together less out of a sense of common philosophy or a unified party platform than out of a common dislike for the Conservatives and their program. The Liberals deeply distrusted "big business interests," while idealizing rural life. Endorsing the farmers' viewpoint on the tariff, they favoured free trade over protection. They also argued for provincial rights.

The Liberal party needed a strong leader, which Alexander Mackenzie was not, to pull its divergent groups together and to provide direction. George Brown had been such a leader—at least for English-speaking Liberals—but he resigned after his defeat in the 1867 election. The fact

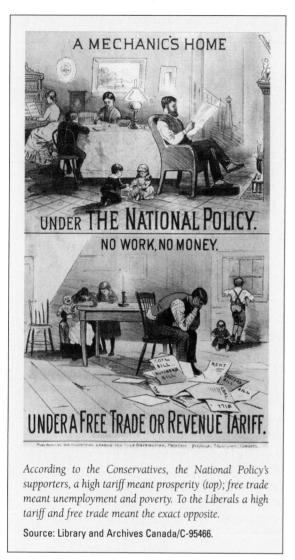

According to the Conservatives, the National Policy's supporters, a high tariff meant prosperity (top); free trade meant unemployment and poverty. To the Liberals a high tariff and free trade meant the exact opposite.

Source: Library and Archives Canada/C-95466.

that a number of influential party members challenged Mackenzie's leadership compounded the problem. Brown lurked in the background; Richard Cartwright, a Conservative defector who left after Macdonald denied him the post of minister of finance, wanted a senior post; Antoine-Aimé Dorion led the party's *rouge* faction and sought the role of Mackenzie's Quebec lieutenant. Finally, Mackenzie faced the enigmatic Edward Blake, former premier of Ontario (1871–72) and a brilliant parliamentary debater, but indecisive about whether to stay in the party.

The Liberals' Political Problems

Mackenzie took office just as Canada entered an economic depression. Two months earlier, the North American and European financial boom of the 1860s and early 1870s broke. As trade declined, the federal debt increased sharply. Mackenzie responded by slowing down the railway-building scheme the Liberal government had inherited from the Conservatives, despite British Columbia's threat to leave the union over the government's broken promises. One of the major expenditures the Liberals incurred came from the establishment of the Royal Military College at Kingston in 1876.

Due to the Dominion's economic depression, the Liberals concentrated on constitutional and political questions. In 1875, they established the Supreme Court of Canada as a national appeal court. While final appeal still rested with the Judicial Committee of the Privy Council in Britain and continued to do so on civil matters until 1949, the Supreme Court became the first Canadian court to review Canadian laws. The Liberals also restricted the powers of the governor general, Britain's representative in Canada, by withdrawing his right to disallow legislation without consulting the Canadian Parliament.

Among political reforms, the Liberals introduced the secret ballot and the practice of holding the entire general election on the same day in each constituency across the country. They also closed the taverns on election day to reduce the possibility of buying votes for drinks. Contested elections were transferred out of the hands of parliamentarians and into the courts. Mackenzie and his cabinet extended the federal franchise effectively to all non-Native males, whether they held property or not. The Liberals also ended the system of dual representation that allowed an individual to hold a federal and a provincial seat simultaneously.

The National Policy of John A. Macdonald

The Mackenzie administration lacked an economic agenda. It had wanted a reciprocity treaty with the United States similar to the one signed in 1854, and had in 1874 successfully drafted such a treaty. But the American Senate defeated the bill, leaving the Liberals without a viable commercial policy.

The Conservatives found an alternative. On the eve of the 1878 election, a lobbying group of the Canadian Manufacturers' Association convinced John A. Macdonald and the Conservative party to accept a protective system of higher tariffs. Increased import duties, they argued, would promote manufacturing in Canada, thus diversifying the Canadian economy. Macdonald pointed out how import duties in Britain and the United States had enabled these countries to advance industrially and that the same could happen in Canada. Macdonald maintained that the creation of an east–west economy by means of a transcontinental railway provided the answer to the depression. Western Canadian farmers could help their Ontario counterparts to feed the growing number of industrial workers in central Canada, who in turn could supply the farmers throughout Canada with agricultural equipment and other manufactured goods. In 1878 the Conservatives returned to power with a majority government.

This policy of nation building—the "national policy," as Macdonald called it—rested on three essentials: the National (capital N) Policy, or high protective tariff; the completion of a transcontinental railway; and the settlement of the West through immigration. It is debatable to what extent the Conservatives envisioned an integrated national policy at the time. In 1879, the Conservatives raised the tariff on textiles, iron and steel products, coal, and petroleum products by 10 to 30 percent, thus achieving their first objective of a high protective tariff. In their budget speech, the Conservatives referred to the tariff as the National Policy, an integral part of the larger "national policy" of nation building. By calling the protective tariff "the National Policy," the Conservatives suggested that all Canadians would benefit.

Debate over the National Policy

Advocates of the National Policy argued that a protective tariff would shift trade from a north–south to an east–west axis. It would provide Canadians with their own national market, thus reducing their dependency on the United States. Furthermore, manufacturers—both Canadian and foreigners building plants in Canada—would ensure more jobs for Canadian workers, technicians, and managers.

In contrast, the Liberals argued that the tariff would erect a fiscal barrier around the country. Furthermore, they maintained that, while the tariff or National Policy was "National" in name, it was regional in interest. It served the needs of central Canadians alone, and more specifically, the needs of the manufacturers and industrialists of the urban centres of Ontario and Quebec, who could live off the bounty of the government. The tariff would serve only to heighten divisions between the various regions of the Dominion, pitting the Maritimes and the West against Ontario and Quebec. Furthermore, it would put the burden of national unity on the hinterland regions, which would become the suppliers of raw materials for the prosperous metropolitan centres of central Canada. In social terms, a corresponding inequality would develop, since workers, farmers, and fishers would have to pay a higher price for consumer goods, whether imported (as a result of the higher tariff) or produced in Canada (as a result of higher production costs). The Liberals drove home the point in a pamphlet they published in 1882:

> The farmer starting to his work has a shoe put on his horse with nails taxed 41 percent; with a hammer taxed 40 percent; cuts a stick with a knife taxed 27-½ percent; hitches his horse to a plough taxed 30 percent; with chains taxed 27-½ percent. He returns to his home at night and lays his wearied limbs on a sheet taxed 30 percent, and covers himself with a blanket on which he has paid 70 percent tax. He rises in the morning, puts on his humble flannel shirt taxed 60 percent, shoes taxed 30 percent, hat taxed 30 percent, reads a chapter from his Bible taxed 7 percent, and kneels to his God on a cheap carpet taxed 30 percent … and then he is expected to thank John A. that he lives under the freest Government under heaven.

The Liberals' National Policy

Despite Liberal opposition at the time of the implementation of the National Policy in 1879, the Liberal party under Wilfrid Laurier adopted its own version of the National Policy in its first budget after coming to power in 1896. As the United States still refused to discuss free trade, the Liberals had little choice. In 1897, W.S. Fielding, the Liberal finance minister, introduced a tariff that maintained high duties on imported goods, such as textiles and iron and steel products coming from the United States, and goods from other countries that restricted the entry of Canadian goods. At the same time, the new policy lowered tariffs to any country admitting Canadian goods at a rate equal to the minimum Canadian tariff. As Britain already adhered to such a policy, it became known as the "British tariff."

Building the Canadian Pacific Railway

A transcontinental railway, an indispensable part of nation building, constituted the second component of the national policy. Settlers wishing to go from Toronto to Manitoba via British territory in the 1870s, for example, had to travel by steamboat across the Great Lakes and over eastern Manitoba's lakes and rivers, with wagon journeys at the portages, then by wagon on the newly completed Dawson Road to Winnipeg, and finally by wagon on rough roads to their destination. The alternative was to go through the United States, where American immigration agents often succeeded in persuading Canadian travellers to settle in the American West. Furthermore, British Columbia's entry into Confederation depended on the "trail of iron" as the only means to link this isolated colony to central Canada. Finally, a transcontinental railway, it was felt, would permit Canada to compete with the United States as a great North American nation.

Government Involvement in Railway Building

Prior to the construction of the Canadian Pacific Railway (CPR), the Canadian government had a history of involvement in railway building. In the 1840s and 1850s, the government of the Canadas had gone into heavy debt to help finance the Grand Trunk Railway and other colonial lines. As part of the Confederation agreement, the Canadian government itself financed the extension of the Grand Trunk line, known as the Intercolonial Railway, from Rivière-du-Loup, the eastern terminus, to Halifax, adding substantially to the Dominion's debt.

Yet, despite the expense of the Intercolonial Railway, the Conservative government embarked on the even more ambitious and riskier railway to the Pacific Ocean. This line, when completed, would be two-thirds longer than any other single railway line then existing in the world. It would run across 5000 km of forest, prairies, and mountains to link together 3.5 million people scattered over vast distances. "An act of insane recklessness," protested Alexander

Prime Minister Laurier with his secretary, M. Boudrias, in the library of his home in Ottawa, now a National Historic Site, 1897.

Source: Library and Archives Canada/C-61705.

Mackenzie in 1872, although his administration would be pressured into continuing the project. The building of the CPR took on the dimensions of a national dream—and, at times, the qualities of a political nightmare.

WHERE HISTORIANS DISAGREE

The National Policy

The national policy of high tariffs, railway building, and development of the West, first established by the Conservative government in the late nineteenth century, generated considerable debate at the time and much debate since among historians and economists. Historian Donald Creighton spoke for many in the central Canadian nationalist tradition in arguing that the national policy, especially the protective tariff of 1879, was an essential component of Canada's growth as an independent nation. Creighton writes: "In international affairs, the tariff asserted the principle of independence as against both Britain and the United States. In domestic matters, it expressed the hope for a new varied and self sufficient national life."[1] Craig Brown notes the success of the national policy in instilling a feeling of nationalism in Canada when traditional national symbols, such as a common language, a common cultural tradition, or a common religion, were absent.[2]

Historian Ben Forster has noted how other factors—besides, or possibly instead of, nationalism—were important in shaping Canada's national policy. He points to a wide range of political and economic factors and interests—including business, industry, agriculture, and government—as all having made a contribution from 1825 to 1879 in shaping the policy.[3]

Economist John Dales has questioned the success of the national policy as a policy of nation building. Dales argues that the national policy was from the beginning a "dismal failure."[4] Railway building became an expensive undertaking for the Canadian taxpayer through heavy government subsidies to the Canadian Pacific Railway Company, established in 1880 to build the transcontinental line. Second, immigration and the settlement of the West did not occur until well after the national policy was in place and then for reasons independent of the national policy itself. Third, the high tariff pitted region against region. It also created an artificial climate for industrial growth that ironically made Canada more, not less, dependent on the United States through a branch-plant economy. Dales also questioned to what extent international economic trends dictated Canadian economic policy.

Historian Michael Bliss agrees that the protective tariff fostered the "Americanization of the Canadian economy," but points out that that was exactly what it was intended to do. "By 1911," he writes, the "concern ... was not to limit what had already been called an American 'invasion' of Canada, but rather to sustain and encourage the branch-plant phenomena."[5]

Some historians in western Canada and the Maritimes have presented the negative impact of the National Policy of tariff protection, especially on their regions. David Bercuson writes, "The ill effects [of the National Policy] abound: high prices for the manufactured products of Central Canada (added to by shipping costs) and the loss to East and West of significant commercial intercourse with New England and the northwestern areas of the United States."[6] It resulted in the growth of industry in central Canada at the expense of the hinterlands.

Economist Kenneth Norrie has countered this viewpoint in reference to western Canada.[7] He argues that the lack of industrial development in the West had nothing to do with the National Policy and everything to do with the West's location—away from the heart of North American development—and its lack of a sufficient population base to make industrialization viable.

The debate on the National Policy received renewed vigour during the national debate over both the Canada–United States and the North American free-trade agreements in the late 1980s and early 1990s. Central to any discussion of the future of Canada, the National Policy will long be a subject of debate.

1   Donald Creighton, *Dominion of the North* (Toronto: Macmillan, 1957), p. 346.

2   Craig Brown, "The Nationalism of the National Policy," in R. Douglas Francis and Donald B. Smith, eds., *Readings in Canadian History: Post-Confederation*, 6th ed. (Toronto: Nelson Thomson Learning, 2002), pp. 3–8.

3   Ben Forster, *A Conjunction of Interests: Business, Politics, and Tariffs, 1825–1879* (Toronto: University of Toronto Press, 1986).

4   John Dales, "Canada's National Policies," in Francis and Smith, eds., *Readings in Canadian History: Post-Confederation* (cited above), pp. 8–17.

5   Michael Bliss, "Canadianizing American Business: The Roots of the Branch Plant," in I. Lumsden, ed., *Close the 49th Parallel Etc.: The Americanization of Canada* (Toronto: University of Toronto Press, 1970), p. 29.

6   David Bercuson, ed., *Canada and the Burden of Unity* (Toronto: Macmillan, 1977), pp. 3–4.

7   Kenneth Norrie, "The National Policy and Prairie Economic Discrimination, 1870–1930," in Donald Akenson, ed., *Canadian Papers in Rural History*, vol. 1 (Gananoque, ON: Langdale, 1978).

Why did the Conservative government agree to undertake this mammoth project? Several compelling reasons explain its decision. First, the United States in the past had threatened to annex the North West and was in a position to do so, especially after the completion of its first transcontinental, the Union Pacific Railway, in 1869. Only with a Canadian railway could the Dominion secure effective control over the region of the North-West Territories that it had acquired in 1869–70. Secondly, the transcontinental railway would enable Canada to be a worthy member of the British empire by being part of a westerly "all red route to the Orient," a route to Asia entirely through British territory. Thirdly, Canadian politicians believed in the resource potential of the North West. Two scientific expeditions into the region, the British Palliser and the Canadian Hind expeditions in the late 1850s, reported that the North West contained millions of hectares of fertile land. Finally, the promise to British Columbia of a transcontinental railway within ten years of the province's entry into Confederation obliged even the Liberal government to build it.

The Search for a Private Company

Macdonald's Conservative government initially favoured a private company to undertake the project. Before the depression of the mid-1870s, two companies competed for the contract: the Interoceanic Company of Toronto, headed by Senator David Macpherson and backed by British financiers; and the Canada Pacific Company, a Montreal consortium under Sir Hugh Allan, president of the Merchants' Bank, with American financial backing. Macdonald favoured a merger of the two companies, but neither Macpherson nor Allan would agree. The government awarded the contract to the Canada Pacific Company in return for generous financial contributions on Allan's part to the Conservative campaign fund in the election of 1872. The resulting Pacific Scandal forced the Macdonald Conservative government to resign and ended the short-lived Canada Pacific Company.

The new Liberal government continued the railway, but only on those sections where settlement warranted construction and only as public money became available, relying on waterways and even American lines to fill the gaps. To move slowly, however, meant reneging on the Conservatives' promise of completing the railway to British Columbia in ten years. Edgar Dewdney, a surveyor and MP for British Columbia, insisted on "The Terms, the Whole Terms and Nothing But the Terms." Already, British Columbia and railways had become inseparable.

When the Conservatives returned to office in 1878, an economic upturn enabled them to find a new private company, the Canadian Pacific Railway Company (CPR), made up of a group associated with the Bank of Montreal, headed by George Stephen, R.B. Angus, and Donald Smith. The syndicate agreed to build the railway across northern Ontario from Callander (near North Bay) to Port Arthur and from Winnipeg to Kamloops by May 1, 1891. In return, the government offered $25 million in financing and 25 million acres (10 million ha) of land consisting of alternate sections not already sold in a belt nearly 40 km wide on both sides of the track across the Prairies. Land not "fit for settlement" could be exchanged for better land elsewhere. The company also obtained free of charge the 1200 km of track already completed or under construction, which had an estimated worth of $31 million. The government promised exemption of construction materials from duty. As well, CPR property and its capital stock would be free from taxation. Its grant of 10 million ha of land remained tax-exempt for 20 years or until sold. Finally, the government agreed to a monopoly clause: no competing line could be built south of the main CPR line until 1900.

In Parliament, Liberals, and even some Conservative backbenchers, questioned the need for such generous terms. The two-month debate that followed proved one of the longest and most bitter in the history of Parliament. As popular historian Pierre Berton has pointed out, more than a million words were spoken, more than in the Bible's Old and New Testaments combined.[1] Yet Macdonald held his party together, and the Conservatives voted down the 25 amendments proposed by the Liberal opposition.

The CPR Route

The new CPR Company decided to alter the route of the railway from that proposed by Sandford Fleming's survey team in the early 1870s along the North Saskatchewan River and through the Yellowhead Pass to a southerly prairie route through Pile O' Bones Creek (Regina), Swift Current, Fort Calgary, and the Kicking Horse Pass. A number of reasons account for this sudden shift. First, the company feared that the American Northern Pacific Railway would siphon off the trade of the southern prairies, bringing the region within the American sphere of influence. Second, Elliott Galt, the son of Alexander Galt, a Father of Confederation, had discovered coal deposits near Lethbridge that could be exploited as a source of fuel for the locomotives on the southern route. Third, John Macoun, a botanist and recent leader of a scientific expedition in the West who had visited the area during the wettest decade in more than a century, reported that the southern prairies were not the desert that John Palliser had earlier described. (Palliser had seen it in the 1850s, one of the driest periods.) Most importantly, the company hoped through the sudden switch to bypass speculators, who had bought up land along the proposed northern route. When speculators attempted to do the same along the southern route—guessing where divisional points and stations might be—the company arbitrarily changed its plans and placed stations and divisional points at spots not originally intended. In this way, the CPR retained control over the land profits to be made in building the railway from Brandon to Revelstoke.

Once the government confirmed the route, construction began. In 1881 the syndicate hired William Cornelius Van Horne, a robust, impetuous, and experienced American engineer, as general manager to oversee construction. Van Horne drove his men without mercy. He boasted that his construction gang, which at one time had 5000 workers and 1700 teams of horses, could lay 800 km of prairie track in a year. When asked the secret of his success, the hardboiled Van Horne replied, "I eat all I can; I drink all I can; I smoke all I can and I don't give a damn for anything." The line reached Calgary in August 1883.

Still ahead lay the difficult mountain terrain. Surveyors had already chosen the Kicking Horse Pass through the Bow River valley, despite its steep incline, as the best route through the Rocky Mountains. Only late in the summer of 1882, however, did Major A.B. Rogers, an experienced railway surveyor, locate a pass that allowed the CPR to cross the more westerly Selkirk Mountains. He insisted that the pass bear his name. Difficulties abounded: laying track along the sides of mountains, blasting tunnels through rock, bridging swift mountain rivers. The construction of the British Columbia section, particularly that built by Andrew Onderdonk from Port Moody on the coast nearly 400 km into the interior, cost enormous amounts of time and money and took the lives of hundreds of the estimated 15 000 Chinese workers who had been hired as cheap labour to do the difficult and dangerous tasks of tunnelling and handling explosives. Chinese Canadians had a saying that "for every foot of railway through the Fraser Canyon, a Chinese worker died." Onderdonk himself estimated that three Chinese died for every kilometre of track that was laid. It is estimated that Chinese labourers saved the CPR $3.5 million.

Construction costs rose because Van Horne insisted on the best materials to ensure long-term use. On Macdonald's insistence, he also had to build along the north shore of Lake Superior instead of relying on the inefficient waterway system or on competing American lines. This meant blasting through hundreds of kilometres of what Van Horne called "engineering

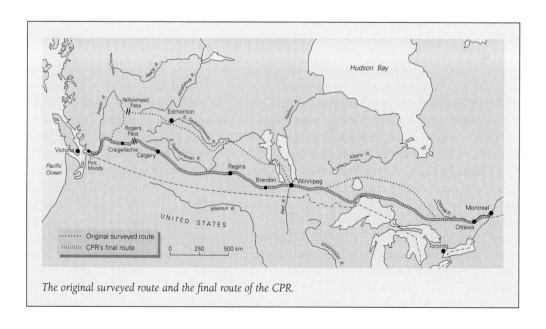

The original surveyed route and the final route of the CPR.

impossibilities"—Precambrian rock. In addition, the company had to buy up eastern lines to connect the Pacific railway with Toronto and Montreal. When the CPR's construction boss was asked about the prospect of not having sufficient funds to complete the project, he replied, "If we haven't got enough, we'll get more, that's all about it." The money did come—from investors, from the sale of stock, and from bank loans. When these sources proved inadequate, the company turned to the only remaining source, the government.

In the summer of 1883, the syndicate needed an estimated $22.5 million—an enormous sum, almost an entire year's revenue for the federal government. Pressed by opposition within his own party against further concessions, Macdonald replied that the CPR might as well ask for the planet Jupiter. But J.H. Pope, Macdonald's secretary, reminded his leader: "The day the Canadian Pacific bursts, the Conservative party bursts the day after." Macdonald convinced his party to agree to another loan, but only after the CPR

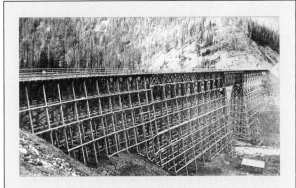

The CPR's Mountain Creek Bridge under construction in the Selkirks. Building the rail line through the mountain ranges proved one of the most challenging tasks facing the Canadian Pacific Railway Company, and cost the lives of hundreds of Chinese navvies.

Source: Glenbow Archives, Calgary, Canada/NA-782-13.

agreed to mortgage the entire main line, all the rolling stock, and everything else connected with the railway. The CPR also promised to make the railway even more political. It would provide more political appointments to jobs; secretly it would back several Conservative newspapers; and it would construct a terminus at Quebec City to please French-Canadian voters. The money kept construction going through 1884, but by the end of that year, the company once again plunged toward bankruptcy.

On the evening of March 26, 1885, George Stephen met with Macdonald to appeal for more government money. The prime minister turned him down. Macdonald knew his party would never agree to another loan. Stephen returned home convinced the railway would, after all, go under. Then, in the morning, came the extraordinary news: the Métis had rebelled under Louis Riel, defeating the North-West Mounted Police in a battle near Duck Lake in the North-

West Territories (see Chapter 4). Macdonald's luck had saved him once again. The uprising justified the railway. That day in Parliament, the government voted to send troops out on the railway to fight Riel and the Métis. It also introduced a bill to finance the remaining mountain section of the railway.

On November 7, 1885, Donald Smith drove in the last spike at Craigellachie, named for a rocky crag in Scotland where Smith grew up—a proud moment for all who had been involved in the project. The American-born Van Horne remarked that "to have built that road would have made a Canadian out of the German Emperor." He also boasted that a train could now make the trip from Montreal to Vancouver in a mere 85 hours, with a first-class ticket costing $123.35 (a railway labourer then earned $2 a day). In 1886, daily mail service was inaugurated across the nation. But the cost of such national pride was

Although Chinese labourers built the BC section of the CPR, there are few contemporary photos of them. This is one, a shot of a Chinese railway camp at Kamloops, British Columbia, 1886.

Source: British Columbia Archives/67609.

The driving of the last spike, November 7, 1885, 9:30 a.m., at Craigellachie, British Columbia. The important CPR financial backer Donald A. Smith (later Lord Strathcona) holds the heavy spike hammer. Behind Smith stands white-bearded Sandford Fleming, former engineer-in-chief, and to the left is the burly figure of W.C. Van Horne, CPR general manager.

Source: Glenbow Archives, Calgary, Canada/NA-218-3.

high. The Pacific railway cost the Canadian government 10.4 million ha of the best prairie land, an estimated $63.5 million in public funds, and government loans of $35 million. Yet as a private company it did very well, and it would by 1905 have capital of $228 million. Was the project worth the effort and the extra expense at the time? The North-West Rebellion of 1885 saved Macdonald from the necessity of answering that question. The CPR allowed for the immediate dispatch of over 3000 troops westward.

Two New Transcontinental Railways

During the economic boom of the Laurier era (1896–1911), Canada added two new transcontinental railways. The first was the Canadian Northern Railway. Begun by Donald Mann and William Mackenzie, two Ontario-born entrepreneurs, the company had built up sufficient rail lines in the West, and sufficient financial strength by 1901 (through the building of branch lines and the incorporation of rival companies' near-defunct charters, which often included substantial land grants—a policy discontinued during the Laurier era) to expand transcontinentally. It applied for financial assistance from the federal government to build from Port Arthur (now Thunder Bay) to Montreal. The second new transcontinental, the Grand Trunk Railway, an eastern-based company, wanted to build a line westward to profit from prairie grain traffic. The logical solution would have been for the two companies to cooperate, but each feared that the other would dominate in any joint venture. At the same time, Laurier believed the country could support three transcontinental railways. He assured Parliament: "This is a time for action. The flood tide is upon us that leads on to fortune; if we let it pass it may never recur again."

The Liberals backed the Grand Trunk. They even offered to build the difficult 2880-km-long eastern section of the railway, at government expense, through Ontario and Quebec to Moncton, New Brunswick. This section, known as the National Transcontinental, would be leased to the Grand Trunk for 50 years at a modest annual rate of 3 percent on construction costs. The first seven years of operation would be rent-free. A new company, the Grand Trunk Pacific, a subsidiary of the Grand Trunk, would build the western section from Winnipeg to the Pacific. The federal government agreed to guarantee 75 percent of the bond money for its construction. Despite such financial support, the line was a failure, especially the British Columbia section— "the most expensive and least remunerative portion of the railway," according to historian Frank Leonard, due to "many actions, 'a thousand blunders,' which senior and junior GTP managers carried out."[2]

Meanwhile, Mann and Mackenzie went ahead with their transcontinental line, convinced that Ottawa would, if they encountered difficulties, assist. As a result, in many areas of the West, these competing lines ran parallel to each other and sometimes within sight of one another. As historian T.D. Regehr notes, "a short distance west of Portage la Prairie, a traveller going north could cross eight parallel east–west lines within the space of 55 km."[3] The Conservative opposition denounced the Liberals' railway-building scheme as a "$200 million vote catcher, designed to carry elections rather than passengers." Ultimately, both lines ended in bankruptcy.

In the meantime, the two companies added 18 000 km of prairie railway—six times more line than the CPR had when completed in 1885. It gave Canada the dubious distinction of having by 1914 more kilometres of rail line per capita than any other country in the world. The new lines also opened up lucrative mining areas in northern Ontario and Quebec, and provided employment for thousands during the construction and operational phases. It remains debatable, however, whether the end result justified the tremendous cost to the Canadian taxpayer.

New Inventions

Other technological inventions in the nineteenth century helped unite the country. In 1884, the first electric telegraph line was built in the United States. Soon other countries, such as Canada, realized the benefits of this new rapid means of communication for business and for pleasure. Then in 1876, Alexander Graham Bell, at the time a Canadian resident, invented the telephone in a successful call between Brantford and Paris, Ontario. Before long, every business and household coveted a telephone. In the late nineteenth century, the energetic Sandford Fleming, dubbed "the Father of Canadian Communications," turned his attention to build first a transatlantic and then a transpacific underwater cable to link Canada to Britain and to the other British possessions in the Pacific. Then in 1901, Guglielmo Marconi picked up the first wireless signal sent across the Atlantic Ocean by erecting an antenna on Signal Hill in St. John's, Newfoundland. Marconi's Wireless Telegraph Company of Canada, created in 1902, operated a transatlantic radio link between Glace Bay, Nova Scotia, and London, England.

Such rapid means of communication and trade heightened the inadequacy of recording time by astronomical calculations in each locality. It proved difficult, for example, to create a train schedule in which the time varied from place to place. So railway companies demanded a standardized approach. It was Fleming once again who "invented" standard time, by dividing the world into 24 time zones and persuading governments throughout the world to standardize time within their own time zones so as to ensure conformity and uniformity.

The arrival of the first CPR passenger train at Vancouver, at the foot of Howe Street, May 23, 1887. The next day marked Queen Victoria's birthday.

Source: Vancouver Public Library/1091.

The Dominion's Strategy for the North West

Development of the West constituted the third component of Macdonald's national policy. Without a populated West, no justification existed for a transcontinental railway. Without a railway, east–west trade could not occur. And without internal trade, the National Policy of tariff protection was meaningless.

In preparation for settlement, the Canadian government surveyed the land into townships similar in size to those in the American West. Each township was 36 square miles (92 km²) and consisted of 36 sections. Each section was one square mile (2.6 km²) and contained 640 acres (259 ha) each. Sections were subdivided into more manageable quarter-sections of 160 acres (65 ha).

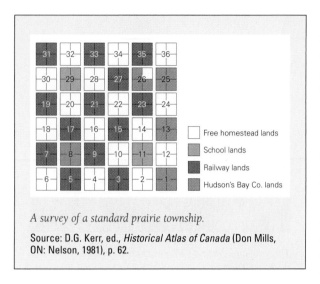

A survey of a standard prairie township.

Source: D.G. Kerr, ed., *Historical Atlas of Canada* (Don Mills, ON: Nelson, 1981), p. 62.

Legend:
- Free homestead lands
- School lands
- Railway lands
- Hudson's Bay Co. lands

Not all land was available for settlement. The HBC received "one twentieth of the land of the fertile belt" as part of the sale of Rupert's Land to the Canadian government in 1869. In Manitoba, the Canadian government appropriated, as part of the Manitoba Act of 1870, 1.5 million acres (600 000 ha), or one-seventh of the new province, for the benefit of the Métis. The CPR received 25 million acres (10 million ha), and other railway companies also received land as part of their contracts until the practice ended in 1894. Additional land was set aside for schools. The remaining land belonged to the federal government to sell or to turn over to private land companies to sell. This latter scheme proved disastrous. Most of the 26 colonization companies in existence in 1883 were owned by friends of Macdonald's government and held up to 3 million acres (1.2 million ha) of land, most of which remained idle either as a result of failed immigration or speculation on the part of the companies that land prices would rise.

To encourage settlement, the government passed the Dominion Lands Act in 1872. It provided a quarter-section free to each head of family or 21-year-old male if he did the following: paid a $10 registration fee, resided on the land for three years, cultivated 30 acres (12 ha), and built a permanent dwelling. At the time, conventional wisdom held that a farm of this size could support a family.

Women's property rights in the West were seriously curtailed. Married women did not qualify for free land under the Dominion Lands Act, and only a few widowed women succeeded in receiving the 160-acre (65-ha) land grant. In 1886, the North-West Territories government abolished a woman's right to the dower—a one-third interest in her husband's property upon widowhood. Western Canadian women protested the dower legislation for over 30 years before it was rescinded in 1917.

Establishing Canadian Law in the North West

To ensure peaceful settlement, the federal government established territorial courts and organized the North-West Mounted Police (NWMP). The 300 "Mounties" began their work in the North West in 1874 after a long, arduous march across the southern prairies. They established important posts throughout the region: Fort Walsh in the Cypress Hills, Fort Macleod on the Old Man River, and Fort Calgary at the junction of the Bow and Elbow rivers. The NWMP administered Canadian law to the Native peoples, curtailed the whisky traders, and assisted the early settlers. Their success lay in what they represented: their red tunics and white helmets symbolized British over American law and tradition, a collective as opposed to an individual authority. As the American writer Wallace Stegner pointed out, "One of the most visible aspects of the international border [in the West] was that it was a colour line: blue below, red above, blue for treachery and unkept promises, red for protection and straight tongue."[4]

Ranching

Ranching became the first major occupation in the newly surrendered western lands, with beef the major export. The foothills region and the southern grasslands, with their short grass, numerous coulees and streams to provide water for livestock, and the winter winds known as *chinooks* that regularly melted the snow and exposed the grass for winter pasture, proved suitable for cattle ranching.

Initially, ranching existed as a small-scale operation. A few Mounties bought small ranches after their three-year enlistment terms expired. They knew the terrain and lifestyle, and had already established contact with the First Nations. They supplied the beef for the NWMP and for the status Indians' rations in the early 1880s, once the prairie buffalo herds had been decimated.

This era of small-scale ranching proved short-lived, however. During the 1880s, "the golden age of ranching," a few wealthy gentlemen ranchers from Ontario, Quebec, France, and Britain established large ranches—the most famous being the Cochrane Ranch, the North West Cattle Company, the Walrond Ranch, and the Oxley Ranch Company—which monopolized the business. Many of the early cowhands, however, came from the United States. The coming of the CPR in 1883, the federal government's embargo on live cattle imports from the United States, and a generous land-lease system that allowed ranchers to lease up to 100 000 acres (40 000 ha) for 21 years at the modest rate of two cents a hectare all benefited the big ranchers.

NWMP Commissioner James Macleod, standing second from right, with his men at Fort Walsh in the Cypress Hills, in what is now southwestern Saskatchewan, in the late 1870s. Macleod treated the Native peoples with dignity and respect. The Blackfoot called him "Stamixotokan," or "Bull's Head," and welcomed his promise of a new order.

Source: Glenbow Archives, Calgary, Canada/NA-52-1.

Immigration and the Settlement of Western Canada

Up until the turn of the century, only a limited number of immigrants entered the North West from outside Canada. Instead, most new settlers in the West were migrants from Ontario, English-speaking Quebec (French-speaking Quebeckers did not move out West in great numbers), and the Maritimes. Being the first to arrive, they became the established commercial and political elite, ensuring that the region became integrated with the rest of the country.

The first immigrants were the Mennonites, descendants of the radical Anabaptists of the Reformation era and followers of Menno Simons (1496–1561), a religious leader in the Netherlands. They left their homes in southern Russia, now Ukraine, as a result of the intense Russification policy of the Tsarist government and its introduction of universal military conscription. These policies went against the sect's religious beliefs in pacifism, noninvolvement with government, and a strict interpretation of the Bible. The Canadian government provided travel assistance and a promise that the Mennonites could settle in communal villages, or *strassendorffs*, and enjoy religious freedom as well as exemption from military service. The 7000 Mennonites who arrived in the 1870s settled on two reserves, one southeast and the other southwest of Winnipeg.

In the mid-1870s, 2000 Icelanders left their homeland, with its limited supply of fertile land and declining fishing industry, to settle on the shores of Lake Winnipeg. They named their new western settlement Gimli, meaning paradise. Floods in 1879 and 1880 forced many to resettle elsewhere in Manitoba or move into the Dakotas. Despite these setbacks, the original settlement prevailed and had even begun to prosper by the turn of the century.

Selected groups of Jewish immigrants came to western Canada in the 1880s. Sir Alexander Galt, Canada's high commissioner in London, joined the archbishop of Canterbury and several titled English gentlemen in aiding victims of Russia's pogroms (massacres of Jews) and offered the Canadian prairies as a refuge. The Canadian government encouraged the new settlers to farm, and they established rural farming communities such as New Jerusalem near Moosomin, and Wapella and Hirsh, Saskatchewan, but few remained in these rural communities. Most chose instead to become small shopowners, merchants, or labourers in urban centres, particularly Winnipeg, Canada's major western city at the turn of the century.

The Mormons were the largest single American group to arrive in western Canada before 1896. Charles Ora Card, a religious leader, entrepreneur, and colonizer from Utah, first led them northward in 1887 to establish farms at Lee's Creek (later renamed Cardston in honour of their leader), Sterling, and Magrath in present-day southern Alberta. The Canadian government encouraged them to settle in the Palliser Triangle area as they had practised dryland farming in Utah. By 1912, some 7000 Mormons lived in Alberta. They built a temple at Cardston, which when completed in 1923 was the only Mormon temple outside of the United States at that time.

An Immigration Boom

Between 1896 and 1914, more than 1 million people immigrated to western Canada in what would be the last great continental land rush, thus ensuring the success of the third component of the "national policy"—settlement of the West. What had changed by 1896 to account for this tremendous influx of immigrants? Both "push" and "pull" factors played a role. The push factors varied as widely as did the migrants themselves. Many left because of limited prospects in their homeland. The industrial revolution in Europe raised the number of births and lowered the death rate thus overpopulating Europe. In the countryside, particularly in eastern Europe, farmers divided their relatively poor agricultural land into smaller parcels to provide for their offspring. In Galicia, the northeastern province of the Austro-Hungarian empire, each peasant family needed about 7 ha for subsistence, yet most farms were only half that size and some families had to get by on less than a hectare. A new class of landless peasants emerged.

Share of Population by Province, Census Years 1871–1911 (percentage of total)

	1871	1881	1891	1901	1911
Maritimes	20.7	20.1	18.2	16.7	13.0
Prince Edward Island	2.5	2.5	2.3	1.9	1.3
Nova Scotia	10.5	10.2	9.3	8.6	6.8
New Brunswick	7.7	7.4	6.6	6.2	4.9
Quebec	32.3	31.4	30.8	30.7	27.8
Ontario	43.9	44.6	43.7	40.6	35.1
Prairie Provinces	0.7	1.4	3.2	7.9	18.4
Manitoba	0.7	1.4	3.2	4.8	6.4
Saskatchewan	—	—	—*	1.7	6.8
Alberta	—	—	—*	1.4	5.2
British Columbia	1.0	1.1	2.0	3.3	5.4
Yukon	—	—	—	0.5	0.1
North-West Territories	1.3	1.3	2.0	0.4	0.1

*Included with North-West Territories.
Source: Calculated from M.C. Urquhart and K.A.H. Buckley, eds., Historical Statistics of Canada *(Toronto: Macmillan, 1965), Series A2-14. Reproduced in Kenneth Norrie and Douglas Owram,* A History of the Canadian Economy, *2nd ed. (Toronto: Harcourt Brace, 1996), chapter 16.*

In the European cities, working-class people lived in cramped slum quarters. The Canadian government's promise of 160 acres (65 ha) of good farmland offered an escape. For the Americans who moved north and the prosperous British immigrants who came on the advice of friends or relatives already in Canada, the move promised adventure, a chance to strike out on their own and to become self-sufficient.

Others, like the Mennonites, Hutterites, and Doukhobors, sought religious freedom. Both Galician Slavs and Jews faced ethnic persecution in the Austro-Hungarian empire. A large number of Asians came to work on the railroads in British Columbia as contract labourers or simply in search of a better way of life. Many immigrants were single men who hoped to make enough money either to return home prosperous or, if they were married, to bring their families to Canada.

The pull factors were equally varied and related to world conditions in general and the Canadian West's attractions in particular. The rapid growth of international trade after 1896 meant jobs. Prosperity also increased demand for raw materials, especially for food for the growing urban population. Farmers in the West could benefit from a ready market and a high price for Canadian wheat. Increased prosperity also meant declining interest rates and lower freight rates, which in turn resulted in higher profits for exports of Canada's bulky natural resources. Most importantly of all, Canada benefited from the closing of the American frontier after 1890. After the best land—especially well-watered land—in the American West ceased to be available, the Canadian prairies became the "last best West."

Improved farming conditions also made the Canadian West attractive. Better strains of wheat, such as Marquis, discovered by the Canadian plant breeder Charles Saunders in 1909, matured earlier than Red Fife, thus enabling it to be grown in northern areas of Alberta and Saskatchewan without risk of frost damage. The price of wheat quadrupled between 1901 and 1921. Better machinery such as the chilled-steel plough (introduced from the United States), improved harrows and seed drills, and tractors and threshers also aided western farmers. A steam-thresher could process more in a day than a farmer could by physical labour for an entire season.

Sifton Promotes the West

Credit also goes to Clifford Sifton, an energetic Manitoba politician with a business background, and Laurier's minister of the interior. He completely reorganized his department by streamlining it, and by bringing it directly under his control. Then he pressured the HBC and the CPR to sell their reserved lands at reasonable rates to prospective settlers. He discontinued the practice of using land grants as incentives to railway promoters. Sifton also simplified the procedure for obtaining a homestead and encouraged settlers to buy up an adjacent section, if available, by allowing them the right to preempt such land—that is, to make an interim claim on it and to purchase it at a reduced rate from the government later on.

His department produced numerous pamphlets—such as *The Wondrous West*; *Canada: Land of Opportunity*; *Prosperity Follows Settlement*; and *The Last Best West*—which contained glorified descriptions of conditions in the Canadian West. In 1896 alone, his department printed 65 000 pamphlets; four years later, the figure reached 1 million. Millions of brochures were sent out to prospective immigrants in the United States and Europe, in over a dozen languages. As well, he advertised in thousands of newspapers, arranged for lecture tours and promotional trips for potential settlers (particularly Americans), and offered bonuses to steamship agents based on the number of immigrants they brought to Canada. Sifton had his agents target mainly young, white, British and American males, followed in preference by young,

"Now Then, All Together." A cartoon in the 1904 Liberal election pamphlet Laurier Does Things *suggests that immigrants, male at least (no women appear), could live together in harmony in Western Canada. It is most unlikely, of course, that a "Frenchman" would want to sing "The Maple Leaf Forever," English-Canada's unofficial anthem. It praises James Wolfe, the English victor at Quebec in 1759. But in propaganda all things are possible, and the cartoon shows a "Frenchman" joining in.*

Source: Saskatchewan Archives Board R-A 12,402.

white British and American females. When insufficient numbers came, he had to target western and eastern Europeans.

Immigrant Groups

British immigrants came mostly on their own and at their own expense. There were exceptions. The Barr colonists, a group of Londoners who came together under the aegis of Reverend Isaac Barr at the turn of the century, settled in the Lloydminster area on the border between Saskatchewan and Alberta. Also, some 80 000 "Home Children" came to Canada between 1867 and 1924 to work as agricultural and domestic servants. They were organized and sent by childcare organizations in England, the largest being the Barnardo Home. Despite some known incidences of gross neglect and child abuse, the government supported the movement and deemed it successful. Most British immigrants adjusted relatively easily to Canadian life. They did not have to learn a new language or radically different customs, and many were relatively well off. Those who lacked farming experience, however, had a more difficult time adjusting. Some drifted into the booming prairie towns in search of work; others first learned how to farm as hired hands. But not all British received a warm welcome; some employment ads read, "No English Need Apply." Canadians resented the haughty attitude of upper-class Englishmen in particular, many of whom refused to fit into Canadian society.

American immigrants were high on Sifton's list of desirable settlers. Although not British, the majority were of Anglo-Saxon extraction. As they already spoke English, they mixed easily with their Canadian neighbours and participated fully in their new communities. As well, many were experienced farmers. Many sold their farms at home at a high price and bought new ones in Canada at a low price. One Iowa farmer, for example, sold his old homestead for $250 per hectare and bought good land in Manitoba for $18 per hectare. Many ex-Canadians returned. About a third of those coming from the United States were newcomers from Europe, such as Germans and Scandinavians who had initially settled in the American West.

In an age of racial-superiority theories, African Americans were not welcomed. While Canadian agents told white Americans that the climate of the North West was mild and healthy, they informed black Americans of the region's rigorous and severe climate. When a group of well-to-do African Americans from Oklahoma crossed into Canada in 1910, local newspapers, especially the Edmonton *Journal* (Edmonton was reported to be their destination), warned of an "invasion of Negroes." In the end, the effort to restrict black immigrants succeeded. Between 1901 and 1911, fewer than 1500 African Americans came to Canada, as against hundreds of thousands of other Americans.

Robert, a Barnardo Boy

Robert[1] was a "Home Child," one of some 80 000 British boys and girls sent to Canada between 1868 and 1925 to work as agricultural and domestic servants. He belonged to the Barnardo Homes, the largest of the child-care organizations in England, begun by Dr. Thomas Barnardo in 1870 in London's East End, to assist waifs, strays, orphans, and street urchins by providing them with a "home." The original Barnardo Home had a sign out in front that read: "No destitute child ever refused admission." While in operation, the Barnardo Homes took in over 30 000 destitute children.

Robert was one of them. He was admitted into the home on November 23, 1921, at the age of 9, along with an older brother, Alfred, and a younger brother, Harold. Another brother, Sidney, was old enough to be on his own. Their mother, Emily, had died from pregnancy complications in 1920, and their father, Edward, a brewer's labourer, died a year later from pneumonia. A maiden aunt, Annie, took them in for a brief time, but when she was unable to care for them any longer, they were admitted to the home. They were given the familiar Barnardo uniform of a tunic, a pair of red-striped trousers, and a hat like that of a Salvation Army officer.

From the beginning, Dr. Barnardo had arranged to send "his" children overseas to "the colonies," where he believed they had a better chance at a new life than in the slums of London. Robert had a choice of going to either Canada or Australia, and chose Canada.

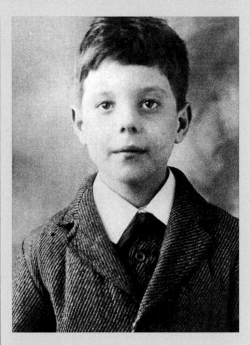

Robert Francis, as a young boy.

Source: R. Douglas Francis.

He and his brother Harold left England on the S.S. *Melita* on September 18, 1924, with the customary "Barnardo trunk" that contained all of their earthly possessions; Alfred stayed in England with Sidney. It was the last time the four brothers would see each other.

Upon arrival in Canada Robert and Harold were sent to the Barnardo's Canadian Office and Distributing Home for Boys in Toronto. From here, they were sent north to Bracebridge to a bush farm in Muskoka, where a widow had requested two boys as farm workers. Like so many Home Children, the boys did not have a good initial experience in Canada. The lady saw them as indentured labourers. They ate separately from the family and slept in an unheated section of the house. They were underfed, and Robert recalled drinking the cow's milk from the bucket before taking it into the house. They attended school but missed many days when needed around the farm. Robert wrote to the officials in Toronto to complain about the harsh conditions, and an inspector came out, but only after informing the lady of his impending visit. Robert recalled that day as the only time he ate with the family and had a scrumptious meal. When the official left, conditions became even more intolerable.

It was customary for employers of Home Children to pay them a wage when they reached the age of 15. When Robert became 15, the lady let the boys go. They were then sent down to the Niagara Peninsula, where a large number of Barnardo boys were located, to assist on the fruit and vegetable farms. Robert's new "home" was a wonderful contrast to his first; the farm owner, Sidney Wright, had been a Barnardo boy himself. Robert got to be part of the family, enjoying the privileges of regular family members. Unfortunately, he was let go when, during the depression, the family could no longer afford him. He moved to another farm in the area, where once again he was treated as "just a Barnardo boy." He stuck it out until he married a local girl whose parents owned a farm, at which time he took over the family farm. The couple had three children and lived in the community for the remainder of their lives.

1   Robert is Robert Francis, the father of one of this textbook's authors.

European Immigrants

The Canadian government had little success in attracting large numbers of western Europeans. France, for example, had a low birth rate and a well-balanced economy that provided ample work for its population. It also had its own colonies to populate, such as Algeria. Moreover, the French government openly discouraged Canadian immigration agents because it feared a future war with Germany, whose population was almost double that of France.

The Scandinavian countries also restricted emigration, fearing the negative result of such migration, especially of skilled workers, on their own economies. Germany prohibited immigration agents within its borders and fined steamship lines for carrying emigrants. Still, between 1901 and 1911, the German population in the three Prairie provinces increased from 46 844 to 147 638. Many of these immigrants came from German-speaking settlements in eastern Europe rather than directly from Germany, and were sponsored by German Roman Catholic organizations, the most successful being the German-American Land Company, a joint religious–lay venture that established the Saskatchewan colonies of St. Peter and St. Joseph.

To get around these emigration restrictions, Clifford Sifton allowed W.T.R. Preston, Canada's immigration inspector in London, to set up a clandestine organization, the North Atlantic Trading Company, in 1899 to work with European shipping agents to bring western Europeans to Canada. Each agent received a $5 bonus for every healthy man, woman, or child over 12 who was a bona fide farmer, farm worker, domestic servant, or accompanying family member. This illegal scheme ended in 1905 after public outcry against undue profiteering, but not before the company had succeeded in bringing in 50 000 emigrants from western Europe.

Immigrants in "Sheepskin Coats"

Sifton encouraged immigrants from eastern Europe, particularly Ukrainians, seeing them as ideal settlers. By World War I, 170 000 Ukrainians had come to Canada from the Austro-Hungarian empire. They left Ukraine for a variety of reasons, but were attracted to Canada for one main reason—*vilni zemli*, or free land. The first group of 4000 Ukrainians—or Galicians, as the immigration agents called them because they came from the province of Galicia—settled at Star and Josefberg, 65 km east of Edmonton. This forested area assured them an abundant supply of wood, a scarce commodity back home. Soon the tightly knit farming communities grew into villages of timber and whitewashed-clay houses with thatched roofs, and distinctive churches with onion-shaped domes.

The Doukhobors

Some 7000 Doukhobors (meaning "spirit wrestlers") came from Russia in the late 1890s because of persecution for their pacifist and anti-tsarist beliefs. Leo Tolstoy, the great Russian novelist, and Peter Kropotkin, a leading Russian anarchist, admired their simple, communal lifestyle and assisted them to emigrate from Russia. James Mavor, a professor of political economy at the University of Toronto and a friend of Kropotkin's, helped settle them in Canada. They founded three colonies, two near Yorkton, Saskatchewan, and another near Saskatoon. They held land collectively, in a special arrangement agreed upon by the Canadian government, and lived in communal villages.

All was peaceful until a radical wing calling itself the Sons of Freedom marched toward Winnipeg in search of Christ and a new earthly paradise, and in expectation of the arrival of their leader, Peter Veregin, recently released from captivity in Russia. The group walked naked through the Doukhobor villages in a quest for a state of purity akin to that of Adam and Eve before the Fall. Public outcry provided an excuse for Frank Oliver, Clifford Sifton's successor as minister of the interior (1905–11), to confiscate half of their Saskatchewan land. He did so on the grounds that the Doukhobors refused to cultivate quarter-sections, to swear allegiance to the Crown, or to register births and deaths. (The federal government had exempted them from these conditions originally.) In protest, 5000 Doukhobors trekked to the Kootenay district near Grand Forks, British Columbia, where Peter Veregin had purchased private land.

Although he tolerated eastern European immigrants as potentially good farmers, Sifton disdained southern Europeans. He believed them to be migratory labourers who would only settle in the urban centres. "I don't want anything done to facilitate Italian immigration," the minister of the interior warned his assistants, as he did not think they would succeed. As a result, those Italian immigrants who did arrive mostly came illegally, through the help of *padros*, or employment agents, who worked with the railway companies and business interests to find work for these unskilled labourers.

Doukhobor women pulling a plough. During their first spring in Canada the Doukhobors had no farm animals. With most of their men away working on railway construction to earn money for the community, the women hitched themselves to the plough.

Source: Saskatchewan Archives Board #SPA R-B 1964(1).

Asian Immigrants

Asian immigration occurred mainly on the West Coast. In the 1850s, at the time of the Fraser River gold rush, the first Chinese, Chang Tsoo and Ah Hong, arrived. They were followed about 20 years later

The tax certificate for Lau Shong (or Shing), 1912, for $500, the amount required to bring in Chinese immigrants.

Source: Library and Archives Canada/C-96443.

by a small number of Japanese. By 1911, nearly 10 percent of British Columbia's population was Asian. To restrict further immigration, the federal government imposed a head tax on all Chinese immigrants, first of $50 in 1885, which rose to $100 in 1900 and then to $500 by 1903. Still, many paid the tax, enabling Ottawa to collect $4 381 550 in head taxes from Chinese between 1885 and 1908. The government was prevented from imposing a similar tax on the Japanese because Japan was a military ally of Britain and a major trading partner of Britain and Canada. Instead, the Canadian and Japanese governments mutually agreed to restrict Japanese immigrants to Canada to 400 a year.

The head tax succeeded in reducing overall Chinese immigration, particularly female immigrants, since many married men could not afford to bring their wives, and few single men could pay the tax for single women who might become their wives. Some companies, such as the railways, paid the head tax, or simply brought in Chinese males illegally because they worked hard and for low wages. Asians also worked in mining, land clearing, public works, lumbering, salmon canning, and market gardening.

A few immigrants came from India. As British subjects, they had a special claim for entry into another country within the British empire. Dr. Sundar Singh spoke for his Sikh community when he reminded the Empire Club in 1912: "We are subjects of the same Empire." But West Coast citizens opposed their entry. In May 1914, the ship the *Komagata Maru* brought nearly 400 Punjabis, mostly Sikhs, to Vancouver. But for two months, port authorities refused them entry. In the end, the Punjabis were forced back to India, amid cries of "White Canada forever" and the refrain of "Rule Britannia."

Sikh mineworkers at CPR station, Frank, Crow's Nest Pass, Alberta, 1903.
Source: Library and Archives Canada/PA 125112.

Nativist Attitudes

With the arrival of various ethnic groups in significant numbers at the turn of the century, concern arose as to their place in Canadian society. Few English Canadians were as tolerant as the western Canadian reformer and author Nellie McClung. In her book, *In Times Like These*, she wrote:

> Among the people of the world in the years to come, we will ask no greater heritage for our country than to be known as the land of the Fair Deal, where every race, colour and creed will be given exactly the same chance—for immigrants "the Land of the Second Chance."

A theory of the proper ethnic hierarchy developed among English Canadians. As ethnic historian Howard Palmer notes, it was based on each group's "physical and cultural distance from London (England) and the degree to which [its] skin pigmentation conformed to Anglo-Saxon white."[5] Not surprisingly, the British and Americans, for the most part "Anglo-Saxon" Protestants, stood at the top of the list of desirable immigrants. Next came the northern and western Europeans, particularly Scandinavians, Germans, and Dutch, considered by many English Canadians to have the best qualities of "Anglo-Saxons" and welcomed. After the "chosen races" came the central and eastern Europeans, generally respected as industrious people and good farmers. Ukrainians and Doukhobors were less tolerated among the eastern Europeans because of their exclusiveness and "strange" customs. Lowest in the hierarchy of European immigrants came Jews and southern Europeans, both considered difficult to assimilate and regarded as poor farmers. Ranked well below Europeans came those of African background and Asians (Japanese, Chinese, and South Asians)—all believed to be inassimilable.

Asians faced overt discrimination. While many Chinese immigrants were kept out by the head tax and Japanese immigrants by a quota system, those Asians who did enter the country remained marginalized, being denied the franchise in the western provinces, barred from the professions, and subjected to discrimination in housing and in access to public places. They also faced physical persecution. In 1907, for example, the Asiatic Exclusion League of Vancouver led a march of 10 000 people through Chinatown, brandishing sticks, stones, bricks, and bottles, and damaging buildings and assaulting residents. They entered the Japanese quarters, too, but were pushed out. It took the police four hours to control the crowd. The government responded to the violence by further restricting Asian immigration rather than dealing with the recalcitrants.

Both the Liberal and the Conservative administrations put intense pressure on First Nation communities to surrender reserve land. A number of illegal losses of reserve lands occurred, particularly in the last years of Laurier's administration. Frank Oliver, as Laurier's minister of Indian affairs and minister of the interior, passed a law in 1908 that allowed the government to remove Native people from reserves near towns of more than 8000 residents. Then, in 1911, he amended the Indian Act to allow companies and municipalities to expropriate reserve land for roads, railroads, or other public purposes.

Underlying these racist attitudes, so blatantly expressed at all levels of Canadian society at the turn of the century, were differing views of the ideal Canadian society. Few English Canadians at this time thought in terms of a culturally pluralistic society. Most could not even believe that a nation of two languages was viable or desirable. "Anglo-Saxons" simply believed that they were at the pinnacle of human "civilization." Thus they sought to create a homogeneous culture based on British-Canadian customs and the English language. They looked to the churches and especially the schools to inculcate these values and one language. Most English-speaking Canadians believed that "foreign" immigrants could only become Canadians by abandoning their own customs and language so as to assimilate.

By 1914, the era of nation building was complete with a national economic policy: the National Policy, or high tariff; the completion of the transcontinental Canadian Pacific Railway; and settlement of the West through large-scale immigration. But certain groups, classes, and regions of the country felt alienated or neglected. Their discontent contributed to a new era of protest and a resurgence of regionalism.

In September 1907, a mob of 10 000, incited by the Asiatic Exclusion League, invaded Vancouver's Chinatown, and then moved into the Japanese quarter of the city. The photo shows the damage to a Japanese-Canadian grocery store. The Japanese men easily pushed back the mob that rushed into their neighborhood.

Source: William Lyon Mackenzie King Collection/Library and Archives Canada/C-14118.

NOTES

1. Pierre Berton, *The National Dream* (Toronto: McClelland & Stewart, 1970), p. 363.

2. Frank Leonard, *A Thousand Blunders: The Grand Trunk Pacific Railway and Northern British Columbia* (Vancouver: University of British Columbia Press, 1996), pp. 4–5.

3. T.D. Regehr, "Triple Tracking," *Horizon Canada* 7 (1986), p. 1878.

4. Wallace Stegner, *Wolf Willow: A History, a Story, and a Memory of the Lost Plains Frontier* (New York: Viking, 1966), p. 101.

5. Howard Palmer, "Reluctant Hosts: Anglo-Canadian Views of Multiculturalism in the Twentieth Century," in R. Douglas Francis and Donald B. Smith, eds., *Readings in Canadian History: Post-Confederation*, 7th ed. (Toronto: Thomson Nelson, 2006), p. 176.

BEYOND THE BOOK

Weblinks

CPR: The Scottish Connection
http://www.mccord-museum.qc.ca/en/keys/webtours/VQ_P2_18_EN
An exhibit of contributions and connections of Scottish Canadians to the Canadian Pacific Railway.

North-West Mounted Police
http://www.rcmp-grc.gc.ca/history/marchwest_e.htm
Commissioner George Arthur French's diary of the North-West Mounted Police's initial march to Western Canada.

Immigrant Voyage Stories
http://ist.uwaterloo.ca/~marj/genealogy/voyages/arcadia.html
An account of Ukrainian Dmytro Romanchych of his voyage across the Atlantic to immigrate to Canada in 1897.

Immigration from Asia
http://www.canadiana.org/citm/specifique/asian_e.html
Digitized versions of the Chinese Immigration Act over time, as well as other documents regarding immigration and immigrants from Asia.

Sir Sanford Fleming
http://www.histori.ca/minutes/minute.do?id=10182
A public service television video detailing Sir Sanford Fleming and his inventions.

Films & Novels

The Days of Whiskey Gap. Directed by Colin Low. 1961.

Kobzar's Children: A Century of Untold Ukrainian Stories. By Marsha Skrypuch. 2006.

Under the Willow Tree: Pioneer Chinese Women in Canada. Directed by Dora Nipp. 1997.

RELATED READINGS

The relevant articles from R. Douglas Francis and Donald B. Smith, eds., *Readings in Canadian History: Post-Confederation*, 7th ed. (Toronto: Thomson Nelson, 2006), for this chapter are Craig Brown, "The Nationalism of the National Policy," pp. 24–28; A.A. den Otter, "The Philosophy of Railways: Conclusions and Conjectures," pp. 29–52; and Howard Palmer, "Reluctant Hosts: Anglo-Canadian Views of Multiculturalism in the Twentieth Century," pp. 175–188.

BIBLIOGRAPHY

The nationalism of the Canada First movement is discussed in a chapter in F.H. Underhill, *The Image of Confederation* (Toronto: Canadian Broadcasting Corporation, 1964); and in David Gagan, "The Relevance of 'Canada First,'" *Journal of Canadian Studies* 5 (November 1970): 36–44. On the rising French-Canadian nationalism of the 1870s see Jean-Paul Bernard, *Les Rouges: libéralisme, nationalisme et anti-cléricalisme au milieu du XIXe siècle* (Montreal: Presses de l'Université du Québec, 1971); Nive Voisine and Jean Hamelin, eds., *Les ultramontains canadiens-français* (Montreal: Boréal Express, 1985); Arthur Silver, *The French-Canadian Idea of Confederation, 1864–1900*, 2nd ed. (Toronto: University of Toronto Press, 1997); and "The Clerical Offensive" in Susan Mann, *The Dream of Nation: A Social and Intellectual History of Quebec*, 2nd ed. (Montreal/Kingston: McGill-Queen's University Press, 2002), pp. 115–31.

Dale Thomson's *Alexander Mackenzie: Clear Grit* (Toronto: Macmillan, 1960) gives a good portrait of Canada's second prime minister. On Edward Blake see F.H. Underhill, "Edward Blake," in C.T. Bissell, ed., *Our Living Traditions* (Toronto: University of Toronto Press, 1957), pp. 3–28; and Joseph Schull's two-volume biography, *Edward Blake: The Man of the Other Way* (Toronto: Macmillan, 1975) and *Edward Blake: Leader in Exile* (Toronto: Macmillan, 1976). The ideas underlying Canadian liberalism in the 1870s are examined by F.H. Underhill in "The Political Ideas of the Upper Canadian Reformers, 1867–1878," in his *In Search of Canadian Liberalism* (Toronto: Macmillan, 1960), pp. 68–84; and by W.R. Graham in "Liberal Nationalism in the 1870's," *Canadian Historical Association Report* (1946): 101–19. On the politics of the Laurier era see R.C. Brown and R. Cook, *Canada, 1896–1921: A Nation Transformed* (Toronto: McClelland & Stewart, 1974); and three biographies of Laurier: Joseph Schull, *Laurier: The First Canadian* (Toronto: Macmillan, 1965); Richard Clippendale, *Laurier: His Life and World* (Toronto: McGraw-Hill Ryerson, 1979); and Réal Bélanger, *Wilfrid Laurier: quand la politique devient passion* (Quebec City: Presses de l'Université Laval, 1986).

On the national policy see Ben Forster, *A Conjunction of Interests: Business, Politics, and Tariffs, 1825–1879* (Toronto: University of Toronto Press, 1986); R.C. Brown, *Canada's National Policy, 1883–1900: A Study in Canadian–American Relations* (Princeton, NJ: Princeton University Press, 1964); and John Dales, *The Protective Tariff in Canada's Development* (Toronto: University of Toronto Press, 1966). The *Journal of Canadian Studies* 14 (Autumn 1979) is devoted to "The National Policy, 1879–1979."

Pierre Berton's two-volume popular study, *The National Dream: The Great Railway, 1871–1881* (Toronto: McClelland & Stewart, 1970) and *The Last Spike: The Great Railway, 1881–1885* (Toronto: McClelland & Stewart, 1974), describes the building of the Canadian Pacific Railway. For a less nationalistic view of the railway see A.A. den Otter, *The Philosophy of Railways: The Transcontinental Railway Idea in British North America* (Toronto: University of Toronto Press, 1997). On the Chinese contribution to the building of the CPR, see Paul Yee, *Building the Railway: The Chinese and the CPR* (Toronto: Umbrella Press, 1999).

On railway building during the Laurier era consult T.D. Regehr, *The Canadian Northern Railway: Pioneer Road of the Northern Prairies, 1895–1918* (Toronto: Macmillan, 1976); and G.R. Stevens, *Canadian National Railways*, 2 vols. (Toronto: Clarke Irwin, 1960). On the Grand Trunk Pacific see Frank Leonard, *A Thousand Blunders: The Grand Trunk Pacific Railway and Northern British Columbia* (Vancouver: University of British Columbia Press, 1996). In *The Canadian Pacific Railway and the Development of Western Canada* (Montreal/Kingston: McGill-Queen's University Press, 1989), John A. Eagle examines the CPR's contributions to western Canadian economic growth between 1896 and 1914. On the relationship of railways and government see Ken Cruikshank, *Close Ties: Railway, Government, and the Board of Railway Commissioners, 1851–1933* (Montreal/Kingston: McGill-Queen's University Press, 1991). Suzanne Zeller's *Inventing Canada: Early Victorian Science and the Idea of a Transcontinental Nation* (Toronto: University of Toronto Press, 1987) examines the role of scientists in shaping the idea of a transcontinental nation.

On the development of the Canadian West in the 1870s and 1880s see Gerald Friesen, *The Canadian Prairies: A History* (Toronto: University of Toronto Press, 1984). On settlement patterns in the West see Chester Martin, *"Dominion Lands" Policy*, published in an abridged form (Toronto: Macmillan, 1973). For an account of homesteading see the essays in David C. Jones and Ian Macpherson, eds., *Building Beyond the Homestead: Rural History on the Prairies* (Calgary: University of Calgary Press,

1985). A detailed study of settlement in one prairie town is Paul Voisey, *Vulcan: The Making of a Prairie Community* (Toronto: University of Toronto Press, 1988). For a discussion of the North-West Mounted Police see R.C. Macleod, *The North-West Mounted Police and Law Enforcement, 1873–1905* (Toronto: University of Toronto Press, 1976). William Baker has edited a collection of articles on the early NWMP in *The Mounted Police and Prairie Society, 1873–1919* (Regina: Canadian Plains Research Center, 1998). On ranching see David Breen, *The Canadian Prairie West and the Ranching Frontier, 1874–1924* (Toronto: University of Toronto Press, 1983); Warren Elofson, *Cowboys, Gentlemen and Cattle Thieves* (Montreal/ Kingston: McGill-Queen's University Press, 2000); and his *Frontier Cattle Ranching in the Land and Times of Charlie Russell* (Montreal/Kingston: McGill-Queen's University Press, 2004); and Simon Evans, Sarah Carter, and Bill Yeo, eds., *Cowboys, Ranchers and the Cattle Business: Cross-Border Perspectives on Ranching History* (Calgary: University of Calgary Press, 2000).

Overviews of immigration to western Canada are available in R.C. Brown and R. Cook's chapter "Opening Up the Land of Opportunity," in *Canada, 1896–1921: A Nation Transformed* (Toronto: McClelland & Stewart, 1974); Pierre Berton's *The Promised Land: Settling the West, 1896–1914* (Toronto: McClelland & Stewart, 1984); Gerald Friesen's *The Canadian Prairies: A History* (cited above); and the relevant chapters in Ninette Kelley and Michael Trebilcock, *The Making of the Mosaic: A History of Canadian Immigration Policy* (Toronto: University of Toronto Press, 1998). See as well Paul Robert Magocsi, ed., *Encyclopedia of Canada's Peoples* (Toronto: University of Toronto Press for the Multicultural Society of Ontario, 1999).

On immigration to western Canada in the pre-1896 era see Norman Macdonald, *Canada: Immigration and Colonization, 1841–1903* (Toronto: Macmillan, 1966); and the relevant articles in Franca Iacovetta et al., *A Nation of Immigrants: Women, Workers, and Communities in Canadian History, 1840S–1960s* (Toronto: University of Toronto Press, 1998). Robert Painchaud reviews early French-speaking settlement in *Un rêve français dans le peuplement de la Prairie* (Saint-Boniface, MB: Éditions des Plaines, 1987). Royden K. Loewen, *Family, Church, and Market: A Mennonite Community in the Old and the New Worlds, 1850–1930* (Toronto: University of Toronto Press, 1993) describes the Mennonite community in western Canada in the late nineteenth century. Clifford Sifton's role in promoting immigration to the West is examined in D.J. Hall's two-volume biography, *Clifford Sifton*, vol. 1, *The Young Napoleon, 1861–1900* (Vancouver: University of British Columbia Press, 1981), and vol. 2, *The Lonely Eminence, 1901–1929* (Vancouver: University of British Columbia Press, 1985).

The immigration of British home children is the subject of Joy Parr's *Labouring Children: British Immigrant Apprentices to Canada, 1869–1924* (Montreal/Kingston: McGill-Queen's University Press, 1980); and Kenneth Bagnell's *The Little Immigrants: The Orphans Who Came to Canada*, rev. ed. (Toronto: Dundurn Press, 2002). On American farmers' immigration to western Canada see Carl Bicha, *The American Farmer and the Canadian West, 1896–1914* (Lawrence, KS: Coronado Press, 1968); and Harold Troper, *Only Farmers Need Apply* (Toronto: Griffin House, 1972). European immigration is discussed in Donald Avery, *"Dangerous Foreigners": European Immigrant Workers and Labour Radicalism in Canada, 1896–1932* (Toronto: McClelland & Stewart, 1979). The European immigrants' perspective can be gleaned from John Marlyn's novel, *Under the Ribs of Death* (Toronto: McClelland & Stewart, 1957); and from R.F. Harney and H. Troper's *Immigrants: A Portrait of the Urban Experience, 1890–1930* (Toronto: Van Nostrand Reinhold, 1975).

Black immigration to western Canada is covered in Robin Winks, *The Blacks in Canada: A History*, 2nd ed. (Montreal/Kingston: McGill-Queen's University Press, 1997). On Asian immigration to British Columbia in the pre–World War I era see Jin Tan and Patricia E. Roy, *The Chinese in Canada* (Ottawa: Canadian Historical Association, 1985); Peter Ward, *White Canada Forever: Popular Attitudes and Public Policy Toward Orientals in British Columbia*, 3rd ed. (Montreal/Kingston: McGill-Queen's University Press, 2002); Patricia Roy, *A White Man's Province: British Columbia Politicians and Chinese and Japanese Immigrants, 1885–1914* (Vancouver: University of British Columbia Press, 1989); and Hugh Johnston, *The Voyage of the Komagata Maru: The Sikh Challenge to Canada's Colour Bar* (Delhi: Oxford University Press, 1979). On Nativist attitudes see Howard Palmer, *Patterns of Prejudice: A History of Nativism in Alberta* (Toronto: McClelland & Stewart, 1982).

Chapter Four

THE FRAGILE UNION: THE RESURGENCE OF REGIONALISM

TIME LINE

1872	Oliver Mowat elected premier of Ontario and begins the provincial-rights movement
1885	Outbreak of the North-West Rebellion under Louis Riel Execution of Louis Riel
1886	Parti national formed in Quebec under Honoré Mercier
1887	First interprovincial premiers' conference held
1888	Jesuits' Estates Act passed in Quebec
1889	Manitoba Schools Question controversy begins
1891	Federal election focuses on issue of Canadian–American relations Sir John A. Macdonald dies
1896	Liberal party comes to power under Wilfrid Laurier
1897	Laurier–Greenway compromise on Manitoba Schools Question
1905	Saskatchewan and Alberta become provinces Autonomy Bills passed

We have come to a period in the history of this country when premature dissolution seems to be at hand." So wrote Wilfrid Laurier, the official leader of the opposition, in the early 1890s. The Canadian experiment in nation building appeared to be a failure. Bickering between Ottawa and the Dominion's seven provinces had become endemic. A provincial-rights movement flourished in Ontario; secessionist sentiments resurfaced in Nova Scotia; and regional protest arose in the North West resulting in rebellion in 1885. In Quebec, French-Canadian nationalist feeling strengthened in reaction to the execution of Louis Riel, and in the course of the debate concerning the Jesuits' Estates Act and Manitoba's denominational schools. As well, a deep economic depression resulted in one million people leaving for the United States in the 1880s. No one seemed to know the solution to Canada's problems; some, like Laurier, questioned whether a solution existed.

The Provincial-Rights Movement in Ontario

Oliver Mowat, Liberal premier of Ontario from 1872 to 1896, can rightfully be considered the "father of provincial rights." He endorsed the concept known as the provincial-compact theory—a belief that Confederation constituted a compact entered into by the provinces of their own volition, and one that could be altered only with their consent. As premier of Ontario, Mowat continued the policy of Edward Blake, his predecessor, of making the province dominant within the federation. One opportunity to do so arose over the question of the boundary line between Ontario and Manitoba.

The Ontario Boundary Dispute

The origins of the Ontario–Manitoba boundary dispute dated back to pre-Confederation days. The British had never established a precise boundary line between Rupert's Land and the colony of Upper Canada (Ontario). Mowat argued that Ontario's western boundary should run due north from the source of the Mississippi River, which was slightly west of Lake of the Woods at a place called Rat Portage (present-day Kenora). He referred to western explorations during the French regime to justify his claim. In contrast, Macdonald and the federal Conservatives wanted to draw the boundary between Ontario and Manitoba near Port Arthur on Lake Superior. Macdonald wanted to restrict Ontario's size so as to lessen its influence in Confederation.

The issue remained unresolved when the federal Liberals came to power in 1873. The following year, the two Liberal governments agreed to establish an arbitration board, which ruled in favour of Ontario. But before the board's decision became law, the federal Liberals were defeated in 1878 and the newly elected Conservatives refused to ratify the arbitrators' award. Instead, in 1881 Macdonald unilaterally awarded the disputed territory—from Lake of the Woods eastward to Thunder Bay—to Manitoba. Since the federal government owned Manitoba's natural resources, it was in a position to control the land and the mineral rights. The prime minister then granted timber rights to logging companies in the disputed area.

After two years of legal chaos, both governments agreed to submit the issue to the Judicial Committee of the Privy Council in London, the supreme legal authority in the British empire. Mowat himself pleaded Ontario's case, and won. In 1884 the Judicial Committee fixed the

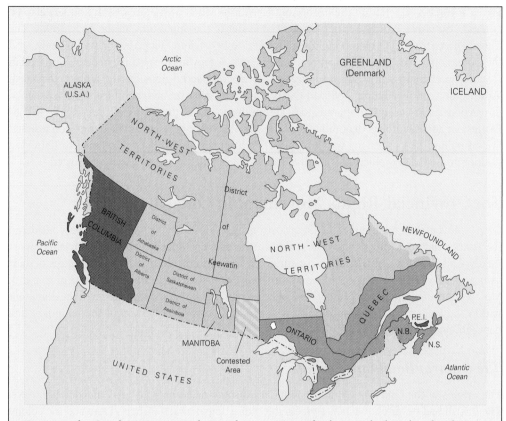

For years, the Canadian, Ontario, and Manitoba governments fought over the boundary line between Ontario and Manitoba. This map of Canada in 1882 shows the contested area.

Source: Based on information taken from National Topographic System map sheet number MCR 2306.
© 1969, Her Majesty the Queen in Right of Canada with permission of Energy, Mines and Resources Canada.

western limits of Ontario at the northwest angle of Lake of the Woods (the present boundary). Still John A. Macdonald delayed. Not until 1889 did the federal government confirm Ontario's boundaries and its right to the natural resources within the disputed territory.

Powers of the Lieutenant Governor and Federal Disallowance

Mowat won a series of victories in other disputes with the federal government, notably over the powers of the lieutenant governor, and the federal power of disallowance (the right granted to the federal government in the BNA Act to disallow any provincial law considered to conflict with federal law). According to the BNA Act, the federal government appointed lieutenant governors, paid their salaries, and had the right to dismiss them at any time. At the time of Confederation, Macdonald had believed this would keep provincial policies in harmony with national objectives.

Mowat argued that the lieutenant governor had the same position in the province as the governor general in the federal government. In his view, the provinces were to coordinate sovereignties on a par with the federal government on constitutional matters. Once again the Judicial Committee of the Privy Council upheld Mowat's position. In its ruling of 1892, it declared that a lieutenant governor "is as much the representative of Her Majesty, for all purposes of provincial government, as the Governor-General himself for all purposes of the Dominion Government."

The Ontario premier advanced provincial interests on yet another front. He argued that the provinces had certain legal powers before Confederation that they retained after 1867; one was the right to issue liquor licences. In 1884 the Ontario government passed the Act Respecting Licensing Duties, which the federal government immediately disallowed. Ontario took the dispute to court in the case of *Hodge v. the Queen*. The Judicial Committee sustained Ontario's position, holding that the provinces had full authority in their own realm of legal jurisdiction. Thus, by 1896 and the end of Conservative rule, Mowat had succeeded in strengthening provincial powers and Ontario's rights, at the expense of the federal government.

Protest in Atlantic Canada

Mowat had provincial-rights allies in Atlantic Canada. The anti-confederate sentiments of the mid-1860s reemerged in the 1880s as Maritimers protested their perceived inferior position in the new Dominion. The custom, for example, of flying flags at half-mast on July 1, which first began in 1867, continued in many Atlantic communities.

The Maritimes faced difficult economic times in the 1880s. The Conservatives' high protective tariff of 1879 contributed to regional dissatisfaction. Fish and lobster exports had dropped a staggering 75 percent in the early 1880s when the Americans raised their import duty on Maritime fish in response to the high Canadian tariff. Shipbuilding declined, as iron steamers replaced wooden sailing ships. Yarmouth, for example, once a thriving centre of Nova Scotia's shipbuilding industry, built only six vessels in 1880, four in 1884, and none in 1887. Many Nova Scotians left in search of jobs elsewhere.

Secession Threats in Nova Scotia

From 1878 to 1884, Nova Scotia's Conservative government asked Ottawa for financial assistance. But Macdonald's top priority remained the CPR and the development of the West. The unwillingness of Ottawa to help contributed to the Liberals' provincial victory in 1884 on a wave of anti-confederate sentiment.

W.S. Fielding, the new premier, also attempted to extract larger subsidies from Ottawa. When he proved no more successful than his Conservative predecessor, he introduced a secessionist resolution in the Nova Scotia legislature in 1886. The premier appealed to the other Maritime provinces to secede as well and to create an independent Maritime nation.

The other two provinces declined. New Brunswick saw Nova Scotia's offer of Maritime union as a ploy to benefit Halifax. New Brunswick had also just received federal financial support for a rail line to Saint John. Prince Edward Island feared the loss of its autonomy in a close Maritime union. Fielding himself retreated, despite a stunning victory of 29 of the 39 seats in the provincial election of 1886. The would-be separatist sensed insufficient support within the province. At the same time, his pressure tactics worked: the federal Conservative government lowered freight rates and offered generous financial assistance for railway building in the province.

Newfoundland Considers Joining Confederation

In Newfoundland, major economic changes in the late nineteenth century led to renewed interest in union with Canada once again. The fishing industry, which by 1885 employed nine out of ten of the island's work force and accounted for nearly all of its exports, experienced a serious slump. Between the early 1880s and the late 1890s, industry earnings fell by a third as a result of decreased exports to the United States and increased competition from other fishing nations, such as Norway, Denmark, and France.

The Newfoundland government successfully negotiated a reciprocity agreement with the United States in 1890, only to have the Colonial Office in Britain veto it. The Colonial Office had acted on advice from the Canadian government that protested that the agreement, if ratified, would hurt the fishing industry within the Maritimes.

Newfoundland also experienced financial troubles. In 1894, the colony witnessed a bank crash. A year later the Newfoundland government defaulted on interest payments on its loans. Premier Whiteway approached the Canadian government about discussing terms of union. Although only a few years earlier, Ottawa had offered Newfoundlanders generous terms, by 1895 the political climate had changed. Prime Minister Mackenzie Bowell feared that better terms for Newfoundland would reopen appeals from other provinces. Whiteway also found little enthusiasm on the island for union. Had not Canada scuttled Newfoundland's reciprocity negotiations with the United States? The talks broke down, and Newfoundland waited another half-century before joining Confederation.

Discontent in the North West

Macdonald faced problems in the North West as well as in the Maritimes. In Manitoba, settlers complained that the lack of transportation competition in the West kept freight rates high. They paid more to ship their goods than did central or eastern Canadians, as the monopoly clause, that prohibited competitive lines for 20 years after the completion of the CPR, gave the railway free rein to charge exorbitant prices.

The Manitoba government responded by chartering competitive lines to the American border. The federal government disallowed these provincial charters on the grounds that they were not in the "national interest." The new Liberal premier, Thomas Greenway, then began building a railway from Winnipeg south to Emerson to connect with American lines. He warned Ottawa that, if federal politicians opposed it, he would solicit American financial—and, if need be, military—support. The federal government gave in, abandoned its policy of disallowance, and bought out the CPR monopoly.

The most serious challenge arose farther west. The First Nations, particularly the Crees in the Treaty Number Six area, in what is now central Alberta and Saskatchewan, felt betrayed by the federal government's failure to keep its treaty promises of providing food rations in time of scarcity. The government had not anticipated that the buffalo would disappear so quickly and had willingly inserted the "famine clause" in Treaty Number Six in 1876. Despite its promise, however, the debt-ridden federal government did little, aside from supplying insufficient amounts of poor-quality food. The First Nations peoples also resented the government's refusal to allow them to choose their own reserve lands, as promised in the treaty. Ottawa prevented the establishment of large concentrations of reserves in the Cypress Hills area and then around Battleford.

The Métis in the region resented Ottawa's failure to act on their land claims. After the Red River resistance of 1869–70, many of the Manitoba Métis moved to the South Saskatchewan River Valley, especially around the village that became known as Batoche. Once again, their livelihoods appeared threatened as settlers moved in. They appealed to the federal government to recognize their land claims and to allow them to keep their river-lot system instead of

Gabriel Dumont, military leader of the Métis in 1885, and previously, in the "buffalo days," their leader in the hunt in the South Saskatchewan River Valley.

Source: Glenbow Archives, Calgary, Canada/ NA-1177-1.

making them conform to the rectangular township plan imposed elsewhere in the territories. By the end of 1884, Ottawa had still not responded to their petitions.

Many of the settlers at Prince Albert, northeast of Batoche, were also discontented. The CPR's decision to reroute the railway through the southern region left them hundreds of kilometres away from a rail link to eastern markets. As well, the more politically active settlers demanded an elected assembly for the North-West Territories and representation in the federal Parliament.

The Return of Louis Riel

The Métis, with the support of the "country-born" (English-speaking mixed-bloods) in the Prince Albert area, welcomed back Louis Riel to lead their protest. They believed that Riel could obtain for the North West what he had for Manitoba fifteen years earlier. But the Riel who returned in 1885 was not the Riel of 1869. During the intervening years, he had been hospitalized in two mental asylums in Quebec and had spent years in exile in the United States. He became convinced that God had chosen him "prophet of the New World," responsible for creating a reformed Roman Catholic state on the prairies. He saw his invited return to western Canada as part of God's plan.

The North-West Rebellion of 1885

Initially, Riel and his followers avoided violent action. They petitioned Ottawa on December 16, 1884, to ask for more liberal treatment for the Native peoples, a land grant for the mixed-bloods, responsible government for the North-West Territories, western representation in Ottawa, a reduction of the tariff, and the construction of a railway to Hudson Bay as an alternative to the CPR. The federal government acknowledged receipt of the petition and promised to appoint a commission to investigate problems in the North West. But apart from making a list of mixed-bloods, it promised no specific action. Moreover, it failed even to mention the Métis grievances.

The University of Toronto's "K" Company, Queen's Own Rifles, shown immediately after their return from the North West, by the doorway of University College. A grateful University honoured its undergraduate soldiers by exempting them from their annual examination, and automatically giving them their academic year.

Source: University of Toronto Archives/A73-0093-002(39).

Subsequently, in mid-March, Riel established a provisional government with himself as president and Gabriel Dumont as adjutant general for the purpose of taking up arms against the federal government as he had done in 1869–70. The Métis leader underestimated, however, how much the situation had changed in fifteen years. In 1885, a federal police force existed in the North-West Territories; thousands of settlers had located there; and a newly completed railway linked the region to central Canada. Moreover, by this point the non-Native settlers in Prince Albert had broken their informal alliance with him and only a small number of First Nations people supported him. As well, the Roman Catholic Church opposed him, denouncing him as a heretic for his unorthodox religious views.

WHERE HISTORIANS DISAGREE

The Causes of the North-West Rebellion of 1885

Earlier generations of English-speaking Canadian historians blamed the North-West Rebellion of 1885 on one man: Louis Riel. The rebel leader incited violence; his actions were those of a madman. In 1905, R.G. MacBeth wrote that "rebellion was rampant with a madman at its head."[1] In contrast, French-Canadian historians saw Riel as a misguided leader acting out of concern for his Métis people amid troubles brought about by the federal government's mismanagement of the North West. Both groups of historians saw Riel and the rebellion largely in terms of the continuing controversy of English Canadians versus French Canadians, Protestants versus Catholics.

Canadian historiography took a new turn in the 1930s. Influenced in part by the "frontier" school of thought, already well established in American historiography, several Canadian historians saw the Métis as frontier hunters and nomads who opposed the advancing frontier of a different cultural group. Historian George F.G. Stanley saw the rebellion of 1885 as a clash between "primitive and civilized peoples."[2] French ethnologist Marcel Giraud also subscribed to this cultural-conflict thesis, while American writer Joseph Kinsey Howard depicted Riel, in his popular undocumented study, as the symbolic leader of all North American Aboriginal people struggling to free themselves from white domination.[3]

Historian W.L. Morton denied that the Métis were "primitive": they were an advanced society, one whose interests and values simply differed from those of other Canadians. Moreover, by 1885, the Métis formed part of a larger western Canadian society that felt aggrieved by the indifference of Ottawa to western concerns. The rebellion of 1885 was therefore more than a Métis uprising incited by one man; it was a resistance by the people of the North West, including, at least initially, the First Nations, the Roman Catholic clergy, and settlers in addition to the Métis. It was the first of a series of western protest movements against central Canada in general, and the federal government in particular, for their failure to address western complaints.

Thomas Flanagan questions whether the Métis had to rebel to force the Conservative government to act. He argues that "the Métis grievances were at least partly of their own making; that the government was on the verge of resolving them when the Rebellion broke out; that Riel's resort to arms could not be explained by the failure of constitutional agitation." Flanagan does not exonerate Ottawa, but claims that the government's mistakes were "in judgment, not part of a calculated campaign to destroy the Métis or deprive them of their rights."[4] Flanagan argues that Riel acted as much out of self-interest or, at least, private motives, as for his Métis followers.

Historian D.N. Sprague has challenged Flanagan's assertion that the government was playing fair. He argues that Métis grievances over land claims in Manitoba during and after the resistance of 1869–70 continued to poison Métis–Ottawa relations in Saskatchewan, where so many Métis had fled when the situation in Manitoba became intolerable. Sprague implies that the federal government deliberately provoked Riel into forming a second provisional government so as to accuse him of treason.

Recently, the debate has shifted away from Riel to the Métis themselves. Why did they follow Riel? The shift in perspective has led to the study of Métis society in an effort to explain what conditions prevailed within the community that would have caused its members to follow Riel into rebellion. Diane Payment has examined Métis society in the South Saskatchewan River valley.[5] Noting that not all Métis supported Riel, historian David Lee examines the reasons why some Métis did and others did not support their leader.[6]

In *Homeland to Hinterland*, Gerhard Ens argues that the economy and society of the Red River Métis underwent dramatic change between 1840 and 1890 from being pre-capitalist and "subsistence" to a dynamic capitalist market economy, based on the buffalo-robe trade, in the North-West Territories. The result was out-migration from the Red River Colony well before 1870. Ens maintains that migration after 1870 was part of this earlier trend as economic opportunities for the Métis in Manitoba continued to decline, along with the added economic difficulties the Métis experienced as a result of the "intolerant actions and behaviour of the incoming Protestant settlers from Ontario,"[7] rather than as a result of any action by the Canadian government. Furthermore, he argues that the Métis who supported Riel in the uprising of 1869–70 came from those Métis who believed Manitoba could still be their economic "homeland." Those who did not simply moved farther west in search of better economic opportunities, but only to reenact, unfortunately, the same scenario fifteen years later in the North-West Rebellion of 1885. By this time, however, the West as a whole had become an economic "hinterland" to central Canada.

1   R.G. MacBeth, *The Making of the Canadian West* (Toronto: W. Biggs, 1905), p. 144.

2   George F.G. Stanley, *The Birth of Western Canada* (London: Longmans, Green, 1936), p. vii.

3   Joseph Kinsey Howard, *Strange Empire: The Story of Louis Riel* (Toronto: James Lewis & Samuel, 1952).

4   Thomas Flanagan, *Riel and the Rebellion: 1885 Reconsidered* (Saskatoon: Western Producer Prairie Books, 1983), pp. 146, 147.

5   Diane Payment, *The Free People—Otipemisiwak: Batoche, Saskatchewan, 1870–1930* (Ottawa: National Historic Parks and Sites Canada, 1990).

6   David Lee, "The Métis Militant Rebels of 1885," in R. Douglas Francis and Donald B. Smith, eds., *Readings in Canadian History: Post-Confederation*, 7th ed. (Toronto: Thomson Nelson, 2006), pp. 80–95.

7   Gerhard Ens, *Homeland to Hinterland: The Changing Worlds of the Red River Métis in the Nineteenth Century* (Toronto: University of Toronto Press, 1996), p. 170.

The Military Campaign

On March 26, 1885, Dumont and his Métis followers successfully routed a group of about 100 settler-volunteers and the North-West Mounted Police at Duck Lake, near Batoche. Subsequently, a band of Crees surrounded Battleford, while militant Cree warriors killed nine people near Frog Lake, northwest of Battleford.

The federal government dispatched troops to the North West on its almost-completed railway. Within a month, more than 3000 troops, under the command of Major General Frederick Middleton, arrived, joining the 2000 volunteers and Mounties already in the North West. Middleton organized the troops in three columns, at Qu'Appelle, Swift Current, and Calgary.

The Métis ambushed Middleton at Fish Creek, south of Batoche, on April 24. The battle ended in a stalemate; the Métis and Native peoples, although poorly equipped, fought superbly. Lieutenant Colonel William Otter successfully relieved Battleford, but on May 2, Poundmaker defeated his force at Cut Knife Hill. Major General Thomas Bland Strange led the Alberta Field Force from Calgary, by way of Edmonton and the North Saskatchewan River, against Big Bear's band at Frenchman's Butte in late May. As at Fish Creek, the encounter was a draw, with both sides retreating at the same time.

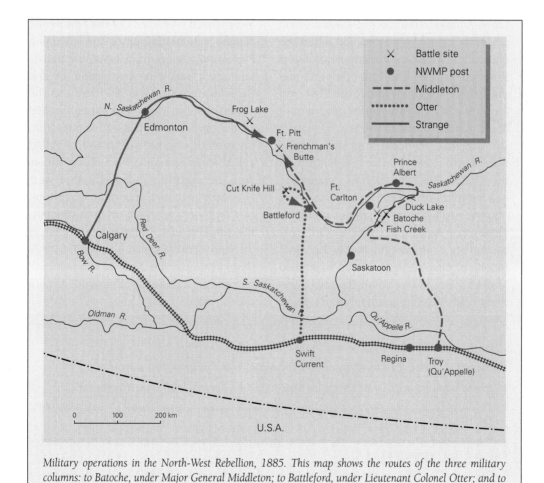

Military operations in the North-West Rebellion, 1885. This map shows the routes of the three military columns: to Batoche, under Major General Middleton; to Battleford, under Lieutenant Colonel Otter; and to the Ft. Pitt area, under Major General Strange.

Big Bear (front row, second from the left) and Poundmaker (front row, far right), shown at their trials, 1885. Father André (back row, second from the right) spent the night before Riel's execution in prayer with him. He walked with him to the scaffold.

Source: Glenbow Archives, Calgary, Canada/NA-3205-11.

The main battle took place at Batoche, Riel's headquarters, beginning on May 9. The three-day standoff ended when, out of frustration, Middleton's troops ignored his command and charged the Métis. The defenders, now out of ammunition, retreated. Riel surrendered on May 15, while Dumont and others fled to the United States.

Poundmaker and Big Bear soon surrendered. Fortunately for the federal government, most of the First Nations peoples opposed violence and favoured a political solution. The First Nations kept their promise not to take up arms against the Crown. Only about 4 percent of them joined Riel. If they and the other Métis communities had joined the uprising, the settlement of the West might very well have been postponed for a decade or more by ongoing warfare.

In the trials that followed, the Canadian government prosecuted more than 125 First Nations people. The First Nations received harsher treatment than the Métis. The government convicted 44 First Nations people, eight of whom were hanged publicly. This mass hanging, the largest in Canadian history, demonstrated Ottawa's determination to punish any challenge to its authority and to send a message to the Aboriginal community against further opposition. Big Bear and Poundmaker each received prison sentences of three years, although both leaders had spoken against participation. Poundmaker had joined only when attacked by the Canadians; Big Bear participated to counter the militants in his band. They were released before their terms ended, because of poor health; both died within a year of their release.

Riel's Trial

A jury of six men, all of British background, tried Louis Riel for treason in a Regina courtroom. Riel pleaded not guilty. His lawyers wanted to fight for acquittal on the grounds of insanity, but he refused to comply. Riel maintained that it was the federal government that was insane.

Louis Riel's address to the jury during his trial at Regina, late July 1885.

Source: Glenbow Archives, Calgary, Canada/NA-1081-3.

"The federal government," he claimed, "besides doing nothing to satisfy the people of this great land, has even hardly been able to answer once or give a single response. That fact indicates an absolute lack of responsibility, and therefore insanity complicated by paralysis." Two doctors—James Wallace of Hamilton and Daniel Clark of Toronto—examined Riel during the trial. Both concluded that Riel was sane, that he could distinguish right from wrong. Dr. François Roy, who had treated Riel at the Beauport asylum in Quebec, testified that Riel was insane and in no condition "to be master of his acts."

Riel's speech in English to the jury eloquently explained his reasons for involvement in the rebellion:

> *No one can say that the Northwest was not suffering last year … but what I have done, and risked, and to which I have exposed myself, rested certainly on the conviction I had to do, was called upon to do something for my country.… I know that through the grace of God I am the founder of Manitoba.… Even if I was going to be sentenced by you, gentlemen of the jury, I have the satisfaction if I die—that if I die I will not be reputed by all men as insane, as a lunatic.… Gentlemen of the jury, my reputation, my liberty, my life are at your discretion.*

The jury deliberated for an hour before reaching its verdict: Riel was guilty of treason.

The Execution of Riel

Only the federal cabinet could commute the court's decision. Appeals for clemency came from Canada, the United States, Britain, and France. Many members of the Orange Order, however, remembered Thomas Scott's execution fifteen years earlier and demanded revenge. In contrast, many in Quebec demanded that the French-speaking Riel be exonerated.

Prime Minister John A. Macdonald twice postponed the execution. The second time, he appointed a medical commission to reexamine the question of Riel's sanity. The commissioners concluded that Riel was sane. November 16, 1885, became the new execution date. On that clear and chilly morning, Riel mounted the gibbet at Regina. The executioner, who had been imprisoned by Riel in Fort Garry in 1869, placed the rope around Riel's neck, the priest performed the last rites, and the trap door was sprung. A Métis, a French-Canadian, and later a western-Canadian martyr was born.

It has been argued that Macdonald decided, in words attributed to him, that "Riel must swing" to keep Ontario loyal to the Conservative party. He gambled that Quebec would continue to give its support to the party. Macdonald's loyal French-Canadian lieutenants, Hector Langevin, Adolphe Caron, and Joseph-Adolphe Chapleau, were denounced as traitors for standing by their leader. Sir John A. Macdonald was burnt in effigy in the streets of Montreal. The Sunday following the hanging of Riel for treason, Wilfrid Laurier, a young Liberal politician, declared at a huge Montreal rally: "If I had been on the banks of the Saskatchewan, I too, would have shouldered a musket." In hindsight, it is evident that Riel's execution contributed to the demise of the Conservatives in Quebec in the 1890s and to the rise of the Liberals.

The North-West Rebellion of 1885 marked a transition on the Prairies; henceforth the settler society would dominate. Many events symbolized the transition: the execution of Riel and the imprisonment of Big Bear and Poundmaker; the use of the newly completed CPR to transport troops west to suppress the insurgents; and the establishment of an elected territorial assembly a year later, in 1886, in which no Métis were present. Possibly the most poignant, however, was the animus generated over the capture of two Ontario women—Theresa Delaney and Theresa Gowanlock—by a group of Cree during the rebellion. In accounts of the capture, confinement, and ultimate release of these two women, they came to embody the virtues of the "civilizers" from the East and, by contrast, the "barbaric" nature of the indigenous Native population, especially Aboriginal women. The liberation of these captives at the hands of the supposedly cruel, treacherous "savages" marked the triumph of the forces of "good" over "evil" and provided a rationale for the "necessary" suppression of the minority by the dominant society.

A HISTORICAL PORTRAIT

Will Jackson (Honoré Jaxon)

Will Jackson, secretary to Louis Riel in 1884–85, was one of the most interesting individuals to emerge from the North-West Rebellion. The former University of Toronto student, labour radical, convert to Baha'i, English-Canadian-turned Métis, spent a lifetime helping others, but died in poverty at the age of 90 in New York City in 1952.

Jackson was born into a Methodist family in Toronto on May 3, 1861. Several years later the family moved to Wingham, about 150 km northwest of Toronto, where his father opened a store. A good student, Will completed high school, and then studied classics for three years at the University of Toronto. His father's sudden bankruptcy, however, prevented Will from completing his final year. In 1882, he followed his family to Prince Albert in the North-West Territories, where Will's father began a farm implement business.

The young Jackson was elected secretary of the local farmers' union. The short man with the loud, booming voice soon became a familiar sight, riding on horseback to meetings throughout the Prince Albert district. Vigorously, he attacked the federal government's harsh land regulations and its maladministration of the North West. He advocated a settlers' alliance with the Métis at neighbouring Batoche, who, concerned about their land claims, had just invited Louis Riel back from the United States. Thus fate brought the two men together. Jackson would support Riel to the end, long after the Prince Albert settlers abandoned Riel.

On May 12, 1885, Canadian troops took Jackson into custody as Riel's secretary and sent him to Regina to be tried. The Regina court committed the prisoner, who was long-haired with a full beard and wore a Métis headband, to the lunatic asylum at Lower Fort Garry. There he wrote his assessment of Riel: "The oppression of the aboriginal has been the crying sin of the white race in America and they have at last found a voice...."

On November 2, 1885, Jackson escaped and crossed the border into the United States. He now identified himself as a Métis and changed his name to the French-sounding Honoré Jaxon. In Chicago, he became a labour organizer and helped the carpenters fight for an eight-hour working day. In 1894 he joined Coxey's Army of unemployed as they marched on Washington, DC. Three years later he converted to Baha'i, the new world religion from Persia, which stressed the simplicity of living and service to suffering human beings.

Honoré Jaxon, sitting by his library, much of which is about to be transported to the New York City dump, December 13, 1951.

Source: Photographer Hal Mathewson, *New York Daily News*, December 13, 1951. *New York Daily News/* N1421873.

Jaxon returned to Canada for two years from 1907 to 1909 but was disillusioned by the old injustices that remained. He went back to the United States and ended up in New York City in the 1920s. He loved the city, with its museums and libraries. His life mission became the establishment of a library for the Aboriginal people of Saskatchewan. To this end throughout the 1930s and 1940s he bought old books and pamphlets and saved newspapers, whatever he considered of value, and stored them in his apartment.

His dream died on December 12, 1951 when his landlord evicted him. His library went first to the street, then to the New York City dump. In poor health and broken in spirit, Honoré Jaxon died in New York one month later, on January 10, 1952.

Rising French-Canadian Nationalism

The aftermath of 1885 contributed to the growing rift between English- and French-speaking Canadians. The Riel controversy intensified the nationalist sentiment of some French-Canadian leaders. They linked French-Canadian nationalism to the struggle for provincial autonomy. Honoré Mercier, leader of the Quebec wing of the Liberal party after 1883, expressed this nationalist position in the mid-1880s. At the same rally in Montreal at which Laurier declared his support for the Métis, Mercier denounced the federal Conservative politicians who had been responsible for Riel's execution: "Riel, our brother, is dead, victim of fanaticism and treason—of the fanaticism of Sir John and some of his friends, of the treason of three of our people who sold their brother to keep their portfolios."

The Quebec Liberal leader appealed to his fellow Quebeckers to form a Parti national, an exclusive French-Canadian party, one that would put French-Canadian interests first: "We felt that the murder of Riel was a declaration of war against Quebec; and that, therefore, French Canadians had a duty to cease their fratricidal quarrels and unite in a crusade to preserve the nation in Quebec from encroaching federal power." Mercier won the provincial election of 1886.

As premier, Mercier endorsed a theory of provincial rights that complemented Oliver Mowat's. T.J.J. Loranger, a Quebec court judge, best expressed Mercier's position in his *Letters upon the Interpretation of the Federal Constitution Known as the British North America Act* (1884). Loranger argued that both levels of government, federal and provincial, were sovereign in their own area of jurisdiction and that the federal government had only limited power to deal with transprovincial concerns.

In 1887, Wilfrid Laurier became the federal Liberal leader. He proposed a French-Canadian nationalism that was an alternative to Mercier's, one that included French Canadians across the country. Initially, this was not so. In the 1860s, for example, Laurier opposed Confederation. But he became reconciled to union in the early 1870s, when elected to the House of Commons, and he began the brilliant career that led him to become prime minister. While he blamed the federal government for neglecting the Métis grievances, he appealed for moderation on both sides. In one of his speeches, Laurier presented a message of toleration reminiscent of that given by Georges-Etienne Cartier at the time of Confederation:

Immediately after Riel's execution on November 16, 1885, French Canadians rose in protest against the federal government. In Montreal, demonstrators burned Sir John A. Macdonald in effigy at the base of the statue of Queen Victoria in Victoria Square.

Source: *Frank Leslie's Illustrated Newspaper*, November 28, 1885. Saskatchewan Archives Board/R-D1776.

> We form here, or wish to form, a nation composed of the most heterogeneous elements, Protestants and Catholics, English and French, German, Irish, Scottish, each, let us not forget, with its own traditions and prejudices. In each one of these opposing elements, however, there is a common point of patriotism, and the only veritable politics is that which dominates this common patriotism, and brings these elements toward a unified goal and common aspirations.

The First Interprovincial Conference

To assist him in his challenge to Ottawa, Mercier called an interprovincial conference in 1887, the first of its kind. Two provinces declined the invitation—British Columbia and Prince Edward Island, both of which had Conservative governments—while the other five provincial Liberal governments accepted. The federal Conservative government ignored the conference, dismissing it as a partisan session of provincial Liberal governments.

The premiers summed up the provincial-rights position. They argued that Confederation was a contract among the British North American colonies that had agreed to establish a new country. Therefore, the provinces should control the federal government. Among their demands were appeals for larger federal subsidies, abolition of the federal power of disallowance, and Senate reform to strengthen provincial power.

A photo of the first interprovincial conference, called by Honoré Mercier in 1887, to challenge the authority of the federal government. The Quebec premier appears seated second from the left. Ontario's Oliver Mowat, the "Father of Provincial Rights," is seated in the centre. W.S. Fielding, who tried during his premiership to take Nova Scotia out of Confederation, is beside Mowat on the right.

Source: Library and Archives Canada/C-11583.

Macdonald refused to meet the premiers, but their protest did have an effect. From this time onward, the prime minister became cautious about using the federal power of disallowance. In 1888, he capitulated on the issue of the Manitoba railway legislation, which allowed Manitoba to build provincial rail lines, and a year later he gave in on the Ontario boundary question.

Cultural and Religious Feuds

Laurier's appeal for unity between English and French Canadians and Protestants and Roman Catholics went unheeded in the ethnically and religiously intolerant atmosphere of the late nineteenth century. Two issues—the Jesuits' Estates Act and the Manitoba Schools Question—revealed just how bitter ethnic relations and religious differences had become.

The Jesuits' Estates Controversy

The dispute over the Jesuits' Estates began in 1888. During the era of New France, the Jesuit order obtained large grants of land. After the conquest and the disbanding of the order by the Pope in the early 1770s, ownership of these properties passed first to the British government and then to the province of Lower Canada. In the early 1840s, Bishop Ignace Bourget brought back the newly established Jesuits to Quebec. The Jesuits appealed to the provincial government to have their property returned or to receive financial compensation for its losses. Premier Mercier appealed to the Pope to act as arbiter. On the basis of the Pope's recommendation, Mercier agreed to distribute $400 000 (a sum well below the actual value of the land) among the Jesuits, Université Laval in Quebec City, and the Catholic dioceses of the province. He awarded a further $60 000 to Protestant postsecondary educational institutions in Quebec. This became the basis of the Jesuits' Estates Act.

Many in Ontario reacted vehemently to the idea of papal intervention. D'Alton McCarthy, an anti-Catholic and a Conservative MP from Ontario, insisted that the Pope had no right to meddle in Canadian affairs. He moved a resolution in the House of Commons to have the federal government disallow the Jesuits' Estates Act. He and his twelve supporters became known as "the noble thirteen" or "the devil's dozen," depending on one's perspective. They considered the Act to be the latest in a series of attempts by the Jesuits and French-speaking Roman Catholics to rule Canada. McCarthy insisted on one common Canadian nationality based on the English language and British Protestant culture. But Prime Minister John A. Macdonald refused to intervene in this provincial matter; as a result, McCarthy and his followers lost their appeal. Still, the battle was far from over. Ethnic and religious tensions also centred on the school question.

The New Brunswick School Question

The first dispute over denominational schools since Confederation occurred in New Brunswick. The BNA Act recognized separate schools that existed *by law* before the union in the four original provinces. Roman Catholic schools existed by custom, not law, in New Brunswick before the union. In 1871 the New Brunswick government proposed legislation to amend the province's Schools Act to introduce a non-sectarian school system, which would deny public support to "separate" parish schools teaching French and providing religious instruction. To New Brunswick's Roman Catholics, both Acadians and Irish, this legislation meant depriving them of a right that they had enjoyed in fact, if not by law, at the time of Confederation. They requested the federal government to disallow the act under section 93 of the BNA Act, which included the right to intervene to protect the educational rights of a minority.

The federal Conservative government refused to intervene. Macdonald argued that the act lay within the province's jurisdiction. Roman Catholics did not lose any rights that they had had *by law* at the union or that they had acquired since. Hence the prime minister refused disallowance, or federal remedial action under section 93. Furthermore, he was reluctant to interfere in education—an area under provincial jurisdiction in the BNA Act. The federal government did make a strong appeal to the New Brunswick legislature to consider minority rights, but stopped at that.

The New Brunswick School Question provided the only precedent for the courts and the politicians when the Manitoba Schools Question arose in the late 1880s and early 1890s; but because it dealt with Roman Catholic schools in a founding province of Confederation whose rights had been written into the original BNA Act, it was not really applicable. Furthermore, the Manitoba Act of 1870 had guaranteed rights and privileges to Catholic and Protestant schools not only in practice but also in law, unlike the case in New Brunswick. So Manitoba's Catholics had a stronger case than did New Brunswick Catholics for school rights.

The Manitoba Schools Question

In Manitoba in 1870, the predominantly Métis population was split almost equally between French- and English-speaking, Roman Catholic and Protestant inhabitants. The Manitoba Act of 1870 had granted language rights to French-speaking and English-speaking Manitobans and school rights on Roman Catholics and Protestants in the province.

By 1890, however, the situation had changed in Manitoba. The English-speaking Protestant population in Manitoba had increased tenfold, greatly outnumbering the French-speaking Métis and French-speakers from eastern Canada. Many French-speaking Métis had left the province. Moreover, French-speaking Canadians from Quebec did not join their English-speaking compatriots to the same extent in moving west in the late nineteenth century, despite a concerted effort by the French-speaking clergy of the Roman Catholic church in the West. Distance helps to explain this. For French-speaking settlers contemplating leaving Quebec, New England was closer and more convenient, and almost everyone in Quebec had relatives or friends living there. Quebeckers could also be assured jobs as factory workers or labourers in New England. Should they wish to farm, opportunities existed in the American West with much easier access than in the Canadian West before the completion of the CPR in 1885. Thus the North West held little appeal for them.

Interference in Manitoba's separate school question came from outside the province. In August 1889, D'Alton McCarthy delivered an emotional speech at Portage la Prairie against denominational schools in Manitoba as undermining the future greatness of Canada. A few months earlier, he had supported the formation of an Equal Rights Association, which claimed in its platform to stand for "equal rights of all religious denominations before the law, special privileges for none," which was a rationale for a single language—English—and a single system of public schools. According to McCarthy and his followers, Canada's minorities, especially the French-Canadian and Métis Roman Catholics in the West, should not have "special concessions." On the same platform as McCarthy at Portage la Prairie sat Joseph Martin, attorney general for the Manitoba government. He pledged his government's support in abolishing the dual school system, as well as French as an official language, in Manitoba.

In 1890, the Manitoba government passed a Schools Act that established a provincial department of education and a system of non-sectarian public schools that alone would receive the provincial grant for education. Denominational schools could still exist, but without government funding. Those contributing to such schools must do so in addition to their public-school taxes. The same session of the legislature abolished French as an official language, contrary to section 23 of the Manitoba Act of 1870.

Main Street and City Hall Square in Winnipeg, about 1897. View looking southward toward Portage and Main. The Winnipeg monument to the Canadians who fought in 1885 appears on the extreme left.

Source: Provincial Archives of Manitoba/Simons Marguerite 5 (N10911).

Manitoba Catholics Fight School Legislation

Discontented Roman Catholics had three options: appeal to the federal government to use its right of disallowance of provincial legislation; take the issue to the courts to have the legislation declared *ultra vires*, or unconstitutional; or appeal to Ottawa to intervene on behalf of the minority through remedial legislation as set out in section 93 of the BNA Act. Eventually, they pursued all three possibilities.

Macdonald resisted using the federal government's right of disallowance, fearing that the Manitoba electorate's disapproval of such an action would strengthen the provincial government's power. He favoured court action and agreed that the federal government pay the legal costs of the appellant. The case, known as *Barrett v. the City of Winnipeg*, went through the provincial court, which upheld the Manitoba government's position, to the Supreme Court of Canada, which upheld the right of the Roman Catholic minority to have state-supported separate schools. Then, the Judicial Committee of the Privy Council in London reversed this decision in favour of the Manitoba government's position. During the same period, the territorial assembly of the North-West Territories in 1892 followed Manitoba's lead in denying the French language official status in the legislature, the courts, and schools—all rights granted in the North-West Territories Act of 1875, as amended in 1877.

One final option remained. The Manitoba Roman Catholics appealed to the federal government for remedial action under section 93 of the BNA Act. The Judicial Committee of the Privy Council eventually ruled that, yes, the federal government had the constitutional right to intervene on behalf of the minority even though the Manitoba law had been judged valid. The Conservatives introduced the remedial legislation bill in Parliament in January 1896. The government established a nine-member board to run the separate-school system, to be supported by the Roman Catholics' own tax monies; the schools in this system would share a portion of the provincial educational grant; and, to ensure proper standards, the separate schools would be inspected regularly and funds would be withheld if they were judged inefficient. Clearly, remedial legislation favoured the Roman Catholic position. But Parliament dissolved on April 23, with the bill still not passed into law. Four days later, Mackenzie Bowell resigned as Conservative leader under pressure from the Orange wing of his party, angered over his handling of the schools question.

The Election of 1896

The Conservatives entered the federal election of 1896 with a new leader, Charles Tupper—the party's fifth leader in five years. After Macdonald's death in 1891, no one seemed capable of holding the party together. The Manitoba Schools Question proved only one of several contentious issues in the election, although an important one. In Quebec, the Conservatives stressed during the election campaign that they had introduced remedial legislation on behalf of the Manitoba Roman Catholics. In English-speaking Canada, Conservative candidates emphasized that the bill was not, and might never become, law. Some English-speaking Conservatives even spoke openly against the party position on this controversial issue. Outside Quebec, the Conservatives also remained on the defensive over their high tariff policy and were being blamed for the country's continuing economic depression.

The Conservative party had mixed opportunities in the election campaign. In Quebec, the Roman Catholic hierarchy issued a pastoral letter appealing to parishioners to vote for candidates who promised to support remedial legislation. But many of the French-Canadian Conservatives who knew of their party's internal split refused to work during the campaign. Israël Tarte, a one-time Conservative organizer, defected to the Liberals.

The Liberals were in an enviable position. As the opposition, they could denounce the Tories without offering concrete alternative policies. On the controversial schools question, for example, Wilfrid Laurier had not taken a strong stand during the stormy parliamentary session of 1896.

During the election campaign, the Liberal leader simply promised that his Liberal government, if elected, would end the dispute through compromise with the Manitoba Liberal government in a way that would respect provincial rights. "If it was in my power," he said in 1895, "and if I had the responsibility, I would try the sunny way." To voters weary of the wrangling between the federal government and the provinces, the "sunny way" of compromise seemed appealing. In Quebec, the Liberals had the advantage of a French-Canadian Roman Catholic leader. Liberal leaders in the province reminded Quebeckers that if they turned Laurier down as prime minister they would never live to a see a French-Canadian prime minister in Ottawa.

The Liberals narrowly won the election of 1896. Outside Quebec, they tied the Conservatives in the number of seats. But in Quebec they obtained two-thirds of the province's share, and, after nearly two decades in opposition, returned to power.

The Laurier–Greenway Compromise

Laurier opened negotiations. He and Manitoba's Premier Greenway struck a compromise: religious instruction would be allowed in the public schools for half an hour at the end of each day. Roman Catholic teachers could be employed in urban schools with 40 Roman Catholic pupils or in rural districts with 25. On the language question it was agreed that, when ten of the pupils in any school system spoke the French language or any language other than English as their native language, the teaching of such pupils would be conducted in English and French or the other language "upon the bilingual system."

The French-Canadian Roman Catholic minority in Manitoba would have obtained more under the Conservatives' remedial legislation. The compromise allowed religious instruction but led to the abolition of the state-supported separate-school system. French would be retained only when sufficient population warranted it; hence, it lost the status of equality with English that it had had under the Manitoba Act of 1870. Moreover, it became a language like any other in Manitoba, all of which were unofficial except English. (In 1916, at the height of World War I, even the bilingual clause of the Laurier–Greenway compromise was abolished, making English the only language of instruction in the province's schools.)

The Roman Catholic hierarchy in Canada accused Laurier of capitulating to the English-Canadian Protestants. Laurier argued that the agreement was the best that could be hoped for, given the Roman Catholics' minority position. Some Canadian bishops appealed to the Pope to intervene on behalf of the Manitoba Roman Catholics. The Pope sent Monsignor Merry del Val to investigate the issue. The papal adviser reported that while the compromise was unsatisfactory, these terms were the best that the Roman Catholics could, under the circumstances, obtain.

The Autonomy Bills

The schools question in the West arose again in 1905, with the creation of the two new provinces of Saskatchewan and Alberta. The original ordinances of the North-West Territories Act of 1875, as amended in 1877, had provided for both Protestant and Roman Catholic schools to receive public funding. As well, both French and English could be used as languages of instruction. In the early 1890s, however, the territorial government made English the official language of instruction in the Roman Catholic school system, restricting French to the primary grades only for French-speaking children. Then, in 1901, the territorial government restricted religious instruction to the last half hour of the school day, as was the case in Manitoba.

When the time came to draw up the Autonomy Bills to bring Saskatchewan and Alberta into existence, Charles Fitzpatrick, the federal minister of justice and a Quebec Roman Catholic, and Henri Bourassa drafted the educational clause to restore the original system of 1877. The clause permitted the free establishment of Roman Catholic and Protestant schools as well as the use of

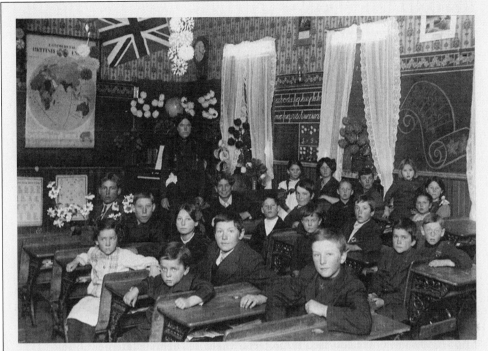

Interior of a school near Vulcan, Alberta, at the turn of the century. Teachers insisted that children from non-English-speaking countries speak English in the classroom. Legally, even French-Canadian students were obliged to do so in Alberta after their first two years of elementary school as a result of ordinances passed by the territorial government in the early 1890s.

Source: Glenbow Archives, Calgary, Canada/NA-748-41.

French in the school system. The powerful Clifford Sifton, who had once been a cabinet minister under Manitoba Premier Greenway, opposed the educational clause, claiming it went against the wishes of the government of the North-West Territories. He resigned from the cabinet in protest.

Laurier intervened and allowed Sifton to redraft the educational clause, although he did not invite him back into the cabinet. Sifton's revised clause restricted the rights of the French-Canadian Roman Catholic minorities to the limited concessions granted in the ordinance of 1901. Laurier accepted the "honourable compromise," as he described the Sifton amendment. But Bourassa denounced it as a sellout. It infringed on the rights of French Canadians as set out in the original North-West Territories Act. He maintained that French-Canadian Roman Catholics in the West should enjoy the same rights that English-Canadian Protestants enjoyed in Quebec. In the end, however, the Sifton amendment became law.

The period from 1880 to 1914 saw a resurgence of regionalism. Provincial-rightists successfully challenged the power of the central government on a number of constitutional issues, thus making Canada in practice a federal state with a more even division of power between the federal and provincial governments. Regional protests arose in the Maritimes with the attempt by Nova Scotia once again to secede from Confederation and in the West over the North-West Rebellion of 1885. As well, English- and French-speaking Canadians feuded over Riel's execution, over the Jesuits' Estates Act in Quebec, and over linguistic and religious rights in schools, first in Manitoba and then in Saskatchewan and Alberta. These disputes contributed to the defeat of the Conservatives in the 1896 election and the coming to power of the Liberals under Wilfrid Laurier.

BEYOND THE BOOK

Weblinks

Manitoba Newspapers

http://manitobia.ca/cocoon/launch/en/newspaperslist
Contains digitized versions of newspapers published in Manitoba beginning in the 1880s. View their accounts of the 1885 rebellion and the Manitoba Schools Question.

Walter F. Stewart Collection

http://web.mala.bc.ca/davies/letters.images/W.F.Stewart/collection.page.htm
Daily journal of Walter F. Stewart, a member of the North-West Mounted Police who fought in the Riel Rebellion of 1885.

Manitoba Schools Question

http://manitobia.ca/cocoon/launch/en/themes/msq
Analysis of the Manitoba Schools Question, including a historical map showing the location of Protestant and Roman Catholic school districts of the time.

Wilfrid Laurier

http://www.collectionscanada.ca/2/4/h4-3175-e.html
A detailed biography of Prime Minister Wilfrid Laurier, including digitized versions of his speeches.

Final Statement of Louis Riel

http://www.law.umkc.edu/faculty/projects/ftrials/riel/rieltrialstatement.html
Louis Riel's final statement given to the jury of his trial in 1885, and his later religious renunciation.

Newfoundland's Confederation Negotiations of 1895

http://www.heritage.nf.ca/law/negotiations.html
Analysis and digitized historical documents regarding the negotiations with Newfoundland to join Confederation in 1895.

Films & Novels

Louis Riel: A Comic-Strip Biography. By Chester Brown. 2004.

The Temptations of Big Bear. By Rudy Henry Wiebe. 1973.

Canada: A People's History—Episode 10: Taking the West. Directed by Bill Cobban. 2001.

Chiefs: The Trial of Poundmaker. Directed by Gil Cardinal. 2002.

RELATED READINGS

Some topics in this chapter can be examined in greater depth in the following articles from R. Douglas Francis and Donald B. Smith, *Readings in Canadian History: Post-Confederation*, 7th ed. (Toronto: Thomson Nelson, 2006): Peter Russell, "Provincial Rights," pp. 56–68; J.R. Miller, "Unity/Diversity: The Canadian Experience; From Confederation to the First World War," pp. 68–76; David Lee, "The Métis Militant Rebels of 1885," pp. 80–95; A. Blair Stonechild, "The Indian View of the 1885 Uprising," pp. 96–108; and Jean Barman, "Taming Aboriginal Sexuality: Gender, Power, and Race in British Columbia, 1850–1900," pp. 154–174.

BIBLIOGRAPHY

For an overview of Dominion–provincial relations in the late nineteenth century see P.B. Waite, *Canada, 1874–1896: Arduous Destiny* (Toronto: McClelland & Stewart, 1971), and the *Report of the Royal Commission on Dominion–Provincial Relations*, Book 1 (Ottawa: J.O. Patenaude, Printer to the King, 1940).

The provincial-rights movement in Ontario is discussed in J.C. Morrison, "Oliver Mowat and the Development of Provincial Rights in Ontario: A Study in Dominion–Provincial Relations, 1867–1896," in *Three History Theses* (Toronto: Ontario Department of Public Records and Archives, 1961); Christopher Armstrong, *The Politics of Federalism: Ontario's Relations with the Federal Government, 1867–1942* (Toronto: University of Toronto Press, 1981); and Paul Romney, *Getting It Wrong: How Canadians Forgot Their Past and Imperilled Confederation* (Toronto: University of Toronto Press, 1999). See, as well, Margaret Evans's biography *Sir Oliver Mowat* (Toronto: University of Toronto Press, 1992). On political protest in Atlantic Canada in the 1880s see Judith Fingard, "The 1880s: Paradoxes of Progress," in E.R. Forbes and D.A. Muise, eds., *The Atlantic Provinces in Confederation* (Toronto: University of Toronto Press, 1993); T.W. Acheson, "The Maritimes and 'Empire Canada,'" in D.J. Bercuson, ed., *Canada and the Burden of Unity* (Toronto: Macmillan, 1977), pp. 87–114; E.R. Forbes, *Aspects of Maritime Regionalism, 1867–1927* (Ottawa: Canadian Historical Association, 1983); and George Rawlyk, ed., *The Atlantic Provinces and the Problem of Confederation* (St. John's: Breakwater Books, 1979). Rawlyk also deals with developments in Newfoundland in the 1880s and 1890s, as does Frederick W. Rowe in *A History of Newfoundland and Labrador* (Toronto: McGraw-Hill Ryerson, 1980). On western Canada see T.D. Regehr, "Western Canada and the Burden of National Transportation Policies," in D.J. Bercuson, ed., *Canada and the Burden of Unity* (Toronto: Macmillan, 1977), pp. 115–41. David Cruise and Alison Griffiths discuss the impact of the CPR rates in *Lords of the Line* (Toronto: Viking, 1988).

The most authoritative account of the North-West Rebellion is Bob Beal and Rob Macleod, *Prairie Fire: The 1885 North-West Rebellion* (Edmonton: Hurtig, 1984). For the First Nations perspective on the 1885 Rebellion see Blair Stonechild and Bill Waiser, *Loyal Till Death: Indians and the North-West Rebellion* (Calgary: Fifth House, 1997). On aspects of the conflict between the First Nations and the Anglo-Canadians on the Prairies see Walter Hildebrandt, *Views from Fort Battleford: Constructed Visions of an Anglo-Canadian West* (Regina: Canadian Plains Research Center, University of Regina, 1994). On the aftermath of 1885 on the Plains Cree, see Edward Ahenakew's *Voices of the Plains Cree* (Toronto: McClelland and Stewart, 1973; Regina: Canadian Plains Research Center, 1995). For the impact of disease, consult Maureen K. Lux, *Medicine That Walks: Disease, Medicine, and Canadian Plains Native People, 1880–1940* (Toronto: University of Toronto Press, 2001). For a historical perspective on the Delaney–Gowanlock captivity see Sarah Carter, *Capturing Women: The Manipulation of Cultural Imagery in Canada's Prairie West* (Montreal/Kingston: McGill-Queen's University Press, 1997). Hugh A. Dempsey explains the participation of Big Bear's band in *Big Bear* (Vancouver: Douglas & McIntyre, 1984), as does J.R. Miller in *Big Bear (Mistahimusqua)* (Toronto: ECW Press, 1996). George Woodcock discusses Gabriel Dumont's role in *Gabriel Dumont* (Edmonton: Hurtig, 1975). On Louis Riel see the readings cited for Chapter 2 of this book, as well as the titles listed in "Where Historians Disagree" in this chapter. A historiographical article is J.R. Miller, "From Riel to the Métis," *Canadian Historical Review* 69(1) (March 1988): 1–20. For the reaction of Ontarians to Riel see A.I. Silver, "Ontario's Alleged Fanaticism in the Riel Affair," *Canadian Historical Review* 69(1) (March 1988): 21–50. All of Riel's writings have been edited by George F.G. Stanley et al., *The Collected Writings of Louis Riel*, 5 vols. (Edmonton: University of Alberta Press, 1985). A number of excellent articles on the events of 1885 are contained in *NeWest Review* 10(9) (May 1985), a special "1885" issue. For a discussion of the military engagement at Batoche see Walter Hildebrandt, *The Battle of Batoche: British Small Warfare and the Entrenched Métis* (Ottawa: National Historic Parks and Sites, Parks Canada, 1985).

George F.G. Stanley reviews the various interpretations of Riel in "The Last Word on Louis Riel—The Man of Several Faces," in F. Laurie Barron and James B. Waldram, eds., *1885 and After: Native Society in Transition* (Regina: Canadian Plains Research Center, University of Regina, 1986), as does Doug Owram in "The Myth of Louis Riel," *Canadian Historical Review* 63(3) (September 1982): 315–36. George Melnyk's *Radical Regionalism* (Edmonton: NeWest, 1982) and his edited collection *Riel to Reform: A History of Protest in Western Canada* (Saskatoon: Fifth House, 1992) examine the roots of western protest and its relationship to regional identity. For an examination of Louis Riel in Canadian culture, see Albert Braz, *The False Traitor: Louis Riel in Canadian Culture* (Toronto: University of Toronto Press, 2003). The extraordinary life of Will Jackson (1861–1952), Riel's secretary in 1884/85, later known in the United States as Honoré Jaxon, is told by Donald B. Smith in *Honoré Jaxon: Prairie Visionary* (Regina: Coteau Books, 2007).

Quebec's views on federal–provincial relations are analyzed in R. Cook, *Provincial Autonomy: Minority Rights and the Compact Theory, 1867–1921* (Ottawa: Queen's Printer, 1969); and Arthur Silver, *The French-Canadian Idea of Confederation, 1864–1900* (Toronto: University of Toronto Press, 1982). See also Mason Wade, *The French Canadians: 1760–1945* (Toronto: Macmillan, 1955), pp. 331–446; and Susan Mann, *The Dream of Nation: A Social and Intellectual History of Quebec*, 2nd ed.(Montreal/ Kingston; McGill-Queen's University Press, 2002), pp. 150–66. Honoré Mercier's views are presented in Gilles Gallichan, *Honoré Mercier: La politique et la culture* (Sillery, PQ: Septentrion, 1994).

J.R. Miller's *Equal Rights: The Jesuits' Estates Act Controversy* (Montreal: McGill-Queen's University Press, 1979) deals with that subject in depth. On the Manitoba schools question and its impact on the election of 1896 consult Paul Crunican, *Priests and Politicians: Manitoba Schools and the Election of 1896* (Toronto: University of Toronto Press, 1974). On Rome's position in the controversy see Roberto Perin, *Rome in Canada: The Vatican and Canadian Affairs in the Late Victorian Age* (Toronto: University of Toronto Press, 1990). Lovell Clark has compiled a collection of sources in *The Manitoba School Question: Majority Rule or Minority Rights* (Toronto: Copp Clark, 1968). On D'Alton McCarthy's role see J.R. Miller, "D'Alton McCarthy, Equal Rights, and the Origins of the Manitoba Schools Question," *Canadian Historical Review* 54 (December 1973): 369–92. Gilbert L. Comeault, "La question des écoles du Manitoba—un nouvel éclairage," *Revue d'histoire de l'Amérique française* 33(1) (June 1979): 3–23, stresses the local origins of the Manitoba schools question. Treatment of the schools question in Alberta and Saskatchewan can be found in Manoly R. Lupul, *The Roman Catholic Church and the North-West School Question: A Study in Church–State Relations in Western Canada* (Toronto: University of Toronto Press, 1974). On Sifton's contribution see D.J. Hall, *Clifford Sifton*, vol. 2, *The Lonely Eminence, 1901–1929* (Vancouver: University of British Columbia Press, 1985).

The politics of the 1890s are discussed in John T. Saywell's introduction to *The Canadian Journal of Lady Aberdeen, 1893–1898* (Toronto: Champlain Society, 1960); Lovell Clark, "Macdonald's Conservative Successors, 1891–1896," in John Moir, ed., *Character and Circumstance: Essays in Honour of Donald Grant Creighton* (Toronto: Macmillan, 1970), pp. 43–62; H.B. Neatby and J.T. Saywell, "Chapleau and the Conservative Party in Quebec," *Canadian Historical Review* 37 (March 1956): 1–22; P.B. Waite, *The Man from Halifax: Sir John Thompson, Prime Minister* (Toronto: University of Toronto Press, 1985); Phillip Buckner, "Sir Charles Tupper," *Dictionary of Canadian Biography*, vol. XIV (1911–1920) (Toronto: University of Toronto Press, 1998): 1014–1023; and H. Blair Neatby, *Laurier and a Liberal Quebec: A Study in Political Management* (Toronto: McClelland & Stewart, 1973). See as well Réal Bélanger's, *Wilfrid Laurier: quand la politique devient passion* (Quebec: Presses de l'Université Laval, 1986).

Birdseye View of Dawson, Yukon Ter., 1903.

Chapter Five

IMPERIALISM, CONTINENTALISM, AND NATIONALISM

TIME LINE

1871	Treaty of Washington signed
1884	Imperial Federation League formed in Canada
1897	Queen Victoria's Diamond Jubilee
1899	Outbreak of the South African War
1903	Founding of the Ligue nationaliste Alaska Boundary Dispute settled
1909	Department of External Affairs established
1910	Naval Service Bill introduced
1911	Reciprocity Treaty negotiated with the United States rejected in federal election Conservatives win federal election under Robert Borden
1912	Conservatives impose closure to pass the Naval Aid Bill

In the late nineteenth century, few Canadians believed that Canada could survive, politically and economically, as a fully independent country. George Ross, Ontario's minister of education and later premier (1899–1905), proposed one option: an increased role in the British empire. "As Canadians," he stated in 1896, "we should teach more of Canada and in teaching Canada we should teach it as only one colony of the vast British empire on whose dominion the sun never sets." Another group of English Canadians favoured instead closer economic or even political association with the United States. Goldwin Smith, a historian-cum-journalist and long-time critic, advanced this position in his controversial book *Canada and the Canadian Question* (1891). A third option, presented by Henri Bourassa of Quebec, gained support among French-speaking Canadians. The Quebec nationalist argued that Canada should formulate its own foreign policy as an autonomous nation within the British empire. All three options were heatedly debated in the context of international events such as the South African war, the naval crisis, and the failed reciprocity agreement with the United States. The first two issues deeply divided French Canadians and English Canadians, while the latter one pitted farmers and workers against industrialists.

The North Atlantic Triangle and the Treaty of Washington

The triangular relationship between Britain, the United States, and Canada broke down in the 1860s. After the North won the U.S. Civil War in 1865, it immediately demanded compensation from Britain for "supporting" the South. The British government had allowed Confederate agents to purchase ships and ammunition in Britain. One British-built warship, the *Alabama*, inflicted heavy losses on American merchant shipping. Also British vessels, such as the *Trent*, had carried Confederate envoys to England to raise money for the Southern cause. As a final irritant, Confederate sympathizers, on at least one occasion, had used British North America to attack the North.

The Americans had contributed to the tensions too. The American Congress cancelled the Reciprocity Treaty in 1866, and some Congressmen assumed that economic collapse north of the border would follow, causing the British North American colonies to seek union with the United States. As well, the American government did nothing to prevent the Fenian Brotherhood, a radical group of Irish-Americans who hoped to capture Canada for use as a bargaining tool for the independence of Ireland, from making raids across the border. The Fenians continued their attacks until 1871. Prominent American leaders also talked openly of annexing Canada as part of their "manifest destiny" to control the North American continent.

Canadian leaders wanted greater control over their internal affairs. They also insisted on a stronger voice within the British empire. At the same time, English Canadians and many French Canadians also saw Britain as their military protector, and welcomed the 15 000 British troops garrisoned in the new Dominion in 1867. It was the British government, wanting to reduce expenses, that insisted on their withdrawal by 1871.

British and American leaders agreed to hold a conference in Washington to settle outstanding disputes between the two countries, in particular the *Alabama* claims. The United States also wanted to bargain for the right to fish in the territorial waters of the Maritime provinces and to use those provinces' ports—privileges denied since 1818, except during the term of the Reciprocity Treaty from 1854 to 1866. Canada hoped to use the fisheries question as leverage to force the Americans to renew limited free trade. In addition, Canada wanted compensation for damages caused by Fenian raids. On the Pacific Ocean, a clear boundary line between Vancouver Island and the American mainland needed to be drawn.

For the first time, a Canadian, Prime Minister John A. Macdonald, attended an international conference as a participant. Although he spoke for Canada, he belonged officially to the five-member British delegation to Washington and represented Britain as well. This dual role placed Macdonald in an awkward position; he realized, "If things go well my share of the kudos will be but small, and if anything goes wrong I will be made the scapegoat at all events so far as Canada is concerned." From Macdonald's perspective in the negotiations, the British proved once again too willing to bargain away Canadian interests for a lasting Anglo–American peace.

The Americans did well by the Treaty of Washington. They succeeded in keeping the question of compensation to Canadians for the Fenian raids off the conference agenda, yet obtained $15.5 million as a settlement for their *Alabama* claims. They won the right to fish in British North American territorial waters in return for a cash payment, subsequently agreed upon by an arbitration committee to be $5.5 million. As well, they obtained free navigation in perpetuity

The Treaty of Washington commissioners in 1871. Prime Minister John A. Macdonald is third from the left. This was the first international conference in which a Canadian leader participated. The settlement confirmed Canada's southern boundary with the United States.

Source: M.B. Brady/Library and Archives Canada/C-2422.

on the St. Lawrence River. The treaty also provided for the arbitration of the San Juan boundary dispute. Through the arbitration process in 1872 the German kaiser decided that the Americans should own the San Juan Islands east of Victoria.

From their perspective, Canadians received very little of a concrete nature: the right to free navigation on three remote Alaskan rivers, and the removal of duties on Canadian fish exported into American markets. Yet, in one respect, Canada did well: through the Treaty of Washington, the United States recognized Canada as a separate nation in North America. Canada no longer needed the British military garrison, as the United States confirmed and recognized Canada's borders.

Macdonald returned from Washington determined to obtain a greater Canadian voice in deciding British imperial policy that affected Canada. The prime minister later appointed Alexander Tilloch Galt, who had briefly served as the Dominion's first finance minister in 1867, as high commissioner for Canada in London. Only reluctantly did the British government approve the new quasi-diplomatic post, and then only on the condition that Canada would not use the term "minister." The delegate became known as a "high commissioner," a title the Canadian diplomatic representatives in the United Kingdom and other Commonwealth countries retain today. Galt's tasks included the promotion of Canada's exports to Britain and of British investment in Canada, as well as the encouragement of British emigration to the Canadian North West.

Continentalism

The Liberals—more so than the Conservatives—favoured stronger continental ties in the 1880s and 1890s. Closer links between the two countries could take many forms. Freer trade, for example, appealed particularly to the exporters of fish, farm products, and timber. Some Liberals simply wanted a return to the Reciprocity Treaty of 1854 or a restricted reciprocity agreement, which would apply to natural products only. Others favoured unrestricted reciprocity, or free trade, in some manufactured goods as well as in natural resources. Still others proposed commercial union—an integrated economic union with a free interchange of all products, a sharing of internal revenue taxes, and a common tariff policy against other countries. At the extreme end of this spectrum came political union.

All of these positions naturally depended on the Americans' openness to some kind of association. In the 1870s, however, protectionists dominated the American Senate, and the Republican administrations turned down Canadian offers to renegotiate a reciprocity treaty.

The Trade Question and the 1891 Election

The trade issue came to a head in the election of 1891. The Liberals worked for closer Canadian–American ties, although they differed on what form they should take. Most extreme was Goldwin Smith who advocated political union with the United States. He regarded Canada as an unnatural country economically, geographically, and culturally. Political expediency alone held it together. Canada's natural destiny lay in a larger North American nation. Smith looked toward continental union as the means to assimilate the French Canadians, whom he regarded as a most backward people. He also wanted to open up the natural north–south trade axis of the continent and to achieve a federation of North America's English-speaking people. Richard Cartwright, former minister of finance in the Mackenzie government, saw commercial union between the two countries, with a common tariff against outsiders, as being in Canada's best interest. By contrast, Edward Blake, former leader of the federal Liberal party (1881–87), opposed unrestricted reciprocity, seeing it as a threat to national interests. Laurier, as party leader, pressured Blake

The cartoon shows Liberal leader, Wilfrid Laurier, and Richard Cartwright, his Liberal financial critic, on a toboggan slipping down the slope of "Unrestricted Reciprocity" with the symbolic Miss Canada between them. With the knife of Reciprocity, Cartwright is cutting the rope that prevents the toboggan from falling into "Annexation." Macdonald, straining to hold the toboggan back, calls for help to save Canada in the forthcoming federal election, March 5, 1891.

Source: Library and Archives Canada/C007369.

into silence on his opposition until after the election, at which time Blake publicly denounced the policy in an open letter to his constituency. In the middle stood Wilfrid Laurier. Commercial union appealed to him in principle but was too extreme for a party platform, so he committed the party to unrestricted reciprocity instead.

Canadian manufacturers opposed any form of reciprocity. In 1887, they published a manifesto warning that reciprocity would adversely affect the infant industries of Canada that were still struggling under the National Policy to survive a recession. Macdonald claimed that unrestricted reciprocity threatened Canada's independence because it would ultimately lead to political union with the United States. He maintained that protectionism was the means to prevent American assimilation and to uphold the British connection. He declared his loyalty to Britain in his popular campaign slogan, "A British subject I was born, and a British subject I will die," and proceeded to drape himself in the British flag.

The 1891 Election Results

The Conservatives won the election of 1891, but only by a narrow majority of 27 seats. They lost seats to the Liberals in close votes in the rural areas, which tended to support free trade, but won most of the urban vote in Ontario and Quebec, where protectionism was strong. They made their real gains, however, in the outlying provinces—"the shreds and patches of Confederation," as the disgruntled Liberal Richard Cartwright called them. The Conservatives won in all three Maritime provinces on the loyalty issue and returned fourteen out of a possible fifteen members in the West. With the open backing of the CPR, they won every seat but one (in Manitoba) along the railway's main line from Vancouver to Montreal. When asked about that one loss, Cornelius Van Horne, president of the CPR, replied that it must have been a case of pure oversight on the CPR's part.

The election of 1891 ended unrestricted reciprocity as a Liberal policy. Two decades would pass before the Liberals would champion "continentalism" once again in the election of 1911.

Imperialism

Many English-speaking Canadians favoured stronger British ties through imperial federation. After 1875, British attitudes to empire changed. Benjamin Disraeli's statement in the 1850s that colonies were "millstones around the neck of the British" had given way to a new imperialism in the late nineteenth century. Indeed, Disraeli himself, as Conservative prime minister, became one of its most ardent supporters, having come to appreciate the importance of colonies in maintaining Britain's military and economic supremacy in the world. In particular, overseas colonies proved important for British hegemony as Germany and Italy became major European powers and as the United States threatened to supplant Britain as the leading English-speaking country in the world.

Rivalry between imperial countries meant competition for colonial markets and for world trade, thus giving an economic emphasis to the new imperialism. The cry from imperialists that "trade follows the flag" led British manufacturers and many in the working class to support imperialism in the late nineteenth century. Depressed economic conditions in England during the 1880s and 1890s strengthened the new imperial movement.

Imperialism, however, represented for many of its followers much more than trade, tariffs, and guns. It was an intellectual and spiritual force. Imperialists believed implicitly in the superiority of the Anglo-Saxon "race." Applying Charles Darwin's theory of evolution in the animal kingdom to society, race theorists argued that some races were born "superior"—were better fit to survive—than others, and that, in Britain and in colonies settled by whites, the Anglo-Saxons constituted the elite. Imperialists argued that their "race's" superior position made it imperative for "Anglo-Saxons" to spread their "virtues"—their British values and Christian beliefs, the two being considered synonymous—to the less fortunate "infidels" of Asia, Africa, and the Pacific. They believed they must take up this "white man's burden," as the British author Rudyard Kipling expressed it.

Women played an important role in the imperialist movement. Organizations such as the Imperial Order Daughters of the Empire (IODE), founded by Margaret Polson Murray during the South African War, became strong advocates of imperial sentiment. Its motto—"One Flag, One Throne, One Country"—summarized its aspirations. Through its first chapters in Fredericton and Montreal, the organization sought to promote the British Empire and British institutions in the schools. By World War I, it would become one of the largest English-Canadian women's voluntary associations. In her fine novel *The Imperialist* (1904), novelist Sara Jeannette Duncan presented an Ontario community that was loyal and attached to Britain, but that rejected substantial imperial commitments.

British women, however, were much more than advocates of imperialism; they were also symbols, or icons, of imperialism, as representatives of the moral, religious, and spiritual components of its ideology. They were the bearers of the finest British civilization and thus the true "empire builders." Their children were the offspring of the dominant race, and thus the means to ensure its survival. English-Canadian imperial literature extolled the virtues of the fairer sex of the empire builders, by contrasting the noble attributes of British women with the "degenerate qualities" of "coloured women" in the subservient colonial society. As well, protecting this "fairer sex" became a pretext for suppressing and controlling the indigenous population. Once again, then, racism and imperialism were fused to accentuate the superiority of the conqueror by emphasizing the inferiority of the conquered, the "others" in the imperial–colonial relationship.

Imperialism as Nationalism

English-Canadian imperialists believed that Canada could offer the British empire much, economically, militarily, and spiritually. In turn, the empire could advance Canada's national interests. In this sense, as historian Carl Berger has written, "imperialism was one form of Canadian nationalism."[1] These imperialists believed that Canada was destined to become the heart of the British empire. Throughout history, they pointed out, all great "races" had come out of northern climates. English-speaking Canadians were the last group of "Anglo-Saxons" to struggle in a cold, rugged, northern climate, and this struggle "in the true north, strong and free" had strengthened their will to survive. It prepared them to assume the mantle of imperial grandeur as it passed from British hands. At the same time English-Canadian imperialists argued that in aiding the empire, Canadians would also be helping themselves. English-Canadian imperialists envisioned imperial federation as a means to free Canada from economic depression, ethnic tension, provincialism, and threatened American annexation, thus enabling it to reach greater heights—"a sense of power" as historian Carl Burger notes—in the world.

Imperialism drew its greatest support in Canada from a small English-speaking social and political elite, mainly Protestant ministers, lawyers, teachers, and politicians. In 1887 they formed a Canadian branch of the Imperial Federation League, an organization begun in Britain three years earlier. Descendants of United Empire Loyalists joined in large numbers, seeing imperialism as the fulfillment of their long-time dream of a "United Empire," which gave the league its greatest support in Ontario and the Maritimes.

A HISTORICAL PORTRAIT

Sara Jeannette Duncan

Sara Jeannette Duncan symbolized the "new woman" of the late nineteenth century. She was the first Canadian woman to become a journalist and counted among her friends two other "exceptional" women: Pauline Johnson, the Mohawk poet; and Augusta Stowe, the daughter of Emily Stowe, the first woman to graduate from a Canadian medical school.

Sara was born in Brantford, Ontario, in 1861. Her parents encouraged her to enjoy "romping and fresh air" and even to play hockey with her brothers. But in terms of career choice for their oldest child, they were quite traditional, encouraging Sara to become a teacher. She attended Normal School but loathed teaching, and decided instead to pursue a career in journalism. Her first breakthrough came in 1882, when a Boston magazine, *Outing*, accepted her account of a trip she and her brother made to Quebec. Two years later, she travelled to the New Orleans Cotton Centennial and sold her account of that journey to a series of Canadian and American newspapers. Her success enabled her to obtain a job as a columnist for the Toronto *Globe*, the first woman to do so.

In 1886, she and a female friend embarked on a world tour—unchaperoned—by going "the wrong way" via Asia rather than Europe. They visited Japan, Ceylon, and India before arriving in England. Duncan participated in what were considered "unladylike activities" for the time: riding a locomotive cowcatcher through the Rockies; travelling by donkey, camel, and elephant in India; and taking a catamaran to Ceylon. Her account of her tour came out in serial form in a popular British magazine as "A Social Departure," and then appeared in book form under the same title. Upon marriage to an English official she met in India, she settled there.

Her finest novel was *The Imperialist*, published in 1904. It combined her intimate knowledge of Canada from growing up in Brantford with her wider knowledge of the British empire, acquired through her world travels. Her novel familiarized Canadians with the British empire and worked to instill in them a love for their own country.

Duncan viewed imperialism along the lines of the Canadian imperialists of her day. She too admired Britain as the mother country, but was repulsed by the materialism and militarism of the British imperialists. What imperialism needed was a new seat of power, and Duncan saw Canada as the logical new location. "In the scrolls of the future it is already written that the centre of the Empire must

Sara Jeannette Duncan was one of the most penetrating observers of Canadian society of her day.

Source: Library and Archives Canada/ C-46447.

shift—and where, if not to Canada?" she has her protagonist, Lorne Murchison, ask rhetorically. The proper imperial tie would boost Canadian nationalism and hence ward off the danger of absorption into the United States. As an ardent nationalist, she held Canada in the highest esteem.

During World War I, Sara Jeannette Duncan moved from India to England. In 1919, she and her husband, who had become a journalist, had an opportunity to accompany Edward, the Prince of Wales, on his Canadian tour. It was her last visit to her homeland. On July 22, 1922, she died of pneumonia. She was buried in England under a gravestone with the simple inscription: "This leaf has blown far."

Leaders of the Canadian Imperial Federation League

The Imperial Federation League attracted some colourful individuals. In Toronto, Colonel George Taylor Denison was the most dynamic member. A descendant of a long line of enthusiasts of the British military tradition, he wrote a book in 1892 entitled *The Struggle for Imperial Unity*. One reviewer claimed it might well have been entitled "How I Saved the Empire." For 30 years, from 1880 to 1910, Denison would be one of Canada's most outspoken exponents for imperial unity.

Two other "Georges"—George Monro Grant and George Parkin—became leaders in the Imperial Federation League. Unlike Denison, they were concerned with the intellectual and spiritual aspects of imperialism. Grant was a Presbyterian minister before becoming in 1877 principal of Queen's University, a position he held until his death in 1902. Grant's imperialism grew out of his religious fervour. He saw imperial unity and Christian unity as one and the same thing, since in his mind British imperialism embodied Protestant Christian values. He admonished "Anglo-Saxons" to serve the empire in distant corners of the globe.

George Parkin argued for the humanitarian side of imperialism. John S. Ewart once described Parkin as "the prince of Imperialists and their first missionary." Parkin never became a minister, but he found an outlet for his missionary zeal in education. First he began teaching high school in his native province. Then, in 1885, he joined the Imperial Federation League and completed three books on the subject of imperialism. In 1896 he was appointed principal of Upper Canada College in Toronto, a position he held until 1902, at which time he became the organizing secretary for the Rhodes Scholarship Trust, an educational fund honouring Cecil Rhodes, the British South African arch-imperialist and mining magnate. The scholarships enabled gifted students from the British empire to attend Oxford University. Parkin used his position to tour the empire to spread the gospel of imperial federation. A bust of Parkin still stands in Rhodes House at Oxford as a reminder of his contribution to the imperialist cause.

Parkin's most important book, *Imperial Federation: The Problem of National Unity* (1892), set out a vision of a single British imperial nation that would unite all Anglo-Saxons in the world as a common cultural group. He viewed the empire as an instrument for the betterment of mankind, providing freedom from ignorance and advancement for the non-white races.

WHERE HISTORIANS DISAGREE

The Nature of Imperialism

Historians have debated the nature and impact of imperialism in Canada's past. Inspired by William Lyon Mackenzie King's efforts to achieve Canadian independence, liberal nationalist historians of the interwar years viewed imperialism as an obstacle in the way of Canada's evolution from colony to nation. Oscar Skelton, later undersecretary of state for external affairs (1925–41), argued that imperialism hindered the growth of Canadian independence. It also caused disunity, as French Canadians could not identify with the imperial vision.[1]

In his writings in the 1930s, liberal-nationalist historian Frank H. Underhill equated imperialism with colonialism. The British connection embroiled Canadians in imperial wars of no direct interest to them. Only later did Underhill see the British empire in positive terms, as a liberal association that had granted self-government to its colonial dependencies and that had been the foundation for the modern British Commonwealth of Nations. Such a positive view became possible only after imperialism had ceased to be an active and pervasive force in the world and in Canadian thought.

In the post–World War II era, Donald G. Creighton and other conservative-nationalist historians looked to the imperial connection as the counterforce to the menacing pull of continentalism, and thus Canada's means of maintaining independence in North America. Creighton depicted John A. Macdonald as the great Canadian statesman who had understood the importance of British imperialism in safeguarding Canada against American continentalism. "The diplomatic and military support of Great Britain," Creighton wrote, "could alone offset the political preponderance of the United States; and Macdonald proposed therefore to bring in the old world to redress the balance of the new."[2] Historian Norman Penlington has argued that English-Canadian imperialists in general had seen the empire as Canada's means to strengthen its position vis-à-vis the United States.[3]

Historian Carl Berger shifted the focus of the debate. He showed that imperialism was more an intellectual than a political, economic, or military phenomenon, that it was primarily a concept in the mind of those who endorsed it. In reality, Berger argued, imperialism was "one variety of Canadian nationalism."[4] Canadian imperialists believed that Canada could achieve a "sense of power" and thus fulfill its destiny as a great nation through the imperial connection.

Berger's argument that imperialism was an indigenous phenomenon promoted largely by an elite of English-Canadian thinkers has been challenged by historian Robert Page. In a review of Berger's book, Page wrote that "external events and a very strong international climate of opinion,"[5] including such phenomena as the popular enthusiasm surrounding Queen Victoria's Diamond Jubilee and the patriotism that came forth during the Boer War, also contributed. Furthermore, Page questions Berger's strictly nationalist and intellectual perspective on imperialism, arguing that a study of the attitudes toward imperialism among businesspeople, for example, would undoubtedly yield a different, more economic, perspective.

1   O.D. Skelton, *The Life and Letters of Sir Wilfrid Laurier* (Toronto: Oxford University Press, 1921).

2   Donald Creighton, "Macdonald and the Anglo-Canadian Alliance," in *Towards the Discovery of Canada: Selected Essays* (Toronto: Macmillan, 1972), p. 223.

3   Norman Penlington, *Canada and Imperialism, 1896–1899* (Toronto: University of Toronto Press, 1965).

4   Carl Berger, *The Sense of Power: Studies in the Ideas of Canadian Imperialism, 1867–1914* (Toronto: University of Toronto Press, 1970), p. 9.

5   Robert Page, "Carl Berger and the Intellectual Origins of Canadian Imperial Thought, 1867–1914," *Journal of Canadian Studies* 5 (August 1970), p. 40.

Stephen Leacock was a younger member of the Imperial Federation League, and later of the British Empire League, as the organization came to be known after 1896. Best remembered as one of Canada's finest humorists, Leacock expressed his serious side in his writings on imperialism. He saw imperial unity as a means by which Canadians could transcend their parochial and narrow provincial concerns to achieve a "Greater Canada," to use the title of one of his writings on imperialism. To him, imperialism was much more than trade and military exploits; it was buying citizenship in the greatest empire the world had ever known—one upon which the sun never set.

These men—Denison, Grant, Parkin, and Leacock—became the intellectual leaders of the imperial movement in Canada in the pre–World War I era. Their writings and public speeches emphasized Canada's interest in distant imperialist wars and in British affairs. They advocated, as well, closer links with the mother country through a transatlantic cable and through the penny post. Large numbers of middle-class English Canadians identified with their message, but French Canadians, Catholic Irish Canadians, the Native peoples, and the growing number of non–"Anglo-Saxon" immigrants did not. Thus, ironically, in their enthusiasm to use imperialism as a means to unite Canadians, these imperialists actually divided Canadians.

Imperialism and Queen Victoria's Diamond Jubilee

British imperialism peaked in the 1890s. Joseph Chamberlain, appointed to the Colonial Office in 1895, personified the imperial spirit and spearheaded the movement. Two years later, Queen Victoria celebrated her Diamond Jubilee—her 60 years as the ruling monarch—in a spectacular celebration to show the world the splendour and the might of the British empire. Representatives from all the colonies, including Canada's new prime minister, Wilfrid Laurier, joined in the military parades and reviews, assemblies of school children, patriotic speeches, unveiling of monuments, and numerous banquets. Special commemorative stamps were issued, among them a Canadian stamp showing a map of the world splashed with red for all the British possessions. The inscription read: "We hold a vaster empire than has been." A year after Queen Victoria's Diamond Jubilee, several provinces established Empire Day on May 23—the day before Queen Victoria's birthday. Ontario, Nova Scotia, and the Protestant schools of Quebec celebrated the occasion in 1898, and other provinces followed suit. The day was designed to use the public schools for promoting patriotic sentiments.

The South African War

In 1899, the British empire extended over a quarter of the earth's land surface and contained nearly a quarter of its people. The Royal Navy, the largest in the world, made Britain the greatest maritime power. When British imperial expansion in southern Africa led to conflict with the Boers—the descendants of European settlers, mainly Protestants from the Netherlands—the result seemed a foregone conclusion. The British assumed they would immediately defeat the two tiny Boer, or Afrikaner, republics: the Transvaal and the Orange Free State. Yet the war turned out quite differently. Initially, in fact, the Afrikaners inflicted a series of defeats on the British. They knew the country, and effectively practised guerrilla warfare techniques. Britain then turned to its dominions, including Canada, for help.

Many English-Canadian imperialists saw the South African war as a struggle between civilization and barbarism. In this struggle, Canadian soldiers were described by one enthusiast as "missionaries togged in khaki, Bibles at the end of guns." They saw their chance to prove their unquestioned loyalty to Britain—to a common Queen, flag, kin, language, and governance. The English-language newspapers, especially those in Montreal and Toronto, demanded immediate Canadian participation. Lord Minto, the governor general, and Major General Edward Hutton, commander of the Canadian militia, worked out plans for a Canadian contingent, without informing Prime Minister Laurier. A cable from Joseph Chamberlain, the British colonial secretary, thanked Canada for its "offer to serve in South Africa." His thanks were premature, however, since the Canadian government had not yet made an official statement of support.

Prime Minister Laurier tried to temper this enthusiasm. While he admired the British empire as the world's leading protector of the liberal values of liberty and justice, he opposed imperial federation. The Canadian cabinet, not the British colonial secretary, should decide Canada's participation, he believed.

The South African war aroused strong anti-imperialistic sentiments in Quebec. If French Canadians sympathized with anyone in the struggle, it was with the Boers, whom they regarded as a kindred oppressed minority. Henri Bourassa, a young politician and brilliant orator like his grandfather, the legendary Louis-Joseph Papineau, leader of the Rebellion of 1837 in Lower Canada, opposed Canadian involvement in this distant imperialist war. Bourassa equated imperialism with militarism and commercialism, and thus condemned the British empire "not because it is British, but because it is Imperial. All empires are hateful. They stand in the way of human liberty, and true progress, intellectual and moral. They serve nothing but brutal instincts and material objects." He was not, however, prepared to advocate Canadian independence, believing that internal divisions between English- and French-speaking Canadians within an independent Canada might lead to annexation to the United States, which he opposed. He favoured an autonomous Canada within the British empire, a country in which the two linguistic groups respected each other.

The Canadian Compromise on the South African War

For two days, Laurier's cabinet met to find a solution. On October 13, 1899, Laurier devised a compromise. He proposed that "in view of the well-known desire of a great many Canadians who are ready to take service under such conditions," the Canadian government would equip and transport a volunteer force of 1000 men for service on the British side. Once in South Africa, however, the troops would become the British government's responsibility and would fight as British soldiers. Laurier reminded imperialists and French Canadians alike that this decision to send troops should not be "construed as a precedent for future action." (Eventually Canada sent 7300 men to South Africa, of whom 245 died overseas, more than half from disease.)

The members of the Prince Edward Island Transvaal contingent before their departure for South Africa. In total, some 7300 Canadian volunteers fought in the South African War (1899–1902). Those English-speaking Canadians who volunteered to fight for Britain in the South African war parallelled, in their enthusiasm, the French-speaking Canadians who came forward to fight as Zouaves for the Pope in Italy in the late 1860s.

Source: Patent and Copyright Office Collection/Library and Archives Canada/C-7983.

Both English-Canadian imperialists and French-Canadian anti-imperialists protested Laurier's compromise. John Willison, editor of the Toronto *Globe*, wanted Canada to assume full responsibility for Canadian troops in South Africa.

In Montreal, a group of McGill students attacked the offices of the antiwar French-language newspapers in the city and fought street battles with French-Canadian university students. Henri Bourassa, on the other hand, denounced Laurier as *un vendu*, a sellout to the English-Canadian imperialists. He warned that the mere fact of sending troops established a dangerous precedent, since Britain would expect support every time the empire got entangled in future wars. He resigned his seat in protest on October 18, 1899, only to be reelected as an independent by acclamation six months later.

In 1902, Joseph Chamberlain, hoping to capitalize on the imperial sentiment generated by the South African war, called a colonial conference to promote imperial federation. But Laurier resisted closer imperial unity. On the eve of the colonial conference, he assured Parliament that he would not "bring Canada into the vortex of militarism which is the curse and blight of Europe." At the conference itself, he steadfastly opposed having Canada become part of a consolidated imperial defence force. He would only agree that Canadians must contribute to their own defence.

To this end Canada assumed responsibility for the British-controlled ports of Halifax and Esquimalt, British Columbia, in 1904. Then in 1909 Joseph Pope, former private secretary to Sir John A. Macdonald and secretary of state after 1896, established the Department of External

Thousands of Torontonians crowded city streets on June 5, 1901 to celebrate the announced end of the South African war, which actually continued until 1902, with the final submission of the Afrikaner troops.

Source: Archives of Ontario, F 1143-1, S 1244, York Pioneer and Historical Society Fonds.

Affairs to deal with aspects of the Dominion's foreign affairs. Laurier believed the department would allow Canada to become more autonomous in its external relations without offending British or English-Canadian imperialists.

Growing French-Canadian Nationalism

Imperialist sentiments in English-speaking Canada contributed to a parallel French-Canadian nationalism in Quebec. In 1903, a group of young French-Canadian nationalists, inspired by Henri Bourassa, founded the Ligue nationaliste and their own newspaper, *Le Nationaliste*, a year later. The organization had a three-point program: Canadian autonomy within the British empire; provincial autonomy within a federal state; and the rational development of Canada's resources. Other French-Canadian nationalists founded the Association catholique de la jeunesse canadienne-française (ACJC), or "Catholic Association of French-Canadian Youth," in 1904. This group, under the leadership of Lionel Groulx, a Catholic priest and teacher, recruited new members from the classical colleges. They saw the Roman Catholic Church as playing an important role in shaping Quebec nationalism.

Jules-Paul Tardivel, a Franco-American born in Kentucky, who came to Quebec in 1868 to study French and then took up the causes of ultramontanism and French-Canadian nationalism, took a more extreme position. In his newspaper, *La Vérité*, and in his futuristic novel *Pour la Patrie* (1895), Tardivel proposed Quebec's separation from Canada to create a Roman Catholic state on the banks of the St. Lawrence River. In an exchange published in 1904, Tardivel and Bourassa outlined their differing conceptions of French Canada. Tardivel distinguished between his exclusive French-Canadian form of nationalism and Bourassa's broader Canadian nationalism. Tardivel wrote: "Our own nationalism is French-Canadian nationalism.... For us our fatherland is—we do not say precisely the Province of Quebec—but French Canada; the nation we wish to see founded at the hour marked by Divine Providence is the French-Canadian nation." Bourassa replied:

> For us the fatherland is all Canada, that is, a federation of distinct races and autonomous provinces. The nation that we wish to see develop is the Canadian nation, composed of French Canadians and English Canadians, that is of two elements separated by language and religion, and by the legal dispositions necessary to the preservation of their respective traditions, but united in a feeling of brotherhood, in a common attachment to the common fatherland.

In this interchange lay the essence of two currents of twentieth-century French-Canadian nationalism: one leading to separatism, the other to a bilingual and bicultural nation.

The Alaska Boundary Dispute

At the turn of the century a new dispute arose between Canada and the United States, this time over the boundary between Alaska and the Yukon Territory. The dispute had its origin in the Anglo–Russian Treaty of 1825, which had established an ambiguous boundary line, "to follow the summit of the mountains situated parallel to the coast," between British and Russian territory running north from Portland Channel. Unfortunately, the territory encompassed many mountain chains and an uneven coast.

The Americans adopted the Russian stance on the border after they purchased Alaska in 1867. They sought a continuous border along the Pacific coast, and after British Columbia joined Confederation in 1871, they denied Canada's claim to several fiords with access to the Yukon.

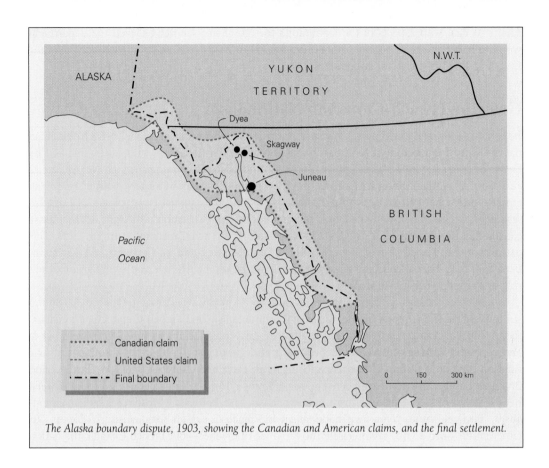

The Alaska boundary dispute, 1903, showing the Canadian and American claims, and the final settlement.

The news that gold had been discovered in the Yukon in 1897 suddenly made the boundary question of utmost importance. Prospectors crossed the mountain passes into the Yukon, and by the summer of 1898, Dawson City had a population of more than 20 000 people, making it temporarily the largest Canadian city west of Winnipeg. In June 1898, the federal government made the Yukon a separate territory with its own commissioner, to help prevent the area from becoming a *de facto* part of Alaska.

Both the Canadians and the Americans, along with the British, agreed to settle the issue through a joint commission. Britain, which continued to have sovereign control over Canada's foreign policy, made the appointments and named five Canadians to the six-member Anglo–Canadian commission. It appeared at first as though a quick settlement could be reached, but negotiations broke down as each side refused to compromise.

To break the deadlock, the three countries agreed in 1902 to appoint a six-member tribunal, three from each side, to review the disputed border. Britain appointed a British judge and two Canadian lawyers for its side. The United States government appointed three members who came to the bargaining table determined to secure the full acceptance of the American claim. Furthermore, President Theodore Roosevelt confidentially informed the British that if the Americans failed to win the case, he would "run the line" on their claim.

In the end, Lord Alverstone, the lone British member of the tribunal, sided with the Americans. He agreed that the boundary line should be around the heads of the inlets, giving the United States territorial control of them. He also agreed to the equal division of the four islands at the mouth of Portland Channel. Thus, in a vote of four to two, the commission favoured this settlement. But the two Canadian commissioners, who opposed, refused to affix their signatures to the agreement.

Miners packing their equipment and supplies up the Chilkoot Pass, 1897–98, on their way to the Klondike gold fields. On reaching the summit, they had to return to get another load. It took many ascents, because the North-West Mounted Police required each miner to have a year's supply (about 500 kg) of provisions upon entering Canada.

Source: E.A. Hegg/Library and Archives Canada/C-5142.

Canadian historians have since debated on what basis Alverstone made his decision. Recently, however, analysts tend to argue that the Canadian position was actually the weaker of the two, while at the same time agreeing that the bellicose Americans weakened their case. Regardless of the merits of the case in hindsight, many Canadians at the time, including the prime minister, considered Alverstone's decision to side with the Americans to be "one of those concessions which have made British diplomacy odious to Canadian people."

Renewed Prospects of Reciprocity with the United States

After the contentious Alaska boundary dispute, Canadian–American relations did actually improve. By 1910, closer trade relations seemed possible. This time the Americans took the initiative to open up negotiations. President William Howard Taft, who came to office in 1909, favoured lower tariffs, arguing that expanding American industries badly needed Canadian raw materials. On January 26, the Liberals made a surprise announcement in Parliament that a reciprocal trade agreement had been reached with the Americans that, in essence, renewed the popular Reciprocity Treaty of 1854. The proposal allowed Canadian natural products free entry into American markets in exchange for letting American manufactured goods into Canada at a lower tariff rate. Contrary to the Reciprocity Treaty of 1854, however, this agreement was to come into effect through concurrent legislation passed by the two governments rather than by treaty, enabling Canada to avoid seeking British approval. The American Congress passed the legislation in July 1911. It remained only for the Canadian parliament to give its approval.

Very quickly, opposition to the reciprocity agreement arose in central Canada. Clifford Sifton, no longer a westerner but rather a well-established Torontonian, led a group of Ontario entrepreneurs who opposed the agreement because they believed it threatened Canada's economic future and its close ties with the British empire. "These resolutions," Sifton warned, "spell retrogression, commercial subordination, the destruction of our national ideals and displacement from our proud position as the rising hope of the British empire." He organized a group of eighteen prominent Toronto manufacturers, industrialists, and financiers to petition the government against the agreement. The group went on to become the core of a newly created Canadian National League. The league published a pamphlet, *The Road to Washington*, in which it warned that the United States intended to annex Canada.

Inopportune statements by imprudent American politicians aided the league's campaign. Champ Clark, speaker-designate of the House of Representatives, said of the agreement: "I am for it, because I hope to see the day when the American flag will float over every square foot of the British North American possessions clear to the North Pole." President Taft himself noted that "Canada stands at the parting of the ways." By this he meant that Canada had to choose between remaining an isolated protectionist country or trading with the Americans. But anti-American proponents in Canada interpreted the statement to mean that Canada had to choose between Britain and the United States. Emotional arguments about loyalty and nationalism replaced economic ones.

The Naval Crisis

The controversy over reciprocity coincided with the contentious naval question. Tension between Germany and Britain increased at the turn of the century. In 1908, the British press warned of Germany's growing naval strength that threatened Britain's control of the high seas. The British Conservative opposition demanded that the British government immediately build eight super-battleships, or dreadnoughts. Many English Canadians insisted that Canada contribute to the cause. French-Canadian nationalists such as Henri Bourassa opposed such a move, claiming it would only lead to greater Canadian involvement in imperial and European wars of no interest to Canada.

Both the Liberals and the Conservatives agreed that in the long term Canada should establish a Canadian navy, rather than contribute funds regularly to the British admiralty. But the two parties differed on the best *short-term* policy. The Conservatives wanted an emergency direct cash contribution to Britain in the present crisis, while Liberals favoured the immediate establishment of a Canadian navy under Canadian command, to be used by Britain in the event of war if the Canadian Parliament approved.

In January 1910, Laurier introduced the Naval Service Bill. It proposed that Canada construct five cruisers and six destroyers and establish a naval college to train Canadian officers. The Canadian government could, "in case of war," place the force under imperial command with the Canadian Parliament's approval.

Opposition to the Naval Service Bill

Although Laurier saw the Naval Service Bill as a suitable compromise, his opponents did not. On the one hand, imperialistically minded conservatives, both federal members of Parliament and provincial premiers, denounced this "tin-pot navy," as they described it, as a disgrace to Canada's role in the empire. On the other hand, Bourassa and the *nationalistes* in Quebec opposed the Naval Service Bill because it went too far; this navy could be used to fight imperial wars of no interest to Canada. "It is the most complete backward step Canada has made in half a century," Bourassa declared. He was in favour of a navy for home defence but not one that would involve Canada in the "whirlpool of militarism." He questioned whether Canada needed a navy at all, since the only threat to the country could come from the United States, with whom Canadians had enjoyed a century of peace. Since 1905, Bourassa's attacks against Laurier had become more strident. By 1907, he had left federal for provincial politics where he attacked the Quebec government's close links with foreign entrepreneurs who wanted to exploit Quebec's natural resources. In 1910, he established a daily newspaper, *Le Devoir*, in which he championed his vision of Canada as an independent member of the British empire, one that placed Canadian interests first. In that year, the *nationalistes* ran a candidate against the Liberals in a by-election in the "safe" seat of Drummond—Arthabaska. Laurier, who had represented the district in the Quebec legislature, campaigned personally on behalf of the Liberal candidate, only to see the *nationalistes* win.

The 1911 Election

During the 1911 federal election campaign, Laurier faced vigorous attacks from both imperialists in Ontario, who branded him a continentalist on the reciprocity issue, and French-Canadian nationalists, who called him an imperialist on the naval issue. "I am neither," an exasperated Laurier protested during an election rally in St. Jean, Quebec, in August. "I am a *Canadian*." His policy, he claimed, was one of "true Canadianism, of moderation, or conciliation." The Liberals, however, tarnished by corruption and inefficient government after fifteen years in office, lost the election. The combined opposition of Ontario imperialists and Quebec nationalists over the issues of reciprocity with the United States and imperial defence deprived Laurier of victory.

Borden's Conservative Government

Robert L. Borden became the new prime minister. His cabinet reflected the practical nature of his government. No single minister stood out as dynamic or memorable, with the possible exceptions of the irascible Sam Hughes, minister of militia and defence, or George Foster, minister of trade and commerce. Yet, collectively, the Borden cabinet ran an efficient government. Limited French-Canadian representation, however, crippled his cabinet in reference to any political issues bearing on Quebec.

One of the government's first decisions concerned the naval issue. Despite strong Quebec opposition, the prime minister, as his own secretary of state for external affairs, introduced the Naval Aid Bill in December 1912. It provided a direct cash contribution of $35 million to Britain to build three dreadnoughts. One of Borden's French-Canadian cabinet ministers resigned in protest, but the prime minister persevered. The Liberals attacked the Naval Aid Bill as a sham and as an inadequate alternative to Laurier's naval program. Eventually, the Conservatives imposed closure—for the first time in Canadian legislative history—to cut off the debate. The Liberals countered by using their strong majority in the Senate to defeat the bill. By this time, the issue had died since military experts questioned the efficiency of dreadnoughts against submarines. Thus, on the eve of World War I, Canada had neither made a contribution to the British navy nor built up a navy of its own.

For half a century after Confederation, Canadians debated the nation's destiny. Many politicians and critics felt that Canada was incapable of being a great nation, which led them to enhance Canada's national status through some form of association with either Britain, in an imperial federation, or the United States, in a continental association. But English Canadians and French Canadians could not agree on the nature and extent of imperial union, while entrepreneurs and farmers disagreed over the nature and extent of a continental connection. At this stage few thought in terms of Canadian independence; most felt that the country was not yet strong enough, or sufficiently united, to be independent.

NOTES

1. Carl Berger, *The Sense of Power: Studies in the Ideas of Canadian Imperialism, 1867–1914* (Toronto: University of Toronto Press, 1970), p. 259.

BEYOND THE BOOK

Weblinks

Canada and the South African War

http://www.civilization.ca/cwm/boer/boerwarhistory_e.html

Personnel profiles, battle descriptions, and other digitized historical records of Canadian soldiers' participation in the South African War.

Boundary Dispute: Executive Council of British Columbia

http://www.canadiana.org/ECO/PageView/14348/0002

This document is a digitized report of the Executive Council of British Columbia regarding the disputed boundary between Canada and Alaska. It is believed to have been published in the late 1880s.

Robert L. Borden

http://www.lac-bac.gc.ca/premiersministres/h4-3200-e.html

A detailed biography of Prime Minister Robert Borden, including digitized versions of his speeches.

Stephen Leacock

http://www.collectionscanada.ca/leacock/index-e.html

A detailed biography of Stephen Leacock, as well as commentaries on his works.

Mail Order Catalogues

http://www.collectionscanada.ca/cmc/index-e.html

Explore digitized mail order catalogues used by families at the turn of the century, such as those published by Eaton's. Click "Browse by Date" or "Browse by Company" to narrow your search.

Films & Novels

The Border Confirmed: The Treaty of Washington. Directed by Ronald Dick and Pierre L'Amare. 1969.

Journey. By James A. Michener. 1994.

RELATED READINGS

The following articles in R. Douglas Francis and Donald B. Smith, eds., *Readings in Canadian History: Post-Confederation,* 7th ed. (Toronto: Thomson Nelson, 2006), relate to this topic: Carl Berger, "Imperialism and Nationalism, 1884–1914: A Conflict in Canadian Thought," pp. 112–16; and J. Levitt, "Henri Bourassa on Imperialism and Bi-culturalism, 1900–1918," pp. 116–27; and Phillip Buckner, "Casting Daylight upon Magic: Reconstructing the Royal Tour of 1901 to Canada," pp. 127–49.

BIBLIOGRAPHY

The most comprehensive survey of Canada's relations with Britain and the United States remains C.P. Stacey, *Canada and the Age of Conflict: A History of Canadian External Relations,* vol. 1, *1867–1921* (Toronto: Macmillan, 1977). See also John Bartlet Brebner, *The North Atlantic Triangle: The Interplay of Canada, the United States and Great Britain* (New Haven, CT: Yale University Press, 1945). W.L. Morton discusses the Treaty of Washington in *The Critical Years: The Union of British North America, 1857–1873* (Toronto: McClelland & Stewart, 1964).

Canadian–American relations in the late nineteenth century are dealt with in John Herd Thompson and Stephen J. Randall, *Canada and the United States: Ambivalent Allies*, 3rd ed. (Montreal/Kingston: McGill-Queen's University Press, 2002); J.L. Granatstein and Norman Hillmer, *For Better or for Worse: Canada and the United States to the 1990s* (Toronto: Copp Clark Pitman, 1991); and C.C. Tansill, *Canadian–American Relations, 1875–1911* (Toronto: The Ryerson Press, 1943). On Canadian-American relations in the context of Anglo-Saxonism, see Edward P. Kohn, *This Kindred People: Canadian-American Relations and the Anglo-Saxon Idea, 1895-1903* (Montreal & Kingston: McGill-Queen's University Press, 2004). Goldwin Smith's *Canada and the Canadian Question* (Toronto: Hunter, Rose, 1891; rep. University of Toronto Press, 1971) is an interesting contemporary statement. Also of importance are W.R. Graham, "Sir Richard Cartwright, Wilfrid Laurier and the Liberal Party Trade Policy, 1887," *Canadian Historical Review* 33 (March 1952): 1–18; F.H. Underhill, "Edward Blake, the Liberal Party and Unrestricted Reciprocity," *Canadian Historical Association, Report* (1939), pp. 133–41; and P.B. Waite, *The Man from Halifax: Sir John Thompson, Prime Minister* (Toronto: University of Toronto Press, 1985). Allan Smith provides a collection of interpretative essays in *Canada—An American Nation?: Essays on Continentalism, Identity, and the Canadian Frame of Mind* (Montreal/Kingston: McGill-Queen's University Press, 1994).

Norman Penlington's *The Alaska Boundary Dispute: A Critical Appraisal* (Toronto: McGraw-Hill Ryerson, 1972) and John Munro's *The Alaska Boundary Dispute* (Toronto: Copp Clark, 1970) cover this issue in Canadian–American relations; the latter is a collection of primary and secondary sources. A third study that touches on the question of Canada's sovereignty in the Yukon dispute is W.R. Morrison's *Showing the Flag: The Mounted Police and Canadian Sovereignty in the North, 1894–1925* (Vancouver: University of British Columbia Press, 1985). In *Land of the Midnight Sun: A History of the Yukon* (Edmonton: Hurtig, 1988), Ken S. Coates and William R. Morrison provide an overview of the territory. For the impact of the Great Rush see Charlene Porsild, *Gamblers and Dreamers: Women, Men, and Community in the Klondike* (Vancouver: University of British Columbia Press, 1998).

Carl Berger's *The Sense of Power: Studies in the Ideas of Canadian Imperialism, 1867–1914* (Toronto: University of Toronto Press, 1970), analyzes the beliefs of English-Canadian imperialists. On the negative side of imperialism see Sarah Carter, *Capturing Women: The Manipulation of Cultural Imagery in Canada's Prairie West* (Montreal/Kingston: McGill-Queen's University Press, 1997). Norman Penlington's *Canada and Imperialism, 1896–1899* (Toronto: University of Toronto Press, 1965), discusses Canadian imperialism in the context of the South African War. A more recent study is Carman Miller, *Painting the Map Red: Canada and the South African War 1899–1902* (Montreal/Kingston: Canadian War Museum, McGill-Queen's University Press, 1992). See also Robert Page, *The Boer War and Canadian Imperialism* (Ottawa: Canadian Historical Association, 1987), and his book on the subject, *Imperialism and Canada, 1895–1903* (Toronto: Holt, Rinehart and Winston, 1972). Useful collections of essays include: Colin M. Coates, ed., *Imperial Canada 1867–1917* (Edinburgh: Centre of Canadian Studies, University of Edinburgh, 1997); *Imperial Relations in the Age of Laurier* (Toronto: University of Toronto Press, 1969), edited by Carl Berger, and Frank H. Underhill's collection of interpretative lectures, *The Image of Confederation* (Toronto: Canadian Broadcasting Corporation, 1964), also edited by Carl Berger. On the Boy Scout movement and imperialism see Robert H. MacDonald, *Sons of the Empire: The Frontier and the Boy Scout Movement, 1890–1918* (Toronto: University of Toronto Press, 1993). On literature and the empire see Barrie Davies, "'We Hold a Vaster Empire Than Has Been': Canadian Literature and the Canadian Empire," *Studies in Canadian Literature* 14(1) (1989): 18–29; and Sara Jeannette Duncan, *The Imperialist* (1904), rep. (Toronto: McClelland & Stewart, 1990). On Duncan's life see Marian Fowler, *Redney: A Life of Sara Jeannette Duncan* (Toronto: Anansi, 1983); and Thomas E. Tausky, *Sara Jeannette Duncan: Novelist of the Empire* (Port Credit, ON: P.D. Meaney, 1980). For a discussion of Duncan's ideas as presented in her writings, see Misao Dean, *A Different Point of View: Sara Jeannette Duncan* (Montreal/Kingston: McGill-Queen's University Press, 1991). On the IODE, see Katie Pickles, *Female Imperialism and National Identity: Imperial Order Daughters of the Empire* (Manchester: Manchester University Press, 2002).

French-Canadian views on imperialism and nationalism during this era can be found in M. Wade, *The French Canadians, 1760–1945* (Toronto: Macmillan, 1955), pp. 447–535; and in Susan Mann, *The Dream of Nation: A Social and Intellectual History of Quebec*, 2nd ed. (Montreal/Kingston: McGill-Queen's University Press, 2002), pp. 167–83. Joseph Levitt's *Henri Bourassa on Imperialism and Bi-culturalism* (Toronto: Copp Clark, 1970) and his pamphlet *Henri Bourassa, Catholic Critic* (Toronto: Canadian Historical Association, 1976) summarize the ideas of this French-Canadian thinker.

The issue of reciprocity in the 1911 election is analyzed in L.E. Ellis, *Reciprocity, 1911: A Study in Canadian–American Relations* (Toronto: The Ryerson Press, 1939). Paul Stevens, ed., *The 1911 General Election: A Study in Canadian Politics* (Toronto: Copp Clark, 1970) provides a selection of primary and secondary sources. On the formation of the Department of External Affairs see John Hilliker, *Canada's Department of External Affairs*, vol. 1, *The Early Years, 1909–1946* (Montreal/Kingston: McGill-Queen's University Press, 1990).

The fortunes of the Conservative party are discussed in R.C. Brown, *Robert Laird Borden: A Biography*, vol. 1, *1854–1914* (Toronto: Macmillan, 1975); and in John English, *The Decline of Politics: The Conservatives and the Party System, 1901–20* (Toronto: University of Toronto Press, 1977).

For maps and charts on the period see the *Historical Atlas of Canada*, vol. 2, *The Land Transformed, 1800–1891*, edited by L.R. Gentilcore et al. (Toronto: University of Toronto Press, 1993); and vol. 3, *Addressing the Twentieth Century, 1891–1961*, edited by Donald Kerr and Deryk W. Holdsworth (Toronto: University of Toronto Press, 1990).

Part 2

URBAN AND INDUSTRIAL CANADA, 1867–1914

INTRODUCTION

At the turn of the century, Canada underwent as rapid and substantial a change to urbanization and industrialization as any other country in the Western world, but in absolute terms, it lagged behind developments in both Britain and the United States. Canada lacked the financial and economic infrastructure, the expertise, and the technology to enable it to keep pace with these vastly more populated countries. Canada did, however, possess an abundance of natural resources now in demand for industrialization: timber, minerals, water power, and land fit for large-scale agricultural production. The exploitation of natural resources, along with manufacturing, allowed the economic expansion that occurred in Canada from 1867 to 1914.

The change was evident by comparing Canada in 1867 with Canada in 1914. In 1867, 80 percent of the population lived on farms or in hamlets or small villages, and worked in primary industries such as farming, fishing, and lumbering. By 1914, nearly 50 percent lived in towns or cities, and worked in secondary or service industries. Such growth fostered optimism in Canada's future, which in turn led to further growth, making the two decades spanning the century, 1890 to 1910, a period of "economic takeoff."

While virtually all Canadians were affected to some degree by the change occurring around them, not all benefited to the same extent from industrialization. Regionally, central Canada—Ontario and Quebec—advanced the most, followed by the West and then the Maritimes. Ethnically, Anglo-Celtic Protestants were more prosperous than other ethnic and cultural groups. In gender terms, males benefited more than females, consistently receiving jobs with higher wages or salaries. Socially, the upper and middle classes enjoyed greater advantages over the lower working class. Indeed, a new class of poor appeared—the urban poor—who were in some respects worse off than their rural counterparts, since they depended on others for the basic necessities of life and lived in slum or run-down areas of towns and cities. Many worked in factories or shops that were hazardous to their health, had monotonous jobs, and faced extended periods without work and thus wages. Often both parents and even older children had to work in order to survive. Fraternal societies, unions, and even taverns attempted to help the working poor, but with limited success.

Middle-class social reformers worried about the negative impact of urbanization and industrialization on Canadian moral values, ethical standards, and social mores. Believing that their values and attitudes were the right ones for the survival of civilization, they attempted to impose them upon the working class. There arose as well in the late nineteenth century a belief in environmental determinism: the conviction that individuals were shaped as much, if not more, by society as by hereditary traits. Thus, social reformers believed that if they could create the perfect society, they could produce perfect individuals who were morally upright, responsible citizens. A host of social reform movements arose to work to create the perfect society. Each group of reformers had its own vision of what constituted the perfect society and how best to achieve it, but together they attempted to mould the new urban and industrial society to desirable ends. As well, some Canadians promoted music, drama, and art to make Canada a more cultured and civilized society, while others favoured popular culture as a means of enjoyment and relaxation from the drudgery and burdens of work.

As a result, Canada in 1914 had become a more sophisticated, prosperous, modern, and complex society than it had been half a century earlier. Still, basic problems of regional, ethnic, social, and gender inequalities continued to plague the country.

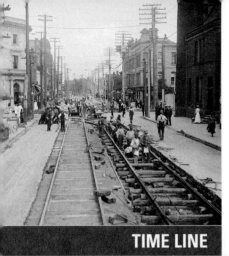

Chapter Six

BOOMTIME: INDUSTRIALIZATION AT THE TURN OF THE CENTURY

TIME LINE	
1869	The beginning of the T. Eaton Company: Timothy Eaton opens his first dry-goods store at Queen and Yonge streets in Toronto
1873	Beginning of an economic recession
1877	Establishment of the Laurentide Company, Canada's first major newsprint company
1883	Discovery of nickel in Sudbury, Ontario
1891	Ontario government establishes a Bureau of Mines
1895	First smelter at Rossland, British Columbia
1902	International Nickel Company of Canada (Inco) incorporated
1904	Over 1800 freight cars passing through Winnipeg a day
1906	Creation of Ontario Hydro
1908	Henry Ford introduces the Model T
1910	Combines Investigation Act passed Federal government establishes the Royal Commission on Industrial Training and Technical Education Steel Company of Canada created
1914	Completion of the Panama Canal

"To visit Canada just now is a bracing experience…. For Canada is conscious, vocally, uproariously conscious, that her day has come…. A single decade has swept away her diffidence, and has replaced it by a spirit of boundless confidence and booming enterprise." So wrote J.A. Hobson, the well-known English economist and journalist, in his *Canada Today*, published in 1906. At last, a number of factors—the success of the national policy increased financial investment in the Canadian economy, better world prices for raw materials, a decline in freight rates, and a positive attitude toward business—combined to enable Canada to undergo its industrial revolution. Industrialization also spurred urbanization. Not all regions experienced uniform and sustained growth. The Maritimes languished, while the West developed as a great agricultural area, and central Canada became the heartland of industrial growth. Even here, industrial growth was uneven. Ontario outperformed Quebec, while in Quebec, the minority Anglophone population greatly predominated over francophone as industrial entrepreneurs.

But overall, Canada entered an age of general prosperity through industrialization and resource extraction that led prime minister Wilfrid Laurier to predict that the twentieth century would be Canada's century.

Canada's Economic Expansion

At the turn of the century, the national policy finally worked as intended. Growth in the primary industries—farming, fishing, lumbering, and mining—increased the demand for secondary industry, such as road construction, rail transportation, and shipbuilding. The CPR and the two new transcontinental railways, the Canadian Northern and Grand Trunk Pacific/National Transcontinental, brought hundreds of thousands of immigrants westward and took away the West's natural resources to eastern markets. Railways were also major employers. By World War I, Canada prided itself on having 55 000 km of track, spanning the country from coast to coast. Equally, a growing rural population in the West required eastern manufactured goods, from agricultural implements to common household items. Stimulated by additional foreign investment, industry and manufacturing expanded to meet the increased demand for consumer goods. Employers needed workers in iron and steel foundries, agricultural-implements works, machine shops, textile and shoe factories, and a host of other manufacturing plants that supplied consumer goods. Service industries, as well as governments (national, provincial, and municipal), became major employers. Indeed, by 1921 as many people worked in service industries as in the primary sector.

Canada's Population (in thousands), 1861–1921

YEAR	NATURAL INCREASE*	IMMIGRATION	EMIGRATION	NET MIGRATION	POPULATION
1861					3230
1861–71	610	260	410	−150	3689
1871–81	690	350	404	−54	4325
1881–91	654	680	826	−146	4833
1891–01	668	250	380	−130	5371
1901–11	1025	1550	740	810	7207
1911–21	1270	1400	1089	311	8788

*Natural increase is the number of births minus the number of deaths.

Source: From Canada: Our Century, Our Story: Ontario Edition, *student text by Fielding/Evans. © 2001. Reprinted with permission of Nelson, a division of Thomson Learning: www.thomsonrights.com. Fax 800-730-2215.*

Financial Investment

At the turn of the century, Canada's abundant natural resources and increasing population made it an attractive country for investment. The federal government provided direct, as well as indirect, financial assistance to private companies. The governments of Quebec and especially Ontario invested heavily in development. They offered bonuses, subsidies, and guarantees to industrialists to locate new plants within their borders. Banks provided another source of internal revenue. Like business corporations, they too consolidated, declining in number from 48 to 18 between 1880 and 1920, although the number of branches increased from 300 to nearly 5000. The three largest—the Bank of Montreal, the Royal Bank (also with its headquarters in Montreal), and the Toronto-based Bank of Commerce—centralized their operations, invested in new industries, and provided capital for entrepreneurs.

Foreign investment increased as well, especially from Britain, since Canada was the preferred country for British capital investment in the Empire. British financiers invested in railways, construction, and industry, chiefly in the form of indirect portfolio investments (loans in the form of bonds). In contrast, American investors preferred ownership to indirect investment. They continued to build branch plants in Canada to avoid tariff restrictions. By 1913, some 450 American-owned branch plants existed in Canada, with assets of over $400 million. Many Americans invested heavily in mining and in the growing pulp and paper industry. Most politicians and Canadians in general looked favourably on American direct investment as an assurance of more jobs in Canadian industries, and as a means to stem the emigration of Canadians to the United States.

Large-scale industrial production required substantial amounts of capital. To encourage investment, Canadian businesses adopted the concept of limited liability. Individual investors contributed only a portion of the necessary sum and, if the company failed, they lost only their own contribution and no more.

Limited liability opened up the investment field. Large corporations—"immortal beings" in terms of commercial law—predominated. In 1902, a handful of consolidated companies existed; by 1912, there were nearly 60. These mergers involved nearly 250 smaller companies. The most noteworthy included: the merger of the Massey and Harris companies in 1890 and then amalgamation of smaller companies (including some American firms) in the following two decades to make the Massey-Harris Company Canada's largest and undisputed producer and exporter of agricultural implements; Dominion Canner Limited, which in 1910 amalgamated 34 smaller canning factories; Canada Cement, a consolidation of eleven cement companies in 1909; and Stelco (the Steel Company of Canada), formed in 1910 out of several small Ontario and Quebec iron and steel mills. The young New Brunswick financier Max Aitken, the son of a Presbyterian minister, who was later to become Sir Max and eventually Lord Beaverbrook and who created Canada Cement and Stelco, became the "merger king" by buying and combining companies to form trusts and larger companies. (Aitken was so skilled at mergers that one friend commented at the time of his death that now he could "set about merging heaven and hell.")

Role of Government in the Economy

As the saying went at the time, the government that governed best governed least. Ottawa did nothing to regulate the monopolies, apart from passing the Combines Investigation Act of 1910. This act allowed government to investigate monopoly price-fixing. But during its nine-year lifespan, the investigation board dealt only with one case. As well, corporations took advantage of the division of powers between the federal, provincial, and municipal governments over regulations to play one government off against the other. This often led to infighting between governments, and to regional divisions and animosity. Clearly business enjoyed a free hand in the boom years before World War I.

Limited state involvement in the economy did occur, however. In the case of Ontario Hydro, public ownership came about because of the need for cheap energy on the part of businesses in Toronto and other southern Ontario towns and cities. When it seemed likely that a small privileged business group alone might harness the tremendous energy power of Niagara Falls, business interests rallied behind Adam Beck, a manufacturer of cigar boxes and the Conservative member for London in the Ontario legislature, to urge the Ontario government to create a Crown corporation of the hydroelectric power industry. Beck's movement succeeded. "From the outset," notes historian H.V. Nelles, "the crusade for public power was a businessmen's movement; they initiated it, formed its devoted, hard-core member-ship, and, most importantly, they provided it with brilliant leadership. By the phrase 'the people's power,' the businessmen meant cheap electricity for the manufacturer, and it was assumed that the entire community would benefit as a result."[1]

Beck, the aggressive founder and promoter of the Hydro-Electric Power Commission of Ontario, built it up until, by the time of his death in 1925, it had become the largest publicly owned power authority in the world. Today, a larger-than-life-sized statue of Beck stands near the Ontario Hydro building on Toronto's University Avenue with the provincial legislature in the background.

Cooking class at a Canadian ladies' college, 1906.

Source: William James Topley/Library and Archives Canada/ PA-42227.

A Positive Attitude Toward Business

The new economy necessitated a new managerial class and a skilled industrial labour force. In many ways, primary schools became training grounds for the workplace. In factory-like institutions, teachers taught young people the values of punctuality, obedience, thrift, and self-discipline—values essential for an industrial society. As historian Michael Cross notes: "Children learned to obey clocks."[2] Girls studied domestic science, while boys learned mechanical skills or how to prepare for business. In 1903, Ontario granted money to schools for shop and domestic-science courses. Under the Industrial Education Act, Ontario established trade schools. The Quebec government also built secondary technical-education schools in Montreal and Quebec City. Nova Scotia opened the Technical University of Nova Scotia in 1907, a postsecondary trades college.

Since education was outside of federal jurisdiction, Ottawa could not intervene directly in the provincial area of technical education. It did, however, establish in 1910 the Royal Commission on Industrial Training and Technical Education, which investigated the current state of Canadian education. Four years of war intervened before the federal government could act on the report. Then, in 1919, the federal Technical Education Act established a fund of $10 million for technical education over the next decade.

At the turn of the century in Canada's "gilded age," Canadians honoured business suc-cesses. In a poll taken in 1908 by the *Canadian Courier*, a major newspaper, nine out of ten of those named "Canada's Top Ten Biggest Men" were captains of industry and railway magnates. The philosophy of Social Darwinism prevailed: survival belonged to the fittest, the successful believed. Their wealth proved their virtue. Many young English-speaking Canadians accepted the theory of the popular American writer Horatio Alger that anyone could rise from rags to riches through hard work, thrift, and self-discipline.

English-speaking Canadians had numerous role models for success: Herbert Holt, the billion-dollar recluse who founded the Montreal Light, Heat and Power Company in 1902 and became president of the Royal Bank; Henry Pellatt, active in the formation of Canadian General Electric and owner of Toronto's Casa Loma, one of the most palatial residences in North America; Joseph W. Flavelle, president of the William Davies Meat Packaging Plant in Toronto and chair of the Bank of Commerce and the National Trust Company; Francis H. Clergue, founder of the Algoma Steel Company of Sault Ste. Marie, Ontario; Patrick Burns, owner of the Burns Meat Packing Company of Calgary; and Max Aitken, a millionaire by the age of 30, who used his Royal Securities Corporation as an investment bank to fund his own mergers. Novelist Allan Sullivan was so enamoured of Francis H. Clergue's success in utilizing the rapids at Sault Ste. Marie to create the Algoma Steel Company that he wrote a novel entitled *The Rapids* about Clergue, whose identity was only thinly veiled by calling the "hero" Clark and the site of his enterprise, St. Marys. Sullivan extolled Clergue's virtues as a visionary and morally upright business entrepreneur.

Few Canadian merchants eclipsed the success of Timothy Eaton, who opened his Toronto dry-goods store at Yonge and Queen streets in 1869. He introduced two new revolutionary practices to Canadian merchandising. First, he accepted cash only. Second, he promised "money refunded if goods not satisfactory." Eaton also knew the value of advertising and took out full-page ads in the Toronto newspapers. By 1882, his business had grown to such an extent that he transformed his operation with a department store that eventually would have three floors, 35 departments, electric lights (the first in a Canadian store), the first elevator, and the first store restaurant-café. In the late 1880s, he introduced evening closings at 6 p.m., and, in the summer months, a Saturday afternoon holiday. Next he started an Eaton's mail-order catalogue, a volume soon to be termed "the Prairie Bible" in western Canada. By the time of his death in 1907 at age 72, Timothy Eaton employed over 9000 people. His "empire" extended across the country and the world, often undermining local retailers who found it difficult to compete.

Some Canadian entrepreneurs built up industrial empires beyond Canadian shores, especially in the Caribbean, Mexico, Brazil, and Spain. Brazilian Traction (later Brascan, but always best known to Brazilians simply as "The Light") became a Canadian business success story. "The Light" combined Canadian entrepreneurship, American engineering power, and European capital. As its underwriters, the company had such prominent Toronto capitalists as William Mackenzie, George Cox, Joseph Flavelle, E.R. Wood, Henry Pellatt, and A.E. Ames. Other Canadian-owned companies in foreign lands included the Mexican Light and Power Company in Mexico City; the West Indies Electric Company in Kingston, Jamaica; the Havana Electric Railway Company in Cuba; and the Demerara Electric Company in Georgetown, British Guiana. These industrial empires in Canada and abroad were worth millions of dollars and employed tens of thousands of workers.

Rise of a Managerial Class

Canadian entrepreneurs and other corporate leaders relied on a new, skilled managerial class to run the complex, day-to-day operations of their expanded business: increased production data, costs, personnel, and internal communications. These managers were often trained in "scientific management," a term coined by the American Frederick W. Taylor. "Scientific managers" used workers to complete simple and routine jobs at a proficient speed for a minimum wage. Indeed, a process of "deskilling" occurred. Employers used new technology to break down skills into more narrowly specialized tasks that could be performed by less skilled, lower-paid workers—in some industries by women and children. Concerned only with growth and profit, they gave little thought to the aesthetics of the workplace, the needs of workers, or the possibility of profit sharing. Work was judged only in terms of efficiency. Offices, as they became automated with the introduction of such devices as typewriters, the Hollerith punchcard machines, and the

Burrough adding machine, resembled factories in terms of routine production. Technology and efficiency became the new watchwords of success and progress.

Beneath this managerial class and closely supervised by it came the clerical workers who carried out the daily routine office jobs. Increasingly, women performed the mechanized and highly specialized jobs. Women clerks did not replace male clerks, but rather ended up doing inferior clerical work under them. This "feminization of clerical work" occurred at a rapid rate in the decade from 1910 to 1920, when clerical positions in general more than doubled. Women acquired most of the new typewriting jobs. During the war years (1914–1918), in particular, females replaced male clerks who went off to war. By 1920, male managers and female secretaries had become the norm in most offices.

COMMUNITY PORTRAIT

The T. Eaton Company: A Community Store

Timothy Eaton's ability to create Canada's most successful department store by the early twentieth century was due to a variety of factors, but clearly one of the most important was his ability to create a sense of community among his employees. They proudly identified themselves as "Eatonians," an identity that not only linked them to Timothy Eaton and his family but also to a community of fellow workers who had one thing in common: they were employees—or what Eaton preferred to call "associates"—of the T. Eaton Company.

Eaton's modest upbringing on a farm outside Ballymena in Northern Ireland, and his own harsh beginning in retail as a young man, made him sympathetic to his employees in a paternalistic way. "The Governor," as he became known, cultivated a close personal relationship with his staff, his "loyal subjects," that engendered respect, cooperation, and enthusiasm on their part. Stories became legendary of his kindness and generosity to loyal workers who experienced financial difficulties. Employees absent from work for extended periods of time due to illness continued to receive their pay, often along with an order of coal to keep them warm if the illness occurred in the winter months. During one

Photo of a woman touching the boot of the statue of Timothy Eaton in the Winnipeg downtown Eaton's store. People rubbed the boot for good luck.

Source: *Winnipeg Free Press*, October 23, 2002, p. A5.

particularly severe winter, Eaton set aside $3000 to assist workers who were in need of help. "When it's gone, let me know," he informed his accountant, as he was prepared to provide more money.

When his Toronto store at the corner of Queen and Yonge became too large for him to supervise his staff by himself, and when other stores opened across the country, Eaton hired managers. He handpicked and trained them himself to ensure that they felt an identity with the company and also that they treated those under them with respect. "When you discover a young person doing anything which he or she should be corrected for," he informed managers, "speak to them alone and never before customers." Employees dismissed for errors in judgment often gained reinstatement when they apologized. "The Governor" personally held meetings in his store at which employees could air grievances and suggest ways to improve good relations (and thus increase sales). As he reminded his managers: "None of us are too wise to learn, even from our juniors." To cultivate the sense of community, Eaton provided his "associates" with additional benefits such as a 10 percent discount on merchandise, low-interest loans to those wishing to buy a home, a welfare department, a pension and life insurance plan, and deposit accounts with generous interest rates.

Timothy Eaton cultivated the same strong sense of community among his customers, many of whom also considered themselves "Eatonians." As one store brochure stated: "The Eaton Spirit is the combined faith and enthusiastic loyalty we have for the store and for our fellow employees.... [T]he spirit of the store too, demands the customer's satisfaction at any cost." With the beginning of the Eaton's catalogue in 1884, the "wider community" of Eatonians stretched across the country. One enthusiastic Westerner proclaimed that "the Eaton catalogue is as much a Western institution as the wheat itself." During World War I, the catalogue even cultivated a sense of community among Canadian soldiers on the front. Some soldiers found half-charred copies of the catalogue in training camps, and in hastily abandoned buildings or even in trenches at the front. Among soldiers, the catalogue became known as "The Wish Book" since soldiers ordered items that they wished to own, such as a wristwatch—and that Eaton's often provided at no cost—or dreamed of having when they returned home.

When Eaton died on January 31, 1907, several thousand of his employees followed the funeral entourage from Timothy Eaton Methodist Church to the Mount Pleasant Cemetery. In 1919, twelve years after his death, and on the occasion of the fiftieth anniversary of the founding of the T. Eaton store, company employees presented a life-sized bronze statue of Timothy Eaton for the main store as a gift to the Eaton family. A copy of the statue was also given to the main Western Canadian store in Winnipeg. From that day on, passersby would rub the toe of the left shoe to the point of making it shiny, hoping that Eaton's good fortune might rub off on them.

The T. Eaton Company remained in operation until 1999, when it filed for bankruptcy. Its demise came when the company no longer engendered the sense of community loyalty that its founder had so successfully cultivated.

FURTHER READING

Joy L. Santink, *Timothy Eaton and the Rise of His Department Store* (Toronto: University of Toronto Press, 1990).

Rod McQueen, *The Eatons: The Rise and Fall of Canada's Royal Family*, rev. ed. (Toronto: Stoddart, 1999).

Patricia Phenix, *Eatonians: The Story of the Family Behind the Family* (Toronto: McClelland and Stewart, 2002).

Urbanization

Industrialization accelerated urbanization. Industrial growth required factories, large banks, commercial institutions, and transportation services in large urban centres. These institutions in turn required workers and employees. During the period from 1890 to 1920, Montreal and Toronto, the two largest and most advanced industrial cities, almost tripled their population, each surpassing the half-million mark. But the most rapid urban growth in this time period occurred in the West, thanks mainly to large-scale immigration. Winnipeg's population increased sevenfold; Vancouver's, twelvefold (growing at a rate of 1000 new residents per month in the peak year of 1910); and Calgary's, sixteenfold. Of all the major western cities, though, Saskatoon eclipsed the rest in rate of growth, rising from several hundred to nearly 10 000 people in the first decade of the new century. From 1901 to 1911, the Canadian urban population increased 63 percent. In 1901, Canada had 58 urban centres with a population greater than 5000; by 1911, that number had grown to 90.

Stenographer pool, land department, CPR Department of National Resources, Calgary, 1915. Women did clerical work at the turn of the century, but became ghettoized at the lowest levels of office work. Note the dominance of paper on every desk.

Source: Glenbow Archives, Calgary, Canada/NA-5055-1.

Canadian urban centres became heartlands that controlled their surrounding hinterlands, providing the rural inhabitants with manufactured goods and services; but these centres themselves became hinterlands dependent on larger cities beyond Canadian borders. Montreal and Toronto, for example, the only two Canadian metropolises that were not hinterlands of other Canadian cities, were dependent on metropolitan centres outside Canada such as London, New York, and Chicago.

The dominance of Montreal and Toronto as urban centres dated back to the mid-nineteenth century and the railway boom. After 1885 and the completion of the CPR, Montreal's and Toronto's influence reached to the Pacific. Their real growth, however, occurred in the 1890s and early 1900s, due to rapid industrialization.

Economic Development in the East and West

The nature and extent of industrial and urban growth varied across the country. In Newfoundland, the economy remained highly dependent on the cod and sail fisheries as the major industries, employing 85 percent of the Island's population in the late nineteenth century. A serious decline in both industries, however, prompted Sir William Whiteway's government in the early 1890s to implement a Newfoundland version of Canada's National Policy, "the Policy of Progress." Its centrepiece consisted of a railroad across the island that, like the CPR, would link east and west coasts, and stimulated industrial growth. A moderate tariff would in turn protect small manufacturers in St. John's. But with a bank failure in 1894, financing of the railroad came under Canadian control when the Robert G. Reid company of Montreal underwrote the costs. As well, the iron ore deposits on the island were shipped out to Cape Breton rather than processed at home.

In the Maritimes, the resource-based economy lost some of its momentum. The West Indies sugar trade fell dramatically in the 1870s, when a world glut of sugar caused prices to collapse, resulting in a decline in trade between Nova Scotia and the West Indies. In the same decade Britain's demand for Maritime lumber and wooden ships fell, seriously weakening Nova Scotia's and New Brunswick's economies. An industrial economy developed to supplement the region's resource economy. Businesspeople in Nova Scotia, for instance, invested in steel products, such as steel rails and locomotives, to take advantage of the Cape Breton coal fields. At one point in the early 1880s, thanks in large part to the Intercolonial Railway, the National Policy of tariff protection, and a vigorous iron and steel industry, Nova Scotia's industrial growth on a per capita basis actually outstripped that of Ontario and Quebec.

In the long run, however, the Maritimes' industrial expansion faltered. Some historians have pointed out that the region lacked resources as extensive or diverse as, for example, Ontario's. Although Cape Breton had coal, timber, iron ore, and fish, its agriculture could not compete. Distance from the large markets of central Canada and the small regional population in Atlantic Canada combined to create a significant obstacle to expansion for factories in the region. Furthermore, Maritime investors, like their Canadian counterparts elsewhere, saw western and central Canadian development as potentially more lucrative. Local banks, for example, themselves swallowed up by central-Canadian-owned banks, invested outside the region. As well, the "Boston States" acted as a magnet drawing population from the Maritime provinces, causing one Maritime historian to conclude that the pull to the south "may have resulted in the decapitation of Maritime society."[3]

As industrialization proceeded so slowly, Maritime cities grew at a slower rate than those elsewhere. Halifax's population increased by only 16 000 people between 1871 and 1911 to a total of 46 619, while that of Saint John, New Brunswick, actually declined, then regained a modest number of inhabitants, to bring its population to 42 500 by 1911. These cities remained small, with modest hinterlands of their own, and, in time, dependants of Montreal and, to a lesser extent, of Toronto.

A view of Victoria harbour in 1886. During the 1890s, a new building code limited downtown construction to brick or stone buildings, resulting in the pulling down of the city's deteriorating structures, like the ones shown here.

Source: William Molson Macpherson Collection/Library and Archives Canada/PA-62200.

Growth in the West

British Columbia's economy shifted from its Pacific orientation (southward to California) toward central Canada, thanks to the completion of the CPR. The provincial economy remained still predominantly resource-based: mining, forestry, fisheries, and agriculture. Mining speculation ran at a fever pitch by the turn of the century—so much so, a local journalist noted, that British Columbia was cursed with a "class of crooks who prefer to mine the public instead of the ground." Extraction of lode gold and silver began in the Slocan and Boundary districts in the 1890s, but copper, lead, and zinc superseded precious metals after 1900. The smelting, or refining, of these base metals required large-scale smelters. The first successful smelter opened near the Rossland mines at Trail Creek in 1895, and a second, Cominco, in the Kootenays. Coal mining, especially in and around Nanaimo on Vancouver Island, also contributed to the province's economy.

Then, as now, forestry outdistanced mining in terms of both wealth and employment. Logging increased by an astonishing 400 percent between 1900 and 1910, and wood-product manufacturing provided numerous jobs. Until 1912, and the passage of the Forestry Act, trees were cut without concern for reforestation or the preservation of Crown land.

Fisheries, especially the salmon fisheries, expanded and consolidated in a highly competitive business that pitted Natives, Euro-Canadians, and Japanese-Canadians against each other. Denied treaties, the First Nations were excluded by the newcomers from their ancestral fisheries used for consumption and trade. British Columbia Packers Association emerged as the most powerful salmon packing company after 1902 and used the most modern technology, including the "Iron Chink"—a racist term applied to the butchering machine for processed fish that replaced work previously done by Chinese- and Japanese-Canadian workers. The small port of Steveston became known as the sockeye capital of the world.

Agriculture was slow to get established in British Columbia, but by World War I it ranked second to forestry in terms of output. Fruit farming was the most commercially viable, especially after the introduction of refrigerated rail cars at the turn of the century, since much of the fruit was exported. Even manufacturing grew in the late nineteenth century, outdistancing that of the Prairie provinces and almost reaching Ontario standards. In 1880, British Columbians contributed over 1 percent of the net value of Canadian manufactures; by 1890, the figure was close to 5 percent, more than equal to the growth of its share of the national population. Still, the province's distance from the centre of the industrial development in central Canada, combined with the high freight rates and the small regional market, prevented the province from becoming a substantial and ongoing secondary-manufacturing base. Rather, British Columbia, like the Maritimes, became another hinterland region.

On the Prairies, wheat was king. The world demand for wheat after 1896 opened up areas on the northern fringe and in the arid Palliser Triangle to production, thus increasing substantially both the wheat lands and yields. In 1901, 55 000 prairie farms occupied 15.4 million acres (6.2 million ha), of which 70 percent was in wheat; by 1911, 200 000 farms occupied over 58 million acres (9 million ha), of which 59 percent was in wheat. In terms of yields, that amounted to a record 208 million bushels in 1911. Such growth justified and necessitated new rail lines, especially to service the new areas of settlement. Rail lines in the region doubled from 1885 to 1900, to 6000 km, and then tripled again to 18 000 km by 1913. But the Prairies faced the same problem that British Columbia and the Maritimes faced: too small a regional market to foster substantial secondary manufacturing. Thus, as the National Policy made inevitable, the Prairies became subservient to central Canada in terms of economic growth and dominance.

A view of Victoria harbour 25 years later, in 1910. Construction on the impressive new legislative buildings shown in the background began in 1893.

Source: William H. Gibson/National Archives of Canada/ PA-59895.

Rise of Cities in the West

Victoria and Vancouver vied for dominance in West Coast trade. Vancouver won out by 1914 because of the excellent dock and terminal facilities on Burrard Inlet and its role as the western terminus of the CPR. This new status fostered the growth of transportation, wholesaling, and resource companies in the city. By 1914, its population reached 155 000, while that of Victoria, the provincial capital, stood at only 35 000. Again, such growth necessitated a variety of retail, manufacturing, and professional services. The completion of the Panama Canal in 1914 enabled Vancouver to surpass Winnipeg as Canada's major western city; prairie farmers could now ship wheat to European markets through Vancouver and the Panama Canal. On the eve of World War I, Vancouver stood between two worlds. As historian Robert McDonald notes: "At one level Vancouver functioned as a metropolitan city, managing resource industries, directing transportation and commerce, and providing a growing range of business and professional services for the region. At another it continued to be a city on the frontier, a new society different from Burrard Inlet's nineteenth-century lumber communities yet still subject to the vicissitudes of a regional economy narrowly based on resource extraction and promotion."[4] Such urban developments proceeded without regard to First Nations' land claims.

Urbanization occurred at a rapid rate on the Prairies. In 1870, at the time of the region's incorporation into Confederation, no urban centres existed in the region; by 1911, there were seventeen incorporated cities and 150 incorporated towns. Five dominant cities emerged by 1914: Winnipeg, Saskatoon, Regina, Edmonton, and Calgary. Each serviced a surrounding agricultural hinterland.

Winnipeg's location as the "gateway to the West" with rail links to the East made the entire West its hinterland. Thanks to this strategic location, it became the third-largest manufacturing city in pre–World War I Canada. Nicknamed the "Hub City," it stood at the junction of three transcontinental railways. It processed rural agricultural products and, in return, sold construction materials to settlers—lumber, bricks, finished steel, and cement, as well as some manufactured goods. The city employed thousands in its rail yards, the largest in the world by 1904, with as many as 1800 freight cars passing through in a single day. But the eastern cities in turn dominated even Winnipeg. Ultimately, all western rail lines led to Montreal and Toronto.

Industrialization and Urbanization in Central Canada

At the turn of the century, industrialization occurred largely in Ontario and Quebec. In 1900, both provinces together produced over four-fifths (82 percent) of the total value of Canadian manufacturing. Ontario's growth initially was based on small-scale consumer goods industries in a series of towns and cities throughout southern Ontario that "fed" the demands of a booming agricultural hinterland economy. These industries depended chiefly on coal as a source of energy and on iron production. In both cases, Ontario had an advantage over Quebec because of the province's proximity to the Pennsylvania coal fields and the Minnesota iron ranges. But Canada created its own iron and steel companies that increased production sixfold between 1877 and

An immigrant woman and her children waiting on a curb in front of the imposing CPR Station in Winnipeg, around 1909. Almost everyone who came west came through this station, built in 1904. In 1992 the Aboriginal Centre of Winnipeg Inc. bought the building. The refurbished Aboriginal Centre is now a modern office space.

Source: The United Church Archives, Toronto/93.049P/3111N.

1910 and another tenfold by 1913, producing one million tons of iron at peak production. Already by 1911, iron and steel industries outdistanced the traditional dominant industry of textiles in terms of both production and employment. Also, a network of rail lines crisscrossed Ontario, linking the numerous towns and cities to the rural countryside and to other urban centres. Thus by the turn of the century, Ontario already had numerous manufacturing centres scattered from Windsor to Cornwall—London, Berlin (later Kitchener), Guelph, and Peterborough, with the largest concentration at the western end of Lake Ontario, including Toronto, Hamilton, Brantford, St. Catharines, and Niagara Falls. These centres produced tariff-protected goods such as engines, farm implements, stoves, furniture, and canned goods. Hamilton, a steel-producing town, became as well the home of large railcar shops. But most of Ontario's largest head offices, financial institutions, factories, and warehouses were located in Toronto. Historian Peter A. Baskerville notes that in the first decade of the twentieth century alone "manufacturing output in Ontario's major cities almost doubled—the greatest increase of any time before World War II."[5]

In Quebec, much of the new industry was small-scale and labour-intensive. Quebec had only two major manufacturing and industrial cities: Montreal and Quebec City. A few small textile towns grew up in the Eastern Townships, but most did not develop into manufacturing centres comparable to the smaller towns and cities of Ontario. The province instead concentrated on the small-scale manufacturing of shoes, textiles, lumber, and foodstuffs (flour, sugar, dairy products)—light industries utilizing cheap and abundant labour for a limited domestic market. These industries were concentrated near the rail facilities of the two main cities of Montreal and Quebec City. Montreal had the advantage here over Quebec City, the latter becoming more isolated from the major canals and rail networks without a bridge over the St. Lawrence. Montreal also had the majority of financial institutions to provide capital for businesses in the city. Quebec City's shipbuilding had greatly declined by the late nineteenth century.

According to economic historians, Albert Faucher and Maurice Lamontagne, a second industrial revolution began in 1911, when hydroelectric power replaced steam as the main source of industrial energy. Now pulp and paper, and later minerals, became the new resource products. Even during this "second industrial revolution" Ontario continued to outperform Quebec, thanks to mineral production, the pulp and paper mills in the Ontario north, and hydroelectric power, especially in and around Niagara Falls.

Still, in the Laurentian Shield, Quebec had vast spruce forests for the pulp and paper industry, and an abundance of water power for electricity. Between 1900 and 1910, power production in the province tripled. The pulp and paper industry experienced similar phenomenal growth in the same period due to American demand for newsprint. Unencumbered by a perceived need to make treaties with the First Nations to the north, pulp and paper operations pushed northwards. The federal government did conclude Treaty Nine with the First Nations of Northern Ontario in 1905/06 (and 1930), but Northern Quebec remained unsurrendered land until the last quarter of the twentieth century.

Initially, the pulp produced by Canadian-based companies went for processing in the United States. But at the turn of the century the Quebec government, at the urging of Quebec nationalists, placed an embargo on exports of pulp from Crown lands. Subsequently, Quebec pulp mills began producing their own newsprint for export. The Laurentide Company, established in 1877, became Canada's first and largest newsprint maker at the time. By 1914, Quebec had become a leading industrial province. More than two-thirds of its population worked in non-agricultural activities, and roughly one-half of its population lived in urban centres.

The Uniqueness of Quebec's Industrial Development

For French Canadians, Quebec's industrialization had a unique and disturbing aspect: they had almost no control over it. In 1910, of Canada's entrepreneurs, only one out of 40 was French-speaking. French Canadians were the labourers, not the owners of industry. Exceptions existed— Senator Louis Forget and his nephew Sir Rodolphe Forget, powerful financiers and investors in Quebec industries; Senator Frédéric-Liguori Béique, director of the Banque d'Hochelaga and later president of the Banque Canadienne Nationale; Alfred Dubuc, owner of the Chicoutimi Pulp Company in the Saguenay valley; and Georges Amyot, an influential textile magnate—but these men stood out as the exceptions.

Was this imbalance due to French Canadians' limited pool of capital? Perhaps in part, but French-speaking Canadians in the Dominion faced a larger obstacle: the language of business was English. Historian Michel Brunet has argued that in the early twentieth century "the Quebec English-speaking business community constituted a select private club into which only a few assimilated former French Canadians were admitted."[6]

Education might also have been a factor. The Roman Catholic church tended to emphasize a humanistic education, particularly at the classical college level, over science and commerce. The Quebec government tried to correct this imbalance by offering financial support for the establishment of technical schools. In 1907 it created the École des Hautes Études Commerciales (HEC), a university-level business school. Yet, many graduates still faced the need to work in English, at least at the managerial level.

The French-Canadian Response to Industrialism

French Canadians differed on the question of French-Canadian involvement in industrialization. Jules-Paul Tardivel, the ultramontane nationalist and editor of the newspaper *La Vérité*, best expressed the viewpoint of those wanting to avoid involvement: "It is not necessary for us to possess industry and money.... We would no longer be French Canadians but Americans like the others…. To cling to the soil, to raise large families, to maintain the hearths of spiritual and intellectual life, that must be our role in America."

Others, like Errol Bouchette, a French-Canadian economist, urged Quebeckers to accept industrialism as the best means to survive in North America. Not even agriculture could survive, he argued, if outsiders controlled the rest of Quebec's economy. "Emparons-nous de l'industrie" (Let us take over industry!) was his rallying cry.

"New Ontario"

Industrialization advanced fastest and farthest in southern Ontario, especially in the period from 1890 to 1914, which economic historian Ian Drummond calls the province's "heroic age."[7] The high protective tariff helped, as did the extensive railway system that tied the industrial core at the western end of Lake Ontario to the rest of the province, and to all of Canada. But another decisive factor was the wealth of timber and minerals in northern Ontario. Suddenly this area— "New Ontario"—ceased to be perceived as an unproductive wasteland of rocks, lakes, and muskeg, and was seen instead in terms of its resource potential. Several northern Ontario towns and minerals became synonymous: Sudbury—nickel; Cobalt—silver; Timmins—gold. By 1914, the mineral-resource base of northern Ontario had become accessible through rail transport to major urban centres outside the region.

Mining required sophisticated and expensive equipment and large consolidated companies. In nickel production, for example, the ore had to be mined from the rock and then burned in the open air to concentrate the metal and reduce the sulphur content. Unfortunately, the environmental cost of development was high. The miners cleared the land of trees to fuel the roasting process, while sulphur and arsenic fumes escaped from the smokestacks into the atmosphere and poisoned the surrounding vegetation. A Bureau of Forestry was created in 1898, but it had limited influence in regulating the cutting of forest reserves in the region.

WHERE HISTORIANS DISAGREE

Industrial Growth in Quebec

During the Quiet Revolution of the 1960s, Quebec historians began to question why Quebec appeared to lag behind Ontario in terms of industrial growth, and to question as well why French Canadians lagged behind the minority English Canadians as the owners of industry in the province. These questions have led historians to look back at the beginning of industrialization in Quebec for answers.

In the early 1950s two Quebec economists, Albert Faucher and Maurice Lamontagne, argued that Canadian industrialization occurred in two stages, or two "industrial revolutions"—one from 1866 to 1911, the other after 1911. In the first, industrial growth depended chiefly on the ability to produce iron and steel, resources that Quebec had in short supply and that were unavailable nearby. Ontario, by contrast, benefited from its proximity to the Pennsylvania coal fields and the Minnesota iron ranges. In the second stage, growth depended on the availability of hydroelectric power, which by 1911 had become the new source of industrial energy. Here Quebec was well blessed, but by this time Ontario had already developed an industrial infrastructure, and Quebec could not catch up.

Other economic historians have questioned Faucher and Lamontagne's identification of the "industrial takeoff" period in Quebec. John Dales contends that hydroelectricity experienced its greatest growth—310 percent—in the first decade of the twentieth century.[1] André Raynauld argues that in some decades, such as the period 1910–20, Ontario accelerated faster than Quebec, but that over the extended period 1870–1957, the two provincial economies grew at almost parallel rates, each one taking its turn as the leader in industrial growth. Thus, overall, Quebec did not lag behind.[2]

Historians H.V. Nelles and C. Armstrong agree. They argue that by 1920, both Ontario and Quebec produced the same quantity of hydroelectric power. But the two provinces differed in the nature of control of this key energy source. In Ontario it was publicly owned through Ontario Hydro, thus making it available to a larger industrial base, whereas in Quebec two very large privately owned companies controlled profits and alone benefited.[3]

Economic historian John Isbister looks to the differing agricultural economies of the two provinces for his explanation. Quebec produced insufficient surplus food to serve its urban centres. Agriculture was in the province "a subsistence sector, economically isolated, not integrated into the wider market system," unlike in Ontario. Cultural explanations, according to Isbister, explain the difference; Quebec had "a different attitude toward the farming life. The Quebec *habitant* was a peasant, poor and self-sufficient, not a man of business."[4] Only in the twentieth century would this attitude change, and by then Ontario farmers had surged ahead.

More recently, Quebec historians Paul-André Linteau, René Durocher, and Jean-Claude Robert have questioned whether Quebec industrialized at a slower pace than Ontario even at the turn of the century. They argue that by dwelling on the resource-oriented industries, historians and economists have overlooked the sustained growth in manufacturing in Quebec at the turn of the century, which shows the period to be one of industrial takeoff.[5]

The second question—why French-speaking Quebeckers failed to become the leaders of industry in their own province—has also proven to be contentious. Historians Maurice Séguin and Michel Brunet blame the Conquest of 1759–60 for the disadvantage. They contend that New France had a dynamic business class, but that its members were forced to return to France after the conquest because of poor business opportunities under the British conquerors. With the departure of the French bourgeoisie, British interests stepped in, causing French Canadians to lose their economic role from that point onward.[6]

Historian Fernand Ouellet has challenged this interpretation.[7] He denies the existence of a viable business class in New France. Rather the French Canadians' nonprogressive business mentality led to British commercial superiority. In any event, the two sides agree that anglophone business interests already controlled the economy of Quebec in the nineteenth century.

Current debate has revolved around the question of how this small Anglo minority was able to maintain its favoured position. Some historians blame the church-dominated educational system, with its emphasis on a classical education rather than on training in science and commerce, for the failure of French-speaking Canadians to succeed in business. But recent research does not entirely bear this out. Some science and commerce courses were in fact part of the school curriculum in Quebec.[8] Historians Craig Brown and Ramsay Cook argue that where the church and the schools erred was in putting nationalism ahead of practical economic considerations: "Education ... had a moral and patriotic function, to which practical training for economic life was secondary."[9] Historians Paul-André Linteau, René Durocher, and Jean-Claude Robert explain the gap in industrial leadership of French-Canadian businesspeople in terms of limited technological know-how. Unlike English-speaking immigrants in Quebec, whose contact with their place of origin provided them with important business links and an international perspective, French Canadians lacked an "information network."[10] Their contacts and know-how never extended beyond the confines of Quebec.

1   John Dales, *Hydroelectricity and Industrial Development in Quebec, 1898–1940* (Cambridge, MA: Harvard University Press, 1957).

2   André Raynauld, *Croissance et structure économique de la Province de Québec* (Quebec: Ministère de l'industrie et du commerce, 1961).

3   H.V. Nelles and C. Armstrong, "Contrasting Development of the Hydro-Electric Industry in the Montreal and Toronto Regions, 1900–1930," in Douglas McCalla, ed., *The Development of Canadian Capitalism: Essays in Business History* (Toronto: Copp Clark Pitman, 1990), pp. 167–190.

4   John Isbister, "Agriculture, Balanced Growth, and Social Change in Central Canada Since 1850: An Interpretation," in Douglas McCalla, ed., *Perspectives on Canadian Economic History* (Toronto: Copp Clark Pitman, 1987), p. 67.

5   Paul-André Linteau, René Durocher, and Jean-Claude Robert, *Quebec: A History 1867–1929* (Toronto: James Lorimer, 1983).

6   Maurice Séguin, "The Conquest and French-Canadian Economic Life," translated from "La Conquête et la vie économique des Canadiens," *Action nationale*, 28 (1947): 308–26, in Dale Miquelon, ed., *Society and Conquest: The Debate on the Bourgeoisie and Social Change in French Canada, 1700–1850* (Toronto: Copp Clark Publishing, 1977), pp. 67–80; and Michel Brunet, "The British Conquest and the Decline of the French-Canadian Bourgeoisie," translated from "La Conquête anglaise et la déchéance de la bourgeoisie canadienne," in *La Présence anglaise et les Canadiens* (Montreal: Beauchemin, 1958), pp. 49–109; also in Miquelon, *Society and Conquest*, pp. 143–61.

7   See the conclusion of Fernand Ouellet's *Histoire économique et sociale du Québec 1760–1850* (Montreal: Fides, 1966), pp. 539–596. This work is available in translation, *Economic and Social History of Quebec 1760–1850* (Toronto: Gage, 1980), pp. 547–609.

8   W.J. Ryan, *The Clergy and Economic Growth in Quebec, 1896–1914* (Quebec: Presses de l'Université Laval, 1966).

9   R.C. Brown and R. Cook, *Canada, 1896–1921: A Nation Transformed* (Toronto: McClelland and Stewart, 1974), p. 132.

10 Linteau, Durocher, and Robert, *Quebec: A History, 1867–1929*, p. 404.

The investment capital and technical skill required for large-scale production led to consolidated companies. In 1902, the Canadian Copper Company at Sudbury amalgamated with several smaller American companies to form the International Nickel Company of Canada (Inco). In the Porcupine district, three large companies—Hollinger (Canadian-owned), Dome (American-owned), and McIntyre (Canadian-owned after 1915)—soon controlled 90 percent of the gold production. In Sault Ste. Marie, F.H. Clergue, an American-born entrepreneur, built an industrial empire, the Consolidated Lake Superior Company, by using largely American capital.

The Ontario government assisted promoters. During Mowat's time as premier (1872–1896), the Ontario government invested heavily in the north for a handsome return of some $17 000 000, enabling the Ontario government to be debt-free at a time that most other provincial governments had large deficits. In 1891, in response to the recommendations of a royal

The building of two new transcontinental railways across northern Ontario in the early twentieth century opened up vast areas of the Native peoples' hunting and trapping grounds to settlement and resource development. It also eliminated the Native peoples' jobs as freighters. The photo shows HBC Native voyageurs on their way to Flying Post with supplies from Biscotasing on the CPR, northwest of Sudbury, around 1900.

Source: Archives of Ontario/Acc. #10144.

commission on Ontario's mineral resources, the government established the Bureau of Mines "to collect and publish information and statistics on the mineral resources and mining industry." It also established the School of Mining at Queen's University in the early 1890s (later merged into the university's Faculty of Applied Sciences). As well, the provincial government handed out loans, railway land grants, timber leases, and mineral rights. Only when production began did the province demand royalty payments. By 1904, one-quarter of the province's revenue came from mining and another quarter from forestry.

Mining Towns in Northern Ontario

A host of mining towns arose. Some, such as Golden City, Elk Lake, and South Porcupine, were little more than camps made up of shacks and log cabins; others became company towns, built and owned by the town's only employer. Only a few, such as Sudbury and Timmins, became main service or distribution centres for the entire region. All of these northern Ontario mining communities depended on the capricious rise and fall of world metal prices. In time they came under the dominance of Toronto, the provincial capital, their main supply base, the focus of their rail transport, and the source of money for many of the mining and forestry companies.

From 1880 to 1914, Canada underwent its industrial revolution as a result of the success of the national policy, large-scale financial investment from within the country and abroad, and a new, more positive attitude toward business. Manufacturing and large-scale industrial production, and accompanying urban growth, meant increased prosperity and an overall higher standard of living. But not all regions of the country, nor all social classes, benefited equally from the economic expansion. The social costs of rapid change were high.

NOTES

1. H.V. Nelles, *The Politics of Development: Forests, Mines and Hydro-Electric Power in Ontario, 1849–1941* (Toronto: Macmillan, 1974), pp. 248–49.

2. Michael Cross, "The Canadian Worker in the Early Industrial Age," in Gregory S. Kealey and W.J.C. Cherwinski, eds., *Lectures in Canadian Labour and Working-Class History* (St. John's: Canadian Committee on Labour History and New Hogtown Press, 1985), p. 49.

3. Judith Fingard, "The 1880s: Paradoxes of Progress," in E.R. Forbes and D.A. Muise, eds., *The Atlantic Provinces in Confederation* (Toronto: University of Toronto Press, 1993), p. 97.

4. Robert A.J. McDonald, *Making Vancouver: Class, Status, and Social Boundaries, 1863–1913* (Vancouver: University of British Columbia Press, 1996), p. 148.

5. Peter A. Baskerville, *Ontario: Image, Identity and Power* (Toronto: Oxford University Press, 2002), p. 157.

6. Michel Brunet, "The French Canadians' Search for a Fatherland," in Peter Russell, ed., *Nationalism in Canada* (Toronto: McGraw-Hill, 1966), p. 55.

7. Ian Drummond, *Progress Without Planning: The Economic History of Ontario from Confederation to the Second World War* (Toronto: University of Toronto Press, 1987), p. 104.

BEYOND THE BOOK

Weblinks

Montreal: The Industrial City
http://www.mccord-museum.qc.ca/en/keys/webtours/VQ_P2_14_EN
Digitized photographs, maps, and advertisements describe the growing industrial city of Montreal at the turn of the century.

Urban Growth of Victoria, British Columbia
http://www.vihistory.ca/content/documents/victoria.by-law.124.php
This bylaw passed in 1890 expanded the boundaries of the City of Victoria to keep up with its marked growth.

Urbanization and Industrialization of the West
http://www.collectionscanada.ca/canadian-west/052903/05290302_e.html
This website contains historical photographs and industrial diagrams that illustrate the industrialization and urbanization of the West.

Cobalt: The Town with a Silver Lining
http://www.cobalt.ca/history.htm
A brief history of the mining town Cobalt, Ontario, from the discovery of silver to the present.

Films & Novels

Eaton's: A Canadian Saga. Directed by John McGreevy. 2003.

RELATED READINGS

The following articles in R. Douglas Francis and Donald B. Smith, eds., *Readings in Canadian History: Post-Confederation*, 7th ed. (Toronto: Thomson Nelson, 2006), deal with topics relevant to this chapter: Robert A.J. McDonald, "'Holy Retreat' or 'Practical Breathing Spot'?: Class Perceptions of Vancouver's Stanley Park, 1910–1913," pp. 298–316; and Stephen Davies, "'Reckless Walking Must Be Discouraged': The Automobile Revolution and the Shaping of Modern Urban Canada to 1930," pp. 316–326.

BIBLIOGRAPHY

Michael Bliss's *Northern Enterprise: Five Centuries of Canadian Business* (Toronto: McClelland & Stewart, 1987) provides a comprehensive history of Canadian business. See, as well, Graham Taylor and Peter Baskerville, *A Concise History of Business in Canada* (Toronto: Oxford University Press, 1994). On economic developments consult Kenneth Norrie and Douglas Owram, *A History of the Canadian Economy*, 3rd ed. (Toronto: Nelson, 2002). Two chapters—"The Triumph of Enterprise" and "French Canada and the New Industrial Order"—in R.C. Brown and R. Cook, *Canada, 1896–1921: A Nation Transformed* (Toronto: McClelland & Stewart, 1974) deal with industrialization and urbanization in English and French Canada, respectively. On Quebec consult also Paul-André Linteau, René Durocher, and Jean-Claude Robert, *Quebec: A History, 1867–1929* (Toronto: James Lorimer, 1983); and Susan Mann, *The Dream of Nation: A Social and Intellectual History of Quebec*, 2nd ed. (Montreal/Kingston: McGill-Queen's University Press, 2002), pp. 132–49 and 167–83. On the links between industrialization and immigration policy, see Ninette Kelley and Michael Trebilecock, *The Making of the Mosaic: A History of Canadian Immigration Policy* (Toronto: University of Toronto Press, 1998).

Michael Bliss deals with Canadian business's attitudes in *A Living Profit: Studies in the Social History of Canadian Businessmen, 1883–1914* (Toronto: McClelland & Stewart, 1974). Fernande Roy has studied the economic outlook of francophones in Montreal in *Progrès, harmonie, liberté: le libéralisme des milieux d'affaires francophones à Montréal au tournant du siècle* (Montreal: Boréal Express, 1988). Joy L. Santink's *Timothy Eaton and the Rise of His Department Store* (Toronto: University of Toronto Press, 1990) is an important study of this prominent Canadian merchant. Lord Beaverbrook's dealings are discussed in Gregory P. Marchildon, *Profits and Politics: Beaverbrook and the Gilded Age of Canadian Finances* (Toronto: University of Toronto Press, 1996). For a general debate on industrialism in Ontario consult Ian Drummond, Louis P. Cain, and Majorie Cohen, "CHR Dialogue: Ontario's Industrial Revolution," *Canadian Historical Review* 69(3) (September 1988): 283–314.

On industrialization in the Maritimes see T.W. Acheson, D. Frank, and J. Frost, *Industrialization and the Underdevelopment in the Maritimes, 1880 to 1930* (Toronto: Garamond Press, 1985); Kris Inwood, *Farm, Factory and Fortune: New Studies in the Economic History of the Maritime Provinces* (Fredericton: Acadiensis Press, 1993); the relevant chapters in E.R. Forbes and D.A. Muise, eds., *The Atlantic Provinces in Confederation* (Toronto: University of Toronto Press, 1993); and W. Acheson, "The National Policy and the Industrialization of the Maritimes, 1880–1910," in G. Stelter and A.F.J. Artibise, eds., *The Canadian City: Essays in Urban and Social History* (Toronto: McClelland & Stewart, 1977; rev. ed., Ottawa: Carleton University Press, 1984), pp. 93–124. On industrialization and rural society, see Daniel Samson, ed., *Contested Countryside: Rural Workers and Modern Society in Atlantic Canada, 1800–1950* (Fredericton: Acadiensis Press, 1994) For Newfoundland see David Alexander, "Economic Growth in the Atlantic Region, 1880–1940," in E. Seager, L. Fisher, and S. Pierson, comp., *Atlantic Canada and Confederation: Essays in Canadian Political Economy* (Toronto: University of Toronto Press, 1983), pp. 51–78; and the relevant sections of Margaret R. Conrad and James K. Hiller, *Atlantic Canada: A Region in the Making* (Toronto: University of Toronto Press, 2001). On the impact of out-migration on industrialization, see Patricia Thornton, "The Problem of Out-Migration from Atlantic Canada, 1871–1921: A New Outlook," *Acadiensis* 15(1) (Autumn 1985): 3–34.

On British Columbia see Allen Saeger, "The Resource Economy, 1871–1921," in Hugh J.M. Johnston, ed., *The Pacific Province: A History of British Columbia* (Vancouver: Douglas & McIntyre, 1996), pp. 205–52; Frank Leonard, *A Thousand Blunders* (Vancouver: University of British Columbia Press,

1996); Jeremy Mouat, *Roaring Days: Rossland's Mines and the History of British Columbia* (Vancouver: University of British Columbia Press, 1995); and Martin Robin, *The Rush for Spoils: The Company Province, 1871–1913* (Toronto: McClelland & Stewart, 1972).

Studies in English of industrialization in Quebec include A. Faucher and M. Lamontagne, "History of Industrial Development," in M. Rioux and Y. Martin, eds., *French-Canadian Society* (Toronto: McClelland & Stewart, 1964), pp. 257–71; J.H. Dales, *Hydroelectricity and Industrial Development in Quebec, 1898–1940* (Cambridge, MA: Harvard University Press, 1957); and W.J. Ryan, *The Clergy and Economic Growth in Quebec, 1896–1914* (Quebec: Presses de l'Université Laval, 1966). See, as well, John Dickinson and Brian Young, *A Short History of Quebec*, 3rd ed. (Montreal/Kingston: McGill-Queen's University Press, 2003). For information on Quebec's banks consult Ronald Rudin, *Banking en français* (Toronto: University of Toronto Press, 1985); and, for background on its credit unions, Ronald Rudin, *In Whose Interest? Quebec's Caisses populaires, 1900–1945* (Montreal/Kingston: McGill-Queen's University Press, 1990).

For Ontario's resource development see H.V. Nelles, *The Politics of Development: Forests, Mines and Hydro-Electric Power in Ontario, 1849–1941* (Toronto: Macmillan, 1974); Duncan McDowall, *Steel at the Sault: Francis H. Clergue, Sir James Dunn, and Algoma Steel Corporation, 1901–1956* (Toronto: University of Toronto Press, 1984); and Jean L. Manore, *Cross-Currents: Hydroelectricity and the Engineering of Northern Ontario* (Waterloo, ON: Wilfrid Laurier University Press, 1999).

For the impact of industrialization and urbanization and resource developments on the Native peoples in Ontario consult Edward S. Rogers and Donald B. Smith, eds., *Aboriginal Ontario* (Toronto: Dundurn Press, 1994); and for British Columbia, Rolf Knight, *Indians at Work: An Informal History of Native Labour in British Columbia, 1848–1930* (Vancouver: New Star Books, 1996). Also of importance for Canada as a whole is Christopher Armstrong and H.V. Nelles, *Monopoly's Moment: The Organization and Regulation of Canadian Utilities, 1830–1930* (Philadelphia: Temple University Press, 1986). On Canadian investment abroad the following studies are important: C. Armstrong and H.V. Nelles, *Southern Exposure: Canadian Promoters in Latin America and the Caribbean, 1896–1930* (Toronto: University of Toronto Press, 1988); and Duncan McDowall, *The Light: Brazilian Traction, Light and Power Company Limited, 1899–1945* (Toronto: University of Toronto Press, 1988).

On urbanization see J.M.S. Careless's booklet *The Rise of Cities in Canada Before 1914* (Ottawa: Canadian Historical Association, 1978), and his *Frontier and Metropolis: Regions, Cities and Identities in Canada before 1914* (Toronto: University of Toronto Press, 1989). Consult as well Richard Preston, "The Evolution of Urban Canada: The Post-1867 Period," in R.M. Irving, ed., *Readings in Canadian Geography*, 3rd ed. (Toronto: Holt, Rinehart and Winston, 1978), pp. 19–46; and the collection of articles in Stelter and Artibise, eds., *The Canadian City* (cited earlier). The Canadian Museum of Civilization has sponsored eight volumes in its series of histories of major Canadian cities: *Regina* (1989) by J. William Brennan, *Ottawa* (1986) by John H. Taylor, *Winnipeg* (1977) by Alan Artibise, *Calgary* (1978) by Max Foran, *Vancouver* (1980) by Patricia Roy, *Hamilton* (1982) by John C. Weaver, *Toronto to 1918* (1983) by J.M.S. Careless, and *Toronto since 1918* (1985) by James Lemon.

For a detailed study of urbanization in the Maritimes, see J.M.S. Careless, "Aspects of Metropolitanism in Atlantic Canada," in M. Wade, ed., *Regionalism in the Canadian Community, 1867–1967* (Toronto: University of Toronto Press, 1969), pp. 117–29. On British Columbia see Robert A.J. McDonald, *Making Vancouver: Class, Status, and Social Boundaries, 1863–1913* (Vancouver: University of British Columbia Press, 1996); and Norbert McDonald, *Distant Neighbors: A Comparative History of Seattle and Vancouver* (Lincoln, NE: University of Nebraska Press, 1987). On the Prairies consult Paul Voisey, "The Urbanization of the Canadian Prairies, 1871–1916," *Histoire Sociale/Social History* 8 (1975): 77–101; A.F.J. Artibise, "The Urban West: The Evolution of Prairie Towns and Cities in 1930," *Prairie Forum* 4 (1979): 237–62; and A.F.J. Artibise, ed., *Town and City: Aspects of Western Canadian Urban Development* (Regina: Canadian Plains Research Center, University of Regina, 1981).

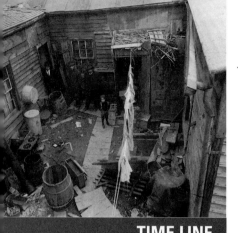

Chapter Seven

THE IMPACT
OF URBAN AND
INDUSTRIAL GROWTH

TIME LINE	
1872	Trade Union Act passed
1879	Beginning of the Provincial Workmen's Association for coal miners in Nova Scotia
1883	Founding of the Trades and Labor Congress of Canada (TLC)
1889	Royal Commission on the Relations of Labour and Capital issues report
1892	Criminal Code outlaws contraceptives
1894	Labour Day established as a national holiday
1897	Herbert Ames publishes *City Below the Hill*, a sociological study of Montreal
1900	Department of Labour established
1905	Founding of the Industrial Workers of the World (IWW), or "Wobblies," as the trade union became known
1907	The Industrial Disputes Investigation Act passed
1908	The Fishermen's Protective Union is founded in Newfoundland by William Ford Coaker
1913	Publication of John MacDougall's *Rural Life in Canada: Its Trends and Tasks* Ontario Housing Act enacted
1914	Workmen's Compensation Act passed in Ontario
1917	The Order of Sleeping Car Porters, the first African-Canadian railway union, formed in North America

Industrialization and urbanization transformed the lifestyles of Canadians. In rural areas, they contributed to the migration of younger members of farm families into the towns and cities in search of work. Farming, too, became more a business enterprise than a way of life. Machinery replaced people, and tasks became more routine. First Nations people in all regions of the country, but especially in the north, had to adjust to increased competition from other interest groups. In the cities, rural migration, along with immigration, led to the rise of large working-class districts in the congested and polluted city centre.

Increasingly, urban workers worked outside the home in factories or offices that were often sub-standard in terms of cleanliness and safety. They worked long hours for meagre pay. Women and some working-class children worked for lower wages even when doing the same job as men. Workers looked to charitable institutions for assistance, fraternal organizations and clubs for camaraderie and identity, and unions for better wages and working conditions. While overall, Canadians enjoyed a higher standard of living in 1914 than they did in 1867, social and gender inequality and sub-standard living and working conditions persisted, causing social reformers to target these concerns.

The Impact on Rural Society

On the eve of Canada's urban and industrial revolution, farming remained a fairly stable occupation, with the family farm a relatively self-sufficient unit. Farm families produced a substantial amount of the food they consumed and sold the surplus. Farmers tried still to pass their farms down from generation to generation, usually to the eldest son. Many younger sons worked to save money to purchase their own farms. Farmers' daughters helped on the family farm in preparation for marriage—preferably, their parents hoped, to a young farmer in the district.

Industrialization altered the rural lifestyle. The introduction of labour-saving machines—hay mowers, reapers, threshers, and tractors—enabled a farmer to bring more land under cultivation. A mechanical haymower, for example, allowed a farmer to cut 10 acres (4 ha) a day, or 40 times as much as had been the case previously. By 1900, farmers, who used labour-saving machinery, produced a bushel of wheat in one-hundredth of the time required only 30 years earlier. Now a farmer required greater revenue from the farm to pay for the expensive equipment he used. Large-scale farms became common. Dairy and fruit farming also became agribusiness. As well, improved and increased rail and steamship service that included cold-storage facilities and lower freight rates made it possible for Canadian farmers to sell their produce abroad—in Britain, for example.

The nature of work changed. It became more routine and specialized. Farmers also began to take over what had previously been considered women's work. Economist Marjorie Cohen notes, "As large dairy herds developed, dairying ceased to be a part-time occupation for farm women and more and more became the major work of males on the farms."[1] Large-scale dairy farms produced the milk to supply cheese factories that, by 1901, produced 40 percent of Canadian cheese. As was the case with cheese, the production of butter and the canning of fruit, traditionally women's work, now occurred in factories instead of on farms.

Mechanization also reduced the number of older children needed to work the farm. This encouraged some youth to seek jobs or at least to work seasonally in the cities. Better-paying jobs and better working conditions also lured the younger generation from the land. Rural depopulation became a concern. Many social commentators, such as John MacDougall, a minister from Spencerville, Ontario, whose lectures on rural life were incorporated in *Rural Life in Canada: Its Trends and Tasks* (1913), warned of the dire consequences of a declining rural population. Like MacDougall, society at large continued to associate rural living with good moral values.

The Impact on First Nations People

On the West Coast, salmon processing came under the control of the British Columbia Packers Association after 1902. The company replaced Aboriginal people with Japanese as fishers, boat builders, and processors, since the latter would work for lower wages, could be relied on for year-round fishing, and were less prone to strike. Asians also replaced First Nations people in the canneries, although both groups were subordinate to Euro-Canadians as managers. The introduction of modern assembly line and processing equipment eliminated jobs in general in fish-processing plants.

First Nations peoples were adversely affected by commercialization in the northern fur trade. Initially, at the turn of the century, this was not the case. Rising prices and increased demand for furs in Europe created a lucrative market. New companies, such as the Revillon Frères of Paris and the Northern Trading Company, undermined the Hudson's Bay Company's monopoly, resulting in increased demand, higher prices, and cash fur buying. Prosperity had its downside, however. The influx of non-Aboriginal hunters and trappers led to increased competition, and a rapid decline in furs. The federal and provincial governments introduced conservation methods and laws to provide protection for wildlife, but they failed to appreciate the Aboriginal peoples' commercial, ceremonial, and subsistence needs and treaty rights in those areas under treaty.

The loss of trading and employment opportunities within the fur industry would not have been so dramatic if the northern First Nations people and Métis had had viable alternative means of livelihood, but they did not. Even such traditional alternatives as working on

This shot by Robert Reford of the interior of a salmon cannery, on the Skeena River in northwestern British Columbia, shows four First Nation women doing butchering work.

Source: Library and Archives Canada/PA-118162.

the railroads, supplying the railway ties, or working in mining areas as aboveground workers erecting buildings, clearing sites, and constructing roads were increasingly given to new immigrants. "By mid-century," historian Arthur Ray notes, "many northern Native groups were probably more dependent on hunting and trapping than they had been at anytime since the late eighteenth century."[2]

Life in the Industrial City

As a result of industrialization, cities became more socially stratified, with working-class districts physically separated from middle- and upper-class areas. Formerly, prosperous and low-income people lived side by side; no exclusive neighbourhoods existed. In a western city such as Calgary or Edmonton, for example, people in mansions looked out on plank or dusty sidewalks, and occasionally on a stray cow. The urban "elite" in the late nineteenth century wanted their homes close to their businesses or places of work. But with the arrival of the electric streetcar and the automobile, the middle and upper classes had an option. They could leave the inner city for suburban districts away from downtown congestion and pollution.

The city centres became both business and industrial districts, in which the majority of the working class lived. A number of long-established cultural institutions, such as churches and social clubs, were removed from the city centre and relocated in more luxurious and pleasant suburban areas. Many city centres became ghettoized and undesirable places to live. The Commission of Conservation, established by the federal government in 1909, noted in its *Annual Report* in 1914:

> Industrial smoke disfigures buildings, impairs the health of the population, renders the city filthy, destroys any beauty with which it may naturally be endowed and tends, therefore, to make it a squalid and undesirable place of residence, and this at a time when economic influences are forcing into cities an ever increasing proportion of our population.

In Montreal and Toronto, the two largest and most industrialized Canadian cities, most working-class people rented rooms in either boarding or tenement houses—old wooden cottages or two-storey buildings with little or no yard area. Rent could be as high as $10 or $12 a month for basement rooms, roughly 25 percent of an unskilled worker's wages. Some philanthropists, such as Toronto's Sir Joseph Flavelle and Hart Massey, subsidized workers' houses near their factories. In 1913, the Ontario government passed the Ontario Housing Act to provide municipal support for upgraded working-class districts. But before World War I, most working-class families had to face intractable landlords on their own. Few families owned their own houses, since house prices remained well beyond the means of the ordinary worker.

An average working-class family of five typically lived in a one-or-two-room flat: damp, unventilated, inadequately lighted, and poorly heated. Overcrowding remained a constant problem. In Toronto, for example, rapid growth led to a housing shortage. Some families lived in hastily constructed shacks, in backyard tents, or even on the street. In summer, a stench rose from the cesspools and outdoor privies.

Wife beating and the sexual abuse of children occurred among all social classes but was particularly pronounced in working-class families. Very often such violence in working-class districts was associated with drinking, unemployment, and destitution. Wives had little legal recourse, because male-dominated courts rarely challenged the husband's proprietary right over his wife's person and her sexuality. If anything, judges questioned the woman's character. Because of high legal costs, divorce also remained out of the question for most abused women.

A slum courtyard in Toronto. Several dwellings opened out onto this common space used for hanging wash, storage, and as a play area for children. Note the buildings are constructed of wood with tar paper roofs. Photo taken November 26, 1913.

Source: City of Toronto Archives, Series 372, Sub series 32, Item 259.

Children, particularly those of the working class, enjoyed fewer rights and privileges than did women at the turn of the century. They had to assume family responsibilities at an early age, and to grow up and mature quickly. In Montreal, a maximum grade three education was common for working-class children. In Ontario in 1871, John Sandfield Macdonald's Liberal government had passed legislation that made school attendance compulsory to the age of 16, but the law was not rigorously enforced. Children had to enter the work force as soon as possible (age 11 or 12 being the norm) to supplement the family income. The census of 1871 reveals that 25 percent of boys and 10 percent of girls between the ages of 11 and 15 held jobs outside the home; these statistics did not include boys hired to do odd jobs or girls working as domestics. In the 1880s Ontario and Quebec passed Factory Acts prohibiting the hiring of boys under 12 and girls under 14, but they had little impact due to poor enforcement and the difficulty of taking recalcitrant factory owners to court. Those children unfortunate enough to end up in court were more likely to be penalized than protected, and sent to harsh probationary institutions, such as the Toronto Mercer Reformatory or the Vancouver Boys' Industrial School.

Recent research enables us to make some generalizations about those children most likely to work outside the home and those who stayed home in Montreal, Canada's most industrialized city. Young daughters were less likely than young sons to be employed outside the home, since girls, by the age of 15 or 16, made only half to two-thirds of the wages paid to boys of the same age for doing a similar job. Patriarchal attitudes militated against daughters working in factories. As well, girls up to the age of 16 were required at home to help run the household and tend to younger family members. Still, poorer working-class families had to send their daughters out to work because of economic necessity.

Untreated waste from Toronto, and virtually every other municipality in the Great Lakes area, in both Canada and the United States, polluted the region's water systems.

Source: City of Toronto Archives Fonds 1244, Item 1122A.

Working Conditions in Canada's Cities

Industrialization created harsh working conditions. In times of demand the average labourer spent at least ten to twelve hours a day, six days a week, at work. Factories were poorly ventilated, noisy, and dirty. Factory foremen ran the factory to ensure maximum efficiency. They often fined workers for tardiness or for talking to fellow workers on the job. Industrial accidents and deaths occurred frequently.

Job security did not exist. Victims of industrial accidents had no workers' compensation. Layoffs, especially during the slower winter months, occurred regularly. Even in good times, unemployment was common, a byproduct of the capitalist system. Before the federal government introduced unemployment insurance in 1940, layoffs meant months of subsistence without wages.

Still, urban life had its attractions. Young people, both men and women, left the farm in increasing numbers to find work in the congested, noisy cities. While the working hours were long, they were still shorter than those on the farm, with at least Sunday and, sometimes, Saturday afternoon off. Factory wages also tended to be higher than farm wages. As well, cities had taverns, sports events, music halls, and, soon, the cinema for entertainment.

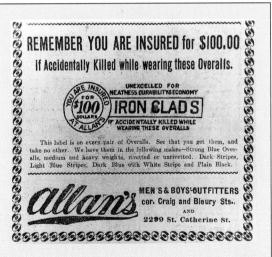

Photo of advertisement from the Montreal Star, *April 4, 1903. At the time, the average labourer made less than $11 a week.*

Source: National Library of Canada/18635.

The Standard of Living

The cost of living in urban centres rose continually and outpaced urban wages. The federal Department of Labour issued "typical weekly expenditure" budgets listing those items necessary for a family of five to enjoy a minimum standard of living. Although it allowed for only 0.6 kg of fresh meat per week per person, less than a litre of milk a day for a family of five, and no fresh vegetables or fruit, this minimum was more than the average working-class family could afford. In 1901, the estimated cost of living was $13.38 a week. But, at best, the average male worker could, without layoffs, make $425 a year in 1901, or an average of $8.25 a week. (The modern definition of poverty is any individual or family having to spend more than 70 percent of total income on basic needs such as food, fuel, and shelter.) Thus, many working-class families needed at least two incomes to stay above the poverty line.

Women in the Workplace

At the turn of the century, women made up about one-seventh of the paid work force. Usually they worked outside the home only between the ages of 14, the youngest age permissible for girls to work after 1885, and 24, the normal marrying age. After marriage, they rarely returned to paid work, unless widowhood, desertion, or illness in the family forced them to do so. The routine of housework—rearing children, cleaning, cooking, washing, mending, and shopping—meant full and exhausting days in an era before labour-saving devices. Marriage, motherhood, and domesticity remained intertwined in the minds of most women, no matter to which class they belonged. This was considered women's "proper sphere." Men dominated the "public sphere." Nevertheless, many women supplemented the family income by taking in boarders, doing part-time sewing, or doing laundry.

The most economically pressed mothers had no choice but to work outside the home in female-related jobs in textile factories, as waitresses, or as domestics. Women without familial support had to find work. In these cases, they had to rely on friends, neighbours, relatives, or on working-class associations to assist with children. Sometimes immigrant women could count on the support of ethnic groups to provide mutual aid and, occasionally, employment agencies. Increasingly, however, there arose a segment of working women who were single, non-immigrant girls, popularly known as "working girls," who performed non-domestic waged work outside the home. Being single, young, independent, and alone, they became the concern of moral reformers who saw them as a threat to the ideal Canadian society as made up of morally upright, married, and motherly women.

Middle-class women depended on domestic help at the turn of the century. Families were larger then, homes harder to keep clean, and food preparation much more time-consuming. Domestics tended to be young girls from rural areas or immigrant women. Indeed, the demand for domestic servants was so great that they were considered "preferred" immigrants. In 1891, 40 percent of all women working outside the home were employed as domestics.

Domestic servants, if working away from the protection of family or friends, were vulnerable to sexual exploitation. The most typical response of those victimized was simply to leave. Not in one case, however. Carrie Davies, an 18-year-old servant of Charles Albert Massey, a member of the farm machinery family founded by Hart Massey, opposed his sexual advances and finally shot and killed him. About a thousand sympathetic supporters in Ontario contributed to her trial-defence fund in 1915. The jury acquitted her for murdering her employer.

Women preferred factory work to domestic service because of higher wages and shorter hours. Still, in 1900, most women worked up to 60 hours a week. Textile and shoe factories hired women because they could pay them lower wages (approximately half of what men

This store at the turn of the century shows the diversity of items available to those who had money to purchase them, including Jell-O, which had just come on the market in 1897. Note the method of displaying goods at the time, from floor to ceiling.

Source: Provincial Archives of New Brunswick/P18-163.

earned) and because they were better workers for the type of work to be done. Women made up about two-thirds of the work force in the textile industry in 1880 and almost half by 1900. Historian Jacques Rouillard describes the exhausting working conditions in a textile factory:

> *It was not so much the physical effort required by the machines, as the tremendous speeds at which they functioned and the attention they demanded, which taxed the nervous system of the worker. The noise caused by the hundreds of weaving machines as well as the high degree of humidity in the spinning and weaving rooms were especially irritating. This damp atmosphere, maintained to keep the thread from breaking, resulted in fatigue among the workers and often led to loss of appetite and anemia. Many of the young women had to quit their jobs, unable to overcome the tension they suffered in this atmosphere.[3]*

A HISTORICAL PORTRAIT

Emily Jennings Stowe

Emily Jennings Stowe became the first female public-school principal in Upper Canada, and, immediately after Confederation, the first Canadian woman to practise medicine openly. She was also one of the country's first suffragists.

Born near Norwich, Upper Canada on May 1, 1831, Emily came from a Quaker background. Since the Society of Friends (Quakers) gave women the same status as men, she grew up in an atmosphere of gender equality. Her struggle to achieve equality for women began in 1852 when she applied for admission to Victoria College in Cobourg. Refused on the grounds that she was female, she then applied successfully to the Toronto Normal School. She graduated with first-class honours in 1854. She taught until her marriage in 1856 to John Stowe, owner of a carriage business in neighbouring Mount Pleasant.

Shortly after the birth of their third child in 1863, John Stowe contracted tuberculosis and had to leave the family for treatment. With the financial help of the Jennings family, and the support of her sister, Cornelia, who agreed to care for Emily's children, Emily Stowe prepared for a medical career.

Barred from medical school in Canada because she was female, Emily enrolled at the New York Medical College for Women, a homeopathic (or natural medicine) institution in New York City. She graduated in 1867. But when she returned to Canada, the College of Physicians and Surgeons refused to certify her. So for over a decade she practised medicine in Toronto without a licence. She was not prosecuted for doing so, but was charged in 1879 with having performed an abortion. In the lengthy trial that followed, she successfully defended her qualifications, skill, and professional conduct. After her acquittal, the College of Physicians and Surgeons granted her a medical licence.

Dr. Stowe helped to organize the Women's Medical College in Toronto (the forerunner of Women's College Hospital) in 1883. That same year, her daughter Augusta achieved her mother's own goal of 20 years earlier—she obtained a medical degree from the University of Toronto. Augusta Stowe became the first woman to receive a Canadian medical degree.

Emily Stowe treated her husband on terms of perfect equality. When John Stowe regained his health, she supported him while he retrained as a dentist. After his graduation, the Stowes practised side by side at 111 Church Street in Toronto, until Emily retired in 1893.

While in New York City as a medical student, Emily Stowe became interested in feminist causes. Upon her return to Canada she launched the Toronto Women's Literary Club, a pseudonym for a suffrage group, the first in Canada. It issued a magazine, *The Citizen*, that championed women's education and enfranchisement. In 1883, the group reconstituted itself as the Canadian Woman's Suffrage Association. Six years later, the group helped to form the Dominion Women's Enfranchisement Association. Dr. Stowe became its first president, a position she held until her death in 1903.

In a note she wrote in 1896, Emily Stowe provided her own best epitaph: "My career has been one of much struggle characterised by the usual persecution which attends everyone who pioneers a new movement or steps out of line with established custom."

Women sought in particular office jobs away from the noise and pressure of the factory. By the turn of the century, women were employed in most of the clerical jobs. Conventional wisdom held that women's "natural" feminine characteristics—sympathy, adaptability, courtesy, and even nimble fingers—made them particularly suitable for clerical work. Male clerks, however, retained the senior managerial positions. Women also worked as department-store clerks or telephone operators, two of the most "feminized" occupations at the turn of the century.

After domestic, factory, and office work, teaching was the most important female occupation. The public schools had greatly expanded in the late nineteenth century. At the turn of the

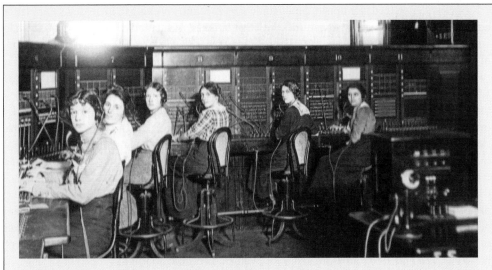

Amherst, Nova Scotia Telephone Exchange, around 1909. Telephone operators belonged to the elite of female clerical workers.

Source: Cumberland County Museum, 184-78-2.

century, women constituted three-quarters of the teaching profession. Teaching was considered an acceptable occupation for women, and one that allowed for the possibility of some upward social mobility, although it provided little financial security. Women received low salaries and had little chance of advancing to become department heads or principals. Generally, female teachers were expected to give up their teaching positions if they married.

A small number of women worked as nurses. Thanks to Florence Nightingale's campaign, nursing had become a respectable occupation at the turn of the century although not yet recognized as a profession. Many gravitated toward the Victorian Order of Nurses (VON), formed in 1897, as a model public-health nursing service. Only a handful of women entered Canadian medical schools. For one thing, few hospitals would provide them with hospital privileges after graduation. Unable to attract enough patients, a number of Canada's early female doctors became medical missionaries overseas instead. In all the professions that women entered in small numbers at the turn of the century, they experienced lower pay than men, lack of control over their work, and pressure to quit once they married.

Health

Frequent illness complicated the normal daily problems of living and working. Montreal in particular remained a most unhealthy city in which to live, especially for children. At the turn of the century, approximately one out of every four infants died before the age of one. Urban reformers claimed that only one other city in the world exceeded this death rate—Calcutta. City inhabitants suffered from impure water, unpasteurized milk, and the limited use of vaccines for smallpox, diphtheria, and tuberculosis. Families had neither sick benefits nor hospital or life insurance to protect them. Women were expected to provide essential health care at home. Nevertheless, Ontario established a Board of Health in 1882, modelled on Britain's Public Health Act of 1875, to carry out preventive measures. The other provinces followed suit by 1909.

Society denounced attempts to limit family size. A country seeking to increase its population had a stake in encouraging women to have large families. Limitation of family size, especially among those of British stock, was considered "race suicide." Section 179 of the Criminal Code of Canada, prepared in 1892, read: "Everyone is guilty of an indictable offence and liable to two years' imprisonment who knowingly, without lawful excuse or justification, offers to sell, advertise, publish an advertisement of or has for sale or disposal any medicine, drug or article intended or represented as a means of preventing conception or causing abortion." Despite such threats, many married women, anxious to limit their family size, sought birth-control information. Many lacked even the basic information taught to children today in elementary school. But as historian Angus McLaren has written: "Doctors would not discuss the merits of the most reliable forms of contraception—the condom, douche, and pessary—because they associated them with the libertine, the prostitute, and the midwife."[4] A few doctors, and a greater number of hacks, performed abortions, but since abortions were illegal it is difficult to know how many occurred. As well, some women had self-induced abortions. Statistics of women who died from improper abortions are available for a later period and speak to the magnitude of the problem; between 1926 and 1946, an estimated 4000 women died from abortions.

Charitable and Social Institutions for the Working Class

At the turn of the century, churches and private philanthropic organizations administered limited charitable help. Early in the century, Toronto had more than 50 charitable organizations and 20 churches providing relief to the poor. Montreal had nearly 30 shelters and outdoor-relief agencies for the poor, as well as about a dozen old-age homes and a dozen orphanages. Between 1900 and 1911, these institutions provided relief for 2000–3000 families in their respective cities every year—usually a meal of soup, bread, and tea, and a bath and a bed. Generally society held that, with the exception of the handicapped and the aged, individuals alone remained responsible for their plight. Thus charities provided only temporary relief as a stopgap measure.

Skilled workers looked to fraternal organizations for financial and emotional support. Associations and lodges such as the Orange Lodge, the Masons, the Oddfellows, and the Independent Order of Foresters, along with sporting clubs for baseball, snowshoeing, rowing, and lacrosse, gave their male members a sense of importance and self-worth and a feeling of camaraderie. Females could not belong to the fraternal or sporting clubs, but in some instances, such as the Oddfellows, women could belong to a parallel organization, such as the Rebekahs. Some associations had mutual-aid plans to care for sick members and to assist widows and orphans in the event of a member's death. They also gave workers a means to express publicly and collectively their discontent with industrial capitalism by supporting parades through the streets of towns and cities to show both solidarity and defiance. Association life was, as labour historian Bryan Palmer notes, "a realm apart from the troubled conflicts of the workplace"[5] and an important phase on the road to a working-class consciousness.

In a study of the mining communities on Vancouver Island in the mid-to-late nineteenth century, the first working-class community in British Columbia's history, historian John Belshaw notes their transition from "British" to "Canadian" and particularly British Columbians. He argues that as these communities matured through industrialization and urbanization, they took on more North American qualities. Drinking became a favourite pastime, but it came up against the opposition of employers, social reformers, and even union leaders who wanted to eliminate "demon rum." Sports and other recreational activities also became popular working-class activities, independent of, rather than directed by, middle-class reformers. As well, miners identified more with fraternal associations than with unions, because the former provided a source of identity and support for miners beyond the workplace. Belshaw dispels the myth of

British Columbia miners being more rebellious and radical than miners elsewhere in Canada. He concludes: "Skills, custom, and security were the principal 'British' watchwords, not rebellion, racism, revolution, or socialism."[6]

Unions

Between 1850 and 1890, labour unions took root in Canada. At first, most unions were local, dispersed across the country, and specialized. Initially, the government refused to grant them legal recognition or to accept workers' right to collective bargaining. The first victory came in 1872, after more than 100 Toronto printers stayed off the job for almost two months. They went on strike for a nine-hour day, protesting that "nine hours a day, six days a week is enough for any man to work." George Brown, who had been one of the Fathers of Confederation, and was now editor of the Toronto *Globe*, opposed the strikers. But his arch-rival, Prime Minister John A. Macdonald, enacted the Trade Union Act, which recognized the right of unions to exist and to organize without fear of prosecution as illegal associations, so long as they registered with the government. Helped by the act, the Toronto printers eventually won better wages and a 54-hour work week. The implementation, at the same time, of the Criminal Law Amendment Act, however, constituted a step backward. This act imposed severe penalties, including a prison sentence, for most forms of picketing and union pressure. Picketing remained illegal in Canada until 1934.

In the late nineteenth century, only a minority of Canadian workers belonged to unions, and those who did affiliated with a variety of groups, among which three stand out: the Knights of Labor; the Provincial Workmen's Association; and the American Federation of Labor.

Knights of Labor procession, King Street, Hamilton, 1885. Parades were an expression of workers' solidarity and a means to achieve public recognition.

Source: W. Farmer/Library and Archives Canada/PA-103086.

Young Cape Breton miners at the pit head, 1903. Allie, on the far left, was a boy of only nine, who worked as a trapperboy. He opened and closed the door for horses bringing coal carts out of the mine. Every week he worked a thirteen-hour shift, six days a week, for 55 cents a day. Canada's industrial revolution depended on coal, and Cape Breton Island contained the richest coal deposits in eastern Canada. By 1901, it produced half of Canada's coal.

Source: Beaton Institute, University College of Cape Breton.

The Knights of Labor, an American organization founded in 1869, enjoyed its greatest success among workers in Ontario and Quebec, although it had branches across the country. Its secret rituals enjoyed great popularity among its followers. At the moment of greatest expansion, it had more than 450 assemblies and over 20 000 members across Canada. The Knights believed in developing a working-class consciousness through the organization of workers by industry rather than by craft. The organization used its newspapers, the *Pallidium of Labour* and the *Labour Advocate*, to educate the working class to its ideals. The Knights' platform urged, wherever possible, arbitration instead of strikes, an eight-hour day, an end to child labour, the passage of health and safety legislation, and equal pay for equal work. As an industrial, rather than a craft union, the Knights took in semiskilled and unskilled workers as well as women and blacks, although not Asians.

Most unions refused to support women, arguing that by improving women's wages they encouraged women to remain at work, where they took jobs away from men. Despite such a general negative attitude, some unions, such as the Knights of Labor and others, attempted to organize female telephone operators, retail clerks, laundry workers, waitresses, and even domestics. In some industries, women formed their own unions. In the garment industry, for example, a number of women joined locals of the International Ladies' Garment Workers Union. Their success in this particular industry might have come partially from the support of male trade unionists who needed their female counterparts to mount effective strikes. Still, unionized women workers remained more the exception than the rule.

Most unions also refused to support visible minorities such as blacks and Asians, seeing them as cheap labour that would undermine unionization. Since these minorities ended up working only part-time or seasonal jobs, it was difficult for them to form their own unions. One exception was the occupation of railroad employees. In 1917, porters formed the Order of Sleeping Car Porters—the first African-Canadian railway union in North America. Many of its members came from Africville, an African-Canadian neighbourhood in Halifax, while others were more recent immigrants from the American South and the Caribbean. Although the Canadian Brotherhood of Railway Employees initially refused to accept the union, it did so in 1919, making it the first craft union to lift racial restrictions on memberships.

The Provincial Workmen's Association, founded in 1879 by the coal miners of Springfield, Nova Scotia, became the Maritime equivalent of the Knights of Labor, and Canada's first industrial union. After a slow beginning, it became recognized as the voice of the coal miners, and later represented other Maritime workers in seeking protection and compensation. In 1909, however, the Scottish immigrant James Bryson McLachlan helped introduce to Cape Breton a more militant union, a branch of the American-based United Mine Workers of America. Ten years later, the miners at last gained the eight-hour day and made important gains in their standard of living.

In Newfoundland, William Ford Coaker, a local fisher, founded the Fishermen's Protective Union (FPU) in 1908 to protect fishers from the vagaries of curing weather, fish migration, and volatile markets. Its motto was "To each his own," believing fishers did not enjoy the benefits of their own labour nor the right to a decent living. The objective of the union was "to promote the commercial welfare of the fishermen" by securing the highest price for their fish and lowest price for their supplies. In addition, Coaker advocated a "national plan" that consisted of free and compulsory education, a night-school system, nondenominational education in small outposts, outpost hospitals, and universal old-age pensions. The FPU turned to politics to attempt to achieve its objectives, and won eight seats in the Newfoundland Legislature in the 1913 election.

Initially, the Knights of Labor controlled the Trades and Labor Congress of Canada (TLC), the central labour organization founded in 1883 by the Toronto Trades and Labor Council as a successor to the Canadian Labor Union (1873–77). Originally it brought together trade unionists from Ontario only. By 1900, however, it had become a Dominion-wide organization.

The TLC moved away from the Knights' approach to reform and organization by industry when it established strong ties with the American Federation of Labor (AFL), a strictly craft-union organization. The conservative leadership of the AFL believed that the primary purpose of unions should be simply to improve the material benefits of its workers—better wages and hours and safer working conditions—rather than to radically reform the capitalist system. It expelled industrial unions such as the Knights from its membership.

With the decline of the Knights of Labor in the early twentieth century, unskilled workers looked increasingly to politics or radical unions to achieve their objectives. Some worked to create an independent socialist party, while others, who had given up hope that the AFL would become more militant, supported radical unions, such as the Industrial Workers of the World (IWW), founded in 1905. The "Wobblies," as they became known, attempted to organize all workers, regardless of their trade, skill, or sex, into one large union for the purpose of calling a general strike to bring down the capitalist system. The first sentence of their constitution revealed their view of North American society: "The working class and the employing class have nothing in common." The IWW had little impact in eastern Canada but greater success in western Canada.

In the West, the philosophy of individualism remained entrenched, resulting in a lack of sympathy for any form of collective action. Yet generally conditions remained poor for western workers. Wages were exceptionally low, inflation high, employment sporadic, especially in the primary industries, and working conditions, especially in the mines and railway camps, atrocious. Large-scale immigration into the region proved both the strength and weakness of unions in the region. On the one hand, immigration provided a large pool of unskilled workers who hindered the growth of unions by their willingness to work as "scabs" for low wages. On the other hand, many European, and especially British, immigrants were well versed in socialist ideas and experienced in union organizations and contributed greatly to labour protest and union building in Canada.

In Quebec, the Roman Catholic Church assisted in providing church-affiliated unions as an alternative to what it considered to be socialist and anti-clerical international unions that undermined the church's position among the working class. The clergy first intervened directly in a labour dispute in the Quebec shoe-workers' strike of 1906. One year later, the church founded a union. Its successor would be the Confédération des Travailleurs Catholiques du Canada (CTCC), an exclusively Roman Catholic organization founded in 1921, with a priest, as chaplain, effectively in charge of each local.

Limitations of Unions in the Prewar Era

In general, unions had limited success prior to World War I. As late as 1911, less than one-tenth of the national work force belonged to unions. Most unskilled workers and virtually all women remained non-unionized. Unions were also divided, and their leaders suspicious of one another. Furthermore, unions had few rights. Employers could still fire union workers at will or demand that workers sign contracts in which they promised not to join a union. As well, employers brought in immigrant labourers on the condition that they work as strikebreakers or for extremely low wages. Workers fought back by pressuring the Laurier government to pass the Alien Labour Act in 1908, which prohibited "any person, company, partnership, or corporation, in any manner to pre-pay the transportation of, or in any other way to assist or solicit the importation of immigration of any alien or foreigner into Canada under control or agreement." But the act was rarely enforced and had no impact on controlling companies wanting cheap labour. Unions also faced a hostile and indifferent managerial class. The views of one Montreal mill manager, as reported in *La Presse* in 1908, characterized the general attitude of managers to workers: "It was not at all his concern whether his employees could live on the wages he paid them. If they don't like it, they can go work somewhere else."

Nevertheless, unions did organize strikes—1000 disputes were recorded between 1900 and 1911, mainly in the manufacturing, construction, transportation, and mining industries. Workers protested against low wages, inadequate working conditions, and managerial tyranny. But most strikes, however, ended without workers gaining any significant concessions. Many of them erupted into physical violence, with the government calling out the militia to end them. This happened on more than 30 occasions before 1914.

Governments clearly favoured business interests over workers. The same government that supported employers by means of tariffs or other economic incentives argued against intervention on behalf of workers on the basis of a laissez-faire philosophy. The federal Conservative government did, however, establish the Royal Commission on the Relations of Labour and Capital, which in its report in 1889 documented the negative impact of the industrial revolution. Few reforms resulted from the report, although in 1894, the Conservatives officially established Labour Day, the first Monday of September, as a national holiday for working people.

The Laurier Liberal government created the Department of Labour in 1900 to prevent and settle strikes as well as to enforce a fair wage policy. In 1907 it also passed the Industrial Disputes Investigation Act, which prohibited strikes and lockouts in mines or public utilities until a three-member board had investigated the dispute. The Ontario government under James Whitney introduced the Workmen's Compensation Act in 1914, but only after the act met with the approval of employers, who realized that they would also benefit from government compensation to injured workers.

Skilled workers tried to gain influence through politics. They set out their own agenda, such as the sixteen-point program of the Trades and Labor Congress passed at its meeting in 1898, in which they demanded free compulsory education, an eight-hour day, a minimum wage, tax reform, public ownership of railways and telegraphs, extension of the franchise, abolition of the Senate, prohibition of prison and contract labour, legislative elimination of child labour, and opposition to Chinese immigration—the Chinese being perceived as a threat to labour's employment opportunities and wages. Then they tried to pressure the two traditional parties to adopt some or all of their recommendations. When this approach failed, they fielded their own labour candidates in federal, provincial, and municipal elections. While a few were elected, most labour politicians had limited success and impact, particularly at the federal and provincial levels. Greater success occurred at the municipal level. By 1920, fully 271 working-class candidates ran for political office in 44 municipalities. One hundred and eleven were elected, including labour mayors in Fort William, Port Arthur, Sault Ste. Marie, and Moncton. But overall, workers had a weak political voice in the pre–World War I era.

At the turn of the century, Canadians lived well by world standards, but social injustice and inequalities persisted. Farming had undergone significant change. The family farm had to adjust to mechanization, higher costs, fewer workers, and routine and specialized jobs. Many left the land for the growing urban centres. Cities became socially and physically stratified, with working-class districts in the city centre and middle-class areas in the surrounding suburbs. Both male and female workers lived in cramped quarters and worked long hours, under poor conditions, in factories and offices. In times of need, they looked to charitable and social institutions, and ultimately to unions, for assistance. By the early twentieth century the injustices had become so noticeable that they gained public attention, especially among a rising group of middle-class social reformers.

NOTES

1. Marjorie Griffin Cohen, *Women's Work, Markets, and Economic Development in Nineteenth-Century Ontario* (Toronto: University of Toronto Press, 1988), p. 106.

2. Arthur J. Ray, *I Have Lived Here Since the World Began* (Toronto: Key Porter, 1996), p. 291.

3. Jacques Rouillard, "A Life So Threadbare," *Horizon Canada* 25 (1985): 594.

4. Angus McLaren, "A Motherhood Issue," *Horizon Canada* 87 (1986): 2074.

5. Bryan Palmer, *Working-Class Experience: The Rise and Reconstitution of Canadian Labour, 1800–1980* (Toronto: Butterworths, 1983), p. 80.

6. John Douglas Belshaw, *Colonization and Community: The Vancouver Island Coalfield and the Making of the British Columbian Working Class* (Montreal/Kingston: McGill-Queen's University Press, 2002), p. 214.

BEYOND THE BOOK

Weblinks

The Lions Gate Bridge

http://www.mccord-museum.qc.ca/en/keys/webtours/GE_P4_3_EN

A virtual exhibit with digitized photographs and artifacts regarding the building of the Lions Gate Bridge in Vancouver, British Columbia in the 1930s.

Growing Up Healthy in Urbanized Quebec

http://www.mccord-museum.qc.ca/en/keys/webtours/VQ_P4_4_EN

This exhibit describes the effects of urbanization on the health of young people growing up in urban Quebec in the early 1900s. It also explores public health measures implemented to aid them.

Philanthropy: Responses to New Pressures

http://www.musee-mccord.qc.ca/en/keys/webtours/VQ_P3_7_EN

This photographic exhibit describes social philanthropic efforts made primarily in Quebec over the period 1896 to 1919.

Mackenzie King and Labour

http://www.collectionscanada.ca/king/053201/053201130201_e.html

This article describes Prime Minister Mackenzie King's positions on labour, industry, and social justice.

1880s Newfoundland

http://www.collectionscanada.ca/eppp-archive/100/200/301/ic/can_digital_collections/nfld/index.html

Photographs of Newfoundland in the 1880s. Includes images of St. John's, fishing communities, and other rural locations.

Films & Novels

Canada: A People's History—Episode 11: The Great Transformation. Directed by Halya Kuchmij and Andrew Burnstein. 2001.

RELATED READINGS

The following article in R. Douglas Francis and Donald B. Smith, eds., *Readings in Canadian History: Post-Confederation*, 7th ed. (Toronto: Thomson Nelson, 2006), is relevant to this chapter: Bettina Bradbury, "Gender at Work at Home: Family Decisions, the Labour Market, and Girls' Contributions to the Family Economy," pp. 210–26.

BIBLIOGRAPHY

Recent revisionist histories that examine the dynamics between rural life and urban and industrial growth are: Daniel Samson, ed., *Contested Countryside: Rural Workers and Modern Society in Atlantic Canada, 1800–1950* (Fredericton: Acadiensis Press, 1994); R. W. Sandwell, ed., *Beyond the City Limits: Rural History in British Columbia* (Vancouver: UBC Press, 1999); Kenneth Michael Sylvester, *The Limits of Rural Capitalism: Family, Culture and Markets in Montcalm, Manitoba, 1870–1940* (Toronto: University of Toronto Press, 2001).

On the impact of industrialization and commercialization on the First Nations see Arthur Ray, *I Have Lived Here Since the World Began* (Toronto: Key Porter, 1996); Diane Newell, *Tangled Webs of History: Indians and the Law in Canada's Pacific Coast Fisheries* (Toronto: University of Toronto Press, 1993); Bruce Hodgins and Jamie Benidickson, *The Temagami Experience: Recreation, Resources, and Aboriginal Rights in the Northern Ontario Wilderness* (Toronto: University of Toronto Press, 1989); and Kerry Abel, *Drum Songs: Glimpses of Dene History* (Montreal/Kingston: McGill-Queen's University Press, 1993).

Working-class life in the major industrial city of Montreal at the turn of the century is discussed in T.J. Copp, *The Anatomy of Poverty: The Condition of the Working Class in Montreal, 1897–1929* (Toronto: McClelland & Stewart, 1974); and in J. Rouillard, *Les syndicats nationaux au Québec de 1900 à 1930* (Quebec: Presses de l'Université Laval, 1979); as well as in his *Histoire du syndicalisme québécois* (Montreal: Boréal Express, 1989). For family life in Montreal see Bettina Bradbury, *Working Families: Age, Gender and Daily Survival in Industrializing Montreal* (Toronto: McClelland & Stewart, 1993). For Toronto see Gregory Kealey, *Toronto Workers Respond to Industrial Capitalism, 1867–1892* (Toronto: University of Toronto Press, 1980); and Michael Piva, *The Conditions of the Working Class in Toronto, 1900–1921* (Ottawa: University of Ottawa Press, 1979). On epidemics see Michael Bliss, *Plague: A Story of Smallpox in Montreal* (Toronto: HarperCollins, 1991). For the unemployed, see Peter Baskerville and Eric W. Sager, *Unwilling Idlers: The Urban Unemployed and Their Families in Late Victorian Canada* (Toronto: University of Toronto Press, 1998). On the experience of ethnic minorities, see Franca Iacovetta et al., eds., *A Nation of Immigrants: Women, Workers, and Communities in Canadian History, 1840s–1960s* (Toronto: University of Toronto Press, 1998).

On women workers see the relevant sections in Alison Prentice et al., *Canadian Women: A History*, 2nd ed. (Toronto: Harcourt Brace, 1996); the relevant essays in Veronica Strong-Boag, Mona Gleason, and Adele Perry, eds., *Rethinking Canada: The Promise of Women's History*, 4th ed. (Toronto: Oxford University Press, 2002); Marjorie Griffin Cohen, *Women's Work: Markets and Economic Development in Nineteenth-Century Ontario* (Toronto: University of Toronto Press, 1988); and Graham S. Lowe, *Women in the Administrative Revolution: The Feminization of Clerical Work* (Toronto: University of Toronto Press, 1987). Mary Kinnear, ed., *First Days, Fighting Days: Women in Manitoba History* (Regina: Canadian Plains Research Center, University of Regina, 1987), contains several essays on women workers. See also J. Acton et al., eds., *Women at Work: Ontario, 1850–1930* (Toronto: Canadian Women's Educational Press, 1974); and Wayne Roberts, *Honest Womanhood: Feminism, Femininity and Class Consciousness Among Toronto Working Women, 1893 to 1914* (Toronto: New Hogtown Press, 1976). A comparative study of men and women workers in the two Ontario towns of Paris and Hanover is provided in

Joy Parr, *The Gender of Breadwinners: Women, Men, and Change in Two Industrial Towns, 1880–1950* (Toronto: University of Toronto Press, 1990). For the Maritimes see Janet Guildford and Suzanne Morton, *Separate Spheres: Women's Worlds in the 19th-Century Maritimes* (Fredericton: Acadiensis Press, 1994). For women in the professions, see Mary Kinnear, *In Subordination: Professional Women, 1870–1970* (Montreal/Kingston: McGill-Queen's University Press, 1995). Gender conflict is reviewed in Franca Iacovetta and Mariana Valverde, eds., *Gender Conflicts: New Essays in Women's History* (Toronto: University of Toronto Press, 1992).

On working families see Bettina Bradbury, ed., *Canadian Family History: Selected Readings* (Toronto: Copp Clark Pitman, 1992); and R. Marvin McInnis, "Women, Work and Childbearing: Ontario in the Second Half of the Nineteenth Century," *Histoire sociale/Social History* 24(48) (November 1991): 237–62. Women's dealings with the law are the subject of Constance Backhouse's *Petticoats and Prejudice: Women and Law in Nineteenth Century Canada* (Toronto: The Osgoode Society, 1991). On changing notions of sexuality see Gary Kinsman, *The Regulation of Desire: Homo and Hetero Sexualities in Canada*, 2nd ed. (Montreal: Black Rose Books, 1996); Sharon Dale, *Lesbians in Canada* (Toronto: Between the Lines, 1990); and Angus McLaren and Arlene Tigar McLaren, *The Bedroom and the State: The Changing Practices and Politics of Contraception and Abortion in Canada, 1880–1980* (Toronto: McClelland & Stewart, 1986). McLaren has also written a short popular article, "A Motherhood Issue," *Horizon Canada* 87 (1986): 2072–77, on birth control in Canada in the late nineteenth and early twentieth centuries.

The labour movement is discussed in Craig Heron, *The Canadian Labour Movement: A Short History*, rev. ed. (Toronto: James Lorimer, 1996); Bryan Palmer, *Working-Class Experience: Rethinking the History of Canadian Labour, 1800–1991* (Toronto: McClelland & Stewart, 1992); and Desmond Morton with Terry Copp, *Working People: An Illustrated History of the Canadian Labour Movement* (Toronto: Summerhill Press, 1990). Also useful is Laurel Sefton MacDowell and Ian Radforth, eds., *Canadian Working Class History: Selected Readings* (Toronto: Canadian Scholars' Press, 1992); and G. Kealey and P. Warrian, eds., *Essays in Canadian Working-Class History* (Toronto: McClelland & Stewart, 1976). On the Provincial Workmen's Association see Ian McKay, "'By Wisdom, Wile or War': The Provincial Workmen's Association and the Struggle for Working-Class Independence in Nova Scotia, 1879–97," *Labour/Le Travail* 18 (Fall 1986): 13–62; and for the Fishermen's Protective Union, see Ian D.H. McDonald, *"To Each His Own": William Coaker and the Fishermen's Protective Union in Newfoundland Politics, 1908–1945* (St. John's: ISER, Memorial University, 1987). David Frank has written *J.B. McLachlan: A Biography—The Story of a Legendary Labour Leader and the Cape Breton Miners* (Toronto: James Lorimer, 1999). On the making of a working-class community in the coalfields of Vancouver Island, see John Douglas Belshaw, *Colonization and Community: The Vancouver Island Coalfield and the Making of the British Columbian Working Class* (Montreal/Kingston: McGill-Queen's University Press, 2002). Women and unions are discussed in Julie White, *Sisters and Solidarity: Women and Unions in Canada* (Toronto: Thompson Educational, 1993). D. Owen Carrigan, *Crime and Punishment in Canada: A History* (Toronto: McClelland & Stewart, 1991) deals with this important subject. On the Order of Sleeping Car Porters union, see Sarah-Jane (Saje) Mathieu, "North of the Colour Line: Sleeping Car Porters and the Battle Against Jim Crow on Canadian Rails, 1880–1920," *Labour/Le Travail*, 47 (Spring, 2001): 9–41. For race relations, see Constance Backhouse, *Colour-Coded: A Legal History of Racism in Canada, 1900–1950* (Toronto: University of Toronto Press, 1999).

Chapter Eight

AN ERA OF SOCIAL REFORM: 1890–1914

TIME LINE

1874	Founding of the Woman's Christian Temperance Union (WCTU)
1875	New Brunswick's Mount Allison University is the first university in the British Empire to grant a degree to a woman, Grace Annie Lockhart
1877	The Toronto Women's Literary Club becomes the first Canadian women's suffrage organization
1878	Canadian Temperance Act (Scott Act) passed
1885	Banff National Park established
1887	Establishment of the first bird sanctuary in North America at Last Mountain Lake, North-west Territories
1893	National Council of Women North-West Territories established, the first official voice of the Canadian women's movement Wilfred Grenville begins his mission in Newfoundland and Labrador Algonquin Provincial Park established in Ontario
1894	Fred Victor Mission founded in Toronto
1895	Reading Camp Association, forerunner of Frontier College, created by Alfred Fitzpatrick
1897	The first Women's Institute founded near Stoney Creek, Ontario
1898	National Referendum on prohibition held
1900	Alphonse Desjardins begins his *caisses populaires*, or credit unions, in Quebec
1903	Founding of the Ligue nationaliste in Quebec
1904	Founding of the Association catholique de la jeunesse canadienne-française (ACJC)
1909	Jack Miner establishes his bird sanctuary in Kingsville, Ontario
1911	Founding of the École Sociale Populaire (ESP)

Various social reform movements arose to correct injustices brought about by large-scale industrialization and rapid urbanization at the turn of the century. Each offered its own solution. In English-speaking Canada, social gospellers demanded that religion be more concerned with improving social conditions in this life for all Canadians than worrying about salvation in the afterlife. In Quebec, religious reformers turned to the traditional institutions of the Roman Catholic church and the family as the best means to achieve social reform. Educational reformers favoured child-centred schools that prepared children with good work habits and strong morals for the new industrial age. Urban reformers were inspired to create the perfect city, with a pleasing architecture, the elimination of ghettos, and proper social services. Conservationists campaigned to preserve wildlife and the wilderness. Women reformers fought for political equality on the belief that women would use the power of the ballot to bring about social reform. They also spearheaded the prohibition movement to eliminate "demon drink," which they saw as one of the root causes of social ills. Together, these reformers made positive changes in Canadian society, but their ultimate goal of an ideal reformed Canada still eluded them on the eve of World War I.

The Social Gospel Movement in English Canada

The social gospel movement, part of a larger movement of religious revival in Britain and the United States, aimed at directly applying Christianity to correct society's ills. It sought to create a perfect "Kingdom of God on Earth." The movement developed partially in response to a crisis in religious beliefs challenged by the Darwinian concept of evolution. In *The Origin of Species* (1859) and *The Descent of Man* (1871), Charles Darwin, an English naturalist, advanced his theory that humans had evolved, over millions of years, from earlier forms of life in the animal kingdom. Darwin's arguments challenged the orthodox Christian belief that God created humans in his own likeness and as special beings during the six days of creation. From their reading of the Book of Genesis, some Christians even provided a precise date for creation, 4004 B.C.

At the same time that science challenged contemporary Christian theology, a new philosophy of "higher criticism" presented the Bible as literature—a document written by humans, and therefore not the divine and absolute word of God. The Bible thus contained moral and religious, but not historical and scientific, truths. The rise of the social sciences also challenged the authority of religion. These new ideas and movements undermined many traditional Christian theological teachings and led to new definitions of faith. In response, a number of church leaders directed their attention away from theological questions to social issues. The new emerging industrialized Canada had a host of social problems that needed to be addressed.

Social gospellers regarded people as inherently good. If individuals erred, they did so, not because of any basic weakness or maliciousness of character, but because of their environment. Social gospellers believed in environmental determinism. If they could improve social conditions, then people's character would change for the good, which would result in an ideal Christian society.

Social gospellers wanted the church to concern itself with social problems: prostitution, alcoholism, and intolerable living and working conditions, rather than with such "personal sins" as drunkenness, sex, and slovenliness. The Reverend S.D. Chown of the Methodist church summed up the new attitude in a lecture in 1905: "The first duty of a Christian is to be a citizen, or a man amongst men. We are under no obligation to get into heaven, that is a matter entirely of our own option; but we are under obligation to quit sin and to bring heaven down to this earth." Social gospellers strove to create in this world a humane society based on the Christian principles of love, charity, humanity, brotherhood, and democracy.

British and American developments influenced the Canadian social reformers. In Britain, for example, the Fabian Society, a group of social thinkers, labour leaders, and university professors committed to improving society, helped to create the British Labour party. In the United States

A Salvation Army meeting in Calgary, late August 1887. Meetings featured testimony, prayer, music, and song. The Salvation Army, begun by General William Booth in England, came to Canada in 1882.

Source: Library and Archives Canada/ C-14426.

the Progressives, a middle-class reform movement, exposed social ills in American urban and industrial society. Canadian social gospellers often combined British and American models to design their own reform program. Yet, while united in their aspiration to improve the quality of life, social gospellers were divided on the means to do so. As many ways to regenerate and reform society existed as there were regenerators and reformers.

What one might call the "direct action group" of regenerators worked to give immediate assistance to society's destitute through the establishment of missions and settlement houses. In 1890, the Reverend D.J. Macdonnell founded St. Andrews Institute in Toronto to bring the Presbyterian church closer to the working people. Four years later, with financial assistance from the wealthy Massey family of Toronto, a group of Methodists founded the Fred Victor Mission in Toronto, named in memory of Fred Victor Massey (1867–90). In Newfoundland, Dr. Wilfred Grenfell, who had trained as a doctor in London's notoriously poor East End, established his Grenfell Mission in 1893 to help improve the appalling social conditions he found in northern Newfoundland outposts and along the Labrador coast. He challenged church leaders to provide better schooling; merchant capitalists to provide greater financial support to fishers and their families; and politicians to provide more hospitals. His efforts led to the establishment of a Newfoundland public health movement that addressed in particular the serious tuberculosis epidemic in the British colony.

Sara Libby Carson started the first settlement house in 1902 and helped found the Toronto and McGill University settlements. Similar settlement houses in Britain, and especially Jane Addams's Hull House in Chicago, which offered classes in music and art and provided a gymnasium and day nursery, inspired McGill's and the University of Toronto's programs. By 1920, at least thirteen settlement houses existed in Canada, offering the basic necessities of food and shelter and, often, a night school and a library. Many provided medical care. Others included gymnasiums, clubrooms, savings banks, and nurseries.

The Army of Salvation, better known as the Salvation Army, started by William Booth in England, also established centres in Canada at the turn of the century to help the poor. They modelled themselves after the regular army. Their members wore military-style uniforms and insignia. The ministers were called "officers," and the converts were "soldiers." At their peak, their "field force" enlisted nearly 150 000 in Canada to fight sin and poverty. Among their "field force" were a number of women—"Hallelujah lasses"—who preached on street corners and worked in shelters and homes to alleviate the misery of their "sisters."

Some reformers, labelled social purity activists, concerned themselves with issues of vice, such as gambling and prostitution (often referred to as "the social evil"), along with homosexuality, venereal disease, "feeblemindedness" (which they believed resulted from masturbation), and abortion. They sought to regulate and legislate sexual relations as a means to ensure racial purity and social control. English-Canadian social purists feared that with the influx of large numbers of "foreigners," into Canada, non-regulated sex would dilute the dominant and superior Anglo-Celtic "race." Rev. S.D. Chown linked the two when he commented, "The immigration question is the most vital one in Canada today, as it has to do with the purity of our national life-blood."

Social control took many forms. Churches hired "morality experts" to address, or had ministers preach on, moral concerns such as extramarital sex, masturbation, homosexuality, prostitution, and abortion. Rev. W.J. Hunter reportedly lectured to as many as 1500 men a night at St. James Methodist Church in Montreal on such topics. Rev. C. Sharp told his Toronto congregation in 1908: "God abhors the spirit as prevalent nowadays which condemns mother-hood," in reference to the feminist and women's suffrage movement. "How it must grieve Him when He sees what we call race suicide; when He sees the problems of married life approached lightly and wantonly, based on nothing higher and nobler than mere luxury, and gratification of passion." The Methodist and Presbyterian churches established social reform agencies under the umbrella of the Moral and Social Reform Council of Canada, established in 1907, which later changed its name to the Social Service Council of Canada. The Methodist church also recommended and distributed sex manuals, especially the popular eight-volume "Self and Sex" series. The Woman's Christian Temperance Union (WCTU) hired purity reformers such as William Lund Clark, Arthur Beall, and Beatrice Brigden to tour schools to warn young people against self-abuse and promiscuity. Clark recommended that "they drink neither tea nor coffee and refrain from dancing and that they seek improved ventilation and take frequent baths." The WCTU also built homes for "fallen women."

Increasingly, however, regulation of sex moved from the church, the family, and the local community to the state. Cities hired social workers, experts on prisons, and psychiatrists to present the latest "scientific" theories, to educate the public on proper moral standards, and to work with the "sexual deviants" in the jails and mental institutions. Some social theorists, known as eugenicists, argued for selective breeding by preventing people deemed to have undesirable mental and physical traits from reproducing. All too often the "unfit" and "inferior" were also foreigners, thus adding an ethnic component to the eugenics movement. Some cities, such as Toronto, under its reform mayor William Howland, established morality departments to arrest and prosecute anyone involved in prostitution or in same-sex relationships. The department targeted in particular single young women—"working girls"—who frequented amusement parks and dancehalls, where they became easy prey for lusty young men, or pimps.

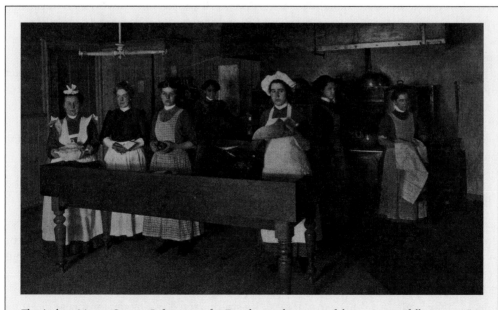

The Andrew Mercer Ontario Reformatory for Females taught virtues of domesticity to "fallen women." In prison strict time-management was instituted to encourage regular work habits.

Source: Ontario prisons, Annual Report of the Inspector of Prisons and Public Charities, [Sessional Papers] 35 (1903), 87. This appears as an illustration in Carolyn Strange, *Toronto's Girl Problem: The Perils and Pleasures of the City, 1880–1930*, p. 87.

The courts assisted the state in regulating morality. In 1892, the Criminal Code was formulated to include a comprehensive system of offences to "protect" young girls and women by imposing stiff penalties of up to 14 years on brothel operators and those who enticed women into prostitution. It also legislated against "gross indecency," which referred to homosexual acts. Punishment was set at a minimum of five years, with provisions for whipping. In 1907, the federal government passed the Juvenile Delinquents Act, which created separate courts and different punishments for young offenders than for adults. These courts, like the morality squad and the sexual purists, aimed to regulate sex for the "good of society" and for the "purity of the race." Juvenile courts, however, actually worked to the detriment of children, contrary to the intentions of their founders, since accused children lost many of the rights of due process and faced more indiscriminate sentencing than the accused in adult courts. Often the courts committed them to industrial or training schools, like Toronto's Mercer Reformatory, where they were lectured on morality while receiving agricultural, manual, or domestic training.

A second group of social gospellers worked to change people's attitudes. They believed that attitudes of greed, competition, and materialism caused society's problems. Through education, people could learn of the greater benefits of living in a society governed by Christian principles of love, charity, brotherhood, and democracy. In 1918, William Lyon Mackenzie King, then a young Canadian labour conciliator but in one year to become the leader of the federal Liberal party, published *Industry and Humanity*. He sought moral regeneration through the application of Christian principles. Social salvation, he argued, would come to a society that practised the ethical laws of Christianity.

The third group believed in state intervention. They argued that the concept of laissez-faire—the belief that governments should not upset the natural laws of the marketplace—had been used by the wealthy in society to exploit the poor. They advocated, instead, state intervention. An activist government operating on Christian principles of cooperation, democracy, and brotherhood would ensure that all people—not just an elite—benefited from the well-being of society. Government involvement was needed to provide essential social services and welfare assistance for the unemployed and the disabled, and to regulate industry and nationalize key industries to ensure that they served the public good.

For a few social gospellers, such as J.S. Woodsworth—then a Methodist minister, later the founder of the Co-operative Commonwealth Federation (CCF)—these innovative reforms served only as a prelude to a more fundamental restructuring of society. Woodsworth believed that the "ideal Kingdom of Jesus" was a socialist paradise where everyone worked for the well-being of the whole rather than for its individual parts. True social reform meant replacing the profit motive of capitalism with Christian charity through socialism.

Impact of the Social Gospel Movement

The social gospel movement raised public awareness of urban and industrial injustices. Social gospellers also contributed to other social reform movements, such as prohibition, women's suffrage, urban reform, and labour movements. The social gospel gave reformers a religious zeal, to bring God's kingdom here on earth. Their efforts contributed to the passing of Ontario's Workmen's Compensation Act in 1914, which established financial benefits for individuals injured in the workplace. Later expanded, the legislation served as a model for similar measures in Nova Scotia (1915), British Columbia (1916), Alberta (1918), and New Brunswick (1918). Social reformers also played a role in the passage in 1916 of the Manitoba Pensions Act, which provided a basic allowance to widowed, divorced, or deserted wives with children. Ultimately, the social gospel movement contributed to the rise of the CCF in the early 1930s. Social gospellers prepared the way for the establishment of our modern social welfare system.

Religious and social historians have debated whether the social gospel movement gave religion a new beginning, or hastened its decline. They are in agreement in seeing the social gospel movement as an era of religious reevaluation, but differ in judging the result. One group, the religious revivalists, see the social gospel movement as a time of renewal and rebirth for the Protestant faith, giving it a new purpose. Another group, the secularists, argue instead that social gospellers, in attempting to make religion more relevant to everyday concerns and thus to move it away from abstract, theological issues, ironically denied religion its distinctive spiritual function and traditional role. Religious leaders became indistinguishable from social scientists. In essence, they argue, the clergy became lay sociologists; the sacred became secular. Still another group argues that the mainline churches simply accommodated their faith to the new age particularly to the rise of the social sciences, thus enabling churches to remain active agents of social change well into the twentieth century.

By World War I, social reform appeared to be shifting from a religious and social gospel approach to a secular and scientific approach. Reformers were more increasingly professionally trained in the social sciences rather than schooled in religion. Social activists were replaced by social workers and sociologists; moral purists replaced by doctors and psychiatrists in the medical profession and by lawyers and judges in the legal profession. These new professionals relied on surveys as a "scientific" way of documenting problems. They also allied themselves with the state to bring about far-ranging social change, thus contributing to increased government control over the regulation of individuals, even in their private lives.

Roman Catholic Social Action in Quebec

The origins of social reform in Quebec lay in the Roman Catholic church's emphasis on personal humanity and on its principles of social justice and Christian charity. In his encyclical *Rerum Novarum* (1891), Pope Leo XIII urged that "some opportune remedy be found quickly for the misery and wretchedness pressing so unjustly on the majority of the working class." Catholic social reformers in Quebec believed that the Catholic faith constituted the "remedy." They believed that the family and the church, rather than the state, were the best institutions to deal with social problems. The ideal Christian social order, church leaders argued, rested on the family and the French-Canadian nation. Thus in Quebec, Roman Catholic values and French-Canadian nationalism became intertwined with social reform.

Role of the Church in Social Reform in Quebec

The Roman Catholic church initiated and supported various social-reform movements in Quebec. In 1911, for example, the Jesuits founded the Montreal-based École Sociale Populaire (ESP) to develop a social doctrine for the church. The ESP published pamphlets, organized study groups and retreats, and worked to sensitize the clergy to the social needs of their parishioners. In 1902, priests at Université Laval established the Société du parler français to increase French Canadians' awareness of French vocabulary in a largely English-language-oriented urban and industrial society and to eliminate anglicisms in business and industry.

In the classical colleges, religious instructors created the Association catholique de la jeunesse canadienne-française (ACJC) in 1904. It sought to encourage among Quebec's youth a unique French-Canadian and Catholic response to the province's social problems. The popular young Abbé Lionel Groulx of Valleyfield became the chief leader of the ACJC. In 1907, the Quebec diocese started a newspaper in Quebec City, *L'Action sociale*, later renamed *L'Action catholique*, that addressed social problems. It campaigned for the prohibition of alcohol or at least strict government control of the manufacturing and sale of alcoholic beverages. It also called for the abolition of movie theatres to protect Catholics from possible "corruption."

Many priests supported the *caisses populaires*, the credit unions founded in 1900 by Alphonse Desjardins, as their way of improving Quebec society. Desjardins believed that a lack of capital handicapped French Canadians in business. He established his savings and lending cooperatives to assist French-Canadian enterprises to get started in the hopes of improving the living standards of the working class and of bringing economic liberation to the Quebec people. By 1907, the *caisses* had sufficient assets to establish new cooperative ventures. By the time of Desjardins's death in 1920, more than 200 *caisses populaires* existed, mainly in Quebec but also among French-speaking Canadians in Ontario, Manitoba, and Saskatchewan, as well as among Franco-Americans in New England.

French-Canadian priests also promoted Catholic unions for Quebec workers (see Chapter 7). Church leaders feared that workers in secular unions, especially American-controlled ones, would become too materialistic and too socialistic in their outlook. The church rejected the idea of organizing workers along class lines, favouring instead Roman Catholic unions based on a spirit of Christian charity and employer–employee cooperation.

The church also lent its moral support to the Ligue nationaliste, a middle-class group of reformers founded in 1903. Besides concerning themselves with Canada's position in the British empire and Quebec's status within Canada, they formulated a French-Canadian and largely Catholic response to problems arising out of Quebec's urbanization and industrialization on the assumption that French Canadians needed to retain their identity in an increasingly secularized society. They believed in the family as the fundamental social unit of society and in Christian values as the bulwark of society. Thus they viewed individual or family businesses as compatible with Roman Catholic teachings, while opposing large-scale capitalism, which, they felt, was guided by mercenary concerns. The state, they argued, should curtail the excessive monopolization of big business by preventing private control of utilities. Ultimately, they favoured a society based on Christian values of cooperation and a concern for the public good.

Educational Reformers

Perceptions of education, like religion, changed during the reform era. Earlier, educators had concerned themselves with preparing children for the workplace by teaching good work habits. They viewed children as miniature adults, to be placed into adult society. By the turn of the century, however, a new generation of educators, strongly influenced by Friedrich Froebel, a European philosopher, advocated a child-oriented education that treated children as children, not miniature adults, by providing them with love and by protecting them from the harsh realities of adult life.

To some educational reformers, kindergartens provided the answer. James L. Hughes, a Toronto school inspector, and his future wife, Ada Marean, established the first Canadian public-school kindergarten in 1883 to provide, in Froebel's words, "reverent love for the child, profound respect for his individuality … and freedom and self-activity as the condition of most perfect growth physically, intellectually, and spiritually." Four years later, in 1887, Ontario formally incorporated kindergartens into the public-school system. The Free Kindergarten Association in Winnipeg advocated the same for Manitoba, arguing that "the proper education of children during the first seven years of their lives" did "much to reduce poverty and crime in any community."

In Montreal and Quebec City, nuns ran *salles d'asile* or day-care centres for children of working parents. Between 1898 and 1902, more than 10 000 children attended. In addition to these centres, which offered care on a daily basis, orphanages, provincial asylums, and homes for the poor also provided care for children of destitute families.

Other educational reformers worked for different objectives. Some called for temperance education to warn children of the evils of alcohol, while others asked for social programs in public health and in physical and mental hygiene. Reformers also advocated practical or "manual training" in farming and industrial work to prepare children for future jobs. They were successful in getting a number of provinces to introduce technical courses in domestic science, gardening, and shop or industrial arts.

All educational reformers appreciated the importance of extended and free schooling. They succeeded by 1905 in getting all provinces except Quebec to legislate free schooling and compulsory attendance for youngsters up to the age of 12. School attendance, especially in elementary school and increasingly in secondary schools too, soared, doubling from 1891 to 1921.

Two exceptional educational reformers were John Kelso and Alfred Fitzpatrick. Kelso, a young police reporter for the Toronto *World*, was concerned about the street urchins who could not be reached through the regular educational system. He quit journalism to begin the Humane Society. When its members seemed only marginally interested in the plight of children, he began yet another organization, the Children's Aid Society. In 1899, Rev. Alfred Fitzpatrick, a Presbyterian minister from Nova Scotia, created the Reading Camp Association, later called Frontier College, to bring education to immigrant workers in the lumber shanties and railway bunkhouses across northern Canada. Fitzgerald recruited university-student volunteers to give night classes in the "three Rs" and in basic civics. One of the young men whose social conscience was aroused by his work in the camps was Norman Bethune, later renowned for his medical work in Spain and China in the 1930s.

Norman Bethune (third from the left), a labourer/teacher with Frontier College, near Whitefish on the north shore of Georgian Bay, 1911. Bethune would become famous for his medical assistance during the 1930s, first to Spanish civilians during the Spanish Civil War and then to communist Chinese fighting against Japanese invaders.

Source: Frontier College Collection/Library and Archives Canada/C-56826.

The Urban Reform Movement

Urban reformers formed an important part of the social-reform movement. Inspired by the "City Beautiful" movement in the United States and Europe, they believed that reform must include the urban environment—the physical structure of the city, its aesthetic nature, and the quality of its municipal government. According to historian Paul Rutherford, what united urban reformers was "less a single creed and more a common approach to a wide variety of urban problems."[1] They worked to transform the existing urban environment into a humane and beautiful one.

The earliest urban reformers included newspaper editors who concentrated on the sordid side of urban life. Through their sensational and inexpensive newspapers (the penny press), among them Montreal's *Daily Star* and *La Presse* and Toronto's *Telegram* and *World*, the editors appealed to readers' emotions both to sell newspapers and to raise public concern over child abuse, slums, prostitution, and political corruption. Seldom did they have concrete solutions to offer.

The Children's Aid Society, founded by John Kelso, opened its first shelter in Toronto in 1892. This photo of the shelter was taken in the mid-1890s.

Source: City of Toronto Archives/SCI-3.

Reform-minded businesspeople and concerned citizens also helped raise public consciousness. Herbert Ames financed a sociological study of a working-class ward in Montreal, entitled *The City Below the Hill* (1897). G.A. Nantel wrote *La métropole de demain*, a grandiose scheme for the better governance of Montreal. Samuel Wickett spoke and wrote in Toronto regularly on the importance of efficient and expert municipal governments as the first step to urban reform. In Winnipeg, J.S. Woodsworth wrote the highly acclaimed *My Neighbour* (1911), about the problems of living in the modern city.

A host of professionals—engineers, architects, surveyors, medical people, and urban planners—offered advice on how to create the perfect city. Architects emphasized the need for stately buildings, while urban planners stressed parks, treed boulevards, and adequate housing. Medical professionals argued for clean water and air, and campaigned for pasteurized milk.

These urban reformers had limited success in the pre–World War I era because vested interests strongly opposed their proposals. Developers, for example, saw little profit in expensive urban renewal. Nor were badly funded municipal governments prepared to act, for the reforms suggested often came at a high price, which would result in increased taxes. As well, the Canadian public, suspicious of experts, was not ready to follow their lead toward urban reform.

Wilderness and Wildlife Conservation

The idea of conservation emerged slowly in Canada. The popular Canadian naturalist Farley Mowat recalls in his book *Sea of Slaughter* a story about his grandfather, Gil Mowat. "One autumn weekend in 1884, he and three companions left on a weekend duck hunting trip. They left armed with double-barrelled 10-gauge shotguns. They returned with 140 canvasbacks, 227 redheads, about 20 scaups, 84 blacks, about five dozen teal, and enough additional assorted kinds to quite literally fill the four-wheeled farm wagon that brought them and their trophies home."[2] Out of pride, the men took photographs of their kill. No one questioned their excessive kill.

In 1885, the federal government reserved to the Crown more than 26 km² of land around the mineral springs near the railway station of Banff. It would protect the hot springs and the scenery from private exploitation. Ottawa had taken the first step in the creation of Canada's national parks. Two years later, it extended the area to 675 km². It then officially turned the reserve into a national park, Rocky Mountains Park (renamed Banff in 1930). Banff began as a recreation park rather than a conservation area, although the latter would soon become its chief function.

In 1887, the first bird sanctuary in North America opened at Last Mountain Lake, in present-day Saskatchewan. In 1893, the Ontario government established Algonquin Park, south of North Bay, as the province's first wilderness area. Other provinces followed Ontario's example in establishing their own provincial parks.

By the early twentieth century, the overexploitation of the country's wildlife was becoming obvious. Major improvements in firearm technology, combined with the rapidly increasing commercial value of certain types of wildlife, led to the extermination of certain species. The Plains bison herds disappeared on the Canadian side of the border as early as 1879. By 1900, the great prairie herds of pronghorn antelope declined to a tiny fraction of their original number. Hunted thoroughly, the passenger pigeon had vanished from Nova Scotia by 1857, from Manitoba by 1898, and from Ontario by 1902. (The last surviving member of this once abundant species died in an Ohio zoo in 1912.) By 1900, trumpeter swans had disappeared from eastern Canada, as had wild turkeys before them. The upper-middle and upper classes purchased cottages in the Georgian Bay and Muskoka areas of Ontario, the Lake of the Woods region near the Manitoba–Ontario border, the Laurentians and Murray Bay in Quebec, and the Bras d'Or Lakes on Nova Scotia's Cape Breton Island, putting pressure on these wilderness areas.

Slowly, a conservation mentality developed, cultivated by back-to-nature movements, such as the Alpine Club and Field-Naturalists' Clubs. Woodcraft Clubs, and the Boy Scout and Girl Guides movements, promoted the importance of a wilderness experience for good health, spiritual rejuvenation, and refuge from hectic city life. Schools in British Columbia, Nova Scotia, Ontario, and Alberta initiated nature study classes in the first decade of the twentieth century through the initiative of naturalists' societies, farm organizations, and experimental farms.

The federal government responded slowly to the need for conservation. It established the Commission of Conservation (1909–21), which helped to secure the passage in 1917 of the Canada–United States Migratory Birds Convention Treaty, an agreement that was supposed to ensure international protection for migratory bird populations throughout their ranges. The commission hired James Harkin as national parks branch commissioner in 1911 to oversee Canada's existing national parks and establish new ones. In 1919, the Canadian government convened the first national wildlife conference to discuss with the provinces how best to conserve the country's wildlife.

Later, in the 1930s, the popularity of Grey Owl (born Archie Belaney) assisted the conservation movement. Through his books, films, and lectures, he advocated the protection of Canada's wilderness and wildlife. When the young Belaney first arrived at Lake Temagami in northeastern Ontario from England in 1907, he met the Ojibwa, whose identity he assumed. He came to learn about their view of the universe and its inhabitants, and discovered that one of the fundamental differences between his inherent beliefs and those of his assumed people was their notion of what was "human." To the Native peoples, all animals, fowls, fish, trees, and stones were endowed with immortal spirits and possessed supernatural powers. Humans were a part of this animated world, not its master. Much of what he later wrote as Grey Owl in the 1930s attacked the well-worn and much-abused biblical notion that humans should "have dominion over" all creatures.

Women and Social Reform

By the 1890s a "new woman" had appeared, demanding an active role in society; middle-class women found that opportunity through social reform movements. Local, provincial, and national women's organizations such as the Woman's Christian Temperance Union, the National Council of Women, the Young Women's Christian Association (YWCA), and the Dominion Women's Enfranchisement Association assisted women in reaching out to society. By 1912 an estimated one out of every eight adult women—the majority of them middle-aged, middle-class, English-speaking Protestants—belonged to a women's group, thus making these organizations influential agents of social change.

The bicycle aided the liberation of the new woman. This popular vehicle enabled women to abandon restricting, ankle-length, tight skirts in favour of comfortable, loose-fitting clothes such as bloomers, which were loose trousers gathered at the knees. The clergy voiced their concerns about the impact of the bicycle on morals, since women could now go out without chaperones.

Grey Owl

Archie Belaney was born in Hastings, Sussex, England, on September 18, 1888. Abandoned by his parents, he was raised by two maiden aunts, the Misses Belaney. From early boyhood he was fascinated by North American Indians and dreamt of living among them. His aunts, however, wanted him to take up a profession after leaving grammar school. But finally they gave their consent for him to emigrate to Canada. Archie left in 1906. Apart from two years abroad with the Canadian army in World War I, he spent the remainder of his life as a trapper, guide, and later conservationist, in northern Canada.

In 1910, he married Angele Egwuna, an Ojibwa woman from Lake Temagami, Ontario. She taught him how to canoe, trap, and to speak some Ojibwa. But the marriage did not last. Knowing nothing of a stable family relationship, he followed in his father's footsteps and abandoned his wife and their young daughter in 1912. Several other relationships followed over the next quarter of a century, the most important being with Gertrude Bernard, whom he called Anahareo, a beautiful young Iroquois woman whom he married in a traditional Aboriginal ceremony in northern Quebec. She convinced him in the late 1920s to abandon trapping and to work and write for the conservation of Canada's wildlife and forests.

In his articles and books, Belaney wrote as Grey Owl. The *Canadian Who's Who* of 1936–37 summarized his romantic stories about his origins: "Born encampment, State of Sonora, Mexico; son of George, a native of Scotland, and Kathrine (Cochise) Belaney; a half-breed Apache Indian ... adopted as blood brother by

Grey Owl and a beaver, June 1931.

Source: Glenbow Archives, Calgary, Canada/ NA-4868-213.

Ojibway tribe, 1920 ... speaks Ojibway but has forgotten Apache." Impressed by his first articles, the Canadian government invited Grey Owl to join the Canadian Parks Branch as a "caretaker of park animals." His first book, *Men of the Last Frontier*, a collection of his published stories and others, appeared in 1931. Three years later came *Pilgrims of the Wild*, a moving account of his life with Anahareo and their struggle to preserve wildlife and the wilderness. Two other books followed, the children's book *The Adventures of Sajo and Her Beaver People* (1935) and *Tales of an Empty Cabin* (1936).

His books became bestsellers. Films were made with him at Prince Albert

National Park in Saskatchewan. The public loved the fact that the beaver built their lodge outside—and partially inside—his cabin. He made two lecture tours of Britain, each of several months' duration. During his last visit, in December 1937, the tall, hawk-faced man dressed in buckskin performed at Buckingham Palace for the royal family. No one discovered his true identity, not even in Hastings, which he visited twice. His aunts knew, but, intensely proud of him, they kept his secret.

Physically the tours were demanding, and the constant threat of exposure was very great. Shortly after Grey Owl's return to Beaver Lodge in early April 1938, totally exhausted and run down, he was rushed to hospital in Prince Albert, where he died on April 13. Swift detective work in Canada and England in the weeks after his death revealed his true identity. His contributions as a writer and spokesperson for conservation received new recognition in the 1970s, when the preservation of the natural environment became a recognized concern.

Most women accepted the prevailing "scientific" stereotyping of them as womanly and motherly. Consequently they accepted the belief that their primary task was to maintain the home. A battery of books on proper mothering reinforced this belief. But a few women came to believe that their maternal instincts should be used to reform society. "Rocking the cradle for the world" was how Nellie McClung, an influential reformer, saw women's new role. These reform-minded women argued that men had controlled society for ages without making any appreciable improvements; now it was their turn. As McClung explained it:

> *Women must be made to feel their responsibilities. All this protective love, their instinctive mother love, must be organized in some way, and made effective. There is enough of it in the world to do away with all the evils which war upon childhood: undernourishment, slum conditions, child labour, drunkenness. Women could abolish all these if they wanted to.*

The women's reform movement fought for better education for women. It was in the Maritimes that the first woman was admitted to a university. In 1875, Mount Allison University in Sackville, New Brunswick, conferred a bachelor's degree in science and literature to Grace Annie Lockhart. She, in fact, became the first woman in the British empire to receive a university degree. The University of Toronto followed Mount Allison, first opening its doors to women in 1884. Many male professors opposed the decision. Daniel Wilson, a professor of history and English literature, considered that a mixed class posed serious problems in the teaching of Shakespeare—because of the sexual allusions in several of the playwright's works. His objection was overruled.

Adelaide (Hunter) Hoodless helped to further the women's cause in another way. Born in 1858, the twelfth child in the family, she apparently received little education beyond elementary school. She married John Hoodless, a wealthy furniture manufacturer. Their

Two women cyclists, Flo and Jessie McLennan, Owen Sound, Ontario. Bicycles liberated women from restrictive clothing—and from chaperones.

Source: Glenbow Archives, Calgary, Canada/ NA-2685-61.

Mount Allison University graduates, 1875. Grace Annie Lockhart, the lone woman in this photo, was the first woman in the British Empire to receive a university degree from a recognized university.

Source: Mount Allison University Archives/005 540.

fourth child, a son, died in 1889, at the age of 18 months, from the unpasteurized milk that farmers delivered in open cans, which exposed it to bacterial contamination. Seeing an urgent need to teach women nutrition and proper health measures, she offered domestic science or home-economics classes through the YWCA. Later the dedicated reformer assisted in having the subject introduced in the schools and, eventually, at the Ontario Agricultural College in Guelph and at McGill University. In 1897, she started the first Women's Institute near Stoney Creek, south of Hamilton, Ontario—an equivalent, for women, of the Farmers' Institutes. The new organization helped women to increase their knowledge of farm and household management.

Thanks to Hoodless's unflagging efforts, the University of Toronto eventually created the School of Household Economics. Hoodless also helped found the Victorian Order of Nurses to offer nursing and housekeeping services to impoverished invalids. Although she worked to improve women's role in society, Adelaide Hoodless parted company with the suffragists on the "vote question." She believed that a woman's primary role was to be a wife and mother and that the vote would not aid them in this task. In fact, she feared that the right to vote might lead to the breakdown of home and family.

The Women's Suffrage Movement

Many women reformers saw the right to vote as the means by which women could obtain the power to reform society. The women's suffrage movement began in Ontario with leaders such as Dr. Emily (Jennings) Stowe. But if Ontario launched the first suffrage movement, further momentum came from the prairie provinces. In the newer settler society of the West, women had found a greater degree of equality. In establishing a homestead and building a farm, women worked alongside their husbands, although prairie wives had to fight their husbands for an equal right to the family farm. Early on, they won the support of western farm organizations that also struggled for national recognition and were, therefore, better able to empathize with women's efforts for equality. The prairie farmers' newspaper, the *Grain Growers' Guide*, founded in 1908, added a women's column to its paper in 1911, while the Grain Growers' Association of Manitoba, Saskatchewan, and Alberta endorsed women's suffrage as early as 1912.

The presence of a large immigrant population on the Prairies helped the suffrage cause in a somewhat perverse way. Women suffragists protested against giving recent male immigrants the vote while denying it to long-standing Canadian female citizens. As one suffragist bluntly put it: "What an outrage to deny to the highest-minded, most cultured native-born lady of Canada what is cheerfully granted to the lowest-browed most imbruted foreign hobo that chooses to visit our shores."

The West had several outspoken women actively involved in the struggle for female suffrage, such as Henrietta Edwards, Emily Murphy, Louise McKinney, Nellie McClung, and Irene Parlby. Perhaps Nellie McClung, with her gift for oratory, her energy, and her delightful sense of humour, best epitomized the suffrage movement. Her spirited leadership rallied many others to the cause of women's suffrage.

Canadian gender history, though a relatively new field of historical study, has already raised a healthy historical debate. One contentious issue has been the primary motive behind the women's reform movement. The first historians to write on the subject in the 1960s and early 1970s argued that women reformers sought only the right to vote—women's suffrage—believing that political equality would bring about an era of societal reform. This narrow focus on the ballot box seemed to explain why the movement for reform died out so rapidly in the 1920s, once women's suffrage had been achieved.

Some historians see women's reform as part of a greater "progressive reform" movement that went well beyond a concern for the enfranchisement of women. In his introduction to a reprint of Catharine L. Cleverdon's classic study, *The Woman Suffrage Movement in Canada*, Ramsay Cook linked women's reform to the larger social gospel movement. "The suffragists were a part of a more general, middle-class reform movement that was concerned to remove a wide range of injustices and evils that afflicted the country."[1] Other historians question this idealized image of women reformers as being motivated purely by religious zeal. Veronica Strong-Boag argues that power, fame, and influence motivated them, at least those associated with the influential National Council of Women of Canada. She notes that "the female relatives of Canada's powerful men, energized by a changing external environment and by their own recent access to higher education and the professions, had few formal ways of expressing their complementary desires for national leadership and influence."[2] In short, these middle-class women reformers worried more about their own position of power in society than about the disadvantaged.

Carol Bacchi applied the feminist theories of the 1980s to the leaders of the suffrage movement in the 1910s, and found the suffragists wanting.[3] They were middle-class reformers more than they were feminists, and as such were more conservative than radical in outlook. They succeeded in getting the vote for women, according to Bacchi, only because men in positions of power at the time realized that giving women the right to vote would not upset the status quo. In a review of Bacchi's book,[4] which was based essentially on a study only of women leaders in Montreal, Toronto, and the Prairies, historian Ernest Forbes, relying on his own work on Halifax women reformers, challenged her conclusions. In Halifax, at least, according to Forbes, suffrage leaders were feminists before they were reformers, and used their position to encourage women to get out of the home, and even provided them with opportunities to do so. In this respect, they were "revolutionary" in aspiration. Furthermore, he argued that although Halifax suffragists were from the middle class, they addressed working-class issues. Thus Forbes appealed for more "local studies" to help draw a definitive conclusion about suffragists on a national level.

Historian Margot Iris Dudley took up Forbes's challenge and examined the women's suffrage movement in

Newfoundland.[5] She discovered a group of women reformers who crossed class lines and even religious divisions between Catholics and Protestants, and who allied themselves with the International Alliance of Women, based in London, England. Her study brought into question the assumption that the women's suffrage movement in Canada was middle-class, Protestant, and narrowly national.

More recently, some women historians have concentrated on the 1920s to see whether the women's reform movement died out after political emancipation as previously believed. Historians Linda Kealey and Joan Sangster have studied a group of "radical women" in the 1920s to show that, for these women, left-wing politics became the means to achieve real change, something that was not possible in the more conservative social-reform movement.[6] Nevertheless, these women had to adopt male tactics and abandon the "private sphere" in order to succeed in the traditionally male-dominated "public sphere."

Veronica Strong-Boag reentered the debate to argue that the real struggle for reform did not take place in politics—in the public sphere—but rather in a highly politicized private sphere. "Theirs was the feminism of the workplace, day-to-day life. It was not for the most part an organized movement as the campaign for enfranchisement had been, but it flowed from a similar awareness of women's oppression and a desire to end it."[7] Strong-Boag's study underlines the need to rethink the categories of political/apolitical, public/private, and male/female.

Linda Kealey appeals for a broader definition of "public" and "political" in dealing with women reformers to include "the home, the neighbourhood, and the community, as well as ... the union, the party, or the workplace."[8] She argues that some socialist women reformers were concerned with women workers as wage earners or working-class wives and mothers, while others advocated a radical transformation of the industrial capitalist system. In either case, they succeeded in bringing working-class women's issues into the public domain, despite opposition from men and even middle-class female reformers.

Janice Newton shows how Canadian women reformers within the socialist movement rejected the middle-class obsession of the suffragists to get the vote and instead worked for equality of working-class women through such organizations as the Canadian Socialists League, the Socialist Party of Canada, and the Social Democratic Party.[9]

Monda Halpern has examined social reform among Ontario farm women. She argues that farm women spoke the language of "social feminism," which she defines as being "informed by domestic community needs and values." She identifies those values as nurturing, cooperation, love, and peace, ones that are closely allied with maternal feminism and cultivated through farm women's roles as wives and mothers. According to Halpern, farm women applied these values in the public domain to such success that they challenged the patriarchal system and values, and in the end had a greater impact on social reform than the equity feminists, such as the suffragists.[10]

It is ironic that just as Canadian women obtained a political voice, First Nations women were denied one. Under their traditional system of governance, for example, the women of the Six Nations (Iroquois) Confederacy chose the Confederacy's chiefs, but under the Indian Act of 1880, they did not even have a vote in community decisions. This topic deserves to be studied.

1   Ramsay Cook, "Introduction" to Catharine L. Cleverdon, *The Woman Suffrage Movement in Canada* (Toronto: University of Toronto Press, 1950; rep. 1974), p. xvii.

2   Veronica Strong-Boag, *The Parliament of Women: The National Council of Women of Canada, 1893–1929* (Ottawa: Canadian Museum of Civilization, 1976), p. 410.

3   Carol Bacchi, *Liberation Deferred? The Ideas of the English Canadian Suffragists, 1877–1918* (Toronto: University of Toronto Press, 1983).

4   Ernest Forbes, "The Ideas of Carol Bacchi and the Suffragists of Halifax," *Atlantis* 10(2) (Spring 1985): 119–26.

5   Margot Iris Dudley, "The Radius of Her Influence for Good: The Rise and Triumph of the Women's Suffrage Movement in Newfoundland, 1909–1925," in Linda Kealey, ed., *Pursuing Equality: Historical Perspectives on Women in Newfoundland and Labrador* (St. John's: Institute of Social and Economic Research, Memorial University, 1993).

6   Linda Kealey and Joan Sangster, *Beyond the Vote: Canadian Women and Politics* (Toronto: University of Toronto Press, 1989).

7   Veronica Strong-Boag, "Pulling in Double Harness or Hauling a Double Load: Women, Work and Feminism on the Canadian Prairies," *Journal of Canadian Studies* 21 (Fall 1986): 34.

8   Linda Kealey, *Enlisting Women for the Cause: Women, Labour, and the Left in Canada, 1890–1920* (Toronto: University of Toronto Press, 1988), p. 10.

9   Janice Newton, *The Feminist Challenge to the Canadian Left, 1900–1918* (Montreal/Kingston: McGill-Queen's University Press, 1995).

10 Monda Halpern, *And on That Farm He Had a Wife: Ontario Farm Women and Feminism, 1900–1970* (Montreal/Kingston: McGill-Queen's University Press, 2001), p. 8.

Nellie (Mooney) McClung was born in Ontario in 1873 but educated in Manitoba, where her family began homesteading in 1880. After attending Winnipeg Normal School and teaching for several years, she married Wes McClung, a pharmacist and later an insurance company manager, in 1896. Her fiancé promised her before marriage that he would not stand in the way of her writing career, a promise he kept. Between 1897 and 1911, she had four sons and a daughter, but still found time to write—first poems, sketches, and editorials for Sunday school publications, and later adult stories in leading North American magazines. Early on, her interest in reform led her to write her best-selling novel, *Sowing Seeds in Danny*. In 1912, she joined the Winnipeg Political Equality League, whose president was Lillian Beynon Thomas, another reformer. Nellie wrote her witty but powerful social commentary on suffrage, *In Times Like These*, for the 1916 election in Manitoba, in which suffrage was the major issue. The suffragists made their first breakthrough in that election when the Liberals came to power. The new government introduced a suffrage bill, making Manitoba the first province in Canada to grant women the vote.

Presentation of a petition by the Winnipeg Political Equality League for the Enfranchisement of Women, December 23, 1915. Mrs. Amelia Burritt, then 93 years old, gave the document to the provincial government. In 1916, Manitoba became Canada's first province to grant women the franchise.

Source: Provincial Archives of Manitoba/Events 173/3 (N9905).

Women Reformers in Quebec

Women involved in social reform in Quebec had a more difficult battle than their sisters in English-speaking Canada, since French-Canadian tradition cast women almost exclusively in the role of mothers and domestic guardians. Archbishop Bruchési of Montreal defined *féminisme* as "the zealous pursuit by woman of all the noble causes in the sphere that Providence has assigned to her." He added: "There will be no talk in your meetings of the emancipation of woman, of the neglect of her rights, of her having been relegated to the shadows, of the responsibilities, public offices and professions to which she should be admitted on an equal basis with man."

Despite such stern warnings, several French-Canadian women spoke out for the feminist cause, often through membership in the local council of the National Council of Women of Canada. In 1907, Marie Lacoste Gérin-Lajoie, Caroline Béique, and Josephine Dandurand founded the Fédération nationale Saint-Jean-Baptiste to consolidate Quebec women's activities in charitable associations, in education, and in the work force. Marie Lacoste Gérin-Lajoie directed the federation's activities for the first 20 years. The federation offered a forum for Quebec women to fight for a variety of causes, including the pasteurizing of milk to reduce infant mortality, better working conditions for women, and the elimination of alcoholism and prostitution. It also contributed to better women teachers' pensions, improved working conditions for women in factories and stores, increased home-economics courses, and established pure milk depots.

The federation, along with the Sisters of the Congregation of Notre Dame, petitioned Mgr. Bruchési to obtain approval for a classical college for women. The bishop agreed only when the newspaper *La Patrie* announced the opening of a French *lycée*, a lay-administered classical college for women. In 1908, Bruchési granted his permission to the Congregation of Notre Dame to open the École d'enseignement supérieur pour les filles. But the École had to wait until 1926 before gaining the right to call itself a *collège*; it then became the Collège Marguerite-Bourgeoys named after the founder of the Sisters of the Congregation of Notre Dame. In 1910, Marie Gérin-Lajoie, the daughter of Marie Lacoste Gérin-Lajoie, became the École's first graduate. She had the further distinction of coming first in the provincial university-entrance examinations for the province, much to the consternation of the all-male examiners. But she did not obtain the award; since women could not attend university, they gave first prize to the male who placed second.

Marie Lacoste Gérin-Lajoie led the fight for women's suffrage in Quebec. She obtained her legal education by studying from her father's law books and under his supervision. Shocked to learn that the legal status of a woman was that of an adjunct of her husband, with no personal financial or civil independence, she initially considered refusing her future husband's marriage proposal. Only after her suitor pledged his support for the equality of the sexes did she accept. She spent her early married life writing a legal handbook for women while raising her children.

With an English-speaking colleague, Marie Lacoste Gérin-Lajoie created the Provincial Franchise Committee in 1921 to put pressure on Quebec politicians to grant women the franchise. The committee had no success, and ironically the strongest opposition often came from other women who saw women's suffrage as a threat to their identity as wives and mothers. The fatal blow came when in 1922 the Archbishop of Montreal expressed his disapproval of women voters. In protest, Marie Lacoste Gérin-Lajoie resigned her post as head of the francophone section of the Provincial Franchise Committee, although she continued to promote women's rights. Women in Quebec did not obtain the provincial franchise until 1940, a generation later than women in other provinces.

The Prohibition Movement

Throughout Canada, many women reformers worked for prohibition. "Demon drink," they argued, wrecked home life and led to inefficiency at work. Prohibitionists argued that the only way to eradicate drinking was to prohibit it through government legislation. They reminded governments that they had a right and an obligation to pass laws for the good of society.

The division of jurisdiction over alcohol between the federal and provincial governments complicated the question. The federal government had the power to restrict the manufacture of, and interprovincial trade in, alcoholic beverages. Provincial governments controlled retail sales. Thus, prohibitionists had to apply pressure on both levels of government.

They achieved an initial victory in 1878 with the passage of the Canadian Temperance Act, popularly known as the Scott Act, which allowed the residents of each municipality or county to decide by a simple majority vote whether their constituency would be "wet" or "dry." To prohibitionists, this measure did not go far enough, since it still left open the possibility of wet constituencies. They demanded that governments outlaw the liquor trade completely. The federal Conservative government delayed acting on this contentious issue until the mid-1890s, when it established the Royal Commission on the Liquor Traffic. Before the Commission set out its recommendations, a federal election ensued. During the election campaign of 1896, Laurier and the Liberals promised a plebiscite on the question of prohibition if they gained office. When they won, the prohibitionists held them to their promise.

The results of Canada's first plebiscite were split. Every province except Quebec voted on the dry side. But voter turnout throughout Canada had been low—only 44 percent. Furthermore, of those who did vote, only a small majority of about 13 000 had favoured prohibition. Laurier used these "indecisive" results to avoid enacting legislation that he feared would divide the nation. The Liberals' refusal to follow through on their promise angered the prohibitionists and gave them even greater resolve to banish alcohol.

Protestant churches provided many of the leaders of the prohibition movement. For them, the struggle became part of a religious battle. They urged drinkers to sign "the pledge" card, by which they promised, "by the help of God, to abstain from the use of all intoxicating drinks as a beverage."

The Woman's Christian Temperance Union (WCTU), formed in Ontario in 1874, but quickly becoming a national organization with some 16 000 members by 1914, focussed on the importance of the home and the sanctity of the family. It identified alcoholism as the greatest single cause of domestic violence and divorce. Initially, the WCTU campaigned for prohibition by issuing petitions, circulating literature, and giving speeches. But WCTU members soon developed a new strategy. If women had the right to vote, they argued, alcohol abuse would end. As Mrs. Jacob Spence, first superintendent of the Ontario WCTU's Franchise Department, noted, "The liquor sellers are not afraid of our conventions but they are afraid of our ballots." Prohibition and women's suffrage became mutually supportive causes.

The vision of a purified Anglo-Saxon society inspired many prohibitionists. Drunkenness became associated with "foreigners," whom reformers saw as too liberal in their drinking. Controlling alcohol offered a means of regulating them and of ensuring their conformity in an otherwise heterogeneous society. The greatest support for prohibition came, therefore, from the majority of British descent, who believed themselves superior to other groups that succumbed to alcohol.

Despite their efforts, however, prohibitionists remained in the minority before World War I. On the eve of the Great War, only Prince Edward Island had implemented provincial prohibition, while on the national level the federal government had resisted pressure to restrict the production and interprovincial distribution of "demon rum" and all liquor in general.

Between 1880 and 1914, social-reform movements arose to correct the injustices brought about by large-scale industrialization and rapid urbanization. Each group of reformers had a different solution and its own blueprint for creating the ideal Canadian society. On the eve of World War I, they had accomplished much, but they still fell short of their ultimate goal of social regeneration. The war would spur many of these reforms forward, particularly women's suffrage and prohibition.

NOTES

1. Paul Rutherford, "Tomorrow's Metropolis: The Urban Reform Movement in Canada, 1880–1920," in G.A. Stelter and A.F.J. Artibise, eds., *The Canadian City: Essays in Urban History* (Toronto: McClelland & Stewart, 1977), p. 370.

2. Farley Mowat, *Sea of Slaughter* (Toronto: McClelland & Stewart, 1984), p. 69.

BEYOND THE BOOK

Weblinks

Prohibition, Women's Suffrage in Alberta

http://www.abheritage.ca/abpolitics/people/influ_prohibition.html
A multimedia history of the prohibition and women's suffrage movements in Alberta.

Canada's National Parks

http://www.pc.gc.ca/progs/np-pn/index_E.asp
A history of each of Canada's National Parks. Also describes their ecology and other park characteristics.

The Women's Christian Temperance Union

http://www.abheritage.ca/famous5/achievements/mckinney_WCTU.html
A detailed history of the Women's Christian Temperance Union and its role with prohibition in Canada. Includes many digitized historical photographs and WCTU publications.

J.S. Woodsworth

http://www.canadianencyclopedia.ca/index.cfm?PgNm=TCE&Params=A1ARTA0008704
A detailed biography of J.S. Woodsworth, a prominent Canadian social reformer of the early twentieth century. Includes links to related sites.

Films & Novels

Prairie Women. Directed by Barbara Evans. 1987.

BIBLIOGRAPHY

Chapters 15 and 16 in R.C. Brown and R. Cook, *Canada, 1896–1921: A Nation Transformed* (Toronto: McClelland & Stewart, 1974) provide an overview of the social-reform movements. The social gospel is studied by Richard Allen, *The Social Passion: Religion and Social Reform in Canada, 1914–28* (Toronto: University of Toronto Press, 1971); and Ramsay Cook, *The Regenerators: Social Criticism in Late Victorian English Canada* (Toronto: University of Toronto Press, 1985). On the social gospeller J.J. Kelso see Andrew Jones and Leonard Rutman, *In the Children's Aid: J.J. Kelso and Child Welfare in Ontario* (Toronto: University of Toronto Press, 1981). On Wilfred Grenfell, consult Ronald Rompkey, *Grenfell of Labrador: A Biography* (Toronto: University of Toronto Press, 1991). Kenneth McNaught's study of J.S. Woodsworth, *A Prophet in Politics* (Toronto: University of Toronto Press, 1959), reviews the life of this important social gospel figure. For background to religious life in Ontario at the turn of the century see John Webster Grant, *A Profusion of Spires: Religion in Nineteenth-Century Ontario* (Toronto: University of Toronto Press, 1988); and William Westfall, *Two Worlds: The Protestant Culture of Nineteenth-Century Ontario* (Montreal/Kingston: McGill-Queen's University Press, 1989). For a history of social policy and practice, see Alvin Finkel, *Social Policy and Practice in Canada: A History* (Waterloo: Wilfrid Laurier University Press, 2006).

On religion and moral reform consult Mariana Valverde, *The Age of Light, Soap, and Water: Moral Reform in English Canada, 1885–1925* (Toronto: McClelland & Stewart, 1991); Carolyn Strange, *Toronto's Girl Problem: The Perils and Pleasures of the City, 1880–1930* (Toronto: University of Toronto Press,

1995). On the question of secularism versus religious renewal see Phyllis D. Airhart, *Serving the Present Age: Revivalism, Progressivism and the Methodist Tradition in Canada* (Montreal/Kingston: McGill-Queen's University Press, 1992); David B. Marshall, *Secularizing the Faith: Canadian Protestant Clergy and the Crisis of Belief, 1850–1940* (Toronto: University of Toronto Press, 1992); and John G. Stackhouse, Jr., *Canadian Evangelicalism in the Twentieth Century* (Toronto: University of Toronto Press, 1993). On Canadian women in foreign missions see Rosemary R. Gagan, *A Sensitive Independence: Canadian Methodist Women Missionaries in Canada and the Orient, 1881–1925* (Montreal/Kingston: McGill-Queen's University Press, 1992); and Ruth Compton Brower, *New Women for God: Canadian Presbyterian Women and India Missions, 1876–1914* (Toronto: University of Toronto Press, 1990). See as well Hamish Ion, *The Cross and the Rising Sun: The Canadian Protestant Missionary Movement in the Japanese Empire, 1872–1931* (Waterloo, ON: Wilfrid Laurier University Press, 1989).

Educational reform in the context of social reform is the subject of Neil Sutherland's *Children in English-Canadian Society* (Toronto: University of Toronto Press, 1976). The public-library movement is discussed in Lorne Bruce, *Free Books for All: The Public Library Movement in Ontario, 1850–1930* (Toronto: Dundurn Press, 1994). On higher education see Paul Axelrod and John Reid, eds., *Youth, University and Canadian Society: Essays in the Social History of Higher Education* (Montreal/Kingston: McGill-Queen's University Press, 1989) and for Ontario, A.B. McKillop, *Matters of Mind: The University in Ontario, 1791–1951* (Toronto: University of Toronto Press, 1994). Paul Rutherford's "Tomorrow's Metropolis: The Urban Reform Movement in Canada, 1880–1920," *Canadian Historical Association Report* (1971): 203–24, and his edited anthology, *Saving the Canadian City, 1880–1920* (Toronto: University of Toronto Press, 1974), deal with urban reform. See, as well, G. Stelter and A. Artibise, eds., *The Canadian City: Essays in Urban History* (Toronto: McClelland & Stewart, 1977), pp. 337–418.

Janet Foster discusses the early conservation movement in *Working for Wildlife: The Beginning of Preservation in Canada* (Toronto: University of Toronto Press, 1978). On the federal Commission on Conservation see Michel F. Girard, *L'Écologisme retrouvé: essor et déclin de la Commission de la conservation du Canada* (Ottawa: Les Presses de l'Université d'Ottawa, 1994). For the history of Ontario's provincial parks see Gerald Killan, *Protected Places: A History of Ontario's Provincial System* (Toronto: Dundurn Press, 1993). Farley Mowat's *Sea of Slaughter* (Toronto: McClelland & Stewart, 1984) recounts the destruction of fish and game in northeastern North America. John Wadland recounts the career of naturalist-writer Ernest Thompson Seton in *Man in Nature and the Progressive Era, 1880–1915* (New York: Arno Press, 1978). Donald Smith's *From the Land of Shadows: The Making of Grey Owl* (Saskatoon: Western Producer Prairie Books, 1990) tells the story of the transformation of trapper Archie Belaney to conservationist Grey Owl. Bruce Hodgins and Jamie Benidickson have written one of the first Canadian environmental histories, a study of the Temagami area in northeastern Ontario: *The Temagami Experience: Recreation, Resources and Aboriginal Rights in the Northern Ontario Wilderness* (Toronto: University of Toronto Press, 1989). On the conservation movement in the Canadian West, see George Colpitts, *Game in the Garden: A Human History of Wildlife in Western Canada to 1940* (Vancouver: UBC Press, 2002) and Flinton L. Evans, *The War on Weeds in the Prairie West: An Environmental History* (Calgary: University of Calgary Press, 2002). For British Columbia, see Matthew D. Evenden, *Fish Versus Power: An Environmental History of the Fraser River* (Cambridge: Cambridge University Press, 2004). Chad and Pam Gaffield, eds., provide a useful collection of articles in *Consuming Canada: Readings in Environmental History* (Toronto: Copp Clark, 1995).

For women and social reform see Chapter 7, "The 'Woman Movement,'" in Alison Prentice et al., *Canadian Women: A History*, 2nd ed. (Toronto: Harcourt Brace, 1996); Linda Kealey, ed., *A Not Unreasonable Claim: Women and Reform in Canada, 1880–1920* (Toronto: Canadian Women's Educational Press, 1979), and Micheline Dumont et al., *Quebec Women: A History* (Toronto: Women's Press, 1987). Biographical sketches of Emily Jennings Stowe and Adelaide Hunter Hoodless appear in volume 13 of the *Dictionary of Canadian Biography* (Toronto: University of Toronto Press, 1994), written by Gina Feldberg (pp. 506–10) and Terry Crowley (pp. 488–93), respectively. A recent good biography of Nellie McClung is Mary E. Hallett and Marilyn Davis, *Firing the Heather: The Life and Times of Nellie McClung* (Saskatoon: Fifth House, 1993). On farm women and social reform, see Monda Halpern, *And On That Farm He Had a Wife: Ontario Farm Women and Feminism, 1900–1970* (Montreal/Kingston: McGill-Queen's University

Press, 2001). The story of Marie Gérin-Lajoie and her daughter is told in Hélène Pelletier-Baillargeon, *Marie Gérin-Lajoie* (Montreal: Boréal Express, 1985). On the suffrage movement consult Carol Bacchi, *Liberation Deferred? The Ideas of the English-Canadian Suffragists, 1877–1918* (Toronto: University of Toronto Press, 1983); and Catharine L. Cleverdon, *The Woman Suffrage Movement in Canada: The Start of Liberation, 1900–20* (Toronto: University of Toronto Press, 1974 [1950]). On women socialist reformers see Janice Newton, *The Feminist Challenge to the Canadian Left, 1900–1918* (Montreal/Kingston: McGill-Queen's University Press, 1995); and Linda Kealey, *Enlisting Women for the Cause: Women, Labour, and the Left in Canada, 1890–1920* (Toronto: University of Toronto Press, 1998). On the impact of the medical profession on women and reform see Wendy Mitchinson, *The Nature of Their Bodies* (Toronto: University of Toronto Press, 1991) and her *Giving Birth in Canada, 1900–1950* (Toronto: University of Toronto Press, 2002).

Prohibition in the Maritimes is examined in E. Forbes, "Prohibition and the Social Gospel in Nova Scotia," *Acadiensis* 1 (1971): 11–36; in Ontario, in Gerald Hallowell, *Prohibition in Ontario, 1919–1923* (Toronto: Ontario Historical Society, 1972); and on the Prairies, in James Gray, *Booze: The Impact of Whiskey on the Prairie West* (Toronto: Macmillan, 1972). On the Woman's Christian Temperance Union see Wendy Mitchinson, "The WCTU," in *A Not Unreasonable Claim* (cited earlier); and Sharon Anne Cooke, *"Through Sunshine and Shadow": The Woman's Christian Temperance Union, Evangelicalism, and Reform in Ontario 1874–1930* (Montreal/Kingston: McGill-Queen's University Press, 1995).

Paul-André Linteau, René Durocher, and Jean-Claude Robert, *Quebec: A History, 1867–1929* (Toronto: James Lorimer, 1983); and Susan Mann, *The Dream of Nation: A Social and Intellectual History of Quebec*, 2nd ed. (Montreal/Kingston: McGill-Queen's University Press, 2002), discuss social reform in Quebec. Jean Hamelin and Nicole Gagnon, *Histoire du catholicisme québécois; le XXe siècle*, vol. 1, *1898–1940* (Montreal: Boréal Express, 1984), discuss the role of the Quebec church in social reform. Joseph Levitt's *Henri Bourassa and the Golden Calf* (Ottawa: University of Ottawa Press, 1969) analyzes the views of the Ligue nationaliste on social questions. On the *caisses populaires* see Ronald Rudin, *In Whose Interest? Quebec's Caisses Populaires, 1900–1945* (Montreal/Kingston: McGill-Queen's University Press, 1990); and the short sketch by Yves Roby, "A People's Bank," *Horizon Canada* 65 (1986): 1550–55.

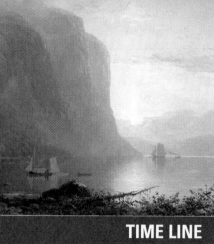

Chapter Nine

CULTURE: 1867–1914

Culture refers to activities associated with education and leisure. In the late nineteenth and early twentieth centuries, it was expressed in what are today the fine arts—music, drama, and the visual arts—along with literature. Already, however, a form of popular culture was emerging—culture that appealed to the rising middle class and growing working class. The middle class found enjoyment in such leisure activities as roller skating and dancing, or attending movie theatres and fairs. The working class also increasingly enjoyed the same activities, but was more inclined to find enjoyment and camaraderie in taverns, picnics, and festivities. All three social groups—upper, middle, and lower—enjoyed sport, although the kinds of sport they participated in and supported varied. By 1914, popular culture had surpassed elite culture, and professional sport prevailed over amateur sport. In both cases—popular culture and professional sport—Canadian culture became more Americanized as a result. First Nations people did not share in mainstream Canadian culture, except as contributors to fairs if Aboriginal participation benefited the host society, or in sport, in which First Nations people excelled. The same was true of ethnic Canadians, until there existed a critical mass of immigrants to force recognition and a host society willing to value their contribution to a vibrant Canadian culture.

Elite or Upper-Class Culture

Elite or upper-class culture refers to the cultural interests and activities of the social elite in Canadian society. This elite had more time for leisure and cultural activities than the middle and lower classes enjoyed. They also saw culture as a way of transferring and maintaining the values, beliefs, and ideals of British society into Canada. For the Canadian cultural elite, cultural activities were one way to ensure a continuity with the mother country and Western civilization, thus offsetting the limitations of living in an isolated part of the world where harsh conditions militated against cultural sophistication and where living next door to the United States posed a constant threat.

Music

While music was the most widespread of cultural activities in the late nineteenth century in both English-speaking and French-speaking Canada, only a few choral groups or orchestras achieved national fame or performed at the level of comparable groups in European society. The James Street Baptist Church Choir in Toronto, consisting of 250 voices and led by choirmaster Augustus Stephen Vogt, had a national reputation. Out of Vogt's choir came the nucleus of the famous Toronto Mendelssohn Choir, which Vogt himself conducted from its founding in 1894 until 1917. In Quebec, the Montreal Oratorio Society, formed in 1864, acquired both a national and an international reputation by the turn of the century, as did the Société musicale des Montagnards Canadiens and Les Orphéonistes de Montréal. These choirs and their audiences favoured oratorios, cantatas, and masses, especially works by Bach, Handel, Haydn, and Beethoven.

Notable Canadian composers included Guillaume Couture, organist and conductor of the Montreal Philharmonic Society, known for his religious compositions, and William Reed, who composed the organ recital *Grand Choeur in D Major*, considered to

Meeting of the Philharmonic Society, Hamilton 1877.
Source: Library and Archives Canada/C-066220.

Canada's opera superstar, Marie Lajeunesse, better known by her stage name, Emma Albani.

Source: William Hicock Low, Marie-Emma Lajeunesse, *Dit Madame Albani*, oil on canvas, 226.4 × 126.2 cm, Musée national des beaux-arts du Québec, 49.83, Patrick Altman, photographer.

be one of the finest organ works written by a Canadian. By far the most popular was Calixa Lavallée. His fame came from his music for "O Canada" in 1880, first performed at the request of the Société Saint-Jean-Baptiste in Quebec City. It was an immediate hit. Only after Lavallée's death did his other compositions come to light and begin to be performed. The English-Canadian equivalent of "O Canada" was "The Maple Leaf Forever," originally a patriotic poem written for a poetry contest in Montreal, in which it won second prize, and then set to music by Alexander Muir, a Toronto school principal.

Local church choruses, bands, and orchestras proliferated in the late nineteenth century. Almost every city in Canada had singing groups such as the Orpheus Club in Halifax, Nova Scotia, or the Oratorio Society in Saint John, New Brunswick. Many of the brass bands formed around militia camps as a form of local entertainment for the troops. But some of the most impressive were in Indian residential schools as a means to impose discipline and order. The Septuor Haydn chamber ensemble, consisting of a string quintet, flute, and piano, and conducted by Arthur Lavigne of Quebec City, was founded in 1871. By 1903, it had grown into the city's Société symphonique.

Opera appealed to the upper class. Tour companies performed a variety of operas from grand to ballad and comic. Most of these tours originated in Europe and then came to North America. Cities in the Maritimes and central Canada were part of the North American circuit, along with such American cities as Boston, New York, Chicago, and Philadelphia. By the turn of the twentieth century, the major cities of Montreal, Quebec City, and Toronto had their own local opera company.

The nineteenth century is often referred to in musical circles as the "age of the virtuoso"— a time when gifted soloists astounded the public with superb performances. Canada became home to five world-class soloists: Frantz Jehin-Prume, an outstanding violinist from Belgium who became concertmaster of the Montreal Philharmonic Society; Luigi von Kunits from Vienna, who accepted an invitation in 1912 to teach at the Canadian Academy of Music in Toronto; and Calgary-born Kathleen Parlow, an internationally renowned violinist, who toured Europe, Russia, North America, and Asia.

Canada's most internationally known virtuoso was Emma Albani. Born Marie Lajeunesse in Chambly, near Montreal, in 1847, she adopted the stage name Emma Albani while on a European tour in the early 1870s. The French-Canadian diva sang at the best opera houses in Europe. In 1886, the British critic Eduard Hanslick wrote of her, "By far the best singer at Covent Garden this season, if not the only important one." She made various visits from her home in England to Canada—in 1883, 1889, and a grand tour from Halifax to Victoria in 1896–97.

Calixa Lavallée

Calixa Lavallée, the composer of "O Canada," was born on December 28, 1842 in Verchères, Canada East, the son of Augustin and Charlotte-Caroline Lavallée. His father, a blacksmith by trade, was talented musically, and taught Calixa to play the piano, organ, violin, and cornet. Calixa's own musical talent advanced when the family moved to St. Hyacinthe, and he took piano lessons with Paul Letonal and Charles Sabater, two distinguished French pianists who for some time resided in Lower Canada.

At age fifteen, Lavallée left Canada to seek his fortune in the United States. A piano competition in New Orleans, in which he won first prize, resulted in a tour of South America, Mexico, and the West Indies as an accompanist for a Spanish violinist. In 1861, he became a musician in the Union army, a position that lasted only one year, when he was discharged after being wounded in the battle of Antietam, in Maryland. In 1867, he married Josephine Gently, an American, and settled in Boston where he became a composer, teacher, and virtuoso performer.

The talented musician returned to Montreal in 1872. The following year, with financial support from a wealthy friend, he went to Paris to advance his study of piano and to take classes in harmony and composition. Two years later, Lavallée

Calixa Lavallée, the composer of "O Canada." Canada's national anthem since 1980 was originally composed in 1880 for St. Jean Baptiste Day, now recognized as Quebec's national holiday.

Source: *Heritage Canada* 5(2) (May 1979): 13.

returned to his native Quebec where he became a well-known composer and choirmaster.

Lavallée was asked to compose a national song for the convention of the French-Canadian patriotic organization, the Société Saint-Jean-Baptiste in 1880 in Quebec City. He took the words of a patriotic poem written by judge Adolphe-Basile Routhier, and set them to music; the result was "O Canada." The song soon became popular throughout Quebec, and, decades later, in several versions in English-speaking Canada as well. On July 1, 1980, a century after its creation, Parliament made "O Canada," in both its French and its officially approved English version, Canada's national anthem.

A great honour, but a century earlier Lavallée's financial position had become so precarious that he had felt he could no longer support himself and his family comfortably in Canada. He returned to the United States, settling permanently. Ironically, the composer of "O Canada" publicly declared himself in favour of Canada joining the United States.

He died in Boston in 1891. Forty-two years later, in 1933, a group of Lavallée's admirers brought his body back to Montreal and had it interred in the Côte-des-Neiges Cemetery after a funeral service at the majestic Notre-Dame Basilica. Thus did the gifted composer belatedly receive the public recognition he deserved.

Visual Arts

In 1860, on the occasion of the official opening of the Victoria Bridge, a magnificent structure that spanned the St. Lawrence River from Montreal to Longueuil, the government of the Canadas held a "Great Exhibition" of Canadian art in Montreal. The exhibition contained paintings by Quebec's famed Cornelius Kreighoff, known for his quaint depictions of habitant life, and by Charles Jones Way, a younger artist from England whose majestic paintings of Canadian scenery caught the eye of the Prince of Wales upon his visit to British North America that year. Also on exhibit were photographs by William Notman, a Scot who by 1860 had established a thriving photograph studio in downtown Montreal. In the 1860s and 1870s, the Notmans opened over a dozen branches in Ottawa, Saint John, Halifax, and even several eastern American cities. Many of Canada's aspiring artists of the day began their careers in Notman's Studio.

After the "Great Exhibition," English-speaking artists in the city formed the Art Association of Montreal. It became the nucleus for the Society of Canadian Artists, founded in 1867. Many of its members were recent immigrants. John Bell-Smith, an English artist who had arrived in Montreal a year earlier, became its first president. The society held its first exhibition in 1868. It contained works by the elite of Montreal artists: C.J. Way; John A. Fraser, a Scot who had worked for the Notman Studio before striking out on his own; Otto Jacobi, a Prussian who came to Montreal in 1860, in search of adventure and new opportunities; Adolph Vogt, another German who arrived in 1865 via Philadelphia and quickly acquired a reputation as "a very promising young artist"; William Raphael, a German Jew, best known for his *Behind Bonsecours Market, Montreal* (1866), a painting depicting life on the Montreal wharfs; Harry Sandham, a native Montrealer and a young employee of Notman's Studio; and Allan Edson, from the Eastern Townships. The society set an ambitious goal: to foster a pan-Canadian artistic tradition so as to make Canadian artists known both within Canada and abroad.

Shortly after the formation of the Montreal society, the Ontario Society of Artists formed in 1872. These Toronto-based artists were caught up in the pan-Canadianism of the Canada First Movement. Seven of them met at the home of John A. Fraser, who had moved from Montreal to Toronto to launch the new society. They promised to do everything in their power to promote Canadian art, including holding annual exhibitions of their works and working toward the building of a permanent public art gallery in Toronto.

Out of these two societies, the one in Montreal and the other in Toronto, came the beginnings of the Canadian Academy of the Arts, founded in 1880 with the help of Governor General Lord Lorne. A year later, Queen Victoria officially prefixed "Royal" to its title. Lucius O'Brien became its first president, a position he held for ten years. Women countered with their own organization, the Women's Art Association. Established in 1890, it soon spawned branches throughout the country to support women artists.

Lucius R. O'Brien, Sunrise on the Saguenay, *1880. This painting, first exhibited at the opening of the Royal Canadian Academy of the Arts in 1880, won O'Brien much praise and recognition.* Sunrise *is traditionally considered to have been the first work entered into the collection of the National Gallery of Canada.*

Source: National Gallery of Canada, Ottawa. Royal Canadian Academy of Arts diploma work, deposited by the artist, Toronto, 1880.

O'Brien and the Royal Canadian Academy of the Arts embodied the new spirit of the age. Born at Shanty Bay near Barrie, Ontario, and educated at Upper Canada College in Toronto, O'Brien first painted scenes of his home region of Lake Simcoe. But he clearly "felt a calling to reflect the majesty beauty of his native land,"[1] according to his biographer, and sought opportunities to paint the diverse Canadian landscape. He was among the first Toronto artists to travel on the Intercolonial Railway in 1877 to paint the areas of southern Quebec and the Baie des Chaleurs region of New Brunswick through which it passed. One of O'Brien's most famous paintings, *Sunrise on the Saguenay* (1880), came out of these trips. He exhibited it at the opening exhibition of the Royal Canadian Academy of the Arts in 1880, and it dominated the exhibition.

Lucius O'Brien was also the chief Canadian contributor, with almost one-quarter of the 500 illustrations, to the two-volume *Picturesque Canada,* the most ambitious publishing project of the day when launched in 1876. The book was based on the highly successful *Picturesque America.* Two Americans, the Belden brothers of Chicago, launched the project. The investors employed Americans who had worked on the previous book on the United States to complete three-quarters of the Canadian illustrations. O'Brien was, in fact, the token Canadian—the Belden brothers claimed that Canadian artists were not experienced enough in preparing work for the volumes, a viewpoint that caused an uproar in the Canadian art community!

George Monro Grant, principal of Queen's University and a Canadian art enthusiast, edited the *Picturesque Canada* text. He overlooked the American visual contributions and instead underscored the importance of the volumes for the growth of a pan-Canadian nationalism. "I

Many art galleries in the late nineteenth century had to rely on a coal stove for "climate control."

believe that a work that would represent its characteristic scenery and the history and life of its people," he wrote, "would not only make us better known to ourselves and to strangers, but would also stimulate national sentiment and contribute to the rightful development of the nation." Grant's text and O'Brien's paintings together reflected the growing national spirit of English-speaking Canadians who looked to the Canadian landscape for the essence and the soul of Canada. (Individuals like Grant did not, however, look to the First Nations for future strength for Canada. In *Picturesque Canada*, the principal of Queen's University himself contributed the article on "The North-West Manitoba," in which he wrote: "The Indians of Manitoba are gradually disappearing before the stronger races.")

While some Canadian artists were looking for Canada's identity in its landscape, others found it in its country folk. Many of these artists, who emerged in the 1880s and 1890s, were trained in Europe, especially in Paris, considered at the time to be the art centre of Europe. They returned to Canada prepared to apply European art styles and subject matter to Canadian scenes. Some of them were taken in particular by the French Barbizon school that looked for the essence of a country in its habitants. Wyatt Eaton of Quebec was influenced by Millet's paintings of French peasants in rural settings, such as his *Woman with a Lamp*, *The Angelus*, and *The Gleaner*; he took the Quebec habitant as his subject. Horatio Walker of Listowel, Ontario, did a six-month walking tour along the St. Lawrence River from Montreal to Quebec City in which he painted scenes of French-Canadian farmers and farm life. Homer Watson, who grew up in Doon, a hamlet in the Grand River valley of Ontario, did the same for Ontario rural folk. Walker and Watson were joined by William Brymner, Paul Peel, and George Reid, other Ontario artists who had studied in Paris, as well as Robert Harris of Prince Edward Island. Peel would become one of Canada's best-known painters in Europe in the late nineteenth century.

Canadian artists got an opportunity for international fame when the British government invited Canada to contribute paintings to a Colonial and Indian Exhibition in London, England in 1886, the year preceding Queen Victoria's Golden Jubilee. The Canadian display included works by such established painters as Vogt, Raphael, Fraser, and O'Brien. But it was the paintings of the younger, Paris-trained, group that caught the attention of British art critics.

At the turn of the twentieth century, English-Canadian art came of age. James Wilson Morrice and Maurice Cullen, both from English-speaking Quebec, became the leading Canadian practitioners of European Impressionism and Post-Impressionism. Morrice was born into a wealthy, established Montreal family. After a brief schooling in law at the University of Toronto, he discovered art to be his real passion. In 1890 he sailed for Europe, on the advice of Sir William Van Horne, the manager of the Canadian Pacific Railway and an art connoisseur, who spoke glowingly of young Morrice's artistic talents to Morrice's father. Morrice won instant international acclaim. His works were purchased by a number of the great European galleries as well as by the French government and Parisian art connoisseurs. Ironically, he was hardly known in Canada.

Morrice's contemporary, the Newfoundland-born Maurice Cullen, influenced a whole generation of Canadian painters with Impressionism. After an unsuccessful initial career in business in Montreal, he left for Paris in 1888 to practise sculpture. There he met the great French Impressionists, especially Monet. Five Cullen canvases were exhibited in the 1894 Salon. The

Philippe Hébert, one of Canada's best known monumental sculptors, loved the history of New France. He appears here in his Montreal studio with a plaster model (on the left of the photo), of his famous Sans Merci: *a depiction of the struggle of an early French settler with a reaping hook in his hand against a First Nations warrior.*

Source: Louis-Philippe Hébert à l'atelier avec le groupe "Sans Merci" au premier plan, 1910–11, Musée national des beaux-arts du Québec, Fonds Héberts (H-21/H-17).

following year he was elected to the distinguished Société Nationale des Beaux-Arts. Yet, despite such recognition in Europe, he returned to Canada in 1895. His acceptance at home was slow and difficult. His work would inspire A.Y. Jackson, a young Montreal avant-garde artist of the time and a future member of the Group of Seven. Speaking on behalf of the Group of Seven, Jackson once said of Morrice: "To us he was a hero."

Canadian Literature

English-Canadian poetry became established in the 1880s. The "Confederation Poets"—the name literary critics have given to the four poets Charles G.D. Roberts, Bliss Carman, Archibald Lampman, and Duncan Campbell Scott—gave a spiritual dimension to Confederation. Roberts's first volume of poetry, *Orion and Other Poems*, inspired Lampman, who later wrote: "It seemed to me a wonderful thing that such a work could be done by a Canadian, by a young man, one of ourselves." The Confederation Poets sought the essence of Canada in nature—in the physical world of rocks, streams, and woods, and in the country lifestyle of the farmer and lumberjack. They depicted nature in the highly romantic terms of the British Romantic poets who inspired them, such as Wordsworth, Keats, and Shelley. In Canada, they were the literary equivalent of the Canada First Movement, and of the Canadian Academy of the Arts, seeking to discover the soul of the new nation.

Bliss Carman (left) and Charles G. D. Roberts (right), two of the "Confederation Poets," were cousins.

Source: PANB Miscellaneous Photograph Collection: P37-402.

Isabella Valancy Crawford also drew inspiration from the Canadian landscape. She depicted nature as half-human, as possessing a soul that was very much in tune with the human soul. In her mind, both "souls" struggled with love and death—common themes in her nature poetry.

Pauline Johnson became the most famous female poet in the late nineteenth century. Born the daughter of a Mohawk chief and his English wife, Johnson—or Tekahionwake, her Mohawk name—celebrated her Iroquois heritage while at the same time expressing a Canadian, and an imperial, feeling. In her poem "Canadian Born" she expressed her imperialistic fervour:

> *The Dutch may have their Holland, the Spaniard have his Spain, The Yankee to the south*
> *of us must south of us remain; For not a man dare lift a hand against the men who brag*
> *That they were born in Canada beneath the British flag.*

In Quebec, a generation of poets used François-Xavier Garneau's magisterial *Histoire du Canada*, published between 1845 and 1848, along with folklore, patriotic feeling, and religion, as themes for their poetry. Not surprisingly, survival, or *la survivance*, became an overriding concern in their poems. Octave Crémazie, for example, expressed the patriotic sentiment of his fellow citizens for their French-Canadian nation and looked to its past under the French empire for their moments of greatness. In the same way, Louis Fréchette, considered the unofficial poet laureate of nineteenth-century French Canada, wrote a series of patriotic poems, *La Légende d'un Peuple* (1887), inspired by dramatic moments of Canada's past from the arrival of Jacques Cartier to the hanging of Louis Riel.

Quebec's poetry came into its own with the École littéraire de Montréal. Founded in 1895, it received acclaim for its poetry, which broke free of the patriotic-romantic verse that then dominated. Its most famous member was Émile Nelligan. This poet of genius produced some

170 poems when he was between the ages of 17 and 20. Perhaps his best known is "Le Vaisseau d'or" (Ship of Gold). Unlike other members of the "École," Nelligan found his inspiration for poetry less in romantic nature, historical subjects, or patriotic fervour, and more in what Wordsworth called "the still, sad music of humanity," the poetry of the spirit. Exhausted and ill, Nelligan lost his grip on reason in 1899, at the age of 21, and spent the last 41 years of his life in mental institutions. His poetry is still widely read in Quebec, where he enjoys today almost legendary status.

Notable English-Canadian novelists and short-story writers emerged in the late nineteenth century. Both Charles G.D. Roberts and Ernest Thompson Seton had popular reputations for their realistic animal stories. Seton was born in England, raised in Ontario, and lived in Manitoba in the early 1880s before leaving permanently for the United States in 1896. He published his first collection of animal stories, *Wild Animals I Have Known*, in 1898. Eight years later his classic of children's literature, *Two Little Savages*, based on his boyhood experiences of "playing Indian" in Ontario, was published.

Many of the best Canadian novels had regional settings. Norman Duncan's *The Way of the Sea* (1903) and Theodore Goodridge Roberts's *The Harbour Master* (1913) were set in Newfoundland. Lucy Maud Montgomery's first novel, *Anne of Green Gables* (1908), captured the spirit of her native province of Prince Edward Island through her beloved orphan character, Anne Shirley. An instant success, the novel made her, and the island, world-famous. Gilbert Parker's *The Seats of the Mighty* (1898), a historical novel about New France, became an international bestseller. Popular French-Canadian novels of the Quebec rural countryside appeared, one of the most popular being Ernest Choquette's *Claude Paysan* (1899). But Charles Chiniquy outdistanced all of his Quebec contemporaries in terms of the number of editions and translations of his works. His *The Priest, the Woman and the Confessional* (1875), *Fifty Years in the Church of Rome* (1885), and *Forty Years in the Church of Christ* (1899) were popular among Protestant extremists throughout the world because of their vitriolic attacks on the Roman Catholic church.

Stephen Leacock acquired international recognition as one of the great humorists writing in the English language. *Sunshine Sketches of a Little Town* (1912), an affectionate satire of small-town Ontario life in the fictitious town of Mariposa, and *Arcadian Adventures of the Idle Rich* (1914), a parody of city life, were the best known of about 60 books that earned Leacock a reputation as the "Mark Twain of the British Empire." But there was more to Leacock's novels than humour; he questioned the values and virtues of liberal capitalism and advocated a more humane and spiritual society.

In the West, the settlement of the prairies provided a rich subject and inspiration for a generation of Prairie novelists. Authors such as Ralph Connor (Charles Gordon), Robert Stead, Nellie McClung, and Janey Canuck (Emily Murphy) wrote of the settlement experience

Pauline Johnson was one of Canada's greatest performers in the late nineteenth and early twentieth centuries. She travelled across the Dominion many times on tour. When one old dowager asked the Mohawk poet if her father really was an Indian, she replied, "Was your father really a white man?"

Source: Library and Archives Canada/ C-85125.

Émile Nelligan (1879–1941), the legendary Quebec poet and member of the École littéraire de Montréal. The intense young man already was confined to a mental asylum at the time this photo was taken in 1904.

Source: Library and Archives Canada/ C-88566.

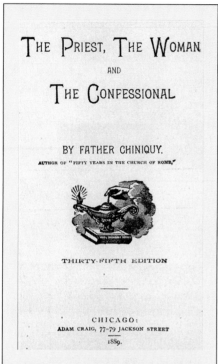

Father Chiniquy alleged in this major work that the confessions of female parishioners caused some Roman Catholic priests to end their vows of celibacy. This certainly had been his own experience and led to his excommunication. The Protestants embraced him when he began his furious campaign against the "Church of Rome." He made few converts in French Canada.

of the Canadian prairies with highly utopian depictions of the West. The phenomenally successful novels of Ralph Connor sold in the millions and had a larger audience outside the country than within it. He made his reputation with his first novel, *The Sky Pilot* (1899), the story of a North-West Mounted Police officer. All of his western novels capitalized on the romance, adventure, and physical beauty of the early West. His novels also dealt with the familiar theme of good, simple-hearted Christians challenged by scoffers and non-believers who, in the end, were won over to the purer life. In British Columbia, Martin Allen Grainger's *Woodsmen of the West* (1908) captured life in the logging industry on the West Coast. Robert Service's verse, published in his *Songs of a Sourdough* (1907), *The Spell of the Yukon* (1907), and *Ballads of a Cheechako* (1909), established his reputation as a writer of humorous ballads.

Canadian Theatre

English-Canadian theatre grew slowly in the period from 1867 to 1914 and was restricted to the major urban centres. In Montreal, the New Dominion Theatre opened in 1873 to cater to professional drama touring groups. It succumbed, however, to vaudeville or music hall troupes by 1876, a reflection of the type of culture in demand at the time. In Toronto, a new Grand Opera House opened in 1880, which, along with the Princess Theatre and the Academy of Music, housed most of the important cultural events that came to Toronto between 1880 and 1914. These theatre houses welcomed American and British touring companies.

The prevailing mood in late-nineteenth-century English Canada, according to the theatre historian Murray Edwards, was "essentially anti-theatre."[2] Few Canadians attended productions, fewer still supported their actors, and theatre productions were seldom reported in the local newspapers. One reason for such a low opinion of acting was its association with "immorality and debauchery" in the mind of church leaders. The stage was regarded "as the gate of Hell," according to Edwards. While this may have been the perception of leaders of public opinion, it was not always the views of theatregoers. Sarah Bernhardt, the flamboyant French actress, succeeded in "packing the house" no matter where she performed in the country.

By the turn of the century, theatre had become well established, thanks to large-scale urbanization and industrialization. However, it remained a foreign phenomenon. American money built most of the new theatres, and American touring companies provided nearly all the English-language entertainment. These large American companies toured North America, including Canada, and put on the same productions in different cities, regardless of the locale. They made no attempt to use local talent, and in fact discouraged the growth of indigenous talent by getting Canadians accustomed to looking beyond Canada's borders for theatrical talent.

Some patrons of the arts became concerned about the "Americanization of English-Canadian theatre." But instead of supporting Canadian actors, they brought in British touring groups. For a while, in the period 1910–1914, a battle existed between these two external groups for the domination of Canadian theatre. With the outbreak of war, however, the British "theatrical

The Sherman Grand Theatre opened in Calgary, in February 1912, at the height of the city's pre–World War I economic boom. From 1901 to 1911 the city's population grew from 4000 to 44 000. The Grand, with a "stage one foot larger than that of the Royal Alexandra in Toronto," served as Calgary's centre for the performing arts for over a generation.

Source: Illustration from *The Western Standard*, June 12, 1913. Glenbow Library.

invasion" of Canada ended. The Great War also curtailed American productions in Canada. By this time, according to Murray Edwards, the time to cultivate an indigenous theatre had passed. Only in the interwar years would a respectable Canadian theatre develop, in competition with the new moving-picture industry.

Quebec plays often had a political theme to them. In May 1880, Louis Fréchette's *Papineau* appeared at Montreal's Académie de Musique, and his *Retour de l'exilé (The Return of the Exile)* played in June of the same year. Both plays concerned the heroes and events of 1837–38 and advocated a reconciliation of French and English, while holding out hope of the *Canadiens* one day freeing themselves from British rule. Another play, *Un Bonheur en attire un autre (One Piece of Luck Attracts Another)*, written by Félix-Gabriel Marchand, premier of Quebec between 1897 and 1900, was performed in 1883 at "a benefit for the families of those killed during the 1837/38 Rebellion."

At the same time, the Saint-Jean-Baptiste Society organized *soirées de famille* (family nights) in which young aspiring actors and actresses put on local plays under the guise of "elocution lessons" so as to ward off any interference from the Roman Catholic church. Unfortunately, these *soirées* lasted only three years. Yet another blow to French-Canadian theatre occurred in 1909, when the municipal government of Montreal levied an amusement tax. Attendance dropped, and many reputable and long-established theatres, including the historic Académie de Musique, closed their doors.

An appreciative audience watching a movie at the Innisfail Opera House, Innisfail, Alberta, 1910.

Source: Glenbow Archives, Calgary, Canada/NA-1709-23.

The Promotion of Canadian Culture

Canada's viceroys played an important role in promoting English-Canadian and French-Canadian culture. They saw the promotion of Canadian culture as an integral part of the promotion of Canada as a nation, a form of nation building. Just as Canadian leaders believed that the Canadian economy needed state intervention in the form of the National Policy to grow, so too they believed that Canadian culture required state assistance to mature free of American and British competition.

Government assistance took a variety of forms. Some Canadian viceroys, for example, bought and displayed Canadian art in their official residence. Lord Dufferin, Canada's third governor general (1872–78), went further. He laid the groundwork for the establishment of the Royal Canadian Academy of the Arts, modelled after the British Royal Academy. Dufferin's successor, the Marquis of Lorne, brought the Academy, along with the National Gallery of Canada, its successor, into existence in the early 1880s.

For the first 30 years, the National Gallery housed only government purchases, donations, bequests, and commissions. Then, in 1907, the federal government established the three-person Advisory Arts Council to promote "the growth of a true taste and general interest in public arts amongst the people of Canada." Three years later, the gallery's first full-time curator, Eric Brown, arrived from England. In the 1910s, Brown encouraged Canadian artists to develop works "along national lines." He helped begin the Canadian War Memorial Fund, which sponsored Canadian artists to go abroad to paint the carnage of World War I.

The prosperity and expansion at the turn of the century led to new government initiatives. Governor General Earl Grey sponsored the Earl Grey Musical and Dramatic Trophy Competition, which held national competitions in different Canadian cities yearly in an effort to promote and elevate the quality of Canadian talent. Grey, a fervent imperialist, also sponsored lecture tours to promote the British empire both within Canada and abroad. Stephen Leacock, who toured Canada, Great Britain, Australia, New Zealand, and South Africa in 1907, became one of the beneficiaries. Grey purchased an entire printing of Robert Stead's book *The Empire Builders* (1908) because he liked its imperial message. To promote the study of Canadian and British history, Grey founded the Historical Landmark Association of Canada, the precursor of the Historical

Sites Board of Canada, in 1907. It had as its mandate the establishment of national historic sites such as the Plains of Abraham, a difficult site to interpret due to strong and conflicting feelings on the part of anglophones and francophones.

By the turn of the century, Canadian governors general and the public could rely on a growing business community for some financial support of the arts. The Canadian Pacific Railway Company hired artists in the 1880s to create works of art for their hotels, chateaus, railcars, and offices and to design their promotional posters. Later it gave Dominion Drama Festival finalists a round-trip ticket to Ottawa for the price of a one-way fare to make it possible for the finalists to participate in the annual competitions. For writers and dramatists it often provided free passes to enable authors to read their works across the country and dramatists to stage their plays.

Private family businesses also supported the arts—the wealthy Massey family of Toronto, in particular. As early as the 1870s, the Massey Manufacturing Company established a company band—the Massey Concert Band—a glee club, an employees' orchestra, and even a literary magazine, *Massey's Illustrated*, published between 1882 and 1895. As well, the Massey family purchased a number of church organs for Methodist churches in Toronto. In 1894, Hart Massey built the magnificent Massey Hall, with a seating capacity of 4000, and underwrote the costs of the Toronto Symphony Orchestra and the Toronto Mendelssohn Choir. The family business would continue its generous patronage under Hart's grandson, Vincent, in the interwar years.

Popular Culture

Historians of popular culture have debated what constitutes popular culture and who defines it. Lawrence W. Levine, one of the leading authorities of American popular culture, describes popular culture as "culture that is *popular*." By popular, he means, "culture that is widely accessible and widely accessed; widely disseminated, and widely viewed or heard or read."[3] He notes that such diffusion generally occurred in the late nineteenth and early twentieth centuries by such media of communication as national magazines and syndicated newspapers, and then by the 1920s through radio and film as well. These media allowed for mass production and widespread dissemination and thus led to the rise of mass culture. With regard to the second question of debate, who defines popular culture, the issue has focused on the producers versus the consumers of popular culture. Do the producers of popular culture dictate what is popular and a passive audience accept their choice? Or is the audience of popular culture discerning as to what they accept or reject? The answer appears to be a blending of the two. Clearly the producers of popular culture have a great influence in shaping that culture until a discerning audience emerges. Then the audience takes an active role in choosing what it likes and dislikes.

In Canada, both the producers and the consumers of popular culture were in short supply at least until the turn of the twentieth century if not until the beginning of World War I. What was needed was more leisure time. "Leisure" has been defined in two ways historically: as synonymous with cultural enrichment and learning and as "free time." The Greek word for leisure is *schole*, whence originates the English word "school and learning," thus associating leisure with learning and cultural enrichment. More common today is the second meaning of leisure: free time, meaning time free from working. This concept emerged out of the Industrial Revolution, when work occurred for defined periods of time, leaving demarcated periods of time for non-work-related activities. Mass media arose to fill this leisure time with activity. Some cultural historians have seen the move to fill leisure time as a form of control not unlike that of work time. Since Canada did not experience its "industrial revolution" until the decades spanning the twentieth century, it is only then that the media of communication emerged to disseminate the material of popular culture and to cultivate a sufficiently large national audience.

Mass Newspapers

In the late nineteenth century, most newspapers were local rather than national, the product of a particular city or town and serving its urban audience and surrounding rural hinterland. News tended to be of local interest. By the turn of the century, however, new technology enabled newspapers to widen their coverage to national and international events and to reach a wider and larger audience. Historian David Sutherland notes that by the early twentieth century "steam-powered production machinery, cheap newsprint, telegraph communications, a comprehensive rail network, and efficient postal delivery combined to create the penny-a-copy urban daily which made information gleaned worldwide available to more and more Canadians."[4] Some of the more popular mass-produced newspapers were the Montreal *Star* and *La Presse* in Montreal and the *Telegraph*, the *World*, the *News*, and the *Star* in Toronto. These inexpensive and independent newspapers, whose product was known as "yellow journalism," or "the people's press," altered the nature of news. It became less informational and more sensational, focusing on subjects of popular interest such as war and crime. They also began to include advertisements from large department stores that catered to the "masses," such as Eaton's, as a means of defraying production costs. According to cultural historian Paul Rutherford, these publications promoted Canadian nationalism; he identifies three key ideas that all the popular newspapers emphasized—nationalism, progress, and democracy—claiming all three ideas were interrelated.

Mass Magazines

In the late nineteenth century, few Canadian magazines existed, but there was a host of American ones. One observer of cultural practices in Canada noted in 1907 that one of the popular American magazines (probably *Saturday Evening Post*) had a Canadian circulation of 60 000—more than all the major Canadian magazines combined. They contained an abundance of advertising to absorb the cost of production and to keep prices low. They also targeted the rising middle class by including numerous articles of a personal nature. These American imports hindered the growth of a *Canadian* popular culture. Only in the interwar years would popular Canadian magazines appear to rival the American ones, and then they often depended on the American magazines for feature articles.

Canadian Cinema

Movie theatres made their debut in Canada at the turn of the century. The first permanent movie house, the Edison Electric Theatre, opened on Cordova Street in Vancouver in 1902. Winnipeg's Unique and Dreamland followed in 1903, Montreal's Ouimetoscope (an impressive 1000-seat cinema named after Ernest Ouimet, its owner) in 1904, and the York Theatre in Saint John, New Brunswick in 1906. These theatres charged their customers a nickel, hence the name "nickelodeon" for these early movie theatres.

Developing a Canadian movie industry was a constant battle. Quebec cinematographers looked to Europe, especially France, for inspiration, content, and support, while cinematographers in the rest of Canada looked to the United States. The challenge, particularly for English-speaking cinematographers, was to carve out a unique Canadian perspective in films from that of Hollywood. As well, not unlike other areas of popular culture, the Canadian state used support for cinematography as a way of state control of the enterprise.

James Freer, a farmer from the Brandon area of Manitoba, became Canada's first indigenous cinematographer. He filmed agricultural subjects in 1897, with the blessing of the Canadian government and the Canadian Pacific Railway Company, as promotion literature to attract settlers, especially from the British Isles, to the Canadian West. At the turn of the century, Freer toured the British Isles with his moving pictures that showed the potential of the Canadian West. At the same time, a number of "scenic" films were done of popular and exotic Canadian sites, which paralleled illustrations in many of the weekly or monthly "illustrated news" magazines. Since these films resembled photographs or pictures, they were called "moving pictures."

Hiawatha, the Messiah of the Ojibway (1903) became the first single-reel film produced in Canada. It was filmed on a First Nations reserve in Ontario, using Aboriginal performers. But the inspiration for the film was American: based on renowned American poet Henry Wadsworth Longfellow's *The Song of Hiawatha*. The film's appeal, according to the cultural historian George Melnyk, was its ability to "fit the colonizing culture's late-nineteenth- and early-twentieth-century fascination with Native Americans and their supposed doomed way of life."[5]

Four Canadian film companies between 1912 and 1914 produced films on Canadian subjects in an effort to create a Canadian-based fictional narrative, quickly becoming the popular style of film of the day. The British American Film Company produced *The Battle of the Long Sault*, about an Iroquois attack on Montreal in 1660. A Montreal production company made *Madelaine de Verchères*, about a Quebec heroine who defended a fort against the Iroquois. The All-Red Feather Company did *The War Pigeon*, an account of the War of 1812, while the Canadian Bioscope Company made *Evangeline*, based on another of Longfellow's popular poems. Each company had its moment of glory, but quickly died out in the competition with more sophisticated and well-funded Hollywood feature films. Many Canadian filmmakers headed south, and along with them Canadian actors. The most famous of these actors was Gladys Mary Smith—or to use her stage name, Mary Pickford. She became "America's Sweetheart," coming to symbolize female youthful feminine beauty. In the end, Canadian cinema suffered the fate of other forms of popular culture in Canada in the pre–World War I era: insufficient producers and consumers to sustain a uniquely Canadian film industry.

Mary Pickford (1893–1979). The Canadian-born golden-haired girl, nicknamed "America's sweetheart," became the most popular movie actress of her time. Alfred Cheney Johnston, the official photographer of the Ziegfeld Follies, took this photo in 1920.

Source: Library and Archives Canada/ PA-185967.

Sport

Sport evolved in the half-century after Confederation from an activity for the elite to a popular form of culture for the middle and lower classes. It also went from being amateur to professional, and along with this transition, from being solely Canadian to being American-dominated.

Amateur Sport

Amateur sport clubs existed in major urban centres at the time of Confederation in such sports as hunting, curling, golf, lawn tennis, and, in port cities, yachting. They provided social meeting places for Canada's political, economic, and commercial elites. Membership was often restricted to people with certain ethnic, religious, and educational backgrounds and denied to racial minorities. But wealth and social position also became criteria for entrance, allowing entry to a new professional and business class, such as lawyers, doctors, entrepreneurs, and

Women's field hockey team. Photographed by Walter Gage, between 1900 and 1910.

Source: Courtenay and District Museum and Archives/ 990.24.139 .

bank managers. Women were active in these clubs, although in a clearly defined and subservient role, while racial minorities were barred entirely. They were forced to create their own teams and clubs. In Nova Scotia, African Canadians in the community of Africville, on the outskirts of Halifax, formed their own baseball and hockey teams; while on the West Coast, Japanese formed a baseball team, called the Asahi. Out of these organizations came a number of key figures in the development of amateur sport.

Organized team sport, such as football, baseball, lacrosse, and ice hockey, grew as well in popularity. As people settled in urban centres and worked clearly defined hours in factories or offices, they had more time for sport. Better transportation facilities and communication links also enabled intercity competition. The standardization of rules in sport, in turn, led to the creation of local, provincial, and national associations. The Amateur Athletic Union of Canada became the first truly national association when it formed in 1909. By 1912, it already included 1300 clubs and over 100 000 individual members, and regulated all aspects of amateur sport.

A few women athletes formed their own clubs and teams by the 1890s in such vigorous sports as basketball, ice hockey, and baseball. The Young Women's Christian Association, which first emerged in the 1890s in the large urban centre, assisted by providing athletic facilities and club houses for young, urbanized working girls. Most girls and young women, however, pursued athletic interests and team sport in the sanctum of schools, colleges, and universities until a more receptive audience for women athletes and more public facilities were available.

Social reformers reacted to women's involvement in sport in two ways. Some of them, concerned about the demise of the Anglo-Saxon race with the influx of large numbers of non-Anglo-Saxon immigrants and the decline of the birth rate among the white Anglo-Saxon Protestant (WASP) population, urged Anglo-Canadian women to improve their health through physical activity in expectation of having healthy, robust children. Other social reformers, equating sport with qualities of manliness and masculinity, saw athletic women as challenging this exclusively male domain. Some even went so far as to associate masculinity with Christian morality. These were the advocates of "muscular Christianity," believing that through athleticism and rugged team sport, young Anglo-Canadian males would become robust, vigorous fighters for their faith, their country, and the British Empire.

Team Sport

Although football made its debut in Canada in the late nineteenth century, it became a recognized national sport when Governor General Earl Grey donated the cup that bears his name in 1909. At first the sport remained largely the preserve of an anglophone Canadian elite associated with universities in the larger cities of central Canada. Only in the first decade of the twentieth century did football spread to the smaller towns of Ontario and the Prairies. It also became more of a spectator sport. In so doing, it became more "Americanized," except that it retained the oval ball and the rules of rugby—both Canadian contributions to the game. Soccer also was played,

Smirle Lawson of the Varsity Blues hurdles the McGill defence in October 1909. The University of Toronto went on to defeat Toronto Parkdale that fall, to win the first Grey Cup.

Source: Canadian Football Hall of Fame and Museum.

particularly by British immigrants. In 1904, the Galt Football Club represented Canada at the Olympic Games in St. Louis, Missouri, and won the soccer gold medal.

Baseball, the most Americanized sport in Canada, became the most Canadian sport in terms of those who either played or watched the game, because it required minimal facilities. During the 1870s, baseball clubs emerged in all parts of Canada, and intra-town leagues became popular by the 1880s. In rural areas, baseball was played only occasionally, when the farm work allowed it. Very often it was during a picnic or other gathering associated with celebrations, such as May 24 (later Victoria Day), Dominion Day, and Labour Day.

Many Canadians considered lacrosse Canada's national sport. The National Lacrosse Association, founded in 1867, and its slogan—"*Our* Country and *Our* Game"—certainly claimed that status. George Beers, a Montreal dentist, promoted it as such when he wrote in 1867: "We may find that lacrosse will do as much for our young Dominion as the Olympian games did for Greece or cricket for our Motherland." Lacrosse was also closely associated with the game of baggataway, which was played by several First Nations. On the very day of Canada's creation, Kahnawake took the Dominion lacrosse title—at the time, the equivalent of world championship—by defeating the Montreal Lacrosse Club 3 to 2. The First Nations in eastern North America originated the sport, but non-Aboriginals had altered the game by drawing up new "rules." Even so, the Kahnawake team defeated the Montreal team while playing under the non-Aboriginal rules.

Lacrosse had a sporadic history before 1914. After an enthusiastic beginning in the 1860s, it ebbed in the early 1870s as a result of the presence of "rowdy" or undesirable elements at many of the matches. The game revived in the 1880s but also changed from amateur to professional. This change could be seen in the shift from exhibition games, arranged occasionally, to system-atized leagues that met and competed on a regular basis for spectators. The game also became a "national" sport, with teams located in urban centres across the country, although the sport lacked a national association until 1912.

Ice hockey had already become *the* Canadian sport by World War I. The first regulated game dates back to 1875 in Montreal, when two nine-man teams from the Montreal Football

Choosing sides, boys before a hockey game, Sarnia, Ontario, December 29, 1908.

Source: Photo by John Boyd. Library and Archives Canada/ PA-60732.

Club, looking for some winter training, confronted each other. Companies that sponsored the local "amateur" teams hired the first professional players, who were thus paid both to work and to play hockey. Already players earned more money from hockey than from their regular work. Many of the early teams began in Canada's mining, lumbering, and farming towns, resulting in tough games and ferocious intercommunity rivalry. The sport caught on quickly. By 1880, the number of players per side had been reduced from nine to seven, and a standardized set of rules was also in place. Montreal held the "world championship" in 1883, in which the McGill University team was victorious.

Three years later, in 1886, the Amateur Hockey Association of Canada formed. Initially the association was made up of clubs from Montreal, Quebec City, and Ottawa only. Teams from these three cities dominated hockey between 1883 and 1893, the year Lord Stanley, governor general of Canada, donated the coveted Stanley Cup to the champion team, the Montreal Amateur Association team. The Ottawa Hockey Club, usually referred to as simply "the Ottawas," later known as "the Silver Seven," and finally renamed "the Senators," won many Stanley Cups. Between 1893 and 1914, three of the original teams won 19 of the 22 competitions.

A group of colleges, universities, and military and athletic clubs founded the Ontario Hockey Association in 1890. Similar associations sprang up in the Maritimes and the West. Montreal had more than 100 hockey clubs in 1895, and by 1905, hockey teams existed across Canada. The cities of Saint John, Montreal, Ottawa, Toronto, and Edmonton even had a few women's teams.

In 1904, the International Hockey League (IHL) formed, consisting of five communities in the United States and Ontario. It lasted only three years, however, due to the difficulty of getting professional players, because local elite Canadian leagues professionalized players to prevent

Ottawa's "Silver Seven," winners of the 1905 Stanley Cup, shown in the centre of the photo.

Source: Library and Archives Canada/Credit: Thomas Patrick Gorman/Thomas Patrick Gorman fonds/PA-91046.

them from migrating to the IHL. In 1909, this organization was replaced by the National Hockey Association, the forerunner of today's National Hockey League, which launched its inaugural season with seven teams: three from Montreal, one of which was the Canadiens, the new French-Canadian team, with other teams from Ottawa, Renfrew, Haileybury, and Cobalt. They employed professional players. By 1912, the three small-town teams had folded, victims of rising costs. The league now consisted of two teams from Montreal, two new ones from Toronto, and a team from both Ottawa and Quebec City. Also by 1912, the first artificial-ice rinks appeared, making playing conditions more stable and also allowing ice hockey to become a West Coast sport. A Pacific Coast Hockey Association formed, which, in 1917, affiliated with the National Hockey Association to create the National Hockey League (NHL).

In four major sports in Canada at the turn of the century—football, baseball, lacrosse, and ice hockey—professionalization had taken over by World War I. Good players could make a living from sports alone, because there now existed a group of people, mostly middle class, willing and able to support spectator sports. From this point onward, money and victory overrode gentlemanly conduct and pleasure as the objectives of sports. Sports had become a business. Even the newest sport, basketball, invented only in 1891 by James Naismith, a Canadian physical education instructor at the School of Christian Workers in Springfield, Massachusetts, later became professionalized. These team sports also reflected the dominant cultural values of a competitive urban and industrial society.

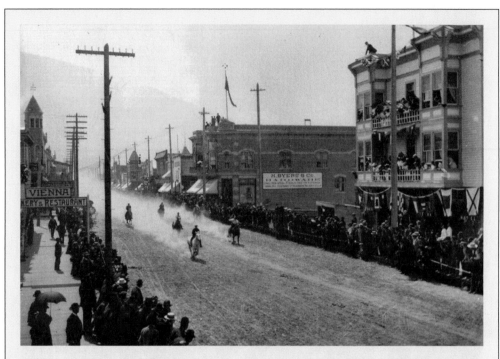

Residents of Nelson, British Columbia, celebrated Dominion Day in 1898 with a horse race down the town's main street.

Source: British Columbia Archives/HP-6225.

Middle-Class Culture

At the turn of the century, the middle class had more time and money for leisure. Middle-class male leisure activity often crossed class lines to incorporate working-class men as well. What united them was male bonding more than class affiliation. Such willingness to cross class lines was less frequent among women; middle-class women had their own separate and acceptable social organizations, including the church, which they deemed "respectable." They would have nothing to do with working-class associations, including the Salvation Army (which they regarded as a working-class religion), roller-skating rinks, or dance halls. Yet these places gave working-class women a sense of identity and a great deal of enjoyment.

In the cities, leisure centres arose, such as roller-skating rinks, dance halls, amusement parks and theatres, and fairs. The most popular in the Victorian era became Toronto's Industrial Exhibition, the forerunner of the Canadian National Exhibition. Founded in 1879, it entertained a broad segment of the populace of Toronto and its surrounding towns in the last few weeks of summer. Keith Walden points out that, while it entertained, the exhibition also

Methodist Ladies' Aid Society, Metcalfe, Ontario, around 1900.

Source: Library and Archives Canada/PA 103926.

helped to "shape understanding in a society being altered profoundly by industrial capitalist production, technological developments, and new ideas and values, including consumerism."[6] Industrial fairs expressed the perspective of the dominant or hegemonic groups in society, usually the industrial and mercantile members of the rising middle class. These fairs and exhibitions in the larger urban centres provided "respectable" leisure to the rising middle class.

Working-Class Culture

A working-class culture fully emerged in both English-speaking and French-speaking Canada in the late nineteenth century. It took shape through a proliferation of associations, societies, clubs, and lodges that had formed earlier but took on a new importance as they replaced institutions of self-help (mechanics' institutes) and community protection (finance companies). They provided a place where male workers (female workers could not belong) of common background and interests could meet and enjoy each other's company. Taverns served the same purpose in larger urban centres. Joe Beef's Canteen, established in Montreal in the 1860s by Charles McKiernan, an Irish Protestant ex-soldier, became one such place. Because of its rowdy atmosphere, the establishment was the target of reform zealots. But for casual labourers, the unemployed, and transients it provided a haven from the harsh realities of daily life in the slums and factories. The Canteen offered its working-class clientele food, drink, and accommodation—a blanket and access to a tub, a barber, "medical" advice, and "cures"—all for ten cents.

By the 1880s, larger working-class associations such as the Knights of Labor assumed the role that Joe Beef's Canteen and other, similar establishments, such as Dan Black's Tavern in Hamilton, had played. Through the American-based organization's ritualistic procedure of secret pledges, obedience, and committed charity, working men and women bonded and shared a sense of pride. Festivals, dinners, picnics, and workers' balls provided social gatherings to "cement the bonds of unity." Until the Knights' decline in the 1890s, workers held labour parades and demonstrations, often drawing thousands to such events from both towns and cities, thus providing visual reminders of labour's strength and solidarity.

The many working-class societies, clubs, lodges, and associations of the pre–World War I era, the taverns like Joe Beef's in Montreal, and the Knights of Labor all helped to build a working-class culture.

Aboriginal Culture

Although many English and French Canadians in the late nineteenth century had a sentimental regard for the First Nations peoples, it did not extend to a belief that they had a right to keep their ancestral cultures and religions. When John A. Macdonald proposed the creation of a separate Department of Indian Affairs in 1880, he noted judiciously: "We must remember that they are the original owners of the soil, of which they have been dispossessed by the covetousness or ambition of our ancestors. Perhaps, if Columbus had not discovered this continent—had left them alone—they would have worked out a tolerable civilization of their own." Yet, in the same speech, Macdonald went on to justify the need for a Department of Indian Affairs "to advance the interests of the Indians, civilizing them and putting them in the condition of white men."

These views were in keeping with the age. Canadians, like the rest of the Western world, believed that the First Nations were inferior and therefore had to be assimilated into the "superior" Western European culture. Edward Blake, former premier of Ontario and federal leader of the Liberal party prior to Wilfrid Laurier, described the First Nations peoples in 1888 as "an inferior race, and in an inferior state of civilization." This negative perspective justified suppressing any aspect of Aboriginal culture that might get in the way of achieving assimilation. Thus, while English

The Six Nations Council, around 1910. After Sir John A. Macdonald gave his speech to the Council a quarter of a century earlier on the value of becoming citizens, it was translated into Mohawk. A council speaker then replied that they need not become Canadian citizens because they already constituted a sovereign nation with their own political institutions.

Source: Department of Indian Affairs and Northern Development Collection/Library and Archives Canada/ C-33643.

and French Canadians at the turn of the century concerned themselves with cultivating their own cultural traditions, they failed to have the same regard and concern for the culture of the First Nations.

Yet, with a peculiar twist of irony, as Canadians believed that the First Nations were about to disappear, they became more fascinated with this "quaint" and disappearing "race." They wanted to include First Nations ceremonies and customs in their country fairs and stampedes. This worked against the federal government's policy of assimilation, and not surprisingly, the government undermined such popularizing of traditional First Nations customs and ceremonies. Thus when organizers of the Dominion Exhibition, the forerunner of the Calgary Stampede, invited a number of First Nations people to participate, Frank Pedley, the deputy superintendent-general of Indian affairs, appealed to the minister of agriculture not to give any financial support to the exhibition unless the organizers cancelled the "Indian performance." Unfortunately, for Pedley, he was too late, as the contribution had already been made.

The Huron Community of Wendake

When the French first visited the Wendake people in the early seventeenth century, they lived on a small peninsula between the Georgian Bay and Lake Simcoe in southern Ontario. The French called them "Huron." By the early 1650s, the Iroquois from present-day New York State drove the Huron from their territory. A small group of them retreated to the region around Quebec City. In 1697, they moved to their new home of Lorette, or Wendake, near the St. Charles River, only 15 km north of Quebec. They continued to practise their traditional slash-and-burn agriculture, and to live in bark longhouses.

Two hundred years later, Léon Gérin, a French-Canadian federal civil servant and pioneer sociologist, visited Wendake. He found a community of about 400 people who, in terms of their housing, dress, and religion, appeared to be almost identical to their French-Canadian neighbours. The village consisted of fifty houses or so, low-roofed wooden buildings, small whitewashed structures in double rows, as in the French-Canadian tradition. Some homes had very small gardens beside them, while others were placed so closely together that no room existed for a garden. Encroachments by non-Native settlers had reduced the village site itself to a very small tract. The Hurons also had a reserve for hunting as well as a timber tract, but neither was adjacent to the village site. In terms of dress, only one old Huron woman, in her nineties, dressed in her traditional costume of the last century. The men dressed like the French Canadians around them, but, for special occasions, the chiefs and leading men wore their traditional native costumes. Apart from a handful of Protestants, all the Hurons were Roman Catholics; one, Prosper Vincent, had become a priest. L'Abbé Vincent could not speak Huron, but he was one of the last members of the community to know a number of Huron dances and songs.

The Hurons at Wendake spoke exactly the same French as the French Canadians around them, with the identical accent and expressions. The use of Huron as a daily language had effectively died out half a century earlier. Other changes had occurred. No longer, for example, were the clans as important as they had once been. In the past one obtained one's clan identification from one's mother, but now a number of Huron men had married French-Canadian women, thus in essence ending female lineage.

Their immediate locality was not well adapted to agriculture, and as a result, the Huron gradually abandoned their farming activities. Some Huron still practised hunting, trapping, and guiding, but the vast majority worked in the village itself, especially in the manufacturing of moccasins and snowshoes. On average, 10 to 15 000 hides were cut annually at Wendake. In 1898, the Hurons made 140 000 pairs of moccasins and about 7000 pairs of snowshoes. The improved transportation system of the late nineteenth century allowed for the expansion of the market for the sale of these items throughout Canada and the United States.

In 1869, the federal "Act for the graduate enfranchisement of Indians," later incorporated into the federal Indian Act of 1876, made rules that further eroded the community's Native traditions. The Act ruled that when an Indian woman married a non-Indian, or someone that was not under the Indian Act, she automatically lost her Indian status. The same would be true for their children. It did stipulate that when a non-Indian woman married an Indian under the Indian Act, she gained Indian status, as did any future children they might have. But the Indian Department worked to achieve the complete assimilation of the Huron into the surrounding French-Canadian population by encouraging the "enfranchisement" or voluntary giving up of Indian status by adult Huron males. (Under Bill C-31 in 1985, Canada gave up enfranchisement, and amended the Indian Act to permit those who had given up or lost their status to regain it.)

Despite such changes, Gérin also found evidence that the Wendake Huron were determined to resist assimilation and to maintain their unique Native traditions and customs. For example, they still held all their land communally. They also fought to maintain their traditional hunting rights, and resisted the leasing of reserve lands in their hunting grounds to sport clubs. Gérin found that the

"Our people are at peace." The Wendake Huron chief Ovide Sioui, at left, accepts the pipe from Six Nations (Iroquois chief) Andrew Staats, in centre. In early August 1921 the Hurons and the Iroquois made peace at the tercentenary commemoration of Champlain's landing at Penetanguishene, on the Georgian Bay in Ontario.

Source: Toronto Reference Library/T 33409.

Wendake Huron saw themselves as a culturally separate community, different and distinct from the larger French-speaking community because of their Huron roots and traditions. They refused to abandon their First Nation status, and Wendake.

FURTHER READING

Léon Gérin, "The Hurons of Lorette," an offprint from the *Transactions of the Ottawa Literary and Scientific Society*. Read June 26, 1900, 69–92.

Denys Delâge, sous la direction de, "Les Hurons de Wendake," special issue of *Recherche amérindiennes au Québec*, 30, 3 (2000): 3-97.

Denis Vaugeois, sous la direction de, *Les Hurons de Lorette. Léon Gérin. Jean-Charles Falardeau. Christian Morissonneau. Denys Delâge. Marcel Trudel. Cornelius Jaenen. Alain Beaulieu* (Sillery, Québec: Les editions du Septentrion, 1996).

By the turn of the century, the cultural traditions of other ethnic groups also emerged, as immigrants came in large numbers and brought their customs, ceremonies, and special festivities with them. The fact that many of these customs were frowned upon by the host society did not prevent newly arrived ethnic groups from enjoying their own customs within their own communities.

In the years 1867 to 1914, Canadian culture proved to be a delicate but persistent enterprise. Most cultural endeavours began as amateur and local and only slowly evolved into being professional and national. As well, elite culture increasingly gave way to popular culture. However, just as Canada was slow to cultivate a national political culture, so too the country only gradually developed a national popular culture, beginning in the pre–World War I era, gaining strength in the interwar years, but really reaching strength only in the post–World War II period.

NOTES

1. Dennis Reid, "Lucius Richard O'Brien," *Dictionary of Canadian Biography*, vol. 12, *1891–1900* (Toronto: University of Toronto Press, 1990), p. 793.

2. Murray D. Edwards, *A Stage in Our Past: English-Language Theatre in Eastern Canada from the 1790s to 1914* (Toronto: University of Toronto Press, 1968), p. 28.

3. Lawrence W. Levine, "The Folklore of Industrial Society: Popular Culture and Its Audiences," *AHR Forum, American Historical Review* 97(5) (December 1992): 1373.

4. R. Louis Gentilcore et al., eds., *Historical Atlas of Canada*, vol. 2 (Toronto: University of Toronto Press, 1993), p. 133.

5. George Melnyk, *One Hundred Years of Canadian Cinema* (Toronto: University of Toronto Press, 2004), p. 21.

6. Keith Walden, *Becoming Modern in Toronto: The Industrial Exhibition and the Shaping of a Late Victorian Culture* (Toronto: University of Toronto Press, 1997), p. xi.

BEYOND THE BOOK

Weblinks

Pauline Johnson

http://www.humanities.mcmaster.ca/~pjohnson/home.html
Digitized materials of the work and life of Pauline Johnson, poet and entertainer at the turn of the century.

Pastimes of Yesteryear

http://www.musee-mccord.qc.ca/en/keys/webtours/VQ_P3_5_EN
This photographic exhibit describes the common pastimes of people in Quebec around the years 1896 and 1919. Sports, dances, and other forms of leisure or recreation are explored.

Hockey in 1899

http://www.collectionscanada.ca/hockey/index-e.html
Read "Hockey: Canada's Royal Winter Game," Arthur Farrell's 1899 handbook about how to play the sport.

English-Canadian Literature

http://www.canadiana.org/ECO/Browse?brange=collection&Language=en&id=session
This collection contains digitized copies of over 800 works of early Canadian drama, fiction, biography, and exploration accounts written before 1900. Select "English Canadian Literature" to browse the collection, and then "Show Advanced Options" to search by date.

Sheet Music from Canada's Past

http://www.collectionscanada.ca/sheetmusic/index-e.html
This site explores Canada's musical heritage with essays, digitized song albums, and audio files of early Canadian recordings.

Sophie Puckette

http://asalive.archivesalberta.org:8080/access/asa/documents/display/GLEN-117
Digitized school records, marriage certificate, and other possessions of Sophie Puckette. Puckette was an American immigrant who settled in Innisfail, Alberta in the early 1900s.

Films & Novels

The Journals of Knud Rasmussen. Directed by Zacharias Kunuk. 2006.

RELATED READINGS

In R. Douglas Francis and Donald B. Smith, eds., *Readings in Canadian History: Post-Confederation*, 7th ed. (Toronto: Thomson Nelson, 2006), the following articles relate to material covered in this chapter: Peter DeLottinville, "Joe Beef of Montreal: Working-Class Culture and the Tavern, 1869–1889," pp. 226–46; Nancy B. Bouchier, "Idealized Middle-Class Sport for a Young Nation: Lacrosse in Nineteenth-Century Ontario Towns, 1871–1891," pp. 250–68; Colin D. Howell, "Gendered Baselines: The Tour of the Chicago Blackstockings," pp. 268–85; and Helen Lenskyj, "Femininity First: Sport and Physical Education for Ontario Girls, 1890–1930," pp. 285–97.

BIBLIOGRAPHY

A synthesis of the arts in Canada has yet to be written. For an overview consult Maria Tippett's *Making Culture: English-Canadian Institutions and the Arts Before the Massey Commission* (Toronto: University of Toronto Press, 1990). For the Laurier era see, as well, Robert J. Lamb, *The Arts in Canada During the Age of Laurier: Papers from a Conference Held at the Edmonton Art Gallery* (Edmonton: University of Alberta Press, 1988). The *Dictionary of Canadian Biography*, vols. 9–14, has very good biographical sketches of some of the major cultural figures of this period. For a contemporary commentary on the cultural divisions of French-speaking and English-speaking Canadians at the turn of the century see André Siegfried, *The Race Question in Canada* (Toronto: McClelland & Stewart, 1966 [1907]). On the role of the Canadian Clubs in promoting culture consult Russell R. Merifield, *Speaking of Canada: The Centennial History of the Canadian Clubs* (Toronto: McClelland & Stewart, 1993). An analysis of the tercentenary celebration of the founding of Quebec can be found in H.V. Nelles, *The Art of Nation-Building: Pageantry and Spectacle at Quebec's Tercentenary* (Toronto: University of Toronto Press, 1999).

Music is discussed in Helmut Kallmann, *A History of Music in Canada, 1534–1914* (Toronto: University of Toronto Press, 1960); and his edited *Encyclopedia of Music in Canada*, 2nd ed. (Toronto: University of Toronto Press, 1992); Timothy J. McGee's *The Music of Canada* (New York: W.W. Norton, 1985); and, for the early twentieth century, George A. Proctor, *Canadian Music of the Twentieth Century: An Introduction* (Toronto: University of Toronto Press, 1980). For Quebec see, as well, Annette Lasalle-Leduc's *Music in French Canada* (Quebec: Ministry of Cultural Affairs, 1967).

On the history of painting consult J. Russell Harper, *Painting in Canada: A History*, 2nd ed. (Toronto: University of Toronto Press, 1966); and Dennis Reid, *A Concise History of Canadian Painting*, 2nd ed. (Toronto: Oxford University Press, 1988). On landscape painting in the late nineteenth century see Dennis Reid, *"Our Own Country Canada": Being an Account of the National Aspirations of the Principal Landscape Artists in Montreal and Toronto, 1860–1890* (Ottawa: National Gallery of Canada, 1980). For Quebec see, as well, Guy Viau, *Modern Painting in French Canada* (Quebec: Department of Cultural Affairs, 1967). David Karel's *Horatio Walker* (Quebec: Musée du Québec, 1987) looks at the life and paintings of this artist. For a review of the renowned sculptor Philippe Hébert, see Bruno Hébert, *Philippe Hébert* (Montreal: Fides, 1973); and also Yves Lacasse, "Philippe Hébert," in the *Dictionary of Canadian Biography*, vol. 14, *1911–1920* (Toronto: University of Toronto Press, 1998): 467–470. For a review of photography see Roger Hall, Gordon Dobbs, and Stanley Triggs, *The World of William Notman: The Nineteenth Century Through a Master Lens* (Toronto: McClelland & Stewart, 1993). For architecture consult Harold Kalman, *A Concise History of Canadian Architecture* (Toronto: Oxford University Press, 2000).

Literary history is well documented in Carl F. Klinck, ed., *Literary History of Canada*, 2nd ed. (Toronto: University of Toronto Press, 1976); and Eugene Benson and William Toye, eds., *The Oxford*

Companion to Canadian Literature, 2nd ed. (Toronto: Oxford University Press, 1997). For Quebec see Guy Sylvestre, *Literature in French Canada* (Quebec: Department of Cultural Affairs, 1967). Recent interest in First Nations literature has led to several new studies of Pauline Johnson. Three of these are: Sheila M.F. Johnson, *Buckskin and Broadcloth: A Celebration of E. Pauline Johnson—Tekahionwake 1861–1913* (Toronto: National Heritage Books, 1997); Veronica Strong-Boag and Carol Gerson, *Paddling Her Own Canoe: The Times and Texts of E. Pauline Johnson* (Toronto: University of Toronto Press, 2000); and Charlotte Gray, *Flint and Feather: The Life and Times of E. Pauline Johnson, Tekahionwake* (Toronto: Harper Flamingo, 2002). The life of Charles Chiniquy is told by Marcel Trudel in *Chiniquy* (Trois-Rivières: Editions du Bien Public, 1955). On John William Dawson, see Susan Sheets-Pyenson, *John William Dawson: Faith, Hope, and Science* (Montreal/Kingston: McGill-Queen's University Press, 1996).

For the history of Canadian theatre in English-speaking Canada see Murray D. Edwards, *A Stage in Our Past: English-Language Theatre in Eastern Canada from the 1790s to 1914* (Toronto: University of Toronto Press, 1968). For western Canada, consult E. Ross Stuart, *The History of Prairie Theatre: The Development of Theatre in Alberta, Manitoba and Saskatchewan 1833–1982* (Toronto: Simon and Pierre, 1984); and Eugene Benson and L.W. Conolly, eds., *The Oxford Companion to Canadian Theatre* (Toronto: Oxford University Press, 1989). For Quebec see Elaine F. Nardocchio, *Theatre and Politics in Modern Québec* (Edmonton: University of Alberta Press, 1986); and Jean Hamelin, *The Theatre in French Canada* (Quebec: Department of Cultural Affairs, 1967). On the colourful performances of Sarah Bernhardt, see Ramon Hathorn's lecture to Canada House in London, *Sarah Bernhardt's Canadian Visits* (Leeds: University of Leeds for Canada House, 1992).

Canadian folklore is discussed in Edith Fowke, *Folklore of Canada* (Toronto: McClelland & Stewart, 1990), her *Canadian Folklore* (Toronto: Oxford University Press, 1988), and Paul Rutherford's *A Victorian Authority: The Daily Press in Late Nineteenth-Century Canada* (Toronto: University of Toronto Press, 1982).

On popular culture, see Mary Vipond, *The Mass Media in Canada* (Toronto: James Lorimer & Co, 1989), and for cinema, George Melnyk, *One Hundred Years of Canada Cinema* (Toronto: University of Toronto Press, 2004). Clarence Karr, *Authors and Audience: Popular Canadian Fiction in the Early Twentieth Century* (Montreal/Kingston: McGill-Queen's University Press, 2000), and for the West, Frances W. Kaye, *Hiding the Audience: Viewing Arts and Arts Institutions on the Prairies* (Edmonton: University of Alberta Press, 2003).

For sport in Canada see Alan Metcalfe, *Canada Learns to Play: The Emergence of Organized Sports, 1807–1914* (Toronto: McClelland & Stewart, 1987); and Colin Howell, *Blood, Sweat, and Cheers: Sport in the Making of Modern Canada* (Toronto: University of Toronto Press, 2001). See, as well, the relevant essays in Morris Mott, ed., *Sports in Canada: Historical Readings* (Mississauga, ON: Copp Clark Pitman, 1989). On hockey see Daniel Mason, "The International Hockey League and the Professionalization of Ice Hockey, 1904–1907," *Journal of Sport History* 25(1) (Spring 1978): 1–17; William Houston, *Pride and Glory: 100 Years of the Stanley Cup* (Toronto: McGraw-Hill Ryerson, 1992); and Dan Diamond, ed., *The Official National Hockey League 75th Anniversary Commemorative Book* (Toronto: Firefly Books, 1991). On lacrosse, see Donald Fisher, *Lacrosse: A History of the Game* (Baltimore, MD: Johns Hopkins University Press, 2002). For women and sport, see M. Ann Hall, *The Girl and the Game: A History of Women's Sport in Canada* (Peterborough: Broadview Press, 2002).

For a discussion of an emerging middle-class culture in English-speaking Canada, see Lynne Marks, *Revivals and Roller Rinks: Religion, Leisure, and Identity in Late Nineteenth Century Small-Town Ontario* (Toronto: University of Toronto Press, 1996); and Keith Walden, *Becoming Modern in Toronto: The Industrial Exhibition and the Shaping of a Late Victorian Culture* (Toronto: University of Toronto Press, 1997).

On working-class culture the best source is Bryan Palmer, *Working-Class Experience: The Rise and Reconstitution of Canadian Labour 1880–1991*, 2nd ed. (Toronto: Butterworths, 1993). An insightful article on taverns and working-class culture is Peter de Lottinville, "Joe Beef of Montreal: Working-Class Culture and the Tavern, 1869–1889," reprinted in R. Douglas Francis and Donald B. Smith, eds., *Readings in Canadian History: Post-Confederation*, 7th ed. (Toronto: Nelson Thomson, 2006), pp. 226-246.

Among the best studies of the impact of the dominant society on the First Nations are Katherine Pettipas, *Severing the Ties That Bind: Government Repression of Indigenous Religious Ceremonies on the Prairies* (Winnipeg: University of Manitoba Press, 1994); Brian E. Titley, *A Narrow Vision: Duncan Campbell Scott and the Administration of Indian Affairs in Canada* (Vancouver: University of British Columbia Press, 1986); and Edward Ahenakew, *Voices of the Plains Cree* (Toronto: McClelland & Stewart, 1973). For an overview, see Olive P. Dickason, *Canada's First Nations: A History of Founding Peoples from Earliest Times*, 3rd ed. (Don Mills, ON: Oxford University Press, 2002); J. R. Miller, *Skyscrapers Hide the Heavens: A History of Indian–White Relations in Canada*, 3rd ed. (Toronto: University of Toronto Press, 2000); and Arthur J. Ray, *I Have Lived Here Since the World Began* (Toronto: Key Porter, 1996).

Part

3

THE IMPACT OF TWO WORLD WARS AND THE GREAT DEPRESSION, 1914–45

INTRODUCTION

Like two bookends on a shelf, two world wars enclose the years 1914–45.

The country felt the impact of these wars in a number of ways. In human terms, Canada sent over 600 000 men into battle in World War I, of which 60 000 died. In World War II, the country sent one million with 40 000 deaths. An even greater number returned home maimed in body and in mind from both wars. Canadian soldiers, sailors, and pilots distinguished themselves in battle, thus contributing greatly to the Allied cause, and advanced Canada's national recognition abroad.

During World War I, energy was directed principally toward the production of war-related materials. Since insufficient numbers of men were available to work in the factories and munitions plants, more women were called upon to work outside the home. This did not, however, result in gender equality in the workplace, although it did contribute to women getting the franchise. Women continued to face wage discrimination and were the first to be let go when the economy lagged. War also had a significant impact on all Canadians. The state intervened in the lives of Canadian citizens to a greater extent than ever before: regulating and restricting what people could buy; dictating wages and working conditions; introducing new forms of revenue, such as the income tax and the sale of victory bonds; and reallocating resources to maximize war production. Politically the Borden government created a Union party in 1917 made up of Conservatives and a number of English-Canadian Liberals as a united war effort. It implemented military conscription. Conscription divided English-speaking and French-speaking Canadians to an unprecedented degree and left a legacy of bitterness that endured long after the war was over.

After a period of recession in the postwar years, economic prosperity returned by the mid-1920s. A new economy of pulp and paper, mineral production, and the manufacturing of consumer goods replaced the old wheat economy. But the age-old regional, cultural, ethnic, gender, and class divisions remained. Politically, the two traditional parties survived the war, but a new third party, the Progressive party, challenged them. A new political tradition of federal multiparty rule began. Internationally, Canada took control over its foreign relations and achieved constitutional autonomy from Great Britain.

The Great Depression of the 1930s affected the country profoundly. It occurred at the same time as severe climatic conditions in the Canadian West, making this one of the hardest-hit regions of the country. New political parties, and new radical left- and right-wing movements, emerged, desperate to find a solution to the economic crisis. The magnitude of the Depression forced Mackenzie King's government to appoint a Royal Commission on Dominion-Provincial Relations in an attempt to find a solution to the tension between the two levels of government.

World War II might have ended the depression, but it plunged the country into something even more horrific. Although Mackenzie King's government was reluctant to get involved in the war on a major scale, it had no alternative as Hitler's army swept through western Europe. Once again, women were called upon to work outside the home for the war effort. This time they experienced greater gender equality than they did during World War I, but not without a struggle. Internationally, Canada had to confront changing relations with Britain and the United States. The signing of the Ogdensburg Agreement with the United States in August 1940 saw Canada agree to join in Canadian–American defence of North America. This proved to be the turning point from an era of British alliance to American protection.

The Canada that emerged from World War II in 1945 proved as different from the Canada that entered World War I as the Canada of 1867.

Chapter Ten

CANADA IN THE GREAT WAR

TIME LINE

1914	World War I begins Parliament passes War Measures Act First Division of the Canadian Expeditionary Force leaves for England
1915	Battle at Ypres Salient John McCrae writes "In Flanders Fields"
1916	Battle of the Somme Battle of Beaumont-Hamel "Bilingual" schools abolished in Manitoba Women in the four western provinces are the first to get the right to vote provincially
1917	Battle of Vimy Ridge Canadian Defence Force established Military Service Act (the conscription bill) becomes law Election of Union government under Robert Borden Halifax explosion Creation of Canadian National Railways (CNR) "Temporary" income tax introduced
1918	Establishment of Department of Soldiers' Civil Re-establishment, the Women's Bureau, and the Food Board Union government imposes national prohibition Canadian soldiers enter Mons Armistice signed ending World War I Women over the age of 21 (except female status Indians and female Asians) get the right to vote in Canada Outbreak of Spanish flu epidemic

World War I marked a turning point in Canadian development. Between 1914 and 1918, Canada sent some 625 000 men to the war front and several hundred women as nurses to assist—an enormous contribution for a nation of only eight million people. The Canadian Expeditionary Force fought valiantly in a number of key battles, but at great human cost. One in ten of those who fought on the battlefields of Europe died in the service of their country; an even greater number were wounded in the deadly trench warfare. The numbers were even higher proportionately for Newfoundlanders; an estimated one out of four died. During the war, the government intervened in the affairs of the state to an unprecedented degree: regulating the production, distribution, sale, and consumption of such essential resources as coal, wood, and gas fuels; establishing such institutions as the Canadian National railways and the Canadian Wheat Board; and financing the war through a federal income tax and the sale of Victory Bonds. Women assisted the war effort through millions of hours of volunteer work, and by filling vacancies in factories and offices left by men who went overseas. The war initially united Canadians but then divided them. Prime Minister Borden established a Union government for a united war effort, but then immediately implemented conscription that deeply divided French Canadians and English Canadians. Workers and industrialists quarrelled about who was making the greatest contribution to the war effort. Social reformers, particularly women suffragists and prohibitionists, used the war as a catalyst for their causes. During the war, Canadian leaders succeeded in bringing the Canadian troops under Canadian command, and insisted on a more active role in deciding imperial war policy. At the end of the war, they fought for Canadian independent participation in the peace conference and for membership in the League of Nations.

Crowds swarmed into downtown Calgary the night war was declared, August 4, 1914.

Source: Calgary Herald.

Canada Joins the War Effort

The murder of Archduke Ferdinand, heir to the Austro–Hungarian throne, by a young Serbian nationalist in June 1914 began a chain of events that led to World War I. The European powers' intricate network of alliances and agreements forced them into war. Austria attacked Serbia, an ally of Russia. Germany backed Austria, while France came to the defence of Russia. Britain, the ally of France—which in turn was allied to Russia—had promised to defend Belgium's neutrality. When Germany invaded Belgium, Britain declared war. As a member of the British empire, Canada was automatically at war.

Initially, Canadians united behind the war effort. When Borden summoned Parliament for a special war session on August 18, he told a cheering House of Commons: "As to our duty, we are all agreed, we stand shoulder to shoulder with Britain and the other British Dominions in this quarrel." Throughout the country loyal demonstrations occurred, involving impromptu parades, flag-waving, and, in the streets of Montreal, the singing of "La Marseillaise" and "Rule Britannia." Even the anti-imperialist Henri Bourassa initially supported Canadian participation, seeing the survival of France and Britain as vital to Canada. Many believed that the Allies would achieve a quick victory—by Christmas. Most English-speaking Canadians viewed the war in black-and-white terms: good versus evil; democracy versus tyranny; the Anglo-Saxons versus the "Huns." This dichotomy continued throughout the war years. Newspapers, magazines, and films would report on the war in a way that brought it "home" to the average Canadian citizen, and in such a way as to distance "us" from "them," being the enemy. Such identification was important to create a national consensus to galvanize *all* Canadians behind the war effort and to help them get through four painful years.

Canada prepared for war. Unanimously Parliament passed the War Measures Act in 1914, which gave the cabinet the right to suspend the civil liberties of anyone suspected of collaborating with the enemy and to regulate any area of society deemed essential for the conduct of the war. Under the act, Ottawa required all those classified as "enemy aliens"—people who held citizenship in enemy countries, mostly German and Austro–Hungarian immigrants—to carry identity cards and to report once a month to the local police or to the Royal North-West Mounted Police. Ottawa interned those who were considered dangerous, as well as anyone who refused to register. It established 24 internment camps, from Halifax to Nanaimo. In very basic camps, such as the one at Castle Mountain in Banff National Park, the internees worked for 25 cents a day for six days a week. The imprisoned labourers, mainly Ukrainians, helped to build roads, paths, and tourist sites such as the Banff golf course. Despite notification from the British Foreign Office in January 1915 that Ukrainians from Galicia and Bukovyna (the areas of the Ukraine under Austro–Hungarian rule) should be given preferential treatment as "friendly aliens," the internment of Ukrainians and some other eastern Europeans continued.

Among those interned was a Russian revolutionary who had been taken off a Norwegian ship in Halifax harbour while travelling from New York. After his release, Leon Trotsky joined V.I. Lenin in Petrograd, Russia, to lead the Bolshevik Revolution. During his one-month detainment at Amherst, Nova Scotia, in April 1917, he preached revolution to the 800 internees there. During the war, the Canadian government imprisoned about 8000 individuals. In 1918, a further order in council forbade the printing, publishing, or possession of any publication in an enemy language without a licence from the secretary of state.

The Canadian Expeditionary Force

Canada's permanent army in July 1914 numbered only 3000, with an additional 60 000 men in the militia. Their military training consisted of possibly one or two nights at the local armoury supplemented by an annual seven- or ten-day training period at summer camp. Its navy

As subjects of Canada's enemy the Austro-Hungarian Empire, many "enemy aliens," most of them ethnic Ukrainians, faced internment. These men were interned at Castle Mountain, Banff National Park.

Source: Glenbow Archives/NA-1870-6.

consisted of only two antiquated British cruisers, the *Niobe* and the *Rainbow*, and Canada did not have enough sailors even to serve these two. As a result of Canadian participation in the South African War over a decade earlier, the country still had a number of trained officers with actual experience on the battlefield. Cadet training had also been implemented in schools and some universities in most provinces. Sam Hughes, who had been a "volunteer" since the age of 12, and had fought in the South African War, served as the minister of militia in Robert Borden's government. He had also worked in his own determined way to build up the volunteer sector of the Canadian militia between 1911 and 1913. It was the volunteer nature of the Canadian Corps and the absence of class divisions that proved to be one of the great strengths of the Canadian army in the Great War.

At first, tens of thousands of young men answered the call for volunteers. Some came forward convinced of the righteousness of the Allied cause; others looked for adventure, and others for a job during a time of economic depression. Within two months, 30 000 Canadian volunteers were trained at Valcartier, a military camp 25 km northwest of Quebec City. Here Hughes placed them into numbered battalions of about 1000 men, then into brigades, and finally into divisions to be sent overseas. Pleased by the enlistment results and anticipating a short war, Prime Minister Borden promised that he would not implement conscription.

The First Division of the Canadian Expeditionary Force of some 36 000 sailed for England on October 3, 1914, the largest convoy ever to cross the Atlantic until that time. More than

60 percent of the troops, known as "Hughes's Boys" after Sam Hughes, were recent British immigrants, mostly unmarried, frequently unemployed, and emotionally close to Britain. Native-born Canadians of British stock made up 25 percent of the soldiers. The remainder included French Canadians, non-British immigrants, and Native Canadians. Among the Force were 101 volunteer nurses.

A "White Man's War"

From the beginning, the war was considered a "white man's war." As in other allied armies, the Canadian army discouraged visible minorities from enlisting. When fifty African Canadians from Sydney, Nova Scotia, attempted to enlist, the recruiting officers told them: "This is not for you fellows, this is a white man's war." They then pressed for a totally African-Canadian battalion. Major-General Willoughby Gwatkin, Canada's chief of the General Staff, agreed, but only if the battalion were officered by "white men." Daniel Sutherland, a contractor from Nova Scotia experienced in railway construction, commanded the No. 2 Construction Battalion (Coloured), the only African-Canadian battalion in Canadian military history. The unit recruited from across the country, but the majority of its 700 members came from Nova Scotia. Nearly 600 of them went overseas to southern France, but on a separate transport ship so as to avoid "offending the susceptibility of other troops." They joined the Canadian Forestry Corps where they played an important role in the lumber camps. The battalion engendered pride in the African-Canadian community both at the time and since.

A group of soldiers, many of them Ontario Native people, before going overseas in World War I. Photo taken in the North Bay area.

Source: Archives of Ontario/Acc. 9164 S15159.

Canadian Patriotic Fund poster.

Source: Toronto Reference Library.

Japanese Canadians also faced discrimination in their effort to enlist. When Canadian military authorities denied them the right to join regular units, the Canadian–Japanese Association of Vancouver raised an exclusively Japanese unit. The 227 enlistees drilled at their own expense, but under British veteran and militia captain R.S. Colquhoun. Eventually 185 of them served overseas in different battalions.

First Nations men faced similar obstacles. The Canadian Militia Council forbade the enlistment of status Indians on the belief that "Germans might refuse to extend to them the privileges of civilized warfare." Still, they persisted. Sam Hughes permitted them to establish their own units so long as they were under the watchful eye of "white" officers who could cultivate their "natural" talents as fighters and marksmen. The 114th became an all–First Nations unit, but it was broken up upon arrival in England, its members dispersed to various battalions, where many ended up doing labour duty. A few joined the front lines. Corporal Henry (Ducky) Norwest from Alberta became one of the most celebrated Canadian snipers of the First World War. Francis Pegahmagabow, an Ojibwa from Parry Island in Georgian Bay, was awarded the military medal plus two bars for bravery in Belgium and France.

By 1917, the Canadian authorities, now desperate for all possible human power, lifted restrictions on the enlistment of visible minorities. In the end, a significant number enlisted: some 3500 First Nations (registered Indians under the Indian Act), probably several thousand Métis, over 1000 African Canadians, and several hundred Japanese Canadians. Unfortunately, they gained little in return for their service. At war's end, they were still denied respect and equality.

Canadian troops trained on Salisbury Plain in southern England. That first winter of the war proved the wettest in years—over a 75-day period, only five days were dry. Heavy mists and occasional snow curtailed training. The troops' inadequate army clothing contributed to illness and poor morale. Then, in February 1915, the 1st Canadian Division, as it became known, joined the British army under the command of Lieutenant General E.A.H. Alderson for action in Flanders, in northwestern Belgium and adjacent France.

As late as February 1915, many Canadians, including many of English Canada's most respected opinion makers, still regarded the war romantically. In an address on February 23, Maurice Hutton, principal of University College at the University of Toronto, saluted the students and faculty who were going off to fight in France. In his mellifluous Oxford accent he promised, "You will not regret it. When you return your romance will not vanish with your youth. You will have fought in the great war, you will have joined in the liberation of the world." Those already in the killing fields of Flanders knew the reality of the Great War.

The Nature of the Great War

From the outset it became a war of attrition, one designed to kill as many of the enemy as possible. The fundamental concept of war remained Napoleonic. Like the French emperor a century earlier, the belligerent parties tried to destroy the main enemy army. They made no attempt to hit a tactical point, and in fact *blitzkrieg* tactics would only develop in the last months of the war.

As early as October 1914, deadlock had developed on the Western Front. Neither side could make a breakthrough. The two opposing sides faced each other, across a narrow "No Man's Land," in deep trenches stretching from Switzerland to the North Sea. Four years of trench warfare began, fought over an area no bigger than southern Ontario. From the beginning, the Canadian troops were singled out for their skill at trench raiding. It was the Princess Patricias who first used the tactic of surprise attacks on enemy trenches at night in the first battle of St. Eloi in February 1915, and their success greatly boosted the morale of the Canadian Corps.

On the Western Front, all soldiers faced the same intolerable conditions: mud, vermin, rotten food, and the stench of rotting flesh. The soldiers spent hours digging trenches, tunnels,

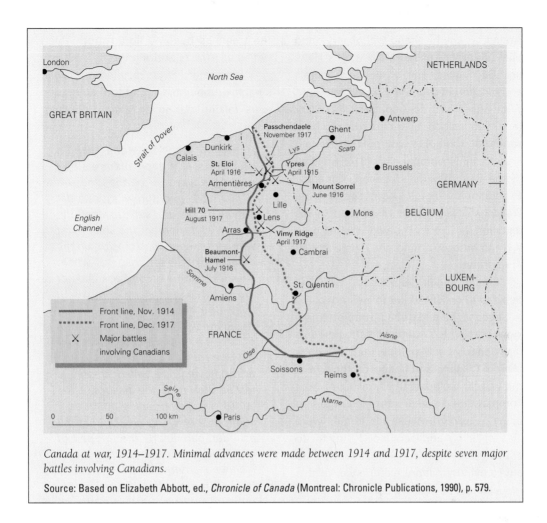

Canada at war, 1914–1917. Minimal advances were made between 1914 and 1917, despite seven major battles involving Canadians.

Source: Based on Elizabeth Abbott, ed., *Chronicle of Canada* (Montreal: Chronicle Publications, 1990), p. 579.

dugouts, and underground shelters, only to have them washed away by the rain and mud or abandoned in haste. Then there was the noise. As Canadian military historian John Swettenham has written, "It has been likened to an infernal orchestra made up of ear-splitting crashes from heavy artillery, the deeper roar of mined charges, the flailing crack of field pieces, the higher-pitched note of rifles, the ghastly staccato rattle of machine-guns, the shriek and wail of shells, and the insect zip and whine of bullets, but no words can ever describe it adequately."[1]

A HISTORICAL PORTRAIT

Private Fraser

"I do make Oath that I will be faithful and bear true Allegiance to His Majesty George the Fifth, His Heirs and Successors, and that I will as in duty bound honestly and faithfully defend His Majesty, His Heirs and Successors, in Person, Crown and Dignity, against all enemies, and will observe and obey all orders of His Majesty, His Heirs and Successors, and of all the Generals and officers set over me. So help me God." With those words—repeated in every recruiting station by hundreds of thousands of Canadian volunteers—Donald Fraser, on November 14, 1914, enlisted in the 31st (Alberta) Battalion, Canadian Expeditionary Force. Aged 32, Private Fraser was older than most men in his battalion, but he shared with the majority a common background: they were British immigrants.

Fraser never explained why he decided to enlist. Although well educated in Scotland, he had drifted from job to job since coming to Canada in 1906, first as a farm labourer in Manitoba, then as a bank clerk in Calgary, and finally, on the eve of the war, as a clerk with a Vancouver trust company. He chose to return to Calgary to enlist, possibly because his friends were also enlisting and persuaded him to do so. There is no evidence that Fraser had any previous military experience; in this respect, too, he was typical.

Fraser's battalion was equipped, put through elementary military drill and discipline, and sent overseas to England in mid-May 1915. After four months of "drills and manoeuvres, trench digging ... courses of special instruction in bayonet fighting, grenade throwing, machine-gunnery, musketry, signalling and map reading," they left on September 16 for France. By the end of the month they huddled in the trenches, "small, damp and cold and overrun with rats." Later he describes the mud: "For want of sunshine and wind, it is impossible for the ground to dry up and after a while we learn that it is useless trying to keep the trenches passable. The rain loosens the earth and the sides cave in. With additional rain the bottom of the trenches become liquid mud which defies all efforts at drainage."

Years later Fraser recalled one close scrape with death. He and four comrades were talking during an enemy shelling. Then,

a report that sounded like a premature or a short made us bolt out of the way.... I rounded the end of the wall and threw myself flat behind it on the side nearest the line. At that moment the shell burst with a tremendous explosion on the other side of the sandbag wall where I was standing a second ago and not more than a yard away from where I lay. The report of the explosion dazed me and I was hit with all sorts of debris as they fell on me in their downward course. The concussion or whatever it is called created a terrific strain on the tissues. I felt as if I was being pulled apart, as if some unseen thing was tearing me asunder, particularly the top part of my body, and especially the head. I know I could not have stood a fraction more without bursting, the outward pull on the tissue was so immense.

Although wounded again at Passchendaele in late 1917, Fraser was one of the lucky ones: he survived, recovered by and large, and received his honourable discharge. Of the 4500 officers and men from Private Fraser's battalion who served in World War I, nearly 1000 were killed.

In Calgary in 1919, he married Caroline Mackintosh, a young woman he had known in Scotland, and they had a family. Years later, in the early 1980s, his daughter recalled a comment of her mother's: "He [Donald] lost quite a bit of his strength and vigour, and thus led a quieter life than he ordinarily would have. Also, he was unable to travel any great distance without feeling unwell." Private Donald Fraser died in 1946. Canadian military historian Reginald Roy edited his war diary, *The Journal of Private Fraser, 1914–1918* (Victoria: Sono Nis Press), which was published in 1985. In his preface, Roy describes it as "one of the most vivid personal descriptions of trench life by a Canadian soldier I have ever read."

Amid these horrors came something worse—chemical warfare. The Germans first used chlorine gas, a greenish substance that caused coughing, choking, and burning eyes and skin, on April 22, 1915, at the Battle of Ypres. One Canadian officer described it vividly: "A great wall of green gas about 15 or 20 feet high was on top of us. Captain McLaren gave an order to get handkerchiefs, soak them and tie them around our mouths and noses." A British soldier later recalled what he saw when he and his contingent arrived to relieve the Canadians: "We stopped at a ditch at a first-aid clearing station. There were about 200 to 300 men lying in that ditch. Some were clawing their throats. Their brass buttons were green. Their bodies were swelled. Some of them were still alive. Some were still writhing on the ground, their tongues hanging out." Half of the men in surgeon John McCrae's brigade were killed or wounded. While waiting on the rear step of an ambulance for the wounded to arrive, he wrote a poem. "In Flanders Fields" became the most popular poem of the Great War and made the poppy flower the enduring symbol of those who died.

At Ypres, the Canadians made their reputation by preventing a German breakthrough in the Allied lines to drive to the English Channel. But nearly 2000 Canadians lay dead, with another 3410 wounded and 775 taken prisoner, out of a total divisional fighting strength of 10 000. After Ypres, historian Daniel Dancocks explains, "there was no more bravado about an early victory over the Hun, no more fears of missing out on 'the fun.'"[2]

In 1915 and 1916, three more Canadian divisions joined the 1st Canadian Division in France. Lieutenant General Sir Julian Byng, a British regular officer, replaced Alderson as commander of the Canadian Corps. There was also a change of equipment. The Canadian-built Ross rifle, insisted upon by Sam Hughes, jammed in trench warfare. "The least thing would jam it," one soldier wrote, "—a speck of dust, a shower of rain, even a burst of rapid fire. Very often there was difficulty in loading. The Ross Rifle was a standing joke amongst the Imperial troops." In the spring of 1916, the Canadian cabinet overruled Hughes and officially replaced the Ross rifle with the better-built British Lee-Enfield.

The Ross rifle affair highlighted the incompetence of Sam Hughes as minister of militia and defence. The governor general, the Duke of Connaught, once privately described the controversial and eccentric cabinet minister as a "conceited lunatic." Accused of corruption, of failure to attend to his departmental duties, and of incompetence in handling the administration of the war, Hughes had his responsibilities reduced by Prime Minister Borden. J.W. Flavelle, general manager of the William Davies Packing Company, took over the Imperial Munitions Board, which was responsible for producing munitions in Canada for Britain. By 1917, the board oversaw 60 factories and a quarter of a million workers who produced $2 million a day worth of shells, ships, fuses, and even airplanes. R.B. Bennett, a Calgary lawyer and Conservative member of Parliament, chaired the National Service Board, established in the fall of 1916 to increase recruiting. Sir George Perley, the high commissioner to Britain, took charge of the newly created Ministry of Overseas Military Forces to deal with the troops in Britain and at the war front. Finally, in November 1916, Borden sacked Sam Hughes, chiefly for openly criticizing the prime minister.

The Interventionist State

The war led Ottawa to intervene in Canada's economic, social, and military affairs to an unprecedented degree. Borden's reform of the civil service on the eve of the war helped make the transition easier. His government had implemented regulations that raised the requirements for entry into the civil service. As well, the government in 1912 had passed the Canadian Grain Act, which established the government-controlled Board of Grain Commissioners to supervise, inspect, and regulate grain sales. Thus, in 1917, when the Allied demands for Canadian wheat made it imperative for Canada to step up production and export, the government could intervene further without difficulty. Through the newly created Board of Grain Supervisors (after 1919 the Canadian Wheat Board), the government regulated all aspects of the production and distribution of wheat. Hectarage in wheat doubled, and the price per bushel increased by more than 50 percent. But one of the disadvantages was that the West was seen only as a wheat-growing area, causing it to be overlooked for munitions manufacturing or any form of manufacturing or industrial production. Thus, while towns and cities in other regions, especially central Canada, prospered from war contracts, western cities did not.

The government also regulated the production, distribution, sale, and consumption of coal, wood, and gas fuels. As military historian Desmond Morton notes, "Canadians learned to live with unprecedented government controls and involvement in their daily lives. Food and fuel shortages led to 'Meatless Fridays' and 'Fuelless Sundays.'"[3] Government regulations reminded Canadians of their need to contribute, whether on the war front or the home front. As well, the government nationalized two new transcontinental railways, the Canadian Northern and the Grand Trunk Pacific. Both tottered on the edge of bankruptcy by 1915, when a royal commission recommended government takeover to avoid a total collapse. Between 1917 and 1920, the Canadian government incorporated these railways into the publicly owned Canadian National Railways (CNR).

Naturally, such federal government intervention created resentment and accusations of favouritism. Western Canadians accused Flavelle's Imperial Munitions Board of favouring central Canadian firms over those from the West. Maritimers complained of military ships being built in Quebec rather than in Maritime ports. Workers resented the federal government's War Labour Policy, passed in 1918, that prohibited strikes and lockouts. They believed upper-class Canadians were not making the same sacrifices. Farmers and labourers demanded that wealth as well as manpower be conscripted for the war effort.

Financing the War

At the outbreak of war, the federal government depended on revenue from the tariff and the sale of federal bonds to finance the war effort. But as imports declined and as New York replaced London as the main underwriter of Canadian bonds, the government had to look for additional money to fund the war. It sold "Victory Bonds," which proved to be immensely popular—more than 1 million Canadians purchased the bonds by war's end, generating close to $2 million in revenue. The government also introduced another important innovation: direct taxation. First it imposed a business-profits tax; then, in 1917, it imposed its first federal income tax—3 percent for a family earning more than $3000 or an individual earning more than $1500. Ottawa promised that the new tax would only remain for the duration of the war. While these new sources of revenue helped, costs continued to outdistance revenue, forcing the government to borrow vast sums at home and abroad, at high interest rates. The national debt increased fivefold, from $463 million in 1913 to $2.46 billion by 1918.

The increased cost of living hurt people on fixed incomes and cancelled the benefits workers received from increased wages. Workers joined trade unions in an effort to increase their bargaining power. The unions in turn staged strikes.

Women and the War

Women made major contributions to the war effort. Twenty-five hundred women served as nursing sisters in the Canadian Army Medical Corps, working overseas at station hospitals, on hospital ships, and on ambulance trains. Forty-three died in the service of Canada. Margaret Macdonald, director of the army nursing sisters, received the Royal Red Cross and the Florence Nightingale Medal for her effort, while Matron Ethel Ridley was invested into the Order of the British Empire for her efforts as principal matron in France.

Women also contributed millions of hours of unpaid labour to the war effort through their work for voluntary organizations, including the Imperial Order Daughters of the Empire (IODE), Red Cross clubs, the Great War Veterans' Association, the Next-of-Kin Association, the YWCA, and the Women's Patriotic Leagues. They rolled bandages and knitted socks, mitts, sweaters, and scarves for the troops; raised money to send cigarettes and candy overseas; and marshalled support for the cause, not least by persuading wives and mothers to allow their men to enlist. Volunteering was a way to express patriotism to mediate fear and grief, and to demonstrate worthiness. They headed the Canadian Patriotic Fund, established in 1914 to assist families of soldiers overseas. They lobbied for mothers' pensions, day nurseries, and health inspection. By 1918, the government established federal agencies, such as the Women's Bureau and the Food Board, to assist them in the war effort. Children were encouraged to help by growing "victory gardens."

Unmarried women entered the work force in large numbers, as did some married women, to ease the wartime labour shortage. On farms, in factories, and in offices, women filled positions previously occupied by men. In summertime, the YWCA recruited hundreds of female volunteers in the cities and towns to help on farms. The Women's Canadian Club organized a Women's Emergency Corps to recruit women for the munitions-production industries. In its first year of operation, more than 35 000 Ontario and Quebec women signed up.

In wartime industries, however, gender discrimination remained: lower wages for women, lack of union support, and inadequate day-care facilities. Still, tens of thousands of women filled jobs previously closed to them, even in such male-dominated industries as railways and steel production. A number of women used their new bargaining position to raise social issues such as women's suffrage, child labour, and conditions in jails and asylums.

Fighting on the Battlefields of Europe

On June 1, 1916, Canadian soldiers contributed to the Battle of Sorrel in the Ypres Salient, a small triangular

Canadian nursing sisters at 1st Canadian Field Hospital, Etaples, France. They are helping to clean up after a German bombing killed three nurses, June 1918.

Source: Library and Archives Canada/ PA-3747.

area around Ypres. The Germans began an intense artillery barrage that enabled them to break through the Allied lines to capture Mount Sorrel. Arthur Currie led the First Division troops that began the counterattack. By June 13th, the Canadian Corps had recaptured all that had been lost to the Germans, a great victory but at the loss of 8000 men in just 12 days of fighting.

A month later, Canadian and Newfoundland soldiers joined British and French soldiers in the massive but ill-conceived Battle of the Somme against heavily fortified German positions. On July 1, the first day of the Big Push or Grand Assault at Beaumont-Hamel, the Newfoundland Regiment suffered 720 casualties—three-quarters of the unit. It was the greatest single disaster in Newfoundland's history, and the heaviest loss by any army on any single day in the history of the Great War. Among the casualties was Owen Steele, a 29-year-old lieutenant from St. John's whose published diary is the best account of the Newfoundland experience in the first two years of the war, first at Gallipoli, the regiment's baptism of fire, and then at the Battle of the Somme. Britain recognized Newfoundland's efforts by awarding its regiment the title "Royal." At the end of the war, the people of Newfoundland purchased the land at Beaumont-Hamel, and erected a statute of a lone bull caribou, the regiment's emblem. For Newfoundlanders, the battle, commemorated annually on July 1, came to represent what Vimy Ridge did for Canadians.

Canadian soldiers made their major contribution to the Battle of the Somme in the assault on the Regina Trench, a shallow ditch on the outskirts of the town of Courcelette. The Royal 22nd Regiment, the famous "Vandoos," led the attack. Their commanding officer, Lieutenant-Colonel Thomas Tremblay, wrote: "If hell is as bad as what I have seen at Courcelette, I would not wish my worst enemies to go there." After a week of fierce fighting and heavy casualties, the Canadians captured the Regina Trench and the town of Courcelette. This battle was one of the last—and few victories—in the infamous Battle of the Somme in which, during the three-month period, the Canadian Corps lost close to 2500 men.

Canada's finest hour came in the Battle of Vimy Ridge. On Easter Monday, April 9, 1917, some 70 000 Canadian soldiers, under the command of Julian Byng, along with British units, made a major attack against the German-held Vimy Ridge. Earlier in the war, both the British and French armies, with heavy losses, had failed to dislodge the Germans. This time, the Canadians took it. A Paris newspaper described Vimy as "Canada's Easter gift to France." In

Canada's Enlistment/Casualty Rate, 1917

MONTH	ENLISTMENTS	CASUALTIES
January	9 194	4 396
February	6 809	1 250
March	6 640	6 161
April	5 530	13 477
May	6 407	13 457
June	6 348	7 931
July	3 882	7 906
August	3 177	13 232
September	3 588	10 990
October	4 884	5 929
November	4 019	30 741
December	3 921	7 476
Total	**64 339**	**122 946**

Source: From Canada: Our Century, Our Story: Ontario Edition, *Student text by Fielding/Evans. 2001. Reprinted with permission of Nelson, a division of Thomson Learning: www.thomsonrights.com. Fax 800-730-2215.*

Cyril Barraud, The Stretcher-Bearer Party, *about 1918. The stretcher bearers administered essential first aid before transporting the wounded. In the background soldiers carry duckboard, which they used to bridge trenches and to provide a secure footing in the mud.*

Source: Cyril Barraud, *The Stretcher-Bearer Party*, AN: 19710261-0019, Beaverbrook Collection of War Art, © Canadian War Museum (CWM).

an editorial headlined "Well Done Canada," the New York *Tribune* wrote that "every American will feel a thrill of admiration and a touch of honest envy at the achievement of the Canadian troops…. No praise of the Canadian achievement can be excessive." David Lloyd George, the British prime minister, recalled in his memoirs: "The Canadians played a part of such distinction … that thenceforth they were marked out as storm troops; for the remainder of the war they were brought along to head the assault in one great battle after another." The cost for such praise and national honour was devastating: 3598 killed and 7004 wounded.

Canadians and Newfoundlanders also served with distinction in the air and on the sea. Canada did not have an air force of its own, but some 2500 Canadian flyers, trained in Canada by the Royal Flying Corps after 1917, joined the Royal Air Force (RAF). A number became high-scoring "aces," such as British Columbia's Raymond Collishaw, Manitoba's "Billy" Barker, Ontario's Roy Brown (credited with shooting down the notorious Baron von Richthofen—the "Red Baron"—in April 1918), and the legendary Billy Bishop, who was credited with shooting down 72 German fighters, earning him a Victoria Cross. But casualties were high. As the British never issued parachutes in World War I, there were no parachute escapes for Canadians from burning or disabled aircraft. The airplanes, too, were very flimsy; more pilots died in crash landings than in the air. Canadians wanting to serve at sea joined the Royal Canadian Navy, under the command of the British Royal Navy. Some 8800 Canadians and 200 Newfoundlanders joined. Among their duties was the patrolling of Canadian and Newfoundland waters against German U-boats (submarines).

"Invite Us to Your Councils"

As the war progressed, Canadian politicians demanded a greater voice in Britain's war policy. At the outset of the war, the British government treated Canada and the other dominions as colonial subordinates, neglecting to consult with them about war strategy or even to keep them informed of developments. When Prime Minister Borden first requested a stronger voice for Canada, Bonar Law, the colonial secretary (who by chance had been born in New Brunswick) replied curtly: "I fully recognize the right of the Canadian government to have some share of the

On June 10, 1916, the 102nd Battalion embarked for overseas from Comox, Vancouver Island. The whole Courtenay–Comox community came to the harbour to see them off.

Source: Courtenay and District Museum and Archives/ P215-1141.

control in a war in which Canada is playing so great a part. I am, however, not able to see any way in which this could be practically done."

When David Lloyd George became prime minister in December 1916, he found a way. He invited the dominion prime ministers to London to meet as an Imperial War Cabinet, a group consisting of the British War Cabinet and dominion representation. There, in March 1917, for the first time, Borden learned about the Allied position, discussed strategy, and, most important, became involved in the decision-making process.

The Imperial War Conference met simultaneously with the Imperial War Cabinet. The representatives passed a host of resolutions, one of which recognized in theory the equality of the dominions with one another and with Britain. It stated that Britain and the dominions agreed that their new constitutional status "should be based upon a full recognition of the dominions as autonomous nations of an Imperial Commonwealth."

Borden also gradually replaced British senior officers with Canadian commanders. Then in June of 1917, Arthur Currie, the commander of the First Canadian Infantry Division, was appointed commander of the entire Canadian Corps.

Recruitment

With continuous high casualties in Europe, Ottawa stepped up its recruitment drive. In his New Year's Day address of 1916, Borden announced his "sacred promise" that Canada would send a total of 500 000 to the war front, double the current numbers. Initially, it appeared that the government could honour its commitment. In January alone, nearly 30 000 volunteers enlisted. By June 1916, the total number of wartime recruitments numbered over 300 000. Then recruitment dropped off dramatically. In summer, farmers needed young men to help on the farms. Munitions factories were in need of more workers. The government responded by establishing the National Service Board, which had a mandate to "determine whether the services of any man of military age are more valuable to the state in his present occupation than in military duties and either to permit or forbid his enlistment." The government assigned registration cards to every male of military age. It concluded that 475 000 potential recruits existed.

Borden next established the Canadian Defence Force in the spring of 1917. This force was designed to get men who opposed fighting overseas to sign up for home defence. They would replace those already in uniform who were willing to serve on the war front. This last desperate attempt to get more troops without conscription failed. In the first month of operation, fewer than 200 signed up for home defence.

National Disunity

As voluntary enlistment dried up, complaints arose about those groups who appeared reluctant to give their full support to the war effort. Once again, this exposed the geological fault line that divided French and English Canadians. Several reasons can be given for the coolness of

French Canadians to the war effort. To them, the war was alien and remote. They had few or no emotional ties to Britain or even to France. Few of the officers at the Royal Military College in Kingston, the training school for military officers, were French-speaking, since English remained the sole language of instruction. In Quebec, an English-speaking elite with little sympathy for, and even less contact with, French Canadians headed the recruitment effort.

Sam Hughes, the minister of militia and defence who was of Orange Irish descent, did little to encourage French-Canadian enlistment. He placed French Canadians in English-speaking units and seldom appointed or promoted French Canadians to the rank of officer. Initially, apart from the one French-language battalion, the famed "Vandoos" (the Royal 22nd Regiment of Quebec), English ruled as the language of the army.

The Ontario Schools Question

The question of language rights for French Canadians outside Quebec also poisoned relations between French-speaking and English-speaking Canadians during the war years. This time the controversy centred on Ontario. By 1910, French Canadians, who had been moving into northern and eastern Ontario since the late nineteenth century, made up nearly 10 percent of Ontario's population. These Franco-Ontarians appealed to the Ontario government to protect their bilingual schools (or "English–French schools," as they were called) and to promote French-language interests.

These English–French schools came under attack from both the Orange Order and Irish Catholics. The Orange Order believed that the use of the French language in schools undermined the unity of Canada and of the British empire. Irish Catholics feared that language concessions to French Catholics would give French Canadians control of the separate-school system. The Irish Catholics favoured Roman Catholic—but not bilingual—schools. Bishop Michael Fallon of London, Ontario, led the Irish Catholic opposition. He viewed the bilingual school system as one that "teaches neither English nor French, encourages incompetency, gives a prize to hypocrisy, and breeds ignorance."

James Whitney, the Ontario premier, appointed a commission to investigate. The commissioners pointed out the inadequate training of many teachers in the English–French schools but stopped short of making any recommendations to solve the problem. In 1912, the Whitney government implemented Instruction 17, or "Regulation 17," which made English the official language of instruction and restricted French to the first two years of elementary school. It also established a commission to enforce its policy. Both the government and opposition, apart from the handful of French-speaking members, agreed with the policy. In 1913, Whitney amended Regulation 17 to permit French as a subject of study for one hour a day. Franco-Ontarians took the government to court on the ruling. While waiting for the Judicial Committee of the Privy Council to deliberate, both sides dug in.

French-speaking Canadians in Ontario and Quebec reacted. At the Guigues school in Ottawa, an "army" of French-speaking mothers, brandishing long hatpins, stood ready to prevent any entry by authorities to remove the bilingual teachers. In Quebec, Henri Bourassa denounced the Ontario government as more Prussian than the Prussians: French Canadians need not go to Europe to fight the enemy; it resided next door. Bourassa carried his message into Ontario. Everywhere he went in Ontario, he met hostility from English-speaking Canadians. In Ottawa, for example, an army sergeant climbed up on to the platform during his speech at the Russell Theatre and insisted that Bourassa wave a Union Jack. In the momentary hush, Bourassa replied, "I am ready to wave the British flag in liberty, but I shall not do so under threats." The curtain fell as the crowd rushed the stage. Bourassa escaped through a back door and calmly finished his speech for friends and newspaper reporters in the lobby of the neighbouring Château Laurier hotel.

The Ontario schools controversy dragged on for years, during which time Franco-Ontarians were deprived of schooling in their own language. Not until 1927 did the Ontario government find a solution: each school designated for bilingual education would be considered on its merits by a departmental committee.

The wartime hysteria poisoned relations with various ethnic groups. Whereas prior to the war, Germans were considered ideal immigrants, now they were vilified as "blood-crazed madmen." The Canadian propaganda machine, through newspaper editorials, books, advertisements, movies, songs, and church sermons, ensured that this image of the enemy prevailed. It also presented the counterimage of the Allies, and especially the Canadian soldiers, as brave and noble warriors. Such propaganda played out in various ways. In Berlin, Ontario, the city government held a plebiscite on whether to change the name of this city. Although over two-thirds of the city's population was of German descent, it was decided, by a narrow vote, to rename the city "Kitchener," after the British military hero who drowned at sea on June 5, 1916.

The Conscription Crisis

In the spring of 1917, Prime Minister Borden visited Canadian soldiers in British hospitals and at the front while attending a meeting of the Imperial War Cabinet in London. The desperate situation and the British pressure on Canada to increase its commitment of men convinced him to break his promise at the outset of the war not to introduce conscription for overseas military service. He informed his cabinet of the decision. His French-speaking ministers warned that conscription would "kill them and the party for 25 years" in Quebec but that they would stand behind him in his decision.

The prime minister favoured a coalition government of Conservatives and Liberals as the best means to introduce compulsory service, so he approached Wilfrid Laurier, leader of the Liberal Party, about the possibility. Laurier faced a major dilemma. While he agreed with the need for a coalition government for the war's duration, he opposed a union government that would introduce conscription, which neither he nor his Quebec followers favoured. "I oppose this bill," he warned when the Conservatives introduced the Military Service Act in Parliament, "because it has in it the seeds of discord and disunion, because it is an obstacle and bar to that union of heart and soul without which it is impossible to hope that this Confederation will attain the aims and ends that were had in view when Confederation was effected."

Opposition to Conscription

The Military Service Act, the official title of the conscription bill, became law in July 1917, although recruitment did not get under way until January 1918, after the election of a coalition government. Throughout the summer of 1917, anti-conscriptionist riots broke out in Montreal. Crowds marched through the streets yelling "*À bas Borden*" (Down with Borden) and "*Vive la révolution*" (Long live the revolution). Soldiers passing through Quebec in the winter of 1917–18 were pelted with rotten vegetables, ice, and stones when they taunted French-Canadian youth for not being in uniform. More riots followed in the spring of 1918, upon the actual implementation of conscription. The most serious riot, an armed clash in Quebec City on the Easter weekend, left four French-Canadian civilians dead and ten soldiers wounded. Fortunately, the war ended a half-year later, or the violence might have escalated.

Others besides French Canadians opposed conscription. Farmers resented their sons' forced departure from the farm, where they contributed to the war effort through food production. Workers saw military conscription as the first step toward the hated compulsory industrial service, forcing them to remain at one job for the war's duration. Both groups demanded the "conscription of wealth," heavier taxes on the rich and the nationalization of banks and industries, to ensure that financiers and businesspeople made the same sacrifice.

Some pacifist groups, such as the Quakers and the Mennonites, opposed wars as inherently evil and immoral. They upheld their beliefs despite being branded "slackers" by pro-conscriptionists. Others without a religious affiliation opposed war as a wasteful and destructive means of settling world problems. The Canadian Women's Peace Party, forerunner of the Women's International League for Peace and Freedom, championed peace under the leadership, ironically, of Laura Hughes, cousin of Sam Hughes, and Alice Chown, niece of S.D. Chown, superintendent of the Methodist church and an ardent supporter of the war. They advocated a non-violent struggle at home rather than war abroad as a means to reform society in order to root out the inherent causes of violence and war.

Union Government and the Election of 1917

Despite Laurier's refusal to join Borden in a coalition government, Borden did convince a number of Liberal members of Parliament and provincial Liberal leaders—including Alberta premier Arthur Sifton (Clifford's brother) and Newton W. Rowell, leader of the Liberal opposition in Ontario—to join his Union government. Then he dissolved Parliament and called an election.

Before dissolving Parliament, the Unionists implemented two bills to strengthen their chances at the polls. The Military Voters Act enfranchised all members of the armed forces, no matter how long or short a time they had lived in Canada. The governing party could use the soldiers' vote in whatever constituency it wished, where a constituency was not indicated. The Wartime Elections Act gave the vote to Canadian women who were mothers, wives, sisters, or daughters of servicemen (this did not apply to female relatives of status Indian servicemen), but denied the vote to conscientious objectors and to naturalized Canadians from enemy countries who had settled in Canada after 1902. Arthur Meighen, the solicitor general, reasoned that these aliens had been banned from enlisting and so should not have the right to vote. He also realized that new Canadians tended to vote Liberal.

Both the Unionists and the Liberals fought the election largely along cultural lines. A Unionist election poster claimed that a vote for Laurier was a vote for Bourassa, the Kaiser, and the Germans. A group of Union supporters issued a map of Canada with Quebec in black, the "foul blot" on the country. On the Sunday before the election, an estimated three-quarters of the Protestant ministers across Canada responded to a Unionist circular, appealing for support of the Union party in their sermons.

In Quebec, political leaders painted conscriptionists as a greater danger to the country than the Germans.

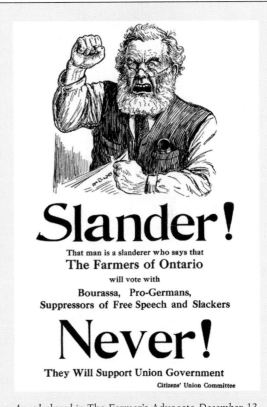

An ad placed in The Farmer's Advocate *December 13, 1917*, by the "Citizens' Union Committee." The federal election of December 1917 was one of the most divisive in Canadian history as a result of the implementation of the Military Service Act, or conscription bill, that past summer.

Source: Courtesy University Archives, Killam Memorial Library, Dalhousie University.

The view from Halifax's waterfront after the great explosion caused by the collision of a Belgian vessel with a French munitions ship, December 6, 1917. The blast, the subsequent tidal wave, and raging fire killed over 1600 people and injured 9000, including 200 blinded by flying glass.

Source: Library and Archives Canada/C-19951.

Bourassa and the *nationalistes* argued that Canada had done enough for the war. "Every Canadian who wishes to combat conscription with an effective logic," Bourassa declared, "must have the courage to say and to repeat everywhere: No Conscription! No Enrolment!"

The outcome of the election proved predictable. The Union party won two-thirds of the constituencies outside of Quebec but only three seats, all in English-speaking ridings, in the province. Ninety percent of the soldiers' vote went to the Union government. The federal government was now literally an English-Canadian government.

Shortly before the 1917 election, the citizens of Halifax experienced the impact of the war in an immediate and devastating way. Early in the morning of December 6, 1917, a massive explosion occurred in Halifax harbour when a Belgian relief ship, the *Imo*, collided with a French munitions ship, the *Mont Blanc*. In an instant, the city of Halifax was destroyed: over 1600 people were killed, and 9000—nearly one person in five—were injured, and some 20 000 left without adequate shelter for the winter, as a result of the blast, or the resulting fires and tidal wave. It would take months for the people of Halifax to rebuild their city. Until the explosion of the atom bomb on Hiroshima in 1945, the Halifax explosion might have been the largest non-natural explosion in history, certainly in a city.

The War and Social Reform

The war greatly advanced the cause of social reform. English-Canadian reformers argued that just as the troops fought for a noble cause on the battlefront, so should those at home—against materialism, alcoholism, and corruption. Social gospellers saw the war as the final struggle for bringing God's kingdom to earth. As superintendent S.D. Chown of the Methodist church told a church conference on "The Church, the War and Patriotism," "the war is a divine challenge to build the Tabernacle of God amongst men."

The Success of Women's Suffrage and Prohibition

Women's suffrage and prohibition both gained support during the war. Women reformers argued that men's aggressive nature, often aggravated by alcohol, had caused the worldwide cataclysm. If women had the right to vote and an opportunity to rule, wars would cease. They also pointed out the inconsistency of fighting for democracy abroad while denying women the democratic right to vote at home.

In 1916, the four western provinces granted women the right to vote in provincial elections. Ontario followed in 1917, Nova Scotia in 1918, New Brunswick in 1919, Prince Edward Island in 1922, and Quebec in 1940.

Federally, the franchise came in three stages: the Military Voters Act of 1917 awarded the vote to women serving in the armed forces or as nurses in the war; the Wartime Elections Act extended voting privileges to women, aged 21 years and over, whose fathers, husbands, or sons served overseas; and finally, in 1918, all women, recognized as British citizens in Canada, over the age of 21, gained the right to vote federally. Still excluded from the franchise were status Indians, Asians, and conscientious objectors, including Mennonites and Hutterites.

The war also helped the cause of prohibition, at least temporarily. Prohibitionists equated their struggle with that of the men at the front. As well, prohibitionists criticized human and material resources being wasted to make liquor at this time of critical shortage. The prohibitionists' first victory came in 1915, when the Saskatchewan Liberal government closed all bars, saloons, and liquor stores. Immediately, this move brought liquor under the control of provincially operated outlets. Alberta went further by endorsing outright provincial prohibition later the same year. Manitoba followed in early 1916. By the end of 1917, every provincial government except Quebec had implemented prohibition legislation. In 1918, the newly elected federal Union government imposed prohibition on Quebec. Within a week of his electoral victory in December 1917, Prime Minister Borden moved to prohibit the manufacture, importation, and transportation of any beverage containing more than 2.5 percent alcohol.

French-Canadian Reformers During the War Years

French-Canadian clerics and laypeople pressed for social, not political, reform during the war period. In 1917, Father Joseph-Papin Archambault, of the Jesuit-inspired École sociale populaire, issued a tract, *La question sociale et nos devoirs de catholiques*, in which he appealed to Roman Catholics to reach out to the working class. In 1920, he began the Semaines sociales, an annual week-long meeting of clerics and laypeople to discuss social questions.

In Bourassa's view, French-Canadian regeneration had to remain linked to Canadian Roman Catholic reform in general. At the turn of the century, most French-Canadian nationalists, including Bourassa, looked to all of Canada as their homeland. After the conscription crisis of 1917, however, perspectives changed. A small group of nationalists, led by Abbé Lionel Groulx, advanced the idea of an independent, Roman Catholic, and rural French-Canadian nation in the St. Lawrence valley. As historian Mason Wade wrote of Groulx in the early 1920s: "For him the French Canadians possessed most of the essential attributes of a nation, and their attainment of political independence would be a normal part of their coming of age as a people."[4]

English-Canadian Reformers and the War

English-Canadian reformers regarded the Allied victory as the beginning of a regeneration for a "New Canada." Some wrote books associating war with reform. In *The New Christianity* (1920), Salem Bland, a leading figure in the social gospel movement and a professor at Wesley College in Winnipeg, presented his vision of a socialist Canada operating on the Christian principles of love, equality, brotherhood, and democracy through a new labour church. Stephen Leacock, the political economist-cum-humorist, had doubts about the utopian nature of socialism. In his *Unsolved Riddle of Social Justice* (1920), he favoured instead legislation designed to make the workplace more appealing. In *Wake Up Canada* (1919), C.W. Paterson saw educational reform as the answer to society's ills. Two agrarian reformers, W.G. Good in *Production and Taxation in Canada* (1919) and William Irvine in *The Farmers in Politics* (1920), proposed rural values as the ideal of the future. William Lyon Mackenzie King welcomed the new urban-industrial society in *Industry and Humanity* (1918), provided that "regenerated men" directed it on Christian principles of cooperation and brotherhood.

Final Year of the War

Meanwhile, the situation in Europe deteriorated. In October 1917, revolution broke out in Russia, and by November, Lenin led the Bolsheviks to power in Russia. They immediately made peace with Germany. Now the Germans could concentrate on the Western Front. The Germans' unrestricted submarine warfare in the North Atlantic brought the United States into the war against Germany in April 1917, but American troops would not be mobilized in force in Europe until the summer of 1918. In October and November, the Allies suffered hundreds of thousands of casualties in the last phase of Field-Marshal Haig's Flanders offensive, including 16 000 Canadian deaths in the battle of Passchendaele, an attempt to take an insignificant ridge in a sea of mud. Finally, in the spring of 1918, came the all-out German counteroffensive, launched before American troops entered the front lines. Once again the Allies faced defeat. Only with the Germans' "black day" at Amiens on August 8, 1918, the beginning of the final "Hundred Days" campaign, did the Allies turn the tide. The Canadian Corps under Currie's command played a key role in the final assault. With victories at Drocourt-Quéant, Cambrai, and Valenciennes, the Canadians pushed on to the city of Mons. As the site of Britain's first defeat at the hands of the Germans in 1914, the recapture of Mons on the night of November 10 held symbolic importance. The next morning at 11 a.m., the Germans surrendered and signed the Armistice. The "Great War" was over.

Parade in Calgary celebrating the armistice and the end of World War I, November 11, 1918. Because of the influenza epidemic, the Alberta government had two weeks earlier ordered all citizens to wear masks when outside their homes.

Source: Glenbow Archives, Calgary, Canada/NA-431-5.

The war ended too late for Private George Lawrence Price. He became the last Canadian soldier killed when a sniper wounded him fatally at Mons three seconds before the ceasefire came into effect at 11 a.m. Local citizens commemorated his tragic death by displaying, at the Mons War Museum, a replica of the Canadian soldier's headstone at the neighbouring St. Symphorien Military Cemetery.

Few Canadian conscripts ever fought on the battlefield in the Great War. While the implementation of conscription put 100 000 more men into the army by the war's end, only one-quarter of them reached the front before the armistice. In hindsight, one wonders whether conscription was worth the price. Yet, in Borden's defence, no one in late 1917 could have predicted that the long-drawn-out war would finally end one year later. Overall, some 600 000 Canadians fought in the Great War; 60 000 of them died.

The Canadian Corps proved itself in the Great War. In assessing its success, historians have pointed to its volunteer nature, the absence of class distinctions and of preconceived rules of conduct of military operations (both of which hindered the established European armies), the fact that the Corps stayed together during the war, the rural and small-town roots of many of the soldiers who were used to a rugged lifestyle, and finally the fact that Canadian soldiers had something to prove: a pride in being Canadian.

COMMUNITY PORTRAIT

The Canadian Corps: A Community of Soldiers

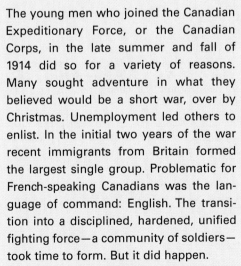

The young men who joined the Canadian Expeditionary Force, or the Canadian Corps, in the late summer and fall of 1914 did so for a variety of reasons. Many sought adventure in what they believed would be a short war, over by Christmas. Unemployment led others to enlist. In the initial two years of the war recent immigrants from Britain formed the largest single group. Problematic for French-speaking Canadians was the language of command: English. The transition into a disciplined, hardened, unified fighting force—a community of soldiers—took time to form. But it did happen.

Many of the Canadian-born recruits came from farming backgrounds or from small rural hamlets or villages, with a propensity to work together for a common cause. The fact that these young men trained together and, in most cases, fought together at the war front reinforced the feeling of camaraderie and the sense of themselves as a community of soldiers. Uniting them as well was the realization that they faced death together at the hands of a common enemy. In an open letter to his cousin Henri Bourassa, Talbot Papineau, a member of the Corps, noted how working together and facing death together forged a sense of community. Canadian soldiers, he wrote in 1916, "are being knit together into a new existence, because when men stand side by side and endure a soldier's life and face together a soldier's death, they are united in bonds almost as strong as the closest of blood ties." English-born Greg Neale, a farmer from Lloydminister on the Saskatchewan-Alberta border, recalled how he found a sense of community in the military. "For years, and especially for an impressionable boy, all my relations were there. Your battalion was there, your company was there, your platoon was there. You belonged to them. You were an identifiable person."

The Canadian Corps also had the good fortune of having commanders who reinforced this sense of unity and community. Julian Byng, who took command of the Corps in May 1916, although British, bonded with his men and worked alongside them to the point where they became identified as "the Byng Boys." When Canadian-born Major-General Arthur Currie, a former real estate agent from Victoria, replaced Byng in the spring of 1917, an even closer bond of unity and community as Canadian soldiers formed. Currie insisted that the Canadian Corps be kept together as a fighting force under Canadian command for the duration of the war.

At Vimy Ridge on Easter Monday, 1917, all four Divisions of the Canadian Corps fought together for the first time. In preparation for that battle, they had trained together down to the minutest detail. They knew that the Corps' success depended on the interconnection and cooperation of the individual soldiers. Harold Innis, later an outstanding social scientist at the University of Toronto, noted the importance of working together as a community of soldiers. Reflecting on his war experience, he recalled that all soldiers realized "other men's lives depended to an important extent on how much work we did." Together, at Vimy, the Canadian Corps had captured the all-important Ridge from the Germans. Earlier attempts by both the British and French had failed. For many Canadian soldiers, it was the defining moment. Greg Clark, later a leading columnist for the *Toronto Daily Star*, recalled it best in a CBC radio interview entitled "In Flanders Fields." Although he realized that the losses at Vimy had been horrendous, for him the Vimy campaign and the war in general had enlarged him in mind and spirit. He attributed his individual survival and the overall success of operations such as Vimy "to the community of men closest to him."

FURTHER READING

Ted Barris, *Victory at Vimy: Canada Comes of Age, April 9–12, 1917* (Toronto: Thomas Allen Publishers, 2007).

Pierre Berton, *Vimy* (Toronto: McClelland and Stewart, 1986).

Terry Copp, "The Military Effort, 1914–1918," in David Mackenzie, ed., *Canada and the First World War: Essays in Honour of Robert Craig Brown* (Toronto: University of Toronto Press, 2005), pp. 35–61.

Jonathan Vance, *Death So Noble: Memory, Meaning, and the First World War* (Vancouver: UBC Press, 1997).

Demobilization

In 1919, the Canadian government faced insurrection among its soldiers stationed in demobilization camps in Britain and Europe, as rumours spread of favouritism and deliberate delays in arranging for returns. To alleviate the tension, army officials began educational classes. When this initiative proved ineffective, the Young Men's Christian Association (YMCA) established the Khaki University in the summer of 1918 under acting president Henry M. Tory, president of the

University of Alberta. Its main campus was in Ripon, a medieval cathedral town in Yorkshire, with additional classes held at University College, London and, after the Armistice, at the University of Bonn, Germany. But soldiers simply wanted to get home as quickly as possible and get on with their lives.

To coordinate the demobilization effort, the Canadian government created in early 1918 the Department of Soldiers' Civil Re-establishment. Even its personnel, however, were unprepared for the difficulties involved in arranging for 300 000 troops to return and be integrated back into society. When they returned to Canada to a lack of appreciation for their sacrifices and few jobs, veterans protested. They used their association, the Great War Veterans' Association (GWVA), the forerunner of the Canadian Legion, to press the government to give preferential treatment to veterans, to provide pensions for those who were disabled, to help financially wives and children of dead soldiers, and to provide proper medical care to veterans.

The problem of treating disabled soldiers paled in comparison with an even greater domestic crisis at the end of the war: the Spanish influenza epidemic, brought back home almost certainly by returning soldiers. The first major outbreak occurred in September 1918 in Quebec. In some

For What? *by Frederick Varley, one of the four war artists who later joined the Group of Seven. Varley's bleak painting of a burial party at work behind the front lines makes a horrible statement on the futility of war.*

Source: F.H. Varley, *For What?* AN: 19710261-0770, Beaverbrook Collection of War Art © Canadian War Museum (CWM).

cities, people were ordered to wear gauze masks in public; in others, theatres and schools were closed, public meetings were banned, and church services were cancelled in an effort to check the deadly disease. Labrador was devastated by the influenza, with a third of the Inuit dying between November 1918 and January 1919. Since there was no known cure, people tried all kinds of home remedies, from camphorated oil on the chest to Epsom salts and even salted herring around the neck, while volunteers fought the dreaded disease in makeshift hospitals. In the fall of 1919, the federal government established the Department of Health to deal with the epidemic. Eventually an estimated 50 000 Canadians died from this "silent enemy"—almost as many as had died in the Great War itself.

The wartime rhetoric that the war would lead to a better Canada, a glorious nation of peace and prosperity, rang hollow in 1918. The war had strained English-Canadian and French-Canadian relations to an unprecedented extent, leading for the first time to the formation of national parties along ethnic rather than political lines. Equally, the war had taxed the nation's capacity in both industrial production and human resources. While Canada had made important strides on the road to nationhood, it had done so at great expense. The total of all Canadian casualties—killed, missing, prisoners of war, or wounded—had reached a quarter of a million people.

Canada had also lost its optimism. Fifteen years earlier, Prime Minister Wilfrid Laurier had predicted that the twentieth century would be Canada's, just as the nineteenth century had been that of the United States. In 1919, Laurier died. His vision had perished before he died, another casualty of the killing fields of Europe.

NOTES

1. John Swettenham, *To Seize the Victory: The Canadian Corps in World War I* (Toronto: Ryerson Press, 1965), p. 106.

2. Daniel Dancocks, *Welcome to Flanders Fields: The First Canadian Battle of the Great War, Ypres, 1915* (Toronto: McClelland & Stewart, 1988), p. 249.

3. Desmond Morton, "World War I," *The Canadian Encyclopedia*, vol. 4, 2nd ed. (Edmonton: Hurtig, 1988), p. 2343.

4. Mason Wade, *The French Canadians, 1760–1967*, 2 vols. (Toronto: Macmillan, 1968), vol. 2, p. 872.

BEYOND THE BOOK

Weblinks

Allied Propaganda Art in World War I

http://www.royalalbertamuseum.ca/vexhibit/warpost/english/exhibit.htm
An exhibit containing dozens of scanned Allied propaganda posters used in World War I, and analysis of them.

The First World War: Canada Remembers

http://archives.cbc.ca/IDD-1-71-2425/conflict_war/firstworldwar
Video and radio testimonials of soldiers and their experiences in combat in World War I.

An Echo in My Heart

http://ca.geocities.com/echoinmyheart@rogers.com
Detailed digitized letters written between Evelyn Albright and Frederick Albright. The Albrights were married in Canada in 1914, and Frederick enlisted and was sent overseas in 1917. The letters span 1910 to 1917.

Canadian Nurses in World War I

http://web.mala.bc.ca/davies/letters.images/Armstrong_collection.htm
This site contains over 70 photographs from nurse Constance Philip detailing her time as a nurse in World War I as part of the Canadian Army Medical Corps.

The Cobourg World

http://www.canadianletters.ca/CobourgMain.php
A database of digitized letters from Canadian soldiers, as published in wartime in the *Cobourg World*, a local newspaper in Cobourg, Ontario.

Wanted! 500,000 Canadians

http://www.mccord-museum.qc.ca/en/keys/webtours/GE_P3_1_EN
A virtual exhibit detailing Canadian recruitment efforts for the Canadian Expeditionary Force in World War I.

Films & Novels

Shattered City: The Halifax Explosion. CBC. 2003.

The Great War. CBC. 2007.

"*For King and Empire.*" Video Service Corp. 2007.

RELATED READINGS

The following articles in R. Douglas Francis and Donald B. Smith, eds., *Readings in Canadian History: Post-Confederation*, 7th ed. (Toronto: Thomson Nelson, 2006) relate to topics in this chapter: James W. St. G. Walker, "Race and Recruitment in World War I: Enlistment of Visible Minorities in the Canadian Expeditionary Force," pp. 188–205; "An Open Letter from Capt. Talbot Papineau to Mr. Henri Bourassa" and "Mr. Bourassa's Reply to Capt. Talbot Papineau's Letter," pp. 260–71; Will R. Bird, "Ghosts Have Warm Hands," pp. 341–47; and Ronald G. Haycock, "Recruiting, 1914–1916," pp. 347–66.

BIBLIOGRAPHY

For overviews of Canada during World War I, see Desmond Morton and J.L. Garanatstein, *Marching to Armageddon: Canada and the Great War, 1914–1919* (Toronto: Lester & Orpen Dennys, 1989); Daniel Dancocks, *Spearhead to Victory: Canada and the Great War* (Edmonton: Hurtig, 1987); R.C. Brown and R. Cook, *Canada, 1896–1921: A Nation Transformed* (Toronto: McClelland & Stewart, 1974), pp. 212–294; and Bill Freeman and Richard Nielson, *Far From Home: Canadians in the First World War* (Toronto: McGraw-Hill Ryerson, 1999). A valuable collection of essays is David Mackenzie, ed., *Canada and the First World War: Essays in Honour of Robert Craig Brown* (Toronto: University of Toronto Press, 2005), as is Marc Milner, ed., *Canadian Military History: Selected Readings* (Toronto: Copp Clark Pitman, 1993). On Robert Borden see R.C. Brown, *Robert Laird Borden: A Biography*, 2 vols. (Toronto: Macmillan, 1975, 1980); and John English, *Borden: His Life and World* (Toronto: McGraw-Hill Ryerson, 1977). For a study of party and politics during the Borden era, consult John English, *The Decline of Politics: The Conservatives and the Party System, 1901–1920* (Toronto: University of Toronto Press, 1977). Joseph Schull's *Laurier: The First Canadian* (Toronto: Macmillan, 1965) and O.D. Skelton's *The Life and Letters of Sir Wilfrid Laurier* (Toronto: Oxford University Press, 1921) deal with the leader of the opposition in the war years. The best short summary of Laurier is that by Quebec historian Réal Bélanger in the *Dictionary of Canadian Biography*, vol. 14, *1911–1920* (Toronto: University of Toronto Press, 1998), pp. 610–28.

John Swettenham, *To Seize the Victory* (Toronto: Ryerson Press, 1965) and Robert James Steel, *The Men Who Marched Away: Canada's Infantry in the First World War, 1914–1918* (St. Catharines: Vanwell, 1989) describe Canadian involvement at the front, as does Sandra Gwyn's *Tapestry of War: Politics and Passion: Canada's Coming of Age in the Great War* (Toronto: HarperCollins, 1992). On Canada's involvement in the Ypres Salient, see Daniel Dancocks, *Welcome to Flanders Fields: The First Canadian Battle of the Great War, Ypres, 1915* (Toronto: McClelland & Stewart, 1988). Pierre Berton tells the story of Canada's greatest battle in *Vimy* (Toronto: McClelland & Stewart, 1986). G.W.L. Nicholson, *The Fighting Newfoundlander: A History of the Royal Newfoundland Regiment* (Ottawa: Government of Newfoundland, 1964) recounts Newfoundland's contribution to the Allied army. For a personal account, see David R. Facey-Crowther, ed., *Lieutenant Owen William Steele of the Newfoundland Regiment: Diary and Letters* (Montreal/Kingston: McGill-Queen's University Press, 2002). Jean-Pierre Gagnon's *Le 22e bataillon (canadien-français) 1914–1919: Étude sociomilitaire* (Quebec: Presses de l'Université Laval, 1987) reviews the story of the famous "Vandoos" in World War I. On Canada's first military commander consult A.M.J. Hyatt, *General Sir Arthur Currie: A Military Biography* (Toronto: University of Toronto Press, 1987). On Sam Hughes, see Ronald G. Haycock, *Sam Hughes: The Public Career of a Controversial Canadian, 1885–1916* (Waterloo, ON: Wilfrid Laurier University Press, 1986). On the Canadian air force, see S.F. Wise, *Canadian Airmen and the First World War* (Toronto: University of Toronto Press, 1980); and for the navy, Michael L. Hadley and Roger Sarty, *Tin-Pots and Pirate Ships: Canadian Naval Forces and German Sea Raiders 1880–1918* (Montreal/Kingston: McGill-Queen's University Press, 1991).

On ethnic relations during the War, see John Herd Thompson, *Ethnic Minorities During Two World Wars* (Ottawa: Canadian Historical Association, 1991). James W. St. G. Walker looks at race relations in the Canadian army in "Race and Recruitment in World War I: Enlistment of Visible Minorities in the Canadian Expeditionary Force," *Canadian Historical Review* 70(1) (March 1989): 1–26. On the only African-Canadian battalion see John G. Armstrong, "The Unwelcome Sacrifice: A Black Unit in the

Canadian Expeditionary Force, 1917–19," in N.F. Dreisziger, ed., *Ethnic Armies: Polyethnic Armed Forces from the Time of the Hapsburgs to the Age of the Superpowers* (Waterloo, ON: Wilfrid Laurier University Press, 1990), pp. 178–97; and Calvin Ruck, *The Black Battalion, 1916–1920: Canada's Best Kept Military Secret* (Halifax: Nimbus, 1987). On First Nations soldiers see Fred Gaffen, *Forgotten Soldiers* (Penticton, BC: Theytus Books, 1985); and James Dempsey's *Warriors of the King: Prairie Indians in World War I* (Regina: Canadian Plains Research Center, 1999). On Canadian internment camps, see Bill Waiser, *Park Prisoners: The Untold Story of Western Canada's National Parks, 1915–1946* (Saskatoon: Fifth House Publishing, 1995). On Ukrainian internments, see Frances Swyripa and John Herd Thompson, eds., *Loyalties in Conflict: Ukrainians in Canada During the Great War* (Edmonton: Canadian Institute of Ukrainian Studies, 1983); and Lubormyr Luciuk, *A Time for Atonement: Canada's First National Internment Operations and the Ukrainian Canadians, 1914–1920* (Kingston: Limestone Press, 1988). For information about the nearly 4000 Canadians held in German prison camps in World War I, see Desmond Morton, *Silent Battle: Canadian Prisoners of War in Germany, 1914–1919* (Toronto: Lester, 1992). Morton has also written *When Your Number's Up: The Canadian Soldier in the First World War* (Toronto: Random House, 1993), a valuable perspective on the war from the vantage point of those who served at the front. The role of propaganda on the war effort is examined in Jeffrey A. Keshen, *Propaganda and Censorship During Canada's Great War* (Edmonton: University of Alberta Press, 1996).

In the shaping of the war on the home front, see Robert Rutherdale, *Hometown Horizons: Local Responses to Canada's Great War* (Vancouver: UBC Press, 2006), and Ian Miller, *Our Glory and Our Grief: Torontonians and the Great War* (Toronto: University of Toronto Press, 2002). On voluntary contributions, see Desmond Morton, *Fight or Pay: Soldiers' Families in the Great War* (Vancouver: UBC Press, 2004).

The question of government intervention in the state during the war is discussed in R. Cuff, "Organizing for War: Canada and the United States During World War I," *Canadian Historical Association Report* (1969): 141–56. On the nationalization of the railways see T.D. Regehr, *The Canadian Northern Railway* (Toronto: Macmillan, 1976); and R.B. Fleming, *The Railway King of Canada: Sir William Mackenzie, 1849–1923* (Vancouver: University of British Columbia Press, 1991). Women's contributions to the war effort are discussed in the relevant sections of Alison Prentice et al., *Canadian Women: A History*, 2nd ed. (Toronto: Harcourt Brace, 1996); Marjorie Barron Norris, *Sister Heroines: The Roseate Glow of Wartime Nursing 1914–1918* (Calgary: Bunker to Bunker Publishing, 2002); and Ceta Ramkhalawonsingh, "Women During the Great War," in J. Acton et al., eds., *Women at Work: Ontario, 1850–1930* (Toronto: Canadian Women's Educational Press, 1974), pp. 261–308. The Halifax explosion is well documented in Alan D. Ruffman and Colin D. Howell, eds., *Ground Zero: A Reassessment of the 1917 Explosion in Halifax Harbour* (Halifax: Nimbus, 1994).

The conscription crisis is covered in J.L. Granatstein and J.M. Hitsman, *Broken Promises: A History of Conscription in Canada* (Toronto: Copp Clark Pitman, 1985 [1977]); and C. Berger, ed., *Conscription 1917* (Toronto: University of Toronto Press, 1969). Mason Wade examines French-Canadian attitudes toward the war in *The French Canadians: 1760–1945* (Toronto: Macmillan, 1955). Students should also consult Elizabeth Armstrong, *The Crisis of Quebec, 1914–1918* (Toronto: McClelland & Stewart, 1974 [1937]). The Canadian peace movement is studied in Thomas Socknat, *Witness Against War: Pacifism in Canada, 1900–1945* (Toronto: University of Toronto Press, 1987). Often forgotten are the veterans; consult D. Morton and G. Wright, *Winning the Second Battle: Canadian Veterans and the Return to Civilian Life, 1915–1930* (Toronto: University of Toronto Press, 1987).

For the Ontario schools questions, see Chad Gaffield, *Language, Schooling, and Cultural Conflict: The Origins of the French-Language Controversy in Ontario* (Montreal/Kingston: McGill-Queen's University Press, 1987); and the articles by Marilyn Barber and Margaret Prang in R.C. Brown, ed., *Minorities, Schools, and Politics* (Toronto: University of Toronto Press, 1969).

For the impact of World War I on social reform, consult John Herd Thompson, "'The Beginning of our Regeneration': The Great War and Western Canadian Reform Movements," *Canadian Historical Association Historical Papers* (1972): 227–45, and his study *The Harvests of War: The Prairie West, 1914–1919* (Toronto: McClelland & Stewart, 1978).

On Canadian imperial and foreign relations during and immediately after the war, see R.C. Brown's biography of Borden (cited earlier) and his "Sir Robert Borden, the Great War and Anglo-Canadian Relations," in J.S. Moir, ed., *Character and Circumstance* (Toronto: Macmillan, 1970), pp. 201–24; as well as C.P. Stacey, *Canada and the Age of Conflict*, vol. 1, *1867–1921* (Toronto: Macmillan, 1977). On the flu epidemic of 1918 see Eileen Pettigrew, *The Silent Enemy* (Saskatoon: Western Producer Prairie Books, 1983).

Sandra Gwyn's *Tapestry of War: Politics and Passion: Canada's Coming of Age in the Great War* (Toronto: HarperCollins, 1992) examines the significance of the war for Canada's advancement; while Jonathan F. Vance looks at the construction of a myth of the Great War in *Death So Noble: Memory, Meaning and the First World War* (Vancouver: UBC Press, 1997).

Donald Kerr and Deryck W. Holdsworth, eds., *Historical Atlas of Canada*, vol. 3, *Addressing the Twentieth Century, 1891–1961* (Toronto: Nelson, 1990) contains a wealth of detail in the form of maps and charts on Canadian society in the early twentieth century.

Chapter Eleven

CANADA, 1919–29: A DECADE OF ADJUSTMENT

TIME LINE

1919	Canada participates in the Paris Peace Conference and joins the League of Nations Sir Wilfrid Laurier dies Winnipeg General Strike
1920	Formation of the Maritime Rights movement Founding of the Group of Seven
1921	Liberals come to power under William Lyon Mackenzie King Newly formed Progressive Party wins 65 seats in federal Parliament Agnes Macphail becomes the first woman elected in a federal election Founding of the Communist Party of Canada
1922	Founding of the Canadian Historical Association Insulin made available for the treatment of diabetes
1923	Canada, not Britain, signs the Halibut Treaty with the United States Federal government bans Chinese immigration
1925	United Church of Canada established
1926	Balfour Declaration signed recognizing the dominions, including Canada, as autonomous nations in the British Commonwealth of Nations King–Byng controversy
1927	Federal government introduces old age pension program National Museum of Canada created
1928	Percy Williams wins two gold medals at the Amsterdam Olympics, making him "the world's fastest runner"
1929	The Privy Council's decision in the Persons Case recognizes women in Canada as "persons" for legal purposes

The decade from 1919 to 1929 was one of adjustment to new postwar conditions and dramatic shifts in politics, economics, and social and cultural developments. Canada experienced its first general strike in Winnipeg in 1919. In politics, both major federal political parties chose new leaders, and regional protest movements surfaced in the Maritimes and the West, as these hinterland regions demanded a stronger voice in the "New Canada" of the postwar era. In foreign affairs, Canada took a number of steps on the road from colony to nation. Economically, Canadians looked increasingly to the United States rather than to Britain for both financial needs and foreign trade. Consumer goods became major items of trade. The nature of the Canadian economy also shifted from a preponderance on wheat to the newer staples of pulp and paper and base metals. In the area of transportation and communications, the automobile industry grew at an astonishing rate, as did all the essentials for the industry such as roads and service stations. Aviation expanded, allowing for regular air-mail service, and opening up the North. By far the most popular communication invention was the telephone, making regular communication possible and ending isolation for many families. Social reform had a brief flurry in the immediate postwar era, as many visionaries put forward proposals for a "New Canada." But it died out by the mid-1920s when the hoped-for changes never occurred, and as a result of economic prosperity. Women still fought for recognition and rights, but in the economic and the legal rather than in the political sphere. Labour unions struggled for recognition and increased membership. Cultural activities flourished in English-speaking and French-speaking Canada, but because of the language differences few points of common contact existed. Popular culture thrived with the advent of radio and the "talkies" in the film industry. Both areas faced greater American domination during the decade. Canadian sport also became more professional and Americanized, the two going together.

The Winnipeg General Strike

Widespread social unrest followed the armistice. Strikes broke out from Halifax to Vancouver as workers tried to make up for the restraints applied in wartime and to protect themselves in an inflationary economy. At the annual meeting of the Trades and Labor Congress in Quebec City in 1918, the western delegates broke rank with the conservative eastern members who controlled the meeting. A month later, the Western Labour Conference called for a single industrial union, the One Big Union (OBU), at its meeting in Calgary. But before its organizers could hold the founding convention, new developments broke out in Winnipeg. On May 1, 1919, metalworkers' and builders' unions struck for better wages and improved working conditions. Other Winnipeg union workers, including police officers, firefighters, and telephone and telegraph operators, joined them on May 15, swelling the numbers of strikers to some 30 000, thus enabling them virtually to close down the city. To provide essential services and to regulate the strike, the organizers created a central strike committee. Business and government officials saw this committee, with its power to dictate what went on in the city, as the beginnings of a "Bolshevik uprising." They countered by creating the Citizens' Committee of 1000, an anti-strike organization. Meanwhile, sympathy strikes of varying degrees of success broke out from Prince Rupert, British Columbia, to Sydney, Nova Scotia.

Fearing that the strike would spread to other centres, the federal government intervened. Arthur Meighen, the minister of justice and minister of the interior, and Gideon Robertson, acting minister of labour, arrived in Winnipeg to assess the situation. They came already convinced that the strike was a conspiracy. Meighen described the strike leaders as "revolutionists of varying degrees and types, from crazy idealists down to ordinary thieves, with the better part, perhaps, of the latter type."

On the night of June 16, Meighen ordered the Royal North-West Mounted Police to arrest ten of the Winnipeg strike leaders, along with labour newspaper editors, including J.S. Woodsworth, and some returned soldiers. In protest, the strikers organized a silent parade on Saturday, June 21. Violence erupted, and the mayor of Winnipeg called in the Mounties to disperse the crowd. The confrontation saw one man killed and another wounded and many others injured. "Bloody Saturday," as it became known, ended with the dispersal of the workers and the establishment of military control of the city. The strike collapsed. On June 26, the strike committee called off the strike, without the workers having gained any of their objectives. The strike did convince them, however, that they must send their own labour representatives to Parliament—individuals such as the social reformer J.S. Woodsworth, who had edited their strike paper, and who would be elected to Parliament as a labour MP for Winnipeg in the federal election of 1921.

WHERE HISTORIANS DISAGREE

The Winnipeg General Strike

Canadian labour and working-class historians agree on the importance of the Winnipeg General Strike of 1919, but on very little else. Initially, the historiography reflected the opposing ideological perspectives of the two sides at the time: the strike opponents seeing it as a revolution aimed at creating a Soviet-style regime in Canada, its supporters seeing it as a legitimate tool by which workers could obtain collective bargaining to secure better wages and working conditions.

Historian D.C. Masters wrote the first scholarly study, *The Winnipeg General Strike*. He emphasized the British background of the strike leaders so as to reinforce the legitimacy of the strike within the British democratic tradition and denied any connection between the strike and the One Big Union (OBU) (often seen as an attempt to create a working-class solidarity as a prelude to a Bolshevik-style revolution). He also challenged those who saw the strike as a spontaneous uprising, claiming "it came at the end of a series of controversies which had raged in a crescendo since at least 1917." Thus, he concluded that "there was no seditious conspiracy and that the strike was what it purported to be, an effort to secure the principle of collective bargaining."[1]

In contrast, sociologist S.D. Clark emphasized the importance of the One Big Union in his introduction to D.C. Masters's study, which was part of a series under Clark's general editorship. Clark saw the OBU, along with the Progressive party among western farmers, as "expressions of protest against eastern dominance ... in the tradition of American frontier radicalism."[2] In this respect, Clark concluded, "the movement was revolutionary"—ironically, a direct contradiction to the conclusion that Masters, whose book Clark was introducing, had drawn!

Historian David Bercuson provided the first comprehensive study of the general strike in *Confrontation at Winnipeg*. He traced the roots of the strike back to labour unrest in the city in 1906, if not to the turn of the century. The massive influx of immigrants came at a time of major social and industrial changes that turned

Winnipeg into a city sharply divided along class lines. Bercuson denied that the strikers were revolutionaries; instead they were striking for legitimate working-class concerns. But, he argued, the fact that they failed to achieve their objectives set back "the cause of labour for at least another generation."[3] Fellow labour historian Irving Abella concurred. "Labour's trauma started at Winnipeg in 1919," he wrote. "With the suppression of the Winnipeg General Strike ... the rapid demise of organized labour in Canada began."[4]

In *Winnipeg 1919: The Strikers' Own History of the Winnipeg General Strike*, historian Norman Penner disagreed with this assessment of the strike's aftermath. To Penner, the strike was above all a political struggle for recognition and rights, and from this perspective, the epic event was "a watershed in the evolution of Canada." "[F]or more than a year," he wrote, "the Winnipeg General Strike and the trials of its leaders kept the labour movement in a constant state of agitation and turmoil which succeeded in translating the economic struggle into a political victory.... Hence the Winnipeg General Strike must be seen as part of the cumulative impact of labour on Canadian life, a constant force which accounts for labour's strength and status in Canada today."[5]

Bercuson introduced a new issue into the debate in an article that examined the strike in the context of the larger issue of western labour radicalism.[6] He argued that western workers were more radical than elsewhere in the country because of unique western frontier conditions, including immigrants who came with utopian dreams of a better lifestyle, only to find themselves up against ruthless and repressive industrialists who thwarted their hopes. Failed expectations, Bercuson argued, were a sure cause for radicalism.

He concluded that the Canadian western industrial frontier bred class consciousness and radical working-class attitudes rather than equality and harmony.

Labour historian Greg Kealey vehemently disagreed with Bercuson's theory that the West was more radical than the rest of the country. Also, Kealey questioned Bercuson's implication that the Winnipeg General Strike could only have occurred in Winnipeg, the most urban of societies. Kealey pointed out that that year was punctuated by strikes and labour unrest throughout the country; in fact, labour unrest in Canada in 1919 was really part of an international working-class solidarity. He went on to argue as well that the strike was part of "larger structural changes in capitalist organization on both a national and international scale."[7] Seen from this wider perspective, the strike was not a failure, but only a momentary defeat before labour emerged even stronger in the move toward industrial unionism in the 1940s.

Bercuson dismissed Kealey's argument in the course of a historiographical chapter appearing in a revised edition of *Confrontation at Winnipeg*. He claimed that evidence of numerous strikes and/or revolts across the country did not constitute proof of working-class revolt. Few of these strikes were "politically motivated and those that were—the Vancouver general strike, for example—were dismal failures." Nor had Kealey proven that the strikers were consciously trying to overthrow capitalism. Kealey's essay, he claimed, was "little more than pamphleteering. He is rallying the revolutionary troops; he is certainly not advancing scholarship." Then Bercuson criticized Marxist history in general as reading back into the past the present dreams of workers. In the case of the Winnipeg General Strike, there was no evidence of any connection whatever between the strike and the rise of industrial unionism in the 1940s, and "only the most slender thread connecting the strike to the rise of the CCF."[8] As for the significance of the Winnipeg General Strike in Canadian history, it lay in "its unique occurrence that took place for particular reasons and which had specific consequences" and not for some "hidden inner meaning" found only in the minds of historians.

Bryan Palmer entered the debate to argue that the significance of the strike lay in the fact that it reflected both "the continuity of class struggle and the changes that had taken place as a consequence of the twentieth-century conditions of monopoly capital, state intervention, and labour market segmentation.[9] Craig Heron agreed with those labour historians who saw the strike as only one of a series of strikes between 1917 and 1925 in industrial centres across the country, where "workers formed their own organizations, marched off the job in record numbers, engaged in defiant acts of solidarity, and made bold new demands."[10] He urged labour historians to study the ethnic and gender component of workers' revolts.

The debate on what happened in Winnipeg in 1919 and its consequences continues. Clearly, though, the strike remains the best-known example of a general strike in Canadian history.

1 D.C. Masters, *The Winnipeg General Strike* (Toronto: University of Toronto Press, 1950), pp. 127, 134.

2 S.D. Clark, "Introduction" to Masters, *The Winnipeg General Strike*, p. viii.

3 David Bercuson, *Confrontation at Winnipeg* (Montreal/Kingston: McGill-Queen's University Press, 1974), p. 176.

4 Irving Abella, "Introduction" to *On Strike: Six Key Labour Struggles in Canada, 1919–1949*, ed. by Irving Abella (Toronto: James Lewis & Samuel Publishers, 1974), p. xii.

5 Norman Penner, *Winnipeg 1919: The Strikers' Own History of the Winnipeg General Strike*, 2nd ed. (Toronto: James Lorimer, 1975), pp. xxiii, vii–viii.

6 D.J. Bercuson, "Labour Radicalism and the Western Industrial Frontier: 1897–1919," *Canadian Historical Review* LVIII, 2 (June 1977): 154–75.

7 Gregory Kealey, "1919: The Canadian Labour Revolt," *Labour/Le Travail* 13 (Spring 1984): 15.

8 Bercuson, *Confrontation at Winnipeg*, rev. ed. (Montreal/Kingston: McGill-Queen's University Press, 1990), pp. 202, 205.

9 Bryan Palmer, *Working-Class Experience: Rethinking the History of Canadian Labour, 1880–1991* (Toronto: McClelland & Stewart, 1993), p. 180.

10 Craig Heron, "Introduction" to *The Workers' Revolt in Canada, 1917–1925*, ed. by Craig Heron (Toronto: University of Toronto Press, 1998), p. 4.

New Postwar Political Leaders

Beginning in 1919, new men replaced veteran national leaders from the prewar era in the two major parties. William Lyon Mackenzie King succeeded Wilfrid Laurier, who died in February 1919, as Liberal leader, while Arthur Meighen became the Conservative leader and acting prime minister after Robert Borden's resignation in July 1920.

The Liberals chose King at a leadership convention, the first in the country's history, in August 1919. King's loyalty to Laurier during the conscription crisis put him in good favour in the party, especially in Quebec. As well, King appeared to represent change. Grandson of

"Bloody Saturday," June 21, 1919, a violent confrontation that occurred between peaceful marchers and the Mounties and special police during the Winnipeg General Strike. Note the burning streetcar.

Source: David Miller Collection/Library and Archives Canada/C-33392.

William Lyon Mackenzie, leader of the Rebellion of 1837 in Upper Canada, he saw himself as a reformer. After graduating from the universities of Toronto, Chicago, and Harvard, with a Ph.D. in political economy from the latter university, he first served as deputy minister of labour. Then in 1908, shortly after his election to the House of Commons, he became Laurier's minister of labour. Defeated in the election of 1911, King returned to the United States to work for the Rockefeller Foundation as a labour conciliator. On the basis of his experiences in the civil service and in industrial relations he wrote *Industry and Humanity* (1918), a discussion of the labour question in Canada. Although convoluted and moralistic, the book did address the pressing problem in the postwar era of the impact of industrialism on society. It established King as an authority on contemporary social and economic issues, and assisted in his winning the leadership of the Liberal party.

The Conservatives met in caucus, rather than in convention, to choose Arthur Meighen as Borden's successor in July 1920. Meighen had attended the University of Toronto at the same time as King. Upon graduation, Meighen moved west to Portage la Prairie, Manitoba, to practise law. He entered federal politics in the election of 1908, the same year that his future rival, King, was first elected. Meighen, an outstanding parliamentary debater, became solicitor general in 1913 and minister of the interior in 1917.

Meighen had, however, by the time he gained leadership of the party, become identified with several of the Conservative and, after 1917, the Union government's controversial policies. He had drafted the conscription bill, which lost him support in Quebec and among farmers in English-speaking Canada. Farm youth, who had been exempt from conscription immediately before the election of 1917, suddenly became eligible after its passage. Meighen also introduced the Wartime Elections Act, which denied the vote to Canadians who had emigrated from enemy countries after 1902—thus losing him part of the ethnic vote. In 1919, he intervened against the workers in the Winnipeg General Strike, angering this political group. That the Conservative caucus still chose Meighen as their leader attests to his influence in the party, but also reveals the party's loss of touch with political reality.

These two leaders had completely opposite approaches to politics. King sought the road of least resistance and the middle path of compromise. To him, right answers did not exist in politics, only answers that seemed better because they offended fewer people. As a result he often spoke in ambiguities and in generalities. Meighen, by contrast, stated his position clearly and unequivocally. He upheld principles over compromise and believed that Canadians should be made to see the truth as he saw it. To him, every problem had a solution, and he clearly articulated solutions often without regard for the possible political repercussions. Each man despised the other.

Regional Protest: The Maritime Rights Movement and the Progressives

In 1920, both new party leaders faced the problem of regional protest movements in eastern and western Canada. In eastern Canada, the Maritime Rights movement arose in an effort to obtain greater Maritime regional voice in national politics, while in the West, farmers created their own third party, the Progressive party, to deal with regional complaints.

The Maritime Rights Movement

In the 1920s, Maritimers witnessed a dramatic decline in their region's influence in Confederation. Politically, their number of seats in the House of Commons fell by one-quarter (to 31) between 1882 and 1921, as a result of the relative depopulation of the Maritimes, as thousands left the region in search of work. Given that the size of the House of Commons increased substantially during this period, as other regions grew in population, the percentage drop was even greater. Economically, manufacturing companies in the region reestablished themselves in the larger markets of central Canada in order to become more competitive. Both Canadian Car and Foundry of Amherst, Nova Scotia and the Maritime Nail Company of Saint John, New Brunswick, for example, transferred operations to Montreal in 1921.

A decline in demand for Cape Breton coal and steel hurt that regional industry. The conversion to oil for heating and power had lost markets for Cape Breton's coal. Shipbuilding also went into decline in the Maritimes as Canada competed with Britain and the United States for international sales. The vital Canadian rail market for steel rails collapsed when railway construction ceased in the postwar era. Unemployment became widespread in Cape Breton's heavy-steel industry. The British Empire Steel Company (BESCO), created from a merger of Nova Scotia's coal, steel, and shipbuilding industries, verged on bankruptcy. It responded by attempting to cut miners' and steelworkers' wages. This touched off in 1921 one of the most intense labour disputes in Maritime history. The provincial government had to call in troops to keep order in New Waterford, Cape Breton Island.

The Maritimes also suffered from tariff reductions throughout the 1920s that had formerly protected its industries. A rise in freight rates, of 200 percent or more, on the Intercolonial Railway equally hurt the region's economy. When the Canadian government nationalized the Intercolonial Railway as part of the Canadian National Railways (CNR), it moved the Intercolonial's head office from Moncton, New Brunswick to Montreal. The railway thus ceased to promote regional interests and became part of a national system.

Individually the Maritime provinces seemed powerless to stem the economic decline, but Maritime leaders believed that collectively their chances would be better. A.P. Paterson, a grocer from Saint John, New Brunswick, led a group of influential business and professional people in launching the Maritime Rights movement. He offered a rationale for the movement in a pamphlet, *The True Story of Confederation*, in which he put forward his version of the compact theory of Confederation. He argued that all Canadians should bear the extra economic costs experienced by any region as a result of its disadvantageous geographical location. Convinced that a study of history would reinforce his argument, Paterson helped to fund the establishment of a department of history at the University of New Brunswick.

The Maritime Rights movement demanded increased federal subsidies for the Maritime provinces, more national and international trade through the ports of Halifax and Saint John, and improved tariff protection to strengthen the region's steel and coal industries. The movement's demand for a tariff increase put the Maritimes in opposition to the Prairies that wanted a lower tariff. By deciding to work for change through the traditional two-party system rather than through a third party, the Maritime Rights movement differed from the prairie Progressive movement.

"*Wooing the West.*" *Cartoonist Donald McRitchie echoes the Maritimers' complaints that the Mackenzie King government favoured the West's regional demands over their own. From the* Halifax Herald, *October 3, 1925.*

Source: Reprinted with permission from The Halifax Herald Ltd.

In the election campaign of 1921, the movement pressed Maritime Liberal candidates to swear that if elected they would "advocate and stand by Maritime rights first, last and all the time." Although taking this pledge helped the federal Liberals to win all but six of the Maritime constituencies, the Maritime members of Parliament could not keep their promises. Mackenzie King's Liberal minority government depended too much on Prairie support to be able to cater to Maritime needs, and especially to raise the tariff.

Disillusioned, Maritime voters switched to the Conservatives in the next federal election in 1925, giving the party all but three of the 31 seats. Unfortunately for Maritimers, the Liberals returned to power in 1926. King diffused the Maritime Rights movement by establishing a royal commission to investigate the group's complaints. The Duncan Commission (headed by British jurist Sir Arthur Rae Duncan) recommended major changes for the Maritimes, such as a 20 percent reduction in all rail rates, aid to the steel and coal industries, and increased federal subsidies. The Liberal government, however, ended up making only minor changes. In the meantime, the Maritime Rights movement had disbanded.

The Progressive Movement

At the turn of the century, western farmers attacked the two traditional parties for neglecting western demands. They wanted reduced freight rates comparable to those in central Canada, an end to the eastern-owned grain-elevator companies' monopoly of the grain trade, an increase in the Canadian Pacific Railway's boxcar allotment for grain trade, a railway to Hudson Bay to rival the CPR, and most of all, a reduction in the tariff.

During the Laurier era (1896–1911), western farmers had gained some of their demands. The Liberal government passed the Crow's Nest Pass Agreement in 1897, by which the CPR reduced eastbound freight rates on grain and flour and westbound rates on a list of manufactured goods. In return, the CPR obtained a government subsidy to build a branch line from Lethbridge through the Crow's Nest Pass to Nelson, British Columbia. The new line enabled the CPR to exploit southern Alberta's and British Columbia's mining fields. Ottawa also passed the Manitoba Grain Act in 1900, which improved grain storage at loading platforms and warehouses. Then, in 1902, in the famous Sintaluta case, named after the town in Saskatchewan where the legal challenge arose, the Territorial Grain Growers' Association won its fight against the CPR for failure to provide adequate boxcars for grain shipment at peak periods.

These victories still left the western farmers' fundamental problem unresolved. The same economic structure—most notably the tariff, which for western farmers symbolized the inequity of Confederation—remained in place. Farmers resented having to buy their agricultural implements and materials in a closed, protected market and to sell their wheat in an open, competitive one. The tariff, they felt, worked against their best interest, and they demanded that Parliament repeal it. After the Liberals' defeat in 1911 on the question of reciprocity with the United States, many farmers talked openly of creating a third party.

Then the war intervened. Out of loyalty, farmers rallied behind the traditional parties. With the election of a "non-partisan" Union government in 1917, farmers hoped that it would remove the tariff. When it failed to do so, Thomas Crerar, a Manitoba farmer, one-time president of the Grain Growers' Grain Company and minister of agriculture in the Union government, resigned from the cabinet in June 1919. Nine other western Unionist MPs followed. They formed the nucleus of a new National Progressive party.

Farmer candidates did well in the provincial elections held immediately after the war. In Ontario, where rural depopulation posed a serious problem, the dissident United Farmers of Ontario won the election of 1919, much to their surprise. Neither the premier, E.C. Drury, a

Arch Dales's cartoon in the Grain Growers' Guide *in 1915 conveys western farmers' views of Canada's political and economic reality.*

Source: Glenbow Archives, Calgary, Canada/NA 3055-24.

farmer from Simcoe County directly north of Toronto, nor most of his party members had had any previous legislative experience. In Alberta, in the provincial election of 1921, the United Farmers of Alberta (UFA) swept out the incumbent Liberal party, which had been in office since 1905. The women's section of the UFA—the United Farm Women of Alberta (UFWA)—under their leader, Irene Parlby, helped the UFA win the election. The UFA won considerable support in southern Alberta, where farmers experienced extreme drought conditions, as bad as they would experience during the Great Depression of the 1930s. In Manitoba, a "Progressive" group of United Farmers formed the government in 1922 under John Bracken.

The Progressives also ran farmer candidates in many constituencies across the country in the 1921 federal election. The results of that election revealed the political divisions within the country. No party secured a majority, and the three largest parties—the Liberals, Conservatives, and Progressives—each held the majority of its seats in one or two regions of the country only, with a very poor showing elsewhere. The incumbent prime minister Arthur Meighen suffered a humiliating defeat by winning only 50 seats, two-thirds of them in Ontario. Mackenzie King and the Liberals won 116 seats, two short of a majority. They won every Quebec riding and did well in the Maritimes, but west of the Ottawa River held only 26 seats. The Progressives won an amazing 65 seats. They swept the West, winning 39 of the 56 seats, and also gained a significant 24 in Ontario, but the new party had no seats in Quebec and just one in the Maritimes. Five independents were elected, of whom two agreed to work together to represent labour interests. At the opening of the parliamentary session, Alberta's William Irvine informed the House of Commons: "I wish to state that Mr. Woodsworth is the leader of the labour group … and I am the group." For the first time in Canadian history, the Canadian public elected a House of Commons divided along regional lines.

The Progressives in Decline

Despite its impressive political strength, the Progressive party was weakened by a split between a Manitoba-based wing under Crerar and an Alberta-based wing under Henry Wise Wood, an American populist farmer who came to Alberta in 1905 and became president of the United Farmers of Alberta (UFA) in 1916. Crerar wanted the Progressives to act as a pressure group to force the minority Liberal government to implement policies favourable to farmers. He hoped the Progressives would vote in unison, in essence as a party. Wood, in contrast, seeing political parties as inherently evil, wanted to abolish them altogether, in favour of "group government" based on all occupational groups in society. Wood argued that society naturally divided into several economic interest groups, of which the farmers constituted one—the largest on the Prairies. If each group obtained representation in Parliament, the laws passed would reflect the interests of all rather than those of the particular group that happened to control the party. In this way, group cooperation would replace party competition.

Unable to resolve their differences, the divided Progressives proved politically ineffective. They declined the role of official opposition even though, as the second-largest party in the House of Commons, they warranted it. Then, in 1922, Crerar resigned as leader, claiming he could not work with Wood. Robert Forke, Crerar's successor, had no better luck at uniting the party. One of his alleged followers commented that Forke "does not control one Progressive vote other than his own, and he is not always sure about that."

The divisions revealed the Progressives as little more than a loose federation of regional groups with insubstantial roots in British Columbia, Quebec, and the Maritimes, and with deep divisions within their two regions of strength—the Prairies and Ontario. The party continued to lose political strength throughout the 1920s. By the election of 1930, they had become a spent force.

In many respects, the Progressives attempted the impossible: to base a party solely on farmers at a time of rural depopulation. They wanted to preserve the family farm, to uphold rural values, and to ensure the political dominance of agricultural interests in an increasingly urban and industrial society. Still, the spirit of the Progressives lived on in the philosophy of populism and in the tradition of western protest. Two new western-Canada-based parties in the 1930s—the Co-operative Commonwealth Federation and the Social Credit movement—succeeded them.

The Election of 1925

From 1921 until 1925, Mackenzie King's minority government ruled precariously, relying on the support of the moderate Progressives. To win over the Progressives, King's Liberal government gradually reduced tariffs and restored the preferential freight rates contained in the Crow's Nest Pass Agreement of 1897, suspended during the war years. In terms of other legislation, however, the Liberals did little. Historians John Thompson and Allen Seager note that "it is impossible to point to a single conspicuous legislative achievement between 1922 and 1925,"[1] but in fairness to King on the tariff issue, it must be acknowledged that he had difficulty trying to reconcile the anti-tariff views of the Progressives and the pro-tariff position of the Maritime Rights movement.

The Liberals lost heavily in the election of 1925. Their numbers fell from 116 to 99 in a House of Commons with 245 members. The prime minister lost his seat, as did eight other cabinet ministers. Only in Quebec did the Liberals retain their numbers. The Conservatives more than doubled their number of seats, to 116, doing exceptionally well in the Maritimes and in Ontario. The Progressives, divided into moderate and radical wings, saw their strength decline by almost two-thirds, to 24 seats.

The King–Byng Affair

Despite his party's setback, King was determined to stay in office, believing he could win enough support from the moderates among the Progressives to win a loss-of-confidence vote. In the throne speech, King made further concessions to westerners by promising a farm-loan program, the immediate completion of a rail link from the prairies to Hudson Bay, the transfer of the natural resources of the three Prairie provinces to their own control, and tariff revisions. To gain the support of J.S. Woodsworth and his followers, King promised an old-age pension plan.

The situation looked encouraging for the Liberals until a customs department scandal broke. Civil servants had received payoffs for allowing liquor smuggling into the United States, where prohibition remained in force. The Progressives, champions of purity in government, could no longer support the Liberals.

Realizing that his government faced certain defeat, King decided to circumvent normal parliamentary procedure. He asked the governor general, Lord Byng, to dissolve Parliament and call an election before a loss-of-confidence vote could be taken in the House. The prime minister had the constitutional right to make such a request, but the governor general, Lord Byng, equally had the right to refuse it—and he did. King promptly resigned as prime minister and announced to a surprised House of Commons on Monday, June 28, that the country was without a government. The governor general then asked Meighen, as leader of the opposition, to form a government. Meighen agreed. The new Conservative government lasted only three days before being defeated by a single vote, giving Meighen the dubious honour of presiding over the shortest-lived government since Confederation. Now, the governor general had no choice but to dissolve Parliament and call the election that he had denied King a few days earlier.

In the 1926 election, King maintained that the governor general had acted unconstitutionally. By refusing to take the advice of his elected representative, he had tried to reduce Canada "from the status of a self-governing Dominion to the status of a Crown Colony." King's strategy worked; it enabled him to sidestep the customs scandal, which Meighen claimed was the real issue in the election. The collapse of the Progressives allowed the Liberals to make substantial gains in the West. New promises to Ontario and the Maritimes ensured greater success there too. In this way, King won his first majority government.

From Colony to Nation

In the decade from 1919 to 1929, Canada made important advancement to autonomy from Great Britain. Prime minister Robert Borden took the first steps along the road from colony to nation in the immediate postwar era. It was Mackenzie King, however, who made the greatest advancements.

Immediate Postwar Advancements

Prime Minister Robert Borden was determined to ensure that Canada benefited from its major contribution to the war through enhanced national status. First he pressed for dominion representation in the British empire delegation at the Paris Peace Conference of 1919, which met to settle the war. The United States questioned why Canada should be involved in the settlement at all, until it was pointed out by the Canadian delegates that Canada had lost more men than the United States in the war. The Big Five (Britain, the United States, France, Italy, and Japan) wanted to make the important decisions, with the "lesser states" involved only in decisions directly affecting them. Borden found this unacceptable, and he won representation for Canada as a power in its own right at the Paris Peace Conference, in addition to its collective representation as a member of the British empire delegation.

Borden also insisted on Canada's right to membership in the League of Nations' General Assembly as well as eligibility for membership in the governing council of the new international body. Once in the League of Nations, however, Canada wanted to limit its commitment. It opposed article 10 of the league's charter, the heart of its collective security system, which bound members to come to the aid of other league members in times of attack. Borden feared that this agreement would commit Canadians to involvement in world disputes that were of no interest to them. (In the end, article 10 remained in place.)

After 1921, King's Liberal government made significant advances in foreign policy. He sought to avoid commitments abroad that might force Canada into imperial wars. To achieve this objective, King delegated himself minister of external affairs and appointed O.D. Skelton, a Queen's University political economist whose outlook on foreign affairs complemented his own, as his undersecretary of state for external affairs, a position Skelton held until his death in 1941.

King's government reduced military expenditures and the size of the Canadian armed forces in the early 1920s. Along with the other Western democracies, Canada consistently opposed any attempt to strengthen the military aspects of the League of Nations. Canada, it might be said, was in the league but not of the league. Frequently, Canadian delegates, with King's support, reminded fellow league members of the hundred years of peaceful relations between Canada and the United States. "We think in terms of peace," Senator Dandurand told the league assembly, "while Europe, an armed camp, thinks in terms of war." Canadians, he went on to say, "live in a fire-proof house, far from inflammable material. A vast ocean separates us from Europe." The implication was that Canada could, and should, be isolationist.

The Chanak Crisis and the Halibut Treaty

As an isolationist, King reacted negatively to British attempts to establish a common imperial foreign policy. The test case became the Chanak crisis. Under the Treaty of Sèvres, one of the treaties ending World War I, the British government agreed to maintain troops in Chanak, Turkey, to ensure the neutrality of the Dardanelles, the strategic straits linking the Black Sea to the Mediterranean. In 1922, Turkish nationalists attempted to oust British troops from the region.

British leaders appealed for a concerted imperial response. King replied that only the Canadian Parliament could decide Canadian participation. Parliament happened not to be in session, and he was in no hurry to summon it. In contrast, opposition leader Arthur Meighen, did not mince words. "Ready, aye, ready we stand by you" should have been Canada's answer, he claimed. By the time Parliament met, the crisis had passed. The Liberal government's refusal of automatic support in the Chanak crisis ended the attempt on Britain's part to define a common imperial policy.

The Halibut Treaty of 1923, a Canadian–American agreement relating to fishing rights on the Pacific coast, became the next step on the road to greater Canadian autonomy. By tradition, only agents of the British government signed treaties affecting the dominions. King resented this "badge of colonialism" and decided to use the treaty to assert Canada's diplomatic independence. He arranged for Ernest Lapointe, minister of marine and fisheries, to be the sole signatory for Canada. The British reluctantly consented, fearing that opposition would prompt Canada to establish its own diplomatic relations with Washington, which would lead to even greater disruption.

The Balfour Declaration

King and the leaders of other dominions now sought a formal proclamation that would recognize their equality with Britain. That came with the Balfour Declaration, signed at the Imperial Conference of 1926. It recognized the dominions as "autonomous communities within the British empire, equal in status, in no way subordinate to one another in any respect of their domestic or external affairs, though united by a common allegiance to the Crown, and freely associated as members of the British Commonwealth of Nations."

In keeping with its recognized equality, Canada established legations or embassies overseas. In 1927, Ottawa opened a legation in Washington, and the United States opened one in Ottawa. Canada also exchanged representatives with Paris and Tokyo in 1928. Britain posted a high commissioner in Ottawa, who henceforth replaced the governor general as the British government's representative in Canada. Canada had already had a high commissioner in London since 1884.

The Statute of Westminster

The final step to securing full Canadian autonomy occurred in 1931 with the signing of the Statute of Westminster. This act prohibited the British Parliament from declaring any law passed by the Canadian Parliament as being *ultra vires*, or unconstitutional, except for laws amending the British North America Act. Canada insisted on continued British approval for these laws because of the failure of the federal and provincial governments to agree on an amending formula among themselves. Some constitutional authorities have viewed the Statute of Westminster as Canada's equivalent of the American Declaration of Independence because it made Canada constitutionally independent of Britain, except in regard to any laws amending the BNA Act. Where it differed, however, was the means: by negotiation rather than by revolution. The Statute of Westminster also continued to recognize Canada's, and the other dominions', allegiance to

Britain through a common sovereign. While the act captured over a decade of moves by Canada to assert its autonomy from Great Britain, it did not lead to Canadian independence.

The Economics of Adjustment

Instability marked the Canadian economy in the 1920s. A volatile international situation and, within Canada, a transition from the old staple economy of fish, timber, and wheat to a new resource economy of pulp and paper, mining, and consumer production meant adjustment. In the first two years of the decade Canada faced a serious business depression. This was followed by a couple of years of slow growth before a five-year boom, beginning in 1925.

The postwar world economy shifted dramatically. Weakened by war, Britain no longer continued as the financial and economic world leader; it devalued its pound sterling. In contrast, the buoyant American economy increased the value of the American dollar. For Canada, the transition proved especially difficult because of its traditional dependency on British markets for trade and on British financial institutions for investment money. Within a brief decade, beginning in 1914, British investment fell to less than 46 percent of the total foreign investment in Canada. In contrast, American investment increased to 51 percent. "Never again," economic historians Kenneth Norrie and Douglas Owram write, "would the mother country come close to the United States in its investment in Canada."[2]

Canadians had to adjust to the differing approach of American, as opposed to British, investors. The British preferred indirect investment in the form of bonds and debentures, whereas American investors favoured equity investment (purchasing common shares) and direct control through branch plants. At the time, few Canadians questioned American economic intervention, as they welcomed American investment of any kind. Canadians also increased substantially their exports to the United States. In 1923, for the first time, Canadians exported more to the United States than to Britain.

During this transition and as a result of the postwar depression, a number of Canadian banks and companies closed or underwent restructuring to avoid collapse. The Home Bank, with its 71 branches across the country, folded in 1923. The Merchant Bank, the Bank of Ottawa, and the Bank of Hamilton sought mergers or were taken over by more stable institutions to avoid similar failures. (This instability benefited the larger banks, because people looked to them for sound investment.) As well, many companies, nearly 4000 in 1922, went bankrupt. Unemployment in the primary sector rose substantially.

A Brief Economic Boom

By 1925, the economy had rebounded. The booming American economy and an easing of U.S. protectionist policies increased demand for the traditional Canadian staples of wheat and lumber, as well as the newer staples of pulp and paper and base metals. As freight rates and tariffs declined, prices rose. Farmers increased their hectarages of wheat production and established wheat pools, beginning in 1923, to market abundant crops. Annually, western farmers hired more than 50 000 harvesters from eastern Canada. The crop in 1928 proved to be the largest on record—567 million bushels. Prices also remained high during these years. Vancouver benefited from the wheat boom as prairie farmers increasingly shipped their wheat via Vancouver and the Panama Canal to Europe. By 1925, Vancouver had six storage elevators with a capacity of 6.9 million bushels.

This time the wheat boom of the mid-1920s did not lead to another era of expansion for wheat farmers; rather, it signalled the final phase of the long cycle of nation building based on the wheat economy. Canadian wheat farmers now had to compete with other wheat-growing regions, such as Argentina, Australia, and the Soviet Union, for a shrinking world market as wheat consumption declined.

Pulp and paper became Canada's leading new export. At the beginning of the 1920s, paper mills in Canada produced 938 million tons of newsprint; by the end of the decade, this production increased more than threefold to 2981 million tons—enough to print 40 billion newspapers a year. Much of the demand came from the United States, where mass-produced daily newspapers needed cheap newsprint. American branch-plant mills in Canada produced most of the newsprint. Several factors contributed to this decision: the availability of inexpensive pulpwood; cheap hydroelectric power; good transportation facilities; and lower American import duties. Politics also played a part; provincial governments either placed an embargo on the export of pulpwood from Crown lands within their borders or imposed a stumpage charge on the number of trees cut, an amount that declined if the producers made the pulp in Canada.

Along with increased production came consolidation. By the end of the decade, three giant companies—International, Abitibi, and Canadian Power and Paper—controlled over half of the pulp production, while the next three largest companies controlled another quarter. Americans owned more than one-third of Canada's pulp production.

Mining followed a similar pattern. After a sluggish period in the early 1920s, it revived as a result of an American demand for Canadian-based metals to produce such consumer goods as automobiles, radios, and electrical appliances. In Quebec, mineral production increased nearly thirtyfold from 1898 to 1929. Whole new areas, such as Noranda (a name combining the words "North" and "Canada"), Rouyn, Malartic, Val d'Or, and Bourlamaque, opened up with the discovery of new lodes of copper, zinc, lead, and precious metals. In British Columbia, Cominco developed new flotation techniques to mill base metals, which revived a dying industry. In Manitoba, a Canadian–American group, incorporated as Hudson Bay Mining and Smelting, refined the ore at Flin Flon, about 100 km north of The Pas, and at Lynn Lake, still farther north. Ontario benefited greatly from the rich mineral deposits in its northland. The nickel companies in the Sudbury area doubled production during the 1920s, thanks in part to the decision of the Canadian government in 1922 to create nickel coinage. Inco, the International Nickel Company of Canada, controlled more than 90 percent of world production.

Hydroelectric production quadrupled in the mid-1920s, providing power for the pulp and paper industry and for the refineries. This energy source was particularly important for the production of aluminum from bauxite ore, a process that required substantial amounts of electricity. Provincial governments realized the importance of hydroelectric power for industrialization and the high cost involved in building hydroelectric plants. Ontario nationalized private companies and included them in Ontario Hydro. In Quebec, the industry remained in private hands but developed with the provincial government's financial support.

A Revolution in Transportation and Communications

Growth in the primary sector—wheat, timber, and minerals—multiplied markets in the secondary sector. The most spectacular secondary growth occurred in the automotive industry. Next to the United States, Canada became "the most motorized country on the globe." The numbers of cars, trucks, buses, and motorcycles on Canadian roads tripled from 408 000 in 1920 to 1.235 million a decade later, while the total capital investment in the industry more than doubled, from $40 million to $98 million.

Initially, Canada produced its own cars. At one time as many as 70 small companies manufactured, assembled, or sold automobiles in Canada. By the 1920s, this period ended as Canadian companies failed to keep pace with their automated American counterparts, that mass-produced less expensive models. Eventually, the Canadian car manufacturers sold out to the American giants. In 1904, Gordon McGregor of the Walkerville Wagon Works obtained a franchise for Canada and the British empire from the Ford Company of America to establish the Ford Company of Canada. Sam McLaughlin used American technology, expertise, and money to begin producing McLaughlin cars in Oshawa, Ontario, and then sold his company in 1918 to General Motors of America. From 1923 onward, the Canadian branch of General Motors oversaw the production of the entire line of GM models, including Chevrolets and Cadillacs, and sold them throughout Canada and the Commonwealth. Chrysler, the last of the "Big Three" manufacturers to appear in Canada, came when the American automobile tycoon Walter P. Chrysler bought out the ailing Maxwell-Chalmers company of Windsor in 1925 to establish the Chrysler Company of Canada. By the end of the decade, the American "Big Three" manufactured three-quarters of the cars purchased in Canada.

Canadians had already begun, in the words of historian Arthur Lower, to worship "the great god CAR."[3] By the end of the decade, one-quarter of all potential owners had an automobile. The car revolutionized the Canadian landscape as the railway had done 70 years earlier. Roads again became important, and in the cities, paved streets became commonplace. In 1925, Canada had 75 200 km of surfaced roads; by 1930, this had almost doubled (128 000 km). Tire companies and factories emerged to produce tires and spare parts, service stations sprang up, and tourism prospered. The car made it easier to get to vacation areas—where there were roads.

Aviation also expanded greatly in the 1920s. Veteran World War I flying aces, using surplus war planes, opened up the North. They flew geologists and prospectors into remote areas of

Traffic congestion on Toronto's Yonge Street in 1929. Streetcars had to contend with automobiles in ever-increasing numbers.

Source: Library and Archives Canada/RD 1004.

Airplanes sharply reduced travel time. In 1934, travellers from Fort McMurray in northern Alberta to Great Bear Lake in the Northwest Territories could choose between 30 days by steamboat or eight hours by plane.

Source: *Canadian Geographical Journal* 10(5) (May 1935): 241.

the Canadian Shield and provided service to isolated northern settlements. These pilots travelled by visual flying; lacking proper maps, they had to stay at low altitudes to spot familiar landmarks. In 1924, Laurentide Air Services began Canada's first regular air-mail service, into the Quebec gold fields at Rouyn–Noranda. Other companies followed, and for several years the Canadian government permitted each company to print and issue its own postage stamps.

Important communications inventions became popular in the 1920s. The telephone became a standard household item by the 1920s. With party lines, eavesdropping ("rubbernecking," as it was called then) became a national pastime. Radio, the great communications invention of the 1920s, helped to end isolation and loneliness. The first scheduled broadcast in North America took place in Montreal in May 1920, when station XWA (later CFCF) relayed a musical program to a Royal Society of Canada meeting in Ottawa. Others were quick to realize the potential of this new invention. By mid-decade, there were numerous stations (most of them small and low-powered) across the country.

Service Industries

Service industries grew to meet the demand of the new consumer age. Retailing, wholesaling, insurance, and banking needs meant more offices and a vast amount of paperwork. The number of managerial and clerical positions grew to keep pace. Mass production, thanks to improved technology, contributed to lower consumer prices. Effective advertising kept consumer goods in the public mind, heightening the demand. Chain stores became popular, accounting for 90 percent of sales by the end of the decade. Their wide array of material goods appealed to every taste. The Canadian T. Eaton Company competed effectively with such American chain stores as Kresge's, Woolworth's, and Metropolitan. Large supermarkets, such as Safeway, Dominion, Overwaitea, A&P, Loblaws, and IGA, began replacing the small corner-grocery store and offering a larger variety of food items and cheaper prices. Women dominated as retail clerks in these large grocery and department stores, but not at the managerial level.

Disillusionment and the Decline of Reform

The initial euphoria and the hope for world peace following the "war to end wars" died quickly after the armistice. Across the globe many nations, instead of emerging into freedom and liberty, slipped back into tyranny and oppression. The new millennium, embodied in American President Woodrow Wilson's fourteen-point program to ensure world peace forever, never arrived. Canadians' awareness of the failed peace contributed to their disillusionment. On November 12, 1924, the *Varsity*, the student newspaper at the University of Toronto, summarized the Armistice Day address of history professor G.M. Smith, a distinguished soldier and the winner of the Military Cross in the Great War:

> *The idealism of youth, and its enthusiasm in fighting for what they considered a good cause, the optimistic spirit which filled the people during the war and reached its climax when*

the Armistice was signed, all this is shattered by the six years aftermath. The fourteen points became the fourteen disappointments and self-determination has become selfish-determination.

Reform declined, in part because each of the reform movements had achieved many of its goals. By 1921, workers had a higher standard of living and had achieved better recognition from employers. Women had the franchise federally and in most provinces. Prohibitionists had succeeded in eliminating legalized drinking. Educational reformers' achievements included better schools, children staying in school longer, and better-qualified teachers. Yet, in a sense, all these groups had failed in their ultimate objective: a new, regenerated, harmonious, and utopian Canada.

Prohibition and Women's Suffrage

In some instances, a reaction to reform set in. Prohibitionists, for example, saw the provincial temperance acts removed one by one. By the end of the 1920s, government-regulated outlets sold liquor in every province except Prince Edward Island. Ironically, returned soldiers—the very people prohibitionists had used to fight *for* prohibition during the war years—played a large part in ending prohibition, as they demanded legalized drinking.

The women's suffrage movement had obtained the vote, but the electorate returned few women to either federal or provincial governments. Agnes Macphail became the only woman elected in the federal election of 1921 and was Canada's first woman member of Parliament. She served until her defeat in 1940, and then sat for several years in the Ontario legislature as a CCF member. Only one other woman, Martha Black, sat in the House of Commons in the interwar years, representing her husband's Yukon constituency from 1935 to 1940, when he was incapacitated by poor health. Provincially, women did better at entering politics, although the results were a far cry from their expectations. By 1940, only nine women sat in provincial legislatures, all of them in the four western provinces. Mary Ellen Smith of British Columbia held the distinction of being the first woman cabinet minister in the British empire when she was appointed in 1921 as minister without portfolio. However, she held the position for only nine months before resigning. Even the usually optimistic Nellie McClung expressed the disillusionment of the time: "When women were given the vote in 1916–17 … we were obsessed with the belief that we could cleanse and purify the world by law…. But when all was over, and the smoke of battle cleared away, something happened to us. Our forces, so well organized for the campaign, began to dwindle."

Women faced continued discrimination. Not until 1929, for example, were women considered "persons" in the act stipulating eligibility for the Canadian Senate and a variety of other privileged bodies. In the famous "Persons Case," five Alberta women reformers—Emily Murphy, the first woman police magistrate in the British empire; Irene Parlby, who became in 1921 the first woman cabinet minister in Alberta; Nellie McClung, a member of the Alberta legislature; and Henrietta Edwards and Louise McKinney, two suffragists and prohibitionists—succeeded in securing a favourable decision from the Judicial Committee of the Privy Council that women were "persons" and thus eligible for membership in all Canadian legislative bodies.

Urban reform languished in the interwar years, in part because the middle-class group most involved in reform began to move out of the city centres and into the suburbs. Suburbanization occurred at an astonishing rate in the 1920s with the development of tramlines and the increasing popularity of the automobile.

Social gospellers within the mainstream churches retreated during the prosperous 1920s, as churchgoers became more concerned with personal prosperity and individual salvation than with social regeneration. Church reformers within the Methodist, Presbyterian, and Congregationalist churches did succeed in 1925 in creating the United Church of Canada. They hoped that this new church would rejuvenate the reformers' zeal and challenge the secularization of Canadian society. But when the new church did challenge society, it appeared to some as too radical and reform-minded. They left and joined fundamentalist churches that upheld more traditional values and beliefs, or they became members of conservative sects and cults.

L'Action Française

In the 1920s, conservative elements in Quebec's Roman Catholic community reacted to the growing secularization of society. Abbé Lionel Groulx, the editor of *L'Action française*, which had only 5000 subscribers at its peak (but was widely read by nationalist elites), saw the onslaught of urban and industrial society as anathema to everything French Canadians believed in: the church, the family, and the French-Canadian nation. In his journal, Groulx launched an all-out attack—*l'action française*—on those forces that he believed were contributing to the anglicization and Americanization of Quebec.

L'Action française called for greater French-Canadian control of Quebec's modern industrial economy. While contributors to the magazine deplored the economic weakness of French Canadians, most of them still believed that agriculture should be the cornerstone of the French-Canadian economy. They opposed the growing urban migration, especially to Montreal. To *l'action française*, the migration threatened the very existence of the French Canadians as traditionally rural, agricultural people.

Historian Susan Mann summarized the movement's outlook: "Cities bred standardization, homogeneity, and ultimately, they suspected, assimilation."[4] To counter this urbanization, *l'action française* stressed the traditional values of the land, the church, and the nation. Groulx placed a special responsibility on women as guardians of the home and the family. In 1922, *l'action française* flirted with the idea of political independence for Quebec, but it returned by the late 1920s to the position that French Canadians should have more rights within Confederation.

Women in the 1920s

Women made only modest gains in the 1920s. Few had the opportunity for a secondary education; in 1929, only a quarter of the national secondary-school student body were women. Of the few who entered the professions, most became teachers or nurses, while only a handful became physicians, lawyers, or professors, and a very tiny number, engineers. Nursing took on a new importance in the 1920s in light of the tremendous contribution nurses made during the war and the Spanish influenza epidemic that followed it. In 1919, the University of British Columbia offered the first university-degree program in nursing. Similar programs followed at the University of Toronto and McGill University in the 1920s.

Women who worked outside the home in industry or business—20 percent of the labour force in 1929—held traditional female jobs as secretaries, sales clerks in department stores, and domestics. Others worked on assembly lines in textile or tobacco factories, canneries, or fish plants. In these jobs, women earned considerably less than men doing the same job. Economic equality, like political equality, remained an elusive goal for women.

Unions did little to organize working women, even in the female-dominated industries. Seldom did they support women on strike. Some union locals included males and females, but even when unions included women, they usually subordinated their interests to men's. Agreements with employers commonly included lower female wage scales. In some cases, male-dominated unions demanded equal pay for women and men—not to combat discrimination against women but rather to ensure that employers would have no financial reason to replace male employees with females.

Although many farms were becoming more mechanized in the 1920s, the farmhouses remained basic. Prairie farm wives were also expected to help outside the house at critical times of the year, while they continued caring for the children, cooking, cleaning, laundering, and sewing. According to historian Veronica Strong-Boag, prairie women were not "pulling in double harness" but "hauling a double load."[5] Rural reform leaders advocated household-science courses, cooperation, and the use of more household appliances as ways of alleviating the burden.

Urban middle-class women enjoyed a higher standard of living than their rural counterparts. Many benefited from modern labour-saving devices such as refrigerators, electric stoves, and vacuum cleaners, and from such luxuries as electricity and running water. Ironically, these "conveniences" increased the amount of time women spent in the home. In many cases conveniences simply raised the standards expected of women in the home.

A battery of "how to parent" books made child rearing more rigorous and scientific in the 1920s. In some of the books, children were viewed as "little machines" to be scheduled routinely for basic activities of eating, eliminating, and bathing. Dr. Helen McMurchy, chief of the newly created Child Welfare Division in 1919, reminded women

Elsie Hall, class of 1920, first woman graduate of the College of Law, University of Saskatchewan.

Source: College of Law, University of Saskatchewan.

that "being a mother is the highest of all professions and the most extensive of all undertakings." To prepare them for their new role, girls were encouraged to stay in school longer and to concentrate on domestic-science courses. The few women who dared to "break out" and be unconventional—the "flappers"—dressed more freely, smoked in public, and—most daring of all—drank at parties. The birth-control movement began in Vancouver in 1923 with the formation of the Canadian Birth Control League, the idea inspired by the visit of the American birth-control advocate Margaret Sanger. Women, however, had to wait until the 1930s for any birth-control clinics to open.

Social Assistance

Limited social assistance programs prevailed in the 1920s. The Department of Soldiers' Civil Re-establishment, the federal government agency responsible for veterans' affairs, administered military pensions along with retraining and employment programs. However, 80 percent of the applicants were rejected on the grounds that they were physically able to return to their previous employment. Veterans with mental disorders were seldom considered disabled and therefore denied assistance.

In 1925, Mackenzie King's minority Liberal government promised to work with the provinces in a jointly funded program of old-age pensions in return for political support from J.S. Woodsworth and his followers to keep the government in power.

Georgina McKay and friends near Prince Albert, Saskatchewan, each enjoying a smoke. In the 1920s women flaunted smoking cigarettes as a sign of liberation.

Source: Saskatchewan Archives Board/R-A1259.

The government fell before King could fulfill his promise, but he moved on legislation when reelected in 1926. The federal legislation was very restrictive. It provided pensions only for people over 70 whose annual income was no more than $125. Some provinces imposed further restrictions such as applicants having no other assets that could be sold to provide a subsistence income and no relatives to care for them, and were unable to work.

Social work began as a profession in the 1920s. In 1922, the Canadian Welfare Council under the direction of Charlotte Whitton offered one perspective on social work. Its main concern was care of children. Then in 1926, the Canadian Association of Social Workers became the professional body for social workers. Their constitution set out their mission: "to promote professional standards, encourage proper and adequate training, and cultivate an informed public opinion which will recognize the professional and technical nature of social work."

The First Nations People

The experience of the First Nations peoples in the 1920s varied across Canada. In the northern forested areas, the First Nations and Métis suffered greatly when boom prices for furs led to an influx of non-Aboriginal trappers. As well, intensive trapping resulted in a serious depletion in the numbers of beaver. Wage labour, however, partially compensated for the loss of income from trapping, now necessary to buy trade goods and store food. Some First Nations and Métis people worked as tourist guides, in commercial fishing, as miners, railway workers, and loggers. In the south, farming on the reserves declined as heavy expenditures became necessary for the new farm machinery. Among the Iroquois, high-steel rigging, although dangerous work, remained popular and lucrative. On the Pacific coast, First Nations people could obtain jobs in logging and commercial fishing. A number of independent First Nations operators owned and operated gas-powered gillnetters, trollers, and seine boats.

A HISTORICAL PORTRAIT

Onondeyoh (Fred Loft)

Fred Loft, or Onondeyoh ("Beautiful Mountain"), a Mohawk in the Ontario civil service, sought the improvement of the system of education offered to the First Nations. Immediately after World War I, the Mohawk veteran established the League of Indians of Canada, the country's first pan-Indian political association.

Fred Loft was born February 3, 1861, on the Six Nations Reserve near Brantford, Ontario. His parents (who spoke English as well as Mohawk) were devoted Anglicans. Fred attended a local school until the age of 12, when he boarded for a year at the Mohawk Institute, an Indian residential school in Brantford. Bitterly, he remembered the horrific experience: "I recall the times when working in the fields, I was actually too hungry to be able to walk, let alone work…. In winter the rooms and beds were so cold that it took half the night before I got warm enough to fall asleep."

Anxious to get the best education possible, he attended high school in the neighbouring non-Native community of Caledonia. After graduation, he won a scholarship to the Ontario Business College in Belleville. After briefly working as a journalist for a Brantford paper, he obtained a job as an accountant in the bursar's office at the Provincial Lunatic Asylum in Toronto, where he stayed for forty years.

In 1898, the Mohawk civil servant met and married Affa Northcote Geare, a lively, energetic woman of British descent, eleven years younger than he. In 1899, Affa gave birth to twins, one of whom died in 1902. Another daughter was born in 1904. For many years the family depended on Affa for extras. She had a sharp business sense; she bought and sold houses, rented to roomers, and owned stock.

The Lofts had an active life, with season tickets to two Toronto theatres. Fred participated in the Masons and the United Empire Loyalist Association and was active in the militia. Every Sunday he attended church. He also returned regularly to the Six Nations Reserve to visit his family. His daughters spent many summers at the family farm. Unsuccessfully, the Six Nations Council requested the federal government to select him in 1907, and again in 1917, as their superintendent.

As a staunch supporter of Britain, Fred Loft had visited Ontario Indian reserves during World War I to encourage Aboriginal recruitment. Anxious to go overseas himself, he served as an officer in France in the Canadian Forestry Corps.

Upon his return from Europe, the Mohawk veteran founded the League of Indians of Canada. The first annual meetings were held in Ontario, then in Manitoba (1920), Saskatchewan (1921), and Alberta (1922). Problems surfaced immediately. Money was short, and correspondence itself proved difficult. As Fred Loft stated, "The sad want of better schooling is evidenced by the fact that scarcely five percent of the adult population on reserves are capable of corresponding intelligently.... This is a most unfortunate admission to be made after 75 years of school work among Indians of Eastern Canada at least." The Department of Indian Affairs' unrelenting opposition to the league, and Loft's poor health in the early 1930s, further weakened it.

At the time of Fred Loft's death in 1934, the league, apart from its western Canadian branches, had come to a complete stop. But Onondeyoh's attempt to form a pan-Indian political organization in Canada would succeed a generation later: today Canada has the Assembly of First Nations, formerly the National Indian Brotherhood, founded in the 1960s.

The federal government's control over the First Nations reached new heights in the 1920s, particularly in southern Canada. In the North, Treaty Eleven, signed in the Mackenzie Valley in 1921, left First Nations with greater freedom because it did not oblige them to settle on reserves.

Labour in the 1920s

Labour unions faced difficult times in the 1920s, as business leaders attempted to limit trade unions' effectiveness. Wage cuts, industrial consolidation, improved technology, and managerial efficiency all weakened the labour movement. Workers retaliated by staging strikes, many of them ending in physical violence. For example, 22 000 coal miners, mainly in Alberta, walked out on strike in August 1922. In 1923, a confrontation occurred in the coal mines

Fred Loft with his company of First Nation soldiers in the Forestry Corps, Canadian Expeditionary Force, Windsor Park, England, July 1917.

Source: Photo courtesy of the late Affa Loft Matteson, daughter of Fred Loft.

of Nova Scotia. James B. McLachlan, the militant Scottish immigrant worker and socialist who had helped found the Amalgamated Mine Workers of Nova Scotia in 1917, led the strike against BESCO, the leading steel company in the region. "War is on us, class war," he proclaimed in one of his fiery speeches. The company's vice-president replied: "Let them stay out two months or six months, it matters not; eventually they will come crawling back." The company eventually mobilized its security force to break up the strike. The workers won some limited concessions, but a legacy of hatred remained. In most other strikes across the country, strikers failed to improve wages or working conditions. As a result, union membership plummeted by more than one-third by mid-decade, reaching a low of 260 000 members.

Unions were also divided. The conservative Trades and Labor Congress (TLC) continued to favour craft unions and to advocate advancement only through conciliation and government intervention. Thus the TLC refused to back the strikers against BESCO. When Samuel Gompers, the founder of the American Federation of Labor (AFL) and the inspiration behind the TLC, died later that year, McLachlan, invited to the funeral, replied: "Sorry, duties will not permit me to attend, but I heartily approve of the event." In 1927, a new militant All-Canadian Congress of Labour (ACCL) union was established. It favoured industry-wide unions and strike action.

In Quebec, some workers and farmers joined Roman Catholic unions, guided by priests and sanctioned by the church. These unions attempted to isolate their members from the more secular and often socialistic "foreign"—American or English-Canadian—unions. The Confédération des travailleurs catholiques du Canada (CTCC) brought 20 000 workers from a variety of industries and occupations into its organization in 1921. The Union catholique des cultivateurs (UCC) in 1924 had a membership of 13 000 farmers. By the 1930s, the UCC had joined with the clergy to organize farmers' wives and to compete with the state-sponsored Cercles de fermières. Throughout the 1920s, the CTCC and the UCC together never succeeded, however, in attracting much more than one-quarter of the total Quebec union membership.

Cultural Developments

Upper-class cultural life flourished in the 1920s in both English-speaking and French-speaking Canada. Arthur Lismer, one of the Group of Seven artists, later recalled: "After 1919, most creative people, whether in painting, writing or music, began to have a guilty feeling that Canada was as yet unwritten, unpainted, unsung.... In 1920 there was a job to be done." French-Canadian artists, writers, and performers shared the same aspiration, although in their case Quebec tended to be their frame of reference. Popular culture also flourished especially with the advent of radio in the 1920s.

Visual Arts

In English-speaking Canada, the Group of Seven dominated contemporary art. The original members—Frank Carmichael, Lawren Harris, A.Y. Jackson, Frank Johnston, Arthur Lismer, J.E.H. MacDonald, and F.H. Varley—had met before the war. Most had worked for the Toronto commercial-art company Grip, and belonged to the Arts and Letters Club. Artist Tom Thomson was part of this circle of friends, but he drowned in a canoe accident in Algonquin Park in 1917 before the group formed. In the year of his death, he produced *The Jack Pine* and *The West Wind*, two paintings that have become icons of Canadian art, reproduced on stamps, on posters, and in art books. Thomson became an inspiration and patron saint for the Group of Seven, when it formed officially in early 1920.

The first Group of Seven exhibition was held in May 1920. The exhibition catalogue claimed that art must reflect "the spirit of a nation's growth." The Group of Seven believed that "spirit" could best be found in the land—in the trees, rocks, and lakes of the Ontario northland. They depicted the land in brilliant mosaics of bright colours. For the Group of Seven, the Ontario northland symbolized the nation the same way the West did in the American tradition—a mythical land that became a metaphor for the Canadian people. As well, the "North" represented a counterforce to the "South," especially the United States, where urbanization, industrialism, and materialism threatened to undermine the Canadian spirit.

Some art critics at the time denounced the group's paintings as belonging to the "Hot Mush School" and its members as "paint slingers." The Group of Seven thrived on the criticism. It indicated that their art challenged the establishment and broke new ground. The group found a strong supporter in Eric Brown, director of the National Gallery in Ottawa, who selected their paintings to represent Canadian art at the British Empire Exhibition at Wembley in 1924. By the time the Group of Seven disbanded in 1931, their members were, in the words of historian Douglas Cole, "elevated to the status of Canadian cultural heroes and their work enshrined as national icons,"[6] even though their best-known paintings depicted only one region of Ontario, the Algoma district, a section south of the 49th parallel. As well, recently environmental historians have taken the Group of Seven to task for allowing their paintings of wilderness to be used by government officials and commercial tourist companies to promote tourism.

COMMUNITY PORTRAIT

The Arts and Letters Club as a Cultural Community

Founded in 1908, Toronto's Arts and Letters Club brought together writers, architects, musicians, artists, and dramatists, with a minority membership of nonprofessionals "with artistic tastes and inclinations" to promote an appreciation of the arts. The membership, restricted to men, expanded rapidly in the 1910s to comprise a significant number of the Toronto arts community; it also included several wealthy Toronto entrepreneurs, friends of the arts. These entrepreneurs greatly assisted an emerging group of artists, who in 1920 became the "Group of Seven." Art historian Peter Mellen notes that "the friendly atmosphere of the club" provided the members of the Group of Seven "with an opportunity to meet Toronto's wealthy elite, who were to become their first patrons" (p. 19). These entrepreneurs found in the Club a haven from the purely commercial nature of modern Toronto. In the words of Augustus Bridle, a founding member, the Club's president in 1913– 14, and author of *The Story of the Club* (1945), the Club provided for all its members "absolute escape from all that otherwise made Toronto" (p. 10).

The members consciously created a sense of community through the Club's location, its decor, and the members' activities. Members believed that poverty would help to draw them together as a community. Hence, despite the wealth of a number of Club members, they chose very modest locations for their headquarters. Their first locale was a garret next door to the Brown Betty restaurant, which was opposite—not in—the opulent King Edward Hotel. It consisted of one room and a cubbyhole in which to make coffee. Evicted ten months later, Club members moved to the old Assize Court room behind No. 1 Police Station, "the most impressive, inaccessible room in Toronto." Bridle boasted that "just before the inaugural dinner day we had neither gas in the kitchen nor electricity in the hall" (p. 2). Yet the event was a great hit as members rallied in support.

In the 1920s, the Club leased St. George's Hall at 14 Elm Street, where it remains today. According to Bridle, each move heightened the mythical belief in the spirit of community that had prevailed in the previous locale, and made Club members determined to create a similar ambience in the new locale. So the first thing Club members did in their St. George location was to build a "collegiate-gothic fireplace." Then they commissioned Club member artist George Reid to paint a mural panel of the Club's Viking crest on the adjacent wall to the fireplace. The crest had been the work of artist J.E.H. MacDonald, who joined the Club in 1911. It consisted of a "Viking ship with the sails full spread before the rising sun to remind us of the open sea and the great adventure."

Club members performed rituals along medieval lines, drawing examples in particular from "the brotherhood of medieval monks" (p. 39), according to Bridle, believing that in medieval times a sense of community and camaraderie existed that was lacking in modern times. Members also purchased a farm to which they could retreat from the stresses of modern life. Camping and canoeing, and other Club activities, contributed to a life of simplicity and friendship, they believed. As well, Club members got involved in social reform activities in Toronto to enhance the sense of community in the city at large. Of particular importance to members, especially for University of Toronto political economist James Mavor, was the Guild of Civic Art.

Nearly a century after its founding, the Club continues to have a sense of community, but with one notable change: women can now be members. In 1986, the Club finally purchased its current location, St. George's Hall at 14 Elm Street.

FURTHER READING

Augustus Bridle, *The Story of the Club* (Toronto: The Arts & Letters Club, 1945).

Peter Mellen, *The Group of Seven* (Toronto: McClelland and Stewart, 1970).

Charles C.H. Hill, *The Group of Seven: Art for a Nation* (Toronto: McClelland and Stewart, 1995).

Karen Leslie Knutson, "Absolute Escape from All That Otherwise Made Toronto: Antimodernism at the Arts and Letters Club, 1908–1920," MA thesis, Queen's University, 1995.

Arts and Letters Club website, http://www.artsandlettersclub.ca.

In British Columbia, Emily Carr had begun in 1908 to visit First Nations communities along the Pacific coast and in the interior of the province. She painted scenes of their villages, buildings, and totem poles. Unable to support herself by her painting alone, she ran a boarding house in Victoria. In 1927 she made a trip to eastern Canada where she met Lawren Harris and other members of the Group of Seven. Her contact with the group, particularly Lawren Harris, gave a fresh direction to her work. After first viewing Harris's works, she wrote: "Oh, God, what have I seen? Where have I been? Something has spoken to the very soul of me, wonderful, mighty, not of this world."

In 1932, at age 57, Carr launched into the most productive period of her artistic career. She emphasized nature themes over First Nations subjects in her paintings. When she suffered a heart attack in 1937, she turned to writing. Her first book, *Klee Wyck*, described her early painting trips to First Nations communities. It won her the governor general's award for general literature in 1941. Klee Wyck, meaning "Laughing One," was the name given Emily Carr by the Nuu-chah-nulth (formerly known as Nootka) people at Ucluelet on the west coast of Vancouver Island.

On the Prairies, Lionel LeMoine FitzGerald, of Winnipeg, and Illingworth Kerr, from Lumsden, Saskatchewan, captured the region's uniqueness on canvas. In the Maritimes, a group of local artists arranged for their own exhibition and issued their own magazine, *Maritime Art*, which by 1940 had become Canada's first full-fledged art magazine. This Maritime group assisted Jack Humphrey and Miller Brittain, both born and raised in Saint John, New Brunswick, where they spent most of their lives, in becoming internationally recognized Maritime artists.

Sculptors Francis Loring and Florence Wyle, together with Elizabeth Wyn Wood and two male sculptors, established the Sculptors Society of Canada in 1928. Sculptors benefited in the 1920s from the postwar enthusiasm for public memorials.

Literature

A new literary culture emerged in the 1920s. In English-speaking Canada, two new journals appeared to capture and epitomize the cultural renaissance: the *Canadian Forum* and the *Canadian Historical Review*.

Members of the Group of Seven at 1920 luncheon at the Arts and Letters Club. From left to right: Fred Varley, A.Y. Jackson, and Lawren Harris; Barker Fairley, a strong supporter of the Group but not a member; Frank Johnston, Arthur Lismer, and J.E.H. MacDonald. Absent was Frank Carmichael.

Source: Photo by Arthur Goss, The Arts and Letters Club, Toronto.

The West Wind, by Tom Thomson, 1917, one of his best-known paintings. Thomson died in a canoe accident in Algonquin Park in 1917, and thus was not a founding member of the Group of Seven when it formed in 1920. He did, however, serve as an inspiration for the Group.

Source: Art Gallery of Ontario, Toronto. Gift of the Canadian Club of Toronto, 1926.

In the inaugural issue of the *Canadian Forum* in 1920, the editors promised that the journal would "trace and value those developments of arts and letters which are distinctively Canadian." Equally, the *Canadian Historical Review* noted in an article on "The Growth of Canadian National Feeling" in the second issue that the "central fact in Canadian history" has been the evolution of a "national consciousness." The Canadian Authors' Association (CAA), founded in 1921 for the purpose of using literature "to articulate a national identity and to foster a sense of community within the country," aided young English-Canadian writers in publishing their works. The CAA sponsored summer schools and gave literary prizes. These nationalistic journals and organizations reflected the growing political nationalism of the period, as Canada emerged from colony to nation. They also, however, served to counteract the growing Americanization of Canadian culture. Cultural historian Mary Vipond notes: "By 1925 it was estimated that for every domestic magazine sold in Canada, eight were imported from the United States—a total of around fifty million copies per year."[7]

In poetry, E.J. (Ned) Pratt of Newfoundland introduced modernism into Canadian poetry in his *Newfoundland Verse* (1923). A professor of English at Victoria College, University of Toronto, Pratt used familiar Canadian scenes or events, often from his native Newfoundland, as the subjects for his poems and elevated them to mythical proportions. Pratt inspired a younger generation of English-Canadian poets.

Frederick Philip Grove in the early 1920s, rafting on Lake Winnipeg with his daughter, May. He was actually Felix Paul Greve, a German translator and writer who faked his own suicide in 1909 by appearing to throw himself off a boat. Having successfully escaped his creditors, three years later he surfaced as Frederick Philip Grove in Manitoba. In his lifetime no one in Canada knew his real identity. The true story was only revealed 25 years after his death, when D.O. Spettigue published his biography of Grove, FPG: The European Years (1973).

Source: University of Manitoba Archives and Special Collections, The Libraries/PC 2, No. 10.

At McGill University, a group of young, rebellious poets known as the "Montreal group"—F.R. Scott, A.J.M. Smith, A.M. Klein, and Leo Kennedy—endorsed the modernist movement. They wrote in free verse, discarded the norms of punctuation, and chose their subject material in the modern city. They began two small literary journals, the *McGill Fortnightly Review* (1925–27) and the *Canadian Mercury* (1928–29), as vehicles for their works.

In French-speaking Quebec, a group of young poets challenged the establishment in the pages of *Le Nigog*, the first arts magazine in Quebec, founded by architect Fernand Préfontaine, writer Robert de Roquebrune, and musician Léo-Paul Morin. Ironically, although this group and the "Montreal group" resided in the same city, they worked in isolation from one another.

Most novels of the 1920s continued to be romantic and escapist. Mazo de la Roche's *Jalna* (1927) chronicled the life of the fictional Whiteoaks family. Her romantic depiction of rural Ontario life sold close to 100 000 copies within a few months of publication, resulting in sixteen sequels. Three novels, however, stood out for their realism: Frederick Philip Grove's *Settlers of the Marsh* (1925), in which Grove explored the inner psychic tension of a Norwegian settler on the Prairies; Martha Ostenso's *Wild Geese* (1925), about the tyrannical patriarch Caleb Gare, who aims to dominate both his land and his family and in the process destroys himself; and R.J.C. Stead's *Grain* (1926), which describes the tensions that farm boy Gander Stake faces in having to choose between life on the farm and in the city.

Music

The University of Toronto's Faculty of Music opened in 1919. The university also housed the Hart House String Quartet, founded in 1924 by Vincent Massey, of the influential Massey family. The

Masseys also continued to support Massey Hall, the location of many musical performances, including the concerts of the Toronto Symphony Orchestra. Schools of Music also began at McGill in 1920, and at Laval in 1922.

The real innovation in music occurred through radio broadcasting. Many Canadian musicians got their start on radio. Radio was used effectively to celebrate the Diamond Jubilee of Confederation in 1927. Beginning in 1929, the Toronto Symphony Orchestra performed 25 concerts over the radio, the last of which was devoted entirely to music by Canadian composers. The concerts could be heard throughout the country.

By 1930, some 60 radio stations existed across the country. Offerings were sparse, as no station transmitted for more than a few hours a day. Programs consisted mainly of news, lectures, or recorded music, compared with the comedies, drama, and live variety of American programs. English-speaking Canadians fortunate enough to be close to the international border listened to American radio stations, which carried popular programs and had stronger transmitters. Rather than compete, Canadian stations themselves bought the right to broadcast these American shows. By 1930, an estimated 80 percent of the programs Canadians listened to came from the United States.

Concerned about the negative impact on Canadian culture of the Americanization of radio broadcasting in Canada, the Canadian government established a royal commission—the Aird Commission—to review public broadcasting. The Aird report recommended that broadcasting become a public monopoly, without competitors and with limited commercial content. The Canadian Radio League, founded by English-Canadian nationalists Alan Plaunt, Graham Spry, and Brooke Claxton, concurred. They hoped, as did the members of the Aird Commission, that public broadcasting would help unite Canadians. Out of their efforts came the Canadian Broadcasting Corporation (CBC) in the 1930s.

Popular Culture

English-speaking Canadian popular culture became more Americanized in the 1920s. American-style service clubs such as Rotary, Lions, Kiwanis, and Gyro gained in popularity, although the uniquely Canadian organization the Kinsmen, founded in 1920 in Hamilton, Ontario, held its own. (Half a century later, the Kinsmen would become Canada's largest national service organization.)

Movie Industry

Popular culture and Americanization combined most noticeably in the movie industry in the 1920s. Initially, it did not appear that this would be the case. Between 1919 and 1923, Canada had a thriving domestic feature film industry that used Canadian settings, casts, and crews. The country also had its own famous movie maker, Ernest Shipman. Born in Hull, Quebec in 1871, he produced seven successful feature films between 1919 and 1922 based on Canadian wilderness tales by such popular authors as James Oliver Curwood who coined the phrase "God's Country" to describe the Canadian wilderness, and Ralph Connor with his popular novels such as *The Foreigner* and *The Man from Glengarry*. Canada even had its own chain of theatres by 1922 owned by the Allen brothers of Brantford, Ontario but with their company headquarters in Calgary, Alberta.

Thereafter, the Canadian movie industry went into a precipitous decline. Shipman tried unsuccessfully to break into the Hollywood movie scene. He was also a victim of the transition in the 1920s from independent movie producers to corporate producers. Canadian companies succumbed to the "Big Five" studios in Hollywood—Paramount, MGM, Warner

Nell Shipman with a friend in Back to God's Country *(1919).*

Source: Library and Archives Canada/MISA-4857.

Brothers, Fox, and RKO. By 1929, these five companies produced and distributed 90 percent of all feature films in North America. The introduction of the "talkies" in 1927 strengthened the American stronghold on Canadian filmmaking because of the high cost involved in producing them. As well, in 1923, the Famous Players Canadian Corporation bought out the Allen theatre chain. The Canadian government refused to intervene to save the feature film industry in Canada; government officials were only interested in promotional propaganda films and documentaries.

In Quebec, filmmaking faced its own challenges. In January 1927, a tragic fire at the Laurier Palace theatre in Montreal killed 78 people, mostly children. The Quebec government reacted by prohibiting children under the age of 16 from attending the cinema—a law that remained in effect until 1967. The film industry also faced opposition from the Roman Catholic church, which saw movies as immoral and an insidious form of Americanization of French-Canadian culture. The Quebec government also established a strict censor board to screen all films for immoralities.

Sport

The professionalization of Canadian sport continued in the 1920s. This meant indoor stadiums, artificial ice, and large payrolls. It also meant greater Americanization. At the beginning of the 1920s, professional hockey was solely Canadian. The Pacific Coast League (formed in 1911), the Western Canadian League (begun in 1921), and the National Hockey League (NHL, inaugurated in 1917) alone competed for the coveted Stanley Cup. Then the NHL expanded into the lucrative urban market of the United States. By 1927, the NHL consisted of five American and five Canadian teams. The Ottawa Senators dominated the NHL in the early years of the decade, winning the Stanley Cup four times.

The NHL dominated hockey throughout the 1920s. It paid the average player $900 a year, with a few exceptional players earning upwards of $10 000. Although interest in the amateur trophies—the Allan Cup and the Memorial Cup—continued in the smaller centres, the focus remained on the NHL even after the league shrank to six teams, with only two of the teams being Canadian: the Toronto Maple Leafs and the Montreal Canadiens. Almost all the NHL players were Canadians.

New trophies were donated throughout the decade: the Hart Trophy, for most valuable team player; the Lady Byng Trophy, donated by the governor general's wife, to the player exhibiting the highest sportsmanship and gentlemanly conduct; the Vezina Trophy, to the goaltender allowing the fewest goals against his team; and the Prince of Wales Trophy, awarded to the season's NHL playoff champion team.

In other sport, a number of Canadian amateurs won international recognition. Track and field athlete Percy Williams won a gold medal at the 1928 Olympics. Williams acquired the reputation of being "the world's fastest human." George Young made a name for Canada in swimming by winning the 32 km race from the California mainland to Catalina Island. In the Maritimes, Captain Angus Walters won the International Fisherman's Trophy three years in succession—in 1921, 1922, and 1923. His schooner, the *Bluenose* (the nickname for Nova Scotians), which never lost a race, was immortalized on the Canadian dime.

Women athletics came into its own in the 1920s enabling women to take control of their own sports. Certainly the success of the Edmonton Grads women's basketball team—setting a world record by winning 502 games and losing only 20 between the team's inception in 1915 and when it disbanded in 1940—helped to promote women in sport. So too did the success of Canadian women in the Olympic Games. In 1928 summer Olympics in Amsterdam, Canada's "Matchless Six," women competitors, won more points than any other nation, including a gold medal for Ethel Catherwood in track and field to match that of Percy William for men's track and field in the same games. Just as professional men's sport teams emerged in the 1920s, so did professional women's sport teams, especially in basketball, ice hockey, and softball. Working-class women formed their own athletic clubs, organizations, and leagues. Some companies that employed large numbers of young, single women, such as Eaton's and the Hudson's Bay Company, provided recreational and athletic facilities. By 1926, sufficient numbers of women's sport teams existed to form the Women's Amateur Athletic Federation of Canada with a nation-wide membership of 1200. It regulated all women's sport.

The Bluenose *in full sail—Canada's most famous ship. Winner of the International Fisherman's Trophy for three successive years (1921, 1922, 1923), the schooner became immortalized in 1937 with its reproduction on the Canadian dime.*

Source: Commercial Photo Service (Halifax)/Library and Archives Canada/PA-41990.

In the decade from 1919 to 1929, Mackenzie King and his Liberal party dominated politics. King succeeded in diffusing the Maritime Rights movement in the East and undermining the Progressive movement in the West. He also moved Canada along the road to autonomy. Women and labour unions made gains, but both groups were still far from achieving a position of equality in Canadian society. The First Nations remained very much dominated by the federal government. Culturally, English Canadians and French Canadians made important advances, but in terms of popular culture, both groups, especially English Canadians, came increasingly under American influence. Few Canadians suspected, as the decade came to an end, that it would be followed by the worst depression in world history.

NOTES

1. John Herd Thompson with Allen Seager, *Canada 1922–1939: Decades of Discord* (Toronto: McClelland & Stewart, 1985), p. 112.

2. Kenneth Norrie and Douglas Owram, *A History of the Canadian Economy*, 3rd ed. (Toronto: Nelson, 2002), p. 322.

3. A.R.M. Lower, *Canadians in the Making: A Social History of Canada* (Toronto: Longmans, Green, 1958), p. 424.

4. Susan Mann, *The Dream of Nation: A Social and Intellectual History of Quebec*, 2nd ed. (Montreal/Kingston: McGill-Queen's University Press, 2002), p. 223.

5. Veronica Strong-Boag, "Pulling in Double Harness or Hauling a Double Load: Women, Work and Feminism on the Canadian Prairie," *Journal of Canadian Studies* 21 (Fall 1986): 36.

6. Douglas Cole, "Artists, Patrons and Public: An Enquiry into the Success of the Group of Seven," *Journal of Canadian Studies* 13(2) (1978): 76.

7. Mary Vipond, *The Mass Media in Canada* (Toronto: James Lorimer & Co., 1989), p. 24.

BEYOND THE BOOK

Weblinks

William Lyon Mackenzie King Diaries
http://king.collectionscanada.ca/EN/default.asp
Digitized diaries of the Prime Minister of Canada William Lyon Mackenzie King.

CPR Farmers' Protest
http://asalive.archivesalberta.org:8080/access/asa/documents/display/GLEN-111
Digitized newspaper articles and files regarding protests by farmers in southeastern Alberta regarding their farming conditions on CPR land.

United Farm Women of Alberta: Records
http://asalive.archivesalberta.org:8080/access/asa/documents/display/GLEN-223
Digitized minutes, a membership list, and cash records of a rural women's group near Pibroch, Alberta in the late 1920s.

King–Byng Affair Letters
http://northernblue.ca/canchan/cantext/modpolit/1926king.html
Digitized letters between Prime Minister King and Lord Byng at the time of their conflict.

Indian Affairs Annual Reports: The 1920s
http://www.collectionscanada.ca/indianaffairs/index-e.html
Digitized copies of the annual reports of the federal Department of Indian Affairs during the 1920s.

The Famous 5
http://www.collectionscanada.ca/famous5/index-e.html
Digitized letters by the Famous 5, an account of the "Persons Case," and further resources about Henrietta Muir Edwards, Emily Murphy, Louise McKinney, Irene Parlby, and Nellie McClung.

Films & Novels

In the Skin of a Lion. By Michael Ondaatje. 1987.

RELATED READINGS

The following article from R. Douglas Francis and Donald B. Smith, eds., *Readings in Canadian History: Post-Confederation*, 7th ed. (Toronto: Thomson Nelson, 2006), deals with a topic pertaining to the 1920s in greater depth: Craig Heron and Myer Siemiatycki, "The Great War, the State, and Working-Class Canada," pp. 370- 90.

BIBLIOGRAPHY

On the Winnipeg General Strike see "Where Historians Disagree: The Winnipeg General Strike" in this chapter. See as well, Kenneth McNaught and David Bercuson, *The Winnipeg Strike: 1919* (Toronto: Longman, 1974); and with regard to the One Big Union, David Bercuson, *Fools and Wisemen: The Rise and Fall of the One Big Union* (Toronto: McGraw-Hill Ryerson, 1978). To examine the Winnipeg General Strike in the wider perspective of strikes elsewhere in Canada, see Craig Heron, ed., *The Workers' Revolt in Canada, 1917–1925* (Toronto: University of Toronto Press, 1998).

For an overview of the 1920s, consult John Herd Thompson with Allen Seager, *Canada, 1922–1939: Decades of Discord* (Toronto: McClelland & Stewart, 1985). Robert Bothwell, Ian Drummond, and John English supply considerable material on the 1920s in *Canada, 1900–1945* (Toronto: University of Toronto Press, 1987). For the Maritime provinces see Margaret R. Conrad and James K. Hiller, *Atlantic Canada: A Region in the Making* (Don Mills, ON: Oxford University Press, 2001); and David Frank, "The 1920s: Class and Region, Resistance and Accommodation," in E.R. Forbes and D.A. Muise, eds., *The Atlantic Provinces in Confederation* (Toronto: University of Toronto Press, 1993).

On Mackenzie King's political life in the 1920s see the latter part of R.M. Dawson, *William Lyon Mackenzie King: A Political Biography*, vol. 1, *1874–1923* (Toronto: University of Toronto Press, 1958); and H.B. Neatby, *The Lonely Heights*, vol. 2, *1924–1932* (Toronto: University of Toronto Press, 1980). A popular study is J.L. Granatstein's *Mackenzie King: His Life and World* (Toronto: McGraw-Hill Ryerson, 1977). On King's association with the West, see Robert A. Wardhaugh, *Mackenzie King and the Prairie West* (Toronto: University of Toronto Press, 2000). Roger Graham's *Arthur Meighen: A Biography*, vol. 2, *And Fortune Fled* (Toronto: Clarke Irwin, 1963), and his pamphlet *Arthur Meighen* (Ottawa: Canadian Historical Association, 1965), deal with King's political rival in the 1920s. On political scandal in the 1920s, consult T.D. Regehr, *The Beauharnois Scandal: A Story of Canadian Entrepreneurship and Politics* (Toronto: University of Toronto Press, 1989). On the liquor trade of the time see Craig Heron, *Booze: A Distilled History* (Toronto: Between the Lines, 2003).

Maritime protest in the 1920s is discussed in E.R. Forbes, *The Maritime Rights Movement, 1919–27: A Study in Canadian Regionalism* (Montreal/Kingston: McGill-Queen's University Press, 1979); and David J. Bercuson, ed., *Canada and the Burden of Unity* (Toronto: Macmillan, 1977). David Frank, "Class Conflict in the Coal Industry: Cape Breton 1922," in G.S. Kealey and P. Warrian, eds., *Essays in Canadian Working-Class History* (Toronto: McClelland & Stewart, 1976), pp. 161–84, recounts the story of labour strife on Cape Breton Island. On the Progressive movement see the relevant chapters in Gerald Friesen, *The Canadian Prairies: A History* (Toronto: University of Toronto Press, 1987); John Thompson, *Forging the Prairie West: The Illustrated History of Canada* (Toronto: Oxford, 1998); Walter Young, *Democracy and Discontent* (Toronto: Ryerson Press, 1969); and W.L. Morton, *The Progressive Party in Canada* (Toronto: University of Toronto Press, 1950). On the United Farmers of Ontario, see Kerry A. Badgley, *Ringing In the Common Good: The United Farmers of Ontario, 1914–1926* (Montreal/Kingston: McGill-Queen's University Press, 2000); and for the United Farmers of Alberta, see Bradford James Rennie, *The Rise of Agrarian Democracy: The United Farmers and Farm Women of Alberta, 1909–1921* (Toronto: University of

Toronto Press, 2000). J.E. Rea's *T.A. Crerar: A Political Life* (Montreal/Kingston: McGill-Queen's University Press, 1997) is a biography of this important Western farm leader. On the plight of Prairie farmers in the 1920s, see David Jones, *Empire of Dust: Settling and Abandoning the Prairie Dry Belt* (Edmonton: University of Alberta Press, 1987). On the King–Byng affair, consult the King and Meighen biographies cited in the previous paragraph and Roger Graham, *The King–Byng Affair, 1926* (Toronto: Copp Clark, 1967).

On the economics of the 1920s see the chapter "The Stuttering Twenties," in Michael Bliss, *Northern Enterprise: Five Centuries of Canadian Business* (Toronto: McClelland & Stewart, 1987) and Kenneth Norrie and Douglas Owram, *A History of the Canadian Economy*, 2nd ed. (Toronto: Harcourt Brace, 1996). Consult, as well, Tom Traves, *The State and Enterprise: Canadian Manufacturers and the Federal Government, 1917–31* (Toronto: University of Toronto Press, 1979). For Quebec see Paul-André Linteau, René Durocher, and Jean-Claude Robert, *Quebec: A History, 1867–1929* (Toronto: James Lorimer, 1983).

Church union is considered in John W. Grant, *The Canadian Experience of Church Union* (London: John Knox Press, 1967); opposition to church union is the subject of N. Keith Clifford, *The Resistance to Church Union, 1904–1939* (Vancouver: University of British Columbia Press, 1985). Susan Mann Trofimenkoff's *Action Française: French-Canadian Nationalism in the Twenties* (Toronto: University of Toronto Press, 1975) analyzes this French-Canadian group. Society in western Canada is discussed in James Gray, *The Roar of the Twenties* (Toronto: Macmillan, 1975).

On women in the 1920s consult Veronica Strong-Boag, *The New Day Recalled: Lives of Girls and Women in English Canada, 1919–1939* (Toronto: Copp Clark Pitman, 1988); Susan Mann Trofimenkoff and Alison Prentice, eds., *The Neglected Majority: Essays in Canadian Women's History*, vol. 1 (Toronto: McClelland & Stewart, 1977) and vol. 2 (1985) and Suzanne Morton, *Ideal Surroundings: Domestic Life in a Working-Class Suburb in the 1920s* (Toronto: University of Toronto Press, 1995). Women and politics is discussed in Linda Kealey and Joan Sangster, eds., *Beyond the Vote: Canadian Women and Politics* (Toronto: University of Toronto Press, 1989). On Canada's first woman MP see Terry Crowley, *Agnes Macphail and the Politics of Equality* (Toronto: James Lorimer, 1990). On Quebec women see, as well, Micheline Dumont et al., *Quebec Women: A History* (Toronto: Women's Press, 1987) and Susan Mann, *The Dream of Nation: A Social and Intellectual History of Quebec*, 2nd ed. (Montreal/Kingston: McGill-Queen's University Press, 2002). For Ontario see Janice Acton et al., eds., *Women at Work: Ontario, 1850–1930* (Toronto: Canadian Women's Educational Press, 1974) and, for the Prairies, Veronica Strong-Boag, "Pulling in Double Harness or Hauling a Double Load: Women, Work and Feminism on the Canadian Prairie," *Journal of Canadian Studies* 21 (Fall 1986): 32–52. On the topic of eugenics see Angus McLaren, *Our Own Master Race* (Toronto: McClelland & Stewart, 1990).

On social assistance and the rise of social work in the 1920s, see the relevant section in Alvin Finkel, *Social Policy and Practice in Canada: A History* (Waterloo: Wilfrid Laurier University Press, 2006), Ken Moffat, *A Poetics of Social Work: Personal Agency and Social Transformation in Canada, 1920–1939* (Toronto: University of Toronto Press, 2001); and selected articles in Raymond B. Blake and Jeff Keshen, eds., *Social Welfare Policy in Canada: Historical Readings* (Toronto: Copp Clark, 1995). On the impact of suburbia in the interwar years, see Richard Harris, *Creeping Conformity: How Canada Became Suburban, 1900–1960* (Toronto: University of Toronto Press, 2004). Canadian culture is dealt with in "The Conundrum of Culture," in *Canada, 1922–1939* (as cited earlier), pp. 158–92, and Carl Klinck, ed., *Literary History of Canada: Canadian Literature in English*, 2nd ed. (Toronto: University of Toronto Press, 1976). On cultural nationalism see Mary Vipond, *The Mass Media in Canada* (Toronto: James Lorimer, 1992). For the Maritimes see, as well, Gwendolyn Davies, *Myth and Milieu: Atlantic Literature and Culture, 1918–1939* (Fredericton: Acadiensis Press, 1993); and Ian McKay, *The Quest of the Folk: Antimodernism and Cultural Selection in Twentieth-Century Nova Scotia* (Montreal/Kingston: McGill-Queen's University Press, 1994).

Painting in the interwar years is discussed in J. Russell Harper, *Painting in Canada: A History*, 2nd ed. (Toronto: University of Toronto Press, 1977); Dennis Reid, *A Concise History of Canadian Painting*, 2nd ed. (Toronto: Oxford University Press, 1988); and Ann Davis, *The Logic of Ecstasy: Canadian Mystical Painting, 1920–1940* (Toronto: University of Toronto Press, 1992). On the Group of

Seven consult Peter Mellen, *The Group of Seven* (Toronto: McClelland & Stewart, 1970) and Charles C. Hill, *The Group of Seven: Art for a Nation* (Ottawa: National Gallery of Canada, 1995).

On theatre in Quebec see Elaine F. Nardocchio, *Theatre and Politics in Modern Quebec* (Edmonton: University of Alberta Press, 1986) and Jean Hamelin, *The Theatre in French Canada, 1936–1966* (Quebec: Department of Cultural Affairs, 1968). For music see Timothy J. McGee, *The Music of Canada* (New York: W.W. Norton, 1985) and George A. Proctor, *Canadian Music of the Twentieth Century* (Toronto: University of Toronto Press, 1980).

On popular entertainment in the West see Don Wetherell and Irene Kmet, *Useful Pleasures: The Shaping of Leisure in Alberta 1896–1945* (Regina: Alberta Culture and Multiculturalism/Canadian Plains Research Center, University of Regina, 1990). Radio is discussed in Mary Vipond, *Listening In: The First Decade of Canadian Broadcasting, 1922–1932* (Montreal/Kingston: McGill-Queen's University Press, 1992). For Canadian sport in general, see Colin Howell, *Blood, Sweat, and Cheers: Sport in the Making of Modern Canada* (Toronto: University of Toronto Press, 2001); and for women and sport, M. Ann Hall, *The Girl and the Game: A History of Women's Sport in Canada* (Peterborough: Broadview Press, 2002).

Important reviews of First Nations history in the interwar years include Arthur Ray, *The Canadian Fur Trade in the Industrial Age* (Toronto: University of Toronto Press, 1990) and his *I Have Lived Here Since the World Began* (Toronto: Key Porter, 1996); Stan Cuthand, "The Native Peoples of the Prairie Provinces in the 1920s and 1930s," in Ian A.L. Getty and Donald B. Smith, eds., *One Century Later: Western Canadian Reserve Indians Since Treaty 7* (Vancouver: University of British Columbia Press, 1978), pp. 31–42; and John Leonard Taylor, *Canadian Indian Policy During the Inter-War Years, 1918–1939* (Ottawa: Indian and Northern Affairs Canada, 1984); On Indian residential schools during this period, see J.R. Miller, *Shingwauk's Vision: A History of Native Residential Schools* (Toronto: University of Toronto Press, 1996) and John S. Milloy, *A National Crime: The Canadian Government and the Residential School System, 1879 to 1986* (Winnipeg: University of Manitoba Press, 1999). For working conditions of First Nations people, see Rolf Knight, *Indians at Work: An Informal History of Native Indian Labour in British Columbia, 1853–1930* (Vancouver: New Star Books, 1978). For developments among the First Nations, see Edward Ahenakew, *Voices of the Plains Cree* (Toronto: McClelland & Stewart, 1973); and for those among the Métis in Western Canada, consult Murray Dobbin, *The One-and-a-Half Men: The Story of Jim Brady and Malcolm Norris, Métis Patriots of the 20th Century* (Vancouver: New Star Books, 1981). A helpful study of northern developments remains René Fumoleau, *As Long as This Land Shall Last: A History of Treaty 8 and Treaty 11, 1870–1939* (Toronto: McClelland and Stewart, 1973).

Students should consult the excellent maps and charts in Donald Kerr and Deryck W. Holdsworth, eds., *Historical Atlas of Canada*, vol. 3, *Addressing the Twentieth Century, 1891–1961* (Toronto: University of Toronto Press, 1990).

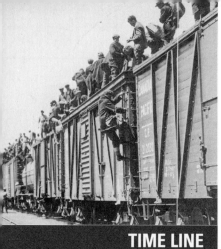

Chapter Twelve

CANADA IN THE GREAT DEPRESSION

TIME LINE

1929	The New York stock market crashes
1930	Conservatives come to power under R.B. Bennett
1931	Statute of Westminster recognizes Canadian autonomy from Britain
1932	Imperial Economic Conference in Ottawa Founding of the Co-operative Commonwealth Federation (CCF) party
1934	Birth of the Dionne quintuplets, the world's first surviving quintuplets
1935	Liberals come to power under Mackenzie King Social Credit party elected in Alberta under William Aberhart On-to-Ottawa Trek by unemployed workers; riots break out in Regina Creation of the Bank of Canada
1936	Founding of the Canadian Broadcasting Corporation (CBC) Maurice Duplessis's Union Nationale party elected in Quebec Dorothea Palmer arrested for distributing birth control literature
1937	General Motors strike in Oshawa Establishment of the Royal Commission on Dominion–Provincial Relations Establishment of the governor general's awards
1939	King George VI and Queen Elizabeth tour Canada

The Great Depression dominated the 1930s. The spectacular crash of the New York stock market in October 1929 signalled the crisis. It was followed by bank failures, a decline in international trade, plummeting commodities prices, spiralling government debts, and massive unemployment.

Canada and the United States experienced the Western world's most severe decline in industrial production and gross national product. Unemployment soared. With no jobs available, thousands of Canadians faced for the first time the degradation of going on public relief. Young single men rode the rails in search of work, and when unable to find work ended up in relief camps under intolerable conditions. People looked to government for answers. First the Conservatives under R.B. Bennett attempted to deal with this unprecedented economic disaster when elected to power in 1930. When they failed to satisfy the Canadian populace, they were ousted for the Liberals under Mackenzie King in 1935. Many Canadians look instead to new third parties, and some even turned to extreme right- and left-wing organizations for solutions. Provincial governments were no more successful at finding solutions. Farm organizations and trade unions attempted to help their members, but with limited success. Women fared no better; in fact, they lost what gains they had made toward economic equality earlier. Some Canadians looked to religion for answers, and a more conservative religious perspective prevailed. Popular culture—particularly movie-going and sport—thrived as temporary diversions from the depressed conditions of everyday life.

The depression certainly had an impact on those who lived through it. Some remember those years as the best of times in terms of social bonding, as people pulled together to help each other; others remember them as the worst of times as they struggled simply to eke out a living.

The Advent of the Great Depression

On October 29, 1929—"Black Tuesday"—the crash of the New York stock market precipitated stock market crashes around the world. Bank failures followed throughout Europe and the United States, causing financial instability. International trade declined as nations imposed high tariffs on foreign trade in an effort to protect industries and workers in their own countries from foreign competition. Worldwide overproduction of commodities such as wheat, newsprint, and metals—all important Canadian exports—caused prices to plummet. Unemployment rose to record highs.

The Great Depression affected the entire Western world. It hit Canada severely, because the national economy had expanded so rapidly and so extensively in the first three decades of the twentieth century. In essence, having risen so high, it had farther to fall. Industrial production fell by over one-third between 1929 and 1932. During the same period, Canada's gross national product sank two-fifths in current dollars. Imports declined in volume by about 55 percent and exports by 25 percent. The unemployment rate soared to a record high of 20 percent of the *total* civilian labour force by 1933.

Within Canada, the Prairie West and British Columbia probably suffered most, because of the dependence of these regions on primary industries, especially wheat production, and their overexpansion in the previous decades. Furthermore, Canada was heavily dependent on one market, the United States, which was greatly affected by the economic downturn and imposed high tariffs in response. Compounding this economic depression, the Prairie West also suffered from a climatic disaster: ten years of exceptional and persistent drought, extreme summer and winter temperatures, unusual weather patterns, and grasshopper infestations. The topsoil turned to dust and blew away. British Columbia contended with high numbers of transients; Vancouver became known as "the Mecca for the unemployed."

Nobody wanted Canada's wheat. From 1928 to 1932 prices fell from $1.29 to $0.34 a bushel for No. 1 Hard, the best wheat on the market. Prices for lesser grades were considerably lower. Also, farmers themselves paid for the cost of shipping the grain to the Lakehead, eroding profit even further. Some western farmers found it cost less to burn their crops than to harvest them.

The wheat pools felt the repercussions. They began in the 1920s advancing (in the fall and winter seasons) a portion of the money expected on next year's crop. This practice was intended to assist farmers in buying seed and getting the wheat crop planted. In the fall and winter of 1928–29, the pools had advanced farmers $1 a bushel. When wheat prices fell below that price in the fall of 1929 and entered a downward spiral for five consecutive years, the wheat pools went bankrupt.

Elsewhere, similar dramatic conditions prevailed in the primary resource sector. Thousands of investors lost everything when mining share prices became worthless. Mines closed down for lack of business. The pulp and paper industry, another major resource industry, had a similar fate to that of wheat and mining. The industry had overexpanded in the 1920s as a result of an insatiable American demand for pulp and paper. Its expenses could only be recouped if the market continued at record highs. When the depression hit, the newsprint market collapsed and, along with it, the pulp and paper industry. According to one industry analyst, by 1933 the pulp and paper industry was operating at only half of its capacity. Even then the bottomed-out prices kept production costs barely above bankruptcy.

Money markets followed. Banks and other financial institutions generously approved loans in the 1920s, hoping to capitalize on the boom. Foreign capital entered the country to take advantage of good times. With the advent of the depression, however, financial investors could not retrieve their money or cover their debts. Foreign investment from Canada's two traditional sources ceased; indeed, Britain and the United States recalled their loans to cover demands at home. Historians Thompson and Seager note that on October 29, "Black Tuesday," "The Toronto Star's index of sixteen key Canadian stocks fell $300 000 000—a million dollars for every minute that markets were open for trading."[1]

Average Canadian investors could not pay loans now recalled by the banks. Nor could they meet their mortgage payments or pay their property taxes. Farmers' debt levels often exceeded their farms' value. Interest payments alone often exceeded an average farmer's annual income. People abandoned their homes and farms, leaving banks with property that no one could afford, and hence had little monetary value.

Companies and factories cut back on wages and employees in an effort to survive. Clerks at Eaton's and Simpson's in Toronto, for example, earned only $10 to $13 a week, while those in Montreal earned much less. Weekly pay for male workers in the furniture industry averaged $10, but "boys" of 19 often earned as little as three dollars. In the textile industry, the Royal Commission on Price Spreads, appointed by the Conservative government in 1934, found shocking conditions: a Quebec home worker earning 5 cents an hour; a seamstress paid $9\frac{1}{2}$ cents for sewing a dozen dresses.

Tens of thousands of workers lost their jobs. By 1933, over 20 percent of the entire Canadian labour force—one worker out of every five—remained unemployed. In some regions of the country, the figures rose as high as 35 percent and even 50 percent. Since no social-security system existed, the unemployed, the destitute, and the sick had to rely on the charity of others, private groups, or government relief.

Dust storm near Lethbridge, Alberta—a familiar sight in Prairie Canada during the "Dirty Thirties."

Source: Glenbow Archives, Calgary, Canada/NA-1831-1.

R.B. Bennett's Policies

At the outset of the Great Depression, the Liberals were in office. Confident of another victory, party organizers remained apathetic and indifferent throughout the election campaign of 1930. The Liberals believed, as did many other politicians in the Western world, that this depression was just another momentary dip in the economy, and therefore saw no need to propose sweeping economic reform during the election campaign. King was also unusually argumentative. In the Parliamentary session just before the election, King was pushed into saying he "would not give a single cent, not a five-cent piece" to any provincial Conservative government, a comment that plagued him throughout the election campaign. In contrast, Richard Bedford Bennett, the exuberant Conservative leader, promised that if elected he could, and would, solve the problems of the depression. He won the election.

Once in power, the new prime minister acted. Bennett introduced a high-tariff policy on manufactured goods as one solution to the depression. But the high tariffs undermined Canada's competitive edge. As a major exporting nation, Canada greatly depended on the export of key staples—wheat, pulp and paper, and minerals—to foreign markets, especially the American market. In 1930, the United States retaliated with the Smoot-Hawley tariff on foreign imports.

Within his first five weeks in office, Bennett introduced the Unemployment Relief Act, which provided $20 million of assistance to the poor—a considerable sum out of a total federal

Eviction in Montreal during the Depression. By 1933 over one-third of the city's francophones were on relief, with many simply forced into the streets.

Source: Library and Archives Canada/C-30811.

budget of $500 million. But Bennett soon discovered that much more was needed. Between 1930 and 1938, Ottawa would provide nearly $350 million in relief for the jobless and for destitute farmers, while municipal and provincial governments added another $650 million. Most of the money went to work-incentive programs, for which municipalities were expected to contribute their share.

The federal government underestimated the destitution of the municipal governments. Already heavily in debt, they, and the provincial governments, had overextended themselves in the boom years of the 1920s. Furthermore, their tax base eroded as people could no longer pay local property taxes. Indeed, all levels of government faced mounting deficits on a decreased tax base. Toronto's budget for relief increased twentyfold between 1929 and 1933. By the outbreak of war, Montreal's per capita debt was twice Toronto's. When the province of Quebec, more tight-fisted toward its towns and cities than other provinces, refused to come to Montreal's rescue, the city was forced to declare bankruptcy in 1940.

Municipal, provincial, and federal governments responded by trying to balance their budgets through cutbacks on services. This, in turn, increased unemployment and slowed down the recovery. Governments had few alternatives, given the magnitude of the debt and their low level of revenue. Also, opportunities to borrow abroad did not exist. All countries faced debt and dealt with it the same way—by trying to balance their budgets.

As the economic crisis continued, Bennett looked to Britain and the other Commonwealth countries for increased trade. In 1932, Canada hosted an Imperial Economic Conference to explore ways to combat the depression. At the conference, Bennett took an aggressive approach. He refused to make concessions to Britain on imports, yet expected the "mother country" to open its markets to Canadian goods. Overall, the conference failed, but Canada did gain a limited preference in the British market for its wheat, lumber, apples, and bacon. In return, Canada gave preference to British manufactured goods by simply raising the level of the general tariff on all but British goods.

Relief

For the first time, thousands of Canadians faced the personal degradation of going on relief—the "pogey," as it was called. In a society built on a philosophy of self-help, relief was an admission that one could no longer fend for oneself. Many people lost their sense of self-worth. The jobless had no choice but to fall back on charity, both public and private.

Those on relief faced the further humiliation of having to acknowledge their failure publicly. They lined up in a church basement or fire hall waiting for relief. When their turn came, they had to proclaim their destitution, and swear that they did not own a car, a radio, or a telephone. Recipients of relief generally had to be in arrears in rent payments and to have received notice of discontinuation of electricity and water service, as well as impending eviction. Then the authorities gave them food vouchers to purchase the minimum necessities at local stores—a further reminder of one's impoverished condition. In Ontario, these relief vouchers averaged $8.07 a person for a week in the winter months. In 1933, North York gave families on relief a maximum of $11.60 a week, although the Toronto Welfare Council estimated that a family of five needed $28.35 a week to maintain an adequate living standard. In Prince Edward Island, relief vouchers amounted to only $1.93, and in New Brunswick they averaged a meagre $1.67.

For relief families, used clothing had to be picked up at a private charity centre. Fuel was often wood cut by people on relief themselves as part of their expected tasks to earn relief money. In the Prairie West—once the "breadbasket of the nation"—food, along with used clothing and fuel, often came in railcar loads from central Canada.

To give those on relief the illusion of working for their relief payments, governments created makeshift jobs known as "boon-doggling." The town of New Toronto, Ontario, for example, required relief workers to haul large stones to vacant lots, where they were smashed and used for road construction. Winnipeg men on relief sawed wood, pulled weeds along city boulevards, and swept the city streets. Rumours abounded of some municipalities that had "relief men" dig holes one day and fill them in the next, simply to keep them occupied.

To avoid drifters coming into town for assistance, most municipalities had lengthy residence requirements to qualify for relief. Recent immigrants now faced a hostile reception. The Immigrant Act allowed for the deportation of immigrants on relief especially if they happened to belong to socialist organizations. Consequently, some municipalities provided the authorities with lists of immigrants who were receiving government assistance. Between 1930 and 1935, Ottawa returned an unprecedented 30 000 immigrants to Europe.

Relief Camps

By 1932, the Great Depression had worsened. More than 1.5 million Canadians (15 percent of the nation's population) depended on relief, and the country seemed ripe for rebellion. Of particular concern were unemployed single men, many of whom "rode the rods" (hopped onto the rods near the axels of freight trains) across Canada in search of work, begged for food and clothing, camped in shantytowns on the outskirts of cities, and lined up at soup kitchens and hostels for food and shelter. General Andrew McNaughton, chief of the Army General Staff, proposed the establishment of relief camps to offer temporary work and prevent dissidence and violence. Beginning in 1932, the federal government established numerous camps across the country, usually in isolated areas distant from major population centres.

During the four-year period that they existed, an estimated 100 000 single, homeless male "volunteers" worked long hours at menial jobs designed simply to keep them busy for a meagre 20 cents a day. Intolerable living conditions in the camps made them ripe for infiltration by communist-led organizations such as the Single Unemployed Workers' Association, an organization funded by the Communist Party of Canada.

The On-to-Ottawa Trek

In the spring of 1935, men in British Columbia work camps jumped the trains en route to Ottawa to protest conditions. They picked up other camp men and unemployed workers along the way. About 2000 trekkers reached Regina before the federal government ordered the RCMP to break up the march. The ensuing confrontation, on Dominion Day, 1935, left one plainclothes policeman dead and numerous strikers and police officers injured. The police arrested 120 of the trekkers and convicted eight of them. Only strike leader Arthur Evans and a few others were permitted to continue to Ottawa, where the unsympathetic Prime Minister Bennett denounced them as "red" agitators and dissidents.

Canada's millionaire prime minister came to represent the callous indifference of the rich to the suffering of the unemployed and destitute, and

A demonstration of strikers at Market Square on the eve of the Regina Riot on Dominion Day, 1935. During the riot, one plainclothes policeman was killed and numerous strikers and police officers were injured.

Source: Dick and Ada Bird Collection/Saskatchewan Archives Board/R-A27560-1.

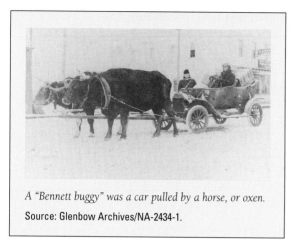

A "Bennett buggy" was a car pulled by a horse, or oxen.

Source: Glenbow Archives/NA-2434-1.

thus became the butt of numerous jokes. People spoke of "Bennett buggies," engineless cars pulled by horses because the owners could not afford gas; "Bennett boroughs," the shantytowns of makeshift "homes" for homeless men; and "Bennett blankets," the newspapers under which transients slept on park benches. Bennett was ridiculed in a parody of the Lord's Prayer:

> *Our Father, who art in Ottawa, Bennett be thy name. Give us this day our bowl of soup and forgive us our trespasses on the CPR and the CNR as we forgive the bulls from chasing us. Lead us not into the hands of the RCMP, nor yet to the relief camp, for thine is the kingdom the power and glory, until there's an election—Amen.*

In fairness to Bennett, beneath his cold exterior existed a warm generosity. Thousands of Canadians wrote personal letters to him expressing their hardships and appealing for help. Very often he sent them money from his own pocket, apparently without any political benefit, since he often insisted on the strictest confidentiality.

Bennett also enacted a number of measures that, over time, strengthened Canada's economy and became permanent structures. He established a central bank, the Bank of Canada, to "promote the economic and financial welfare of the Dominion." His government passed the Natural Products and Marketing Act, which set up a federal marketing board with authority over all "natural products of agriculture and of the forest, sea, lake or river," exported or sold across provincial boundaries. His government also introduced the Canada Grain Board Act, which gave Ottawa control of the marketing of coarse grains, including wheat.

In 1934, Bennett also appointed the Royal Commission on Price Spreads to investigate the buying practices of major department stores and the labour conditions in certain industries. Out of that commission came legislation to institute unemployment insurance and to regulate wages and working hours. Unfortunately, both bills were struck down by the Judicial Committee of the Privy Council as unconstitutional. In 1940, however, the federal government succeeded in implementing an unemployment insurance plan after the British North America Act had been amended to allow for Ottawa's intervention into this traditional field of provincial jurisdiction.

Bennett's "New Deal"

As the election of 1935 approached, Bennett decided to imitate the example of the popular American president, Franklin D. Roosevelt. In a radio address, he announced his "New Deal," a program of reform that his party would introduce if the Conservatives were reelected. It came as a complete surprise, even to his cabinet members, who had not been consulted about the reform package. It included health and unemployment insurance, a maximum work week, financial assistance to farmers to enable them to stay on their farms, and the creation of the Economic Council of Canada to advise the government. (After the election, the Judicial Committee of the Privy Council ruled that many aspects of Bennett's "New Deal" were unconstitutional because they infringed on provincial jurisdiction.)

Many Canadians were skeptical of Bennett's "sudden conversion to reform," especially since none of the legislation was prepared going into the election. The voting public expressed its skepticism and its criticism of the Conservatives in the election of 1935. It returned Mackenzie King's Liberal party to power with a majority government but with a lower percentage of votes than in 1930 when he lost. Political analysts argue that the Liberal victory was more a rejection of Bennett than an endorsement of King. Indeed, in the popular vote, more than 25 percent of Canadians rejected both of the mainline parties to vote for one of the new parties that entered the election.

Third Parties

Two of those new parties began on the Prairies. The Co-operative Commonwealth Federation (CCF) had its beginnings at a national convention in Calgary in August 1932. The CCF drew together dissident groups from a broad spectrum of Canadian society, including farmers, labourers, socialists, academics, and disenchanted Liberals. At the convention the party chose Labour MP J.S. Woodsworth as their leader.

From the beginning, the CCF distanced itself from the two mainline parties by having a clear socialist program to deal with the Great Depression. Woodsworth asked the League for Social Reconstruction (LSR), an organization of left-wing intellectuals who were mostly, although not exclusively, from universities to draft a manifesto for the new party. University of Toronto

The federal CCF caucus meets with its secretary J.S. Woodsworth, who is standing in the centre. On the extreme left sits Tommy Douglas, later Premier of Saskatchewan, and the first leader when the CCF changed its name to the New Democratic Party.

Source: Library and Archives Canada/PA 167544.

historian Frank H. Underhill and McGill University law professor Frank Scott did so. Adopted at the party's second annual convention in Regina in 1933, the "Regina Manifesto" set out a ten-point program for the CCF to follow in its effort to "eradicate capitalism" and create a cooperative commonwealth in Canada. The CCF favoured government control of the economy through the nationalization of the means of production, distribution, and exchange. It also worked for a more equitable distribution of wealth, the creation of a welfare state, and the pursuit of international peace through the League of Nations.

The CCF entered its first federal election in 1935 in high hopes of becoming a major party. Those expectations were dashed when it won only seven seats, all from the West, although the party did win 8.8 percent of the popular vote. Two of those elected—M.J. Coldwell and T.C. "Tommy" Douglas—later became national party leaders. Although weak in representation, the party did come to acquire the reputation of being "the conscience of the House of Commons." Provincially, the CCF did better. The party became the official opposition in British Columbia in 1933, in Saskatchewan in 1934, and in Ontario in 1943; but its real breakthrough came in the midst of World War II, when in 1944 Tommy Douglas led the party to victory in Saskatchewan.

Social Credit

In Alberta, a party quite different from the CCF, the Social Credit party, also began in the midst of the depression. Major C.H. Douglas, a Scottish engineer, first enunciated Social Credit theory in the 1910s. Douglas was concerned about the waste and underutilization of resources in the capitalist system. He did not blame the system, which he admired, but rather the financial institutions that hoarded money, preventing consumers from buying the abundant goods that the capitalist system produced. Douglas's solution was for governments to inject more money into the economy and give it to the people to spend. He used his "A plus B Theorem" to explain his reasoning. "A" represented the wages, salaries, and dividends paid to individuals, while "B" represented all other costs involved in making an item, such as raw materials and bank charges. Together, the two costs would give the "just price" of an item. The problem was, Social Credit theorists argued, that individuals only got the "A" portion. To make up the difference—the "B" portion—a Social Credit government would provide a "national dividend" to every individual to enable him or her to purchase essential goods. To people without sufficient money to buy even the necessities of life, the theory was appealing.

Douglas's theories awaited a popular leader; Alberta provided one, the charismatic William "Bible Bill" Aberhart. Born in Ontario, the son of a dairy farmer, Aberhart came west in 1910. The Ontario teacher became principal of a new high school in Calgary. At the same time, he served as a lay preacher in a local Baptist church. In 1925, the radio station CFCN invited him to give Sunday sermons on their "Voice of the Prairie" program. This opportunity enabled him to reach an estimated 350 000 people with his religious message. With financial contributions from listeners, he built the Prophetic Bible Institute in Calgary, which he later used to distribute Social Credit material.

Aberhart "converted" to Social Credit in the summer of 1932 after the suicide of one of his best students as a result of the depression. Thereafter, he introduced Social Credit economic theory into his weekly sermons. Initially, he hoped one of the established political parties would adopt Social Credit. When they failed to do so, he began his own party on the eve of the 1935 provincial election. He promised each citizen a $25-a-month "basic dividend" to purchase necessities. Helping the party to gain popularity was a sex scandal involving the UFA premier John Brownlee, which destroyed his career.

In the 1935 provincial election Social Credit swept Alberta, winning 56 of the 63 seats. Once in power, the new premier and his party could not implement their election promises. The federal government challenged the constitutional legality of a province issuing its own currency. The party also lacked parliamentary expertise, since the majority of its candidates were political neophytes. Only after the outbreak of war, and especially after the discovery of oil in 1947, did the party become well established under Aberhart's protégé, Ernest Manning, who took over after Aberhart's death in 1943. The party would remain in power until 1971.

The Reconstruction Party

H.H. Stevens, a B.C. member of the Bennett government and head of the Select Committee and then of the Royal Commission on Price Spreads, resigned from the cabinet in October 1934 to begin his own party, the Reconstruction party. He promised "to re-establish Canada's industrial, economic and social life for the benefit of the great majority." In the 1935 election, the Reconstruction party won over 8 percent of the popular vote but elected only one candidate, Stevens. The party reduced Conservative support in various constituencies across the country.

Communists and Fascists

Extreme left- and right-wing political movements, such as the Communist Party and fascist groups, grew during the interwar years. The Communist Party of Canada, founded in 1921 in Guelph, Ontario, thrived in the economic-crisis conditions of the depression, especially among immigrants threatened with deportation. It modelled itself after the Soviet Communist Party. Government repression of the party occurred frequently in the decade by invoking section 98 of the Criminal Code, which made it illegal to advocate "governmental, industrial or economic change within Canada by the use of force, violence or physical injury to persons or property, or by threats of such injury" even if the accused did nothing to bring about such changes. In one crackdown in August 1931, party leader Tim Buck and seven others were arrested. As a result of an attempt on Buck's life in Kingston Penitentiary a year later, the "Toronto Eight," as they became known, emerged as the embattled underdogs. They won sympathy from a number of Canadians who believed in the democratic right of left-wing dissident groups to express their views, even if they disagreed with their ideology.

Most Canadians who wanted radical change during the depression preferred the peaceful, democratic approach of the CCF to the violent, revolutionary change advocated by the communists. On the eve of World War II, the Communist Party supposedly had 16 000 members. But when the Soviet Union signed a non-aggression pact with Adolf Hitler that summer, many members quit the party in protest. In June 1940, the Canadian government declared the Communist Party illegal.

Communist-organized May Day parade in Toronto, May 1, 1934. Note the sign, "Release Tim Buck." The Communist Party of Canada leader had been tried and convicted of sedition. Imprisoned in the Kingston Penitentiary in 1932, he gained his release later in 1934.

Source: City of Toronto Archives, Fonds 1266, Globe and Mail Collection, Item 33196.

Fascists proved less numerous than communists in Canada. The Deutscher Bund Canada, founded in 1934 and led by German Canadians, never had more than 2000 members, while the Canadian Nationalist Party, founded by right-wing militants, and the allied Swastika clubs, added a few thousand more. The Swastika clubs tried to stop Jews from visiting Kew and Balmy Beaches in east Toronto. At McGill University in Montreal, officials conspired to turn away Jewish appli-cants. In Quebec, Adrien Arcand patterned his National Social Christian party along Nazi lines. He claimed to represent the last stand of Roman Catholicism against communists and other "atheist" groups. While Arcand remained a marginal and eccentric character, anti-Semitism found support among nationalist movements in the province, such as the Jeune-Canada and the Ligue d'Action nationale.

Thousands of persecuted Jews fleeing Nazi Germany found Canada's doors firmly closed. A leading member of the immigration department summarized the government's view toward Jewish immigrants, "none was too many." Only a few Canadian leaders, such as Cairine Wilson, Canada's first woman senator and chairperson of the Canadian National Committee on Refugees, denounced Nazi atrocities and urged a liberalization of Canadian immigration regulations. Immigration in total reached an all-time low in the 1930s: only 149 000 immigrants were allowed in during the entire decade, and only 5000 of them were Jews.

Provincial Politics and the Economic Crisis

The depression led to political change in the provinces. In most provinces, voters ousted incumbents, although usually in exchange for governments by well-established, as opposed to new, parties.

An anti-Semitic poster at Sainte-Agathe, a resort area in the Laurentians north of Montreal, 1939.

Source: Library and Archives Canada/PA-107943. Reprinted with permission of *The Gazette*, Montreal.

Newfoundland and the Maritimes

Various problems beset Newfoundland in the 1930s, at the time a British dominion; the most important was the falling price of fish as a result of the depression. In 1932, Sir Richard Squires, the Liberal premier, narrowly escaped being lynched by a mob infuriated by disclo-sures of scandal, as well as by the government's tough relief policies when almost half of the island's labour force was out of work. Indeed, the British navy had to be called in to assist local police in controlling rioters. A new government, the United Newfoundland party, took power after the election of 1932. It obtained further bank loans by arguing that the money was needed to ward off "grave threats of insurrection." A royal commis-sion reviewed the economic crisis and recommended the dissolution of the legislature; Newfoundland reverted to the status of a British colony, and London was obliged to pay off the colony's debts.

Canadians in the Maritime provinces elected Liberal governments in the 1930s and kept them in office until the 1950s. In Nova Scotia, Angus L. Macdonald, a former law professor, became premier in 1933. Practising an activist style of government, "Angus L." implemented old age pensions and began paving provincial roads.

He also appointed a royal commission to investigate Nova Scotia's position in Confederation. Norman Macleod Rogers, who taught political science at Queen's University, drafted the province's submission. It argued for additional compensation for Canada's poorer provinces, since their disadvantageous position resulted from their role in Confederation.

In both New Brunswick and Prince Edward Island, the Liberals came to power on promises of economic and social reform. In New Brunswick, Allison Dysart's government introduced old age pensions, created public works projects, and pressured timber companies into activating their leases or else losing them. In Prince Edward Island, Thane Campbell's government had the distinction of being the first to win every seat in a provincial election. In office, Campbell established a permanent civil service and supported cooperative organizations and marketing boards as its response to the depression.

All three provinces lacked the revenues to complete the promised reforms. New Brunswick, for example, borrowed heavily to finance its massive public works program. Inevitably, other priorities suffered. Education and health services declined to barely half the national average by the end of the 1930s, and illiteracy and infant mortality rates in the province were the highest in the country.

Quebec

In Quebec, the new Union Nationale party, under the leadership of Maurice Duplessis, the Conservative leader, allied his party with a dissident left-wing group within the Liberal party called Action libérale nationale, headed by Paul Gouin, son of former Quebec Liberal premier Lomer Gouin. This "unholy alliance" lasted only long enough to defeat in 1936 the long-standing Liberal government, in power since 1897. Thereafter, the right-wing Duplessis purged his government of the Gouin faction.

Duplessis attacked a number of dissident groups in the province, including socialists, communists, and trade unionists. In 1937 he introduced the "Padlock Law," which made it illegal for any group to use a house or hall "to propagate communism or bolshevism" or to publish or distribute literature "tending to propagate communism." As the bill did not define "communist," it gave the premier a weapon with which to attack any left-wing organization he wished. Duplessis used the law to lock premises suspected of being used for communist activities, to ban publications, and, on a couple of occasions, to arrest dissidents. He attacked union leaders, denouncing them as "dangerous agitators," when unions refused to comply with Quebec's labour laws.

Ontario

Next door in Ontario, in 1934, voters ousted the Conservatives, who had been in office since 1923. They elected the Liberals under their flamboyant leader, "Mitch" Hepburn, whose oratorical skills and quick wit served him well on the political hustings. At one country rally, Hepburn gave his speech from the only available stage, a manure spreader. He remarked that it was the first time he had given an address on a "Conservative platform."

Although initially seen as a reformer, Hepburn soon proved to be reactionary. He sided with industrialists against labourers in a bitter sixteen-day strike against General Motors in Oshawa in 1937. He denounced the United Auto Workers union as "communist inspired," and sent in a government-supported police force, dubbed "Hepburn's Hussars" or "sons of Mitches" to break up the strike. Two of his cabinet ministers, Arthur Roebuck and David Croll, resigned in disgust. Croll proclaimed his "place was marching with the workers rather than riding with General Motors."

Quebec premier Maurice Duplessis meets Ontario premier Mitch Hepburn around 1935.

Source: Library and Archives Canada/C-19527.

British Columbia

In British Columbia, another flamboyant and self-assured provincial Liberal leader, T.D. "Duff" Pattullo, became premier in the midst of the depression. Pattullo had won and lost fortunes in a business career in the Yukon and northern British Columbia before entering politics. He won the election of 1933 on the promise of "work and wages" for every provincial resident. His program became known as the "little New Deal," which promised a provincial health-insurance plan, reduced taxes on lower incomes, public works, unemployment insurance, and an economic council with labour representation to study the problem of unemployment. He also believed in injecting money into the economy by spending on major public works projects, such as the bridge that bears his name and the Alaska Highway. In the words of historian Robin Fisher, his biographer, "The first Pattullo administration offered the most vigorous political response to the depression of any government in Canada."[2] But as in Alberta's case, the government of British Columbia lacked the tax base to make these changes. Pattullo looked to the federal government for loans to help his government fight the "war on poverty." When the Conservative, and then Liberal, administrations in Ottawa refused funding requests, Pattullo failed to follow through on many policies. Nevertheless, he managed to get reelected in 1937, giving his government the distinction of being the only government in Canada to be reelected during the depression. It remained in power until 1941, when it was replaced by a Liberal–Conservative coalition party.

Labour in the Great Depression

Workers became more militant in the desperate conditions of the Great Depression. "Red" trade unions grew, and some affiliated with the Communist Party of Canada. For example, the Workers' Unity League (WUL) was born out of a directive from Moscow that communist-led unions should separate from "reformist" unions, like the All-Canadian Congress of Labour (ACCL), and prepare for the coming world revolution. After signing up workers in mines and shops, the WUL declared strikes to obtain union recognition and better wages and working conditions. At its peak in 1932, the WUL had an estimated 40 000 members. It claimed leadership of most of the strikes across the country in the early 1930s. The WUL also organized the unemployed by establishing workers' councils in various cities and by circulating a petition, eventually signed by 300 000 people, calling for a national non-contributory unemployment-insurance scheme.

Violent confrontation often occurred between police and strikers or between strikebreakers and strikers. The worst was in Estevan, Saskatchewan, in 1931, when 600 coal-mine workers walked out of the mines. The owners denounced the strike as "Communist-led," thus ensuring the support of the politicians and the RCMP. The police opened fire during a strikers' parade, killing three unarmed strikers.

The CIO in Canada

In 1935 a new union, the American-based Congress of Industrial Organizations (CIO), emerged in Canada to "organize the unorganized." The Canadian CIO's greatest success occurred in 1937, when the CIO-inspired United Auto Workers led the strike at the General Motors factory in Oshawa, Ontario. Hepburn intervened to break the strike because he feared a CIO victory would encourage unionization and strikes elsewhere in the province. The CIO also organized Montreal's female garment workers, as well as coal miners in Nova Scotia.

Despite some successes and much publicity, however, the CIO made little headway elsewhere in Canada in the 1930s. Strong opposition came from business and the crafts-dominated Trades and Labor Congress (TLC), which in 1939 expelled the CIO affiliates. The CIO then merged with the weaker All-Canadian Congress of Labour in 1940 to form the Canadian Congress of Labour (CCL).

Women in the 1930s

In the 1930s, women's wages fell dramatically and working conditions deteriorated. Initially, the depression benefited women who wanted to work because they could be hired at half a man's wages. Then came the backlash. Women were attacked for taking jobs away from unemployed men who had wives and families to support. CCF member Agnes Macphail pointed out that the economic system, not women, was to blame for unemployment. She added that many women needed to work if they and their families were to survive.

Women faced difficulties getting relief even if they were eligible for it. In addition, many municipalities opposed giving relief to women. Authorities reasoned that single unemployed women posed no threat to society, as did single unemployed men. Furthermore, they assumed that these women would be cared for by their families. As well, authorities feared that relief to women would contribute to the breakdown of the family. A few single women turned to prostitution as a desperate alternative to dire poverty. Some married women assumed the dual responsibilities of "breadwinner" and sole head of the family, as their husbands left home in search of work or simply deserted their families. Destitute single mothers in Ontario could apply for the Ontario Mothers' Allowance, implemented in 1920, but the amount was meagre, and the recipients became, in essence, wards of the State.

Emphasis was placed on women being wives and mothers as their appropriate roles. Over 90 percent of women eventually married. Once married, they were expected to give up their jobs and take up domestic duties. Marriages seldom ended in divorce. Wife abuse increased, especially during the depression. The police were of little assistance; they usually told victims of abuse simply to make the best of matters and to find comfort in their children.

Family size declined in the 1930s. Infant mortality still remained high by today's standards, due to several factors. Babies born in the winter months had to survive the poor heating in even the best-built residences. Infants also faced a wide range of the "childhood diseases"—measles, mumps, scarlet fever, and whooping cough—illnesses that proved deadly then but are now held in check through public-health programs and by antibiotics.

Birth control was seldom an option women could consider, although by 1937 birth-control clinics existed in Toronto, Hamilton, and Windsor. Also available was A.H. Tyrer's popular book, *Sex, Marriage and Birth Control* (1936). The popular belief of the day was expressed by Dr. Helen McMurchy, director of the Dominion Division of Child Welfare, who described birth control among those of British background as "race suicide." French-Canadian nationalists used the same argument in Quebec. The idea of eugenics—the selective breeding of the fittest and the compulsory sterilization of those considered inferior—gained popularity in the 1930s. Heading the movement was A.R. Kaufman, a wealthy manufacturer, who believed that the "inferior" working class was producing over half of the nation's children. Among them were the "irresponsible, criminal and mentally deficient" who were the source of "most of our social liabilities." His solution was to distribute birth-control information and devices and even to perform surgical operations to restrict or prevent reproduction among certain groups.

A few doctors provided birth-control information and devices, but they did so at the risk of losing their medical licence. Dr. Elizabeth Bagshaw, for example, operated a birth-control clinic for working-class women in Hamilton, Ontario. Dorothea Palmer was arrested in a French-Canadian suburb of Ottawa for distributing contraceptive information. At her trial, where both Tyrer and Kaufman lent support, the judge acquitted her because he believed she had acted "for the public good." The poor, he stated, "are a burden to the taxpayer. They crowd the Juvenile Court. They glut the competitive labour market." For some women, self-induced miscarriages seemed to be the only alternative to unwanted children or children they simply could not afford.

Support for birth control tended often to come from socialist groups. Some women socialists believed that the capitalist system encouraged large families so as to have a cheap source of labour for its factories and cannon fodder for its armies. In 1924, British Columbia socialists founded the Canadian Birth Control League to educate working-class women. In 1929, the Saskatchewan section of the United Farmers of Canada recommended the establishment of birth-control clinics staffed by trained doctors.

The First Nations People in the 1930s

During the 1930s, First Nations and Métis communities faced numerous challenges. As Plains Cree historian Stan Cuthand writes of western Canada in the interwar years: "Conditions on Indian reserves in practically every area—social services, health, education, and living facilities—had deteriorated in the years since the signing of the treaties."[3] The Indian Act's tight regulations remained in full force. But a ray of hope emerged in this decade: political organization. British Columbia had led the way with the formation of the Allied Tribes of British Columbia in 1915, replaced by the more powerful Native Brotherhood of British Columbia in 1931. Fred Loft's League of Indians of Canada, founded after World War I, briefly became the first pan-Indian political organization extending across Canada in the early 1920s. It contributed to the formation of the Indian Association of Alberta in 1929 that also publicized Aboriginal claims.

Liberal Policies

Once back in power after the federal election of 1935, Mackenzie King's Liberals continued some of the Conservatives' policies to cope with the depression and added some of their own. The Liberals, for instance, supported the Bank of Canada as an essential stabilizing force in a time of financial crisis. After the government purchased a majority of the bank's stock, King made its governor responsible to Parliament for monetary policy. But the Liberals altered the Conservatives' high tariff policy. Charles Dunning, the finance minister and former premier of Saskatchewan, negotiated low tariff agreements with both Britain and the United States.

The Prairie Farm Rehabilitation Program

King continued the Conservatives' policy of aid to the drought-stricken farmers of western Canada. The Liberals even extended assistance by implementing the Prairie Farm Rehabilitation Act (PFRA), which provided money to experiment with new farming methods, especially in the dry-belt area of the Palliser Triangle. The experimental farms in the region applied the latest scientific knowledge to attempt to get the soil to regain its productivity. Two innovations followed: first, the Noble plough, invented by Charles Noble of Nobleford, Alberta, which cut the roots of weeds without turning over the topsoil to expose it to sun and wind; second, "trash farming"— instead of ploughing and harrowing their fields to make them look neat and clean, farmers were encouraged to leave the dead plants and grain stubble on the field to prevent wind erosion. The PFRA's program also provided money to build dugouts for spring runoff water for cattle, helped reseed vacant and pasture land, and, in the case of destitute farm families in the Palliser Triangle area, assisted relocation to better farming areas to the north.

The CBC, TCA, and NHA

The Liberals created two innovative national institutions and introduced two important social-security measures in the 1930s. In 1936, they reorganized the Canadian Radio Broadcasting Commission, founded in 1932 to control radio under federal government jurisdiction, into the Canadian Broadcasting Corporation (CBC). According to Graham Spry, whose Canadian Radio League had fought for such an institution, the choice was between "the State or the United States." The government mandated the CBC to regulate private broadcasting and to develop its own network across the country with Canadian content in both official languages. Political scientist Jack McLeod sees the creation of the CBC as "the 20th-century parallel to Macdonald's railway."[4] In 1937, the Liberals established Trans-Canada Air Lines (TCA), the forerunner of Air Canada, as a Crown corporation. Two other federal initiatives proved successful: the Municipal Improvements Assistance Act, which authorized $30 million in federal loans at 2 percent interest for special municipal public-works projects, and the National Housing Act (NHA), which made federally backed mortgages easier to obtain. The NHA provided $30 million worth of mortgages for low-income tenants. It also allowed potential homeowners to borrow at least 60 percent of value for up to 20 to 25 years, and repayment of both interest and principal under a system of blended payments. Historian Richard Harris sees this new financing arrangement as "a key development in suburb development" by allowing more people to buy a home.[5]

The King government also addressed the relief question. It discontinued Bennett's relief camps and instead sent young unemployed males to farms as cheap labour. It established the National Employment Commission to reexamine and restructure the administration of direct relief. In 1867, relief had been a very minor matter, assigned in the BNA Act to the provinces and municipalities. The commission made two important recommendations: first, that the federal government take over unemployment payments because this was too big and expensive an undertaking for municipal or provincial governments; and second, that the government adopt a policy of deficit financing to provide additional relief and stimulate economic growth. King hesitated in acquiring federal responsibility for unemployment and relief, responsibilities that would increase the federal debt load. He also resisted the Keynesian monetary policy of deficit financing, which went against his traditional liberal policies of laissez-faire and a balanced budget.

The Royal Commission on Dominion–Provincial Relations

Before moving on either issue, King created the Royal Commission on Dominion–Provincial Relations to explore all aspects of relations between these two levels of government in light of the current economic crisis. Heralded by the federal government as the most important royal commission in Canadian history, the Rowell–Sirois Commission, as it became known after its head commissioners, N.W. Rowell of Ontario and Joseph Sirois of Quebec, recommended a stronger federal-government economic presence. The decision to launch the commission ran into strong provincial opposition from both Hepburn in Ontario and Duplessis in Quebec. Its report did not appear until 1940; Parliament had just a year earlier imposed the War Measures Act, which gave the government licence to impose many aspects of the report's centralist agenda without consulting the provinces, at least for the duration of the war.

Religion

Many Canadians turned to religion for solace and direction in the depression. The trend was to move away from radical religion, with its emphasis on social reform, to a more conservative faith, with its emphasis on personal salvation and the importance of tradition. Nevertheless, a few radical groups gained some support during the depression. Some socially minded Protestants looked to the Fellowship for a Christian Social Order, founded by members of the United Church, for answers to the economic crisis. Fellowship members insisted that realizing the kingdom of God on Earth meant replacing a bankrupt capitalist system with socialism. Critics of the group complained that too many of its members were more committed to the teachings of Karl Marx than those of Jesus Christ.

Student activists turned to the Student Christian Movement (SCM), an organization begun in 1920 by the YWCA and YMCA. The SCM provided study groups on most Canadian university campuses in the 1930s to discuss social issues and advocate social change. For young girls, the Canadian Girls in Training (CGIT), an organization founded by the YWCA and the Protestant churches in 1917 to train young girls to improve both their lives and those of others, reached its peak of popularity during the depression, when it had an estimated 40 000 members.

Conservative and fundamentalist groups flourished in the decade. Church leaders promised that if people could not find salvation in this world, they could still hope in the afterlife. Disciples of the British Oxford Movement (a predecessor of Moral Rearmament) toured Canada, delivering a message of "revelation, not revolution" to overflow audiences, which on one occasion included R.B. Bennett and his entire cabinet, at Bennett's request.

In Quebec, many in the Roman Catholic church saw the depression as evidence of divine punishment for the sins of humankind—sins that included communism, materialism, urbanization, and even capitalism. They supported a back-to-the-land movement as the best means to combat both unemployment and "moral decrepitude."

WHERE HISTORIANS DISAGREE

Protestantism and Reform in the 1930s

In the late nineteenth and early twentieth centuries, the Protestant churches increasingly advocated and worked for social reform. Essentially, historians have debated whether this move to reform strengthened or weakened the Protestant faith. The decade of the 1930s has been important in this debate, because all churches were called upon to take a more active social role by helping individuals and families who were suffering during the depression.

An earlier generation of religious historians saw a split among the Protestant churches, between conservative and fundamentalist ones that emphasized personal salvation, and liberal and radical ones that stressed social salvation. They also noted a correlation between religious beliefs and political affiliation, at least in regard to new political reform movements and parties on the Prairies in the 1930s. W.E. Mann argued that the greatest support for Social Credit came from the fundamentalist churches and religious sects and cults.[1] Historians David Elliott and Iris Miller disagreed. They argue that the mainline Protestant churches, including those adhering to a liberal theology, most strongly supported Aberhart and his Social Credit movement.[2] Analysts of the Co-operative Commonwealth Federation (CCF) have noted an equally strong religious affiliation. Political scientist Walter Young noted that the party's leadership came largely from the left-wing Methodist church and its offspring, the United Church of Canada.[3] Historian Kenneth McNaught emphasized the importance of Methodism in the life of J.S. Woodsworth, the founding leader of the CCF.[4]

More recently, religious historians have examined the social gospel movement in the Protestant churches in the late nineteenth and early twentieth centuries. Richard Allen argued that industrialization and urbanization created new social problems that required the attention of the Protestant churches.[5] The resulting reform impulse inaugurated an era of revivalism that kept Protestantism alive and active well into the twentieth century. In the 1930s, the Fellowship for a Christian Social Order (FCSO), a socialist group consisting largely of ministers and sons of the manse, brought religion to the CCF.

Historian Ramsay Cook disagreed with Allen. He argued that the social gospel movement undermined the Protestant faith by getting churches involved in social issues that were more secular than sacred. As a result, religion went into a decline that has led to the modern secular society.[6] David Marshall argued that during the Great Depression many clergy appealed for an evangelical revivalism to cope with the social dislocation. But their appeal went unheeded, because "years of accommodating religion with modernism and diluting the supernatural elements of Christianity"[7] left religion a spent force in the 1930s.

The anti-secularists replied, led by historian Michael Gauvreau. He maintained that the Methodist and Presbyterian churches survived the onslaught of secularism in the late nineteenth century through a reformulation of their tradition of evangelicalism to fit the changing times and emerged with a "persistence and vitality" that served them well in the twentieth century. Far from being a spent force, as the secularists argued, Protestantism was alive and well in the twentieth century, and it played a meaningful role in dealing with social concerns in the 1930s. If Protestantism did decline, it was after the Great Depression, Gauvreau argued.[8]

Entering the debate, historian Neil Semple pointed out that to the Methodists everything was sacred because "everything belonged to God," and therefore secularism posed no threat. Furthermore, he suggested looking at the sacred–secular issue not as a linear progression but as something that came and went, somewhat like "waves." One such "wave" occurred in the 1930s, when even social gospellers "underwent a traumatic crisis of faith and sought a spiritual revival for themselves and for the entire church."[9]

The debate is certain to continue as religious historians seek to understand the role of religion in the reform impulse of the late nineteenth and twentieth centuries and the impact of that symbiotic relationship on the Protestant faith.

1   W.E. Mann, *Sect, Cult and Church in Alberta* (Toronto: University of Toronto Press, 1955).

2   David Elliott and Iris Miller, *"Bible Bill": A Biography of William Aberhart* (Edmonton: Reidmore Books, 1987).

3   Walter Young, *The Anatomy of a Party: The National CCF* (Toronto: University of Toronto Press, 1969).

4   Kenneth McNaught, *A Prophet in Politics: A Biography of J.S. Woodsworth* (Toronto: University of Toronto Press, 1959).

5   Richard Allen, *The Social Passion: Religion and Social Reform in Canada, 1914–1928* (Toronto: University of Toronto Press, 1971).

6   Ramsay Cook, *The Regenerators: Social Criticism in Late Victorian English Canada* (Toronto: University of Toronto Press, 1985).

7   David B. Marshall, *Secularizing the Faith: Canadian Protestant Clergy and the Crisis of Belief, 1850–1940* (Toronto: University of Toronto Press, 1992), p. 254.

8   Michael Gauvreau, *The Evangelical Century: College and Creed in English Canada from the Great Revival to the Great Depression* (Montreal/Kingston: McGill-Queen's University Press, 1991).

9   Neil Semple, *The Lord's Domain: The History of Methodism* (Toronto: University of Toronto Press, 1996), p. 448.

The Antigonish Movement

Still others, particularly those in the Maritimes, looked to cooperatives as the answer. In 1931, Pope Pius XI issued his encyclical *Quadragesimo anno*, in which he attacked the competitive nature of capitalism as heartless and cruel, and advocated cooperation instead. His appeal found a receptive audience in the cooperative movement in eastern Canada.

Beginning in the late 1920s and throughout the 1930s, Moses Coady, director of the extension department at St. Francis Xavier University in Antigonish, Nova Scotia, and Jimmy Tompkins, a fellow priest, worked to improve the lives of poor farmers, miners, fishers, and their families. A representative of this young cooperative movement would visit a community and, using local contacts, call a public meeting. A study group would follow to assess the community's economic strengths and weaknesses. After the group's meetings concluded, one or more cooperatives would form to remedy the identifiable weaknesses. The cooperatives might be credit unions, or perhaps cooperatives for selling fish or farm produce. When accused of being too left-wing, Father Coady replied: "I'm not a leftist; I'm where the righteous ought to be."

A Canadian Girls in Training (CGIT) meeting, probably in Toronto, around 1920. The Young Women's Christian Association and the major Protestant denominations established the organization in 1915 to promote the Christian education of girls aged 12 to 17.

Source: Canadian Girls in Training Collection/Library and Archives Canada/PA-125872.

Culture in the 1930s

During the 1930s, popular culture flourished. New forms of entertainment—radio, for instance—allowed a greater choice of escapes from the realities of the depression. Owners of radio sets in English-speaking Canada listened to the comedy show *Amos 'n Andy*, the most popular program of the decade. *Hockey Night in Canada*, with Foster Hewitt, was also a regular favourite. Such recording artists as Willie Eckstein, Percy Faith, and Guy Lombardo and His Royal Canadians got their start on Canadian radio, although by 1940 both Percy Faith and Guy Lombardo had left Canada for larger dance floors in the United States. Lombardo's famous "Auld Lang Syne" had its origins in the Scottish communities of Ontario where he played, but it became synonymous with the American New Year's Eve celebration. Don Messer began playing his "old time" fiddle music on radio in the 1930s, and formed "The Islanders" for CFLY radio in Charlottetown, Prince Edward Island in 1939. French Canadians enjoyed the immensely successful serials written specifically for radio, such as "Le Curé de Village" and "La Pension Velder." Radio variety shows were equally popular programs in Quebec. The songs of "La Bolduc," Mary Travers-Bolduc, enjoyed enormous popularity.

Mass magazines, both Canadian and American, featured stories of wealth and glamour, while films from Hollywood portrayed romance and fantasy. Walt Disney's *Snow White and the Seven Dwarfs* became a box-office hit. While English Canada was looking to Hollywood for its feature films, French Canada was excelling in documentaries. Albert Tessier and Maurice Proulx, two Catholic priests who took an amateur interest in documentaries, did films that glorified Quebec's natural landscape and the life of its rural inhabitants as their contribution to the "back to the land" movement in the province.

The birth of the Dionne quintuplets near Callander, Ontario, in May 1934, attracted worldwide attention and brought over three million people to see a glimpse of them at a special hospital set up to care for them under the auspices of the Ontario government—a government that quickly appreciated the profit to be made from this "tourist attraction." Even this real-life event was a form of escape for the many who came.

Visual Art

In 1933, the Canadian Group of Painters (CGP) formed as an expansion of the Group of Seven. It held its first exhibition that year in Atlantic City, New Jersey. During the 1930s, the group focused its activities in three cities—Toronto, Montreal, and Vancouver. It formed a loose-knit association that provided moral support for artists who were affiliated with it. Younger members included A.J. Casson, Yvonne McKague Housser, Edwin Holgate, Gordon Webber, Isabel McLaughlin, Carl Schaefer, Charles Comfort, Paraskeva Clark, and J.W.G. (Jock) Macdonald. The older members, Arthur Lismer and A.Y. Jackson, the key figures of this new group, linked it directly to the earlier Group of Seven. Art education became an important goal of the CGP. As educational supervisor of the Art Gallery of Toronto, Lismer established the most successful children's art program in North America in the mid-1930s.

Concurrently with the Group of Seven's ascendancy in English-speaking Canada, French-Canadian painters showed a similar fascination with the land. Marc-Aurèle Fortin became a major landscape painter, but his inspiration came from visits to Chicago, Boston, and New York, and later to southern France and northern Italy, where he was especially influenced by the style of the Spanish painter Sorolla y Bastida. His pastoral canvases of the village of Sainte-Rose and of scenes along the north shore of Montreal Island are noted for their subdued colours. After 1935, he began painting in more vibrant, luminous colours. Art critic J. Russell Harper notes: "Fortin accomplished in Quebec what the Group of Seven had accomplished in Ontario: he painted the Quebec landscape as a symbol of the way in which he knew and felt it…. [But] he had one feature which is never found in the work of the Ontario artists: a religious overtone."[6]

Religious subjects also appeared in the early paintings of Jean-Paul Lemieux in the 1930s. He chose colourful Fête-Dieu processions in Quebec streets and other religious events as subjects for his paintings. They too, like Fortin's, were noted for their quiet nostalgia and gentle lyricism.

The period also marked the death of a giant from an earlier era, Marc-Aurèle de Foy Suzor-Côté, in 1937. His obituary in the *Montreal Star* recognized him as "French Canada's greatest painter, and one of her greatest sculptors. His large canvases breathe the very atmosphere and colour of the woods of his beloved Quebec."

Novels

In the 1930s, Morley Callaghan's three novels—*Such Is My Beloved* (1934), *They Shall Inherit the Earth* (1935), and *More Joy in Heaven* (1937)—stood out as good examples of realistic novels, a reaction to the sentimental and romantic literature of an earlier generation. Irene Baird's *Waste Heritage* (1939) dealt with labour unrest and unemployment in Vancouver during the depression. The most outstanding French-Canadian novel in the 1930s was Ringuet's (Philippe Panneton's) *Trente Arpents*, translated into English as *Thirty Acres*, a realistic novel that graphically depicted the transition from rural to urban life in Quebec. It broke with literary tradition in Quebec in describing the French-Canadian farmer as a tragic, rather than heroic, figure. The novel follows the fall of its central character, Euchariste Moisan, from initial prosperity on his farm to a broken man in a New England factory town.

Theatre

During the 1930s in Quebec, several of the best-known French-Canadian playwrights, such as Gratien Gélinas, learned their trade by writing scripts for radio productions, especially for the Canadian Broadcasting Corporation (CBC). But criticism arose once again concerning the propriety of the theatre. When a Parisian company performed the popular but risqué operetta *Phi-Phi* at Montreal's St.-Denis theatre, a judge declared it indecent, closed it down, and levied $15 fines on each of the actors, their agents, and even the orchestra leader.

Although the Roman Catholic church opposed public theatre for entertainment purposes, the clergy did support amateur theatre for educational purposes. Father Émile Legault founded in 1937 a troupe of young actors at Montreal's Collège de Saint-Laurent that from 1938 to 1952 set the pace for a theatrical renaissance in Quebec. With his encouragement, the group moved from an early emphasis on religious theatre to a concentration on classical and contemporary plays. Félix Leclerc, the famous Quebec singer, songwriter, playwright, and actor, acted with the Compagnons de St. Laurent in the early 1940s.

In English Canada, professional theatre languished in the depressed atmosphere of the 1930s. Most theatre groups, which were barely able to hold on during the good times, folded in the depression. Amateur theatre groups took their place. Governor General Lord Bessborough, a theatre enthusiast, assisted amateur theatre by founding in 1932 the Dominion Drama Festival, an annual competition that included amateur societies at the local, regional, and national levels. The best provincial productions went on to national finals, held each year in a different major city. The first competition was held in Ottawa in April 1933, and included 168 participants. During its nearly 40-year existence, the festival inaugurated the careers of a significant number of later-professional actors and actresses.

Young Canadian *(1932), by Charles Comfort. A portrait of fellow-artist Carl Schaefer, whose disillusioned eyes and empty, hanging hands symbolized the Great Depression.*

Source: Hart House, Permanent Collection, University of Toronto.

While professional theatre languished during the 1930s, working-class political theatre emerged. Especially popular was the agitprop troupe (agitprop is a combination of the words "agitation" and "propaganda") theatre used by communist sympathizers to advance class struggle. The conditions of the depression provided both the actors, in the form of unemployed workers and student agitators, and a sympathetic and enthusiastic audience for such theatre.

The Workers' Experimental Theatre became the first agitprop troupe in Canada, and it held its first performance on May 6, 1932, at the Ukrainian Labour Temple. This was followed in the summer of 1933 by three tours through southern Ontario. But their greatest success occurred in December 1933 when the group staged *Eight Men Speak*, a mock trial drama of the arrest two years earlier in 1931 and attempted assassination at the Kingston Penitentiary of Tim Buck, leader of the Communist Party. Many of the actors themselves risked arrest (and in some cases deportation) for taking part in the play, while theatre owners were threatened with having their licences revoked should they permit the play to be staged in their theatre. In the end, only one performance of the entire play was performed to a packed audience of 1500 at the Standard Theatre on Spadina Avenue in Toronto.

Sport

Sport became another form of popular entertainment and a distraction during the depression. In winter, hockey dominated. Hockey stars became household names among sports-minded families: the Toronto Maple Leafs' famous "Kid Line" of Charlie Conacher, Joe Primeau, and Busher Jackson; the legendary Eddie Shore of the Boston Bruins, known for his speed and scoring flair; Francis "King" Clancy of the Toronto Maple Leafs, who once played every position on the ice in a single game; and Howie Morenz of the Montreal Canadiens, with his speed and flashy stick-handling, who was easily the greatest hockey superstar of the 1930s. Shortly after Morenz's tragic death on January 28, 1937, as a result of injuries received in a game, thousands of Montrealers filed past his bier, placed at centre ice in the Montreal Forum.

In summer, baseball continued to be Canada's most popular sport. Every community had a local team, and the larger towns and cities enjoyed franchises in minor professional leagues. As well, Canadians followed American big-league baseball as though it were their own "national" sport and cheered the successes of the legendary Babe Ruth. Canadian baseball fans gathered in front of the newspaper offices to watch the World Series as it was recorded on a scale-modelled baseball diamond, while an announcer described the game as it came in over the wire service.

The Great Depression affected all aspects of Canadian society. Out of desperation, people turned to the government for financial assistance. Governments, in turn, reluctantly accepted new economic and social responsibilities. New political parties appeared, each one offering its own solution to the depression. Women and labourers made only marginal gains. Many turned to religion for guidance. Popular culture flourished as people sought an escape from the harsh reality around them.

NOTES

1. John Herd Thompson with Allen Seager, *Canada, 1922–1939: Decades of Discord* (Toronto: McClelland & Stewart, 1985), p. 194.

2. Robin Fisher and David J. Mitchell, "Patterns of Provincial Politics Since 1916," in Hugh J.M. Johnston, ed., *The Pacific Province: A History of British Columbia* (Vancouver: Douglas & McIntyre, 1996), p. 259.

3. Stan Cuthand, "The Native Peoples of the Prairie Provinces in the 1920's and 1930's," in Ian A.L. Getty and Donald B. Smith, eds., *One Century Later: Western Canadian Reserve Indians Since Treaty 7* (Vancouver: University of British Columbia Press, 1978), p. 41.

4. Jack McLeod, "Taking a Leaf from Sir John's Good Book," *Globe and Mail*, January 11, 1997, p. D-5.

5. Richard Harris, *Creeping Conformity: How Canada Became Suburban, 1900–1960* (Toronto: University of Toronto Press, 2004), p. 11.

6. J. Russell Harper, *Painting in Canada: A History*, 2nd ed. (Toronto: University of Toronto Press, 1977), p. 296.

BEYOND THE BOOK

Weblinks

The Dirty Thirties

http://www.mccord-museum.qc.ca/en/keys/webtours/GE_P4_1_EN

A virtual exhibit of life in the Great Depression in Canada, with digitized photographs and analysis.

An Account of the Great Depression

http://www.junobeach.org/e/2/can-eve-eve-dep-bro-e.htm

A vivid, first-hand account of life as a farmer in the Great Depression by Barry Broadfoot.

Mary Travers-Bolduc

http://www.histori.ca/minutes/minute.do?id=10209

This public service history minute showcases Mary Travers-Bolduc, a popular French Canadian singer in the 1930s.

United Farm Women of Alberta: Monthly Bulletins

http://asalive.archivesalberta.org:8080/access/asa/documents/display/GLEN-247

Digitized monthly bulletins of the United Farm Women of Alberta, covering economic, social welfare, and other topics.

Conditions and Culture in the Great Depression

http://history.cbc.ca/history/?MIval=Section.
html&series_id=1&episode_id=13&chapter_id=1&lang=E

An exploration with photographs and analysis of the conditions and culture of Canadian workers in the Great Depression.

Films & Novels

Clara Callan. By Richard B. Wright. 2002.

Of This Earth: a Mennonite Boyhood in the Boreal Forest. By Rudy Wiebe. 2006.

As for Me and My House. By Sinclair Ross. 1989.

RELATED READINGS

R. Douglas Francis and Donald B. Smith, eds., *Readings in Canadian History: Post-Confederation*, 7th ed. (Toronto: Thomson Nelson, 2006), contains two articles relevant to this chapter: Lara Campbell, "'We Who Have Wallowed in the Mud of Flanders': First World War Veterans, Unemployment and the Development of Social Welfare in Canada, 1929–1939," pp. 390–408; and James Struthers, "Canadian Unemployment Policy in the 1930s," pp. 408–417.

BIBLIOGRAPHY

A popular account of the 1930s is Pierre Berton, *The Great Depression, 1929–1939* (Toronto: McClelland & Stewart, 1990). For a more scholarly account see John Herd Thompson with Allen Seager, *Canada, 1922–1939: Decades of Discord* (Toronto: McClelland & Stewart, 1985). For a good, brief synthesis see Michiel Horn's booklet *The Great Depression of the 1930s in Canada* (Ottawa: Canadian Historical Association, 1984). A.E. Safarian analyzes economic developments in *The Canadian Economy in the Great Depression* (Toronto: University of Toronto Press, 1959). The stock-market crash of 1929 is discussed in Doug Fetherling, *Gold Diggers of 1929: Canada and the Great Stock Market Crash* (Toronto: Macmillan, 1979).

A wealth of material exists on politics in the 1930s. H. Blair Neatby provides an overview in *The Politics of Chaos: Canada in the Thirties* (Toronto: Macmillan, 1972). On R.B. Bennett consult Larry A. Glassford, *Reaction and Reform: The Politics of the Conservative Party Under R.B. Bennett, 1927–1938* (Toronto: University of Toronto Press, 1992). Federal financial measures are studied in Robert B. Bryce, *Maturing in Hard Times: Canada's Department of Finance Through the Great Depression* (Toronto: Institute of Public Administration of Canada, 1986). On the founding of the Bank of Canada and on its first president see Douglas H. Fullerton, *Graham Towers and His Times* (Toronto: McClelland & Stewart, 1986). On the New Deal see J.R.H. Wilbur, ed., *The Bennett New Deal: Fraud or Portent* (Toronto: Copp Clark, 1968).

How Canada dealt with jobless or "radical" immigrants is discussed in Barbara Roberts, *Whence They Came: Deportation from Canada, 1900–1935* (Ottawa: University of Ottawa Press, 1988). James Struthers has studied the relief question in *No Fault of Their Own: Unemployment and the Canadian Welfare State, 1914–1941* (Toronto: University of Toronto Press, 1983), and, for Ontario, his *The Limits of Affluence: Welfare in Ontario, 1920–1970* (Toronto: University of Toronto Press, 1994). See as well Raymond B. Blake and Jeff Keshen, eds., *Social Welfare Policy in Canada: Historical Readings* (Toronto: Copp Clark, 1995); and Cynthia R. Comacchio, *"Nations Are Built of Babies": Saving Ontario's Mothers and Children, 1900–1940* (Montreal/Kingston: McGill-Queen's University Press, 1993).

On the response of Canadians to the depression, see R.D. Francis and H. Ganzevoort, eds., *The Dirty Thirties in Prairie Canada* (Vancouver: Tantalus Research, 1980); Michiel Horn, ed., *The Dirty Thirties: Canadians in the Great Depression* (Toronto: Copp Clark, 1972); James Gray, *The Winter Years* (Toronto: Macmillan, 1990 [1966]), and his *Men Against the Desert* (Saskatoon: Western Producer Prairie Books, 1967); and the poignant L.M. Grayson and Michael Bliss, eds., *The Wretched of Canada: Letters to R.B. Bennett, 1930–1935* (Toronto: University of Toronto Press, 1971). On one memorable episode of the depression see Bill Waiser, *All Hell Can't Stop Us: The On-to-Ottawa Trek and the Regina Riot* (Calgary: Fifth House, 2003). On the relief camps see Laurel Sefton MacDowell, "Relief Camp Workers in Ontario During the Great Depression of the 1930s," *Canadian Historical Review* 76(2) (June 1995): 205–28.

Much material on Canada's socialists is available. Walter Young, *The Anatomy of a Party: The National CCF* (Toronto: University of Toronto Press, 1969), is a good analysis. See also Michiel Horn, *The League for Social Reconstruction: Intellectual Origins of the Democratic Left in Canada, 1931–42* (Toronto: University of Toronto Press, 1980). Biographical works on J.S. Woodsworth include Grace McInnis, *J.S. Woodsworth* (Toronto: Macmillan, 1953); and Kenneth McNaught, *A Prophet in Politics* (Toronto: University of Toronto Press, 1959). Three studies in intellectual history are David Laycock, *Populism and Democratic Thought in the Canadian Prairies, 1919–1945* (Toronto: University of Toronto Press, 1990); Allen Mills, *Fool for Christ: The Political Thought of J.S. Woodsworth* (Toronto: University of Toronto

Press, 1991); and R. Douglas Francis, *Frank H. Underhill: Intellectual Provocateur* (Toronto: University of Toronto Press, 1986).

On Social Credit see David R. Elliott and Iris Miller, *Bible Bill: A Biography of William Aberhart* (Edmonton: Reidmore Books, 1987); and Alvin Finkel, *The Social Credit Phenomenon in Alberta* (Toronto: University of Toronto Press, 1989). Two recent studies have examined anti-Semitism in Social Credit: Bob Hesketh, *Major Douglas and Alberta Social Credit* (Toronto: University of Toronto Press, 1997) and Janice Stingel, *Social Discredit: Anti-Semitism, Social Credit, and the Jewish Response* (Montreal/Kingston: McGill-Queen's University Press, 2000). On the Communist Party see Norman Penner, *Canadian Communism: The Stalin Years and Beyond* (Toronto: Methuen Publications, 1988). Extreme right-wing movements are examined in Martin Robin, *Shades of Right: Nativist and Fascist Politics in Canada, 1920 to 1940* (Toronto: University of Toronto Press, 1991). Esther Delisle discusses anti-Semitism in Quebec in *The Traitor and the Jew: Anti-Semitism and Extreme Right-Wing Nationalism in Quebec from 1929 to 1939* (Montreal: R. Davies, 1993).

On Quebec see Richard Jones's booklet, *Duplessis and the Union Nationale Administration* (Ottawa: Canadian Historical Association, 1983); and the relevant chapters in Paul-André Linteau et al., *Quebec Since 1930* (Toronto: James Lorimer 1991). On the history of the Union Nationale party consult H.F. Quinn, *The Union Nationale*, rev. ed. (Toronto: University of Toronto Press, 1979). For Ontario see John T. Saywell, *"Just Call Me Mitch": The Life of Mitchell F. Hepburn* (Toronto: University of Toronto Press, 1992). On Duff Pattullo in British Columbia consult Robin Fisher, *Duff Pattullo of British Columbia* (Toronto: University of Toronto Press, 1991).

On the social impact of relief consult Dennis Guest, *The Emergence of Social Security in Canada* (Vancouver: University of British Columbia Press, 1980). For a personal memoir see James Gray, *The Winter Years* (Toronto: Macmillan, 1966). Irving Abella and Harold Troper, *None Is Too Many: Canada and the Jews of Europe, 1933–1948*, 3rd ed. (Toronto: Lester, 1991), is a poignant account of Canada's treatment of Jewish refugees. On the growth of suburbia in Canada, see Richard Harris, *Creeping Conformity: How Canada Became Suburban, 1900–1960* (Toronto: University of Toronto Press, 2004).

Labour in the interwar years is discussed in Bryan D. Palmer, *Working-Class Experience: Rethinking the History of Canadian Labour, 1800–1991* (Toronto: McClelland & Stewart, 1992). On the 1930s see Evelyn Dumas, *The Bitter Thirties in Quebec* (Montreal: Black Rose Books, 1975); The Saskatchewan miners' struggle of 1931 is examined in Stephen L. Endicott, *Bienfait: the Saskatchewan Miners' Struggle of '31* (Toronto: University of Toronto Press, 2002).

On women in the 1930s see the relevant chapters in Alison Prentice et al., *Canadian Women: A History*, 2nd ed. (Toronto: Harcourt Brace, 1996); and Veronica Strong-Boag, *The New Day Recalled: Lives of Girls and Women in English Canada, 1919–1939*, rev. ed. (Toronto: Copp Clark Pitman, 1993). The equivalent study for Quebec women is Andrée Lévesque, *Making and Breaking the Rules: Women in Quebec, 1919–1939* (Toronto: McClelland & Stewart, 1994). Consult, as well, articles in Linda Kealey and Joan Sangster, eds., *Beyond the Vote: Canadian Women and Politics* (Toronto: University of Toronto Press, 1989). On gender and the welfare state, see Nancy Christie, *Engendering the State: Family, Work, and Welfare in Canada* (Toronto: University of Toronto Press, 2000) and Margaret Jane Hillyard Little, *"No Car, No Radio, No Liquor Permit": The Moral Regulation of Single Mothers in Ontario, 1920–1977* (Toronto: University of Toronto Press, 1998).

Birth control is the subject of Angus McLaren and Arlene Tigar McLaren, *The Bedroom and the State: The Changing Practices and Politics of Contraception and Abortion in Canada, 1890–1980* (Toronto: McClelland & Stewart, 1986); and Mary F. Bishop, "Vivian Dowding: Birth Control Activist," in Veronica Strong-Boag and Anita Clair Fellman, eds., *Rethinking Canada: The Promise of Women's History* (Toronto: Copp Clark Pitman, 1986), pp. 200–07; and Diane Dodd, "The Canadian Birth Control Movement on Trial, 1936–37," *Histoire sociale/Social History* 16 (November 1983): 411–28. On the Dionne quintuplets see the special issue of the *Journal of Canadian Studies* 29(4) (Winter 1995).

For First Nations in western Canada in the 1930s, two works provide good starting points: Hugh A. Dempsey, *The Gentle Persuader: A Biography of James Gladstone, Indian Senator* (Saskatoon: Western Producer Prairie Books, 1986); and Norma Sluman and Jean Goodwill, *John Tootoosis: A Biography of a Cree Leader* (Ottawa: Golden Dog Press, 1982). Laurie Meijer Dress's chapter "The Origins of the IAA," in the *Indian Association of Alberta: A History of Political Action* (Vancouver: UBC Press, 2002), pp. 9–27 provides a good overview of the 1930s in Alberta. For Ontario, see Robin Jarvis Brownlie, *A Fatherly Eye: Indian Agents, Government Power, and Aboriginal Resistance in Ontario, 1918-1939* (Toronto: Oxford University Press, 2003). J.L. Taylor has written *Canadian Indian Policy During the Interwar Years, 1918–1939* (Ottawa: Department of Indian Affairs and Northern Development, 1984). Murray Dobbin's *The One-and-a-Half Men: The Story of Jim Brady and Malcolm Norris, Métis Patriots of the Twentieth Century* (Vancouver: New Star Books, 1981) is a good study of Métis developments in western Canada in the 1930s.

University education in the 1930s is the subject of Paul Axelrod's *Making a Middle Class: Student Life in English Canada During the Thirties* (Montreal/Kingston: McGill-Queen's University Press, 1990). On religion see J.W. Grant, *The Church in the Canadian Era: The First Century of Confederation* (Burlington, ON: Welch, 1988).

On cultural nationalism in the 1930s see Mary Vipond, *The Mass Media in Canada*, rev. ed. (Toronto: James Lorimer, 1992). For painting see J. Russell Harper, *Painting in Canada: A History*, 2nd ed. (Toronto: University of Toronto Press, 1977); and Dennis Reid, *A Concise History of Canadian Painting*, 2nd ed. (Toronto: Oxford University Press, 1988). On music see George A. Proctor, *Canadian Music of the Twentieth Century* (Toronto: University of Toronto Press, 1980). On theatre in Quebec see Elaine F. Nardocchio, *Theatre and Politics in Modern Quebec* (Edmonton: University of Alberta Press, 1986); and Jean Hamelin, *The Theatre in French Canada (1936–66)* (Quebec: Department of Cultural Affairs, 1968). On working-class theatre see Richard Wright and Robin Endres, eds., *Eight Men Speak and Other Plays from the Canadian Workers' Theatre* (Toronto: New Hogtown Press, 1976). On sport, see the relevant section in Colin D. Howell, *Blood, Sweat, and Cheers: Sport and the Making of Modern Canada* (Toronto: University of Toronto Press, 2001), and for women and sport, M. Ann Hall, *The Girl and the Game: History of Women Sport in Canada* (Peterborough: Broadview Press, 2002).

Chapter Thirteen

CANADA IN WORLD WAR II

TIME LINE

1935	Italian leader Benito Mussolini invades Ethiopia
1939	World War II begins; Canada declares war on Germany
1940	Unemployment insurance scheme begun by federal government Canada and the United States sign the Ogdensburg Agreement
1941	Canadian Women's Army Corps established
1942	Plebiscite on conscription held in April Canadian troops participate in the ill-fated raid on Dieppe
1943	Canadian troops join Allied forces in the invasion of Italy
1944	Family Allowance Act, Canada's first universal social-welfare program, comes into effect Canadian troops participate in the invasion of Normandy Conscription decreed
1945	World War II ends Strike at Ford motor plant in Windsor, Ontario Canada joins the United Nations Organization

During the 1930s, many Canadians felt that their government should use its newly recognized autonomy in international affairs to avoid being dragged into international conflicts. Yet once Britain declared war on Germany in September 1939, doubt no longer existed that Canada would participate. But to what degree? And in what form? Those questions would be answered in the course of often stormy debates. Then, in the final months of the war, Canada assisted in the creation of new institutions that, it was hoped, would preserve peace. The war and its aftermath thus thrust Canada—not always willingly and enthusiastically—into the world arena.

The Canada of 1945 differed greatly from the country that had embarked on war in 1939. The heavy demands of war production catapulted the nation out of economic depression and into rapid growth. As people crowded into the cities in search of jobs, the state took an increasingly active role in providing social services. Canada thus moved toward the creation of a modern welfare state. The war also had profound, though in part temporary, implications for Canadian women. The government needed them to participate in war-related activities, to alleviate labour shortages in the war industries, and to support men in the armed forces.

The war had enduring effects on federal–provincial relations, too. The pendulum of power swung toward Ottawa, as the central government mobilized the economy and controlled national finances to further the war effort. The defenders of provincial autonomy fought back but, more often than not, were forced to retreat. In international affairs, Canada shifted its focus from Britain to the United States as its major ally and trading partner.

Canada's Liberal government successfully weathered war-related problems, including a new conscription crisis. Canadians might not have loved their pompous and aging prime minister, William Lyon Mackenzie King, but they probably recognized his uncanny skill in sensing change and, in any case, they certainly could not agree on who might do a better job.

Neutrality in the 1930s

In the 1930s, Canada used its newly won autonomy in foreign affairs to avoid entanglements overseas. When, for example, Japan invaded Manchuria in 1931, Canada refused to endorse sanctions at the League of Nations. Indeed, the Canadian delegate made a speech judged so pro-Japanese that Japan's diplomatic representative in Ottawa thanked the Canadian government! Similarly, after Italian dictator Benito Mussolini invaded the independent African kingdom of Abyssinia (Ethiopia) in October 1935, Canada's two major political leaders, R.B. Bennett and Mackenzie King, then in the midst of a federal election campaign, both agreed, in spite of political differences, that Canada should not become involved.

Nevertheless, events soon forced the Canadian government to respond to this major test of the League of Nations' ability to curb aggression. Walter Riddell, Canada's advisory officer at the league's headquarters in Geneva, personally favoured strong economic sanctions against Italy. Before receiving specific orders from Ottawa, he proposed including oil and other strategic materials on the embargo list. Prime Minister King, however, wanted above all to avoid Canadian participation in any armed struggles not directly related to the country's own interest. Now, on the advice of O.D. Skelton, undersecretary of state for external affairs, and of Ernest Lapointe, his minister of justice as well as his Quebec lieutenant, King repudiated the "Canada proposal." In his own words, he gave Riddell "a good spanking." Britain and France saved Riddell from further embarrassment when, in exchange for peace, they offered Mussolini the territory he had already overrun in East Africa. A few weeks later, King claimed in the House of Commons that Canada had saved Europe from war.

The Rise of Nazi Germany

Adolf Hitler posed the greatest threat to world peace. Systematically, the Nazi leader, who became chancellor of Germany in 1933, set out to consolidate and to increase Germany's power. First, he reoccupied the hitherto demilitarized zone of the Rhineland in March 1936, in violation of the Treaty of Versailles and the Locarno agreements. Then, in March 1938, he forced the *Anschluss*, or union, upon Austria. Next, he seized the Sudetenland (the western region of Czechoslovakia), a conquest that Britain and France, in their desire to avoid war, accepted at the Munich conference in the fall of 1938. Then, in March 1939, the German leader annexed what remained of Czechoslovakia. Throughout all these acts of aggression, Canada supported Britain and France's policy of appeasement, of making concession after concession.

Mackenzie King visited Hitler in 1937. The Canadian prime minister, convinced of his own divine mission as international peacemaker, described the Führer as "a man of deep sincerity and a genuine patriot"—a modern-day Joan of Arc who would deliver his people. Still, King did tell Hitler that, in the event of war, Canada would support Britain. Hitler, for his part, appeared to convince King that he did not want war but was concerned with the spread of communism. In early 1939, King, who still believed that war could be avoided, wrote to the German chancellor to assure him of their mutual friendship. Indeed, King seemed to fear that London would do more to provoke a war than Berlin.

Reasons for Appeasement

Many supporters of appeasement in Canada saw Hitler and Mussolini as bulwarks against the spread of communism, as defenders of order in an era of chaotic revolution. They viewed General Francisco Franco, the fascist leader who won power in Spain in 1939 after a bitter civil war, in the same light. Rodrigue Cardinal Villeneuve, archbishop of Quebec, reminded his clergy in May 1937 that "dictatorship is better than revolution." To the embarrassment of the Canadian government, which wanted to avoid involvement in Spain, 1250 Canadian volunteers formed the Mackenzie–Papineau battalion to fight for the Spanish republic against Franco's fascists.

Other explanations exist for Canada's support of appeasement. King and his foremost advisers, like Skelton, favoured it out of fear that British policies might undermine Canadian autonomy and draw the country into imperial conflicts, as they had in the past. With his sure political instincts King also knew that another war, just like World War I, risked dividing Canadians in a bitter internal conflict that could destroy national unity as well as his government and the Liberal party.

Furthermore, isolationist sentiment ran deep in Canada, as it did in the United States, which had never even joined the League of Nations. Historian Frank Underhill said it more bluntly than most when he asserted at the time that "all these European troubles are not worth the bones of a Toronto grenadier." Many English-speaking Canadian politicians and professional policy advisers wanted Canada to take, at most, a "back seat" in the international "lunatic asylum," as Loring Christie, an external-affairs adviser, described the world. French Canada, in particular, wanted to keep its distance from Europe. Demographically and sentimentally, French Canadians had long been detached from the Old World.

Finally, a policy of appeasement reflected the belief of many Canadians that the country could have no impact upon events. In 1933, Prime Minister R.B. Bennett wrote candidly to a Toronto clergyman: "Canada is not an important member of the League.... Our military prowess in the next war is regarded as of little concern." With respect to his own role, he added: "What can one man do who represents only ten and a half millions of people?"

Little changed over the remainder of the decade. On the eve of war, Canada had only seven diplomatic missions abroad. In 1938–39, the country's total budget for the armed forces was barely $35 million. The navy had fewer than a dozen fighting ships, and the air force, at best, only 50 modern military aircraft. The professional army had just 4000 troops; the navy, 3000; and the air force, only 1000. Twenty years of neglect had gravely weakened Canada's defences. Clearly, the nation could not even defend its own coasts, let alone dispatch fully equipped and trained forces to Europe.

Canada and the War Against the Axis

On September 1, 1939, German troops invaded Poland. On September 3, Britain and France declared war on Germany. Canada followed a week later, a somewhat belated gesture that symbolically demonstrated the nation's newly acquired sovereignty. A small number of Canadians opposed the war on moral grounds. These included pacifists in the Women's International League for Peace and Freedom and in the CCF. But there was never any real possibility that Canada would remain neutral, as the United States chose to do until the Japanese attacked Pearl Harbor in December 1941. Canada's emotional ties with Britain still remained strong, well after its colonial ties had ended.

Trainee pilots at No. 5 Elementary Flying Training School, Kenyon Field, Lethbridge, August 1940.

Source: Glenbow Archives, *Calgary Herald*, NA-2864-3445.

The British Commonwealth Air Training Plan

The first few months of warfare, described as the "Phoney War," made it possible for the Canadian government to postpone making wrenching decisions concerning the nature of Canada's participation in the conflict. Nevertheless, during this period one vitally important part of Canada's contribution to the war got under way: the British Commonwealth Air Training Plan (BCATP), which was conducted in, and heavily funded by, Canada.

Negotiations with Britain to establish the terms of Canada's involvement proved arduous, even rancorous. As historian Desmond Morton observes, "King's attachment to England did not always extend to Englishmen."[1] The final plan, agreed upon in 1939, gave control of the schools to the Royal Canadian Air Force (RCAF), which the federal government had organized immediately after World War I. The plan had many virtues. This kind of "at home" Canadian participation would be acceptable to French Canadians (although most Quebeckers were automatically disqualified because they did not speak English). It would also avoid the heavy casualties that Canada had suffered in World War I. By the end of the war, the BCATP had trained 130 000 aviators, nearly half the Commonwealth's air crews. The project also gave a tremendous boost to the aeronautics industry and, thanks to the more than $2 billion spent, to the Canadian economy in general.

The War Effort, 1940–42

The Nazis' unexpected invasion of neutral Denmark, Norway, and the Low Countries in the spring of 1940 transformed the war. The rapid German advance led to the near-capture of the entire British Expeditionary Force at Dunkirk. After France fell in June, Britain and its dominions stood alone against the German and Italian aggressors. Overnight, Canada became Britain's chief ally. Until the German invasion of the Soviet Union in June 1941, it remained so. During these dark months, Britain's surrender seemed highly possible.

To assist Britain and combat the Nazis, Canada spared no expense. It built up a much larger army, constructed dozens of warships and hundreds of aircraft, and converted the entire economy to war production. In response to Britain's wartime financial needs, Canada lent, and then gave, huge sums of money—more than $3 billion—through mutual-aid agreements, with no strings attached, although most of the money was spent in Canada on war materials destined for Britain.

Combat action for Canadian troops came first in the Pacific theatre. In hindsight, the federal government had foolishly agreed to reinforce British troops in Hong Kong. Historians W.A.B. Douglas and Brereton Greenhous judge the Canadian prime minister severely: King's "comprehension of strategy and logistics was not very profound and in this essentially military situation his customary political insight deserted him."[2] The British colony fell to the Japanese on Christmas Day, 1941. More than 550 Canadians perished either in the attack or afterwards in the harsh conditions of Japanese slave labour camps. Later, in the Pacific war, Canada played a relatively minor role. Three RCAF squadrons did see action in southeast Asia, but plans to increase Canada's air and sea participation in the Pacific theatre in summer 1945 were cancelled after the Americans dropped atomic bombs on two Japanese cities.

A convoy near Halifax 1941. During the war the Royal Canadian Navy played a major role in defending Allied convoys that transported troops and supplies to Britain.

Source: Library and Archives Canada/DND PA-105344.

Sir Frederick Banting and Pilot Joseph Mackey

Sir Frederick Banting is well known as the discoverer, with Charles Best, of insulin, used in the treatment of diabetes. Joseph Mackey was an American pilot, one of several hundred pilots and crew who worked for Ferry Command, an enterprise set up by the British in Montreal and responsible for flying more than 9000 planes across the Atlantic for delivery in Great Britain.

The first flights began in February 1941. Banting, wanting to go to England, sought space on an aircraft as a passenger. He was assigned to the Lockheed Hudson piloted by Mackey. After bad weather finally cleared, Mackey took off from Gander airport in Newfoundland. Shortly after takeoff, the left engine of Mackey's plane failed. The pilot turned back. Then the right engine lost power and the plane crashed near Musgrave Harbour, Newfoundland. Mackey was injured, but not seriously. The other two crew members were killed. Banting suffered a concussion and internal bleeding. He died a few hours later despite Mackey's efforts to save his life. Three days later, Mackey was finally spotted by a plane and rescued. He later sold his story to a Toronto newspaper and then donated the proceeds to the family of his deceased radio officer.

More than 500 airmen lost their lives while working for Ferry Command, often in crashes of large Liberator bombers used to bring the crews home. About 50 passengers were killed, too. Banting was the first.

This story is told in Carl A. Christie, *Ocean Bridge: The History of RAF Ferry Command* (Toronto: University of Toronto Press, 1995), pp. 62–72.

Canadians in Europe experienced their baptism of fire in August 1942, in the ill-conceived major Allied raid on the French coast at Dieppe. In a few terrible hours, more than 60 percent of the 5000 Canadian participants were killed or captured. The Germans used their documentary film of the slaughter of Canadians on the beach to boost the morale of their own soldiers.

For long months after the tragedy at Dieppe, Canadian troops continued garrison duty in Britain. They were not completely inactive: indeed, thousands of marriages between Canadian servicemen and British women took place. One Montreal journalist commented that the Canadian army was "the first formation in the history of war" in which the birth rate exceeded the death rate!

Canadian–American Wartime Relations

War inevitably drew Canada closer to the United States. In August 1938, President Roosevelt came to Kingston, Ontario, where he pledged that the United States "would not stand idly by if domination of Canadian soil [was] threatened by any other [than the British] empire." This statement pleased King, although Canadian soil was hardly being threatened at that time.

The Ogdensburg Agreement

Two years later, in August 1940, King and Roosevelt signed the Ogdensburg Agreement, which created the Permanent Joint Board on Defence (PJBD), responsible for discussing military questions of mutual interest. As early as 1938, the two countries had begun to exchange military information. In the summer of 1940, King himself pushed for talks on common defence planning. Most Canadians approved of the continental defence tie, as they believed Canada could not rely on its own (then virtually nonexistent) defences or on Britain's. Thus, when Roosevelt proposed the PJBD, King was delighted, although he apparently had some doubts about making the board permanent.

Historians differ in their interpretations of this *rapprochement*. Donald Creighton, always alert to the imperial designs of Canada's southern neighbour, saw the Ogdensburg Agreement as a major step toward the Liberals' surrender of Canadian autonomy. He maintained that King "behaved like a puppet which could be animated only by the President of the United States."[3]

In contrast, J.L. Granatstein and Norman Hillmer have argued that King "wanted to protect Canada and to help Great Britain as much as possible, and he understood and accepted that this obliged him to seek even closer relations with Roosevelt's America."[4] Political scientist James Eayrs has denied that King was manipulated by the charming Roosevelt, seeing him instead as a shrewd politician who astutely exploited his friendship with the American president for the good of the Allies.[5]

During the early months of war, Canada enjoyed some influence in the United States, notably through King's use of quiet diplomacy with the president. For example, King won important modifications to the American Neutrality Act, thus enabling Canada and Britain to purchase military supplies while the United States remained neutral. King knew the limits of his influence, however, and also the limits of an American president's powers in the face of a Congress jealous of its prerogatives.

The Hyde Park Declaration

King and Roosevelt signed a second agreement, the Hyde Park Declaration, at Roosevelt's Hudson River estate on a "grand Sunday" in April 1941. It proved an even more important milestone in Canadian–American relations than the Ogdensburg Agreement.

Canada's wartime economic relations with both Britain and the United States led to this understanding. Since 1939 Britain had ordered ever-increasing amounts of war supplies from Canada and the United States, but it lacked the dollars to pay for them. Meanwhile Canada had accumulated huge deficits in its American trade, largely because of its enormous defence purchases in the United States for equipment destined for Britain. When in 1941 the United States passed the Lend-Lease Act, which exempted Britain from making cash payments on its orders for war materials, Canada worried that it would now lose British business. Britain, for its part, used the threat of shifting orders to the United States to pressure Canada into better terms.

Negotiations with the United States proved arduous. King nevertheless managed to get a reasonably satisfactory agreement: the United States promised to increase its defence purchases in Canada substantially, enabling Canada to make its own purchases of war equipment in the United States. Britain could continue buying Canadian goods and Canada could even get relief, through Lend-Lease, for its American purchases of war supplies to be sent via Canada to Britain. The agreement ended Canada's dollar shortage by 1942. Some scholars see the Hyde Park Declaration as another blow to Canadian independence. In view of Canada's precarious situation, however, the country probably could not have obtained better financial terms.

After Hyde Park, Canada's influence with the United States seriously deteriorated. The American entry into the war in December 1941 substantially changed American perspectives. Relinquishing its isolationism, the United States became more concerned with global rather than hemispheric issues. Canada lost its special status and became a junior partner in the Anglo–American–Russian alliance to defeat the Axis powers from 1942 to 1945.

Reflecting on his wartime service at the Canadian embassy in Washington, external-affairs officer Lester B. Pearson put it bluntly: "We were not consulted about plans and decisions at high levels unless our agreement was essential, and this was seldom." At the outset of the war, Pearson worried that Canada might be squeezed between the United States and Britain. As time went on, he became convinced that the main problem Canada faced was simply being squeezed out! Even at the two wartime conferences held in Quebec City that brought together the British and the American war leaders, Winston Churchill and Franklin D. Roosevelt, Canada acted merely as host. King's presence was largely confined to the official photos.

The Wartime Economy

On the eve of war, more than half a million Canadians—one out of five members of the work force—lacked jobs. Barely a year later, full employment was within sight. The wartime emergency led to large-scale federal economic intervention. Soon Canada produced 4000 airplanes a year, as well as ships, tanks, and huge quantities of shells and guns. Investment in industry doubled between 1939 and 1943. War materials had priority over civilian goods, whose production was severely curtailed.

Just as during World War I, the burgeoning economy generated inflationary pressures. In the spring of 1941, prices spiralled upward at an annual rate of more than 12 percent. In response, Ottawa quickly implemented drastic wage and price controls. The government also resorted to so-called voluntary measures. It exhorted homemakers to put their savings into Victory Bonds and urged merchants to offer customers their change in war savings stamps. The government used the revenue from the bonds and stamps to purchase arms and build bombs. And that—as one patriotic poster proclaimed—was how homemaker "Mrs. Morin bombarded Berlin"! Women also established branches of the Consumers Service that, among other activities, denounced merchants who violated the law. Because of such measures, the cost of living went up very little during the remainder of the war.

Fitting the guns on a 28-ton (25 t) tank at Montreal Locomotive Works, Montreal, around 1942.

Source: Photograph Collection and Library Services Canada/Science and Technology Museum, Image CN 001876.

Rationing

The relative scarcity of various consumer goods led to rationing. The government issued books of coupons and recruited thousands of female volunteers to distribute them to shoppers. Sugar became the first product to be rationed. Later, Ottawa added tea, coffee, butter, meat, and gasoline to the list. Merchants complained about the paperwork required to administer the coupons. As well, a black market in unused coupons flourished, and some farmers sold produce illegally—for a good price. Some people hoarded scarce goods, in spite of the threat of fines. Occasionally, shortages provoked an outcry. When brewers could not supply enough of their favourite beverage, Ontario workers threatened to boycott the sale of Victory Bonds. "No beer, no bonds!" was their warning.

The lack of automobiles and of the gasoline to make them run explains, together with full employment, an enormous increase in the use of urban public transport. During the war, buses and trams were often severely overcrowded. Mothers shopping for food had to compete with commuters for space. The media urged shoppers to avoid travelling at peak hours. Women frequently faced sexual harassment as men complained about "feminine intrusion into their cultural privacy and social space," particularly "their" smoking section at the rear of the bus.[6]

People in business improved their public image, tarnished during the depression years, by helping the federal government organize the country's war production. Hundreds of them trooped off to Ottawa, often for a symbolic annual salary of one dollar. Many worked for the powerful C.D. Howe, minister of munitions and supply, the department in charge of all war procurement. Howe set up numerous Crown corporations and adopted the techniques of private enterprise. He also avoided the accusations of graft and profiteering that had so plagued Robert Borden's government during World War I. Business leaders admired Howe's no-nonsense efficiency and were proud to be called "Howe's boys."

Women and the War Effort

According to traditional Canadian beliefs and practices, married women belonged in the home. War needs, however, forced society to rethink women's roles. At the war's end, pressures for women to return to their domestic occupations intensified but, over time, attitudes changed and more and more women took jobs.

Many women, particularly unmarried women, had worked outside the home long before the war, generally in low-paying occupations such as teaching, office work, retail sales, factory labour in textile and clothing mills, and as domestics. Now, in response to the general labour shortage created by the war, many more women entered the civilian work force, mainly in war-related industries. Through the National Selective Service, set up to coordinate the mobilization of Canada's labour power, the government encouraged female recruitment. Department of Labour advertisements urged women to "roll up [their] sleeves for victory"; the men overseas needed support and women had to "back them up—to bring them back."

Women often did what was traditionally men's work. When a plywood factory opened in Port Alberni on Vancouver Island in 1942 to supply plywood for ammunition boxes and other uses, 80 percent of the workers hired were women. Many of these affectionately nicknamed "plywood girls" had brothers who were in the armed forces.

To attract women to factories from small towns and rural areas, industry and government provided incentives. Employers offered women relatively attractive wages, particularly in war industries; indeed, women's wages increased faster than men's during the war years, although they remained substantially lower. Ottawa temporarily amended the income tax laws to make it possible for husbands to continue to enjoy a full married exemption while their wives earned wages.

At first, the government sought only unmarried women and married women without children, but by 1943 a chronic lack of "manpower" made it essential to recruit mothers, at least for part-time, low-paying service jobs. Child care often caused problems for working women. Most left their children in the care of relatives and friends, but a modest number of government-funded nurseries began operating by 1943, on a temporary basis, in Ontario and Quebec.

Patriotic appeals drew thousands of women into volunteer work. They recuperated and recycled such items as paper, metal, fat, bones, rags, rubber, and glass. They also collected clothes for free distribution and prepared parcels to be sent overseas. Together with their unpaid

Women war workers return home after shift change, Edmonton, 1943.

Source: Library and Archives Canada/National Film Board of Canada fonds/PA-116122.

labour in the home, women's voluntary efforts constituted, in the words of historian Ruth Roach Pierson, "far and away the largest contribution made by Canadian women to the war effort."[7]

Women in the Armed Services

For the first time, women served in the armed services. By the end of the war, 50 000 women had enrolled, but these "Jill Canucks" were not "pistol-packing Mommas" and they did not hurl grenades.[8] The armed services assigned them positions considered proper to their sex and always paid them less than males. They remained subordinate to men of the same rank, and they commanded only other women. A special Canadian Women's Army Corps, created in 1941 and incorporated into the Canadian Army (Active) in late winter 1942, supplied female support staff to release men for combat training and other duties. Auxiliary women's units also existed in the air force and the navy. Unilingual French-speaking women were not accepted because training facilities were available in English only.

Efforts to achieve fairness and equality did not permeate all aspects of life in the services. Male dominance of the military meant a double standard on sexual morality; literature on venereal disease, for example, warned servicemen to beware of "diseased, predatory females," but women received no similar advice regarding "loose men." Pregnancy was cause for an immediate discharge on medical grounds.

Native Peoples and the War

According to the records of the Indian Affairs Branch, over 3000 status Indians enlisted. Most joined the army; indeed, until 1943, navy regulations required that enlistees be "British born subjects, of a white race." Some 200 died in service. These figures do not include the Métis, Inuit, or non-status Indians; military service files gave no information on ethnicity, except in the case of Aboriginal people covered by the Indian Act.

Culture and the State

War also affected cultural life by forging new links between the federal government and the cultural community. The artist Arthur Lismer, the composer Ernest MacMillan, and many Canadian writers sought to make their personal contribution to the war effort by choosing subjects and themes related to the conflict. The National Gallery of Canada sent thousands of reproductions of artists' works to Canadian military establishments in the hope that soldiers' morale would be boosted when they contemplated familiar scenes. Artists and writers also organized associations to work for a postwar "cultural reconstruction" in which the state recognized the importance of assisting the arts community. In 1945, however, neither Ottawa nor the provinces were ready to include culture in their postwar plans.

The War and National Unity

The Canadian government worked to keep support high for the war effort. The National Film Board (NFB), founded in 1939, produced "progressive film propaganda" designed to enhance Canadians' faith in their country. In the same year, Ottawa set up the Bureau of Public Information to promote patriotism and "Canadianism" among all ethnic groups in English-speaking Canada. The need to emphasize Canadian participation was brought home when American newsreels playing in Canadian theatres portrayed the Dieppe raid, in which so many Canadians lost their lives, primarily as an American action. The bureau published hundreds of pamphlets, arranged for news stories, magazine articles, and radio broadcasts, and subsidized "loyal" segments of the foreign-language press.

Private Huron Eldon Brant, member of the Tyendinaga Mohawk community, receiving the Military Medal for bravery at Grammichele, Sicily, 1943, from General Bernard Montgomery. One year later he was shot and killed during an attack near Rimini.

Source: Captain Frank Royal/Library and Archives Canada/ PA-130065.

Wartime Treatment of Minority Ethnic Groups

The federal government also established the Nationalities Branch of the Department of National War Services to attempt to combat widespread anti-immigrant attitudes during the war. With its staff of two, the branch was scarcely an adequate response to a very real problem. As the Wartime Information Board reported in 1943, "It is obvious that prejudice against 'foreigners' in general and Jews in particular has grown."

Ironically, while attempting to unite Canadians, the government meted out harsh treatment to members of ethnic groups whose homelands were at war with Canada, believing that they constituted a danger to the state. Under the War Measures Act, the federal government interned hundreds of German Canadians, although the RCMP found no evidence of domestic subversion. Upon Italy's entry into the war, the RCMP began a "mop-up of Italians," as the *Montreal Star* described the operation. It fingerprinted and photographed thousands of Italian Canadians, and arrested some 700, including tailors, miners, shopkeepers, a United Church minister, and almost all doctors. Businessman James Franceschini was one of those interned at Camp Petawawa; he saw his businesses placed in the hands of the Custodian of Alien Property and the equipment sold off at fire-sale prices to his Montreal competitors. Franceschini's lawyer claimed that these business rivals even intervened to hinder his client's release. A few members of the clergy and university professors questioned the arrests. Most Canadians appeared, by their silence, to acquiesce. Indeed, in Cape Breton, coal miners laid down their tools to force their employer to ban Italians from the mines.

More than any other group, Japanese Canadians bore the brunt of Canadians' animosity. After the Japanese surprise raid on Pearl Harbor in December 1941, which brought fears of an invasion of the Pacific coast, the federal government evacuated the more than 20 000 Japanese and Japanese Canadians living in coastal British Columbia. Evacuees were first housed in the exhibition buildings in Hastings Park, Vancouver, where wooden bunks were installed in horse stalls in the livestock barns. Later, most were transported to camps in the interior of the province, but several hundred males deemed "dangerous" were placed under armed guard at

Japanese Canadians being "relocated" to camps in the interior of British Columbia. More than 20 000 Japanese and Japanese Canadians were moved and their property confiscated and auctioned off after the Japanese attack on Pearl Harbor in December 1941 and throughout the duration of the war.

Source: Tak Toyota/Library and Archives Canada/C-46350.

a camp in the Lake Superior bush country. Those interned saw their property confiscated and auctioned off. Families wishing to stay together had to agree to go to sugar-beet farms in Alberta and Manitoba, where they had to perform the backbreaking labour of sugar-beet topping. After the war, Ottawa resettled the Japanese Canadians across Canada and even attempted to deport thousands—many of whom were Canadian citizens—to Japan. Although the federal government abandoned these plans in 1947, hundreds of Japanese Canadians, embittered by life in Canada, chose to return to Japan.

Most historians view wartime government policy toward the Japanese in Canada as the result of longstanding racial hostility toward this group. "The threat of Japanese subversion was created by the union of traditional racial attitudes and perceptions shaped by the fears and anxieties conjured up by war," writes Peter Ward.[9] A hostile public easily convinced federal politicians to act. Historians Patricia Roy and others, however, have argued that Ottawa carried out the evacuation of the Japanese "as much for their own protection, and, by implication, the protection of Canadians in Japanese hands."[10] Forty years later, the federal government apologized to Japanese Canadians for their wartime treatment and offered financial compensation.

French Canada and the War

French Canada posed a special challenge. Although French Canadians generally accepted participation, as in World War I they remained adamantly opposed to compulsory military service for overseas operations. The stringent Defence of Canada Regulations, which provided for the censorship of antiwar sentiment in the media, attempted to curb opposition to government war policy in Quebec. The CBC also acted as a "propaganda vehicle" in favour of the war effort, but it offered virtually no French-language programs outside Quebec.

Several reasons help to explain French Canada's lack of enthusiasm for the war. During the 1930s many French-Canadian intellectuals showed sympathy for Franco and Mussolini, because the fascist leaders portrayed themselves as stalwart opponents of communism. Members of the clergy also complained of the negative effect that military life had on the morals of soldiers who, as a pastoral letter of 1942 warned, all too often tended to pursue "vile pleasures." Traditionalists predicted that the war would cause the breakup of families because it brought women into the factories. For their part, the defenders of provincial autonomy attacked Ottawa's wartime intrusion into the provincial government's jurisdiction. Furthermore, nationalists denounced the danger of linguistic assimilation by a Canadian army in which the French language was often proscribed.

Most French Canadians, however, simply did not feel immediately concerned by a war in Europe. Having been estranged from France politically, culturally, and demographically for nearly two centuries, they had few ties with that country. They certainly felt no strong loyalty to England. Though most would probably have preferred that Canada remain neutral in 1939, as the United States had done, they agreed to Canada's involvement on the condition that enlistment be voluntary.

Plebiscite of 1942

As the war dragged on and military leaders demanded reinforcements, an increasing number of English-speaking Canadians called for conscription. For one Toronto Tory member of Parliament, that was the only way to get the "disloyal bloody French" to fight. Mackenzie King opposed conscription at almost any cost. Many English-speaking Canadians interpreted King's refusal to consider conscription as putting political advantage, especially his solid support in Quebec, ahead of the war effort. King certainly moved cautiously. In mid-1940, his government decreed national registration, which provided that men be called up for compulsory military training but for home service only. (Since it applied just to unmarried men, the regulation had the unintended effect of provoking hundreds of hurried marriages.) When recruiting for overseas service lagged in 1941, the government decided to retain the conscripts for the duration of the war, in the hope that volunteers in home-defence units would agree to serve overseas. When few signed up, and pressure mounted for King to send more troops, King decided to hold a plebiscite on conscription in April 1942.

Nationalists in Quebec accused the prime minister of betraying his sacred promises concerning conscription. In preparation for the plebiscite, they formed the Ligue pour la défense du Canada to encourage French Canadians to vote "non." The plebiscite question deliberately avoided mentioning the word "conscription." It asked Canadians: "Are you in favour of releasing the Government from any obligations arising out of any past commitments restricting the methods of raising men for military service?" The results of the vote revealed the deep division between Quebec and the rest of Canada. While 72 percent of Quebeckers answered "no," 80 percent of the electorate of the other provinces responded "yes."

Still Mackenzie King delayed. When asked if the time had come to implement conscription, he replied evasively: "Conscription if necessary, but not necessarily conscription." Remembering the disastrous consequences of the conscription crisis of 1917 for national unity and for both major political parties, King hoped that conscription would never be necessary. The government did go one step closer to conscription in the fall of 1942 when it amended the National Resources Mobilization Act (NRMA) to permit the dispatch of conscripts overseas by order in council. Until late 1944, however, Canada continued to rely on voluntary enlistments. Some of the volunteers were NRMA men, "convinced" by moral pressure and even physical abuse to "go active."

A demonstration against conscription in Montreal.

Source: Library and Archives Canada/The Gazette (Montreal) fonds/PA-107910.

Canada Intensifies Its War Effort

In the war on the seas, the Royal Canadian Navy (RCN), which enlisted 100 000 men and 6500 women during the war, took on the responsibility of defending the convoys that transported troops and supplies to Britain. The job was dangerous. Moreover, living conditions on the escorting corvettes were often terrible, as seawater penetrated continually during bad weather. "The smell just got worse and worse," one sailor remembered. "The ship was a floating pigpen of stink. You couldn't get away from it. The butter tasted of it. … The bread smelled of feet and armpits." In the first years of the war, Allied naval losses were staggering; by spring 1943, German U-boats in the North Atlantic had sunk more than 2000 ships, and shipyards were unable to build replacements fast enough. Initially, the Canadian navy had few successes in the anti-submarine war, as a result of inexperience, poor crew training, and deficient technical equipment. But once properly trained and equipped, Canadians played a significant role in the Battle of the Atlantic by sinking, or helping to sink, many German U-boats.

One boat sunk by torpedoes fired from a German U-Boat was the *City of Benares*, en route from England to Canada in September 1940. Among the 400 passengers and crew aboard were 90 English children whose parents had decided to send them to Canada for safety from German bombardments. Only 13 children survived the sinking, half of them on an overcrowded lifeboat that drifted on the stormy North Atlantic for seven days.

On land, Canadian troops saw sustained combat from July 1943. In the mistaken hope that casualties would be light, King pressured British Prime Minister Churchill to allow Canadian forces to join in the Allied invasion of Sicily. In British General (later Field-Marshal) Bernard Montgomery's view, the Canadians behaved "magnificently." Nearly 100 000 Canadian troops took part in the lengthy Italian campaign that followed. Some 6000 Canadian soldiers lost their lives, another 20 000 were wounded, and untold numbers became neuropsychiatric casualties. The fierce battle to capture the strategic town of Ortona alone cost the Canadians 700 dead: they fought from doorway to doorway, from courtyard to courtyard, from rooftop to rooftop, sometimes even moving from house to house without going outside, through a technique of breaking through the walls between houses known as "mouse-holing." Although they faced Germans who often were better armed, the Canadians relentlessly pushed north, breaching the imposing German fortifications of the Gothic Line in September 1944. American journalist Martha Gellhorn noted a special sadness in this bloody combat, which she witnessed: "It is awful to die at the end of summer or in the gentle days of the new autumn when you are young and have fought a long time … and when you know that the war is won anyhow."

Canadians also played a significant role in the Normandy invasion of June 6, 1944. Assisted by the RCN, Canadian troops took an entire German-held beach. The Canadian division suffered greater casualties than the British formations, but it also advanced further inland than any other Allied division on D-Day. Initial successes were made possible by far superior Allied airpower and by the failure of the Germans to mount an immediate counter-attack.

Over the next few weeks, the Canadian army's progress across Normandy was slowed by several costly failures. In possibly the Canadians' worst reversal, a complete battalion, the Canadian Black Watch, was virtually annihilated on July 25 in an unsuccessful attempt to take Verrières Ridge, south of Caen.

Allied bombing errors brought substantial Canadian casualties in the days after the Normandy landings. Moreover, at least 150 Canadian deaths were in reality cold-blooded murders by German soldiers of the Hitler Youth Division, well behind the lines. In one notorious incident, a group of Canadian prisoners was marched to the Abbaye d'Ardennes, where they were shot in the garden after interrogation. Kurt Meyer, the German commander held

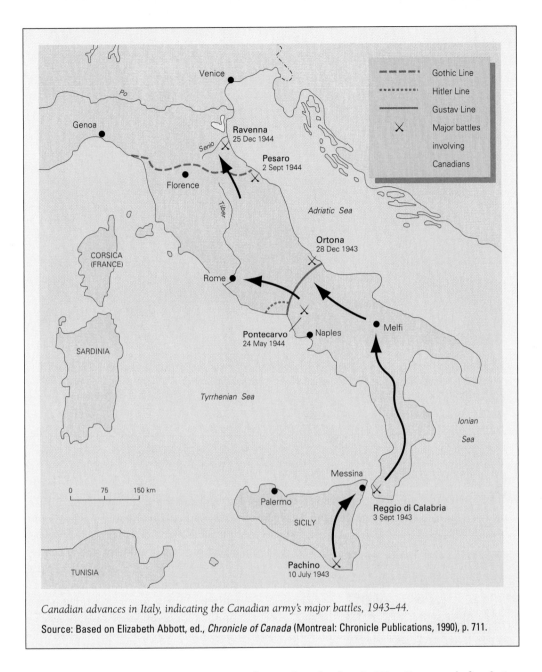

Canadian advances in Italy, indicating the Canadian army's major battles, 1943–44.

Source: Based on Elizabeth Abbott, ed., *Chronicle of Canada* (Montreal: Chronicle Publications, 1990), p. 711.

responsible, did serve some time in prison, first in Canada, then in West Germany, before being released to a hero's welcome in Germany.

The Canadians also organized the bloody sieges of Boulogne, Calais, and Le Havre. Then, in autumn 1944, in dreadful conditions of cold and mud, Canadian troops played a major role in the fight to secure the approaches to the Belgian port city of Antwerp. One effort involved an attempt to dislodge the Germans on Walcheren Island, at the mouth of the Scheldt delta. This approach by land was over a long, bleak rock-and-earth causeway that became a veritable hell for Canadian attackers raked by intense enemy bombardment. After heavy losses, the Canadians managed to establish a bridgehead on the island; then the British modified their strategy and decided to attack elsewhere.

Members of the Fusiliers Mont-Royal Regiment in Falaise, France, just after the Normandy invasion. A Canadian Sherman tank offers the tired infantrymen protection, in the narrow streets of this Norman town, August 1944.

Source: Library and Archives Canada/PA–115568.

Conscription and the End of the War

By late 1944, after one year of the Italian campaign and several months of fighting in France, Canadian officers overseas were demanding reinforcements, particularly the well-trained home-defence conscripts, or NRMA men. The Conservatives, in opposition, urged that the government stop appeasing Quebec and decree conscription. Within the cabinet, Colonel J.L. Ralston, the minister of national defence, who had just returned from a tour of Canadian forces in Europe, also pushed for compulsory military service. King, vexed and still not ready, replaced Ralston with General McNaughton, who promised to continue the voluntary system. As Churchill appealed for fresh troops in the face of the German counteroffensive in late 1944, McNaughton reported that he could not recruit the necessary volunteers. On November 22, just as several of his English-speaking cabinet ministers prepared to resign, King yielded. Canada would again have conscription, and NRMA men would now be sent to Europe.

Few Canadian conscripts ever served overseas, however, and conscription ultimately had no effect on winning the war. In spite of the criticism from both

The town of Leeuwarden, during the liberation of the Netherlands by Canadian troops, April 16, 1945.

Source: Donald I. Grant/Library and Archives Canada/PA-131566.

supporters and opponents of conscription, and perhaps because the criticism came from both ends of the spectrum, King was able to portray himself as a moderate. He and his Liberal party managed to survive the crisis. To their credit, they had limited the ethnic bitterness that occurred in the conscription crisis in 1917.

An Evaluation of Canadian Participation

During the last months of the war, in the late winter and early spring of 1945, Canadian troops participated in the liberation of the Netherlands and in the final offensive against Germany. By the war's end, 250 000 troops had served in the Canadian army in northwestern Europe; more than 11 000 of them died. In addition, from 1942, Canadian aviators conducted thousands of perilous night-bombing missions that destroyed most of Germany's large cities; Canadians eventually made up about a quarter of Bomber Command's crews.

More than 17 000 of the nearly quarter-million Canadians who served in the RCAF lost their lives. All told, more than 1 million Canadians out of a total population of 11.5 million saw military service in Canada and overseas during World War II. About 42 000 were killed, and nearly 55 000 were wounded; many of these would never recover.

Young Canadians, operating under extremely stressful conditions, fulfilled Canada's part in the strategic bomber offensive against Germany. Bomber aircrew suffered the highest wartime casualty rates of all of the branches in Canadian military service.

Source: PL-30121/National Defence. Reproduced with the permission of the Minister of Public Works and Government Services, 2007.

WHERE HISTORIANS DISAGREE

Canadian Participation in the Land War in Northwestern Europe

From the early 1990s, as the media extensively marked the fiftieth anniversary of the events of World War II. Canadian historians showed new interest in that conflict and, in particular, in the role Canadians played in combat in northwestern Europe.

The tragedy at Dieppe in August 1942 has been the subject of several studies. In *Unauthorized Action: Mountbatten and the Dieppe Raid*, Brian Loring Villa assigns responsibility for having ordered the raid to Lord Louis Mountbatten, British Chief of Combined Operations. Villa states that Canadian newspaper magnate Lord Beaverbrook minced no words when he encountered Mountbatten later at a dinner party: "You have murdered thousands of my countrymen.... They have been mown down and their blood is on your hands."[1] But Villa also notes that General A.G.L. McNaughton, commander of Canadian forces in Britain, had delivered numerous bellicose statements. When, at last, an opportunity to use Canadian troops presented itself, McNaughton could scarcely decline the offer. Nor, in spite of his typical caution, could Prime Minister King refuse his authorization. He had to take into account the rising criticism of Canadians who wanted to see their country's troops take a more active part in the struggle.

J.L. Granatstein points his finger at General H.D.G. Crerar, who commanded the 1st Canadian Corps. Crerar, he says, "had come to England convinced that the army had to see action soon, both for its own morale and for domestic Canadian consumption."[2] After Dieppe, Crerar's approach was to rationalize the raid by speaking of lessons learned, an approach that Granatstein says "may even be right."

Peter Henshaw also believes that the Canadian commanders were primarily responsible for the Dieppe fiasco: "Their struggle for autonomy, and for a leading Canadian role in raids, interacted with British interservice rivalries in a way that was decisive for the progress of the planned raid."[3]

Denis and Sheilagh Whitaker, the former a captain at Dieppe, blame British Prime Minister Winston Churchill, who needed to prove to Soviet dictator Joseph Stalin that it was impossible in 1942 to open a second front against the Germans. They argue that Churchill's strategy "was successful, no matter how high the costs."[4] Moreover, the Allies gained essential experience at Dieppe in preparation for D-Day. The lessons learned, they say, "saved countless lives as a result of their far-reaching influence on the success of future operations."[5] W.A.B. Douglas and Brereton Greenhous agree. Because of Dieppe, the Allies realized that "objectives must be more realistic, tactics more sophisticated, and training more rigorous. Communications must be more comprehensive, equipment more appropriate, and, most of all, fire support by sea and air must be overwhelming."[6] For his part, Timothy Balzer has studied how Dieppe was presented to the public. He notes that allied authorities planned in advance to portray any failure as success and to manipulate the press to further this claim. For example, communiqués were to stress the lessons learned before any lessons were learned.[7]

Canadians participated actively in the invasion of Normandy in June 1944 and in the lengthy campaign in northwestern Europe that followed. Canadian

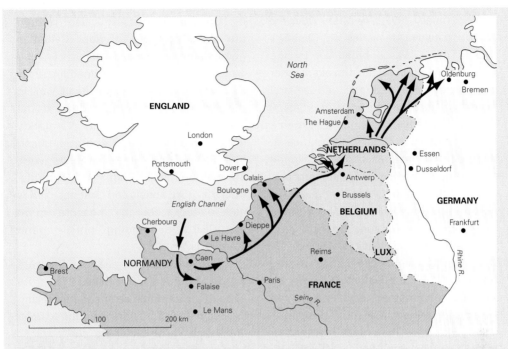

Canadian troop movements in northwestern Europe, 1944–45.

Source: From *Canada: Our Century, Our Story: Ontario Edition*, Student text by Fielding/Evans. 2001. Reprinted with permission of Nelson, a division of Thomson Learning: www.thomsonrights.com. Fax 800-730-2215.

casualties were high. Indeed, in John A. English's view, "the lives of many soldiers were unnecessarily cast away." Who should be blamed? English responds, "those who left them exposed in open wheatfields to be harvested like so many sheaves.... The responsibility must rest with the high command."[8] English argues that, when large-scale training exercises finally began for Canadian soldiers garrisoned in England, senior officers had little idea of how to direct a modern army in field operations. Although many Canadian battalions and armoured regiments were well led and proved successful in battle, at the divisional and brigade levels command was often given to regular army officers of doubtful professional competence.

Historian Terry Copp refutes this rather negative interpretation of Canadian military performance in Normandy. His use of message logs, war diaries, written orders, and other sources leads him to deny that Canadian soldiers were poorly led and poorly trained. True, they did suffer heavier casualties that other Allied units, but they spent more days in close combat. Their performance was extraordinary, Copp concludes, and they made an important contribution to the defeat of the Germans.[9]

In autumn 1944, Allied troops advanced into Belgium but halted at Antwerp, failing to secure the Scheldt estuary and giving the Germans precious time to set up defences and regroup. It was "one of the war's most costly blunders," conclude Denis and Sheilagh Whitaker, and it had a direct bearing on extending the war by many months.[10] Certainly the Canadians paid dearly, sustaining more than 6000 casualties before routing the enemy and clearing the estuary. During these final months of war, says Terry Copp, Canadians experienced both successes and failures. There was no "ascending learning curve."[11]

In January 1992, *The Valour and the Horror*, a television series on Canada's role in World War II broadcast by the CBC and Radio-Canada, provoked bitter controversy. War veterans and several historians accused the writer-producers, Brian and Terence McKenna, of extreme bias and distortion of history. In particular, they felt that the presentation maligned military commanders. A Senate subcommittee held hearings on the series—a gesture some media attacked as a threat to freedom of expression.

Historians S.F. Wise and David J. Bercuson reviewed the series in the framework of an evaluation done by the CBC ombudsman. Both judged the series to be "bad history."[12] Wise took issue with the filmwriters' contention that Canadian atrocities in Normandy were equivalent to those perpetrated by German troops. He also refuted the film's portrayal of poor Canadian generalship. Bercuson, while affirming a general belief that "the Canadian Army as a whole did not acquit itself well in the Normandy fighting," decried the "failure" to put events in Normandy into a broader context and maintained that British and American units were not well prepared either.[13] The ombudsman's report concluded that the series had indeed failed to "measure up to the CBC's demanding policies and standards."[14]

Perhaps historian Graeme Decarie's words of caution were wisest: "The truth ... as this committee seems to be seeking it, does not exist. History is bound to have imbalance, incompleteness and error ... because historians are always selective in the information they use."[15]

---

1   Brian Loring Villa, *Unauthorized Action: Mountbatten and the Dieppe Raid*, 2nd ed. (Toronto: Oxford University Press, 1994), p. 18.

2   J.L. Granatstein, *The Generals: The Canadian Army's Senior Commanders in the Second World War* (Toronto: Stoddart, 1993), p. 102.

3   Peter Henshaw, "The Dieppe Raid: A Product of Misplaced Canadian Nationalism?," *Canadian Historical Review* 77 (1996): 252.

4   Denis and Sheilagh Whitaker, *Dieppe: Tragedy to Triumph* (Toronto: McGraw-Hill Ryerson, 1992), p. 290.

5   Ibid., p. 304.

6   W.A.B. Douglas and Brereton Greenhous, *Out of the Shadows: Canada in the Second World War*, rev. ed. (Toronto: Dundurn Press, 1995), p. 128.

7   Timothy Balzer, "'In Case the Raid is Unsuccessful ...': Selling Dieppe to Canadians," *Canadian Historical Review* 87 (2006): 409–30.

8   John A. English, *The Canadian Army and the Normandy Campaign: A Study of Failure in High Command* (New York: Praeger, 1991), p. 256.

9   Terry Copp, *Fields of Fire: The Canadians in Normandy* (Toronto: University of Toronto Press, 2003).

10 Denis and Sheilagh Whitaker, *Tug of War: The Canadian Victory That Opened Antwerp* (Toronto: Stoddart, 1987), p. 373.

11 Terry Copp, *Cinderella Army: The Canadians in Northwest Europe 1944–1945* (Toronto: University of Toronto Press, 2006), p. 287.

12 S.F Wise and David J. Bercuson, *The Valour and the Horror Revisited* (Montreal/Kingston: McGill-Queen's University Press, 1994), p. 10.

13 Ibid., p. 51.

14 Ibid., p. 72.

15 Quoted in Graham Carr, "Rules of Engagement: Public History and the Drama of Legitimation," *Canadian Historical Review* 86 (2005): 338.

The war caused innumerable personal tragedies, as thousands of Canadians lost a husband, father, son, brother, or fiancé. Sometimes the sad announcement came brutally. One Canadian girl wrote to her soldier boyfriend in France, and after a few weeks the letter came back stamped "Killed in action." The soldiers' return, in some cases after five years of absence, provoked poignant emotions: time brought change, and lengthy absences had often altered perceptions of relationships. The divorce rate rose substantially.

Was Canada's role essential to the Allied victory over the Axis powers? Most historians agree that the Allies would have won even without Canada's participation. Canada's military strength certainly paled in comparison with the resources that its huge southern neighbour was able to mobilize and could continue to count on. Yet, for a small country, Canada's contribution was enormous. In the war in Italy and in northwestern Europe, Canadian forces made a decisive contribution. It is safe to say that, without their aid, the war, and the terrible suffering that it wrought, would have dragged on even longer.

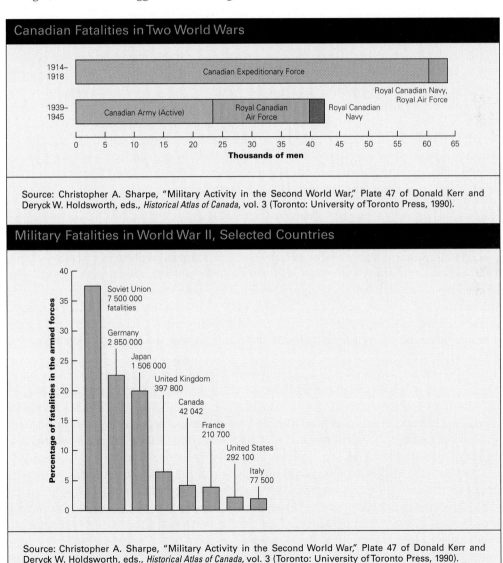

Canadian Fatalities in Two World Wars

Source: Christopher A. Sharpe, "Military Activity in the Second World War," Plate 47 of Donald Kerr and Deryck W. Holdsworth, eds., *Historical Atlas of Canada*, vol. 3 (Toronto: University of Toronto Press, 1990).

Military Fatalities in World War II, Selected Countries

Source: Christopher A. Sharpe, "Military Activity in the Second World War," Plate 47 of Donald Kerr and Deryck W. Holdsworth, eds., *Historical Atlas of Canada*, vol. 3 (Toronto: University of Toronto Press, 1990).

In all, the terrible bloodbath between 1939 and 1945 claimed the lives of nearly 60 million civilians and soldiers.

The Expansion of Unions

Organized labour made significant gains in the war years. Thanks to the war, the labour surplus of the 1930s became a shortage in the early 1940s. As employment rose, so, too, did union membership, particularly in the new industrial unions, which combined all workers in a particular industry in a single union. Between 1940 and 1945, union membership doubled to more than 700 000.

Although the war brought jobs and, in general, higher wages, grievances remained. Employers fiercely resisted union attempts to impose collective bargaining, and many bitter strikes resulted from unions' efforts to ensure recognition. In one case, 3000 shipyard workers in Halifax ceased work for one month in 1944 when their employer refused the automatic checkoff of union dues, a right gained by unions in Nova Scotia in 1937. Sometimes militant workers rebelled against their own union leadership, which they judged too conciliatory. When Cape Breton miners struck unsuccessfully for five months in 1941 for better wages and working conditions and more control over the work process, their rallying cry was "down with Hitler and [United Mine Workers officer] Silby Barrett."[11]

The federal government intervened constantly to prevent strikes that could hurt war production. When workers occupied an aluminum plant in Arvida, Quebec during a work stoppage in July 1941, Ottawa sent in troops to end the strike. To subvert union demands for wage increases, it applied wage controls that labour denounced as inequitable. As historian Laurel Sefton MacDowell's analysis of wartime labour relations has shown, the government felt it necessary, for political reasons, "to conciliate business, its wartime ally in developing the war economy."[12] Business representatives sat on government policy boards; labour did not. Compulsory conciliation often involved interminable delays, a situation that favoured employers. The unions believed that employers alone benefited from this imposed cooperation.

Industrial Conflicts

Workers' growing resentment contributed to a wave of industrial conflicts that peaked in 1943. That year, one union member in three went out on strike and one million working days were lost. A lengthy and very bitter gold-miners' strike in Kirkland Lake, Ontario, in particular, led the archrivals, the Trades and Labor Congress (TLC), an association of skilled craft unions, and the Canadian Congress of Labour (CCL), the leading industrial union, to make joint demands for legislative remedies. Labour's increasing support for the CCF greatly worried Prime Minister King.

The government responded to labour unrest with order in council PC 1003, which recognized the right of workers in industries under federal jurisdiction to join unions and to bargain collectively. It established certification procedures, set out penalties for unfair labour practices by which employers commonly interfered with workers' attempts to set up unions, and established a labour-relations board to administer the law. After the war the federal government adopted new legislation similar to PC 1003, and most provinces passed comparable laws.

A strike at the Ford motor plant in Windsor, Ontario in 1945 also concerned labour security, among other issues. The union wanted an agreement specifying that all employees had to belong to the union and that the company had to deduct union dues from wage cheques—"union shop and checkoff" was the workers' demand. Ford adamantly refused, although across the river, in Dearborn, Michigan, the company had acquiesced on these issues in 1941. To ensure a tight picket line, militant strikers set up a massive automobile blockade in the streets around the plant, imprisoning the vehicles of hundreds of commuters. Federal and provincial authorities as well as the CCL itself intervened, without success.

Finally, both sides agreed to accept binding arbitration. Justice Ivan Rand of the Supreme Court of Canada proposed what became known as the Rand Formula: since all employees benefited from union activities, all should pay union dues, to be collected by the company and remitted to the union. Workers need not join the union, however. Rand also recommended the establishment of a grievance procedure, as well as heavy penalties for unauthorized, or "wildcat," strikes. Although he admitted that a strike was not a "tea party," Rand strongly condemned the workers' motor blockade. He also made a vibrant plea for democratic control of unions and for "enlightened leadership at the top."

The late 1940s saw more dramatic confrontations between labour and management, often in provinces whose governments sided openly with employers. Still, unions felt more secure as the war years ended. The relative labour peace of the 1950s resulted, in part, from these wartime gains.

The State's New Role

The war changed Canada in other ways as well. After the depression, Canadians wanted more economic security. Though the war eliminated unemployment and restored a degree of prosperity, it exacted heavy financial sacrifices from the public. By 1943, as war fatigue set in and increasing Allied success pointed the way to final victory, Canadians reflected on the postwar society they wanted to build. In particular, many wanted governments to introduce measures that would help those in need and establish greater equality within society.

In 1940, with provincial consent and after making a requisite amendment to the British North America Act, the federal government adopted an unemployment-insurance plan whose provisions covered about half the work force. King supported the project because he was "anxious to keep Liberalism in control in Canada [and] not let third parties wrest away from us our rightful place in the matter of social reform." Although the Conservatives tried to project a reformist image with a new leader (John Bracken), a new name (the "Progressive Conservatives"), and proposals for such reforms as a national health scheme, King felt little threat from them. The left, however, troubled him. By September 1943, chiefly as a result of urban support, the CCF had reached 29 percent in the polls—one percentage point ahead of each of the two major parties.

Social-Welfare Measures

A report presented in 1943 by Leonard Marsh, research director for the government's Committee on Reconstruction, urged the immediate creation of a full welfare state. It recommended a comprehensive system of social security, including measures to assist the unemployed, a national health-insurance scheme, old-age pensions, and children's allowances. The federal government, fearful of the costs involved, adopted a cautious and piecemeal approach. In 1944, it introduced a family-allowance program that initially provided monthly payments of $6–$8 to help Canadian mothers support their children. King hoped that the measure would diminish the CCF's popularity. Certain Conservatives, such as Ontario premier George Drew, denounced the project as a "baby bonus" designed to benefit Quebec with its alleged big families, while nationalists in Quebec condemned it as an infringement upon provincial autonomy. Business reacted favourably; it hoped that the allowances would diminish pressure to raise wages.

Housing became a serious problem for increasing numbers of urban Canadians during the war years. As migrants flocked to cities to work in war-related industries, many families lived in garages, empty warehouses, shacks, chicken-coops, "and indeed, in anything that will hold a bed," as one report put it. The influx of military and civilian war workers strained housing facilities in Halifax. By 1943, Montreal claimed it needed 50 000 new dwellings. Unscrupulous landlords gouged tenants, despite the imposition of rent controls.

As the war ended, Canada's rental-controls administrator noted that the country was attempting to solve its shelter problem by "compressing more and more people into the same cubic space." He estimated that at least 200 000 Canadian households were now living "doubled up" or even "tripled up." Ottawa ignored pleas for public intervention to provide low-rental housing; instead, it acted to reduce down payments and to guarantee mortgages in order to stimulate the building of new homes and enable families with moderate incomes to purchase property. It also showed considerable interest in the future of returning soldiers, whom it sought to resettle on small farms by means of the Veterans' Land Act of 1942.

Women in Postwar Canada

In the middle of the war, Ottawa established a special subcommittee to study the role of women in postwar Canada. The members, all women, assumed that many female workers would return to the home. For those who remained employed outside the home, the subcommittee's report recommended expanded employment opportunities, equal pay, better working conditions, and the granting of children's allowances.

These proposals stirred up substantial opposition. Concerned about postwar unemployment, government planners wanted women out of the work force to make room for returning soldiers and workers in shut-down war industries. Unions did not want to see women competing for scarce jobs with their fathers, sons, and future husbands. Polls showed that most Canadians—women as well as men—wanted women back in the home after the war. The war experience was the exception, not the rule. But the House of Commons paid little attention to the report, tabled in early 1944. Other "more pressing" problems had arisen. As historian Gail Cuthbert Brandt wrote, the subcommittee's report was "pigeon-holed and forgotten."[13]

Things appeared to return to "normal" at the end of the war. Women in the armed services were demobilized. Many of the barriers blocking women from the work force went back up again. Historian Susanne Klausen recounts that the "plywood girls" of the Port Alberni plywood factory now became "plywood bags," a derogatory term often used by other women who wished to express their disapproval of young female workers who were occupying jobs that, in their view, should rightfully be given to returning veterans.[14] The proportion of women working outside the home plummeted. Although women slowly began to return to the work force in the early 1950s, not until the 1960s would the proportion of female workers return to what it had been in 1944—27 percent.

The 1945 Election

King's cautious, reformist approach to social problems proved politically sound. With the support of four out of every ten voters, he won the election in 1945, a feat the Liberal leader termed "a miracle." In Quebec, internal strife seriously weakened the nationalist Bloc populaire canadien, a situation that favoured the Liberals. Elsewhere, the extensive anti-socialist propaganda campaign funded by business helped to undermine the CCF's popularity. Canadians seemed to become more conservative as well. They wanted consumer goods such as refrigerators, automobiles, and houses. Nor did they fear that the war's end would plunge the country back into depression. They thus gave little heed to the CCF's Cassandras who warned of impending economic and social doom.

Federal–Provincial Relations: Toward Federal Supremacy

The depression had restricted the autonomy of the provinces, forcing them to rely increasingly on Ottawa for financial assistance. The war created conditions that furthered centralization, as the federal government now took the dominant role in organizing the Canadian economy.

The Rowell–Sirois Report

The Rowell–Sirois Commission on Dominion–Provincial Relations, set up by the King government in 1937, made public its report in May 1940. With the objective of stabilizing provincial finances and giving equal services to all Canadians, the commissioners recommended that Ottawa collect all income taxes and succession duties and, in return, make unconditional grants to the provinces. Disadvantaged provinces should receive special subsidies to enable them to offer social and educational services equivalent to those of other Canadian provinces without having to tax more heavily than the Canadian average. The federal government should also assume all provincial debts.

Provincial autonomists condemned the report as a veritable centralizer's "Bible." They argued that its recommendations would place provincial treasuries at Ottawa's mercy and that the federal government would determine provincial activities by what it was willing to pay out. Premier Mitchell Hepburn of Ontario—a province that would not benefit from the special adjustment grants—attacked the report as "the product of the mind of a few college professors and a Winnipeg newspaperman [John Dafoe] who has had his knife in Ontario ever since he was able to write editorial articles."

Most newspapers reacted favourably. Federal ministers and bureaucrats also endorsed the recommendations strongly, particularly those relating to money. Ottawa wanted to ensure control over fiscal policy to pay for the war as well as to diminish inflationary pressures. It thus urged the provinces to "rent" their tax fields to the federal government.

With no illusions about the outcome, King invited the premiers in January 1941 to discuss the proposals. While some provinces insisted on the need for further study, others rejected Ottawa's plans outright. The conference collapsed in deadlock. Ottawa, however, determinedly pressed ahead. It promised, as a "temporary wartime expedient," that the provinces would have to surrender their income taxes only for the duration of the war, and it proposed to compensate the provinces more generously. All the provinces yielded, although some did so reluctantly.

After 1943, the economic planners in Ottawa, many of whom were disciples of British economist John Maynard Keynes, set forth their designs for the immediate postwar era. They feared that depression might result from the reconversion of the economy to peacetime conditions, just as had occurred after World War I. Moreover, they wanted to make certain that Ottawa could assume the heavy financial responsibilities and increased debt charges resulting from the war. Ottawa, they urged, should thus act as the "balance wheel" of the economy. If it kept its hand firmly on taxation, it could combat cyclical tendencies, either deflationary busts or inflationary booms; it could maintain high and stable employment; and it could offer costly social-security measures to all citizens, thus supporting consumer buying power. For these civil servants, economic, political, and humanitarian objectives dictated that the federal government continue to take charge. It might, however, consult the provinces in areas of their constitutional jurisdiction, such as social services.

The Dominion–Provincial Conference on Reconstruction

In August 1945, immediately before Japan's surrender, Ottawa convened the Dominion–Provincial Conference on Reconstruction. King assured the provinces that he did not want to weaken or subordinate them but rather wished to ensure their "effective financial independence." He intended to do this by convincing them to continue to allow Ottawa to levy all income taxes in return for increased provincial grants, with no strings attached. The federal government also offered to pay part of the cost of a comprehensive health-insurance plan and of old-age pensions, and to expand the coverage of federal unemployment insurance.

Though most provinces reacted positively, the premiers of Ontario, Quebec, and Alberta objected to what they saw as the concentration of financial and administrative powers in the federal government's hands. Historian Alvin Finkel suggests that King actually hoped that the premiers would oppose his plans so that he would have the "necessary excuse" to abandon plans for costly social programs.[15] Ottawa eventually managed to reach agreement on the tax proposals with all but the two largest provinces. The federalism of the next decade remained highly centralized. As economist R.M. Burns put it, during the 1940s and 1950s "the central authority reached its zenith."[16]

The Provinces in the War Years

The war and the after-effects of the depression fostered the uneven development of regional economies and thus contributed to the growth of regionalism in Canada. The war had diversified Canada's manufacturing capacity, as well as further promoting its resource-based industries. Quebec, British Columbia, and especially Ontario made dramatic advances. In Quebec, industries such as chemical products and aluminum refining expanded rapidly. In Ontario, factory employment increased greatly and the exploitation of the province's huge iron-ore deposits began at Steep Rock Lake north of Lake Superior. On the Pacific coast, the port of Vancouver prospered. Its shipyards and those of Victoria employed 30 000 workers at their peak. Prince Rupert became an important supply centre for American bases in Alaska. The military buildup on the West Coast also stimulated British Columbia's economy. By 1943, British Columbians had the highest per capita income of all Canadians. In spite of the war, tourism continued to contribute to Vancouver's development, and wartime promotion ensured that the sector would be poised for rapid postwar expansion.

The North

In 1942, the United States Army Corps of Engineers coordinated the construction teams that built, for defence purposes, a 2500 km highway from Dawson Creek in northeastern British Columbia to Fairbanks, Alaska. The next year the Public Roads Administration, an American civilian agency, directed the transformation of the rough military road into a permanent civilian highway, widening it, extending branch roads to the airstrips, and completing a telegraph line along this American highway built on Canadian soil.

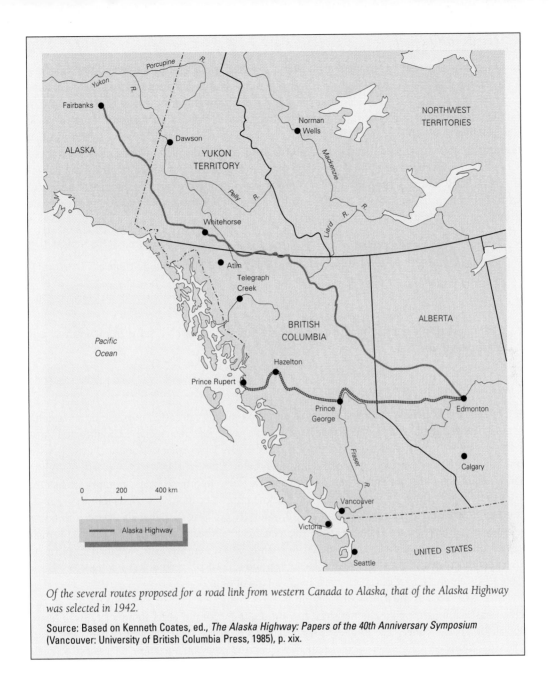

Of the several routes proposed for a road link from western Canada to Alaska, that of the Alaska Highway was selected in 1942.

Source: Based on Kenneth Coates, ed., *The Alaska Highway: Papers of the 40th Anniversary Symposium* (Vancouver: University of British Columbia Press, 1985), p. xix.

The attack on Pearl Harbor also led American defence planners to worry about the threat to energy supplies in the North West; oil tankers now appeared vulnerable to Japanese submarine attack. As a result, the Canadian Oil (Canol) project was begun to pipe oil from the Imperial Oil Company's field at Norman Wells, on the Mackenzie River. The Americans made large-scale expenditures to build a pipeline to Whitehorse, a refinery, and a whole host of subsidiary facilities. This dependable source of oil could then be used in the Pacific war theatre. For three years, thousands of men worked on this second American project on Canadian soil. When the Japanese threat in the Pacific ended, the completed Canol pipeline, now unneeded, was shut down.

Changes in Quebec

In Quebec the Liberals led by Adélard Godbout, elected in 1939, initiated important reforms. Whereas the preceding Union Nationale government of Maurice Duplessis had refused to nationalize the private electric power companies, the Liberal government created Hydro-Québec, a publicly owned hydroelectric utility in the Montreal region. To boost educational levels, it made school attendance obligatory until age fourteen, a measure hitherto opposed by the Roman Catholic clergy, who argued that parents, not the state, should decide how long children went to school. In the Quebec Labour Relations Act, the government set out the rules governing collective bargaining. The bill, supported by the unions, was intended to force companies to negotiate with their unionized employees. In 1940, women in Quebec finally obtained the right to vote provincially. Suffragist Idola Saint-Jean argued forcefully for this right:

> We vote in federal elections as intelligently as women in neighbouring provinces. Why shouldn't we be concerned with problems debated in the provincial parliament? Don't housing, public health and education concern us much more directly than the problems of federal politics?

The legislative assembly finally agreed, despite the vigorous objections of the church and conservative groups.

Ontario: The Return to Conservatism

In Ontario, the impetuous Mitchell Hepburn appeared mainly interested in pursuing a vendetta against fellow Liberal Mackenzie King. At the same time, the provincial CCF attracted support, largely in urban working-class districts. In the 1943 provincial election, the CCF, with one-third of the popular vote, placed second, just behind George Drew's Conservatives. While Drew denounced the socialists, he energetically pursued reform policies, notably in health, education, and housing. Provincial planning became important in areas such as forest conservation, industrial development, and water use. Profoundly pro-British, Drew also wanted to boost immigration from Britain. He established the War Brides Bureau in London to counsel British wives coming to Canada with their soldier husbands. Drew's enthusiastic salesmanship caused Canadian-born British press magnate Max Aitken, now Lord Beaverbrook, to comment: "Look George, is Ontario a part of Canada or Canada a part of Ontario?"

The CCF proved much less threatening in the Ontario election of 1945. In decline in the cities and lacking a rural base, it became, in addition, the victim of fierce denunciations of "state socialism." Party leader E.B. Jolliffe's sensational "revelations," that Drew was maintaining in Ontario "at this very minute, a secret political police, a paid spy organization, a Gestapo" to keep himself in power, backfired. Drew easily won a majority, and Ontario settled into what would become more than 40 years of Conservative government.

The Maritimes and Newfoundland

The war brought fewer economic benefits to Canadians in the three Maritime provinces, although the rise in food prices and the growing demand for minerals and pulp and paper did assist the region. War spending also boosted the regional economy. By 1943, some 75 000 men and women were building and repairing vessels in Maritime shipyards, even at night under floodlights. Halifax became Canada's major port for shipping munitions and other supplies to western Europe.

Historian Ernest Forbes has described the impact of Ottawa's war policies on the Maritimes as "largely negative. While the government did generate economic activity, it created relatively little new industry in the region and even less of a permanent nature."[17] According to Forbes, C.D. Howe believed it was more efficient to develop industry along the St. Lawrence and in the Great Lakes region, a conviction reinforced by the regional prejudices of Howe and his central Canadian political advisers. Nor did provincial governments succeed in obtaining federal funds for necessary infrastructure or private investment in industry. In general, at the war's end, the region appeared ill equipped to undertake any substantial industrial expansion.

Economic weakness meant that governments lacked funds for investment in health and education. In 1945, Prince Edward Island had only half the number of doctors needed to meet the national standard of one doctor per 1000 people. New Brunswick had Canada's highest infant and maternal death rate, and Nova Scotia followed closely. In Prince Edward Island, the great majority of schools had only one room; many needed repair or were beyond repair. Teachers were often poorly qualified, and salaries were low. New Brunswick had Canada's highest illiteracy rate, affecting particularly the province's French-speaking Acadian population. Only after 1940 did the provincial government authorize the use of French-language texts in public schools and recognize the importance of making French the language of instruction in Acadian schools.

After the war an "army" of 40 000 war brides (mainly British) with their 20 000 children, most under the age of three, arrived in Canada.

Source: H.B. Jefferson Collection/Nova Scotia Archives and Record Management/N-820.

Newfoundland's case was somewhat special. At the outbreak of war, low fish prices and uncertain markets left the population of the outports in appalling poverty. The relief rolls overflowed. At first, the war only worsened the situation, resulting in increased taxes and decreased services. Eventually, though, it created a temporary boom in employment through the construction and maintenance of huge American defence projects, especially the bases at Argentia, Gander, and Stephenville. After the British-appointed Commission of Government developed costly plans for postwar reconstruction, Britain came to an understanding with the Canadian government to encourage the island's eventual incorporation into Canada.

The West

The prairie provinces, hard hit by the depression of the 1930s, recovered only slowly. Although war spending brought relatively few jobs to the region, farmers increased their incomes substantially thanks to higher prices, caused largely by the much-increased demand for wheat in Europe, and to improved harvests made possible by better weather conditions. A growing farmers' movement, led by the Canadian Chamber of Agriculture, which had been founded in 1935, set out to defend farmers' interests and improve their lot. Farm incomes had remained much lower than other workers' wages; most rural homes had no indoor plumbing or electricity; and farm villages enjoyed few services.

The war boosted crude-oil production in Alberta, at least until the Turner Valley field near Calgary went into decline after 1942. Coal mines prospered, too, and in Prairie cities the construction industry flourished. But the war did not create the diversified economy that many residents felt the region needed.

Politically, third parties on the Prairies grew stronger, although they tended to moderate their ideology. Social Credit in Alberta, led by William Aberhart until his death in 1943 and then for a quarter-century by his protégé Ernest Manning, denounced socialism and centralization, promised able, businesslike administration, and gently laid Social Credit doctrine to rest. Overt anti-Semites within the party's ranks continued, however, to affirm their views until their expulsion in 1947.

The CCF made inroads in all three prairie provinces, but scored its first victory in Saskatchewan in 1944. Although it had attenuated the socialism of the Regina Manifesto, its ambitious program promised public ownership of natural resources, security of land tenure for farmers, collective bargaining for workers, educational reform, and social services, including a universal socialized health plan. Baptist preacher and CCF leader Tommy Douglas denounced the economic system that he likened to a cream separator: the farmer pours in the milk, the worker turns the handle, and the capitalist, because he owns the machine, "sits on a little stool with the cream spout fixed firmly in his mouth while the farmer and the worker take turns on the skim milk spout." Once in power, the CCF launched major reforms, particularly during its first two years in office, but financial and other factors soon forced it to make pragmatic policy adjustments.

In British Columbia, the old political order also changed. When the Liberals failed to gain a majority in the 1941 election, party members favouring coalition with the Conservatives ousted their leader, Duff Pattullo, whom they sharply criticized for his feuding with Ottawa, his road-building policy, and his abrasive style. The CCF then formed the opposition to the new Liberal–Conservative alliance.

The family of Private Louis Zarowny welcomes him home, at Mewata Stadium in Calgary, in July 1945. Wounded twice, Zarowny served with the Loyal Edmonton Regiment in Italy and Northwestern Europe.

Source: Glenbow Archives, Calgary, Canada/Herald Collection/NA-2864-3448.

Toward a New Internationalism

The war in Europe ended when Germany capitulated in May 1945. By September, Japan also surrendered. Peace brought with it new problems and, in particular, the difficult question of how to maintain it. In contrast to its position after World War I, Canada was ready to accept responsibility in world affairs. Like the other Allied countries, it believed in the necessity of establishing an international organization comparable to, but more effective than, the League of Nations. Canada thus participated in the founding conference of the United Nations at San Francisco in April 1945, where it worked to ensure that both the United States and the Soviet Union became members.

Canada also pushed for world economic and social cooperation. In late 1945, Lester Pearson chaired the founding meeting of the United Nations Food and Agriculture Organization in Quebec City. As a member of the United Nations Relief and Rehabilitation Administration, Canada became a major supplier of aid to war-torn countries, though it had great difficulty convincing the Americans of its right to participate in determining the operations of the association. Canada also joined the International Monetary Fund, as well as the International Civil Aviation Organization, whose headquarters came to Montreal. As external-affairs officer John Holmes commented later, Canada "moved with the tide," trying to avoid letting the Great Powers control everything.[18] Conscious of its position as a rising middle power, Canada attempted, with some success, to get recognition for states like itself. Willingly it recognized that its influence was less than that of the United States, but it wanted the Great Powers to recognize its middle-power status.

World War II changed Canada profoundly, in the country's relations with the world and at home as well. It effectively ended the isolation of the 1930s. Military technology had advanced to the point where Canada could no longer consider itself geographically isolated.

Involvement in world affairs brought benefits but carried a price. Despite Canada's attempts to develop relationships with multilateral associations of states, such involvement meant closer ties to the United States. For supporters of the *rapprochement*, the closer links brought security and economic prosperity through trade and investment. For critics, the triumphant move toward nationhood in the interwar years appeared to have abruptly ended, with Canada being relegated once more to colonial status—this time, as a colony of the United States.

At home, the war created an economic boom that instilled hopes among Canadians for a better life. Trade-union organizations made notable gains, as governments enacted legislation establishing a new framework for the conduct of industrial relations. The entry of large numbers of women into the work force announced a substantial change in their role. With Canada's new federal social programs, Canadians took a significant step in the direction of the welfare state. In federal–provincial relations, Ottawa reasserted a preeminence that endured for two decades. Voters in several provinces elected new governments that stayed in office for lengthy periods. In Ottawa, however, Canadians continued to support King, perhaps because he was, in historian Frank Underhill's words, the leader "who divides us least."[19]

Canada's Minister of External Affairs, Louis St. Laurent and Prime Minister Mackenzie King at the General Assembly of the United Nations Conference on International Organization, San Francisco, May 8, 1945.

Source: Library and Archives Canada/C-22720.

NOTES

1. Desmond Morton, *Canada and War: A Military and Political History* (Toronto: Butterworths, 1981), p. 106.

2. W.A.B. Douglas and Brereton Greenhous, *Out of the Shadows: Canada in the Second World War*, rev. ed. (Toronto: Dundurn Press, 1995), p. 111.

3. Donald Creighton, *The Forked Road: Canada, 1939–1957* (Toronto: McClelland & Stewart, 1976), p. 43.

4. J.L. Granatstein and Norman Hillmer, *For Better or for Worse: Canada and the United States to the 1990s* (Mississauga, ON: Copp Clark Pitman, 1991), p. 144.

5. James Eayrs, *In Defence of Canada*, vol. 2, *Appeasement and Rearmament* (Toronto: University of Toronto Press, 1965), p. 191.

6. Donald F. Davis and Barbara Lorenzkowski, "A Platform for Gender Tensions: Women Working and Riding on Canadian Urban Public Transit in the 1940s," *Canadian Historical Review* 79 (1998): 442–43.

7. Ruth Roach Pierson, *"They're Still Women After All": The Second World War and Canadian Womanhood* (Toronto: McClelland & Stewart, 1986), p. 33.

8. Ruth Roach Pierson, "'Jill Canuck': CWAC of All Trades, But No 'Pistol-Packing Momma,'" *Historical Papers/Communications historiques* (1978): 106–33.

9. W. Peter Ward, *White Canada Forever: Popular Attitudes and Public Policy Toward Orientals in British Columbia* (Montreal/Kingston: McGill-Queen's University Press, 1978), p. 146.

10. Patricia Roy et al., *Mutual Hostages: Canadians and Japanese During the Second World War* (Toronto: University of Toronto Press, 1990), p. 215.

11. Michael Earle, "'Down with Hitler and Silby Barrett': The Cape Breton Miners' Slowdown Strike of 1941," *Acadiensis* 18 (1988): 56–90.

12. Laurel Sefton MacDowell, "The Formation of the Canadian Industrial Relations System During World War Two," *Labour/Le Travail* 3 (1978): 186.

13. Gail Cuthbert Brandt, "'Pigeon-Holed and Forgotten': The Work of the Subcommittee on the Post-War Problems of Women, 1943," *Histoire sociale/Social History* 15 (1983): 239–59.

14. Susanne Klausen, "The Plywood Girls: Women and Gender Ideology at the Port Alberni Plywood Plant, 1942–1991," *Labour/Le Travail* 41 (1998): 199–235.

15. Alvin Finkel, "Paradise Postponed: A Re-examination of the Green Book Proposals of 1945," *Journal of the Canadian Historical Association* 4 (1993): 128.

16. R.M. Burns, *The Acceptable Mean: The Tax Rental Agreements, 1941–1962* (Toronto: Canadian Tax Foundation, 1980), p. 35.

17. Ernest R. Forbes, *Challenging the Regional Stereotype: Essays on the 20th Century Maritimes* (Fredericton: Acadiensis Press, 1989), p. 195.

18. John W. Holmes, *The Shaping of Peace: Canada and the Search for World Order, 1943–1957*, vol. 1 (Toronto: University of Toronto Press, 1979), pp. 235–36.

19. Frank Underhill, "The End of the King Era," *Canadian Forum* (September 1948); reprinted in F.H. Underhill, *In Search of Canadian Liberalism* (Toronto: Macmillan, 1960), p. 127.

BEYOND THE BOOK

Weblinks

Life During the War at McGill University
http://www.archives.mcgill.ca/public/hist_scevents/war/homefront.htm
Digitized pictures and documents detailing student life and war support efforts during World War II.

V-E Day and V-J Day in Toronto
http://www.toronto.ca/archives/ve1.htm
This exhibit of photographs and documents detail the celebrations of citizens in Toronto when the war ended.

Enemy Alien
http://asalive.archivesalberta.org:8080/access/asa/documents/display/GLEN-113
Scanned correspondence and records between the federal government and Angelina Rebaudengo regarding her husband's internment as an enemy alien during the war.

Canadian Letters and Images: World War II
http://www.canadianletters.ca/collections.php?warid=4
A vast database of the letters and photographs of dozens of Canadians who served in World War II.

Political Cartoons in World War II
http://www.mccord-museum.qc.ca/en/keys/webtours/GE_P4_5_EN
An exhibit of digitized political cartoons published in Canadian newspapers in World War II, with a guide to each.

Wartime Shipbuilding in North Vancouver
http://www.mccord-museum.qc.ca/en/keys/webtours/VQ_P4_1_EN
A guided exhibit of photographs of North Vancouver's shipbuilding industry in World War II.

A Soldier's War
http://archives.cbc.ca/IDD-1-71-103/conflict_war/soldiers_ww2
Digitized radio broadcasts from World War II and accounts from soldiers of their experiences.

Films & Novels

Obasan. By Joy Kogawa. 1993.

Love & Duty: Canadian Red Cross Women in World War II. Directed by Shel Piercy. 2002.

Earth and High Heaven. By Gwethalyn Graham. 1944.

Bye Bye Blues. Directed by Anne Wheeler. 1989.

RELATED READINGS

The following articles from R. Douglas Francis and Donald B. Smith, eds., *Readings in Canadian History: Post-Confederation*, 7th ed. (Toronto: Thomson Nelson, 2006), deal with topics relevant to this chapter: James Eayrs, "'A Low Dishonest Decade': Aspects of Canadian External Policy, 1931–1939," pp. 422–34; Jack Granatstein, "Staring into the Abyss," pp. 435–47; and J. Terry Copp, "Battle Exhaustion and the Canadian Soldiers in Normandy," pp. 447–56.

BIBLIOGRAPHY

C.P. Stacey proposes a useful survey of Canadian foreign policy in *Canada and the Age of Conflict: A History of Canadian External Policies*, vol. 2, *1921–1948: The Mackenzie King Era* (Toronto: University of Toronto Press, 1981). R.D. Cuff and J.L. Granatstein review aspects of Canadian–American relations in *Ties That Bind: Canadian–American Relations in Wartime from the Great War to the Cold War*, 2nd ed. (Toronto: Samuel Stevens Hakkert, 1977). J.L. Granatstein, *Canada's War: The Politics of the Mackenzie King Government, 1939–1945* (Toronto: University of Toronto Press, 1975, 1990), is useful on foreign and domestic policy, as are the relevant chapters in Robert Bothwell, Ian Drummond, and John English, *Canada, 1900–1945* (Toronto: University of Toronto Press, 1987). Norman Hillmer et al., eds., present several articles on Canada on the eve of war in *A Country of Limitations: Canada and the World in 1939* (Ottawa: Canadian Committee for the History of the Second World War, 1996).

In addition to works mentioned in this chapter's Where Historians Disagree box, books on Canada's participation in the war include David J. Bercuson, *Maple Leaf Against the Axis: Canada's Second World War* (Toronto: Stoddart, 1995); J.L. Granatstein and Desmond Morton, *A Nation Forged in Fire: Canadians and the Second World War, 1939–1945* (Toronto: Lester & Orpen Dennys, 1989); and appropriate chapters in J.L. Granatstein, *Canada's Army: Waging War and Keeping the Peace* (Toronto: University of Toronto Press, 2002). The soldiers' stories are recounted in Ted Barris and Alex Barris, *Days of Victory: Canadians Remember, 1939–1945* (Toronto: Macmillan, 1995); Desmond Morton and J.L. Granatstein, *Victory 1945: Canadians from War to Peace* (Toronto: HarperCollins, 1995); and Blake Heathcote, *Testaments of Honour: Personal Histories of Canada's War Veterans* (Toronto: Doubleday, 2002).

The Hong Kong debacle is described in Brereton Greenhous, *C-Force to Hong Kong: A Canadian Catastrophe, 1941–1945* (Toronto: Dundurn Press, 1996); and in Oliver Lindsay, *The Battle for Hong Kong, 1941-1945: Hostage to Fortune* (Montreal/Kingston: McGill-Queen's University Press, 2006). Books on the Italian campaign include Daniel G. Dancocks, *The D-Day Dodgers: The Canadians in Italy, 1943–1945* (Toronto: McClelland & Stewart, 1991); and Mark Zuehlke, *The Gothic Line: Canada's Month of Hell in World War II Italy* (Vancouver: Douglas and McIntyre, 2003). Popular accounts of the war in northwest Europe include Ted Barris, *Juno: Canadians at D-Day June 6, 1944* (Toronto: Thomas Allen Publishers, 2004); Mark Zuehlke, *Juno Beach: Canada's D-Day Victory: June 6, 1944* (Vancouver: Douglas & McIntyre, 2004); and George G. Blackburn, *The Guns of Victory: A Soldier's Eye View, Belgium, Holland, and Germany, 1944–45* (Toronto: McClelland & Stewart, 1996).

Canada's military leaders are studied in J.L. Granatstein, *The Generals: The Canadian Army's Senior Commanders in the Second World War* (Toronto: Stoddart, 1993); and in Bernd Horn and Stephen Harris, eds., *Warrior Chiefs: Perspectives on Senior Canadian Military Leaders* (Toronto: Dundurn Press, 2001). Terry Copp and Bill McAndrew study one particular type of battle casualty in *Battle Exhaustion: Soldiers and Psychiatrists in the Canadian Army, 1939–1945* (Montreal/Kingston: McGill-Queen's University Press, 1990). Three books look at the fate of Canadian prisoners of war: Jonathan Vance, *Objects of Concern: Canadian Prisoners of War Through the Twentieth Century* (Vancouver: University of British Columbia Press, 1994); Howard Margolian, *Conduct Unbecoming: The Story of the Murder of Canadian Prisoners of War in Normandy* (Toronto: University of Toronto Press, 1998); and David McIntosh, *Hell on Earth: Aging Faster, Dying Sooner: Canadian Prisoners of the Japanese During World War II* (Toronto: McGraw-Hill Ryerson, 1996). Spencer Dunmore discusses air-force pilot training in *Wings for Victory: The Remarkable Story of the British Air Training Plan in Canada* (Toronto: McClelland & Stewart, 1994). Articles concerning the rehabilitation of returning veterans may be found in Peter Neary and J.L. Granatstein, eds., *The Veterans Charter and Post–World War II Canada* (Montreal/Kingston: McGill-Queen's University Press, 1998). Carolyn Gossage has written a popular history of women in the armed services, *Greatcoats and Glamour Boots: Canadian Women at War, 1939–1945*, rev. ed. (Toronto: Dundurn Press, 2001). On Native participation in the war, see Janice Summerby's illustrated brochure, *Native Soldiers; Foreign Battlefields* (Ottawa: Minister of Supply and Services, 1993).

The history of the Royal Canadian Navy is told in Marc Milner, *North Atlantic Run: The Royal Canadian Navy and the Battle for the Convoys* (Toronto: University of Toronto Press, 1985); Tony German, *The Sea Is at Our Gates: The History of the Canadian Navy* (Toronto: McClelland & Stewart, 1990); and Donald E. Graves, *In Peril on the Sea: The Royal Canadian Navy and the Battle of the Atlantic, 1939–1945* (Toronto: Robin Brass Studio, 2003). Among books recounting the RCN's battle against German U-boats are Michael L. Hadley, *U-Boats Against Canada: German Submarines in Canadian Waters* (Montreal/Kingston: McGill-Queen's University Press, 1985); and Marc Milner, *The U-Boat Hunters: The Royal Canadian Navy and the Offensive Against Germany's Submarines* (Toronto: University of Toronto Press, 1994). The story of the child evacuees from England bound for Canada is told in Tom Nagorski, *Miracles on the Water: The Heroic Survivors of a World War II U-Boat* (New York: Hyperion, 2006). David Zimmerman describes the technical problems encountered by the RCN in developing better-quality radar in *The Great Naval Battle of Ottawa* (Toronto: University of Toronto Press, 1989). Donald Avery studies Canada's contribution to Allied defence research in *The Science of War: Canadian Scientists and Allied Military Technology During the Second World War* (Toronto: University of Toronto Press, 1998). For the role of the RCAF the major work is Brereton Greenhous, Stephen J. Harris, William C. Johnston, and William G.P. Rawling, *The Crucible of War, 1939–1945: The Official History of the Royal Canadian Air Force*, vol. III (Toronto: University of Toronto Press, 1994).

The most thorough study on conscription is J.L. Granatstein and J.M. Hitsman, *Broken Promises: A History of Conscription in Canada*, rev. ed. (Toronto: Copp Clark Pitman, 1985). For an explanation of Quebec's reaction see Richard Jones, "Politics and Culture: The French Canadians and the Second World War," in Sidney Aster, ed., *The Second World War as a National Experience* (Ottawa: Canadian Committee for the History of the Second World War, 1981), pp. 82–91. See also Michael D. Stevenson, *Canada's Greatest Wartime Muddle: National Selective Service and the Mobilization of Human Resources During World War II* (Montreal/Kingston: McGill-Queen's University Press, 2001). Wartime censorship is treated in Claude Beauregard's excellent study, *Guerre et censure au Canada, 1939–1945* (Sillery, QC: Septentrion, 1998). The work of Canadian historians who chronicled the story of the war is described in Tim Cook, *Clio's Warriors: Canadian Historians and the Writing of the World Wars* (Vancouver: UBC Press, 2006).

Social security is discussed in a special issue of the *Journal of Canadian Studies* on "Leonard Marsh and Canadian Social Policy" (vol. 21, 1986). On family allowances see Nancy Christie, *Engendering the State: Family, Work and Welfare in Canada* (Toronto: University of Toronto Press, 2000). Doug Owram examines the evolution of ideas concerning the role of the modern state in *The Government Generation: Canadian Intellectuals and the State, 1900–1945* (Toronto: University of Toronto Press, 1986). Carman Miller looks at the effects of war on the Maritimes in "The 1940s: War and Rehabilitation," in E.R. Forbes and D.A. Muise, eds., *The Atlantic Provinces in Confederation* (Toronto: University of Toronto Press, 1993). Material on Newfoundland may be found in Peter Neary, *Newfoundland in the North Atlantic World, 1929–1949* (Montreal/Kingston: McGill-Queen's University Press, 1988).

On women in wartime see Ruth Roach Pierson, *"They're Still Women After All": The Second World War and Canadian Womanhood* (Toronto: McClelland & Stewart, 1986). For one Toronto woman's experience, see Gunda Lambton, *Sun in Winter: A Toronto Wartime Journal, 1942–1945* (Montreal/Kingston, McGill-Queen's University Press, 2003). Jeffrey A. Keshen analyzes the war's negative social ramifications in *Saints, Sinners, and Soldiers: Canada's Second World War* (Vancouver: UBC Press, 2004). Maria Tippett examines culture in wartime in *Making Culture: English-Canadian Institutions and the Arts Before the Massey Commission* (Toronto: University of Toronto Press, 1990). Aspects of union activity are examined in Desmond Morton with Terry Copp, *Working People: An Illustrated History of the Canadian Labour Movement*, 3rd ed. (Toronto: Summerhill Press, 1990). On the impact of the war on labour–management relations, consult Laurel Sefton MacDowell, *Remember Kirkland Lake: The Gold Miners' Strike of 1941–42*, rev. ed. (Toronto: Canadian Scholars' Press, 2001).

On the treatment of Japanese Canadians consult Ann Gomer Sunahara, *The Politics of Racism: The Uprooting of Japanese Canadians During the Second World War* (Toronto: James Lorimer, 1981); Peter Ward,

White Canada Forever: Popular Attitudes and Public Policy Toward Orientals in British Columbia, 2nd ed. (Montreal/Kingston: McGill-Queen's University Press, 1990); and, for a very different view, Patricia Roy et al., *Mutual Hostages: Canadians and Japanese During the Second World War* (Toronto: University of Toronto Press, 1990). The internment of Italian Canadians is discussed in Franca Iacovetta, Roberto Perin, and Angelo Principe, eds., *Enemies Within: Italian and Other Internees in Canada and Abroad* (Toronto: University of Toronto Press, 2000). Pacifism is examined in Tom Socknat, *Witness Against War: Pacifism in Canada, 1900–1945* (Toronto: University of Toronto Press, 1987). Larry Hannant, *The Infernal Machine: Investigating the Loyalty of Canada's Citizens* (Toronto: University of Toronto Press, 1995), deals with the questions of internal security and civil liberties.

Part

4

MODERN CANADA, 1945 TO THE PRESENT

INTRODUCTION

Canada emerged in the last half of the twentieth century as an important industrial nation and a respected secondary world power. Such achievements brought both benefits and problems. Overall, Canadians have enjoyed one of the highest standards of living of any country in the world, although certain groups within Canadian society remain less favoured and some regions of the country experience greater hardships and fewer advantages than others. How to ensure that all Canadians, regardless of ethnic origin, class, gender, or place of dwelling have equal opportunities continues to be one of the challenges facing Canadian leaders. Canadians have also had to learn to live in a global economy, where they have less control over their economic destiny than ever before. Finally, as the world and Canada face the very serious threats of environmental degradation and declining resources, Canadians are having to consider the consequences of decisions relating to economic development and personal lifestyles.

Internationally, Canada emerged from World War II prepared to play a more active role on the world stage. Caught in the middle of the Cold War between the United States and the Soviet Union, the country chose to play the role of middle power, a role well suited to the country's historic position as the mediator between Britain and the United States. To offset American dominance in the North American defence program, of which Canadians found themselves a part, Canadians have taken an active role in such international

organizations as the United Nations, the British Commonwealth of Nations, and the North Atlantic Treaty Organization (NATO). Still, some foreign policy analysts have criticized Canada for becoming too closely allied to the United States, thus limiting the country's ability to help mediate international disputes.

Politically, the Liberal party's resilience at adapting to change has enabled it to govern Canada during fully three-quarters of the time since the end of World War II. The other traditional party, the Conservatives (formerly the Progressive Conservatives), took power when fatigue with the governing Liberals set in and when it succeeded in moderating its own image. Third parties have also emerged in what has become at times a multiparty system, as a constant reminder that no party has enjoyed complete support from all regions and all groups within the country. Regional parties have been particularly strong in the West and in Quebec, challenging political leaders to find consensus.

As Canada has modernized, it has become more of a consumer society. Culturally, too, it has taken on the attributes of a mass culture, in which the emphasis is on a popular, mass audience. Both of these trends have moved the country, particularly English-speaking Canada, socially and culturally into the American orbit, making it more difficult to maintain a distinctive Canadian identity. Yet, at the same time, regional and local cultural variations as well as a different political culture have continued to challenge these universal homogenizing trends.

Chapter Fourteen

TOWARD A MORE AFFLUENT SOCIETY: 1945–60

TIME LINE	
1947	Oil begins to flow from the first well in the Leduc oil field in Alberta
1949	Newfoundland enters Confederation Canada joins the North Atlantic Treaty Organization Quebec asbestos workers strike for five months
1950	Outbreak of the Korean War
1952	Canada's first television station begins broadcasting in Montreal
1953	Opening of the Stratford (Ontario) Shakespearean Festival
1954	Construction begins on the International Seaway and Power Project on the St. Lawrence River; work is completed in 1959
1956	Founding of the Canadian Labour Congress
1957	Lester Pearson wins Nobel Peace Prize The North American Air Defence Command (NORAD) comes into being Public hospital-insurance program established Liberals defeated by John Diefenbaker's Progressive Conservatives in the federal election Founding of the Canada Council, in support of culture and the arts
1958	Conservatives win a huge majority of seats in federal election
1959	Newfoundland loggers' strike

After a decade of economic depression and six years of war, Canadians wanted to make up for lost time, forget a bleak past, and look toward the future. Workers sought stable jobs and better wages. Consumers wanted cars, household appliances, adequate housing, and more leisure. Yet modest family budgets, limited availability of goods (particularly in the immediate postwar years), and fears that prosperity would not continue, forced them to be patient and prudent. In addition, the insecurity of the recent past made Canadians look increasingly to governments to provide an array of health, educational, and social services as a safety net against misfortune. In regard to the world outside, they took pride in Canada's prestigious role in international organizations, and in the welcome their country extended to immigrants from war-torn and economically ravaged Europe.

Attitudes remained basically conservative. Traditional values and beliefs continued to govern the behaviour of a majority of Canadians. Although more women worked outside the home, long-held notions concerning the role of women in society loosened only gradually. By the late 1950s, however, the old mentality was changing. Slower growth with rising unemployment disrupted the postwar boom. People tired of unimaginative politicians who boasted of past successes and talked in platitudinous generalities. They were now ready to welcome new leaders who would put forth new ideas and propose new solutions.

Economic Nirvana in Canada?

Postwar Canada prospered. *Fortune* magazine called it a "businessman's country." Construction boomed. Total industrial output rose by half in the 1950s, and productivity soared thanks to technological innovation. The lighting of the flame on Leduc no. 1 oil well in a farmer's field near Edmonton on a cold February day in 1947 signalled large-scale job creation and rapid population growth in Alberta. The discovery of large deposits of base metals in northern New Brunswick boosted hopes for significant job creation in that province. In Ontario, demand for a wide array of goods stimulated industrial expansion. The government-owned Polymer Corporation, in Sarnia, Ontario produced fully 10 percent of the world's synthetic rubber, widely used by the rapidly expanding automobile industry.[1] By 1951, 10 percent of the Canadian labour force had jobs related to motor vehicles, mostly in southern Ontario. That same year, the Ford Motor Company announced the construction of a huge plant in the small town of Oakville, just west of Toronto. For a time, Oakville's residents enjoyed the highest per capita incomes in Canada.

The average worker had reason to feel satisfied. Rapid economic growth meant that unemployment rates remained (by contemporary standards) very low: between 2.8 and 5.9 percent. Pay packets for factory workers doubled between 1945 and 1956. In spite of significant increases in the prices of food and consumer goods, workers saw their living standards improve. They also worked less, as the 40-hour week became the norm. In addition, federal transfer payments, such as family allowances and old-age pensions, put more money into consumers' pockets.

The Age of the Consumer

The era of the consumer introduced a new lifestyle. In towns, the iceman with his horsedrawn cart lost his remaining customers as people gradually discarded their iceboxes and equipped their kitchens with electric refrigerators. Coal merchants' sales tumbled as homeowners bought electric ranges and switched to cleaner and more efficient gas and oil heat. Families acquired a variety of new appliances intended to reduce the drudgery of housework. Sales of new automobiles mounted in the 1950s as Canadians bought sleek American Fords and Chevrolets, or slim British Morrises and Austins.

Subdivisions proliferated around major cities. In historian Doug Owram's words, "the rise and triumph of low-density residentially oriented communities was the single most significant urban event of the postwar decades."[2] A million new homes were built between 1945 and 1960. Canadians could buy a bungalow for $15 000 and then borrow the money to pay for it at a fixed rate of just over 4 percent for 25 years. Proud new homeowners hurried to vary the colour of the trim or to plant shrubs in order to distinguish their dwelling from the identical constructions on all sides. Roofs acquired an important new use—as supports for forests of television antennas. Shopping centres sprang up, the first appearing in a Toronto suburb in 1946.

The Environment

More prosperous Canadians posed new threats to the environment as well as having an increased interest in protecting it. In search of new outdoor recreational opportunities, more mobile urban dwellers invaded provincial parks. Existing parks quickly became saturated. In response to this demand, Ontario, for example, embarked upon a major program of park expansion: the number of parks grew from only 8 in 1954 to 94 in 1967. By the late 1950s, however, conservationists worried that increased outdoor recreation threatened the survival of natural areas, and they called for the establishment of nature preserves. In 1959, Ontario adopted the Wilderness Areas Act, which set aside areas of natural, historic, and scenic importance.

Conservation practices had not yet influenced the operations of the forest industry. Harvesting aimed at maximum profits. Clearcutting, facilitated by the mechanization of the industry, was the primary method employed, because it permitted lower labour costs while hugely increasing logging volumes.

Supermarkets became a symbol of postwar prosperity. Woodward's department store, Vancouver, was one of the first in Canada. It included in-store home economists and baby seats in the shopping carts.

Source: Vancouver Public Library/25644.

The Less Advantaged

Yet Canadians were often unhappy when they compared themselves, as they did obsessively, with first-place Americans. Magazines and newspapers featured articles that delved into the revenues and expenses of "typical" Canadian and American families. In 1950, Canadian per capita income was still 40 percent below American levels. Canadians complained that refrigerators costing $400 here could be had for only $275 in the United States. Journalist Blair Fraser remarked that, for Europeans still rebuilding their war-torn economies, second-place Canadians must have seemed like the impoverished tycoon who was down to his last million. Nevertheless, many people of talent, especially entertainers, researchers, and engineers, migrated south, while those who remained behind bemoaned the "brain drain."

Many Canadians saw no boom at all. Few men and far fewer women held the university diplomas that guaranteed good jobs. Salaries were often low, especially for non-unionized workers, immigrants, and women, even taking into account the fact that the dollar's purchasing power was at least ten times what it is today. In the immediate postwar years, most people, like the Montrealers historian Magda Fahrni has studied, probably limited themselves to the "cautious consumption of necessities."[3] In rural Canada before 1950, only a minority of households even had electricity. The 1951 census revealed that half of Canadian families still did not own an electric refrigerator or a vacuum cleaner, 60 percent had no car, 40 percent had no telephone, and 25 percent did not have an electric washing machine. Indeed, one dwelling in three did not have hot and cold running water. Thousands of small farmers, incapable of earning a living, abandoned their land. Incomes of residents of the Atlantic provinces remained nearly 40 percent below the Canadian average. New Brunswick was sharply divided into the impoverished north and east, largely Acadian, and the more favoured south, mostly English-speaking. Thousands of Montrealers with incomes below the poverty line lived in the tenements of St. Henri, which were portrayed poignantly by Gabrielle Roy in her novel *Bonheur d'occasion* (*The Tin Flute* in English). In supposedly French-speaking Quebec, unilingual anglophones enjoyed income levels twice those of unilingual francophones and one-third higher than those of bilingual francophones. In the West, Winnipeg suffered from the decline of old industries, and the relocation of Canadian Pacific Airlines to Vancouver in 1948, which cost the city many jobs.

A number of First Nations people in isolated areas of the country still supported themselves by trapping and fishing; those living in more southern regions, on reserves located in marginal agricultural areas, faced greater difficulties in supporting themselves. Some First Nations and Métis people migrated to urban centres in search of job opportunities; this migration accelerated in the 1960s.

Disadvantaged provinces offered social services of inferior quality. When Newfoundland entered Confederation in 1949, two-thirds of its schools had only one room and lacked electricity and running

Mrs. Hugh Hawkins of Ottawa doing the washing with a traditional labour-intensive wringer washer, 1947. Today young people have heard the expression "through the wringer" but do not know its origin. This is what Mrs. Hawkins is doing in this photo, putting her laundry through the wringer in order to squeeze out the excess water. Modern automatic washers were as yet rarely seen in Canadian homes.

Source: Library and Archives Canada/PA-115254.

water. Rural areas of richer provinces were scarcely better equipped. In Quebec, the wages of primary school teachers, often barely $600 a year, did little to attract talented personnel into the teaching profession. Throughout Canada, the underprivileged, whether unemployed or sick, handicapped or elderly, could not count on the array of social welfare benefits that, in spite of recent cutbacks, still exist today.

A HISTORICAL PORTRAIT

Betty, Ruby, and the Others

At the conclusion of World War II, most working women left the work force and became homemakers for their bread-winner husbands, and full-time mothers of the two, three, or often more children who quickly made their appearance. The gendered division of labour seemed normal and natural. The happiest women were supposedly those whose husbands were able to purchase a modest bungalow on a small lot in one of the dozens of suburbs that sprang up around Canada's cities in the 1950s.

Do the life stories of these ordinary women confirm the myths of contentment in the home in suburbia? Betty's husband bought a bungalow in Cooksville, Ontario, a west Toronto suburb. Betty, who had a B.A. in music and had worked until her marriage, now settled in as a full-time homemaker. Some modern appliances supposedly made her work easier. In 1950, she already had an automatic washer. Historian Joy Parr shows that, in this regard, Betty, an American immigrant, was not typical of her Canadian neighbours, the majority of whom used labour-intensive wringer washers until the mid-1960s. Such washers cost much less, they consumed far less water, and they enabled users to assert more control over the washing process; the wringers, however, did pose some dangers to children's hands![1]

Betty's husband, Dick, commuted to work in downtown Toronto. He did not have a job, he had a "vocation." The distinction signified that Dick viewed his work as "socially important" and that he had to devote virtually all his time to it. Betty was thus often home alone with the children because Dick was away on business. She was convinced that she was doing what was expected of her. "A woman's place is in the home," she repeated. Dick agreed. He was sure that women working outside the home were an important cause of divorce and of juvenile delinquency.

One day Betty decided to begin giving piano lessons at home. Perhaps she merely wanted some extra spending money of her own; perhaps she felt that her musical talents were being wasted; perhaps she was simply bored and lonely. Earnings from the job were modest; indeed, Dick often belittled his wife's efforts. At the same time he did not hesitate, over Betty's protests, to delve into the piano money box when he needed some spare change.

Ruby was another Ontario homemaker in the 1950s. Her sister, Edna Staebler, has edited the letters that Ruby wrote to members of her family. Ruby worried about her appearance—she constantly complained about being overweight. She talked a lot about her children. She also got a job outside the home. In a touching letter to sister Kay, she expounded upon her decision.

I'm so thrilled and so nervous I don't know what to do. I won't sleep a wink tonight I'll bet. You know I've been talking about getting a job for so long because [husband] Fred wasn't earning enough and I guess he got sick of hearing about it.... I finally got up enough nerve to go down to the employment office to see what they could do for me.... I'm to go to Musser's store on Monday afternoon and start selling gloves. I'm so scared. I'll have to make change and fit people and be on my feet all those hours—and what will Fred say when he comes home tonite and I tell him?

Gosh, why did I do it? I could be so comfortable here just watching TV and working on my rug and I wouldn't need many clothes.... If I work ... I'll always be in a rush with my housework and have to make dinner at noon. And I won't be home when the kids get here from school.... (But) it would be good training. And I could use the extra money for so many things we need around here....[2]

"Home dreams" did not fully meet the aspirations of all Canadian women after 1945, as historian Veronica Strong-Boag concludes.[3] Yet much work still needs to be done to reconstitute the life experiences of ordinary women in this period and to reexamine traditional interpretations.

---

1   Joy Parr, *Domestic Goods: The Material, the Moral, and the Economic in the Postwar Years* (Toronto: University of Toronto Press, 1999), Ch. 10.

2   Edna Staebler, ed., *Haven't Any News: Ruby's Letters from the Fifties* (Waterloo, ON: Wilfrid Laurier Press, 1995), p. 58.

3   Veronica Strong-Boag, "Home Dreams: Women and the Suburban Experiment in Canada, 1945–60," *Canadian Historical Review* 72 (1991): 504.

Canada had many second-class citizens, too. The French suffered a linguistic disadvantage, even within Quebec. Women did not enjoy the same employment opportunities as men. Discrimination also afflicted Canada's Aboriginal peoples as well as African Canadians, recent immigrants, and Jews. In 1948, Pierre Berton, a young reporter for *Maclean's*, set out to investigate anti-Semitism. When he attempted to reserve a room at summer resorts north of Toronto, he had much more success using the name "Marshall" than when he identified himself as "Rosenberg." When he replied to a job advertisement as "Greenberg," he was frequently told that the vacancy had been filled. When he telephoned later and said his name was Grimes, the job was still available. To help combat such discrimination through education, the newly founded Canadian Council of Christians and Jews instituted Brotherhood Week, a major program, in 1948. At the same time, various interest groups urged governments to take action to defend minority rights. In 1947, Saskatchewan became the first province in Canada to adopt a comprehensive bill of rights.

Society in this era emphasized family and reproductive heterosexuality, and psychologists warned that overprotective mothers and absent fathers risked provoking homosexual tendencies in their sons. Gays and lesbians faced social stigma as "perverts" and "sex deviates," as well as job discrimination. Immigration law prevented homosexuals from entering Canada. In 1953, lesbian practices were criminalized for the first time. Gay men were often viewed as potential child molesters and, in the climate of the Cold War, as security risks to be purged from government service. By the mid-1960s, RCMP files reportedly contained the names of 7500 homosexuals.

Most homosexuals hid their sexual orientation, except perhaps from a few persons close to them. Yet gay and lesbian networks expanded in Canadian cities. Gay men met in bars, baths, parks, and theatres; indeed newspapers reported frequent arrests in such places. Lesbians socialized at bars that women could frequent and at house parties.

The inequalities suffered by many Canadians engendered increasing discontent. Not clearly articulated in the 1950s, dissatisfaction provoked far-reaching change beginning in the 1960s.

Prosperity and Trade

After demobilization, the federal government worked to convert the Canadian economy back to a free-enterprise system and to avoid a repetition of the severe recession that followed World War I. To achieve this objective, C.D. Howe, Canada's manager of wartime production and now in charge of the country's postwar reconstruction, sold war plants for a fraction of their cost, on condition that they reopen for business. He also wanted to liberalize international trade: only if markets abroad were open, he believed, could a country like Canada, with its economy largely based on exports, prosper. Finally, he urged the government to use tax policy to promote investment and create jobs.

Canada's trade did expand, albeit unevenly. From the late 1940s, the country had a persistently negative trade balance as imports rose faster than exports. The trade balance would have been even worse had prices for Canada's forest products and minerals not remained high. In real terms, Canada exported less in the mid-1950s than at the end of the war. Most Canadian-made manufactured products could not compete in international markets. Canadian production costs remained high because Canadian companies manufactured a wide variety of products in small quantities, and they often relied heavily on imported American components.

As Britain sought to increase its purchases in Europe after World War II, its imports from Canada declined. Canada moved to establish closer economic ties with the United States. Indeed, by 1947, as imports from the United States increased sharply and British regulations made it impossible for Canada to convert into dollars the pounds it earned in trade with Britain, Canada experienced a severe shortage of American dollars. One solution was to negotiate a free-trade agreement with the Americans, in an attempt to boost exports to the United States. But Prime Minister King, recalling Laurier's stinging defeat in the "Reciprocity Election" of 1911, vetoed the project: "I would no more think of, at my time of life and at this stage of my career, attempting any movement of the kind than I would of flying to the South Pole."

A safer move was to try to convince the Americans to permit European countries receiving American aid through the Marshall Plan to use a portion of it to buy Canadian goods. The Americans agreed, thus resolving the dollar crisis. Ottawa also hoped that the General Agreement on Tariffs and Trade (GATT) would come to its aid. This multilateral trade agreement, signed in Geneva in 1947, aimed at stimulating world trade by reducing tariffs. It included accords between Canada and its two principal trading partners, the United States and Britain.

An Investment Boom

Regardless of Canada's rejection of free trade, continental economic integration proceeded apace. Foreign capital poured into Canada, particularly during the Korean War, 1950 to 1953. The Americans sought Canada's resources, as production of some important minerals declined in the United States. Moreover, to gain access to the Canadian market, protected by high tariffs, American multinational corporations established, especially in central Canada, numerous branch plants that manufactured consumer products and industrial goods.

The Royal Commission on Canada's Economic Prospects

Most Canadians assumed that, despite closer economic links with the United States, Canada could maintain its political sovereignty. Some provinces, in their quest for jobs, actively encouraged the entry of foreign capital by keeping taxes and labour costs down. Nevertheless, some observers worried about the "complacency" with which Canadians sold out the country's resources. In particular, the Royal Commission on Canada's Economic Prospects recommended in 1956 that Canada control foreign investment.

Advocates of North American integration argued that multinationals gave jobs to Canadians and helped the country's balance of payments by reducing imports. Howe protested in a speech in 1956 that "had it not been for the enterprise and capital from the United States ... our development would have been slower, and some of the spectacular projects of which we are so proud ... would still be in the future." He called the Royal Commission's preliminary report "manure"—employing, in fact, a more earthy expression.

Investment, both Canadian and foreign, financed several important development projects. Pipelines carried oil and gas from Alberta to markets in Ontario and the United States; a railway nearly 600 km long, running north from Sept-Îles, Quebec, opened up ore-rich Labrador; and the construction of the St. Lawrence Seaway and the Trans-Canada Highway began.

Then the boom ended. By 1958, slow growth raised unemployment to nearly 10 percent. Automation eliminated some jobs. When railways switched to diesel engines, for example, they needed fewer machinists, blacksmiths, and firemen. The high-valued Canadian dollar, which brought a premium when exchanged for an American dollar, hurt exports.

A Government of Efficient Administrators

In the late 1940s and early 1950s, voters wanted politicians who would manage the country efficiently and achieve greater prosperity. They also called upon the state to protect them from the risks of unemployment, illness, and poverty. The Liberal government of businesspeople and administrators largely fulfilled this need. It was a regime that reflected an era.

When William Lyon Mackenzie King finally retired in 1948, he had led the Liberal party for nearly 30 years and could boast of having been the longest-serving prime minister in the history of the British empire. Jurist Frank Scott, who objected indignantly to King's being given credit for everything but putting the oil under Alberta, attributed King's success to his blandness: "He will be remembered wherever men honour ingenuity, ambiguity, inactivity, and political longevity."

Yet many observers of Canadian politics admired King for his accomplishments, even though they disliked him personally and found him uninspiring. He seemed to follow rather than lead, and to be more concerned with his own and the Liberal party's fortunes than with the country's well-being. Nevertheless, he had—like Macdonald and Laurier before him—held the country together effectively through difficult times. His government had also taken the first steps toward establishing a welfare state in Canada.

The St. Laurent Government

Louis St. Laurent, chosen as King's successor in 1948, was a former corporation lawyer from Quebec City and the second French-speaking, though fluently bilingual, prime minister. Denounced in his home province during the war for his approval of military conscription, he was clearly no Quebec nationalist. On constitutional questions he opposed the provincial autonomists in Quebec and elsewhere. In foreign affairs, he appeared more internationalist than most Canadians.

Louis St. Laurent (left) and Prime Minister Mackenzie King (centre), at the national Liberal convention of 1948 at which St. Laurent was chosen to succeed King as Liberal leader and prime minister. In the background is a portrait of former Liberal leader and prime minister Wilfrid Laurier.

The new prime minister followed his predecessor's "accommodative" approach, acting only after consensus had been achieved. While the Progressive Conservatives in opposition suffered from their links with the rabidly Tory "Bay Street interests," and doctrinaire socialists in the CCF vainly preached the need to "share the wealth" so that every family could have "a good kitchen sink and a first-class bathroom," the Liberals continued to occupy the centre of the political spectrum and thus established the consensus so necessary to govern Canada. Prosperity facilitated their task.

Newfoundland Enters Confederation

In 1949, soon after the St. Laurent government took office, Newfoundland became Canada's tenth province. On April 1, the *St. John's Evening Telegram* observed, "Newfoundland slipped as quietly into Confederation last midnight as the grey mist which settled over the capital early this morning."

Confederation had been preceded by months of bitter struggle. Joey Smallwood, leader of the confederate forces, campaigned tirelessly, at times from an old seaplane equipped with loudspeakers, to prove that Newfoundlanders "would be better off in pocket, in stomach, and in health" within Canada. Anti-confederationists denounced those who would "lure Newfoundland into the Canadian mousetrap." They called Smallwood a "Judas" who belittled Newfoundland's good name and lamented that at least Iscariot had had the decency to hang himself.

The referendum held in June 1948 allowed Newfoundlanders to choose among three options: Confederation, favoured by both Britain and Canada; responsible government or dominion status, perhaps leading to economic union with the United States; and the unpopular existing system, by which a commission of British-appointed officials governed Newfoundland. Responsible government won; Confederation placed second. Since no clear majority had emerged, a second referendum was held in July in an atmosphere of sectarian bitterness. Most Roman Catholics, fearing loss of their denominational schools, spoke against Confederation, while many Protestants favoured it. In general, the urban commercial classes opposed Confederation, fearing the competition of the big Canadian department stores (such as Eaton's) and the mail-order companies. The confederates won narrowly this time, with a majority of 52 percent. Canadians and Newfoundlanders now set about negotiating the final terms of union.

Historian David Alexander argues that the decline of the fishing economy, which fell victim to tumbling prices and oversupply, "led Newfoundlanders reluctantly into Confederation."[4] Poverty was endemic: in 1949, the island's citizens had incomes only one-third as high as those of Canadians. Death rates for diseases associated with poverty stood two to three times higher than Canadian rates. Canada's "safety net" of social programs looked inviting.

In addition, Britain clearly desired to quit Newfoundland. In the words of historian Peter Neary, Britain arranged its departure "with a hard logic and clinical precision she would not manage in other parts of her far-flung but now crumbling empire."[5] Yet, Canada also wanted Newfoundland. During World War II, federal civil servants and politicians had discovered the island's strategic and economic importance. Canadians also worried that the United States might seek to strengthen its ties with the island.

Newfoundland's integration into Canada proceeded rapidly. Immediately upon confederation, family allowances and other federal social programs were ready to function. Income levels improved. Yet the federal government did little to favour the province's economic development, and the province simply "shifted its dependence from London to Ottawa."[6]

Federal–Provincial Tensions

The Liberal government's preoccupation with maintaining a buoyant economy had serious implications for Canadian federalism. Civil servants and politicians in Ottawa believed that the federal government should maintain and even strengthen the fiscal and legislative preeminence that it had acquired during the wartime emergency. Disadvantaged provinces had benefited financially. New Brunswick, for example, reaped substantial increases in its revenues when it ceded to Ottawa its right to collect income taxes. But several provinces objected to Ottawa's aggressive centralization. Nova Scotia premier Angus L. Macdonald complained that federal subsidies destroyed provincial independence and transformed the provinces into "mere annuitants of Ottawa." Ontario insisted on its right to formulate its own economic priorities and programs. In Quebec, the Duplessis government feuded continuously with Ottawa over federal tax and spending policies. The province's Royal Commission of Inquiry on Constitutional Problems (the Tremblay Commission) called in 1954 for an end to federal "imperialism" and a return to "true federalism."

Toward a Welfare State

Neither federal–provincial tensions nor the Liberals' moderate conservatism halted Canada's movement toward a welfare state. Canadians were particularly critical of the old-age pensions program instituted by Ottawa in 1927 by which the elderly had to prove need in order to benefit. It was felt that the means test stigmatized the poor and penalized those who had saved. In 1951, after all the provinces had agreed to the requisite constitutional amendment, federal legislation authorized sending old-age-security cheques in the amount of $40 a month to all Canadians over the age of 70 and to needy Canadians over 65. Family allowances, also a universal program covering all children, now took second place. For the government, the family allowances, instituted in 1944, had served their purpose: workers' wages had increased, there had been no postwar depression, and the socialist CCF no longer posed a threat. The government's failure to increase the value of the allowances meant that, with higher living costs because of inflation, their impact on family budgets diminished substantially.

The government also adopted other measures concerning health and welfare. In 1948, Ottawa

A Newfoundland woman votes in the referendum of 1948. Although Newfoundlanders opted for responsible government over union with Canada, the indecisive results forced a second referendum, which the confederationists won. On March 31, 1949, Newfoundland joined Confederation as Canada's tenth province.

Source: C.F. Marshall/Centre for Newfoundland Studies, Queen Elizabeth II Library, Memorial University of Newfoundland.

enacted the National Health Program, which provided for federal grants to each province in the fields of hygiene and health. Unemployment insurance coverage was extended to new categories of workers such as Atlantic fishers. In 1956, after a national publicity campaign by the Canadian Welfare Council, Parliament enacted the Unemployment Assistance Act, a shared-cost program designed to assist employable persons on welfare. Provinces also spent significantly more on welfare as case numbers increased. Yet such aid failed to take into account increased housing and clothing costs. For historian James Struthers, in Ontario "the poor went hungry to pay the rent."[7]

Most Canadians who became ill in the 1950s knew the prohibitive cost of health care. One Montreal businessman, after paying the bills occasioned by his wife's serious illness, commented wryly, "There are two things that can send you to the poorhouse: hospital bills and borrowing from loan sharks. And 90 percent of the borrowing from loan sharks is to pay hospital bills!" Many Canadians tried to cover eventual health costs at least partially by participating in Blue Cross or other doctor-sponsored insurance plans, but at least half of Canadians had no direct coverage for medical care.

Calls for a national health plan were heard constantly. Anxious doctors warned that such a plan would rob them of their independence and interfere with the intimate doctor–patient relationship; they did not however oppose a plan that would cover only hospital care. Several provincial premiers, especially those from the western provinces, most of which had already established hospital insurance, pressured Ottawa into acting. Finally, in 1957, Parliament adopted the Hospital Insurance and Diagnostic Services Act, which provided federal financial assistance to provinces willing to set up a publicly administered hospital-insurance program with universal coverage.

The Golden Age of Canadian Diplomacy

After 1945, Canada had to adapt to a new world power structure. It could no longer rely on a permanently weakened Britain as a counterweight to American influence. To offset growing American power, Canada worked to build strong multilateral institutions. At the same time, it had little desire to let world organizations interfere in its relations with the United States, which it believed it could conduct better alone.

Canada in the Cold War Era

Disappointments were rife in these years, as the postwar era rapidly gave way to the Cold War. At the Paris Peace Conference of 1946, Canada had hoped to play a role in the European settlement commensurate with its contribution to the war effort. The country went virtually unnoticed.

As relations between the United States and the Soviet Union soured, Canadian foreign-affairs officials feared that the often bellicose attitude of the United States would only make matters worse. In the view of external-affairs official John Holmes, the American position was to refuse to negotiate with the Soviet "devil," while Canadians wanted only to make him behave.[8]

Events soon shook Canadians' faith in the West's capacity to reach some kind of reasonable entente with the Soviet Union. In late 1945 Igor Gouzenko, a cipher clerk at the Soviet embassy in Ottawa, defected. He revealed the existence of a Soviet espionage network in Canada that reached into several government agencies. Dana Wilgress, who headed the Canadian mission in Moscow from 1944 to 1947, showed the evolution of Canadian thinking when he denounced the "irresponsible opportunism" of Soviet policies.

The intensification of the Cold War led Canada into ever-closer relations with the United States. Britain's own decline left Canada little choice. "London's impotence," historian Jack

Granatstein argues, compelled Canadian governments to seek "shelter within Uncle Sam's all-encompassing embrace."[9]

Fears of the Soviet Union also led to increased police surveillance of Canadians deemed sympathetic to communism or to left-wing causes in general. For example, the RCMP shadowed Tommy Douglas, the Saskatchewan politician who later became leader of the federal New Democratic party, for thirty years. Some people were censored for their ideological beliefs or unjustly dismissed from their jobs because they were labelled subversives.

The North Atlantic Treaty Organization

As people lost hope that the United Nations could assure world peace through collective security, the Canadian government pushed for an Atlantic alliance for mutual self-defence. The Americans and the British showed interest in the proposal. By December 1948, work began on a draft treaty to form the North Atlantic Treaty Organization (NATO). The United States envisaged a purely military pact, but Canada sought cooperation in other sectors that might eventually unite the Atlantic nations into a closely knit community. For that reason, Canada fought for the inclusion in the draft treaty of an article indicating general economic and social aims.

Canada's interest was clear. Links with western Europe would strengthen Canada in its relationship with the militarily dominant Americans. The so-called "Canadian article" did get into the treaty, in spite of the adamant opposition of the Americans to this product of "typical Canadian moralizing." In March 1949, the House of Commons approved the treaty, and on April 4, in an atmosphere of euphoric optimism, NATO came into existence. But the Canadians' hard-won victory soured quickly, for the "Canadian article" was never put into practice. Rising East–West tensions, especially the outbreak of war in Korea in 1950, turned NATO into an almost exclusively military alliance, soon placed under the American nuclear umbrella. Even so, as historian David J. Bercuson has shown, Canada did indeed make a significant difference to NATO in the alliance's early years "in both the quantity and the quality of its military contribution."[10] Then, as defence spending fell and Canada's priorities became continental, its influence declined.

New Interest in the North

With the development of the Cold War in the late 1940s, the Canadian North again became an area of vital strategic interest to both Canada and the United States. Acting together, the two countries worked to provide a warning system in the event of a Soviet nuclear attack on Canadian and American cities. A chain of more than 40 Distant Early Warning (DEW) Line stations was built in the 1950s across the Arctic, from Alaska to Baffin Island. The DEW Line allowed for four to six hours' warning of a manned Soviet bomber attack across the North Pole. Begun in 1954 and completed in 1957, the system remained in full operation for nearly a decade, until intercontinental ballistic missiles largely replaced the bomber threat. With the warning time now calculated in minutes, the DEW Line lost much of its effectiveness. In 1957, Canada and the United States signed the North American Air Defence Agreement (NORAD), which formally coordinated the two countries' air forces.

The DEW Line and other American proposals revived fears about Canada's sovereignty in the Arctic. Recognizing that one of the surest grounds for Canada's claim would be "effective occupation," the federal government in 1953 arranged for several Inuit families from northern Quebec and Baffin Island to relocate nearly 2000 km away, on Cornwallis and Ellesmere islands in the high Arctic. The migrants lost contact with their communities and, the government's promises aside, found themselves in a much more inhospitable environment than the one they had left behind.

The Commonwealth

In keeping with its desire to balance closer links to the United States with an increased international participation, Canada looked with hope to the evolving British Commonwealth of Nations. Mackenzie King, however, strongly opposed the idea of a uniform Commonwealth foreign policy put forth by certain British politicians; to him, such a plan recalled the days of the empire centralizers. Moreover, the Commonwealth was changing, with the addition of new members such as India, Pakistan, and Sri Lanka (then Ceylon). Canada helped move the Commonwealth in directions that made it an acceptable organization for these new states. It also supported and contributed to the Colombo Plan, which was set up at a meeting of Commonwealth foreign ministers in 1950 to promote economic development in Commonwealth countries in Asia.

Peacekeeping

Canada's early attempts at peacekeeping produced mixed results. In 1950, when communist North Korea invaded South Korea and the United Nations Security Council (which the Soviet Union was boycotting) denounced this act of aggression, Canada contributed a brigade to fight alongside mostly American troops in the name of collective security. Five hundred Canadians lost their lives in the fighting. As the war moved toward a stalemate, Lester B. Pearson, then Canada's secretary of state for external affairs, helped to restrain the "overzealous" Americans from actions that risked bringing China and the Soviet Union into the war. At the same time, as historian John Price has shown, Pearson proved himself to be a "cold warrior par excellence"[11] in his pragmatic support for the pro-American regime in South Korea. Then, in 1954, Canada agreed, with considerable apprehension, to join Poland and India in a three-country International Control Commission to supervise the peace in Indochina where France, the occupying colonial power, had just been defeated by Vietnamese communists.

Finally, in 1956, came what many considered to be Canada's greatest contribution internationally. In October, despite strong American opposition, Israel, together with Britain and France, invaded Egypt, in response to Egypt's nationalization of the Suez Canal. Wary of the dangerous split developing in the western alliance, Pearson proposed the creation of a multinational United Nations emergency peacekeeping force in the region. He then lobbied tirelessly to have the plan accepted by the General Assembly. For his efforts, he won the Nobel Peace Prize in 1957. According to biographer John English, Pearson's initiative "strengthened the United Nations, moderated the tensions between Washington and London, and helped to maintain both the Commonwealth and NATO."[12]

Political Change

When Canadians went to the polls in 1957 to select a government, another Liberal victory seemed likely. Most political observers were surprised when the Progressive Conservatives, under their new leader, John Diefenbaker, won a narrow victory. Stunned Liberals, as cabinet minister J.W. Pickersgill later put it, wondered why they had to suffer a Tory government once in every generation. The CCF, which had restated its original aims in less revolutionary fashion in its Winnipeg Declaration of Principles in 1956, felt bitterly disappointed over its failure to arrest its decline in popularity.

Although the Liberals boasted during the election campaign that voters would not "shoot Santa Claus," not all Canadians were prosperous in 1957. Residents of the Prairies and the Maritimes complained of their regions' underdevelopment. Many senior citizens endorsed Conservative assertions that unindexed old-age pensions were scandalously insufficient. Other voters agreed with Diefenbaker's denunciations in 1956 of the "dictatorial" tactics employed by

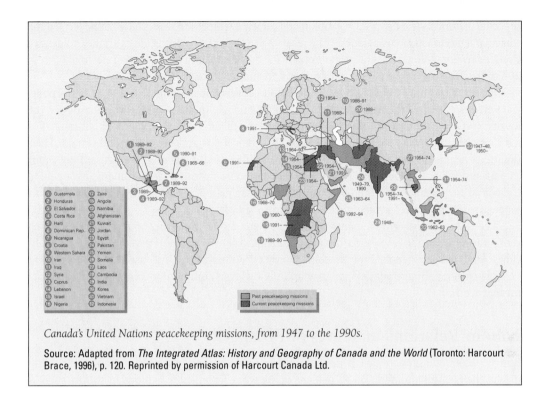

Canada's United Nations peacekeeping missions, from 1947 to the 1990s.

Source: Adapted from *The Integrated Atlas: History and Geography of Canada and the World* (Toronto: Harcourt Brace, 1996), p. 120. Reprinted by permission of Harcourt Canada Ltd.

the Liberals during the pipeline debate in 1956. The government wanted to make an important loan to Trans-Canada Pipe Lines, a private company formed by American and Canadian business interests, to assist in building the western section of a pipeline to carry Alberta gas to central Canadian markets. In a hurry because of a timetable he wanted to respect, Minister of Trade and Commerce C.D. Howe pushed the bill through the House of Commons, unamended, by imposing closure and cutting off debate at each stage. But most of all, many Canadians simply wanted a change from what appeared increasingly to be cold, insensitive, uncreative leadership by an aging Liberal gerontocracy.

The "Diefenbaker Party"

John Diefenbaker surely played a significant role in the success of what became known as the "Diefenbaker party." He was a child of the Prairies, a small-town lawyer, noted for his progressive positions on issues. As the party's new leader, he sought to change voters' traditionally negative image of the Tories. He wrested control of the party from the conservative Toronto business elite and gave it to "outsiders," many of whom came from western Canada. His oratorical talents outshone by far anything the Liberals could muster. At Massey Hall in April 1957, the "modern-day Jeremiah" proclaimed the message to his "fellow Canadians": "This party ... has an appointment today with destiny, to plan and to build for a greater Canada ... one Canada, with equality of opportunity for every citizen and equality for every province."

The new government barely had time to adopt a few popular measures designed to assist the unemployed, Prairie farmers, and Maritimers before Diefenbaker, anxious to form a majority government, called a new election in March 1958. The prime minister then presented his "vision of opportunity" for Canada, a vision based on the development of resources and of the North. Liberal newspapers like the *Toronto Star* mocked Diefenbaker's admittedly vague program as "humbug and flapdoodle served up with an evangelistic flourish." New Liberal leader Lester B. Pearson, whose soporific oratorical style betrayed his diplomatic career, attempted to brush off what he termed the "oracular fervour and circus parades." The result was a Diefenbaker landslide, with the Progressive Conservatives winning what was proportionally the greatest majority in Canadian electoral history: 208 of the 265 seats in the House of Commons, including 50 seats from Quebec.

From the start, the Conservatives had difficulty governing. So long had they sat in the political wilderness that all the new ministers lacked experience. In many cases, they questioned the loyalty of civil servants accustomed to a close working relationship with Liberal politicians. For most Quebec Tory MPs, the triumph of 1958 was their first—and last—electoral victory. Their unilingual Baptist leader from Saskatchewan knew little about Quebec and entrusted no senior cabinet portfolios to Quebeckers. Diefenbaker's vision of northern development, of "opening Canada to its polar reaches," did not capture the imagination of southern Canadians. Liberals mocked what they called a program of "roads from igloo to igloo."

The Conservative government's major problem arose from the country's deteriorating economic situation. It responded to rising unemployment with winter works programs, subsidies, and welfare benefits for seasonal workers. As expenses increased and government receipts declined, budgetary deficits grew and the business community complained of financial mismanagement.

Labour Relations in Times of Prosperity

Postwar economic growth gave a powerful boost to the unions. In 1950, union membership passed the one million mark, or 30 percent of the work force. "Elite" unions in sectors such as heavy manufacturing enjoyed strong bargaining power and succeeded in negotiating high wages. They had frequent recourse to strikes, particularly in the late 1940s. In 1946, for example, one worker in six went on strike, resulting in a total loss of 4.5 million workdays. These strikes aimed at forcing employers to recognize union rights, improve working conditions, and increase salaries. In retaliation, companies frequently hired strikebreakers, and violent confrontations sometimes ensued. Provincial governments supported employers directly through anti-union legislation and the use of the police and the courts.

A campaign poster. John Diefenbaker with his hero, Sir John A. Macdonald.

Source: Diefenbaker Centre poster collection, Diefenbaker Centre, University of Saskatchewan.

Industrial Unrest

Although most workers signed contracts without going on strike and although sickness resulted in far more loss of work time than did strike activity, certain sensational confrontations earned a place in the annals of Canadian working-class history. In one dramatic encounter in 1946, Steel Company of Canada (Stelco) management used airplanes and boats to avoid picket lines and to transport food and supplies to strikebreakers inside its plant at Hamilton, Ontario. In the same year, textile workers, many of them women, struck in Valleyfield, Quebec. Led by Madeleine Parent and Kent Rowley, the strikers obtained recognition for their union only after bloody skirmishes with police. Parent was then convicted of seditious conspiracy and had to wait until 1954 before being acquitted after a new trial.

In 1947, Nova Scotia fishers went on strike against National Sea Products, the monopoly conglomerate, in an attempt to gain union recognition. The company waged a fierce anti-labour campaign and, with assistance from the courts and the provincial government, broke the strike. A year later, the Prince Edward Island government seized a Canada Packers plant during a strike, hired non-union labour, and reopened the plant. It then adopted legislation prohibiting labour affiliation with any union organization outside the province. In 1949, 5000 Quebec asbestos workers struck for five months to improve wages and working conditions. The Duplessis government defended the companies, decertified the union, and sent in special police squads. Some members of the clergy, including Archbishop Joseph Charbonneau of Montreal, defied the government and sided openly with the strikers, one of whose supporters was a young Montreal lawyer, Pierre Elliott Trudeau. Though the settlement gave workers no significant material gains, the strike itself took on great symbolic value: Quebec sociologist Jean-Charles Falardeau even viewed it as a "quasi-revolution."[13]

Conflict continued into the 1950s, a period of consolidation for labour, now that union recognition was more generally assured. Major strikes occurred among loggers, fishers, government employees, and longshoremen in British Columbia, building-trades workers in Halifax and Vancouver, gold miners in Ontario and Quebec, and automobile workers and employees of the International Nickel Company (Inco) in Ontario. In August 1950, 130 000 employees of Canada's two major railways left their jobs, but the government, declaring that "the country cannot afford a railway strike," ordered the workers back. Textile workers at Louiseville, Quebec went out for ten months in 1952, while copper workers at Murdochville, Quebec struck for seven months in 1957 in a violent but vain confrontation. In 1959, Newfoundland loggers, members of the International Woodworkers of America (IWA), went on strike. They wanted better wages, a shorter work day, and camp amenities. Violence broke out when the company recruited fishers to replace strikers. In one skirmish, a policeman suffered fatal injuries. In an effort to break the IWA, Premier Joseph Smallwood set up a union and had the legislature outlaw the IWA in the province. The federal government refused to send the RCMP reinforcements that Smallwood demanded, but the strike nonetheless failed.

Workers Versus Workers

Workers not only fought management and governments, they also feuded with one another for political and personal reasons. On the left, communists and democratic socialists battled each other in fratricidal fury. Both clashed with conservative unionists, who viewed all political links as dangerous for the labour movement.

Anti-communists in the Canadian Congress of Labour (CCL) insisted that, to fight the bosses, "we must get rid of the communists." The CCL thus manoeuvred to oust certain affiliate unions whose executives it charged with being "complete vassals of uncle Joe Stalin." The communist-led Canadian Seamen's Union (CSU) was crushed when the Canadian and American governments combined with the shippers and Trades and Labor Congress (TLC) officers to replace the CSU with the rival Seafarers' International Union (SIU). (After a judicial inquiry later found the SIU guilty of racketeering and a host of other improper practices, Ottawa placed the union under a government trusteeship. Its director, Hal Banks, who had boasted of his ambition to control "everything that floats," forfeited bail and fled to the United States.) Some Canadian unionists thought that the battle against communists merely permitted American unions to reinforce their hold in Canada.

According to historian Irving Abella, the communist purge did little to strengthen the union movement and, in hindsight, was probably "neither necessary nor wise."[14]

Greater labour unity came in 1956, when the TLC and the CCL formed the Canadian Labour Congress (CLC). This union followed the merger in 1955 of the American labour congresses, the AFL and the CIO. The costly raids by TLC and CCL unions on each other, with no total gain in membership, then ended. Claude Jodoin, a well-known Quebec labour leader and president of the TLC, became president of the new million-member CLC. Many of the CLC unions were affiliated with the American AFL-CIO, and they remained subject to American influence. Most Canadian workers, who were employed by American branch companies, found nothing unusual in belonging to American-dominated unions. This, however, was one of the reasons that the Quebec-based CTCC refused to join the CLC.

Although unions made major gains in the postwar period, much work remained. Collective agreements generally left managers with complete authority over the work process on the shop floor. Union organizers had yet to reach vast numbers of workers, especially in the service sector. An attempt to unionize the 12 000 mainly female employees of Eaton's, Canada's largest department store and third-largest employer, failed spectacularly. The increasing bureaucratization of the union movement, fostered by what labour historian Peter McInnis has termed the "excessively legalistic and rigid framework" that came to characterize industrial relations, tended to exclude the rank and file from decisions.[15] Labour legislation in several provinces was unsympathetic to unions. Automation made job security an increasingly serious issue. Worker safety also caused concern: accidents on the job caused nearly five million injuries and more than 12 500 deaths between 1945 and 1959. When fire killed five Italian labourers laying a water main in the Hogg's Hollow district of Toronto, the coroner denounced management's "callous attitude" toward worker safety and noted that "almost all the safety regulations … were violated at one time or another, and many of the regulations were violated continuously."

The Status of Women

After World War II, most Canadians, including a majority of women, thought women—especially married women—should leave the paid work force. Churches stressed family life as a means of countering juvenile delinquency, illegitimate births, and other social ills.

Women who continued in paid employment outside the home still had to perform all the domestic and family chores. One woman journalist explained: "A man whittles himself down to less of a man by consistently performing women's work." Cultural stereotypes reinforced the "traditional" role of women: school textbooks depicted men in interesting careers while portraying women as staying at home, cooking meals, and scolding children. Women's magazines such as *Chatelaine* and the *Canadian Home Journal* contained many articles on sewing, homemaking, gardening, and fashion, but very few on such areas of male hegemony as politics or business. Women were paternalistically excluded from sports judged "unsuitable" for females. Public recreation programs funded hockey and softball far more generously than "activities for women" such as arts and crafts.

Women in the Work Force

Slowly, female participation in the work force increased. In 1951, one paid worker in four was a woman, usually unmarried. During the 1950s the proportion of married women workers also increased, as mothers rejoined the work force after their youngest children enrolled in school.

Most worked as secretaries, nurses, sales personnel, and clerks. As late as 1960, only a handful of women were professionals; they accounted for just 7 percent of doctors, 3 percent of lawyers, and a mere 1 percent of engineers.

For female workers, inequality abounded. Men generally received higher wages than women for performing the same tasks. This so-called "wage differential" was justified by men's role as family breadwinners. Universities paid female professors less than male professors of the same rank and experience. Nor did women have equal opportunity for promotions, even in female-dominated sectors such as teaching. Across Canada, men had a far greater chance of becoming school principals. Minimum wage rates, fixed by governments, were usually lower for women than for men. Wage parity (equal pay for performing the same task) was only beginning to be an issue when Ontario's Female Employees Fair Remuneration Act was passed in 1951. Though the legislation had obvious political value, historian Shirley Tillotson's research shows that it had little tangible effect; the opposition CCF Status of Women Committee called it "a toothless ghost of a real equal pay bill."[16]

Churches such as the United Church of Canada, which accepted women as ministers, nevertheless placed numerous obstacles in the paths of those seeking ordination. United Church moderator James Mutchmor gave Lois Wilson, a minister's wife, reasons for objecting to her ordination: Who would "wear the pants" in the family? Who would have priority in the use of the car? Wilson succeeded in gaining ordination because prominent men supported her. She later became the United Church's first woman moderator.

Only a few women held positions of influence in business or politics in the 1950s. Between 1930 and 1960, the federal government named only seven women senators, while more than 250 men received the coveted lifetime appointment. Few women ran in elections. Those who did generally ran as their party's sacrificial lambs in impossible races. Only in 1957 did a prime minister, John Diefenbaker, appoint a woman to a federal cabinet post—Ellen Fairclough, from Hamilton, Ontario. Fully aware of widespread discriminatory behaviour against women, Fairclough was determined not to let herself be co-opted as an "honorary man." Many observers saw this nomination as only a modest beginning. Charlotte Whitton, Ottawa's feisty mayor, predicted that women were growing so impatient with "the man-made messes of a man-made world" that they would soon insist on a much larger voice in public affairs.

WHERE HISTORIANS DISAGREE

Women and Unions in Postwar Canada

By 1964, 30 percent of hired workers were women, employed mainly in non-unionized sectors of activity, such as clerical and domestic work. Of the barely 16 percent of union members who were women, most worked in industry. What did unionized women seek to obtain from their unions? Did they see themselves simply as workers who, like the men, wanted to improve wages and working conditions? Or did they see themselves primarily as women with objectives that were different from, and at times contradictory to, those of men? And how did men react to the entry of women into "their" workplace?

Labour historians, preoccupied with labour's battles against employers, did not at first ask these questions, particularly as they pertain to the postwar years. Bryan Palmer describes the rise of the communist-led United Electrical, Radio and Machine Workers' Union (UE), whose expansion was fostered by enormous consumer demand for electrical products. The union waged a number of bitter strikes in 1946. Though Palmer notes that a significant part of the UE's membership was female (25 percent by 1954), he does not view their struggle as other than a workers' struggle against the bosses.[1] Craig Heron states that industrial unions of these years had difficulty eliminating the segregation of women into low-wage job ghettos, and then comments, revealingly, that "even if the male unionists' pride had allowed more equity, most men still assumed that women should be at home, supported by a male wage."[2]

In her study of working women in Peterborough, Ontario, Joan Sangster shows how unions and labour disputes have been arenas of both gender conflict and class solidarity.[3] Looking at the UE, she notes that union leadership endorsed gender equality, partly in order to gain women workers' support for the UE's struggle against a rival union. The UE also tried to focus on grievances that could unite men and women, such as more equal pay rates, because men feared the substitution of female for male labour. On other issues, notably the contentious question of merging male and female seniority lists, the union equivocated. Sangster notes also how difficult it was for women to become involved in union activities. While the union itself gave pre-eminence to class rather than to gender, separate organizations for women within unions eventually provided an innovative means for women to demand better working conditions and wages.

Julie Guard has also studied the experience of women within the UE. Like Sangster, she shows that the union was interested primarily in the class struggle, not in women's rights. It made slow progress in endorsing equal pay for women, in spite of women's attempts to prove that low pay for women put a brake on male wages. She too notes that few women participated in union leadership, a fact that men attributed to personal choice rather than to the "inherent gender bias of union structure and culture."[4]

Joy Parr has examined the effect of gender on strike action against a textile company in Paris, Ontario, in 1949. About one-half of the workers were women and, although women were less inclined to join the union than were men, female militancy on the picket line was considerable. Yet, whereas the union itself whipped up male strikers' militancy, female militancy was "forged and sustained in family and neighbourhood relationships" rather than through union organization.[5]

In her study of the United Auto Workers in Canada, Pam Sugiman argues that the traditional view of the UAW as a progressive union that gave vocal support to women's rights in society is only partly true; the UAW also showed persistent gender bias and allowed blatant inequalities to persist in the working environment.[6] Male union officials were reluctant to view the special concerns of female dues-paying members as legitimate union issues. In the immediate postwar years, women did not generally challenge gender ideologies, separate seniority lists, and large pay differentials. Even in the 1950s, women still did not "openly contest their subordination as a sex" although they did develop "a stronger self-identification as wage earners and as unionists."[7] Thanks to improving economic conditions, women became bolder and made use of grievance procedures to protest inadequate wages and to try to improve working conditions.

Gillian Creese has studied the white-collar union at BC Hydro. Although women constituted nearly one-half of the union's membership in the 1950s, union leadership was increasingly dominated by men and contract negotiations represented male concerns and assumptions. Creese says that the union did confront discrimination on an individual level, but that "systematic differentiation that resulted in better jobs and career prospects and higher pay for men was simply not recognized as a form of discrimination."[8] It was only in the late 1970s that a Women's Committee was formed and that many women (but not all) began to challenge masculine privilege and emphasized so-called "women's issues" such as sexual harassment, pay equity, and day care.

Were female unionists as militant as male unionists? Or did they follow the leadership of their husbands at home and their male co-workers? Robert Ventresca has examined the behaviour of women workers, many of them Italian immigrants, in two industrial conflicts in Welland, Ontario. During the lengthy strike at the Lanark auto parts plant in 1964, some women did cross the picket lines; the majority did not. Ventresca contends that most Italian workers demonstrated only weak support for unionization. He concludes that the union focused on "class struggle," not gender (p. 141). Further research will be necessary to understand the "structural and cultural constraints which have historically conditioned labour militancy."[9]

Ester Reiter also sees industrial unions as having functioned traditionally as protectors of male privilege. Yet during the strike against Lanark, the union gave "strong support" to women workers even though it knew that its chances of winning were slight.[10] Reiter argues that working men's class interests led them in this case to support women's struggles. Both the UE and the UAW were engaged in a bitter struggle against a rival union that had been ousted from the Lanark plant by the UE. They supported the Lanark workers, mostly women, because of union interests, not because, or in spite of the fact that, most of the workers were women. As for the women themselves, Reiter concludes: "Their energies in this strike were directed against their unfair treatment as workers, rather than the particular injustices they suffered as women workers."[11]

Interest in the situation of women within postwar unions is relatively recent. Many other case studies will have to be carried out on different aspects of the question before it will be possible to reach general conclusions.

1   Bryan Palmer, *Working Class Experience: Rethinking the History of Canadian Labour, 1800–1991*, 2nd ed. (Toronto: McClelland & Stewart, 1992), p. 287.

2   Craig Heron, *The Canadian Labour Movement: A Short History*, 2nd ed. (Toronto: James Lorimer, 1996), p. 78.

3   Joan Sangster, *Earning Respect: The Lives of Working Women in Small-Town Ontario, 1920–1960* (Toronto: University of Toronto Press, 1995), p. 167.

4   Julie Guard, "Fair Play or Fair Pay? Gender Relations, Class Consciousness, and Union Solidarity in the Canadian UE," *Labour/Le Travail* 37 (1996): 176.

5   Joy Parr, *The Gender of Breadwinners: Women, Men, and Change in Two Industrial Towns, 1880–1950* (Toronto: University of Toronto Press, 1990), p. 108.

6   Pam Sugiman, *Labour's Dilemma: The Gender Politics of Auto Workers in Canada, 1937–1979* (Toronto: University of Toronto Press, 1994), pp. 4–5.

7   Ibid., p. 99.

8   Gillian Creese, *Contracting Masculinity: Gender, Class, and Race in a White-Collar Union, 1944–1994* (Toronto: Oxford University Press, 1999), p. 141.

9   Robert Ventresca, "'Cowering Women, Combative Men?' Femininity, Masculinity and Ethnicity on Strike in Two Southern Ontario Towns, 1964–1966," *Labour/Le Travail* 39 (1997): 142.

10   Ester Reiter, "First-Class Workers Don't Want Second-Class Wages: The Lanark Strike in Dunnville," in Joy Parr, ed., *A Diversity of Women: Ontario, 1945–1980* (Toronto: University of Toronto Press, 1995), p. 170.

11   Ibid., p. 194.

The Baby Boom

With good times, a higher proportion of young adults married. They also married earlier—age 22 for women, a little older for men. As Mary Louise Adams explains, "Marriage was a legitimate avenue of sexual expression for those men and women who felt caught between the incitement to sex in the culture at large and the proscriptions against their own engagement in it. Early marriage was one way to bring changes in sexual behaviour into line with the established moral order."[17]

As Canadian women began, on an impressive scale, to have children, a veritable "baby boom" set in. By 1947, the birth rate had increased to nearly 29 per thousand, and the average family had three or four children. This relatively large contingent of youth, which some demographers have described as the "pig in the python," has had enormous repercussions on Canadian society. The precise nature of the impact would alter with time, as the baby boomers went through childhood, adolescence, young adulthood, and middle age, and then began to enter retirement. The baby boom led to a rapid increase in Canada's population. During the 1950s, births exceeded deaths by three million. Including immigration, the annual growth rate exceeded 3 percent, equivalent to that experienced by many developing countries today.

A wonderful shot of an Edmonton couple by a 1940s car with a handwritten sign on the car, "Just Married Watch Edmonton Grow!" A perfect photo to make the point about the post–World War II Baby Boom—or is it? Buyer beware! This "perfect photo" apparently predates the post–World War II baby boom: if you look closely at the licence plate, you can see that the expiry date reads March 31, 1942.

Source: City of Edmonton Archives/EA-160-898.

Higher Education

Few Canadians attended colleges or universities in the 1950s. In 1951, Canada's institutions of higher learning had only 60 000 students, barely 4 percent of the eligible age group. Only about one university student in four was a woman. Most female students enrolled in programs in education or the liberal arts; few entered the sciences or the professional schools. In Quebec, until 1960, the provincial government denied classical colleges for women the state funds that were made available to all-male colleges. Religious authorities encouraged Quebec women to attend "family institutes," euphemistically nicknamed "schools of happiness," where they would learn to take up the challenges of life in the home. In Toronto, the elite University of Toronto Schools (whose graduates almost all went on to university) admitted no women, even though it was largely state-supported.

In 1951, the Royal Commission on National Development in the Arts, Letters and Sciences, chaired by Vincent Massey, declared that Canadian universities faced "a financial crisis so great as to threaten their future usefulness." It recommended direct federal financial support. Then, in 1956, while the first cohorts of the baby boom generation were still in elementary school, the National Council of Canadian Universities warned that enrolments would soon dramatically increase. The Soviet launching of *Sputnik*, the first space satellite, in 1957, proved an unforeseen boon to Canadian universities. The fear of Soviet scientific superiority convinced many Canadians that governments should invest much more in higher education. Provincial authorities loosened the purse strings and the federal government instituted a system of grants. Facilities for higher education expanded, as several new universities came into being in the late 1950s.

Culture: Canadian Versus American

In the postwar era, Canadian nationalists increasingly felt the dangers of dependence upon American culture. Reduced funding for the Canadian Broadcasting Corporation (CBC) threatened to undermine public broadcasting. Private broadcasters, who wished to offer more American-produced commercial programming, resented the CBC's regulatory role. The federal government also reduced the National Film Board's budget after the war, and private filmmakers sought to obtain the Board's work. Institutions such as the Public Archives of Canada and the National Museum of Canada suffered from lack of coordination, while the country still had no national library. After three-quarters of a century, the National Gallery of Canada still remained in borrowed space.

Cultural associations that enjoyed strong cabinet support convinced the government to establish the Massey Commission. As historian Paul Litt has shown, these associations influenced the commission to obtain the recommendations they wanted.[18] The commissioners agreed that the CBC should retain its supervisory powers over broadcasting. In 1959, however, the Conservative government created instead an independent regulatory body for broadcasting, the Board of Broadcast Governors.

The Massey Commission in 1951 had recommended the establishment of a national arts-funding body, one free of partisan and bureaucratic control. Finally, six years later, the Liberals founded the Canada Council. It gave financial assistance to a multitude of arts organizations, among them ballet companies, theatre troupes (including the Stratford

Zoologist William Rowan lecturing at the University of Alberta, Edmonton, before 1957. Beginning in the 1960s, class sizes would expand to the bursting point with the arrival of the baby boomers at universities.

Source: University of Alberta Archives/Acc. 82-29-37.

Shakespearean Festival), and orchestras. The council also gave grants to writers and scholarships to graduate students. Critics denounced what they viewed as extravagant expenditures, financed by ordinary folk to support longhair, highbrow misfits and freeloaders.

Popular Culture

Prosperity enabled many Canadians to spend lavishly on entertainment. They purchased new longplaying records, often of poor quality and relatively costly. In the late 1940s, they flocked to the movie theatres that had proliferated. The real revolution in the entertainment industry, however, came in the early 1950s with television. Canadians living close to the American border rushed to buy television sets with the standard ten-inch black-and-white screen, at first a status symbol because of the relatively high cost. By 1952, Canada's own television broadcasting began in Toronto and Montreal. It quickly expanded to other cities. Critics warned that television might destroy conversation and make thinking obsolete. The CBC and the French-language Radio Canada countered by airing many news programs, including René Lévesque's current affairs program, "Point de mire." Canadian public broadcasting also presented numerous cultural programs, which attracted small, but influential, audiences.

The advent of television increased popular interest in sport. Armchair spectators marvelled at the exploits of the Edmonton Eskimos' football dynasty. Watching "La Soirée du hockey," or "Hockey Night in Canada," became a popular pastime on Saturday night. Fans avidly discussed the feats of Syl Apps, Maurice "Rocket" Richard, and Gordie Howe, and celebrated the Stanley Cup triumphs of the Toronto Maple Leafs in the late 1940s and of the Montreal Canadiens in the late 1950s. From 1942 to 1967, the National Hockey League (NHL) remained a stable six-team league. The NHL made numerous changes to make television viewing easier. It had ice surfaces painted white and lighting improved, and it dressed on-ice officials in striped jerseys. Canadian performance in international sport brought much less satisfaction, as Canadian teams suffered ignominious defeats in world and Olympic hockey, and sometimes attracted attention for boorish behaviour.

English-speaking Canadians enjoyed newspaper supplements such as the *Star Weekly* and *Weekend*, while French Canadians read a variety of tabloid newspapers. By the end of the 1950s, however, American mass-circulation magazines, among them *Time* and *Reader's Digest* and its French edition, *Sélection du Reader's Digest*, accounted for 75 percent of the Canadian general-interest magazine market.

Most movies were American-made, though some came from Britain or, in the case of the Quebec market, France. The Canadian National Exhibition in Toronto always imported American talent, such as Danny Kaye or Jimmy Durante, as the major attractions for its grand-stand shows. The Calgary Stampede also invited American celebrities such as Bing Crosby, Walt Disney, and Bob Hope to serve as parade marshals.

Although the CBC presented Canadian variety shows such as *Showtime*, which featured dance, song, music, and comedy, it also imported popular American variety shows to boost its ratings and increase its commercial revenues. On Sunday evenings, millions of Canadians loyally watched the most famous and longest-lasting of these, *The Ed Sullivan Show*. Sullivan introduced Elvis Presley and his hip gyrations to Canadians in September 1956. He also boosted the fortunes of Canadian comedians Johnny Wayne and Frank Shuster. Both CBC and private television imported popular American comedies such as *I Love Lucy* and *The Jackie Gleason Show*, and presented contemporary American singers such as Perry Como and Dinah Shore. Baby boom children watched Roy Rogers, Lassie, Walt Disney programs, and the popular American puppet show, *The Howdy Doody Show*. (The author of these lines was once saved in an after-school fight when he reminded his bulky aggressor, seated on top of him, that it was 5:30—"Howdy Doody Time.")

French-language television had more local content. While it beamed a French-speaking *Hopalong Cassidy* and many other programs dubbed in French into Quebec living rooms and kitchens, it also carried original productions, such as the Wednesday-night series adapted from novelist Roger Lemelin's *La famille Plouffe*. Children watched a captivating Quebec-made puppet show called *Pépino*. The CBC's very successful variety show, *Music Hall*, produced in Montreal, featured French stars such as Edith Piaf, Maurice Chevalier, and Charles Aznavour. By 1957, television production in Montreal, historian Susan Mann writes, was "third in the world to New York and Hollywood and second to none in French."[19]

English-Canadian Literature

Canadian literature in both languages came into its own in the post–World War II era. In Montreal, Hugh MacLennan published his celebrated novel *Two Solitudes*, with its theme that Canada's two major linguistic communities needed to demonstrate more mutual tolerance. In Vancouver, Earl Birney, a professor of English at the University of British Columbia and part of a new generation of Canadian poets, published his collection of poems, *Now Is Time*. In *The Mountain and the Valley*, Ernest Buckler examined the dilemma faced by a brilliant and ambitious Nova Scotia boy who found his creativity stifled by his deep attachment to rural life. W.O. Mitchell, in *Who Has Seen the Wind*, interpreted the struggles of a small-town Saskatchewan boy at the time of the depression. Throughout the 1950s, Mitchell produced his highly successful "Jake and the Kid" stories for magazine and radio.

The Schiefners, a farm family living outside Milestone, Saskatchewan, on a Saturday evening in 1956. "Hockey Night in Canada: Toronto Versus Detroit," would be broadcast at 9 p.m.

Source: Library and Archives Canada/Credit: Richard Harrington/National Film Board of Canada fonds/ Accession 1971-271 NPC/ PA-111390.

Mordecai Richler's *The Apprenticeship of Duddy Kravitz*, a portrait of a young Montreal Jewish entrepreneur, established the Montreal author as a successful novelist. Adele Wiseman's first novel, *The Sacrifice*, was strongly influenced by the experiences of her Russian-Jewish parents. In 1951, Morley Callaghan's highly acclaimed *The Loved and the Lost*, set in Montreal, appeared. Robertson Davies gained early recognition as an essayist and brilliant novelist. Poet Dorothy Livesay won governor general's awards for *Day and Night*, in 1944, and *Poems for Peace*, in 1947, while the versatile and flamboyant Irving Layton produced numerous volumes of love poems and prose.

French-Canadian Literature

At the same time, an "aesthetic thaw" came slowly to Quebec. In *Refus global*, a manifesto written in 1948, Paul-Émile Borduas and other signatories condemned Quebec's asphyxiating orthodoxy. The artist's cry for the right to total freedom of expression cost him his teaching job at the École du Meuble in Montreal. He left first for New York, then later settled in Paris. Novelists cast aside traditional themes of religion and rurality. Some, such as Roger Lemelin in *Au pied de la pente douce*, used urban working-class settings. Others, such as Anne Hébert in *Le Torrent* and André Langevin in *Poussière sur la ville*, forcefully portrayed personal dramas. Yves Thériault won international fame with *Agaguk*, a novel about the Inuit. Professional theatre troupes proliferated, with some of their repertories supplied by Quebec playwrights. The play *Tit-Coq*, by Gratien Gélinas, encountered spectacular success. The film that followed attracted 300 000 spectators. Quebec culture seemed to have attained new vibrancy, despite the province's tiny market and few public libraries and bookstores.

Canadians generally continued to cherish conservative values. Books were often censored, particularly when they described sex scenes too explicitly. Censorship in all provinces regulated the movies Canadians saw. The British Columbia Moving Pictures Act, for example, outlawed films "considered injurious to morals or against public welfare, or which may offer evil suggestions to the minds of children." Alberta's censors watched carefully for "any materialistic, undemocratic, un-Christian propaganda disguised as entertainment." Sometimes the cuts produced films probably more objectionable than the original version. One Quebec film featured a scene in which a married man obtained a divorce so that he could pursue a love affair with his girlfriend. The censors in this still very Catholic province cut out the divorce scene—and the couple thus appeared to go on living happily ever after in unwedded bliss!

Religion

Religion "stands out as one of the great gulfs" separating the 1950s from today, writes historian Doug Owram.[20] In that period, the majority of Canadians still attended church or the synagogue regularly. Indeed, a higher proportion of Canadian Protestants belonged to churches and enrolled their children in Sunday schools than had done so in the 1930s. Religion was present in most schools across the country, even in so-called public schools. Pious Quebeckers knelt around the radio after supper for the "Family Rosary" and read the *Annales de Sainte-Anne* or other religious material. Nevertheless, the influence of religion often appeared superficial. Possibly, religious practice was linked more to socialization than to faith. The *United Church Observer* frequently bemoaned the limited commitment of many adherents. Presumably churchgoing Quebeckers bought a million copies each weekend of sex-and-crime tabloids such as *Allo Police*, which flourished in spite of—and possibly because of—the opposition of the Roman Catholic Church. Moreover, historian Michael Gauvreau's research has shown that, under the influence of the more liberal attitudes of women in Catholic Action movements and against the teachings of the church's hierarchy, Quebec women were coming to see marriage as linked to personal fulfillment rather than uniquely directed toward procreation.[21]

The quiet Sundays of English-speaking Canada also came under attack. It was said that in Toronto one could harmlessly fire a cannonball down Yonge Street on a Sunday, and the local press editorialized in favour of the maintenance of Toronto's "typically Canadian" Sunday. But the citizens of "Toronto the Good" voted in favour of Sunday sports in a plebiscite and, in December 1951, elected as their mayor Allan Lamport, a churchgoer who had pledged to make it possible to watch double-headers on Sundays at Maple Leaf Stadium. Across English-speaking Canada, provincial drinking restrictions that determined who could drink, where they could drink, and under what conditions, were increasingly challenged as attitudes changed. In British Columbia, for example, citizens voted in 1952 to authorize the sale of liquor and wine by the glass in cocktail lounges that would be frequented by a well-behaved middle-class clientele. The beer parlours, often viewed as indecent working-class centres of excess, continued to exist, however, with separate sections for men, and for ladies and escorts.[22]

In the late 1940s and the 1950s, Canadian consumers had more money to spend and new products to spend it on. Workers in most regions of the country easily found jobs, and pay scales increased substantially. Governments went about the task of managing economic growth. For a time, Canada's postwar prosperity camouflaged the poverty and inequalities that remained the lot of many Canadians, in spite of the appearance of several new social programs. When, by the late 1950s, the postwar boom appeared to have run its course, new tensions emerged in society. Canadians now seemed to believe that it was time for change.

NOTES

1. Matthew J. Bellamy, *Profiting the Crown: Canada's Polymer Corporation, 1942–1990* (Montreal/Kingston: McGill-Queen's University Press, 2005), p. 89.

2. Doug Owram, "Canadian Domesticity in the Postwar Era," in Peter Neary and J. L. Granatstein, eds., *The Veterans Charter and Post–World War II Canada* (Montreal/Kingston: McGill-Queen's University Press, 1998), p. 213.

3. Magda Fahrni, *Household Politics: Montreal Families and Postwar Reconstruction* (Toronto: University of Toronto Press, 2005), p. 11.

4. David G. Alexander, *Atlantic Canada and Confederation: Essays in Canadian Political Economy* (Toronto: University of Toronto Press, 1983), p. 32.

5. Peter Neary, *Newfoundland in the North Atlantic World, 1929–1949* (Montreal/Kingston: McGill-Queen's University Press, 1988), p. 359.

6. Raymond Blake, *Canadians at Last: Canada Integrates Newfoundland as a Province* (Toronto: University of Toronto Press, 1994), p. 6.

7. James Struthers, *The Limits of Affluence: Welfare in Ontario, 1920–1970* (Toronto: University of Toronto Press, 1994), p. 180.

8. John W. Holmes, *The Shaping of Peace: Canada and the Search for World Order, 1943–1957*, vol. 2 (Toronto: University of Toronto Press, 1982), p. 36.

9. J.L. Granatstein, *How Britain's Weakness Forced Canada into the Arms of the United States* (Toronto: University of Toronto Press, 1989), p. 3.

10. David J. Bercuson, "Canada, NATO, and Rearmament, 1950–1954: Why Canada Made a Difference (But Not for Very Long)," in John English and Norman Hillmer, eds., *Making a Difference? Canada's Foreign Policy in a Changing World Order* (Toronto: Lester, 1992), p. 104.

11. John Price, "The 'Cat's Paw': Canada and the United Nations Temporary Commission on Korea," *Canadian Historical Review* 85 (June 2004): 323.

12. John English, *The Worldly Years: The Life of Lester Pearson*, vol. II, *1949–1972* (Toronto: Knopf Canada, 1992), p. 145.

13. J.-C. Falardeau, *Bulletin des Relations industrielles* 4 (1949), quoted in Fraser Isbester, "Asbestos 1949," in Irving Abella, ed., *On Strike: Six Key Labour Struggles in Canada, 1919–1949* (Toronto: James, Lewis & Samuel Publishers, 1974), p. 163.

14. Irving Abella, *Nationalism, Communism, and Canadian Labour: The CIO, the Communist Party, and the Canadian Congress of Labour, 1935–1956* (Toronto: University of Toronto Press, 1973), p. 221.

15. Peter S. McInnis, *Harnessing Labour Confrontation: Shaping the Postwar Settlement in Canada, 1943–1950* (Toronto: University of Toronto Press, 2002), p. 13.

16. Shirley Tillotson, "Human Rights Law as Prism: Women's Organizations, Unions, and Ontario's Female Employees Fair Remuneration Act, 1951," *Canadian Historical Review* 72 (1991): 532–57.

17. Mary Louise Adams, *The Trouble with Normal: Postwar Youth and the Making of Heterosexuality* (Toronto: University of Toronto Press, 1997), pp. 105–106.

18. Paul Litt, *The Muses, the Masses, and the Massey Commission* (Toronto: University of Toronto Press, 1992).

19. Susan Mann, *The Dream of Nation: A Social and Intellectual History of Quebec* (Montreal/Kingston: McGill-Queen's University Press, 1982, 2002), p. 284.

20. Doug Owram, *Born at the Right Time: A History of the Baby-Boom Generation* (Toronto: University of Toronto Press, 1996), p. 103.

21. Michael Gauvreau, "The Emergence of Personalist Feminism: Catholicism and the Marriage-Preparation Movement in Quebec, 1940–1966," in Nancy Christie, ed., *Households of Faith: Family, Gender, and Community in Canada, 1760–1969* (Montreal/Kingston, McGill-Queen's University Press, 2002), p. 321.

22. Robert A. Campbell, *Sit Down and Drink Your Beer: Regulating Vancouver's Beer Parlours, 1925–1954* (Toronto: University of Toronto Press, 2001).

BEYOND THE BOOK

Weblinks

Life in Postwar Canada

http://archives.cbc.ca/IDD-1-69-1798/life_society/post_war
Radio clips detailing life for soldiers in postwar Canada, and their families. Details education issues for veterans, women in the work force, and the "baby bonus."

Has Confederation Been Good for Newfoundland?

http://archives.cbc.ca/IDD-1-73-564/politics_economy/nfld_confed
This archive of television and radio footage explores Newfoundland's entry into Confederation in 1949, and how it has fared since.

Canada and NATO

http://www.civilization.ca/cwm/nato/nato01_e.html
A history of Canada's involvement in NATO, beginning in 1949.

Madeleine Parent

http://www.histori.ca/minutes/minute.do?id=14861
A Canadian heritage radio minute regarding Madeleine Parent and the 1946 textile workers' strike in Valleyfield, Quebec.

Canada Council for the Arts

http://www.50.canadacouncil.ca/en
Explore the history of the Canada Council for the Arts in this 50th Anniversary retrospective of the organization.

Films & Novels

The Colony of Unrequited Dreams. By Wayne Johnston. 1999.

The Rocket. Directed by Charles Binamé. 2006.

The War Brides: From Romance to Reality. Directed by Anne Hainsworth. 2001.

RELATED READINGS

Two essays in R. Douglas Francis and Donald B. Smith, eds., *Readings in Canadian History: Post-Confederation*, 7th ed. (Toronto: Thomson Nelson, 2006), pertain to topics in this chapter: Veronica Strong-Boag, "Home Dreams: Women and the Suburban Experiment in Canada, 1945–60," pp. 460–81; and Robert Rutherdale, "Fatherhood, Masculinity, and the Good Life During Canada's Baby Boom, 1945–1965," pp. 481–97.

BIBLIOGRAPHY

A general study of this period is Robert Bothwell, Ian Drummond, and John English, *Canada Since 1945: Power, Politics, and Provincialism*, rev. ed. (Toronto: University of Toronto Press, 1989). Doug Owram, *Born at the Right Time: A History of the Baby-Boom Generation* (Toronto: University of Toronto Press, 1996), tells a captivating story. Postwar consumerism is discussed critically in Joy Parr, *Domestic Goods: The Material, the Moral, and the Economic in the Postwar Years* (Toronto: University of Toronto Press, 1999); and in Magda Fahrni, *Household Politics: Montreal Families and Postwar Reconstruction* (Toronto: University of Toronto Press, 2005). Material on economic development may be found in Kenneth Norrie and Douglas Owram, *A History of the Canadian Economy*, 3rd ed. (Toronto: Nelson Thomson, 2002).

Aspects of the welfare state are discussed in Alvin Finkel, *Our Lives: Canada After 1945* (Toronto: James Lorimer, 1997); and in James Struthers, *The Limits of Affluence: Welfare in Ontario, 1920–1970* (Toronto: University of Toronto Press, 1994). The Quebec experience is discussed in Dominique Marshall, *The Social Origins of the Welfare State: Quebec Families, Compulsory Education, and Family Allowances, 1940–1955* (Waterloo, ON: Wilfrid Laurier University Press, 2006). Housing is studied in Richard Harris, *Creeping Conformity: How Canada Became Suburban, 1900–1960* (Toronto: University of Toronto Press, 2004); and in John R. Miron, *Housing in Postwar Canada: Demographic Change, Household Formation, and Housing Demand* (Montreal/Kingston: McGill-Queen's University Press, 1988).

The conservation of nature in the postwar years is examined in George M. Warecki, *Protecting Ontario's Wilderness: A History of Changing Ideas and Preservation Politics, 1927–1973* (New York: Peter Lang, 2000); and Alan MacEachern, *Natural Selections: National Parks in Atlantic Canada, 1935–1970* (Montreal/Kingston: McGill-Queen's University Press, 2001). Richard A. Rajala, *Clearcutting the Pacific Rain Forest: Production, Science and Regulation* (Vancouver: UBC Press, 1998), analyzes forest harvest practices.

Dale C. Thomson presents a biography of Canada's prime minister, 1948–1957, in *Louis St. Laurent, Canadian* (Toronto: Macmillan, 1967). J.L. Granatstein examines the role of federal bureaucrats in *The Ottawa Men: The Civil Service Mandarins, 1935–57* (Toronto: University of Toronto Press, 1998). Studies of provincial politics of this era include Richard Gwyn, *Smallwood: The Unlikely Revolutionary*, rev ed. (Toronto: McClelland and Stewart, 1972, 1999); Roger Graham, *Old Man Ontario: Leslie M. Frost* (Toronto: University of Toronto Press, 1990; A. W. Johnson, *Dream No Little Dreams: A Biography of the Douglas Government of Saskatchewan, 1944–1961* (Toronto: University of Toronto Press, 2004); and, on Alberta, Ted Byfield, ed., *Manning and the Age of Prosperity, 1946–1963* (Edmonton: United Western Communications, 2001). Among several books which examine Newfoundland's entry into Confederation is David MacKenzie, *Inside the Atlantic Triangle: Canada and the Entrance of Newfoundland into Confederation, 1939–1949* (Toronto: University of Toronto Press, 1986).

On Canadian foreign policy of the late 1940s and 1950s see Robert Bothwell, *Alliance and Illusion: Canada and the World, 1945–1984* (Vancouver: UBC Press, 2007); Adam Chapnick's myth-debunking *The Middle Power Project: Canada and the Founding of the United Nations* (Vancouver: UBC Press, 2005); Reg Whitaker and Steve Hewitt, *Canada and the Cold War* (Toronto: James Lorimer, 2003); and Greg Donaghy, ed., *Canada and the Early Cold War, 1943–1957/Le Canada au début de la guerre froide, 1943–1957* (Ottawa: Department of Foreign Affairs and International Trade, 1998). In *Pragmatic Idealism: Canadian Foreign Policy, 1945–1995* (Montreal/Kingston: McGill-Queen's University Press, 1998), Costas Melakopides looks at Canada's involvement in peacekeeping, arms control, and human rights. Critical studies of Canada's participation in the Korean War include William Johnston, *A War of Patrols: Canadian Army Operations in Korea* (Vancouver: UBC Press, 2003); David Bercuson, *Blood on the Hills: The Canadian Army in the Korean War* (Toronto: University of Toronto Press, 1999); and Brent Byron Watson, *Far Eastern Tour: The Canadian Infantry in Korea, 1950–1953* (Montreal/Kingston: McGill-Queen's University Press, 2002). Joseph Levitt examines Canada's role as a "junior partner" in arms-control talks in *Pearson and Canada's Role in Nuclear Disarmament and Arms Control Negotiations, 1945–1957* (Montreal/Kingston: McGill-Queen's University Press, 1993). Postwar trade issues are discussed in B.W. Muirhead, *The Development of Postwar Canadian Trade Policy: The Failure of the Anglo-European Option* (Montreal/Kingston: McGill-Queen's University Press, 1992).

For Canadian–American relations in the defence sector see Joseph T. Jockel's study, *No Boundaries Upstairs: Canada, the United States and the Origins of North American Air Defence, 1945–1958* (Vancouver: University of British Columbia Press, 1987). Craig Stewart looks at one failed Canadian defence initiative in *Shutting Down the National Dream: Avro and the Tragedy of the Arrow* (Toronto: McGraw-Hill Ryerson, 1988). The history of Canada's atomic energy program is discussed in Brian Buckley, *Canada's Early Nuclear Policy: Fate, Chance, and Character* (Montreal/Kingston: McGill-Queen's University Press, 2000). Andrew Richter studies Canada's defence thinking in *Avoiding Armageddon: Canadian Military Strategy and Nuclear Weapons, 1950–63* (Vancouver: UBC Press and Canadian War Museum, 2002). Issues linked to internal security are examined in Amy Knight, *How the Cold War Began: The Gouzenko Affair and the Hunt for Soviet Spies* (Toronto: McClelland & Stewart, 2005); and Reg Whitaker and Gary Marcuse, *Cold War Canada: The Making of a National Insecurity State, 1945–1957* (Toronto: University of Toronto Press, 1994). David MacKenzie's historical booklet, *Canada's Red Scare, 1945–1957* (Ottawa: Canadian Historical Association, 2001), paints a brief portrait of the context. On human rights campaigns, see Ross Lambertson, *Repression and Resistance: Canadian Human Rights Activists, 1930–1960* (Toronto: University of Toronto Press, 2005).

A good business history is Matthew J. Bellamy, *Profiting the Crown: Canada's Polymer Corporation, 1942–1990* (Montreal/Kingston: McGill-Queen's University Press, 2005). For a general presentation of unions of this period, see Bryan D. Palmer, *Working-Class Experience: Rethinking the History of Canadian Labour, 1800–1991*, 2nd ed. (Toronto: McClelland & Stewart, 1992). Peter S. McInnis examines postwar labour–management relations in *Harnessing Labour Confrontation: Shaping the Postwar Settlement in Canada, 1943–1950* (Toronto: University of Toronto Press, 2002). On the history of the Canadian Autoworkers see Charlotte Yates, *From Plant to Politics: The Autoworkers Union in Postwar Canada* (Philadelphia: Temple University Press, 1993). The history of another famous union is told in Andrew Neufeld and Andrew Parnaby, *The IWA in Canada: The Life and Times of an Industrial Union* (Vancouver: IWA Canada/New Star Books, 2000).

Two excellent general syntheses of women's history exist: Micheline Dumont et al., *Quebec Women: A History* (Toronto: Women's Press, 1987); and Alison Prentice et al., *Canadian Women: A History*, 2nd ed. (Toronto: Harcourt Brace, 1996). Patricia T. Rooke and R.L. Schnell, *No Bleeding Heart: Charlotte Whitton, A Feminist on the Right* (Vancouver: University of British Columbia Press, 1987), examines the career of a famous mayor of Ottawa. The issue of female clergy is addressed in Valerie J. Korinek, "No Women Need Apply: The Ordination of Women in the United Church, 1918–65," *Canadian Historical Review* 74 (1993): 473–509. Joan Sangster studies how the justice system dealt with women in *Regulating Girls and Women: Sexuality, Family, and the Law in Ontario, 1920–1960* (Toronto: Oxford University Press, 2001). Veronica Strong-Boag examines the life of suburban women in "Home Dreams: Women and the Suburban Experiment in Canada, 1945–60," *Canadian Historical Review* 72 (1991): 471–504. Valerie Korinek studies a women's magazine in *Roughing It in the Suburbs: Reading <u>Chatelaine</u> Magazine in the Fifties and the Sixties* (Toronto: University of Toronto Press, 2000). The world of fashion is discussed, and abundantly illustrated, in Alexandra Palmer, *Couture and Commerce: The Transatlantic Fashion Trade in the 1950s* (Vancouver: UBC Press, 2001). Several essays on aspects of women's life in Ontario in this period may be found in Joy Parr, ed., *A Diversity of Women: Ontario, 1945–1980* (Toronto: University of Toronto Press, 1995).

Psychology's place in the postwar Canadian family is studied in Mona Gleason, *Normalizing the Ideal: Psychology, Schooling, and the Family in Postwar Canada* (Toronto: University of Toronto Press, 1999). On heterosexuality and homosexuality, see Mary Louise Adams, *The Trouble with Normal: Postwar Youth and the Making of Heterosexuality* (Toronto: University of Toronto Press, 1997); Gary Kinsman, *The Regulation of Desire: Homo and Hetero Sexualities*, 2nd ed. (Montreal: Black Rose Books, 1996); and Richard Cavell, ed., *Love, Hate, and Fear in Canada's Cold War* (Toronto, University of Toronto Press, 2004). William Kaplan recounts the struggle for rights of the Jehovah's Witnesses in *State and Salvation: The Jehovah's Witnesses and Their Fight for Civil Rights* (Toronto: University of Toronto Press, 1989). The changing attitudes of Canadians toward alcohol are examined in Robert A. Campbell, *Sit Down and Drink Your Beer: Regulating Vancouver's Beer Parlours, 1925–1954* (Toronto: University of Toronto Press, 2001).

Paul Litt tells the story of the Massey Commission in *The Muses, the Masses, and the Massey Commission* (Toronto: University of Toronto Press, 1992). Paul Rutherford looks at television fare in *When Television Was Young: Primetime Canada 1952–1967* (Toronto: University of Toronto Press, 1990).

Useful maps and charts on Canada in the World War II and postwar period appear in Donald Kerr and Deryck W. Holdsworth, eds., *Historical Atlas of Canada*, vol. 3, *Addressing the Twentieth Century, 1891–1961* (Toronto: University of Toronto Press, 1990).

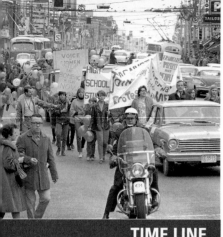

Chapter Fifteen

PROTEST AND REFORM: THE 1960s

Canada experienced profound social, cultural, and political upheavals in the 1960s. Young people, in particular, challenged authority. "A new student class has emerged, aware of its power, ready to act," *Maclean's* proclaimed in November 1967. The universities became centres of protest as demonstrations erupted on campuses. Youth began to reject traditional social and cultural values, and sexual taboos weakened.

Other groups as well wanted to be heard. Women questioned the inequalities of their condition. Labour became more militant in its attacks on the business "establishment." French-speaking Canadians sought linguistic rights that would place them on an equal footing with English-speaking Canadians. An important minority in Quebec believed that only independence could ensure real equality. English-speaking nationalists, particularly in Ontario, denounced the powerful American presence in most aspects of Canadian life. A Native resurgence began in reaction to fears of assimilation and an end to special status. No longer could a small group of middle-aged and elderly men, primarily of British origin and speaking only English, rule Canada politically. A host of new interest groups, with varying agendas, had entered the political forum. For many observers, diversity had now triumphed over unity within Canada.

The economic stability of the postwar years was shaken in the 1960s. As the decade opened, Canada faced the highest unemployment levels since the Great Depression. Although prosperity returned, rapidly rising prices soon became a worry. Economic difficulties led to social problems, and rising popular discontent brought an end to political stability; indeed, in Ottawa, minority governments ruled for much of the decade. Several of the provinces also saw political change. Canadians sought new leaders with new visions.

Traditional Churches Questioned

Canadian society in the 1960s became more secular. In Quebec, the influence of the Roman Catholic church waned as that institution largely abandoned to the state its historic role in education and in social institutions and as church attendance declined. Many clergy left the church's religious orders, and new recruitment fell rapidly.

Elsewhere in Canada, the major Protestant denominations also lost ground. Sunday school attendance in the Protestant churches fell precipitously. In his book *The Comfortable Pew*, author Pierre Berton attacked the churches for their lack of relevance, as they vainly attempted to combat the supporters of beer parlours, Sunday movies, and Sunday sports. Rev. James Mutchmor, the head of the United church's board of evangelism and social service and later moderator of the church, outspokenly denounced the new trends. The "voice against vice" became the most-quoted cleric in Canada in the mid-1960s. Mutchmor's critics mocked: "Let's have much less of Mutchmor!"

As churches attempted to come to terms with change, their congregations often represented a wide spectrum of opinion. Liberal Roman Catholics applauded the decisions of the Vatican II Council, which modernized certain religious practices; more conservative adherents feared the loss of essentials to the faith. Many Protestants who felt that the traditional denominations had become too liberal joined conservative fundamentalist groups such as the Pentecostals, which grew prodigiously. By the late 1960s, a wide variety of sects and cults attracted Canadians.

Youth Protest

Much of the revolt against established social and cultural patterns was superficial. High school boys put away their hair oil and let their hair grow, while their mothers remonstrated with them in vain and barbers lost business. "Flower children" dressed in fringes and beads and displayed psychedelic colours. Blue jeans became the uniform of a generation. Speaking of hair styles and clothing fashions, one Montreal high school principal complained, "These eccentric habits are meant to distract the attention of other students and that's exactly what we don't want." Moustaches, sideburns, and beards adorned the faces of many older male students. Youth denounced age and experience and promised to stay young.

Sexual experimentation flourished, too, as did a drug culture. Student associations called for the legalization of certain "recreational" drugs such as marijuana. Medical opinion was divided over the issue. As historian Marcel Martel has shown, groups such as the police forces had more success than others in shaping public debate and in imposing their choice of policy, which was to keep the status quo.[1]

"Peace and Love"

Young English-speaking Canadians empathized with the peace-and-love message of American folk singers such as Bob Dylan and Joan Baez. But Canadian folk singers, including Ian and Sylvia Tyson, Gordon Lightfoot, and Joni Mitchell, also achieved an international reputation. Ian and Sylvia became popular in the United States at the start of the folk revival in the 1960s, paving the way for other Canadian performers at a time of limited recording opportunities in Canada. Orillia-born Lightfoot began his career in coffee houses and bars; as composer of such pieces as "Early Morning Rain" and "For Lovin' Me," he soon drew crowds to his performances at the Mariposa folk festival and elsewhere. As the decade advanced and interest in folk music waned, Lightfoot enlarged his public by making the transition to pop and country music.

In French Canada, young people flocked to listen to the *chansonniers* who sang, accompanied only by their guitars or the piano, in the *boîtes à chansons* that sprang up across Quebec in the early 1960s. Félix Leclerc and Raymond Lévesque pioneered this form of entertainment. At first, the lyrics dwelt on apolitical themes such as love and nature. Later, as a powerful nationalist current surged through the province, new themes bearing on the historical experience of Quebec's people and their identity dominated singers' repertoires. Gilles Vigneault, who came from Natashquan, a tiny hamlet on the lower north shore of the St. Lawrence River, became one of the most well-known singer-songwriters of the era—and his "Mon pays" became the anthem of nationalist youth. The *chansonniers* soon gave way to popular singers, among whom figured a strong feminine contingent, including Ginette Reno, Renée Claude, Pauline Julien, and Monique Leyrac. Robert Charlebois's audacious creativity, evident in his recording of "Lindberg" in 1968, made him one of the most popular male performers of the era.

Many young Canadians listened avidly to rock music during the 1960s. Enthusiastically they fell

Protest against the war in Vietnam.

Source: Toronto Star Syndicate.

victim to Beatlemania, especially during the shaggy-haired foursome's tour of Canada in September 1964. On September 8, the *Toronto Star* headlined: "200 Girls Swoon in Battle of the Beatles." Vancouver's Empire Stadium saw even greater hysteria, during a concert by the "Fab Four," as hundreds of fans rushed the stage and screams drowned out the singing. Beatle products inundated the market, including Beatle wigs guaranteed to fit all heads. As the decade advanced, a multitude of Canadian rock bands sprang up, usually modelled on British and American groups. But because of the popularity of foreign groups, few Canadian rock-music records appeared. Canadian singers received a substantial boost in 1970, when the Canadian Radio-television and Telecommunications Commission (CRTC) established Canadian-content rules for broadcasters.

Student Revolt

For historian Doug Owram, the 1960s constituted "the moment in history that forever defined the baby boom as a distinct generation."[2] The boomers' centres of activity were the university campuses (although the majority of boomers never went to university), which became centres of protest in the 1960s. Infused with the spirit of "peace and love," Canadian students, like American and western youth in general, picketed in favour of a wide range of reformist causes, and especially against the increasingly bloody war in Vietnam, where the United States had greatly expanded its military campaign in an effort to prevent Communist-dominated North Vietnam from dislodging the pro-American regime in South Vietnam. Nationalist protest took root and flourished, often tended closely by university professors. Academics in the social sciences, particularly in Toronto, prepared research studies to show the extent to which Canada had

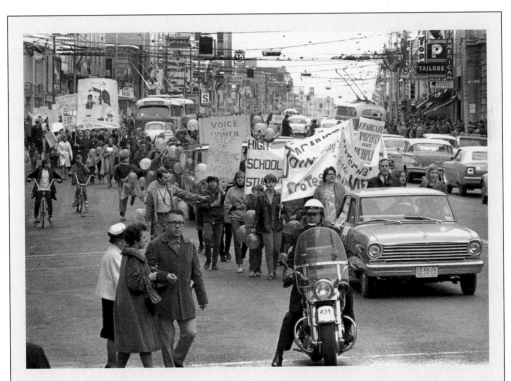

This protest march on Jasper Avenue in Edmonton, October 22, 1967, was aimed mostly against American involvement in Vietnam, but other placards suggest agendas for social justice.

Source: Provincial Archives of Alberta/J127/1.

The magnificent University of Lethbridge, main building, designed by famed architect Arthur Erickson. Construction was completed in 1971.

Source: Courtesy of the University of Lethbridge.

The Montreal campus of the Université du Québec, one of the new universities that sprang up during the 1960s. To build the campus, a church and a convent were torn down. The architects integrated parts of the church's facade into the new structure. Today the Université du Québec has regional affiliates across the province.

Source : Université du Québec à Montréal.

become an American colony, and proposed measures for buying or taking it back. In Quebec's universities, equal fervour was applied to proving that Quebec was a Canadian colony and to devising plans for liberating it.

University protest had political repercussions. In Quebec, where most intellectuals were strong nationalists, it contributed to bringing the language question to the floor of the National Assembly and assisted the rise of the Parti Québécois. In Ottawa, it helped Pierre Elliott Trudeau, who appeared to challenge the establishment and who brought new ideas to the fore, to win the Liberal leadership and the federal election of 1968. In addition, by 1970, the nationalist outcry from many English-Canadian universities, particularly in Ontario, caused the Liberal government in Ottawa to question the continentalism it had espoused in the 1950s.

Students abandoned classes and occupied administrative offices, demanding more active participation in the university community and the recognition of students' rights. At the University of Toronto, for example, students protested against recruiting on campus by Dow Chemical Corporation, a manufacturer of napalm used by the American military during the Vietnam War. Students also staged a sit-in on day care in the Senate chamber, proclaiming that babies had nothing to lose but their diapers. Such protests were all the more visible, in part, because students were now far more numerous. University enrolments doubled during the 1950s, then tripled during the 1960s and 1970s. The parents of baby boomers, many of whom had never finished high school, preached the virtues of a university degree as the key to a bright future.

Higher Education Expands

Provincial governments, convinced that higher education would bring enormous economic benefits to society, dramatically increased spending on universities and established a host of new institutions. British Columbia Premier W.A.C. Bennett told the chairman of B.C. Hydro in 1963: "I want you to be the chancellor of a new university. Select a site and build it and get it going." As a result Simon Fraser University opened in 1965, atop Burnaby Mountain, with 2500 students. (The building was well-known architect Arthur Erickson's first major commission. Some critics later blamed Erickson for student unrest because his design of the campus encouraged student interaction.) In Ontario, York University admitted its first 75 students in 1960; a year later the province gave York 200 ha in northwest Toronto for the building of a campus. Laurentian, Trent, Brock, and Lakehead universities were also set up, as well as Erindale and Scarborough colleges, affiliated with the University of Toronto. Quebec established the public Université du Québec à Montréal with several regional affiliates. The University of Alberta, Calgary branch, became the separate University of Calgary in 1966, while Alberta's third university opened in Lethbridge in 1967. New Brunswick's francophones obtained their own university at Moncton. Regional and community colleges began operations in several provinces. The federal government, which had been making grants directly to the universities since 1951, began in 1966 to make contributions to provincial governments for the financing of postsecondary education. In all, government spending on universities increased sevenfold during the 1960s.

As a result of their rapid growth, universities faced serious shortages of trained staff. English-speaking universities recruited heavily on American campuses. By 1968, fewer than half of the university professors in Canada were Canadians. In that same year, only one of every eight positions filled went to a Canadian. Critics accused universities of ignoring Canadian university graduates in their hiring policies. Celebrated Canadian author Hugh MacLennan, who, years earlier, had been unable to find a teaching position even with degrees from Oxford and Princeton universities, lamented that Canadian universities had embarked on a "program of national suicide." Carleton University professors Robin Mathews and James Steele, after reviewing the statistics on university hiring policies, called for the Canadianization of faculties.

A HISTORICAL PORTRAIT

The Student Radicals at Sir George Williams University

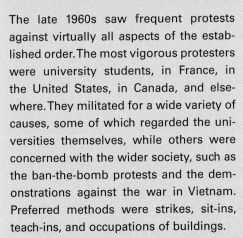

The late 1960s saw frequent protests against virtually all aspects of the established order. The most vigorous protesters were university students, in France, in the United States, in Canada, and elsewhere. They militated for a wide variety of causes, some of which regarded the universities themselves, while others were concerned with the wider society, such as the ban-the-bomb protests and the demonstrations against the war in Vietnam. Preferred methods were strikes, sit-ins, teach-ins, and occupations of buildings.

The great majority of students were not militants but rather passive spectators. Among the militants, some were ready to take extreme measures in defence of causes that appeared increasingly imprecise. The events of February 11, 1969 at Sir George Williams University (today Concordia University) in Montreal appeared to mark a watershed.

"Police rout SGWU militants; $1 million computer centre wrecked." Thus read the *Montreal Star*'s headline that day. The damage figure was revised upward the next day to $2 million, or approximately $10 million in today's dollars.

In December 1968, some students had levelled charges of racism against a biology professor at the university. In early February 1969, they occupied the Faculty Club in the nine-storey Henry Hall Building in support of their cause. At first they succeeded in generating considerable sympathy. Over time, however, the militant group, thanks to new additions, became more radical, and moderates tended to distance themselves. One prominent militant proclaimed that he didn't really care about the charges of racism against the professor. "All we want to do is burn down the university. We want the police to come, we want violence."

Militants then broke into the cafeteria on the seventh floor and hurled chairs and tables down escalators, stairwells, and elevator shafts. As police moved against the crowd, occupants turned on the fire hoses against them, then retreated to the computer centre on the ninth floor. When police attempted to evict them from the centre, militants threw computers, punch cards, tapes, and furniture onto the street, and then set fire to the centre. Outside, other students showed their antagonism to militants by shouting "Burn, burn!"

Police made 90 arrests; those arrested included 42 non-nationals, mainly from the Caribbean and from England. Thirty of those arrested were not even students at Sir George Williams.

The events at Sir George Williams provoked a sharp backlash and a demand for a return to order. Although the *Montreal Star* argued that university administrations were frequently guilty of a lack of responsiveness to honest and often reasonable demands, it denounced what it termed "an indefensible act by student anarchists." When the Quebec student union, UGEQ, declared its complete support for the rioters, SGWU students quit its ranks. Acts of intimidation, disruption, and even violence were occurring at the same time on other campuses. But for historian Doug Owram, the SGWU episode, because of the degree of violence and destruction, "foreshadowed the end of the 1960s era."[1]

---

1 Doug Owram, *Born at the Right Time: A History of the Baby-Boom Generation* (Toronto: University of Toronto Press, 1996), p. 286.

An Interventionist State

Although university teachers and students were among the loudest voices calling for change, Canadians in general endorsed increased state intervention, at all levels, as a necessary tool for reform. They demanded that provincial governments invest heavily in elementary and secondary education, building schools and hiring teachers as enrolments burgeoned thanks to the baby boom generation and to immigration. In Ontario, massive spending increases on education became an explosive political issue as property taxes, largely to pay for schools, soared. In Alberta, revenues from sales of oil and gas enabled the government to spend more money per capita, notably on health and education, than any other province.

Reformers also wanted governments to take measures to protect society's weaker elements, such as the unemployed, older Canadians, people needing expensive medical care, and those living in disadvantaged regions of the country. Citizens also urged the state to act to protect consumers, promote the equality of women, and combat discrimination against minority groups. They pressured municipal governments to improve the quality of life in cities by controlling the heights of buildings, curtailing expressway expansion, expanding urban transit, improving parks and libraries, protecting established neighbourhoods, and fighting urban blight. The cultural lobby requested financial aid to assist Canadian cultural development, while sport organizations urged Ottawa to fund amateur sport and to work to improve Canadian athletes' performances in international competitions.

In response to calls for action, governments also intervened, at least modestly, to supply disadvantaged Canadians with low-income housing. In the late 1940s, large areas of Cabbagetown, a working-class area in Toronto, had been cleared and replaced with three-storey brick apartment buildings with open spaces and playgrounds. The 1960s saw the construction of large apartment buildings in the same area, but with much less space, a situation that gave rise to a variety of social problems. Vancouver's Strathcona area, Halifax's Uniacke Square, and Montreal's Jeanne Mance Park saw similar developments.

Most Canadians dreamed of owning a house in the suburbs. Federal government programs made low-cost mortgages available, provincial governments built roads, and local authorities installed services. The Don Mills community of Toronto, built in 1952–62, served as the prototype of a planned corporate suburb. Around a core area containing a shopping centre and a high school at the intersection of two arterial roads, developers built small apartment buildings and townhouses. Beyond them were four low-density neighbourhood units. Edmonton had its own planned suburb, Mill Woods. Developers made plans for a population of 100 000, which was to live in 23 neighbourhoods that were focused on a town-centre complex containing the necessary services. All large Canadian cities saw suburbs mushroom in the 1960s.

Population Trends

Demographic upheaval also characterized the 1960s as the baby boom of the late 1940s and 1950s fizzled into a "baby bust." In a single decade, the rate of growth of Canada's population dropped by nearly half. Newfoundland's birth rate remained the highest, at 24.3 births per thousand people in 1970; its decline came only in the following decade. Quebec went from having one of the highest birth rates of all the provinces in 1960 to having the lowest rate in 1970, just 16.1 per thousand. The two-child family—the minimum to maintain the current size of the population—briefly became the norm in Canada. Then single-child or childless families became increasingly numerous.

Demographers and sociologists had difficulty explaining the demographic revolution, although other industrialized countries experienced the same phenomenon. Some Quebec analysts attributed the decline in the birth rate to the secularization of Quebec society, but similar trends occurred in all the provinces. Many observers emphasized the availability of better contraceptive methods, particularly the birth-control pill, which became available in Canada in 1966. Contraception and birth-control methods did indeed gain much more exposure and publicity. In 1961, a Toronto couple, Barbara and George Cadbury, founded Planned Parenthood of

Many Canadians dreamt of owning a house in the suburbs. This photo shows the first houses built in Ajax, a small community located between Toronto and Oshawa, just after World War II, around 1948.

Source: *Oshawa Times.* Ajax Public Library/P130-002-001.

Canada, an information and referral service. Only in 1969, however, did Parliament amend Canada's Criminal Code to permit the distribution of birth-control information and devices.

Obviously, Canadians wanted fewer children, and they wanted them later in life. A century earlier, large families had been a necessity—on farms, for example, children meant additional workers and, in general, the extended family cared for its elderly members. In Canada's modern social welfare state, the aged relied less on adult children for financial assistance. As well, the ever-increasing costs of raising and educating them made children seem like financial liabilities. They might also be perceived as a brake on career development.

Changing Family Patterns

A general revolution in family patterns began in the 1960s. Conservative-minded Canadians had long looked askance at the frequency of marriage breakdown in the United States, symbolized by the rapidly moving love lives of glamorous Hollywood stars. After 1968, when Parliament modified Canadian laws, divorce became frequent in Canada, too. By the 1970s, Canada registered one divorce for every three marriages. The trend was particularly apparent in Quebec, where, as in Newfoundland, divorce procedures had previously been exceedingly complicated and divorces rare.

Traditional sexual taboos gradually became more relaxed as society became more tolerant. Clothing-optional beaches such as Wreck Beach in Vancouver made their appearance. Gay and lesbian themes were presented in literature and films. Quebec writer Michel Tremblay introduced gay characters into his plays, while in English-speaking Canada Jane Rule published her first novel, *The Desert of the Heart*, with a lesbian theme. Same-sex relationships became more open after the federal government, promising to stay out of the nation's bedrooms, legalized homosexual practices between consenting adults in private in 1969. Many parliamentarians, favourable to the legislation, nevertheless expressed the view that homosexuals were deviants who needed psychiatric help rather than prison cells. Most Conservative and Social Credit members denounced the changes on religious and moral grounds. While the Canadian Bar Association supported decriminalization, the Canadian Association of Police Chiefs, for its part, vigorously opposed the legislation, asserting that it would lead to "depravity, robbery, and murder." In spite of their apparent victory, gays and lesbians worried that their concerns had now been reduced to narrow issues of criminal-law reform. A coalition of gay and lesbian liberation groups stated that, in spite of the reform, "we are still confronted with discrimination, police harassment, exploitation and pressures to conform which deny our sexuality."

Young people in general began to experiment with different types of living arrangements. For a time, communes were in fashion, although few lasted long. "Living together," or common-law marriage, hitherto frowned upon socially, gained popularity. Some women favoured living together because they opposed marriage in principle as a form of economic servitude—women working without pay—disguised by the myth of romantic love. In most cases, for both women and men, convenience was probably a compelling factor in favour of such unions.

Women: The Long Road Toward Equality

The desire for smaller families symbolized a more general wish by women for a change in their condition. In this age of protest, women's groups began to demand that governments intervene, at both the federal and the provincial levels, to promote equality. Thus began the "second wave" of the women's movement. (The much earlier "first wave" had centred upon women's struggle to obtain the right to vote.)

Women disagreed strongly over the nature of the "ideal woman." Historian Valerie Korinek describes a contest created by *Chatelaine*, Canada's only mass-market women's magazine, a publication that contained numerous feminist articles and editorials. The goal of the contest was to discover Canada's foremost homemaker, "Mrs. Chatelaine," a stay-at-home wife and mother who also did volunteer work and could serve as a role model for readers. Some women, however, proposed other models. One suggested setting up a "Mrs. Slob contest," and named herself as winner. She admitted that she did not always serve nourishing meals, she liked fish and chips, she "entertained" only when her neighbours came in to gab, and she didn't find time to do much volunteer work. She offered her philosophy: "Be happy, don't worry. You do what you can with what you've got when you feel like it."[3]

As the 1960s began, many women felt ready to speak out about the affairs of the country. When *Toronto Star* journalist Lotta Dempsey lamented what appeared to be the increasing danger of nuclear war and wondered where the voice of women was, she hit a raw nerve: hundreds of women turned out for a public meeting at Massey Hall. Thus was born the Voice of Women, whose membership grew to 10 000 in less than a year. Although it was soon racked by internal disputes, the organization, in historian Barbara Roberts's view, had "a 'multiplier effect' on Canadian society out of all proportion to its size and the middle-class character of its membership."[4] Many of its participants later became activists in other women's associations.

Convinced that much more needed to be done, Laura Sabia, president of the Canadian Federation of University Women, called together delegates from 32 women's organizations across Canada who agreed in 1966 to form a new group dedicated to advancing the cause of women. Representatives from this nonpartisan Committee for the Equality of Women in Canada then met members of the federal cabinet to press for the creation of a royal commission on the status of women in Canada. Thérèse Casgrain and other members of the Fédération des femmes du Québec also attended in order to demonstrate that francophone women were making the same demands as their anglophone sisters. Ottawa finally agreed, the following year, to set up a commission, but only after the committee threatened to organize a huge march on the national capital. In general, the media responded negatively to the appointment of the commission, seeing it as a waste of taxpayers' money.

The Royal Commission on the Status of Women, chaired by professional broadcaster Florence Bird, held hearings across Canada and received nearly 500 briefs. Issued in September 1970, the "Bird Report," which one journalist called "a bomb, already primed and ticking," called for a societal change of attitude toward women. It proposed dozens of recommendations concerning women in the workplace, in political life, in education, and in family life.

Women in the Paid Work Force

Male-dominated legislatures did adopt some laws that improved the lot of women. They made divorce simpler and maternity benefits more generous, and they granted tax deductions for child-care expenses. However, women's major demands for change—and, indeed, the changes themselves—occurred in the workplace. In 1961, only one married woman in five was in the labour force, often in part-time employment. Public attitudes still strongly disapproved of married mothers taking paid employment. By 1971, however, as increasing

Canadian Voice of Women in a demonstration for peace, 1960s.

Source: Voices of Women.

numbers of married women sought jobs outside the home, the proportion had risen to one in three. By 1981, it reached one in two.

Women who worked outside the home needed to find some type of day care for their small children. Until the 1960s, it was expected that they would make their own arrangements. Then feminists began to call for affordable state-supported day care that could enable women to exercise their right to work. It would be necessary to wait until the 1970s, however, before even modest state subsidies for provincial day-care centres became available.

Sex segregation in the workplace, resulting in "pink-collar ghettos," still remained the norm. As retail stores proliferated in a consumer-oriented society, many women found jobs as sales clerks. The expansion of health care and education also created traditional employment for women. As office clerical work, too, was considered "women's work," expanding governments hired large numbers of women. Indeed, in the late 1960s, the federal government became the largest employer of women in Canada. Eighty percent of its female employees worked in office or administrative-support jobs. Men dominated in the higher-level, better-paying managerial positions.

Ontario innovated in 1963 by establishing a women's bureau within the provincial Department of Labour. Although primarily responsible for research and public relations, the bureau became interested by the late 1960s in policy development and antidiscrimination initiatives. It thus helped bring about the adoption of the Women's Equal Employment Opportunity Act in 1970. In spite of many loopholes, the law provided for legal unpaid maternity leave and banned the firing of women upon marriage. Business complained that maternity leaves would eventually lead to paid leaves, a kind of "reward for pregnancy"; unions with largely male memberships also showed little enthusiasm for measures to counter discrimination against women.

Women disagreed over the means to effect necessary changes and, indeed, over the changes that they should seek. Some shared the liberal view that legislative reform would give women more equal opportunities. Younger, more radical feminists, inspired by theorists such as the American Kate Millett and the Australian Germaine Greer, believed that only a fundamental transformation of the economic and social structures that perpetuated the dominance of men would end female oppression. This group regarded the Bird Report as far too conservative; indeed, some feminists distrusted the political process itself. From the late 1960s, they waged a militant campaign for women's liberation through newsworthy demonstrations and rallies, in innumerable organized discussions, and in newspapers and other printed literature. Feminists were particularly active on university campuses, where they established women's caucuses of Students for a Democratic Union. Some favoured socialism or Marxism; in Quebec, the Front pour la libération des femmes du Québec also sought national independence.

Labour

In the 1960s radicals in the universities, in the churches, and in the media united in their criticism of the large multinational corporations. They accused these corporations of being the principal villains in society and the prime forces of conservatism. They castigated business in general for its unquenchable thirst for profits and for its failure to display any social or environmental conscience. They flayed developers for destroying old urban neighbourhoods to build luxury highrise apartment buildings and office towers. Finally, in this age of rising inflation and of concern for consumers' rights, they denounced companies for "gouging" consumers by endlessly raising prices.

Attacks on business and on "the establishment" also came from reformist political parties such as the Parti Québécois, with its initial pro-worker bias, and the federal New Democratic Party, launched in 1961, the beneficiary of considerable union support. The major organized assault on business, however, came from unions.

Unions

Canadian workers became increasingly restive during the 1960s. The labour force grew younger as the first cohorts of baby boomers reached the workplace. Many of these new workers had high expectations, which they hoped to realize quickly. As well, in the late 1960s, rising consumer prices made it imperative for workers to obtain generous wage settlements.

The union rank and file vigorously attacked authority. Militant workers frequently rebelled against their conservative leaders by launching wildcat strikes (illegal work stoppages), some of which paid handsome dividends. A lengthy wildcat strike by Inco workers at Sudbury brought miners the highest wages in North America. Another clash at the Stelco plant in Hamilton, with much violence and destruction of property, enabled steelworkers to obtain very substantial wage increases. During an illegal work stoppage on the railways, one striker explained that the "young guys" were "fearless. They don't give a damn for the company or the government or the union. It's a new generation.… We're our own boss now."

Many unionized workers were women. In contrast with the 1950s, when women often hesitated in their resistance to discriminatory practices in the workplace, they now began to wage "a more concerted and organized campaign for gender equality." In this regard, their actions became part of the emerging women's rights movement in the wider society. Results came slowly. In 1968, women employees of General Motors with six years' seniority were being laid off while the company continued to hire new men. One woman vented her frustration with a poem in the newspaper of the local United Auto Workers to which she belonged:

> I read that whole darn paper and never make the grade;
>
> Do they just count the females when union dues are paid?
>
> We wait on recognition and it better show up soon,
>
> I feel more isolated than the men that walked the Moon.
>
> So all you fancy journalists, here's one thing to remember:
>
> I'm classed as just a female, but I'm still a union member.[5]

Workers, often women, in the rapidly growing public sector—teachers, hospital workers, civil servants, municipal employees, and others—also sought to improve salaries and working conditions. They successfully lobbied governments to place them on an equal footing with workers in the private sector, to recognize their right to form unions and, in many cases, to strike. Public-sector unions soon became the largest in Canada and among the most militant. Lengthy work stoppages in the post office, for example, beginning with the postal workers' illegal walkout in 1965, became notorious.

Unlike the American-controlled "international" unions to which many private-sector workers belonged, public-sector unions were entirely Canadian. Indeed, in the climate of rising nationalism that characterized the 1960s and 1970s, some Canadian sections of international unions withdrew and formed their own Canadian unions.

A Cultural Renaissance

Both English-language and French-language cultural expression underwent a transformation in the 1960s. Universal education increased the potential market for cultural products, and higher disposable incomes and more leisure time made it possible for people to enjoy them. Federal and provincial grant agencies gave considerable assistance to cultural endeavours, funding both organizations and individual artists. The Canada Council, for example, helped to finance the activities of the Montreal and Toronto symphony orchestras, several ballet companies, the Stratford Shakespearean Festival, and the Shaw Festival at Niagara-on-the-Lake. Most provinces also invested substantially in libraries, museums, theatres, and concert halls.

Literature

The 1960s saw the rapid growth of a vibrant and diverse literature in both English and French, due in part to Canada Council grants and other federal and provincial government support programs. By 1970, most universities in English-speaking Canada offered courses in Canadian literature in English, as did Quebec universities in French-Canadian literature. New literary periodicals such as *Canadian Literature* and *Liberté* were established to publish and critique Canadian writing. Several new publishing houses also appeared.

Many of the most popular writers of the decade were women. Margaret Laurence, who spent her early life in Neepawa, Manitoba, and then lived in Africa and England for many years, wrote *The Stone Angel* and *A Jest of God*. Both these novels were set in the fictitious town of Manawaka, which bore a close resemblance to Neepawa. Alice Munro, in some of her short stories set in Ontario's Huron County, examined the difficulties experienced by an adolescent girl in coming to terms with her family and with life in a small town. Margaret Atwood, who began her literary career as a poet, in 1966, with the publication of *The Circle Game*, published her first novel, *The Edible Woman*, in 1969, on the theme of women's alienation in a modern consumer society.

A sense of place and of identity was important for many novelists. Ernest Buckler situated his *Ox Bells and Fireflies* in Nova Scotia. Robert Kroetsch, who grew up in rural Alberta, published an "Out West" series of novels before moving mainly into poetry. Rudy Wiebe, a Mennonite from the prairies, set out to explore the tensions between pacifism and war in *Peace Shall Destroy Many*.

The revolution in poetry brought youth to the fore. Indeed, a volume on Canada's fifteen most outstanding poets in 1970 featured only three who were well known before 1960. Irving Layton, a Romanian Jew whose family settled in an impoverished immigrant district in Montreal, filled his poems with his early impressions and experiences. His provocative views on Israel, anti-Semitism, and other subjects attracted much attention. Al Purdy chronicled the geographical and historical complexities of Canada in such volumes as *The Cariboo Horses*, which he wrote after a trip to Baffin Island. Milton Acorn's populist poetry featured left-wing causes popular in this era. In 1964, Acorn helped found the underground magazine *Georgia Straight* in Vancouver. Leonard Cohen of Montreal was also a popular success, both as a poet and as a singer and songwriter. Raymond Souster continued to influence the direction of Canadian poetry by editing the volumes of many poets and by organizing public readings. A number of Canadian poets, including Souster, gave readings at the Bohemian Embassy, a Toronto coffee house established in 1960. (Bell Canada, not yet "hip," listed this establishment in its yellow pages under the general heading "Embassies and consulates.")

Some Quebec authors found their inspiration in the turbulent nationalism of the Quiet Revolution. Poet Fernand Ouellette dwelt upon the alienation and oppression of the Québécois in *Le Soleil sous la mort*, while Jacques Ferron's short stories dealt with the problems of maintaining Quebec's cultural identity. Hubert Aquin wrote *Prochain épisode* while being held in a Montreal psychiatric clinic pending trial on a weapons charge; the novel's narrator, also confined to a psychiatric hospital, awaits trial on charges related to his underground activities as a revolutionary separatist.

Nationalism formed only part of the general theme of liberation being experienced in Quebec during these years. Many novelists examined the emancipation of the person in relation to society. *Une saison dans la vie d'Emmanuel*, which presented a sombre portrait of a tyrannical Quebec family, brought novelist Marie-Claire Blais a wide international audience. Feminist concerns permeated Françoise Loranger's *Encore cinq minutes*, while themes of war, sexual repression, and exploitation of the weak were central to Roch Carrier's highly acclaimed *La guerre, yes sir!*

A deep concern for Aboriginal rights inspired much of the work of Quebec novelist Yves Thériault. In his *Ashini*, the hero, a Montagnais or Innu, commits suicide in the hope that his death will awaken his people from their apathy and bring them to claim their ancestral lands. Playwrights Marcel Dubé and Michel Tremblay made major contributions to French-language theatre; Tremblay's *Les belles-soeurs* violated traditional codes by being the first play to be written entirely in *joual*, or French working-class slang.

Filmmaking

Canada's film industry in both languages underwent substantial development in the 1960s. Through its diverse activities, the National Film Board made both French- and English-speaking Canadians more conscious of their history and culture. In English, producers worked mainly on documentaries. *Memorandum*, an hour-long documentary on Hitler's "Final Solution" to the "Jewish question," helped build an enviable reputation for producer Donald Brittain, who had previously directed *Fields of Sacrifice*, a memorial to Canadians killed in action during World War II. Brittain filmed it on battlefields from Hong Kong to Sicily. Canada's centennial year, 1967, saw other noteworthy productions, including *Labyrinth*, which used the Greek myth of Theseus, who entered a labyrinth to find and kill the Minotaur, to symbolize the universality of a person's journey throughout the world. The lavish film, seen by 1.3 million people at Expo 67 in Montreal, attracted much positive press reaction internationally.

French-language filmmakers experimented with subjects linked to French Canada's social ferment. Denys Arcand's *On est au coton* was a film about the textile industry and workers' fears of unemployment because of factory closures. Pierre Perrault's *L'Acadie! L'Acadie!* featured the struggle by Acadian students at the Université de Moncton for the recognition of language rights. Quebec filmmakers also set about making what one magazine called "maple leaf porno." Denis Héroux produced *Valérie* in 1969, asserting the need to "undress the Quebec female." One-third of Quebec's population went to the movies in 1970 to see Claude Fournier's *Deux femmes en or*, a similar production.

Politics in the Age of Mass Media

Canada's political life in the 1960s also felt the winds of change. Since Confederation, Canadian politics tended to focus increasingly on personalities. Political scientists have attempted to explain this tendency by suggesting that the major political parties generally differ little on questions of basic principle and that "long-standing and well-understood ideological differences do not emerge during campaigns."[6] Parties have offered different leaders, making leadership either a significant asset or a liability for them.

The advent of television in the 1950s undoubtedly increased this focus on the leader. Television became a rapid and effective means of communicating information. Through the news and televised events such as leadership conventions and election campaign debates, it brought politicians into the homes of Canadians. At the same time, as political scientist Frederick J. Fletcher has pointed out, television has inhibited the thoughtful exposition of policies and promoted "simple and flashy promises and one-line put-downs of the opposition."[7] The media have stressed conflict and confrontation in their coverage, emphasizing sensational and exciting occurrences. Prime Minister Lester Pearson once complained that "when we do discuss policies seriously … reporters do not even appear to listen, until we say something controversial or personal, charged with what they regard as news value." In spite of television's particular deficiencies, it began to play a major role in moulding the images—favourable and unfavourable—of politicians.

Politics in Disarray

Federal politics in the early 1960s promoted cynicism among many voters. The country faced grave problems with, at the beginning of the decade, more Canadians out of work than at any time since the Great Depression. Canada also incurred large deficits in foreign trade. The increasing cost of living provoked costly demands from some unions. Relations with the provinces were often difficult, while growing discord also characterized ties with the United States. Yet neither Progressive Conservative leader John Diefenbaker nor Liberal leader Lester B. Pearson appeared to have a vision or long-term plan about what could be done.

Four times these two knights in tarnished armour faced each other on the electoral battlefield; only at the first encounter, in 1958, were they greatly mismatched. In 1962, 1963, and again in 1965, neither won enough seats in the House of Commons to form a majority government. Each made numerous—and costly—promises in attempts to rally more voter support. Some of their techniques, borrowed from Madison Avenue, elicited mockery and disdain. The Liberals, for example, published colouring books portraying Diefenbaker riding backwards on a rocking horse. They also formed a "truth squad" to pursue the Conservatives relentlessly across the country to make sure they told the truth. (The squad lasted three days.) Once elected, Canada's parliamentarians devoted themselves to discussing a seemingly endless succession of alleged scandals. In his memoirs, Pearson gave the title "Politics in Disrepute" to a chapter on the years 1964 and 1965.

John Diefenbaker looks on, as Lester Pearson attempts to uncoil the cord of a translation earpiece. Canada's two French-speaking prime ministers before this period, Wilfrid Laurier and Louis St. Laurent, were both fluently bilingual. After the 1960s, it became much more important for federal anglophone politicians to be able to speak French.

Source: John McNeill.

The Diefenbaker Government (1957–63)

The decade of the 1960s opened with the Progressive Conservatives led by John Diefenbaker in office in Ottawa. Diefenbaker had first come to power in 1957 with a minority government; then, in elections called in 1958, he won a landslide victory. At first, "Dief the Chief" benefited from a remarkably positive image. Different from many previous Conservative leaders in that he was not closely linked to Toronto's financial establishment, Diefenbaker promised to champion the rights of ordinary Canadians. He was also a fiery orator, able to captivate audiences. Yet by 1960, he had acquired a very negative image. In elections held in 1962, he barely managed to retain power with a minority government. A year later the Diefenbaker government was defeated and the Conservatives returned to the opposition benches.

Diefenbaker's Economic Policies

To some extent, the controversial prime minister became a victim of circumstances. After 22 years in opposition, the Conservatives had no experience with the art of governing, nor could they count on the support of many Ottawa bureaucrats whose loyalties lay with the Liberal party. The severe recession of 1960–61, Canada's most serious since the Great Depression of the 1930s, was not Diefenbaker's fault any more than the Great Depression had been R.B. Bennett's, but sharply rising unemployment posed serious challenges for the government, compromised its ability to launch new development policies, and undermined Diefenbaker's popularity. Industry encountered increased difficulty in selling goods to foreign markets, and laid off workers. Worldwide overproduction and declining prices of agricultural products hit Prairie farmers particularly hard.

Diefenbaker finally found markets—in the People's Republic of China, the Soviet Union, and eastern Europe—for most of Canada's surplus grain. Farm income on the Prairies rose significantly, and Conservative popularity in that region remained strong. The Diefenbaker government's attempts to reduce unemployment were less successful. In particular, it raised tariffs and increased spending in the hope of stimulating the economy. Higher tariffs displeased consumers who now found it more expensive to buy American-made goods, while the budget deficits brought on by "irresponsible" spending irked the business and financial community. The minister of finance even had to resort to austerity measures and to arrange emergency credits with the International Monetary Fund.

Even more controversially, in 1962, shortly after announcing why it was inappropriate to peg the Canadian dollar, the government fixed it at a relatively low (for that era) 92.5 cents (U.S.). It hoped that the measure would reduce Canada's trade deficit with the United States. The decision provoked both outright condemnation by importers and enthusiastic approval by exporters. The Liberals protested noisily that devaluation would mean higher prices for consumers. They printed thousands of so-called "Diefenbucks"—92.5-cent dollars adorned with the prime minister's likeness—which they used effectively during the election campaign of June 1962. The dollar's devaluation did indeed stimulate exports, but Canada's balance of payments with the United States remained negative as Canadian subsidiaries of American companies sent back dividends to the United States and Canadian visitors spent heavily there.

Diefenbaker's critics charged him with economic mismanagement as the Canadian economy weakened after 1960. Although Atlantic and western Canada continued to endorse the Conservatives, Ontario and Quebec, and especially the cities, opposed him. By 1962, even traditionally Conservative newspapers such as the Toronto *Globe and Mail* and the Montreal *Gazette*, evoking the business community's loss of confidence in Diefenbaker, were calling for a Liberal government to "get us out of the abyss." Indeed, Diefenbaker lost his majority in Parliament that year. In the next election, in 1963, he lost power to the Liberals, led by Lester B. Pearson. As former Prime Minister Louis St. Laurent's Secretary of State for External Affairs and winner of the prestigious Nobel Peace Prize in 1957, Pearson assuredly had experience in foreign policy and international acclaim. He was less familiar with domestic issues. Moreover he lacked charisma and had difficulty enthusing voters and generating confidence.

Strained Canadian–American Relations

Diefenbaker worried about Canada's increasing economic dependence upon the United States but he lacked the power or the will to effect fundamental changes in economic relationships. Although he promised to divert trade from the United States to Great Britain, he failed to recognize Britain's need to boost trade links with Europe and thus to distance itself from the Commonwealth. Indeed the renewal in 1959 of Canada's defence production treaty with the United States had the effect of stimulating trade, especially in arms, with that country. And when the United States imposed controls on oil imports in support of domestic producers, Canada obtained an exemption from Washington and Albertan oil continued to flow south. Diefenbaker also hoped to reduce American investment in Canada by applying a tax on interest, dividends, and profits sent to nonresidents. In practice, the measure had little effect.

Issues linked to continental defence embittered relations with the United States. Shortly after the 1957 election, Diefenbaker had personally committed Canada to the North American Air Defence Command (NORAD), the continental air-defence alliance headed by an American Air Force general. Then, in 1962–63, in a reversal of his original position, the prime minister refused to accept the nuclear warheads that the Americans wanted installed in their anti-aircraft missiles on Canadian soil. Moreover, he intensely disliked President John F. Kennedy, a feeling the American president reciprocated. Lawrence Martin, at the time *The Globe and Mail*'s Washington correspondent, wrote that Canadian–American relations were plunged into what was, up until then, their "worst state of disrepair in the century."[8]

In these years of renascent Canadian nationalism, Canadians began to agonize over the kind of relationship they wanted with their southern neighbour. Diefenbaker's attempts to reorient Canadian policy reflected the will of part of the electorate, but they also provoked the disgruntlement of many other Canadians, including several of his own cabinet ministers. In addition, as historians John Herd Thompson and Stephen Randall point out, Canadian and American priorities moved increasingly apart. While the United States was determined to confront the Soviet threat and was turning into a warfare state, Canada in the 1960s gave greater priority to advancing the welfare state.[9]

The Conservatives and Quebec

In part, Diefenbaker's downfall arose from the Conservatives' weak basis of support, notably in Quebec, where the party's organization had long been deficient. Diefenbaker's attempts at speaking French were often the subject of ridicule. In particular, his love of the British monarchy; his ferocious loyalty, during the flag debate of 1964, to the Canadian ensign, with the Union Jack in its corner, that served at the time as Canada's unofficial flag; and his championing of "unhyphenated" Canadianism alienated French-speaking Canadians. Moreover, Diefenbaker understood little of Quebec's awakening in the early 1960s. Indeed, Conservatives would struggle unsuccessfully for two decades to deal with the complex "Quebec question." They also quickly found that they could not easily reconcile the interests of urban and rural voters, or those of central Canadians and Canadians living in other provinces.

The government also seemed disorganized and rife with dissension, particularly regarding economic issues and relations with the United States. Diefenbaker complained that enemies from within were plotting to "deliver up my head on a silver platter." Most to blame, in journalist Peter Newman's opinion, was Diefenbaker himself, a "renegade in power" who had conquered a generation and brought only disillusionment.[10]

Third Parties, Right and Left

The rapid decline of federal Conservative strength in Quebec coincided with the rise of a third party in that province. Since the 1930s, Social Credit had remained a fringe group in Quebec. Then, in the 1962 federal election, to the surprise and even stupefaction of most observers, it won one-quarter of the popular vote and 26 seats—one-third of the province's total.

Social Credit's success in the election may be explained partly by Quebeckers' obvious desire for change. A vote for the créditistes was a way of striking back against the establishment. Leader Réal Caouette, an automobile salesman from Rouyn, in northern Quebec, who had joined Social Credit in 1939, carried his crusade through rural and small-town Quebec. He promised a national dividend to all citizens to raise consumers' buying power. He pledged help for the aged, the unemployed, and large families. Most of all he assured voters that they had nothing to lose by trying Social Credit. The fiery orator delivered the same message to weekly television audiences. In addition, party members carried out formidable organizational work, often in the kitchens of ordinary citizens, far from the prying eyes of curious journalists.[11]

Social Credit's success had a considerable impact on federal Liberal fortunes. It seriously reduced the party's strength in Quebec, probably costing it the election in 1962 while ensuring that it could form only a minority government in 1963 and again in 1965.

Less spectacular was the reconstitution of the national CCF. After its very poor showing in the federal election of 1958, the CCF decided to cooperate with the Canadian Labour Congress and with left-wing organizations to form a broad-based movement for social reform. In 1961 these groups launched the New Democratic Party (NDP), choosing Tommy Douglas, then premier of Saskatchewan, as leader. The party program called for jobs, health insurance, free education, and, in a break with the CCF's past tendency to favour a powerful central government, a policy of "cooperative federalism." Financial and organizational difficulties quickly put an end to the euphoria of the new party's first moments. As well, electoral results during the 1960s at both the federal and provincial levels proved disappointing. In particular, even most union members failed to support the NDP, which in turn feared becoming too closely identified with unions. Most workers now saw the Liberal party as the party of social welfare and reform.

The Pearson Years (1963–68)

As the Pearson government took office in 1963, economic recovery seemed well under way. Unemployment dropped to about 5 percent as sales increased and companies began hiring more employees. Even the usually despondent *Globe and Mail* expressed optimism: "Where gloom and doom about the future of Canada has been the governing mood in recent years, there is now buoyancy and optimism." By 1966, however, a new, worrisome trend became evident: prices were moving up more quickly.

Canadians battled inflation in various ways. Angry shoppers boycotted supermarkets, accusing them of price gouging. The members of strong unions in key sectors of the economy, such as transportation, sought massive pay increases. Seaway workers demanded a 35 percent raise over two years and obtained 30 percent. Railway workers struck and won 24 percent spread over three years. Air Canada's machinists went out in support of their demand for 20 percent in one year. These large increases added to inflationary pressures. In 1967, while inflation showed no signs of abating, the economy slowed down noticeably. Economists coined a new word—*stagflation*—to describe the phenomenon of inflation at a time of slow economic growth. First-year economics textbooks insisted that this combination could not occur—but it did, in Canada and throughout much of the world.

Liberal Economic Policies

The Liberals proved incapable of controlling inflation. To little avail, the government urged companies to restrain price increases. It also raised some taxes in an effort to dampen consumer demand. The Conservative opposition's financial critic complained, boldly comparing the Liberal minibudget to then-fashionable miniskirts: "Taxes are getting higher and higher and covering less and less." Most Canadians strongly disagreed with the economists' explanation that inflation was caused by the fact that consumers had too much money to spend.

During the Pearson years, Canadian–American trade relations intensified. The Automotive Products Agreement, signed in 1965, provided for free trade among the manufacturers; Canadian drivers could not, however, bring automobiles back duty-free from the United States. Most economists agree that the "Auto Pact," accompanied by a lower Canadian dollar, brought increased prosperity to southern Ontario, where all of Canada's automobile industry and most of its automotive parts industry are concentrated. Manufacturers now rationalized their production. Canadian plants specialized in producing relatively few models.

Canadians passionately debated the issue of American ownership of Canadian industries in the 1960s. Even when the supposedly pro-American Liberals returned to power in 1963, the problem of foreign investment refused to go away. Walter Gordon, the Liberal finance minister, announced a tax on takeovers of Canadian firms by foreigners, but the ensuing protests from the United States government as well as from Canadian business leaders forced him to retract the proposal. Undaunted, Gordon published in 1966 *A Choice for Canada*, in which he argued that the country would have to choose between political and economic independence or colonial status in the American empire. He also set up a task force on the structure of Canadian industry, chaired by University of Toronto economist Mel Watkins, to study "the significance—both political and economic—of foreign investment."

Prime Minister Lester B. Pearson visits President John F. Kennedy, spring 1963.

Source: Library and Archives Canada/C-90482.

At this time, however, the Liberal government contained very few economic nationalists. Mitchell Sharp, named minister of finance in 1965, did not even want to publish the task force report, while trade and commerce minister Robert Winters assured a San Francisco audience that "Canada welcomes foreign capital regardless of doubt-provoking remarks to the contrary from time to time." Canadians had not yet reached a consensus on the issue.

The Welfare State

The Liberals' management of the economy—critics preferred to speak of "mismanagement"—help explain public dissatisfaction with the government. Still, in other areas, Parliament adopted important and popular legislation in this period. The new laws contributed greatly to entrenching the Canadian welfare state by which Canadians acquired new rights for which all residents, through the state, now became collectively responsible. The Diefenbaker government had already increased old-age pensions; now Ottawa moved to improve its social-security programs for the poor. The year 1966 saw the adoption of the Canada Assistance Act, a coordination of largely existing provincial measures designed to aid persons who were unable to work or were ineligible for unemployment insurance. Although the Pearson government turned down proposals by reformers to establish a national guaranteed income for all Canadians, not only for financial reasons but also because it feared that such a program would reduce incentives to work, it did make low-income pensioners eligible for a guaranteed income supplement.

The most important programs launched by the Liberals concerned pensions and medical care. In 1965, Ottawa established the Canada Pension Plan, a compulsory and completely portable contributory plan paid for by workers and employers. Negotiations with the provinces proved arduous: indeed Quebec chose to set up its own provincial plan, respecting the principles laid down by the federal government; money deposited in the fund was then reinvested.

Canadians increasingly called for the state to provide universal medical care. The Liberals had introduced hospital insurance in 1957 and, by 1961, the Diefenbaker government helped finance provincial plans across Canada. In regard to insuring the costs of medical services, Saskatchewan led the way by establishing a health-insurance plan in 1962. Strongly opposed to the plan, doctors staged a three-week strike before finally capitulating. Debate over constitutional issues and lack of agreement within the federal government slowed action on a Canada-wide program. Only in 1968 did Ottawa enact into law the National Health Insurance Program, also known as Medicare—a national health scheme that provided for financial contributions to provincial plans all of which had to be universal, comprehensive, portable, and publicly administered. Social and health programs proved costly: health expenses alone nearly doubled from $3.3 billion in 1965 to $6 billion in 1970. Ottawa registered what would be its last budgetary surplus for nearly 30 years in 1969–70, a year after Pearson's departure from office.

Pearson's Legacy

In addition to his government's landmark social and health legislation, Lester B. Pearson attempted to find solutions to other problems. He sought to conciliate the provinces and initiated a series of federal–provincial conferences on the Canadian Constitution. In answer to French Canadians' claims for linguistic equality, he set up the Royal Commission on Bilingualism and Biculturalism to study the issue and make recommendations. Also, after weeks of debate in the House of Commons, the Pearson government gave Canadians a national flag.

Pearson's numerous critics reproached the Liberal prime minister for his failure to give the country firm and sure leadership (in the direction they wished). Business considered his election promises irresponsibly costly and blamed him for surrendering too easily to the unions. Labour portrayed itself as the victim, not the cause, of inflation. Canadian nationalists accused him of doing little to counter the Americanization of Canada. In cultural matters, for example, legislation designed to assist Canadian magazines contained important exemptions for the two biggest American magazines in Canada, *Time* and *Reader's Digest*. To defend Canada, Pearson revised his earlier position and authorized nuclear warheads for American missiles in the country. Canadians hotly debated the issue of American ownership of the Canadian economy, but the Pearson government did little to control American investment. Although finance minister Walter Gordon did include proposals to limit foreign investment in his budget in 1963, he had to withdraw them.

Quebec nationalists thought that Pearson was resisting their province's legitimate demands, while strong centralists declared that his concessions to Quebec and the other provinces were balkanizing the country and whetting the appetites of separatists. Monarchists censured him for tolerating creeping republicanism, while French Canadians and new Canadians favoured a loosening of Canada's ties with the British crown. Unhappy residents of the Atlantic provinces thought he was doing little to alleviate regional disparities, and westerners judged him ill attuned to their region's interests. In sum, Pearson endeared himself to virtually none of the regions or major interest groups.

Perhaps Pearson and his Liberal administration should not have been expected to build a consensus on the major questions of the day when Canadians themselves disagreed so strongly on the answers. The 1960s were a time of increasing polarization. In that climate, Pearson manoeuvred with some skill. The policy of "cooperative federalism," by which Ottawa showed greater sensitivity to provincial concerns, was perhaps the best that could be hoped for in a climate of confrontation between Ottawa and the provinces, particularly Quebec. In regard to French–English relations, the establishment of a royal commission, though hardly a solution, appeared a logical step to take. As for the economy and the growing problem of inflation, no obvious long-term solutions existed. Indeed the Canadian government did not have the power to control many of the root causes of inflation, such as the sharp rises in the cost of many products in international markets as well as the huge expenditures associated with the American war in Vietnam. Also, even though the Pearson government did have more than its share of scandals, the prime minister's own conduct remained above suspicion.

Finally, concerning Canada's relations with the United States, Canadians first had to debate options before they could make decisions. Growing American military involvement in Vietnam certainly poisoned relations between the North American neighbours. Rapidly changing circumstances made debate difficult.

Canada's own involvement in the Vietnamese conflict dated from 1954 when, after war in then French Indochina resulted in the division of Vietnam into the Communist North and the pro-Western South, Canada participated in a tripartite commission to supervise the truce. Then, as the Communist presence within South Vietnam intensified, the United States exerted greater pressure on Canada to defend western and American interests on the commission. As North Vietnam continued its incursions, the United States began to bombard North Vietnam and to boost substantially its military presence in the South. Public opposition to the war mounted in Canada (and in the United States). Pearson then made a speech in Philadelphia in April 1965 urging the United States to stop bombing North Vietnam. At a meeting with Pearson immediately afterwards, a furious President Lyndon B. Johnson supposedly seized Pearson by the shirt and told him in earthy language what he thought of this speech delivered in Johnson's own "backyard." As the war escalated, so did Canadian criticism of American actions in Vietnam, but strong domestic opposition to the war now preoccupied the Johnson government far more than foreign criticism.

A Changing Economy

In addition to the ills of unemployment and inflation that Canadians urged their governments to remedy, the country's economy underwent major structural changes during the 1960s. It entered what might be termed a postindustrial era, in which services, such as those provided by governments, schools, hospitals, the communications industry, retail trade, and financial institutions, constituted the largest sector of employment. Manufacturing placed second. Primary industries, including agriculture, came last—a complete reversal of the Canada of 1867.

Such sectors as transportation and communications developed spectacularly as a result of new technologies. Often they had difficulty finding the highly trained personnel they needed. In several other sectors, workers faced painful adjustments in the wake of job losses. Though employees in traditional "soft" industries such as footwear and textiles, hard hit by lost markets and cheap imports, suffered particularly, other industries also faced problems. Shipbuilders, for example, laid off thousands of workers as the federal government reduced subsidies and Canadian shipyards remained internationally uncompetitive.

Declining prices for their products and fierce competition from abroad led Canada's important natural-resource industries to modernize in order to reduce costs. Technological change and market forces led to new challenges in agriculture. Large farms, with the equipment necessary to work more land and boost yields, became the norm. Small farmers lacked the means to make the necessary adjustments. In eastern Canada, for example, as dairies forced farmers to switch from cans to expensive bulk-storage equipment, farmers who kept only a few cows were forced out of business. Many abandoned the land that their families had farmed for generations.

Unequal Growth

Some regions of Canada—southern Ontario and parts of western Canada—prospered during the 1960s. Others, including the Atlantic provinces, much of Quebec, and parts of the Prairies, saw increased unemployment and poverty.

Prosperity in Ontario

The 1950s and 1960s were especially good for Ontario. Demand for a wide variety of goods stimulated industrial expansion, especially in the south. Services—banking, merchandising, education, health, and government—multiplied. The construction industry prospered thanks to strong demand for housing. Governments at all levels invested heavily in building highways and urban expressways. They also promoted urban transit, sponsored electric-power projects, including nuclear-power plants, and completed work on the St. Lawrence Seaway. This intense activity explains why the province's unemployment rate generally stayed below 4 percent from 1945 until 1970. Economist Kenneth Rea calls these the "prosperous years."[12] Rea adds that while the Ontario government might take credit for permitting growth to occur and even, on occasion, stimulating it, the motor pushing Ontario's growth was in fact the private sector.

Western Canada

In the West, the development of natural resources continued apace during the 1960s. Manitoba's government invested heavily in northern development, where it favoured hydroelectric projects, such as the huge installations on the Nelson River, and it attempted to attract private capital through loans and other concessions. Some projects such as the rich Inco mine at Thompson proved successful. Others failed: for instance, the Churchill Forest Industries complex at The Pas, which involved a government loan of $100 million, was halted when the owners disappeared with most of the money. Saskatchewan worked to attract private capital to develop its natural resources including potash and pulp and paper. Alberta's oil production increased when, in 1961, the Diefenbaker government acted to prevent Montreal

On the 56th floor of the Toronto-Dominion Centre, Toronto, April 1966. Constructed from 1963 to 1969, this building was designed by the German-American architect Mies van der Rohe, and reflected the International style of architecture. Skyscrapers like this one came to dominate cityscapes from the 1960s onward.

Source: *The Globe and Mail*/66104-38. Reprinted with permission from The Globe and Mail.

refineries, using less expensive crude oil from Venezuela, from entering the Ontario market. This policy forced Ontario to buy slightly more costly oil from the West.

In British Columbia, a conservative Social Credit government assisted large corporations in consolidating their control of the resource sector by offering them tax concessions, low stumpage rates for timber, and cheap hydroelectricity. It improved highway, maritime, and rail transportation. It extended, at heavy cost, the Pacific Great Eastern Railway, linking the northern interior to the rest of the province. It nationalized the giant B.C. Electric Company and undertook hydro-electric projects. One of these, the gigantic Peace River Dam, built across the Rocky Mountain Trench, created Williston Lake, the province's largest body of water. Bennett also successfully battled with the federal government over the terms of the Columbia River Treaty signed between Canada and the United States in 1961. The premier wanted to sell British Columbia's power allotment from the Columbia dams to the United States, while Ottawa opposed the sale.

The Atlantic Provinces

Economic growth was slow in the Atlantic region; indeed, during the period 1951–71, 15 percent of Atlantic Canada's inhabitants left home in search of work elsewhere. In Prince Edward Island, for example, the traditional "island way of life" increasingly became a myth as many small farmers, unable to compete because of low potato prices, abandoned farming.

Ottawa now paid heed to the complaints of the inhabitants of the Atlantic provinces, who saw themselves as the major victims of Canada's regional disparities. In 1962, John Diefenbaker's Progressive Conservative government set up the Atlantic Development Board to fund projects and improve the region's infrastructure. (Political and patronage considerations often determined its choices.) This initiative, together with equalization grants and other subsidies, facilitated the creation of jobs, albeit often temporary ones, and ensured that the area could offer its citizens services reasonably similar to those provided by wealthier provinces. Then, in 1969, the newly established federal Department of Regional Economic Expansion (DREE) began to offer incentives to encourage companies to locate in less-favoured areas of the country, such as the Atlantic provinces. The department spent money on highway construction, schools, and municipal services, and also attracted some new industry. R. Harley McGee, a student of regional development, saw DREE as "the best approach to both regional development policy and its implementation."[13]

Provincial governments also sought to stimulate economic growth. Nova Scotia's Conservative government created Industrial Estates Limited, with well-known businessman Frank Sobey as its first president, to invest in local enterprises; serious losses, however, notably in stereo equipment and heavy water, followed the investment company's initial successes. For its part, New Brunswick's Liberal government led by Louis Robichaud, the first elected Acadian premier, intervened actively in resource development. When pulp and paper companies failed to use Crown lands they held under long-term lease, the government cancelled their licences and awarded them to other companies. When an American mining company reduced operations in its lead and zinc mine near Bathurst, Robichaud engineered a buyout by Canadian investors, including native son K.C. Irving, who set about building a huge smelter complex.

The Irving family's business interests included 3000 gas stations, trucking and bus lines, shipbuilding, huge forest reserves, paper and saw mills, radio and television stations, and the province's English-language newspapers; these companies employed roughly 25 000 people in New Brunswick. Irving's biographer claimed that "surely no individual in any single Canadian province … ever held so much raw economic power."[14]

Irving's local roots and power gave him considerable bargaining clout with the provincial government, which he exploited to win concessions. Historian James Kenny concludes that

New Brunswick may have escaped dependence on foreign capital, but with Irving it entered into a "new and perhaps more dependent relationship."[15] Irving hired his own companies to perform the construction work on the smelter complex, but delays and ballooning costs finally brought the provincial government to allow a takeover by Noranda. Although the value of the mineral industry increased spectacularly in the 1960s, the industry did not have the desired transforming effects on provincial and local economies.

The Robichaud government also created the Equal Opportunity Program, aimed at improving the lot of the province's poorer citizens, often French-speaking Acadians who lived in rural areas in the north and east; in particular, the government greatly expanded health, social, and educational services. These measures generated fierce opposition among anglophones in the south, who regarded them as proof of a costly Liberal plot to "rob Peter to pay Pierre." A cartoon in one of K.C. Irving's newspapers pictured a despotic Robichaud as a modern Louis XIV, with wild eyes, crown askew, and hand clutching a sword threatening his foes. In spite of opposition from English-speakers, the Robichaud government then moved to adopt the Official Languages Act, which aimed, over time, to give greater linguistic equality to the province's francophones.

New Brunswick Premier Louis Robichaud, the province's first elected Acadian premier. His administration in the 1960s built many hospitals, schools, and public buildings.

Source: Provincial Archives of New Brunswick/P57-15.

Newfoundland and Labrador

After Newfoundland entered Confederation in 1949, the federal government failed to take the necessary steps to restructure the fishing industry, especially the inshore fishery. What Ottawa did do, in the relatively prosperous 1950s, was to extend unemployment insurance coverage to seasonal fishers, a measure that helped increase the number of fishers at a time when the continued health of the industry necessitated significant downsizing.

Joey Smallwood, premier from 1949 until 1972, hoped to carry out an industrial revolution to create thousands of new jobs, stem emigration, and drag the province "kicking and screaming into the twentieth century." He encouraged foreign investment and sponsored projects to develop the province's natural resources, such as iron and pulpwood, as well as Labrador's vast hydroelectric potential at Churchill Falls. There were some successes, but many costly failures.

A HISTORICAL PORTRAIT

Newfoundland Fishers Through Art and Song

Culture transmits, through its diverse forms, the experiences that mark human life. In a plan to fight the poverty rife in Newfoundland's outports, the Smallwood government, mainly during the 1960s, had 250 smaller communities totally evacuated in household resettlement programs involving nearly 30 000 people. Many inhabitants were moved against their will.

Newfoundland artist David Blackwood memorialized the experience in his paintings. One work, titled *Resettlement*, showed an outport family in a boat piled high with their belongings, heading out to sea toward an unknown destination. The painting captured the profound despair of people who had lost all control over their own destiny. Artist Gerry Squires also did several works on the same theme. He commented on one of them, *The House Where Nobody Lives*, which showed one of the thousands of abandoned dwellings: "I still see the fear and the tears when people realized they could never come back."

The experience of relocation was also transmitted through songs that revealed the deep sadness of people at being separated from traditional livelihoods and familiar surroundings:

> No more we'll watch the caplin as they wash upon the sand,
>
> The little fish they used for bait, to fertilize their land;
>
> No more they'll watch their gardens grow or their meadows full of hay,

> Or walk the roads in their working clothes in the good old-fashioned way.[1]

The new communities into which outport residents were transplanted did not offer what had been promised. Songs such as this one revealed the bitterness and frustration of those who had been uprooted and transplanted:

> To a place called Placentia, some of them went
>
> And in finding their new homes their allowances spent
>
> So for jobs they went looking, but they looked all in vain
>
> For the roof had caved in on the Government Game.
>
> It's surely a sad sight, their moving around
>
> Wishing they still lived near the cod-fishing ground
>
> But there's no going back now, there's nothing to gain
>
> Now that they've played in the Government Game.[2]

---

1 Reproduced with permission of Ernie Wilson. © Ernie Wilson.

2 Reproduced with permission of Pat Byrne and Al Pittman. © Pat Byrne and Al Pittman.

Environmental Concerns

Although most Canadians still took a healthy environment for granted in the 1960s, an increasingly vocal minority did begin to realize that industrial development often had deleterious effects upon the physical environment. Critics pointed to pulp and paper companies and smelters in particular as major polluters of the nation's air and water. They urged governments to force such companies to bear some of the huge costs of cleaning up the production process. In Ontario, environmentalists focused their attention on water quality in heavily industrialized areas of the province. The *Hamilton Spectator* complained in 1962: "Sewage, detergents, sludges, chemicals, oil … they all pour into the harbour." Detergent manufacturers vied with each other to create the longest-lasting suds for washing machines and dishwashers. These suds eventually piled up along the shores of lakes and rivers. Finally, in the face of public outcry, the industry regulated itself and developed more biodegradable detergents.

Later, in the 1960s, algae proliferated in southern Ontario's waters, depleting oxygen levels and killing multitudes of fish. The cause was phosphates, again from detergents. At the University of Toronto, antipollution campaigners founded Pollution Probe, staging such events as a mock funeral for Toronto's "dead" Don River. After 1970, governments agreed to take steps to cut phosphate use dramatically in an effort to improve water quality.

Beginning of the Trudeau Era

Many Canadians viewed the Diefenbaker–Pearson years as the culminating point of a bygone and increasingly repugnant brand of politics. Politicians appeared to make countless promises, designed to buy voter support with taxpayers' own money. In this costly contest, each leader tried to outdo the adversary. The public longed for a new style, a new type of leadership, an imaginative and refreshing approach to the complex issues of the day. In 1968, many believed that they had found all this in Pierre Elliott Trudeau.

It was not apparent who might succeed Pearson when the Liberal leader announced his resignation in late 1967. Claude Ryan of *Le Devoir* wrote that the Liberal party was in need of as profound a transformation as the American Democratic party had undergone with Kennedy. A number of intellectuals from central Canada actively promoted Trudeau's candidacy. Trudeau, as justice minister, attracted much attention at the constitutional conference in early 1968, where he jousted with Premier Daniel Johnson of Quebec over the role of the federal government.

Trudeau's Background

Trudeau had been elected for the first time in 1965, when Pearson had convinced him, along with labour leader Jean Marchand and journalist Gérard Pelletier, to enter the House of Commons to help renew Quebec's presence in Ottawa. Prior to that period, Trudeau had generally favoured the NDP and its predecessor, the CCF. During the Duplessis years, Trudeau had been a bitter critic of the Union Nationale regime and, with Pelletier, had established a small-circulation magazine called *Cité libre* to give a voice to liberal-minded Quebeckers. He had also studied at Harvard and the London School of Economics, and he had been a globetrotter. But was he the leader the Liberals needed? Quebec nationalists had no liking for this intellectual who incessantly stigmatized separatism. Business did not have confidence in a candidate who lacked experience in the corporate world; indeed, the business community had its own candidate at the 1968 leadership convention—Robert Winters, one of St. Laurent's appointees to the federal cabinet.

Nevertheless, Trudeau's style and background intrigued delegates at the Ottawa leadership convention. His image was of a wealthy bachelor surrounded by beautiful women. He was athletic, drove a Mercedes-Benz sports car, and often dressed flamboyantly. As *The Globe and Mail* put it: "He is the man we all would like to be: charming, rich, talented, successful." This image was certainly at the basis of the wave of "Trudeaumania" that arose during the Liberal leadership race and reached full height during the June 1968 federal election, which the Liberals won easily.

Trudeau's Program

Trudeau's program differed from both Pearson's and Diefenbaker's. In the 1968 election campaign, he made few specific promises designed to buy blocks of voters with their own money. Rather, he expressed a number of general priorities. He attempted to define the "just society" that

The election of Pierre Elliott Trudeau as Liberal Party leader, spring 1968.

Source: © Library and Archives Canada. Reproduced with the permission of Library and Archives Canada. Library and Archives Canada/Credit: Duncan Cameron/Duncan Cameron fonds/PA-111214.

he wanted Canadians to build: a society whose personal and political liberties were ensured by a charter of rights, a society in which minorities would be sheltered from the caprices of majorities, in which regions and social groups who had not participated fully in the country's material abundance would have greater opportunities. He wanted to discuss with Canadians their country's future. This emphasis on participatory democracy appealed to and attracted many electors. In addition, Trudeau promised a complete revision of Canada's foreign policy in an effort to reorient and reinvigorate Canadian activity abroad.

Trudeau had much to say on the constitutional question as well. When he asked for a strong mandate to oppose the Quebec government's ambitions to play a role in international affairs, Toronto newspapers congratulated him for his "firmness." He vigorously attacked new Conservative leader Robert Stanfield's implicit support for the "two nations" doctrine of a more decentralized Canada. For advocates of a strong central government, here was someone who would stand up to the provinces, which they viewed as continually encroaching upon Ottawa's authority. Trudeau could also promise Quebec that he would promote bilingualism in Canada, notably in the federal civil service, and that he

Expo 67, Montreal 1967—an exciting celebration of Canada's centennial year. Canada put forward its very best and invited the world. Some 50 million visitors attended.

Source: Malak/Library and Archives Canada/C-18536.

would give Quebec and French Canada a major role to play in federal politics. Moreover, like Laurier and St. Laurent before him, he was a French-speaking Canadian. Trudeau's triumphant victory in the 1968 election suggested that he might succeed in building a new consensus among Canadians if he could overcome the Liberals' weakness in the West.

The Canadian Centennial, 1967

The 1960s were a time of celebration as well as confrontation. The highlight of the era was the celebration of Canada's centennial in 1967. Provinces and municipalities vied in organizing festivities to mark the event. Still, typically subdued Canadians gave vent to few of the effusions of American-style patriotism, and many wondered whether the country was going to succeed in holding itself together.

One centennial activity was not restrained: Expo 67, staged on an island in the St. Lawrence River at Montreal. The showpiece event brought together more than 60 nations to celebrate the theme "Man and His World." Fifty million visitors passed through the turnstiles, and governments, both federal and provincial, spared no expense, perhaps unfortunately for the taxpayer.

The Canada of 1970 differed greatly from the country that had timidly embarked on an era of change in the late 1950s. Materially, most Canadians were better off than they had been a decade earlier. They were also better educated and certainly more liberal in their views. Minority groups now defended their interests more vigorously and found that society was at least somewhat more attentive to their claims. For example, the federal government's White Paper, in 1969, designed to end the special status of the First Nations, sparked a wave of protest, and Native Peoples returned to the general public's consciousness.

Many Canadians, particularly older Canadians, found it difficult to accept the rapid pace of change. They criticized what they saw as a general decline in respect for authority and particularly the many excesses that accompanied social transformation. Others felt that the heightened individualism of the era was incompatible with the need to preserve the nation's unity. For the moment, however, these voices of caution had little impact. Indeed the 1970s and 1980s would bring more change against a background of increasing economic difficulties and political disunity.

NOTES

1. Marcel Martel, *Not This Time: Canadians, Public Policy, and the Marijuana Question, 1961–1975* (Toronto: University of Toronto Press, 2006), pp. 198–208.

2. Doug Owram, *Born at the Right Time: A History of the Baby-Boom Generation* (Toronto: University of Toronto Press, 1996), p. 159.

3. Valerie J. Korinek, "'Mrs. Chatelaine' vs. 'Mrs. Slob': Contestants, Correspondents and the *Chatelaine* Community in Action, 1961–1969," *Journal of the Canadian Historical Association/Revue de la Société historique du Canada* 7 (1996): 266.

4. Barbara Roberts, "Women's Peace Activism in Canada," in Linda Kealey and Joan Sangster, eds., *Beyond the Vote: Canadian Women and Politics* (Toronto: University of Toronto Press, 1989), p. 299.

5. Pamela Sugiman, *Labour's Dilemma: The Gender Politics of Auto Workers in Canada, 1937–1979* (Toronto: University of Toronto Press, 1994), p. 136.

6. William P. Irvine, "The Canadian Voter," in Howard R. Penniman, ed., *Canada at the Polls, 1979 and 1980: A Study of the General Elections* (Washington, DC: American Enterprise Institute for Public Policy Research, 1981), p. 67.

7. Frederick J. Fletcher, "Playing the Game: The Mass Media and the 1979 Campaign," in Penniman, op. cit., p. 319.

8. Lawrence Martin, *The Presidents and the Prime Ministers: Washington and Ottawa Face to Face: The Myth of Bilateral Bliss, 1867–1982* (Toronto: PaperJacks, 1983), p. 193.

9. John Herd Thompson and Steven Randall, *Canada and the United States: Ambivalent Allies*, 3rd ed. (Montreal/Kingston: McGill-Queen's University Press, 2002), p. 243.

10. Peter C. Newman, *Renegade in Power: The Diefenbaker Years*, rev. ed. (Toronto: McClelland & Stewart, 1989).

11. Maurice Pinard, *The Rise of a Third Party: A Study in Crisis Politics* (Englewood Cliffs, NJ: Prentice-Hall, 1971), pp. 21–35; Vincent Lemieux, "The Election in Lévis," in John Meisel, ed., *Papers on the 1962 Election* (Toronto: University of Toronto Press, 1964), pp. 33–52.

12. K.J. Rea, *The Prosperous Years: The Economic History of Ontario, 1939–75* (Toronto: University of Toronto Press, 1985).

13. R. Harley McGee, *Getting It Right: Regional Development in Canada* (Montreal/Kingston: McGill-Queen's University Press, 1992), p. xxiv.

14. J.E. Belliveau, *Little Louis and the Giant K.C.*, quoted in Rand Dyck, *Provincial Politics in Canada* (Scarborough, ON: Prentice-Hall, 1986), p. 171.

15. James L. Kenny, "A New Dependency: State, Local Capital, and the Development of New Brunswick's Base Metal Industry, 1960–1970," *Canadian Historical Review* 78 (1977): 38.

BEYOND THE BOOK

Weblinks

Expo 67: A Virtual Experience
http://www.collectionscanada.ca/expo/index-e.html
Explore digitized mementos and documents from the 1967 Expo in Montreal.

The Birth Control Pill
http://archives.cbc.ca/IDD-1-69-572/life_society/pill
A history of the birth control pill in Canada, which came to market in the 1960s.

The Martlet: 1960s
**http://gateway.uvic.ca/archives/featured_collections/uvic_newspapers/
martlet_1960/1960.html**
Explore student life in the 1960s through this digitized collection of the student newspaper of Victoria College (now the University of Victoria) in British Columbia.

Royal Commission on the Status of Women in Canada
**http://www.thecanadianencyclopedia.com/index.cfm?PgNm=TCE&Params=
A1ARTA0007674**
A detailed history of the Royal Commission on the Status of Women in Canada.

Pierre Trudeau
http://www.primeministers.ca/trudeau/bio_3.php
Audio interviews and text accounts of Pierre Trudeau's life and political career.

Films & Novels

Trudeau: The Man, the Myth, the Movie. CBC. 2002.

Canadian Experience—Expo 67: Back to the Future. CBC. 2004.

RELATED READINGS

The following article in R. Douglas Francis and Donald B. Smith, eds., *Readings in Canadian History: Post-Confederation*, 6th ed. (Toronto: Nelson Thomson Learning, 2002), relates to a topic in this chapter: Jennifer Read, "'Let Us Heed the Voice of Youth': Laundry Detergents, Phosphates, and the Emergence of the Environmental Movement in Ontario," pp. 416–35.

BIBLIOGRAPHY

Overviews of the 1960s include Robert Bothwell, Ian Drummond, and John English, *Canada Since 1945: Power, Politics, and Provincialism*, rev. ed. (Toronto: University of Toronto Press, 1989); and J.L. Granatstein, *Canada, 1957–1967: The Years of Uncertainty and Innovation* (Toronto: McClelland & Stewart, 1986). Social history is available in Alvin Finkel, *Social Policy and Practice in Canada: A History* (Waterloo, ON: Wilfrid University Press, 2006). Doug Owram studies the baby boom's effects in *Born at the Right Time: A History of the Baby-Boom Generation* (Toronto: University of Toronto Press, 1996). On Canada's centennial, a highlight of the 1960s, see Gary Miedema, *For Canada's Sake: Public Religion, Centennial Celebrations, and the Remaking of Canada in the 1960s* (Montreal/Kingston: McGill-Queen's University Press, 2005).

David Cameron provides much material on universities in the 1960s in *More Than an Academic Question: Universities, Government, and Public Policy in Canada* (Halifax: Institute for Research on Public Policy, 1991). Drug policy is discussed in Marcel Martel, *Not This Time: Canadians, Public Policy, and the Marijuana Question, 1961–1975* (Toronto: University of Toronto Press, 2006). RCMP espionage on university campuses is treated in Steve Hewitt, *Spying 101: The RCMP's Secret Activities at Canadian Universities, 1917–1997* (Toronto: University of Toronto Press, 2002). Environmental literature relating to the 1960s includes Alan MacEachern, *Natural Selections: National Parks in Atlantic Canada, 1935–1970* (Montreal/Kingston: McGill-Queen's University Press, 2001).

The evolution of Canada's welfare state is discussed in Jacqueline S. Ismael, ed., *The Canadian Welfare State: Evolution and Transition* (Edmonton: University of Alberta Press, 1987); Keith Banting, *The Welfare State and Canadian Federalism*, 2nd ed. (Montreal/Kingston: McGill-Queen's University Press, 1987); and Allan Moscovitch and Jim Albert, eds., *The 'Benevolent' State: The Growth of Welfare in*

Canada (Toronto: Garamond Press, 1987). On the 1960s in particular see Penny E. Bryden, *Planners and Politicians: The Liberal Party and Social Policy, 1957–1968* (Montreal/Kingston: McGill-Queen's University Press, 1997). John R. Miron, ed., studies housing in *House, Home, and Community: Progress in Housing Canadians, 1945–1986* (Montreal/Kingston: McGill-Queen's University Press, 1993).

For further study of Canadian literature, W.H. New, ed., *Encyclopedia of Literature in Canada* (Toronto: University of Toronto Press, 2002) and Eugene Benson and William Toye, *The Oxford Companion to Canadian Literature*, 2nd ed. (Toronto: Oxford University Press, 1997) are indispensable sources. Gary Evans, *In the National Interest: A Chronicle of the National Film Board of Canada from 1949 to 1989* (Toronto: University of Toronto Press, 1991), describes the activity of an important cultural institution. Television is examined in Andrew Stewart and William H.N. Hull, *Canadian Television Policy and the Board of Broadcast Governors, 1958–1968* (Edmonton: University of Alberta Press, 1994). Paul Rutherford offers a lengthy description of television programs of the era in *When Television Was Young: Primetime Canada, 1952–1967* (Toronto: University of Toronto Press, 1990). Ted Magder studies the history of Canadian filmmaking in *Canada's Hollywood: The Canadian State and Feature Films* (Toronto: University of Toronto Press, 1993). Sport history in this period is discussed in Colin Howell, *Blood, Sweat, and Cheers: Sport and the Making of Modern Canada* (Toronto: University of Toronto Press, 2001).

For syntheses of women's history, see the bibliography of Chapter 14. Books that study the role of women in politics include Sydney Sharpe, *The Gilded Ghetto: Women and Political Power in Canada* (Toronto: HarperCollins, 1994); and Sylvia Bashevkin, *Toeing the Lines: Women and Party Politics in English Canada*, 2nd ed. (Toronto: Oxford University Press, 1993). Judith Fingard and Janet Guildford examine women's issues in Halifax in *Mothers of the Municipality: Women, Work, and Social Policy in Post-1945 Halifax* (Toronto: University of Toronto Press, 2005).

How the media responded to the feminist movement is discussed in Barbara Freeman, *The Satellite Sex: The Media and Women's Issues in English Canada, 1966–1971* (Waterloo, ON: Wilfrid Laurier University Press, 2001). On birth control consult Angus McLaren and Arlene Tigar McLaren, *The Bedroom and the State: The Changing Practices and Politics of Contraception and Abortion in Canada, 1880–1980* (Toronto: McClelland & Stewart, 1986). Issues linked to homosexuality are presented in Gary Kinsman, *The Regulation of Desire: Homo and Hetero Sexualities*, 2nd ed. (Montreal: Black Rose Books, 1996); and in Bruce MacDougall, *Queer Judgments: Homosexuality, Expression, and the Courts in Canada* (Toronto: University of Toronto Press, 2000).

A detailed survey of the economy may be found in Kenneth Norrie and Douglas Owram, *A History of the Canadian Economy*, 3rd ed. (Toronto: Nelson, 2002). Dimitry Anastakis, *Auto Pact: Creating a Borderless North American Auto Industry, 1960–1971* (Toronto: University of Toronto Press, 2005) examines a major economic development of the day. Among syntheses of labour history containing material on the 1960s are Craig Heron, *The Canadian Labour Movement: A Short History*, rev. ed. (Toronto: James Lorimer, 1996); Desmond Morton with Terry Copp, *Working People: An Illustrated History of the Canadian Labour Movement*, 3rd ed. (Toronto: Summerhill Press, 1990); and Bryan D. Palmer, *Working-Class Experience: Rethinking the History of Canadian Labour 1800–1991*, 2nd ed. (Toronto: McClelland & Stewart, 1992).

Canadian politicians have been thoroughly studied by political scientists, journalists, and historians, as well as by themselves. Recent works on John Diefenbaker include Garrett Wilson and Kevin Wilson, *Diefenbaker for the Defence* (Toronto: James Lorimer, 1988); and Denis Smith, *Rogue Tory: The Life and Legend of John G. Diefenbaker* (Toronto: Macfarlane Walter & Ross, 1995). Peter Newman offers a "striptease contribution" (in Pearson's words) of the Diefenbaker–Pearson rivalry in *The Distemper of Our Times*, rev. ed. (Toronto: McClelland & Stewart, 1990). On Pearson, consult the diplomat-politician's *Mike: The Memoirs of the Right Honourable Lester B. Pearson*, 3 vols. (Toronto: University of Toronto Press, 1972–75), as well as John English's biography, *The Worldly Years: The Life of Lester Pearson*, vol. 2, *1949–1972* (Toronto: Knopf Canada, 1992). A critical examination of Pearson's legacy may be found in Norman Hillmer, ed., *Pearson: The Unlikely Gladiator* (Montreal/Kingston: McGill-Queen's University Press, 1999).

Pierre Elliott Trudeau's early career is presented in Stephen Clarkson and Christina McCall Newman, *Trudeau and Our Times*, vol. 1, *The Magnificent Obsession* (Toronto: McClelland & Stewart, 1990).

Maurice Pinard analyzes the Social Credit phenomenon in Quebec in *The Rise of a Third Party: A Study in Crisis Politics* (Montreal/Kingston: McGill-Queen's University Press, 1975). On the NDP see Desmond Morton, *The New Democrats, 1961–1986: The Politics of Change* (Toronto: Copp Clark Pitman, 1986). See also William Christian and Colin Campbell, *Political Parties and Ideologies in Canada* (Toronto: McGraw-Hill Ryerson, 1995). English Canada's changing identity is discussed in Philip Buckner, ed., *Canada and the End of Empire*. Vancouver: UBC Press, 2005); and in José E. Igartua, *The Other Quiet Revolution: National Identities in English Canada, 1945–71* (Vancouver: UBC Press, 2006).

On aspects of Canada's international relations, see Robert Bothwell, *Alliance and Illusion: Canada and the World, 1945–1984* (Vancouver: UBC Press, 2007); and John English and Norman Hillmer, eds., *Making a Difference? Canada's Foreign Policy in a Changing World Order* (Toronto: Lester, 1992). Studies of Canadian–American relations with material on the 1960s include J.L. Granatstein and Norman Hillmer, *For Better or for Worse: Canada and the United States to the 1990s* (Toronto: Copp Clark Pitman, 1991); John Herd Thompson and Steven Randall, *Canada and the United States: Ambivalent Allies*, 3rd ed. (Montreal/Kingston: McGill-Queen's University Press, 2002); and, for economic issues, Bruce Muirhead, *Dancing Around the Elephant: Creating a Prosperous Canada in an Era of American Dominance, 1957–1973* (Toronto: University of Toronto Press, 2005).

For a provocative essay on the subject of nationalism, see a new edition of George Grant's classic of the 1960s, *Lament for a Nation: The Defeat of Canadian Nationalism*. Montreal/Kingston: McGill-Queen's University Press, 2005); see also William Christian's biography: *George Grant: A Biography* (Toronto: University of Toronto Press, 1993). On Canada's involvement in the war in Vietnam, consult Douglas Ross, *In the Interests of Peace: Canada and Vietnam, 1954–1973* (Toronto: University of Toronto Press, 1984).

The best overview of the Atlantic provinces is E.R. Forbes and D.A. Muise, eds., *The Atlantic Provinces in Confederation* (Toronto: University of Toronto Press, 1993). Miriam Wright, *A Fishery for Modern Times: The State and the Industrialization of the Newfoundland Fishery, 1934–1968* (Toronto: Oxford University Press, 2001), studies a major economic issue. A general survey of Ontario is available in Randall White: *Ontario, 1610–1985: A Political and Economic History* (Toronto: Dundurn Press, 1985); the province's economy is studied in K.J. Rea, *The Prosperous Years: The Economic History of Ontario, 1939–75* (Toronto: University of Toronto Press, 1985). Overviews of western Canada include Gerald Friesen, *The Canadian Prairies: A History* (Toronto: University of Toronto Press, 1984); John Thompson, *Forging the Prairie West: The Illustrated History of Canada* (Don Mills, ON: Oxford University Press, 1998); and John F. Conway, *The West: The History of a Region in Confederation*, 3rd ed. (Toronto: James Lorimer, 2006). Alberta and British Columbia are studied in Howard and Tamara Palmer, *Alberta: A New History* (Edmonton: Hurtig, 1990); and Jean Barman, *The West Beyond the West: A History of British Columbia*, 3rd ed. (Toronto: University of Toronto Press, 2007), respectively.

Chapter Sixteen

ABORIGINAL CANADA: WORLD WAR II TO THE PRESENT

TIME LINE

1946	Joint House and Senate Committee begins hearings to consider revision of the Indian Act
1951	Parliament passes the new Indian Act
1960	First Nations individuals obtain the right to vote in federal elections without giving up their Indian status
1969	The Liberals introduce their "White Paper" on Indian Affairs in Parliament but later withdraw it due to intense protest
1973	The Supreme Court rules that Aboriginal title exists in Canadian law
1974	The federal government establishes the Office of Native Land Claims to settle First Nations land claims
1975	Signing of the James Bay and Northern Quebec Agreement, the first modern treaty
1982	The Constitutional Act of 1982 affirms, in section 35, the existence of Aboriginal and treaty rights
1985	Parliament amends the Indian Act with Bill C-31, which restores Indian status to those who had lost it
1990	The Oka Crisis
1993	Establishment of the British Columbia Treaty Commission
1996	The Royal Commission on Aboriginal Peoples, established after Oka to examine Native concerns, issues its report
1999	Nunavut becomes a separate territory in the eastern Arctic Launching of the Aboriginal Peoples Television Network
2005	Kelowna Accord agreed upon by the Liberal government of Paul Martin, but not implemented in 2006 by the new Conservative administration of Stephen Harper

Over the last half-century the Native or Indigenous peoples—the Inuit, status Indians, and the Métis—have become the fastest-growing population in Canada. The birth rate among the Inuit and status Indians—who are registered under the federal Indian Act—is twice the national average. This is in contrast with the situation immediately after Confederation, when the Aboriginal population continued to decline due to tuberculosis and other communicable diseases introduced by Europeans. As late as 1932, Diamond Jenness, the distinguished Canadian anthropologist, wrote in *The Indians of Canada*: "Doubtless all the tribes will disappear. Some will endure only a few years longer, others, like the Eskimos, may last several centuries."[1]

The growing perception after World War II that the Indigenous peoples were not "vanishing" led to the development of a more positive attitude in the dominant society. Improved First Nations nutrition and hygiene, as well as continued progress in the prevention and therapy of infectious disease, contributed to increasing numbers. Equally important, particularly from the 1930s onward, was the fact that a new group of politically conscious Aboriginal leaders, with knowledge of the larger society and an ability to articulate their demands in English or French, made their voices heard. The Indian resistance to the federal government's White Paper of 1969, which endorsed assimilation, led to its withdrawal. In the last generation or so the dominant society itself has greatly changed. In contrast with the mid-twentieth century, the Canadian public now appeared receptive to diverse heritages, in particular those of the Indigenous peoples.

The growing number and accompanying migration of many Aboriginal people to urban areas, their visibility, and their political assertiveness, have led to an increasing public awareness of Indigenous issues. The First Nations resistance to the White Paper proved a turning point in Indian and non-Indian relations in Canada. Land claims began in the mid-1970s for over half of Canada. Successful political lobbying in the 1970s contributed to the inclusion of the Aboriginal peoples in Canada's new Constitution in 1982. Widespread recognition of the concept of Aboriginal rights, including Native self-government, followed in the late 1980s and early 1990s. In 1999 the federal government created Nunavut, a separate political jurisdiction in the eastern Arctic, which the Inuit controlled due to their numerical dominance. Astonishing developments have occurred in the field of communications. In 1999 the Aboriginal Peoples Television Network began broadcasting. The First Ministers Conference on Aboriginal Affairs in Kelowna in late November 2005, in the last days of the Liberal administration of Paul Martin, resulted in a five-year, $5 billion plan to improve education, housing, economic development, health and water supplies of the First Nations, Métis and Inuit peoples.

The Yale–Toronto Conference on the North American Indian

The University of Toronto and Yale Conference on the North American Indian that met in Toronto in early September 1939 symbolized the transition from the old to the new Canada on Native issues. The conference, organized by Dr. Tom McIlwraith, the first academic anthropologist employed at a Canadian university (the University of Toronto) and the curator of ethnological collections at the Royal Ontario Museum, was designed "to reveal the conditions today of the white man's Indian wards, and in a scientific, objective and sympathetic spirit, plan with them for their future." Over seventy Canadian and American government officials, missionaries, and academics attended. More importantly, thirteen invited Native people participated. It was the first conference ever held to discuss First Nations welfare and the first scholarly meeting to include Indigenous delegates.

For nearly two weeks, the conference delegates discussed North American Native cultures, reserve economics, health, and education. Perhaps the most revealing information about the First Nations in Canada came from federal government officials who pointed out that, beginning in the mid-1930s, the status Indian population had reversed its previous decline and was increasing annually by 1 percent, thanks to both an increase in the birth rate and a decline in the

The delegates to the Yale–Toronto Conference on the North American Indian, September 1939. This was the first conference held in Canada to discuss Native welfare and the first scholarly conference to include First Nations delegates. The photo was taken on the lawn at the back of the Royal Ontario Museum.

Source: Pringle and Booth/Courtesy of Ken Kidd, a delegate at the conference.

death rate. The conference papers delivered by non-Aboriginal Canadian and American students and administrators of North American Indian policy viewed assimilation as both inevitable and desirable. On the last day of the conference, delegates passed resolutions urging greater attention to "the psychological, social, and economic maladjustments of the Indian populations of the United States and Canada." They established a committee to oversee the publication of the conference's papers and the dissemination of information on North America's Indigenous peoples.

Then a dramatic event occurred. The Native delegates broke from the main group and met separately to pass their own resolutions. They objected to government officials, missionaries, and non-Native sympathizers speaking for them:

> We hereby go on record as hoping that the need for an All Indian Conference on Indian Affairs will be felt by Indian tribes, the delegates to such a conference be limited to bona fide Indian leaders actually living among the Indian people of the reservations and reserves, and further, that such a conference remain free of political, anthropological, missionary, administrative, or other domination.

Unfortunately, their appeal went largely unheard by a Canadian public totally preoccupied by the entry of Canada into World War II, but in retrospect the conference was a turning point.

The Aboriginal Peoples in Wartime

During the war, the status Indian population experienced increased oppression. Acting against verbal promises at several treaty negotiations in western Canada, the federal government initially tried to include status Indians among those eligible for overseas military conscription. Other arbitrary wartime measures included the seizure of reserve lands, the moving of reserve populations, and the revision of band membership lists. When, for example, the federal government decided in 1942 that it needed a military training facility on Lake Huron, it invoked the War Measures Act to appropriate Ontario's Stoney Point Reserve to establish Camp Ipperwash. The Stoney Point people now had to live in the territory of their Kettle Point neighbours.

Financial exigency during the war also contributed to First Nations resentment. To save money and promote self-sufficiency, the Indian Affairs Branch unilaterally proposed a centralization plan designed to remove status Mi'kmaq (Micmac) in Nova Scotia from nineteen small reserves to two large inland ones, one at Eskasoni, 50 km southwest of Sydney, and the other at Shubenacadie, 65 km northwest of Halifax. The abandoned reserves were to be sold. Only mounting First Nations opposition led to the cancellation of the proposal.

In northern Alberta, Malcolm McCrimmon, an Indian Affairs Branch official, created havoc in 1942 when he revised the membership lists in the Lesser Slave Lake agency to trim 700 individuals who he claimed were not "true Indians." He argued that anyone added to the membership list after 1912 needed to prove that his or her father was a "full blood Indian." His action revitalized the already existing First Nations political organization, the Indian Association of Alberta.

These actions undermined the Branch's credibility among the First Nations, as did the fact that its 65 members included only 2 First Nations persons in 1944. Moreover, few of the non-Native Branch officials had any previous experience in Aboriginal affairs.

The war years demoralized the First Nations. They served in great numbers in the war, but were denied benefits given to the other veterans. Furthermore they continued to be legal "wards of the state," without the right to vote. First Nations communities had no control over their reserve land, or money from the sale of their land. Still, the war years contributed to a greater political consciousness among them.

Aboriginal Canada Immediately After World War II

In the interwar years, First Nations people in sparsely populated areas in the North escaped the full weight of the Indian Act. The federal government paid little attention to the First Nations in the Mackenzie valley. During the war, however, the isolation ended for the northern First Nations, Métis, and Inuit. Thousands of armed-service personnel and civilians established military airstrips and radio stations in the North. Small communities arose around these posts. Furthermore, in the late 1940s, with the collapse of the fur market and the unexpected failure to meet the migrating caribou herds, Inuit depended on the federal government for help. Ottawa responded by flying starving families to fur trading posts, where food supplies existed. The federal government also became active in the region in other ways. It brought in nurses and doctors to look after the Inuit refugees coming off the land, and it built hospitals and schools, as well as living quarters. As soon as these non-Native medical personnel, administrators, and teachers arrived, even on a semipermanent basis, the federal government built permanent installations, such as power plants, water and sewer systems, and roads. The small non-Native bureaucracy that administered the social-assistance programs gained enormous control over the Inuit.

For those Inuit who had tuberculosis or other communicable diseases, the government provided medical assistance, such as X-rays and immunization. Those patients requiring immediate hospitalization were sent south by plane or boat. By the 1950s, hundreds had been hospitalized and the Department of Health and Welfare had succeeded in lowering substantially the high mortality rate among the Inuit.

Ottawa now saw its task as bringing the northern First Nations to a level comparable to that of the Inuit in the eastern Arctic. In the Mackenzie valley, the Indigenous peoples had not experienced the same economic collapse as the Inuit had after World War II. Moreover, they already lived in semipermanent camps or cabins around Hudson's Bay Company posts and

Christian missions. Ottawa replaced the mission schools with public schools and provided the same medical services and administrative help as in the eastern Arctic. The government clashed, however, with local chiefs and elders who resented its intrusion into their communities in the Mackenzie valley, who up to this point had run their own affairs.

A New Postwar Attitude Toward the Aboriginal Peoples

After World War II, Canadians developed a more positive attitude toward the Indigenous peoples. Several reasons account for this. First, social scientists discredited the pseudoscientific race theory of the late nineteenth and early twentieth centuries that had held certain "races" to be inherently inferior to others. Second, many Canadians learned through the press and radio, and, in the 1950s, through television, of the impoverished health and living conditions of the northern First Nations and Inuit. Improvements in water and especially air transportation brought even the most remote regions of the Arctic into much closer contact with southern Canada, creating greater awareness of northern conditions. Third, the expansion of the natural-resources frontier took southern Canadians into Aboriginal territory (a situation that brought Aboriginal land claims throughout northern Canada to the public's attention). Fourth, the decolonization movement in Asia and Africa and later the civil-rights movement in the United States in the 1950s and early 1960s contributed to a new consciousness of injustices to minorities, including the Indigenous peoples. Most importantly, Aboriginal leaders, as they had at the Yale–Toronto Conference in 1939, made their opinions known. First Nations political leaders demanded freedom from tutelage, and recognition of their civil rights. Modern technology enabled the new Aboriginal leadership to communicate easily in a new common language, English, and, in parts of southern Quebec, French. By the end of the twentieth century a new leadership skilled in legal argument and media manipulation had emerged to make the First Nations a political force.

After World War II, the Indian Association of Alberta campaigned to have Parliament review the Indian Act. Some veterans' organizations and church groups assisted Aboriginal political leaders in pressuring Ottawa to relax the powerful controls it exercised over the reserves. Had not the First Nations done enough to merit better treatment? Even though they were not recognized as citizens, they had enlisted in large numbers in the Canadian Army in the war.

For the first time, Parliament listened. The Indian Association of Alberta and other provincial Indian organizations participated in the hearings of the Joint Committee of the House of Commons and the Senate on the Indian Act, held from 1946 to 1948. Out of these deliberations came a new revision of the Indian Act in 1951. Assimilation of the First Nations into the mainstream was seen as both inevitable and desirable. The new Indian Act allowed band councils more authority. Women also gained the vote in band council elections. It lifted bans on the potlatch and the Sun Dance. Compulsory enfranchisement for status Indian males was swept away. Yet the new Indian Act's underlying goal remained the assimilation of the status Indian. It made it easier for individuals to give up their Indian status. It also included new provisions to allow the placement of First Nations children in integrated provincial schools. In addition the new act gave provincial authorities responsibility for the welfare of status Indian children.

In the 1960s the provinces became very aggressive in taking Native children from their families, from their communities, and placing them in protective care. Writer Patrick Johnston, the author of *Native Children and the Child Welfare System* (1983), termed this the "Sixties Scoop," in reference to the placement of Aboriginal children in protective custody. In 1955 in British Columbia Native children constituted 1 percent of the children in care, by 1964 the proportion of Native children in care in the province had risen to over 34 percent. Thousands of Indigenous children were removed and settled into foster and adopted homes across North America.

Johnston's study mentions that Manitoba became the last province to impose a moratorium on the export of children, but this only occurred in 1982. Today in various provinces the First Nations communities must, by legislation, be notified if First Nations children are apprehended.

By the 1970s, Ottawa had phased out most of the residential schools (the last federal residential school closed in 1986) and had integrated First Nations children into provincially controlled programs. But integrated schooling did not prove entirely successful. Its shortcomings led a number of bands in the early 1970s to call for community control of their schools. Blue Quills, near St. Paul, Alberta, became the first band-controlled school in 1970. Others followed, and in 1973 the federal government endorsed First Nations–controlled schools.

Gradually the federal government softened its hard line on local band government. In 1960, for example, the Walpole Island band council in southwestern Ontario assumed responsibility for road improvements and other public works on the reserve. Five years later, the same band council gained control over the administration of its own local affairs. By 1966, approximately one-third of all bands in Ontario administered their own welfare services. Other bands created their own police forces, as Walpole Island did in 1967.

Since the 1970s increased attention has been paid to distinctive needs, and participation of Aboriginal people in the justice system, but admittedly great challenges remain. Horrific stories include that of Donald Marshall, Jr., a Mi'kmaq teenager who was wrongly convicted and imprisoned for murder in 1972. Marshall spent eleven years in prison until a reexamination of the case led to his acquittal in 1983. A judicial inquiry after his release revealed anti-Mi'kmaq prejudice embedded in every aspect of the justice system.

During the 1960s, the dominant society showed a greater sensitivity to some Aboriginal issues. Gradually the provinces granted the provincial franchise to status Indians. In 1960, Ottawa extended the right to vote in federal elections to all status Indians (at that time approximately three out of four could not vote in federal elections), without requiring First Nations people to give up their Indian status. The federally appointed Hawthorn Commission on the Indian reported in the mid-1960s. It found that the First Nations occupied the lowest economic rung on Canada's economic ladder. The report concluded that "in addition to the normal rights and duties of citizenship, Indians possess certain additional rights as charter members of the Canadian community." After the publication of the report, Prime Minister Lester Pearson committed his government to revising the Indian Act, after prior consultation with First Nations people.

The federal government, now having adopted a more supportive role toward the Aboriginal peoples, helped to build a pavilion for the First Nations at Montreal's Expo 67. The Indigenous organizers of the pavilion used the building to tell Aboriginal Canada's story to non-Natives. At the entrance, this message greeted visitors: "The Indian people's destiny will be determined by them and our country, Canada, will be better for it." Inside, visitors saw, in bold script, statements such as "Give us the right to manage our own affairs" and "Help us preserve the moral values, the meaningful way of life, the inheritance of our forefathers." The anti-assimilation messages announced the First Nations' political agenda for the remainder of the century.

Prime Minister John Diefenbaker with Plains Cree at Maple Creek, Saskatchewan, during the 1965 federal election.

Source: Library and Archives Canada/Photograph by Bill Cadzow PA-15486.

From the White Paper of 1969 to the Constitution of 1982

In 1969 the recently elected Liberal government of Pierre Trudeau inadvertently contributed to the Aboriginal resurgence. The Hawthorn Report had recommended that First Nations people be treated as "citizens plus." Trudeau's predecessor, Lester Pearson, had promised that the Indian Act would be revised after prior consultation with Indian people. But, without any meaningful prior consultation, the Trudeau administration now promoted an end to the Indian Act, to the reserves, to "citizens plus." Without any further delay, federal legislation, if Parliament accepted the White Paper on Indian policy, would bring the First Nations immediately into the larger society. The elected band councils would evolve into municipal types of institutions such as those in mainstream Canadian society. The new prime minister in a Vancouver address in early August 1969 stated that he did not believe the treaties should continue forever: "It's inconceivable, I think, that in a given society one section of the society have a treaty with the other section of society."

In the White Paper on Indian policy, Minister of Indian Affairs Jean Chrétien called for the end—within five years—of the Department of Indian Affairs, the repeal of the Indian Act, the elimination of reserves, and the transfer to the provinces of many of the federal government's responsibilities for Indian affairs. Assimilation, the goal of Canadian Indian policy since the country's creation in 1867, remained the spirit of the times. For many non-Aboriginals, assimilation, the end of any special recognition for Aboriginal peoples, was viewed as a progressive policy. The policy objectives of the Saskatchewan CCF under Tommy Douglas and Woodrow Lloyd, 1944–64, were virtually identical to those of the White Paper of 1969. Prime Minister Trudeau also announced his government's refusal to negotiate land settlements for the roughly one-half of the country that was not under treaty.

Immediately in "Indian Country" came incredibly strong resistance to the proposals. The White Paper, in effect, did for the First Nations what Lord Durham's report of 1839 had accomplished for French Canadians, in recommending their eventual assimilation. Just as the French Canadians over a century earlier had rejected the thesis that their progress demanded the elimination of their culture, without delay young, educated First Nations leaders joined ranks with Aboriginal elders. They united to oppose the government's position paper recommending their eventual assimilation. Although unsatisfied with the colonial relationship imposed by the Indian Act, the First Nations leaders realized that the legislation at least recognized their special constitutional status. Without the Indian Act, they risked being absorbed into the mainstream of non-Native Canadian society. The fact that the federal government began to provide core funding for First Nations political organizations in 1970 helped strengthen them. It was in Ottawa's interest to do so, as the existence of strong Indian organizations in Canada helped to keep out radical United States Indian groups like the American Indian Movement (AIM). By forming a united front, First Nations political organizations succeeded in convincing the Liberal government to withdraw the White Paper in March 1971. The provincial and territorial Aboriginal political associations representing status Indians in Canada and the National Indian Brotherhood (founded in 1968, and reorganized in 1982 as the Assembly of First Nations) worked next to secure the constitutional entrenchment of Aboriginal and treaty rights.

Assisting the Native activists in their cause was the decision of the Supreme Court of Canada in the *Nisga'a* case of 1973. Although it went against the Nisga'a on a legal technicality, the Supreme Court did agree that the First Nations held Aboriginal title to their lands. Thus the federal government was obliged to accept comprehensive claims in the areas of Canada where treaties had not been signed, as well as specific claims elsewhere. More limited than comprehensive land claims, specific claims usually relate to demands for compensation or the restitution of land or money on the basis of the unfulfilled terms of an existing treaty, or formal legal agreement with the government. In 1974, Ottawa established an Office of Native Claims, a branch of the Department of Indian Affairs and Northern Development, to rule on Aboriginal claims.

Jean Chrétien, Minister of Indian Affairs, meeting with a delegation from the Indian Association of Alberta and other First Nations groups in Ottawa, June 1970. Prime Minister Trudeau is seated beside Jean Chrétien. The First Nations representatives have just presented the "Red Paper," their response to the government's controversial "White Paper."

The first comprehensive land claim signed immediately after the enactment of the new federal policy in 1974 was the James Bay and Northern Quebec Agreement in 1975. By this treaty, the Cree and Inuit surrendered their Aboriginal rights to over 1 000 000 km^2 of land, an area the size of British Columbia. In return, they gained ownership, in and around their communities, of over 14 000 km^2, an area twice the size of Prince Edward Island, as well as exclusive hunting, fishing, and trapping rights over 150 000 km^2, an area roughly the size of New Brunswick, Nova Scotia, and Prince Edward Island combined. Both the Cree and Inuit and the general public obtained equal access to the rest of the land. The agreement also awarded the Cree and the Inuit $225 million (in 1975 dollars) over a period of 25 years. Recently, in 2002, the Grand Council of the Cree and the Quebec government reached an understanding to extend the original 1975 agreement. In exchange for permitting further hydroelectric development on the Rupert and Eastmain Rivers, the Cree will obtain payments valued at $3.5 billion over a fifty-year period. They would also receive important commitments relating to employment, land, and co-management of the region's resources.

The early and mid-1970s were marked by greater Native activism. In the United States the rise of the Red Power movement led to a series of confrontations, including the lengthy standoff of the American Indian Movement (AIM) with the FBI at the village of Wounded Knee in South Dakota in 1973. In the early and mid-1970s Canada also saw a new level of unrest. In late 1971 Alberta First Nations began a six-month sit-in at the Department of Indian Affairs offices in Edmonton to protest the inferior conditions at reserve schools. Ojibwa (Anishinabeg) occupied Anicinibe Park in Kenora, northwestern Ontario, in the summer of 1974, in a land-claims dispute. A Native caravan from Vancouver, several hundred strong, reached Parliament Hill in September 1974 to protest poor housing and social services on reserves, as well as land-claims issues.

The emergence of constitutional issues after the election of the separatist Parti Québécois in Quebec in 1976 provided an opportunity for constitutional advancement of the Aboriginal peoples in Canada. Native political organizations—the National Indian Brotherhood (which became the Assembly of First Nations in 1982), the first permanent national organization for status Indians; the recently formed Native Council of Canada (now the Congress of Aboriginal Peoples), which represented Métis and off-reserve and non–status Indians; and the Inuit Tapirisat of Canada, the Inuit political organization—entered the constitutional debate. A strong campaign by Aboriginal groups led to the inclusion of section 35(2) in the new Constitution of 1982, guaranteeing Aboriginal rights. The clause gave constitutional protection for the first time in Canadian history to the "existing Aboriginal and treaty rights of the Aboriginal peoples of Canada." Most important of all for the Métis, the new Constitution also identified them, for the first time, as an Aboriginal people with the Indians and Inuit.

First Nations Political Demands from the 1980s to the Present

The definition of Aboriginal rights and the demand for self-government became the major constitutional questions for Aboriginal people in the 1980s and early 1990s. Section 35 of Canada's Constitution of 1982 recognized existing treaty and Aboriginal rights, such as those outlined in the Royal Proclamation of 1763. Yet, at a series of four subsequent First Ministers' Conferences on Aboriginal rights held between 1983 and 1987, the prime minister, the provincial premiers, and Indigenous representatives failed to reach agreement either on a definition of the meaning of the phrase "Aboriginal rights" or on a definition of Aboriginal self-government. In the end the federal and provincial governments refused to recognize that the Indigenous peoples had, on account of their history, an inherent right to self-government. These conferences did, however, give Aboriginal issues a very high public profile. The House of Commons Committee on Indian Self-Government in 1983 endorsed in the Penner Report the concept of full Indian control over matters such as education, child welfare, health care, and band membership. For the first time in a federal document, the term "First Nation" was used.

With the end of the constitutional conferences on Aboriginal rights in 1987, the battleground between Indigenous groups and the federal government shifted back to the courts. From the mid-1980s onward, Supreme Court rulings have provided an expanding interpretation of Aboriginal and treaty rights. In *Guerin* (1984) the court established the concept of a trust-like, or "fiduciary," relationship between the Crown and the Aboriginal peoples. This means that the federal government, as a trustee, is expected to act in all transactions in the best interests of the First Nations it represents. The following year the judges in *Simon* (1985) ruled that Indian treaties must be given a "fair, large and liberal interpretation." In 1990 in the *Sparrow* case, the Supreme Court drew on the Constitutional Act of 1982 to draw up rules to restrict to a minimum government's infringement of Aboriginal and treaty rights.

At the four First Ministers' Conferences on Aboriginal issues in the mid-1980s the question of an Aboriginal right to self-government had remained unresolved. The federal government argued that First Nations self-government would be a right delegated from the Crown. The First Nations objected. They contended that they held inherent sovereignty, that sovereignty belonged to them, and only they could delegate it. They possessed inherent sovereignty from their historical occupation of what was now Canada. It would take another decade of discussion before the federal government in 1995 accepted the right of the inherent right of self-government as a matter of policy. Since 1995 Ottawa has begun negotiations with a number of First Nations to implement Aboriginal self-government in conjunction with existing federal and provincial jurisdictions.

The failure of the Meech Lake Accord in 1990 demonstrated the growing influence of the Aboriginal peoples. The federal government and the provinces agreed in 1987 to respond to Quebec constitutional demands, and its opposition to the 1982 Constitution. But the Accord neglected to address Aboriginal concerns. Elijah Harper, an Aboriginal MLA in the Manitoba legislature, managed, on a technical point, to hold up Manitoba's ratification of the accord past the necessary deadline for its approval. Manitoba's and Newfoundland's failure to ratify it before the final deadline scuttled the Meech Lake Accord.

The Charlottetown Accord, a comprehensive agreement, followed. Unlike Meech, it promised to address the constitutional concerns of the Aboriginal peoples as well as those of Quebec. Aboriginal leaders joined the federal and provincial and territorial leaders in the preliminary talks before the national referendum. The Charlottetown Accord represents the highest point reached to date of recognition of Indigenous issues. It promised recognition of the inherent Aboriginal right of self-government within Canada, and the acceptance of Aboriginal governments as one of Canada's three orders of government. The Accord opened the Senate and the House of Commons to Aboriginal representation. But Canadians had grown weary of the constitutional discussions. The Charlottetown Accord failed to win majority support in the referendum in 1992, even in First Nations communities.

During the 1990s Native protests provided much of the momentum for recognition of Aboriginal issues. The federal government's inability to settle the complex, two-centuries-old land claim of the Mohawks at Kanesatake (Oka) contributed to the outbreak of violence in the summer of 1990. The Mohawks, who had seen their land base sharply reduced over the years to a tiny fraction of its original size, resisted attempts by the town of Oka, 50 km west of Montreal, to extend a golf course over disputed lands. Barricades led to a shootout in which a Quebec provincial police constable died, and then to a 78-day armed standoff between the Mohawks and the federal and Quebec governments. The Oka Crisis was the catalyst for Ottawa's creation of the Royal Commission on Aboriginal Peoples, first promised at the time of the Meech Lake Accord.

The federal government established the Royal Commission on Aboriginal Peoples in April 1991. Four of its seven commissioners were Aboriginal. Its mandate was "to examine the economic, social and cultural situation of the aboriginal peoples of this country."

The commission continued for five and a half years. In late 1996, the commissioners tabled their five-volume final report (roughly 3500 pages) in the House of Commons. Their 440 recommendations covered a wide range of Aboriginal issues, but essentially all focused on four major concerns: the need for a new relationship in Canada between Aboriginal and non-Aboriginal peoples; Aboriginal self-determination through self-government; economic self-sufficiency; and healing for Aboriginal peoples and communities. The report and its accompanying research papers constitute the most in-depth analysis ever undertaken on Aboriginal people in Canada.

The federal government waited 14 months before issuing its reply. In January 1998, it presented its response in a document entitled *Gathering Strength: Canada's Aboriginal Action Plan*. Although the statement committed the federal government to a new approach to Aboriginal policy in Canada, it replied directly to only a few of the commission's recommendations. Significantly, in general terms, Ottawa did accept the treaty relationship as the basis for Canada's relationships with First Nations. (This indeed reveals the new spirit of the times as only thirty years earlier the Hawthorn Report of the mid-1960s, and the 1969 White Paper considered treaties of marginal importance.) Second, *Gathering Strength* promised a more stable, long-term fiscal relationship with Aboriginal groups. Third, in future, it would increase efforts to prepare First Nations for self-government. Fourth, additional access would be given to land and resources. Several months later, the federal government also set aside $350 million to support community-based healing initiatives for First Nations people affected by the legacy of Indian residential schools. Georges Erasmus, former co-chair of the royal commission, became the first chair of the Aboriginal-run, not-for-profit Aboriginal Healing Foundation, established to oversee the management of the fund.

After the presentation of the Royal Commission Report, the federal government engaged in talks with the churches and Assembly of First Nations in hopes of reaching an agreement over the liability for abuses in the residential schools. In November 2005 the Liberal government of Paul Martin signed an agreement-in-principle with the Assembly of First Nations to end 15 000 individual lawsuits of former students and 21 class-action suits. The Conservative government of Stephen Harper subsequently approved the agreement, which will see former residential school students obtain what has been termed a "common experience payment" of $10 000, in addition to $3000 for every year they attended the institutions. The estimated cost of the agreement would be at least $1.9 billion. Further money was set aside to address claims of physical and sexual abuse.

In early 2007 the Conservative government announced that an apology would not be immediately forthcoming to former students of Indian residential schools, as part of its settlement with former residential school students. Instead the federal government has committed $60 million to launch a truth and reconciliation commission on Indian residential schools to raise awareness, and to help reveal the historical record. It will travel across Canada to hear and document stories from former pupils and teachers. After the completion of the approximately five-year study Parliament could then address the question of an apology.

WHERE HISTORIANS DISAGREE

Interpreting the Indian Residential Schools, 1879–1986

For nearly a century a church/state-run system of residential schools worked to assimilate First Nations children into the dominant Euro-Canadian society. Each of the four Christian denominations responsible—the Anglicans, Presbyterians, Roman Catholics, and the United Church—have in recent years formally apologized for their role in this assimilation program. On January 7, 1998, the federal government also apologized in its Statement of Reconciliation:

This system separated many children from their families and communities and prevented them from speaking their own languages and from learning about their heritage and cultures. In the worst cases, it left legacies of personal pain and distress that continue to reverberate in Aboriginal communities to this day. Tragically, some children were the victims of physical and sexual abuse.

John Webster Grant, one of Canada's foremost church historians, was one of the first academics to identify the issue. Writing well before non-Natives had ever heard the term "Indian residential school," he identified a number of its failings. Without any attempt to hide the reality, he explained that many First Nations people fought the forced assimilation: "Resistance to enrollment was widespread, and school burnings were more common than mere accidents would explain."[1] Financial handicaps, poor teachers, unhealthy buildings, few

Cree children attending an Anglican Church school, Lac La Ronge, Saskatchewan, March 1945.

Source: Library and Archives Canada. Photo by Bud Glunz, PA-124110.

amenities, all plagued the system. Yet, he argues, in the face of these difficulties, in an age when non-Native Canadians were as culture-bound as any people of their own time or ours, some schools performed well. "Despite its shortcomings, the residential school evidently met a need."[2]

As historian Scott Trevithick has written of the participants in the debate over residential schools, they "do not fit conveniently into two distinct and opposing camps, but rather find themselves spread out at various places across the playing field."[3] Another early contributor to the discussion in the 1980s was historian Celia Haig-Brown. She examined the record of the Kamloops Indian Residential School in central British Columbia, from the recollections of thirteen former students. From her study, rich in oral testimony, one gains a fuller understanding of the mid-twentieth-century schools, or, at least of the Kamloops school. Reflecting her interviewees' vivid and painful memories she emphasizes, "the injustice of the system which attempted to control and to transform them."[4] Yet, as she points out in her study: "Even with the controls already described well in place, the students found time and space to express themselves and to produce a separate culture of their own within the school."[5]

By 1990 the subject of residential schools began to enter into the general public's consciousness. The statement by Phil Fontaine, then chief of the Assembly of Manitoba Chiefs, that he had suffered sexual abuse as a student at a Manitoba residential school, broke other former students' silence. A number came forward to reveal their own stories of physical, sexual, and emotional abuse. Several years later, in 1996, J.R. Miller published his important study, over ten years in the making, *Shingwauk's Vision: A History of Native Residential Schools.* Among a number of interesting observations he notes that, at the high point of the Indian residential school system, in the early twentieth century, probably about one-third of the eligible Inuit and status Indians of school age attended.[6] He concludes his study with this observation: "it seems clear that the schools performed inadequately in most respects, and in a few areas, wrought profoundly destructive effects on many of their students."[7]

Through the ongoing hearings of the Royal Commission on Aboriginal Peoples in the mid-1990s, the public gained a much greater awareness of the Indian residential system's weaknesses. Historian John S. Milloy, who wrote a report for the Commission on residential schools, later published a full-length study in which he strongly criticized the church–state partnership for its assault on the well-being of the First Nations. Both groups' original good intentions paved the way to a form of absolute hell. "In thought and in deed the establishment of this school system was an act of profound cruelty rooted in non-Aboriginal pride and intolerance and in the certitude and insularity of purported cultural superiority."[8]

Much of the challenge with this topic for academic historians resides in the lack of consensus in the oral evidence. As J.R. Miller wrote: "The existence of former students who hold positive memories of residential school and many others who recall it as a living hell seriously complicates a later age's ability to reach a firm, overall assessment of the problem of abuse in these institutions." He concludes: "In a pathetic sense, that emotional confrontation is also a form of abuse perpetuated indirectly by the residential school system."[9]

1   John Webster Grant, *Moon of Wintertime: Missionaries and the Indians of Canada in Encounter Since 1534* (Toronto: University of Toronto Press, 1984), p. 179.

2   Ibid., p. 183.

3   Scott Trevithick, "Native Residential Schooling in Canada: A Review of Literature," *The Canadian Journal of Native Studies* 18(1) (1998): 53.

4   Celia Haig-Brown, *Resistance and Renewal: Surviving the Indian Residential School* (Vancouver: Tillacum Library, 1988), p. 115.

5   Ibid., p. 88.

6   J.R. Miller, *Shingwauk's Vision: A History of Native Residential Schools* (Toronto: University of Toronto Press, 1996), p. 142.

7   Ibid., p. 418.

8   John S. Milloy, *"A National Crime": The Canadian Government and the Residential School System, 1879 to 1986* (Winnipeg: University of Manitoba Press, 1999), p. 302.

9   Miller, op. cit., pp. 341–42.

The mid-1990s marked the beginning of a treaty process in British Columbia. From its entry into Confederation in 1871 the province had refused to acknowledge that the Aboriginal peoples had any treaty rights or ancestral claims over traditional lands. In 1990 British Columbia made a historic change of policy and agreed to enter into treaty negotiations with First Nations groups. The British Columbia Treaty Commission was established in 1993. Six years later Parliament ratified the Nisga'a Treaty, the first comprehensive claim to be settled south of the Yukon and Northwest Territories since the James Bay Agreement in 1975. The Nisga'a obtained control over 2000 km^2 of their territory, as well as nearly $120 million in compensation for their lost lands.

Currently, fifty First Nations in British Columbia, or about two-thirds of all First Nations people in the province, are involved in negotiations to make similar agreements to that of the Nisga'a. Aboriginal groups potentially might obtain firm title to about 5 percent of the province's land mass, an amount of land that currently corresponds to the Aboriginal proportion of the province's total population. Overall little progress has been made in B.C. treaty negotiations. Since the mid-1990s, in fact, they have been so slow that both the federal and the provincial auditor-general stated in late 2006 that the talks were in danger of being overrun by "the changing legal, economic and political environments."[2]

In 1997 in the *Delgamuukw* case the Supreme Court enlarged and clarified the definition of Aboriginal title in Canada. The court unanimously recognized in this British Columbia case that Aboriginal title could extend over large areas of traditional lands. The landmark decision also accepted the validity of using Aboriginal oral history and testimony from elders in cases involving Aboriginal title.

First Nations land issues have advanced in Saskatchewan, which is, in terms of numbers, one of the most Native of all the provinces. Since the creation of Saskatchewan in 1905 the number of First Nations people has increased tenfold, from roughly 10 000 to 100 000. In the 2001 census just over 130 000 persons identified as Aboriginal in the province, that is, approximately 14 percent of Saskatchewan's total population. (This is approximately four times greater than the total percentage, 3.3, of individuals who self-identified as Aboriginal, Indian, Métis, or Inuit in the 2001 census.) As the First Nations and Métis population in Saskatchewan is considerably younger than the non-Aboriginal, this means that nearly one-quarter of the children in the province are Aboriginal. In the early 1990s the federal government negotiated a $450 million settlement in Saskatchewan for treaty land entitlement.

The settlement, the Saskatchewan Treaty Land Entitlement Framework Agreement, signed in 1992, will compensate for illegal losses of reservation lands in the province. This fund also allows for the granting of additional lands to those communities entitled to larger land areas in their historic treaties. Saskatchewan, for example, has led the way in the creation of urban reserves, or lands located in a municipality or Northern Administrative District, these are primarily to provide urban locations for Aboriginal business. By 2005, twenty-eight urban reserves had been initiated, nine of them located in Saskatchewan cities. In that year more than 1350 people worked in businesses developed on urban reserves in the province.

Another confirmation of the growing legal and political recognition of Aboriginal rights came in the Supreme Court's *Marshall* decision of 1999, in a case involving Mi'kmaq fishing rights initiated by Donald Marshall, Jr., the same individual acquitted in 1983 from a wrongful conviction of homicide reported earlier in this chapter. The court in 1999, in the second Marshall case, ruled that the peace and friendship treaties made in 1760–61 between the Mi'kmaq and the British gave the Mi'kmaq a treaty right to a "moderate livelihood" in the Atlantic commercial fishery. Ottawa's continued attempt to try to regulate the Mi'kmaq fishery resulted in sporadic violence in the 2000 and 2001 fishing seasons, particularly at the Mi'kmaq community of Burnt Church, in New Brunswick's Miramichi Bay. The question of a fair settlement of the legal rights of the Mi'kmaq and the non-Native fishers must still be resolved. The Supreme Court of Canada ruled in *Regina v. Van der Peet* in 1996 that Aboriginal practices are indeed protected, but only those practices that were present before European contact.

Contemporary Aboriginal issues abound in the twenty-first century. The Aboriginal claim of the Cree of Lubicon Lake in northern Alberta remains unresolved. Geographical remoteness kept this community out of Treaty Eight signed in 1899. The Cree of Lubicon Lake have taken their case to the United Nations. But the community's distance from major southern urban centres has denied its claim the same attention as Oka received. The breakdown in negotiations in the 1990s came over the nature of the claim. The federal government will recognize the claim only as an unfulfilled treaty entitlement, a specific claim, based on Treaty Eight. In contrast, the Cree of Lubicon Lake argue that they have unextinguished Aboriginal title, and consequently a comprehensive claim. They want a modern-day treaty similar to that of the James Bay Cree or the Nisga'a in British Columbia.

Land-claims issues remain contentious. In December 2006 the Assembly of First Nations voted to make June 29, 2007 a national day of peaceful protest. Aboriginal marchers on that day expressed great frustration, but, as intended, there were no violent confrontations.

First Nations groups contend that the whole federal claims-resolution process is unfair. Ottawa sets the rules and controls the agenda. Under the existing system, Aboriginal communities lacking sufficient economic resources must obtain research and legal funds from the same government that will decide whether or not to accept their claim for negotiation. Exasperated by lengthy delays, for instance, a group of Six Nations protestors in 2006 began a nonviolent

First Nations people know the important of written as well as oral testimony. The photo shows a First Nations delegation of elders and political leaders from southern Alberta visiting the Library and Archives Canada (then the National Archives of Canada) on December 12, 1995. They came to Ottawa to see the original copy of Treaty Seven.

Source: © Library and Archives Canada. Reproduced with the permission of the Minister of Public Works and Government Services Canada (2007). Library and Archives Canada/Jeffrey Thomas/PA-197997.

occupation of the Douglas Creek Estates, a disputed tract of land, near Caledonia, beside the Grand River Territory in Ontario. In early June 2007 Jim Prentice, the Conservative government's Minister of Indian Affairs, announced a new land-claims policy to speed up land claims. Prime Minister Harper added that the bill, to be cowritten with the Assembly of First Nations and presented to Parliament in the fall of 2007, would "revolutionize" the now discredited settlement process. The new independent tribunal would have the authority to make binding decisions to help clear the backlog of nearly 1000 cases. Ottawa will allot $250 million per year over ten years to fund settlements.

The danger of violence over unresolved land-claims issues remains very real, as Oka showed in 1990. Five years after Oka, a land-claims dispute in Ontario over an Aboriginal burial site at Ipperwash Provincial Park led to an incident in which an Ojibwa protester, Dudley George, was killed. The Ipperwash Inquiry was set up in May 2004 to investigate the events that surrounded the man's death, and also to make recommendations that would attempt to avoid a similar tragedy in the future. Sidney Linden, the commissioner in charge of the Ipperwash Inquiry, in his report of late May 2007, laid the blame for the fatal shooting on the police and governments. He stated as well that "the most urgent priority is for the federal government to return" the land to local First Nations bands "immediately."

Another confrontation occurred in British Columbia in the summer of 1995, at Gustafsen Lake, about 100 km from Williams Lake in central British Columbia. First Nations individuals involved claimed the private ranch land they occupied was a sacred site. however, when the Toronto *Globe and Mail* on August 23 interviewed the administrator for the Cariboo Tribal Council, whose four bands are near the site, he reported: "To the best of our elders' knowledge, it is not a sacred or significant place." Local First Nations people and the forces of law and order formed an unusual alliance. The elected officials of the Tribal Council attempted to negotiate peace with the militants. The national chief of the Assembly of First Nations himself tried, and failed. On September 11, a police operation began, surrounding the militants' camp. Shots were exchanged, and the occupiers surrendered six days later, with no casualties. In the nearly year-long trial that followed, 21 individuals received sentences.

Economic and Social Issues for Aboriginal Canada Since the 1980s

The findings of the Royal Commission on Aboriginal Peoples in the mid-1990s confirmed the continuing economic and social inequality of the Indigenous peoples in Canada. For nearly one-half of the registered Indians living off the reserves, the quality of life is somewhat better, but still substantially below that of the average non-Native Canadian.

Before World War II, nearly all First Nations lived in rural areas. Only the most adventurous or better educated left for the cities, where they found ready employment. When large numbers went to find industrial jobs the situation changed. Many experienced racial discrimination. It took various forms, from the refusal of accommodation to discrimination in hiring processes: last hired, first fired. Those who lacked academic and vocational credentials remained the hardest hit. As Georges Erasmus, co-chair of the Royal Commission on Aboriginal Peoples, said: "Moving from a reserve or rural settlement to the city improves income and employment prospects, but only marginally." To help individuals adjust, Native friendship centres formed in the 1960s and 1970s. Although they did assist Aboriginal people in feeling at home in the city, they could not alter economic conditions.

The Indian and Métis Friendship Centre in Winnipeg, 1960.

Source: Archives of Manitoba, Nan Shipley Collection 74.

Another challenge is Indigenous language retention. The 2005 census reported that only one-quarter of Aboriginal people could conduct a conversation in an Aboriginal language. Maintaining Aboriginal languages in urban areas is difficult when there are not many fluent speakers, and those individuals speak different Aboriginal languages, or different dialects. In urban areas only a tiny percent of Aboriginal children are reported speaking their Indigenous languages at home. It has become an issue even on reserves near urban centres.

Great challenges remain in many sectors. Poverty certainly is a major issue. It, for instance, restricts access to quality health care. While life expectancy for registered Indians at birth continues to improve, and to approach parity with the general Canadian population, a gap of approximately 6.3 years has remained between the registered Indian and Canadian population in 2000. Essential are programs such as the University of Saskatchewan's Aboriginal Access to Nursing Program that trains much-needed Native nurses.

Very serious is the underfunding of child welfare services on reserves. This has contributed to a crisis in 2007, with 27 000 Aboriginal children in foster homes, a figure much higher than the total number of students in Indian residential schools at the high point of their existence in the mid-twentieth century. One out of ten Aboriginal children is in foster care, as against one in two hundred non-Aboriginal children.[3]

The incarceration rate of Native people stands at unacceptably high levels. As Marianne O. Nielsen points out, Canada's Aboriginal population is "seriously and tragically overrepresented among the inmates incarcerated in federal and provincial correctional institutions."[4] The most common reason for Aboriginal people being in prison remains the inability to pay

This cartoon captures the reality of the situation facing many Aboriginal people in the Canadian judicial system.

Source: Malcolm Mayes, *Edmonton Journal*, March 28, 1991, p. A22.

fines imposed by the courts. Lack of familiarity with the Canadian legal system, and with the non-Native society itself, add to the disadvantages of Aboriginal people dealing with the Canadian justice system.

Yet, on the positive side, a number of improvements have been made. For one, the number of individuals identifying themselves as Aboriginal has increased. According to the 2001 census, there were approximately 610 000 Indians, 290 000 Métis and non-status Indians, and 45 000 Inuit in Canada, or 3.3 percent of the overall Canadian population. Interestingly, in the 1996 census there were 800 000 individuals who identified themselves as Aboriginal (Indian, Inuit, or Métis), and just five years later, in 2001, almost a million did. Natural increase cannot explain such numbers.

In addition, when one includes those Canadians with some Aboriginal ancestry, but who did not claim an Aboriginal (Indian, Inuit, or Métis) identity, the number of Aboriginals in Canada is 4.4 percent. These figures establish that many more individuals are self-identifying with their Aboriginal ancestry, indicating an increased pride in their Indigenous heritage.

Education is another area in which significant advances occurred. In 1995 the federal government published data that showed that almost three-quarters of status Indian students reached grade 12, as against only one-fifth in 1970. Similarly the number of status Indians and Inuit in postsecondary education has jumped from 4500 in 1970 to 27 000 in 2000–01. The gap between First Nations and the larger Canadian population has narrowed. The fact that large numbers of First Nations individuals have obtained postsecondary education means they are now role models to their youth, creating additional interest in postsecondary institutions as a way of following new career options.

Over the last quarter-century, numerous Aboriginal authors, artists, and performers have emerged. Writers such as Maria Campbell, Thomson Highway, and Basil Johnston have achieved prominence. They join a growing number of Native artists, such as Robert Davidson, Norval Morrisseau, Daphne Odjig, Bill Reid, and Allen Sapp, who have used art to strengthen and affirm their Aboriginal identity. A number of Inuit artists enjoy a worldwide reputation. The group Kashtin and singer Susan Aglukark have succeeded in the popular music field. Tom Jackson has achieved recognition in both music and acting. Architect Douglas Cardinal has won numerous international awards for his work; he designed the Canadian Museum of Civilization in Hull, Quebec and the National Museum of the American Indian in Washington, DC.

Advancement has occurred on other fronts as well. Over the past decade Aboriginal people have served in many important administrative posts, including CBC board of directors member (John Kim Bell), ombudsman of Ontario (Roberta Jamieson), lieutenant governor of Ontario (James Bartelman), Canadian ambassador to Costa Rica (Dan Goodleaf), and chancellor of Trent University (Mary Simon). Annually the National Aboriginal Achievement Awards, nationally televised since 1994, have recognized the successes of Aboriginal people in Canada.

Great progress has also been made in communications. The Aboriginal Peoples Television Network, started in 1999, has recently received a seven-year licence renewal. Canada has taken a leading role in the world in Aboriginal broadcasting. Northern and Southern communities now can hear their own languages and see their own programming. Lorna Roth, the author of the new study, *Something New in the Air: The Story of First Peoples Television Broadcasting in Canada* (2005), credits this success to the persistent efforts of the Aboriginal peoples to take control of their own media sources, as well as the support of the Canadian Radio-television and Telecommunications Commission (CRTC) with the federal Department of Heritage.

Economic progress has been made in a number of communities over the last two decades. The fact that some First Nations and Inuit people have gained ownership over huge chunks of territory, land where resource companies have huge investments, has helped. The creation of First Nations banking institutions, such as Peace Hills Trust Company in Alberta and the First Nations Bank of Canada, formed by the Saskatchewan Indian Equity Foundation and the Toronto Dominion Bank, are positive developments.

Oil and gas have provided supplementary income to a small number of First Nations communities, such as the Mikisew Cree of northeastern Alberta. This community numbering approximately 2400, has profited from the hundreds of jobs provided by the oil sands development. Since the mid-1980s they have operated a small airline, a construction firm, and an energy service company that provides workers and service contracts to the oil sands developments in the Fort McMurray area.

Several communities have obtained a measure of economic self-sufficiency from running casinos. The economic success of Casino Rama, owned by the Mnjikning First Nations near Orillia, Ontario, has been spectacular. Through a revenue distribution system, the profits of Casino Rama are shared among the First Nations in Ontario. In Regina the Federation of Saskatchewan Indian Nations and the Saskatchewan government run Regina Casino, which ironically occupies the city's former railway station, a destination point in the early twentieth century for immigrants anxious to take over former First Nations land. But gaming has negative sides as well. The host community faces gambling addiction, higher crime levels, and additional stress on their roads.[5] And not all First Nations casinos are, like Casino Rama, big moneymakers.

Tourism and successful small businesses have helped other First Nations communities. An entrepreneurial class is emerging. But great challenges remain. Many status Indians have left their reserves to escape their depressed economic conditions. Many of the over 2350 reserves (and many rural communities of non-status Indians and Métis) are very small, scattered, and distant from large urban areas. Part of the problem stems from the fact that they lack the resources and the necessary infrastructure to sustain their increasing populations.

Since the mid-1980s the number of status Indians has increased substantially on account of the passage of Bill C-31 in 1985. The federal Conservative government of Brian Mulroney proceeded with this legislation, despite its oft-stated commitment to consult first with the First Nation's leadership on constitutional and legislative matters. Ironically it was in the midst of the First Ministers' conferences on Aboriginal issues in the mid-1980s that it acted, in the face of widespread opposition from chiefs from the treaty areas, especially from the treaty areas in the prairie provinces. These leaders predicted the legislation unilaterally imposed upon them would have serious economic and social implications, including their cultural identity, political balance on elected councils, and on language preservation. The Conservative administration replied that Bill C-31 was necessary in order to bring the Indian Act into conformity with the three-year-old Charter of Rights and Freedoms, introduced with the new constitution of 1982. The Charter eliminated such discrimination.

Bill C-31 restored Indian status to most Native women who requested it, in particular to those women who had married non-Indians and subsequently lost their status under the Indian Act. Those who lost their status for other reasons could also apply. It also gave status to their immediate descendants, increasing the number of registered Indians by 115 000 from 1985 to 2001. Reinstatement as a status Indian entitled the individual to receive limited medical care, subsidies for higher education, and exemption from all federal and provincial taxation on monies earned on any reserve. Those gaining membership in a specific Indian band (many bands now control their own individual membership) obtain a share of the band's assets, the right to reside on the band's reserve, all hunting and fishing rights, eligibility for federal loans and grants to establish reserve businesses, and free schooling on the reserve.

Unfortunately, a negative aspect of Bill C-31 had become increasingly evident to many First Nations communities. The grandchildren of women who lost their Indian status following a union to a non-status spouse, and then regained it through Bill C-31, ran a risk of losing it. Indian Status *Tekawennake*, a Six Nations newspaper at Ohsweken, Ontario, wrote in an editorial entitled "Twenty Years After Bill C-31, Our 7th Generation Notions Statistically Doomed: INAC Study" (June 29, 2005): "The main finding of the report is that the trend toward exogamy, or out-marriage, in combination with off-reserve educational opportunities and urbanization, will be far and away more effective in doing away with Indian status than any assimilationist government program ever was." Embedded within the Indian Act are descent rules as to who may or may not inherit status. Under section 6-2 of Bill C-31, the children of a reinstated woman, the first generation, obtain Indian status. However, if these children make a union with a non-status person, their children, the second generation, will not meet the requirements for registration as status Indians.

Women play a prominent role in today's First Nations communities. Of the 633 communities represented by the Assembly of First Nations, over a hundred are led by female Aboriginal chiefs. Half a century ago there was only one woman chief in Canada; now 17 percent are female. Women are also very prominent in their communities as band councillors. In the nonpolitical sector many women work as teachers and social workers in their communities

The Métis, the Inuit, and the Federal Government

The Métis position differs from that of status Indians. The federal government has maintained that Canada's obligations to the Métis ended once it had dealt with the Métis land claim under the Manitoba Act and issued land allowances (or the money equivalent) to the Métis in the North-West Territories in 1885 and in 1899–1900. The federal government contends that the provinces have responsibility for the Métis. A high point of the Métis's political struggle for recognition came when they succeeded in achieving identification as an Aboriginal people in the Constitution Act of 1982. One of the difficulties of describing the Métis, however, lies in the lack of an easy definition of the group's ethnicity. According to historian Jennifer Brown, "Métis as a term has become a net cast over a growing variety of people of mixed European–Indian ancestry. It still refers to the first group widely known as Métis (people of Cree-Ojibwa, French-Canadian descent, largely Roman Catholic, and based on the Canadian prairies), but it now also commonly subsumes others of mixed heritage who have been known as 'halfbreeds,' non-status Indians, or by other labels depending on their historical contexts, occupational classes, and other factors."[6] Both the Native Council of Canada (now the Congress of Aboriginal Peoples) and the Métis National Council, formed in 1983 to represent the five Métis provincial organizations west of Quebec, participated in the Charlottetown Accord discussions in 1992.

A victory for the Métis came in September 2003 with the Supreme Court decision in *Regina v. Powley*. In its decision the Court recognized the status of the Métis people as a distinct Aboriginal group with protected constitutional rights, in this case the right to hunt for food; however, it did not define or specify the scope of the Aboriginal rights of the Métis. This makes it necessary to determine what other Aboriginal rights the Métis are entitled to, or should negotiate, on a wide range of issues from natural resources to health services and taxation.

Of the three Native groups, the Inuit have the best chance of retaining control of their lands, because they constitute over three-quarters of the population in the eastern Arctic. Due to the remoteness of the area and, from a southerner's perspective, the severity of its climate (even with global warming), the Inuit will probably always be the majority on the treeless northern tundra. Nunavut (meaning "our land" in Inuktitut), created in 1999, is now Canada's third territory.

Hunter Steve Powley and his lawyer, Jean Teillet, celebrate after an Ontario court in 1998 for the first time recognized the Métis as a distinct Aboriginal people with protected constitutional rights. Jean Teillet is the great-grandniece of Louis Riel.

Source: CP PHOTO/Sault Star-Keith Stephen.

The Aboriginal North from the 1970s to Today

The northern First Nations and Inuit have contributed greatly to the placing of Aboriginal issues on the public-policy agenda. Until recently, the Yukon Native peoples were assigned a peripheral role, both economically and politically. Native political awareness arose in the Yukon in the late 1960s. Elijah Smith, the late chief of the Champagne Aishihik First Nations, urged his people to start looking for guarantees of their rights to their homeland. In the Yukon, and indeed throughout Canada, a new generation of bilingual Aboriginal leaders, men and women in their twenties, came forward to fight for land claims and an end to the federal government's assimilation policies. In 1973, the Yukon Native Brotherhood (which became the Council of Yukon Indians later that year) began formal talks with the federal government about Aboriginal rights in the Yukon.

Aboriginal demands for political control in the neighbouring Northwest Territories also date back forty years. Discussions began in 1968 to form the first territorial Aboriginal organization, and in the following year sixteen chiefs from sixteen villages founded the Indian Brotherhood of the Northwest Territories, later called the Dene Nation. In 1970, the Committee for the Original Peoples' Entitlement (COPE) was formed in Inuvik to protect the interests of the Inuit in the Mackenzie Delta—or the Inuvialuit, as the Inuit of the western Arctic refer to themselves. In 1971 an Inuit organizing committee formed the Inuit Tapirisat of Canada (originally called the Eskimo Brotherhood), a pan-Inuit organization with a mandate to address questions of northern development and to work to preserve Inuit culture. COPE became one of the regional associations

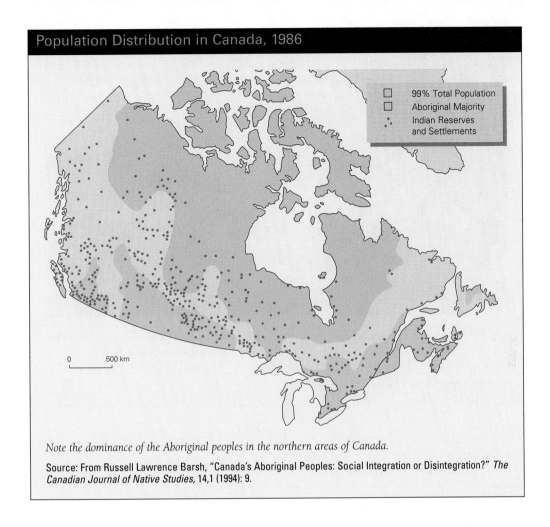

Population Distribution in Canada, 1986

☐ 99% Total Population
☐ Aboriginal Majority
• Indian Reserves
  and Settlements

0   500 km

Note the dominance of the Aboriginal peoples in the northern areas of Canada.

Source: From Russell Lawrence Barsh, "Canada's Aboriginal Peoples: Social Integration or Disintegration?" *The Canadian Journal of Native Studies,* 14,1 (1994): 9.

affiliated with the Inuit Tapirisat of Canada. Later, the Inuit of the eastern and central Arctic established the Tungavik Federation of Nunavut to represent their specific regional concerns. Then, in 1973, the Métis formed their own association, the Métis Association of the Northwest Territories, which eventually joined with the Dene Nation to submit a joint land claim.

The Berger Inquiry, headed by Judge Thomas Berger, in the mid-1970s did a great deal to obtain a national audience for First Nations and Inuit concerns. In 1972, the building of a Canadian pipeline to carry American oil and gas from the vast Prudhoe Bay field on the northeastern coast of Alaska south through the Mackenzie valley seemed a certainty—until a commission was set up to investigate its feasibility. Berger undertook a comprehensive environmental, social, and cultural impact study, holding community hearings, not just in Yellowknife but also in 34 other settlements potentially affected by the pipeline. His final report in 1977 called for the settlement of Native land claims before potentially proceeding and a ten-year delay on the development of the Mackenzie valley pipeline. The report eloquently conveyed the Native peoples' conviction that the North was their own distinct homeland, and not simply a resource frontier for southern Canada. The National Energy Board, the national regulatory body, also rejected the proposed development in the Mackenzie valley.

The Native peoples' concerns contributed to the decision to postpone the pipeline. Several years later, in the early 1980s, a pipeline was built, but only halfway up the valley, to Norman Wells. Today market conditions favour a full northern gas pipeline. With most Aboriginal land

Justice Thomas Berger listens to the residents of Nahanni Butte, an isolated Slavey Dene community of less than a hundred people in the Dehcho region in the southwestern corner of the Northwest Territories, during one of the hearings of the Mackenzie Valley Pipeline Inquiry.

Source: CP PHOTO/Robert Galbraith.

claims now settled, many Native people have dropped their decades-long opposition to the idea of a Mackenzie Valley pipeline.

The development of diamond mines, in which the Aboriginal people have gained jobs, and resource revenue has been welcomed. Three mines have opened, with more planned. The number of First Nations and Inuit people in postsecondary education has jumped with the opening up of skilled and technical jobs.

Nunavut and Denendeh

In 1979, the Aboriginal majority in the legislative assembly of the North-West Territories endorsed the proposed division of the territories. The government of the North-West Territories held a plebiscite on the issue in 1982, in which 56 percent of the votes cast favoured division. Later that year, the federal government accepted the proposal in principle. An Inuit constitutional forum representing Nunavut and a second forum representing the western district, or Denendeh, a northern Athapaskan word meaning "land of the people," were formed to discuss how the territorial division might be accomplished. A major stumbling block became the proposed border between the two jurisdictions. Which one would the Inuvialuit, the Inuit of the western Arctic, decide to join?

Despite blood ties with their fellow Inuit in the east, the Inuvialuit chose to keep their economic links with the west. The adherence of the western Arctic to Denendeh, rich in newly discovered oil and gas potential, greatly pleased the Dene and the Métis. The addition of the 2500 Inuvialuit helped raise the Native population of Denendeh in 1982 to near-equality (15 000) with that of the non-Native population (17 000). On January 15, 1987, leaders of the two constitutional forums confirmed in Iqaluit the decision to divide the North-West Territories. Subsequently the North-West Territories legislative assembly and the federal government approved the territorial division, which occurred on April 1, 1999.

The population of the North-West Territories consisted in the late 1990s of approximately 50 000 people, split almost equally into three groups: Inuit and Inuvialuit, First Nations and Métis, and non-Natives. What is extraordinary about the North-West Territories is the speed with which the Aboriginal people have taken control of the political structures. In 1991, the commissioner of the Northwest Territories was a Métis, his deputy commissioner an Inuk (Inuk is the singular of Inuit), and the government leader a non-Native. The previous two government leaders were a Métis and a First Nations individual. Many Aboriginal people now fill senior administrative posts. Native self-government, the goal of the southern Aboriginal people, is at least partially a reality in the North-West Territories, and now in Nunavut as well.

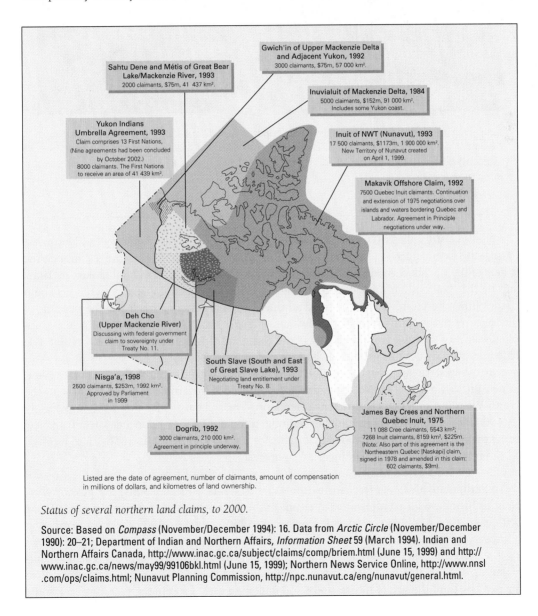

Sahtu Dene and Métis of Great Bear Lake/Mackenzie River, 1993
2000 claimants, $75m, 41 437 km².

Gwich'in of Upper Mackenzie Delta and Adjacent Yukon, 1992
3000 claimants, $75m, 57 000 km².

Inuvialuit of Mackenzie Delta, 1984
5000 claimants, $152m, 91 000 km². Includes some Yukon coast.

Yukon Indians Umbrella Agreement, 1993
Claim comprises 13 First Nations, (Nine agreements had been concluded by October 2002.)
8000 claimants. The First Nations to receive an area of 41 439 km².

Inuit of NWT (Nunavut), 1993
17 500 claimants, $1173m, 1 900 000 km². New Territory of Nunavut created on April 1, 1999.

Makavik Offshore Claim, 1992
7500 Quebec Inuit claimants. Continuation and extension of 1975 negotiations over islands and waters bordering Quebec and Labrador. Agreement in Principle negotiations under way.

Deh Cho (Upper Mackenzie River)
Discussing with federal government claim to sovereignty under Treaty No. 11.

Nisga'a, 1998
2500 claimants, $253m, 1992 km². Approved by Parliament in 1999

South Slave (South and East of Great Slave Lake), 1993
Negotiating land entitlement under Treaty No. 8.

James Bay Crees and Northern Quebec Inuit, 1975
11 088 Cree claimants, 5543 km²; 7268 Inuit claimants, 8159 km², $225m. (Note: Also part of this agreement is the Northeastern Quebec (Naskapi) claim, signed in 1978 and amended in this claim: 602 claimants, $9m).

Dogrib, 1992
3000 claimants, 210 000 km². Agreement in principle underway.

Listed are the date of agreement, number of claimants, amount of compensation in millions of dollars, and kilometres of land ownership.

Status of several northern land claims, to 2000.

Source: Based on *Compass* (November/December 1994): 16. Data from *Arctic Circle* (November/December 1990): 20–21; Department of Indian and Northern Affairs, *Information Sheet* 59 (March 1994). Indian and Northern Affairs Canada, http://www.inac.gc.ca/subject/claims/comp/briem.html (June 15, 1999) and http://www.inac.gc.ca/news/may99/99106bkl.html (June 15, 1999); Northern News Service Online, http://www.nnsl.com/ops/claims.html; Nunavut Planning Commission, http://npc.nunavut.ca/eng/nunavut/general.html.

Court rulings from the 1970s to the present have helped to reestablish an important place for treaty and Aboriginal rights in Canadian society. Since this photo was taken a decade or so ago, the Supreme Court has achieved near–gender equality. The Chief Justice is currently a woman, and three of her eight fellow members are female.

Source: CP Picture Archive.

Nunavut strengthens Canada's sovereignty in the Arctic, as its claims to the Northwest Passage are based largely on the Inuit's use and occupancy of the area. The voyages through the waters of the Canadian Arctic Archipelago by the *Manhattan*, an American oil tanker, in 1969, and by the *Polar Sea*, an American icebreaker, in 1985, awakened Canadians to the uncertain status of their northern waters. The rapid advance of global warming has led to the thinning of the ice cover in the North-West Passage, which will make the Passage a viable commercial shipping route. For the Inuit global warming in the North has already led to rendering their lifestyle based on traditional activities, such as hunting, unpredictable.

In the western Arctic in 1984, COPE, the political organization of the 2500 Inuvialuit, signed the first comprehensive settlement with the federal government in the Yukon and the North-West Territories. In return for surrendering their claim to the title of approximately 345 000 km^2 of land, the Inuvialuit obtained title to about 90 000 km^2 (an area larger than New Brunswick), including subsurface mineral rights for 13 000 km^2 of this area. They also received $152 million (in 1984 dollars) in financial compensation.

By the terms of a tentative agreement between the federal government and the Council of Yukon Indians that was reached in 1994 after 21 years of negotiations, the Yukon's First Nations bands would retain nearly 9 percent of the territory's land mass. In the land-claims settlement, they would also receive approximately $250 million (in 1989 dollars) in cash over a fifteen-year period.

In 1990, the First Nations and Métis of the Mackenzie valley area signed a tentative land-claims agreement. Had both Native groups ratified it, they would have received surface title to an area one-third the size of Alberta and $500 million in cash. Later in the year, however, some individuals rejected what is known as the extinguishment clause in the "agreement-in-principle," requiring them to give up all treaty and Aboriginal rights. In late 1990, the federal government announced that it would negotiate new claims with each of the regions in the Aboriginal territory separately. Parliament accepted the Gwich'in comprehensive land-claims agreement in late 1992, the Sahtu Dene and Métis land-claims agreement in 1993, and the Tlicho (Dogrib) Agreement in 2003, thus settling three of the five regions' land claims.

In the eastern and central Arctic, the Tungavik Federation of Nunavut and the federal government reached an agreement-in-principle in 1990. Three years later, they signed a land-claims settlement that gave the Inuit absolute ownership of parcels of land totalling approximately 350 000 km^2, a territory roughly one-half the size of the province of Saskatchewan. They also received $580 million for relinquishing their Aboriginal claim to 2 000 000 km^2, an area twice the size of the province of Ontario. In 1993, Parliament passed the Nunavut Land Claims Agreement, which in conjunction with the act to create the territory of Nunavut, redrew the map of Canada in April 1999.

Two-thirds of a century ago, Aboriginal issues rarely entered into the consciousness of non-Native Canadians. Few Indigenous people lived in cities. Government paid little attention to national resource expansion into northern Aboriginal-dominated areas of Canada. Treaty rights received little attention. Canadian history texts began with the Europeans' arrival in North America.

Today, while social and economic inequalities persist for many Aboriginal people, improvements have been made. Aboriginal and treaty rights gained protection in the Canadian Constitution of 1982. The Indigenous population, far from diminishing, is growing at about twice the overall Canadian rate. At universities and colleges the number of Aboriginal students has soared. The attitudes of many non-Native Canadians toward Native peoples have changed. Recent Supreme Court decisions, such as *Mikisew Cree First Nation v. Canada* (2005), appear to be emerging as new landmark Aboriginal rights cases, such as the earlier *Delgamuukw* case (1997). The decision in *Mikisew* states that treaty-making, in this case Treaty Eight, is only a step, and that the need for extensive consultation with First Nations that have made treaties continues on public, non-reserve lands.

The resolution of many of the issues involved in the settlement of Indian Residential School claims in 2005 and 2006 shows a new willingness by the dominant society to rectify past injustices. The proposed Kelowna Accord of 2005, reached by the provincial premiers, Indigenous leaders, with the Liberal government of Paul Martin, marked a new level of federal commitment to Aboriginal Canada. It would have directed $5 billion over five years into Aboriginal education, housing, clean water, health services, and economic development. The new Conservative administration of Stephen Harper has not endorsed the initiative. In March 2007 it defended its policy by claiming that its Native spending is $1 billion higher than when the Liberals were in power. To quote the *Report of the Royal Commission on Aboriginal Peoples*, volume 1, *Looking Forward, Looking Back*: "Within a span of 25 years, Aboriginal peoples and their rights have emerged from the shadows, to the sidelines, to occupy centre stage."[7]

NOTES

Many thanks to J. Rick Ponting and Judy Lynch, for their assistance with the revision for the 5th edition of this chapter of *Destinies*. We also thank Ian Getty and Cora Voyageur for their comments on a draft of this version for the 6th edition. Any errors or omissions in both editions remain the responsibility of the authors. Special thanks go to Judy Lynch for making available for the 5th edition an early draft of Michael Cassidy's "Treaties and Aboriginal–Government Relations, 1945–2000." The piece has since been published in David R. Newhouse, Cora J. Voyageur, and Dan Beavon, eds., *Hidden in Plain Sight: Contributions of Aboriginal Peoples to Canadian Identity and Culture* (Toronto: University of Toronto Press, 2005), pp. 38–60.

1. Diamond Jenness, *The Indians of Canada* (Ottawa: King's Printer, 1932), p. 264.

2. As reported in Patrick Brethour, "Band to Withdraw from Treaty Talks," *The Globe and Mail*, March 31, 2007.

3. Campbell Clark, "Natives to Hit Ottawa with Rights Complaint," *The Globe and Mail*, February 5, 2007.

4. Marianne O. Nielsen, "Introduction," in Robert A. Silverman and Marianne O. Nielsen, eds., *Aboriginal Peoples and Canadian Criminal Justice* (Toronto: Harcourt Brace, 1994), p. 3.

5. Yale D. Belanger, *Gambling with the Future: The Evolution of Aboriginal Gaming in Canada* (Saskatoon: Purich Publishing, 2006), p. 100.

6. Jennifer S.H. Brown, "Review of Structural Considerations of Métis Ethnicity: An Archaeological, Architectural and Historical Study by David V. Burley et al.," *Ethnohistory* 41(4) (Fall 1994): 680.

7. Canada, *Report of the Royal Commission on Aboriginal Peoples*, vol. 1, *Looking Forward, Looking Back* (Ottawa: Canada Communication Group Publishing, 1996), p. 216; quoted in Alan C. Cairns, *Citizens Plus: Aboriginal Peoples and the Canadian State* (Vancouver: UBC Press, 2000), p. 3.

BEYOND THE BOOK

Weblinks

Aboriginal Canada Portal
http://www.aboriginalcanada.gc.ca
Portal to information about Aboriginal peoples in Canada. Includes community profiles, government programs, and cultural information.

James Bay Project and the Cree
http://archives.cbc.ca/IDD-1-69-94/life_society/james_bay
A video and audio history of the controversial James Bay Hydroelectric Project and the Cree people.

Aboriginal Peoples Television Network
http://www.aptn.ca
Official website of the Aboriginal Peoples Television Network.

Aboriginals and the Canadian Military: Past, Present, Future
http://www.cda.forces.gc.ca/aborig_conference_autoch/engraph/home_e.asp
Digitized presentations from a 2006 conference regarding Aboriginal contributions to and historical relationships with the Canadian military. The conference was hosted by the Canadian Defence Academy, a division of the Canadian Forces.

First Nations and Inuit Health

http://www.hc-sc.gc.ca/fnih-spni/index_e.html

Describes the health status of First Nations and Inuit peoples, as well as federal health programs focused on this population.

Residential Schools

http://www.wherearethechildren.ca/en/home.html

This site contains a 3D tour of a residential school, transcripts of interviews with individuals who lived in them, and contains historical photographs and other resources.

Films & Novels

Urban Elder. Directed by Robert S. Adams. 1997.

Cree Spoken Here. Directed by Ernest Webb and Neil Diamond. 2001.

Kiss of the Fur Queen. By Tomson Highway. 2000.

RELATED READINGS

R. Douglas Francis and Donald B. Smith, eds., *Readings in Canadian History: Post-Confederation*, 7th ed. (Toronto: Nelson Thomson Learning, 2006), contains the following articles relevant to this chapter: Alan C. Cairns, "Aboriginal Peoples in the Twenty-First Century: A Plea for Realism," pp. 573–89; and Rob Huebert, "Climate Change and Canadian Sovereignty in the Northwest Passage," pp. 603–13.

BIBLIOGRAPHY

Recent surveys of the history of Aboriginal Canada include Olive Patricia Dickason, *Canada's First Nations: A History of Founding Peoples from Earliest Times*, 3rd ed. (Toronto: Oxford University Press, 2002) and her *A Concise History of Canada's First Nations*, adapted by Moira Calder (Toronto: Oxford University Press, 2006); and Arthur J. Ray, *I Have Lived Here Since the World Began: An Illustrated History of Canada's Native People*, rev. ed. (Toronto: Key Porter, 2005). Ted Binnema's "Chronology of Canadian Native History, 1500 to 1992," in Duane Champagne, ed., *The Native North American Almanac* (Detroit: Gale Research Inc., 1994), pp. 103–38, remains useful. An overview of the First Nations in present-day Canada, the United States, and Mexico, appears in Alice B. Kehoe's chapter 10, "First Nations of North America in the Contemporary World," in her *North American Indians, A Comprehensive Account*, 3rd ed. (Upper Saddle River, New Jersey: Pearson Prentice Hall, 2006), pp. 524–54.

For a review of Canadian Indian policy in the early twentieth century, see J.R. Miller. *Skyscrapers Hide the Heavens: A History of Indian–White Relations in Canada*, 3rd ed. (Toronto: University of Toronto Press, 2000); and his *Reflections on Native–Newcomer Relations: Selected Essays* (Toronto: University of Toronto Press, 2004). Unfortunately, there are few historical studies of provincial policies toward Indigenous people; but three contributions are: Paul Tennant, *Aboriginal Peoples and Politics: The Indian Land Question in British Columbia, 1849–1989* (Vancouver: University of British Columbia Press, 1990); F. Laurie Barron, *Walking in Indian Moccasins: The Native Policies of Tommy Douglas and the CCF* (Vancouver: University of British Columbia Press, 1997); and Laurie Meijer Drees, *The Indian Association of Alberta: A History of Political Action* (Vancouver: University of British Columbia Press, 2002). Other valuable introductory studies of the mid-twentieth century include Hugh Dempsey, *The Gentle Persuader: A Biography of James Gladstone, Indian Senator* (Saskatoon: Western Producer Prairie Books, 1986); Harold Cardinal, *The Unjust Society: The Tragedy of Canada's Indians* (Edmonton: Hurtig, 1969; and Vancouver: Douglas and McIntyre, 1999)—a Cree's indictment of Canadian Indian policy; and Edgar Dosman, *Indians: The Urban Dilemma* (Toronto: McClelland & Stewart, 1972).

For an overview of First Nations social welfare issues see Hugh Shewell, *"Enough to Keep Them Alive": Indian Welfare in Canada, 1873–1965* (Toronto: University of Toronto Press, 2004). An older study remains useful, namely Patrick Johnston, *Native Children and the Child Welfare System* (Toronto: James Lorimer, 1983). A regional study of health issues is T. Kue Young's *Health Care and Cultural Change: The Indian Experience in the Central Arctic* (Toronto: University of Toronto Press, 1988). Pat Sandiford Grygier provides a history of the tuberculosis epidemic among the Inuit in the mid-twentieth century in *A Long Way from Home* (Montreal/Kingston: McGill-Queen's University Press, 1994).

For an understanding of the Indian residential schools see J.R. Miller, *Shingwauk's Vision* (Toronto: University of Toronto Press, 1996)—the essential starting point. John S. Milloy examines the schools over a shorter time period in *"A National Crime": The Canadian Government and the Residential School System, 1879 to 1986* (Winnipeg: University of Manitoba Press, 1999). A review of several of the major studies appears in this chapter in "Where Historians Disagree: Interpreting the Indian Residential Schools, 1879–1986." Bernard Schissel and Terry Wotherspoon provide a sociological assessment in *The Legacy of School for Aboriginal People* (Don Mills: Oxford University Press, 2003).

Five recent studies provide good overviews of contemporary Indigenous issues in Canada: James S. Frideres and René R. Gadacz, *Aboriginal Peoples in Canada: Contemporary Conflicts*, 7th ed. (Toronto: Pearson Prentice-Hall, 2005); John Steckley and Bryan D. Cummins, eds., *Full Circle: Canada's First Nations*, 2nd ed. (Toronto: Pearson Prentice Hall, 2007); J.R. Miller, *Lethal Legacy: Current Native Controversies in Canada* (Toronto: McClelland and Stewart, 2004); and David R. Newhouse, Cora J. Voyageur, and Dan Beavon, eds., *Hidden in Plain Sight: Contributions of Aboriginal Peoples to Canadian Identity and Culture* (Toronto: University of Toronto Press, 2005). *Hidden in Plain Sight* is particularly valuable, as it covers treaties, arts and media, literature, justice, culture and identity, sports, and military. *Tapwe: Selected Columns of Doug Cuthand* (Penticton, BC: Theytus Books Ltd., 2005) includes a wide range of articles by a Plains Cree journalist on many contemporary Native issues.

Two treatments of contemporary Aboriginal and non-Aboriginal relations in Canada include: Alan C. Cairns's *Citizens Plus: Aboriginal Peoples and the Canadian State* (Vancouver: UBC Press, 2000); and Tom Flanagan's more controversial *First Nations? Second Thoughts* (Montreal/Kingston: McGill-Queen's University Press, 2000). The latter attacks what Flanagan sees as the prevailing orthodoxy that determines public policy in Canada toward Aboriginal peoples. A welcome addition to the literature is the new book by First Nations academic Dale Turner, a member of the Temagami First Nations in northern Ontario and associate professor of Government and Native American Studies at Dartmouth College in the United States: *This Is Not a Peace Pipe: Towards a Critical Indigenous Philosophy* (Toronto: University of Toronto Press, 2006). An overview of First Nations land claims in Canada is Ken Coates, *Aboriginal Land Claims in Canada: A Regional Perspective* (Toronto: Copp Clark Pitman, 1992). J. Rick Ponting has written *The Nisga'a Treaty: Polling Dynamics and Political Communication in Comparative Context* (Calgary: Broadview Press, 2006).

In *Native Literature in Canada: From the Oral Tradition to the Present* (Toronto: Oxford University Press, 1990), Penny Petrone reviews Aboriginal literature. Students should also consult her two edited collections: *First People, First Voices* (Toronto: University of Toronto Press, 1983) and *Northern Voices: Inuit Writing in English* (Toronto: University of Toronto Press, 1988); and Helmut Lutz, *Contemporary Challenges, Conversations with Canadian Native Authors* (Saskatoon: Fifth House, 1991). For contemporary Indigenous viewpoints on Aboriginal writing, see the section "Literature" in *Hidden in Plain Sight*, ed. David R. Newhouse et al., pp. 169–212.

A great deal of work remains to be done on the history of the Métis in the twentieth century. D. Bruce Sealey and Antoine S. Lussier provide one of the few historical overviews in the final chapters of their study, *The Métis: Canada's Forgotten People* (Winnipeg: Manitoba Métis Federation Press, 1975), pp. 143–94. Olive P. Dickason provides a useful overview in "Aboriginals: Métis," in Paul Magocsi, ed., *Encyclopedia of Canada's Peoples* (Toronto: University of Toronto Press, 1999), pp. 70–79. A recent treatment is George and Terry Goulet, *The Metis: Memorable Events and Memorable Personalities* (Calgary: FabJob Inc., 2006).

A short, well-illustrated overview of Northern history is William R. Morrison's *True North: The Yukon and Northwest Territories* (Toronto: Oxford University Press, 1998). Georges Blondin provides an interesting Dene view of the First Nations' history in the Mackenzie valley in *When the World Was*

New: Stories of the Sahtu Dene (Yellowknife: Outcrop, 1990). Federal policy toward the Inuit is reviewed in Frank J. Tester and Peter Kulchyski, *Tammarniit (Mistakes): Inuit Relocation in the Eastern Arctic, 1939–63* (Vancouver: University of British Columbia Press, 1994). John David Hamilton surveys post–World War II developments in the North in *Arctic Revolution: Social Change in the Northwest Territories, 1935–1994* (Toronto: Dundurn Press, 1994). Keith Brownsey and Michael Howlett, eds., *The Provincial State in Canada: Politics in the Provinces and Territories* (Peterborough, Ontario: Broadview Press, 2000), contains two articles on the Northwest Territories and Nunavut: Peter Clancy, "The Northwest Territories: Old and New Class Politics on the Northern Frontier," pp. 335–68; and Jack Hicks and Graham White, "Nunavut: Inuit Self-Determination Through a Land Claim and Public Government?," pp. 389–439.

Students interested in Aboriginal politics in the last forty years should consult, as a starting point, Sally M. Weaver, *Making Canadian Indian Policy: The Hidden Agenda, 1968–1970* (Toronto: University of Toronto Press, 1981). Studies of important First Nations leaders include: Peter McFarlane's *Brotherhood to Nationhood: George Manuel and the Making of the Modern Indian Movement* (Toronto: Between the Lines, 1993); Roy MacGregor, *Chief: The Fearless Vision of Billy Diamond* (Toronto: Penguin, 1989); and Pauline Comeau's *Elijah: No Ordinary Hero* (Vancouver: Douglas & McIntyre, 1993). Useful for an understanding of contemporary issues are John Bird, Lorraine Land, and Murray Macadam, eds., *Nation to Nation: Aboriginal Sovereignty and the Future of Canada* (Toronto: Irwin, 2002); and J.R. Miller, *Lethal Legacy. Current Native Controversies in Canada* (Toronto: McClelland and Stewart, 2004).

Publications on Indigenous history and contemporary issues are appearing at a fast and furious rate. Interesting new studies on contemporary Aboriginal Canada include the following titles: Blair Stonechild, *The New Buffalo. The Struggle for Aboriginal Post-Secondary Education in Canada* (Winnipeg: University of Manitoba Press, 2006); Yale D. Belanger, *Gambling with the Future: The Evolution of Aboriginal Gaming in Canada* (Saskatoon: Purich Publishing, 2006); Lorna Roth, *Something New in the Air: The Story of First Peoples Television Broadcasting in Canada* (Montreal/Kingston: McGill-Queen's University Press, 2005); *Urban Reserves: Forging New Relationships in Saskatchewan*, eds., F. Laurie Barron and Joseph Garcea (Saskatoon: Purich Publishing Ltd., 1999); and P. Whitney Lackenbauer, *Battle Grounds: The Canadian Military and Aboriginal Lands* (Vancouver: University of British Columbia Press, 2007). Cora Voyageur's new study, *Fire-Keepers of the Twenty-First Century: First Nations Women Chiefs* (Montreal: McGill-Queen's Press), will appear in 2008.

Chapter Seventeen

THE MAKING OF MODERN QUEBEC

Quebec underwent an era of rapid change at all levels in the years after 1960, as the province evolved into a modern, dynamic, secular society. In many ways, Quebec seemed to become more like other regions of North America. Yet, at the same time, most French-speaking Quebeckers (or Québécois, as Quebec francophones now began to style themselves) thought it important that their society reinforce its unique linguistic and cultural character.

Most historians argue that the processes of modernization and secularization began well before 1960, during World War II and even earlier. What changed in 1960 was that a new government showed a readiness to make important reforms. An increasingly interventionist Quebec state became a catalyst for change in nearly all sectors of activity, from the economy and education to health and culture. At the same time, just as elsewhere in the Western world, many Quebeckers demanded and welcomed change.

What undoubtedly attracted outside attention to Quebec after 1960 was the powerful resurgence of nationalism in the province and the profound implications it had for the rest of Canada. When francophones in Quebec complained of being second-class citizens and sought increased recognition for the French language within the federal government and for the French-speaking minorities outside Quebec, English-speaking Canadians had to respond. When various

The battle for Quebec's soul. During the 1995 Quebec referendum debate, Charles Jefferson of Ottawa raised a Canadian flag over a street sign in Montreal. The street, once named Dorchester, a British governor after the conquest, was renamed Boulevard René-Lévesque, for the late Quebec premier, one of the founders of the mainstream separatist movement in Quebec.

Source: CP PHOTO/Robert Galbraith.

political movements and parties vied with one another in claiming greater political autonomy for Quebec—and even sought outright independence—Canada's future appeared to be in doubt. In this regard, the aspirations of many Quebeckers appeared threatening.

Quebec After World War II

Maurice Duplessis and his conservative Union Nationale party first took power in Quebec in 1936, during the Great Depression. Rejected in 1939 by an electorate that believed that the Liberals could best prevent military conscription, Duplessis made a surprising comeback in 1944. Although the Quebec Liberal government of Premier Adélard Godbout adopted a number of important measures while in office, it lost support over issues linked to the war and to the federal Liberals, such as conscription and increasing centralization of power in Ottawa. With Duplessis's return, the Union Nationale began an unbroken sixteen-year reign.

During the period 1945–60, Quebec changed in many respects. The province's population, like Canada's, increased rapidly, by more than 25 percent in the 1950s. Although 400 000 immigrants settled in the province in the years 1946–60, most of the rise in population stemmed from a sharply increased birth rate. In addition, large numbers of rural inhabitants moved to the cities, in search of work.

Quebec also underwent rapid economic growth as investment—much of it foreign—accelerated. The United States not only provided a market, it also supplied development capital for resource industries such as mining. Employment in the principal manufacturing industries also rose significantly, but the major gains in jobs came in the service industries. Thanks to the booming economy, Quebeckers who, like other Canadians, had endured the sacrifices of depression and war now enjoyed greater prosperity.

Traditional ideas and values began to give way. Religious practice declined, particularly in Montreal. Radio and, especially, television introduced new ideas, new norms. As historian Susan Mann explains, "Television brought the world, no longer filtered by press, priest, or politician, into Quebec's kitchens and living rooms."[1] It was incontestably a subversive influence.

Amid these changes, the very conservative Duplessis, supported by traditional elites, emphasized the importance of religious values and of respect for the established order. His government favoured private enterprise, encouraged the entry of foreign (largely American) capital, and kept taxes low. It built roads and bridges, especially in election years, and aided small-scale farmers, from whom it derived its firmest electoral support.

Labour Unrest

Duplessis's policies alienated those Quebeckers who were committed to social change. The premier opposed militant union activity because he believed it deterred investment and economic development. He also saw it as a source of social disorder. As a result, his government designed labour legislation to limit strikes, and provincial labour boards generally showed a pro-employer bias. The government even occasionally used the provincial police to protect strikebreakers or break up demonstrations. It set a low minimum wage for non-unionized workers, which affected large numbers of working women and immigrants. Other glaring inequalities, which the government did little to alleviate, also cast a pall over the general atmosphere of prosperity. Average wages of French Canadians as a group were lower than those of most other ethnic groups in the province.

Opposition to Duplessis

In the 1950s, Duplessis's opponents became increasingly vocal. They included political foes, union leaders, a few members of the clergy, and the newspaper Le Devoir, as well as intellectuals such as Pierre Elliott Trudeau, who, with Gérard Pelletier, published Cité libre, a moderately reformist magazine uncompromisingly hostile to the Union Nationale. Several university professors, among them Dominican priest Georges-Henri Lévesque, dean of the Faculty of Social Sciences at Université Laval, also risked criticizing the government. Although all wanted a more liberal, more modern Quebec, these critics differed considerably in their views on nationalism. Some, like Trudeau, viewed nationalism as necessarily conservative and reactionary, and resulting only in ethnic bitterness and conflict. Others, among them journalist André Laurendeau, who later was co-chair of the Royal Commission on Bilingualism and Biculturalism, saw nationalism as a potentially progressive force.

Duplessis's adversaries also attacked the Union Nationale's corrupt political and electoral behaviour. They showed how the party machine shamelessly extorted money from commercial establishments and entrepreneurs throughout the province, and then used it to buy political support so as to ensure reelection. Election day witnessed such abuses as stuffed ballot boxes, police intervention in favour of government candidates, and "telegraphs," whereby electors voted under false identities. These practices demonstrated clearly, as journalist and future politician Pierre Laporte pointed out in a series of articles after the election of 1956, that Duplessis did not win his elections "by prayers alone."

Progressive elements inside and outside the Roman Catholic Church grew restive as the church hierarchy uncritically supported Duplessis in return for subsidies for church schools, hospitals, and social agencies. As well, critics censured the government for "reactionary" attitudes in labour relations, education, and health. They denounced the common practice of choosing civil servants primarily for their political loyalty. Some critics claimed that the government's economic-development policies resulted in a virtual giveaway of the province's natural resources to foreigners. Others blamed Duplessis for his obstinate refusal to accept federal money to finance necessary social and educational programs. They also decried the Union Nationale's neglect of urban Quebec, a failure made possible by the government's refusal to revise an outdated electoral map that blatantly favoured rural areas. By 1956, some urban ridings had more than 100 000 voters, while many rural ridings, which tended to elect Union Nationale candidates, counted fewer than 10 000.

Anti-Duplessis forces also deplored *le chef's* vendetta against opposition groups. Duplessis sought to discredit opponents by linking them with communism in this era of Cold War characterized by strong anti-Soviet sentiment throughout the West. His government applied the notorious "padlock law" of 1937 that authorized police to lock premises from which alleged communist activities were conducted. In other attacks on civil liberties, the government brought hundreds of Jehovah's Witnesses before the courts for distributing brochures on the streets and had them fined and imprisoned. Moreover, Duplessis often ran the legislative assembly as a personal fiefdom, with total disregard for parliamentary procedure.

Premier Maurice Duplessis, third from left at the front, at the dedication of Ste-Thérèse Bridge, August 18, 1946. To the right, the Most Rev. Joseph Charbonneau. Church and state cooperated to the benefit of each side.

Source: Library and Archives Canada/*The Gazette*/C-53641.

A Reevaluation of the Duplessis Era

In their generally harsh assessment of the Duplessis record, critics often ignored what could be considered mitigating circumstances. Patronage, although rife in the Duplessis regime, had been endemic in Canadian political life at all levels of government from the country's birth. The premier's refusal of federal funds for roads, universities, and other programs appeared negative, but how else could he fight Ottawa's intrusions into areas of provincial jurisdiction? Even Pierre Trudeau supported Duplessis's refusal to accept federal grants for higher education. Duplessis did welcome foreign capital, just as his Liberal predecessors had done. Such investment provided jobs and opened up new areas of the province for development. The government's spending policies were admittedly conservative, but they made it possible to keep taxes and debts low. At the same time, the government did substantially boost spending on social services and education.

Even more telling is the fact that the Union Nationale enjoyed very substantial public support, winning four consecutive elections between 1944 and 1956. Fifty percent of all Quebeckers and more than 60 percent of French-speaking electors voted for the party. Even in 1960, a tiny shift of votes would have assured the Union Nationale's reelection. Yet, by this time, Duplessis, who died in 1959, and Paul Sauvé, his popular, reform-minded successor, who died after scarcely three months in office, were gone, and the once-powerful party appeared a spent force compared with the Liberals, who offered a capable new leader, a dynamic team, and a revitalized program. Perhaps many of those who, in the midst of the Quiet Revolution, viewed the Duplessis era as Quebec's *grande noirceur*, or "Dark Ages," tended to emphasize the sombre realities of the Union Nationale years in order to lend greater credence to their own heady visions and ambitious aspirations.

The Quiet Revolution

The term "Quiet Revolution" was coined by a journalist to describe the years 1960–66, during which Liberal Premier Jean Lesage and his *équipe du tonnerre* brought rapid but nonviolent change to Quebec. In fact, the major changes all occurred before 1964. Nevertheless, some observers with a mind to historical continuity point out that the Union Nationale, when it returned to power in 1966, continued the reforms, as did the Liberals under Robert Bourassa after 1970. The Parti Québécois also had an agenda of reform that it implemented in 1976–80. Thus, it might be said that the Quiet Revolution, in spite of pauses, lasted for two decades.

Although the Liberals came to power with numerous plans for reform in 1960, they had little idea of how much they would be able to accomplish. Lesage's cabinet contained a few progressive individuals, such as René Lévesque and Paul Gérin-Lajoie. It also harboured many solid conservatives who, while they accepted the need for change, did not want to revolutionize Quebec society. When, for example, the Union Nationale attempted in 1960 to discredit its opponents by pointing out that the Liberals threatened the Roman Catholic Church's role in Quebec life, the Liberals countered by publishing biographical sketches of their own candidates that emphasized the number of priests, nuns, and brothers among their relatives. Jean Lesage, for example, was presented as having fought, as a federal minister, for Roman Catholic schools for the "Eskimos" and as having had an audience with Pope Pius XII.

Liberal Reforms

Once in power, the Liberals ended electoral corruption. They also cleaned up much of the petty patronage practised by the Union Nationale, though in so doing they alienated many supporters who wanted a share in the spoils now that their party had at last taken power. Early in its mandate, the government also set up a royal commission, chaired by Monseigneur Alphonse-Marie Parent, of Université Laval, to examine Quebec's educational system. Then it established a provincial ministry of education, thus asserting state control over a sector in which the church had hitherto played such a powerful role. Paul Gérin-Lajoie, the minister, reorganized the province's hundreds of school commissions into 55 regional districts. The government built large, "polyvalent" (comprehensive) secondary schools, improved teacher training, revised curricula, and broadened access to educational facilities. The church retreated. In fact, it had little choice, since it simply did not possess the huge financial and human resources that had to be devoted to schooling in the wake of Quebec's postwar population explosion. Even more serious, in this increasingly secular era, the recruitment of new clergy, both male and female, declined noticeably during the 1950s, and many clergy left the ministry.

Although educational reforms constituted a very important part of the Quiet Revolution, change pervaded Quebec society. In 1962, after heated cabinet debate, René Lévesque convinced Lesage to nationalize the province's private electrical power companies and to merge them with the Crown corporation Hydro-Québec. The giant utility company contributed enormously to the province's development over the next two decades. The government also set up the Société générale de financement to serve as a holding company that would acquire small companies in difficulty. This was but one of a series of initiatives taken to promote a more dynamic francophone presence in an economy dominated by capital from outside the province.

The government improved the financial situation of Quebec's municipalities and established a ministry of cultural affairs with a modest budget. In the important sector of labour relations, it revised the labour code and, significantly, granted most employees in the public sector, with the

Executives from Shawinigan Water and Power taking French lessons after the Liberals nationalized the private hydroelectric companies in Quebec.

Source: Fonds Commission hydroélectrique de Québec 1944–1963 (H2). H21701644. Resources humaines, formation: cours de français délivré aux employés de la Compagnie d'électricité de Shawinigan, 1964. Image no. 32188-2.

exception of police officers and firefighters, the right to strike. Progressive but costly measures in the field of health care included the establishment of a provincial hospitalization insurance plan, one of the Liberals' major electoral promises in 1960. Henceforth Quebeckers could receive hospital care without regard to ability to pay.

Quebec–Ottawa Relations

In his dealings with Ottawa, Lesage adopted a firm autonomist stance. (Autonomists wanted the federal government to abstain from intervening in those fields of jurisdiction, such as education, attributed to the provinces by the constitution of 1867.) Shortly after coming to power, he promised to put an end to conditional subsidies, by which the federal government paid for part of the cost of a program, in an area of provincial concern, in return for setting its conditions; in this way, Ottawa strongly and, in the view of several provinces, unacceptably influenced provincial priorities. Lesage now demanded financial compensation for those federal programs in which Quebec did not participate. He also insisted that Ottawa turn more tax money over to Quebec in view of the province's "prior needs." After the Pearson government in Ottawa unveiled its proposals for the Canada Pension Plan in 1963, Lesage successfully responded with a separate plan for Quebec—one that allowed the province to invest the enormous sums of money generated by such a scheme as it saw fit. The Caisse de dépôt et placement du Québec, set up to administer Quebeckers' "nest egg," became Canada's largest investment fund; it also sponsored the expansion of numerous Quebec firms and helped increase francophone involvement in the province's economy.

The Quiet Revolution altered the face of Quebec dramatically. Sociologist Guy Rocher saw these years as a "cultural transformation," signifying that, beyond the structural reforms, Quebeckers' basic attitudes and values changed significantly.[2] The changes announced the end of what remained of traditional clerical society as the influence of the Roman Catholic Church rapidly waned. Talented authors, musicians, and other artists captured the new spirit in their works (see Chapter 15).

Francophones also acquired a new confidence in themselves that encouraged them to challenge the inequalities they faced. They strongly criticized a Canada in which the federal bureaucracy spoke only English, in which French enjoyed no official recognition in nine provinces, and in which, even in Quebec, French-speakers carried little economic weight. Here indeed were the makings of a new nationalism.

Revolution and Reaction

Perceptions of the Quiet Revolution have varied considerably. Many in the urban middle class have viewed it as the birth of a modern Quebec or, as sociologist Marcel Rioux expressed it poetically, "the reappearance of a spirit of independence that had frozen in the course of the long winter that had endured for more than a century."[3] For this group, the Quiet Revolution signified needed reforms in the important sectors of education, political life, the social services, the civil service, and the economy. A more modern Quebec offered obvious advantages to both them and their children.

By 2000, however, analyses had become more critical, and the almost mythical status given the Quiet Revolution by baby boomers was now hotly contested. Perhaps institutions not linked to the state had suffered too much erosion. Perhaps citizens had become too dependent on an interventionist government, just as they had been in earlier times on an interventionist church. Perhaps the origins of many of the problems which Quebec faced in 2000 could be linked to the failures of the reforms that had been implemented. Education had been democratized, but its quality was often judged to be doubtful. The church had ceased to intervene in family affairs, but the family as an institution was in an increasingly fragile state. The government had intervened vigorously in the economy, but failures had been numerous and costly for taxpayers.

Certainly, in the 1960s, the breathless pace of change upset many more conservative Quebeckers. Rural Quebec felt ignored and grew nostalgic for the Duplessis era. Disadvantaged citizens in French-speaking districts of Montreal also felt bypassed by the major thrust of the Quiet Revolution, as large-scale spending on education and the rapid growth of the civil service did little for them. For some Quebeckers, state interference in the school system meant that religion was being ruthlessly driven out. "Give Jean Lesage breeches and a beard and he'll be a Castro," Union Nationale opposition leader Daniel Johnson warned. In rural Quebec, where hundreds of small schools had been closed and children were being transported long distances by bus to large, impersonal institutions, discontent was rife. After his defeat in 1966, Lesage complained that "education beat us." His biographer, Dale C. Thomson, confirmed that change in this sector "generated more discontent than satisfaction."[4]

The Quiet Revolution engendered big government and bureaucracy, coldly technocratic and often insensitive to the needs of the individual. Higher spending and increased taxes won Lesage the politically disadvantageous nickname of "Ti-jean La Taxe." Militant public-sector labour unions made use of their newly acquired right to strike. The press increasingly criticized Lesage for his "arrogance," a characteristic that came to the fore during the election of 1966, when he campaigned virtually alone.

A small but vocal minority on the left also attacked Lesage. Some urban Quebeckers doubted the government's continuing commitment to reform, especially after 1964. Marxists and socialists called for the overthrow of capitalism. Radical nationalists viewed Lesage's objective of greater autonomy for the province as insufficient. They favoured separation, with the creation of an independent, more interventionist, French-speaking state, as outlined in the program of Pierre Bourgault's Rassemblement pour l'indépendance nationale (RIN).

Return of the Union Nationale to Power

Led by Daniel Johnson, the Union Nationale regained power in 1966, thanks to strong support in rural Quebec and to Lesage's failure to redraw the electoral map. In addition, the fact that the left-wing RIN took votes mostly from the Liberals enabled the Union Nationale to win in several close races. Surprisingly, perhaps, the Union Nationale under Johnson, and then under Jean-Jacques Bertrand, who became premier after Johnson's sudden death in September 1968, did not attempt to undo the Liberals' reforms. In the field of education, Johnson applied the rec-ommendations of the Parent commission and established the Collèges d'enseignement général et professionnel (called CEGEPs), the junior colleges that allowed Quebec students to enrol in occupational programs or to prepare for entrance into the universities. It also established a fourth French-language university, the public Université du Quebec, which opened campuses in regional centres throughout Quebec.

During the late 1960s, the polarization of Quebec society between left and right over issues such as labour–management relations increased. Strike activity, notably in the public sector, grew dramatically, and, as elsewhere in the Western world at this time, protests shook colleges and universities.

The protest movements in Quebec took on a distinct national and cultural hue. Before winning power, Johnson had published a manifesto in which he warned that if French Canada could not achieve equality within Canada, it must seek independence. Johnson wanted more than linguistic equality for French Canadians. In keeping with Quebec's time-honoured political tradition, he also sought greater autonomy for the province. Pointing out that Quebec, the home of more than 80 percent of French-speaking Canadians, represented one of Canada's two major ethnic communities or "nations," Johnson argued that a new constitution should recognize this fact through an appropriate division of powers.

Ottawa and most of the other provinces appeared willing, though not enthusiastic, to discuss the constitutional issue, but Pierre Trudeau, Canada's prime minister after 1968, warned that he would not allow any reduction of federal authority. To Trudeau, the federal government represented all Canadians—not just English-speaking Canadians—and he believed Ottawa could, and should, act to further linguistic equality across the country. Some English-speaking Canadians, however, opposed Quebec's demands from the outset; they had vigorously denounced Trudeau's predecessor, Lester B. Pearson, for appeasing "greedy" provinces and thus helping to "balkanize" the country.

The Debate over Language

Conflict over language was inevitable in Quebec after the Quiet Revolution. Many French-speaking Quebeckers felt that their language did not occupy the position it deserved in the province. While elsewhere in Canada most francophones learned English, the language of the majority, most English-speaking Quebeckers knew little French. By necessity, communication between French- and English-speaking Canadians within Quebec was carried on in the language of the minority. The powerful Montreal business establishment included few French Canadians. Many stores in downtown Montreal failed to offer service to customers in French. Commercial signs in Montreal were often only in English.

Quebec's English-speaking community possessed its own institutions, including Protestant and Catholic schools, universities, newspapers, hospitals, churches, and municipal councils. This was the only province where the linguistic minority—in this case, English-speaking—could function entirely in its own language. No French-speaking minority in the English-speaking provinces came close to occupying such a position. Moreover, census statistics confirmed that French Canadians in most regions outside Quebec were losing their battle against assimilation: in 1971, approximately one-third of Canadians whose mother tongue was French used English as the main language of the home. Only in a few areas of Canada could French-speakers be assured of getting at least part of their education in French. In addition, the language of the workplace in the English-speaking provinces was almost always English.

Since Confederation, Quebec residents had enjoyed the right or privilege of choosing whether their children would be educated in French or English. In practice, however, the great majority of immigrants to Quebec since World War II saw little reason to learn French, and they had enrolled their children in English-language schools to assure their integration into the English-speaking community. Demographers warned that if current trends continued, Montreal would soon have an English-speaking majority. For French-speaking Quebeckers concerned about the survival of their language, "free choice" of the language of education represented a serious threat.

Conflict over English-Language Schools

Conflict over the language of education first erupted in the Montreal Island community of St. Leonard, when the Roman Catholic school board's French-speaking majority voted in 1967 to convert an English-language school, attended mainly by children of Italian origin, into a French-language school. The crisis symbolized the determination of many French-speaking Quebeckers to ensure that children of non-English origin enrolled in French schools. It also demonstrated to the English-speaking community that traditional free choice of the language of education was threatened. Each group pressured the government to support its position. The Union Nationale government ruled against obligatory French-language schools. While Bill 63, which recognized the right of Quebeckers to enrol their children in English-language schools, pleased the non-French population, it unleashed storms of protest among French-speaking Quebeckers. Language thus became a full-fledged political issue.

A Polarized Quebec

The 1970s were a difficult period for Quebeckers. Issues such as language, Quebec's future political status, inflation and other economic problems, union unrest, and generational conflict divided the province. In 1970, in the midst of an economic downturn, the Liberals, led by youthful economist Robert Bourassa, won power.

The new government soon found itself stumbling from crisis to crisis. Shortly after assuming power, it was confronted with the "October Crisis." Since 1963, a revolutionary fringe group, the Front de libération du Québec (FLQ), dedicated to the establishment of an independent, socialist Quebec, had been involved in numerous bank robberies, thefts of dynamite, and bombings. In October 1970, members of the group kidnapped James Richard Cross, a British trade representative in Montreal, and, five days later, Pierre Laporte, a Quebec cabinet minister. (Laporte was subsequently found murdered.) Federal cabinet minutes released in 2001 revealed that certain federal ministers, overwhelmed by events and fearing that Quebec might secede from Canada, wanted to "use the situation in Quebec and the death of Mr. Laporte … to reinforce Canadian unity." Thus, when Bourassa hesitated and seemed to favour negotiations with the terrorists, Ottawa intervened: first, it agreed to dispatch 8000 heavily armed soldiers to Quebec, to guard public buildings and well-known personalities; then, the following day, at 4 o'clock in the morning, it invoked, for the first time in peacetime, the War Measures Act, which enabled police to arrest more than 500 "suspects" on the mere suspicion of their being sympathetic to the revolutionaries. Nearly all those arrested were eventually released, with no charges being laid against them. In 1974, film director Michel Brault produced *Les Ordres*, an internationally acclaimed fictional treatment of the humiliating treatment of prisoners during the October Crisis.

Bourassa appeared equally hesitant in 1971 when, after lengthy discussions on the constitution, he finally said no to the Victoria Charter, a package of constitutional proposals assembled by the federal government, which included an amending formula and a bill of rights. Hopes for a renewed federalism then dissipated. At the same time, Quebec Liberals faced growing animosity from public-sector unions, whose leaders spoke ominously of their desire to overthrow the government and to replace the capitalist system with socialism. Contract negotiations with the unions led to unruly public-service strikes and even, in 1973, to the arrest and imprisonment of the three major union leaders.

Bill 22

Nor could Bourassa avoid dealing with the complex language question. His solution, Bill 22, was aimed at increasing the use of French in the workplace mainly through persuasive measures. With regard to the language of education, the bill gave access to English-language schools to children whose mother tongue was English and to those of non-French origin who could pass a language test. It also created enrolment quotas for English-language schools in each school district. In the end, Bill 22 pleased no one. Nationalists complained that the law would do little to bring immigrants into French-language schools. The English-language community and ethnic groups bitterly denounced the measure as arbitrary and even totalitarian. The issue cost Bourassa support in the election of 1976, which he lost to the Parti Québécois.

Perhaps historians will judge the first Bourassa regime (1970–76) more kindly than did contemporary observers. Bourassa appeared constantly vacillating, but Quebeckers were so sharply polarized on so many issues that major decisions risked alienating large sectors of the electorate. Defenders of the multibillion-dollar James Bay hydroelectric project have argued that its economic advantages have outweighed damage caused to the northern environment and that a substantial financial award compensated for the loss of livelihood sustained by the Cree communities of northern Quebec. Was this choice worse than the recourse to nuclear power then favoured by the Parti Québécois? Others point to the provincial medicare program, financed in part by federal monies, or the Quebec Charter of Rights and Freedoms, designed to combat discrimination.

The Growth of Nationalism

Quebec nationalism had been intensifying since the late 1960s, with calls for constitutional reform, stricter language legislation in Quebec, more bilingualism in the federal government, and an increased francophone presence in Quebec's economy. Some English-language journalists blamed a few individuals for this heightened nationalism, accusing Jean Lesage and Daniel Johnson of undermining Quebeckers' loyalty through their aggressive stance in relations with Ottawa. They also censured French President Charles de Gaulle for the support he appeared to give the cause of independence in his celebrated cry of "Vive le Québec libre!" during a brief speech from the balcony of Montreal's city hall during the Expo 67 celebrations.

While some politicians may have adopted nationalist slogans to gain votes in elections, the real roots of protest went much deeper. Nationalism has been a force in Quebec since at least the early nineteenth century; although its themes varied over time, it was not a new phenomenon in the 1960s.

Contemporary nationalists, however, tended to be members of the new middle class, including teachers, civil servants, and journalists; some even came from the business and professional communities. Critics have pointed out that these groups had a vested interest in nationalist causes. A bilingual civil service in Ottawa, for example, would create job openings for francophones. But these nationalists also resented the inferior position that French-speakers occupied in Canada and, to a certain extent, in Quebec itself. Events elsewhere in the world also influenced them. The movements of national liberation in Africa and Asia, and the struggle of African Americans for civil rights, reminded many French Canadians of what they perceived to be their own condition. In one poignant autobiographical account, *Nègres blancs d'Amérique* (titled *White Niggers of America* in English translation), journalist and FLQ theorist Pierre Vallières portrayed French-Canadian workers as cheap labour, as exploited second-class citizens who had no control over their own society and economy.

"Vive la France! Vive le Québec! Vive le Québec libre!" The crowd roared with approval when French President Charles de Gaulle made his famous remark at Montreal's City Hall, July 24, 1967, in support of an independent Quebec.

Source: CP Picture Archive.

The Rise of the Parti Québécois

Nationalism escalated in the late 1960s. In 1967, René Lévesque, dissatisfied with the Liberals' constitutional policies, quit the party; the following year, he founded the Parti Québécois (PQ). Lévesque had the prestige and stature needed to rally the great majority of nationalists.

The rise of the PQ was striking. Quickly realizing that only a small minority of Quebeckers considered themselves unconditional independentists, party leaders set out to convince more moderate federalist nationalists that independence would greatly improve their lot. While in opposition, the PQ successfully linked nationalism to a variety of progressive social causes, enabling it to build a relatively broad coalition of supporters. Unions, increasingly hostile to the Bourassa government, now came to see an independent Quebec as one in which workers would be better treated. As for feminists, historian Susan Mann has emphasized how much they had in common with nationalists.[5] Their origins, social class, and occupations were often similar. Both sought more status and desired greater autonomy. For many radical feminists, an independent socialist Quebec was the key to the liberation of women. The Parti Québécois, with so many reformist measures written into its program, was perhaps the tool to help bring this about.

The *péquistes'* electoral gains confirmed the success of this strategy. The party won one-quarter of the vote in the first election it contested in 1970. In that election, economic problems, particularly a high unemployment rate, caused Quebeckers to favour the Liberal party, whose leader, Robert Bourassa, promised to create 100 000 jobs. Three years later, although the Liberals took virtually all the seats in the National Assembly, PQ support rose to one-third. Then, in 1976, with slightly more than 40 percent of the vote, the PQ won an election contested by three major parties.

Many *péquistes* saw their victory as a vote for independence, the first step in the march toward national liberation. Certainly, the "happening" in the Paul Sauvé Arena in Montreal on the night of November 15, as party militants savoured victory, showed vividly that hopes were high. Other observers, however, saw the PQ success simply as a vote for good government and against the scandal-ridden Bourassa regime. The PQ had, after all, promised that it would not try to separate Quebec from Canada until the decision was approved in a referendum. Most voters therefore believed that they had voted only for a change in government.

Quebec Under the Parti Québécois

The new PQ government pursued reforms that continued the Quiet Revolution of the 1960s. In order to democratize Quebec politics and prevent powerful interests from "buying" favourable legislation, it overhauled the electoral law to prohibit large—mainly corporate—contributions to political parties. The government also introduced a no-fault system of automobile insurance, covering all personal injuries sustained; private companies continued to insure drivers for damage to vehicles. It brought in agricultural zoning legislation designed to protect increasingly scarce good farmland, much of which had disappeared due to urban sprawl since World War II. It set up a dental care plan for children, adopted new legislation to protect consumers, and froze tuition fees for university students at the lowest levels in Canada. It also supported unions through an anti-strikebreaking law, a move that management bitterly opposed. In 1977 it amended the Quebec Charter of Rights to make Quebec the first Canadian province to protect gays and lesbians from discrimination.

René Lévesque at the Paul Sauvé Arena, Montreal, on the night of the Quebec election, October 29, 1973. His recently created Parti Québécois won 33 percent of the popular vote in that election, but only six seats. By 1976, the party would be in power.

Source: © Library and Archives Canada. Reproduced with the permission of Library and Archives Canada. Source: Library and Archives Canada/Credit: Duncan Cameron/ Duncan Cameron fonds/PA-115039.

Bill 101

In contrast to Bourassa's vacillation on the language question, the Parti Québécois's stance seemed clear. In 1977, the government adopted Bill 101, a charter of the French language, which was intended to make Quebec as overwhelmingly French as Ontario was English. This controversial legislation opened English-language schools only to children who had at least one parent educated in English in Quebec. That "objective" criterion was used because of the impossibility of verifying a child's mother tongue, one of the conditions used by Bourassa's Bill 22, to determine admission. French, with a few exceptions, was to become the language of the workplace. Professionals were required to have a knowledge of the French language. Most signs were to be posted in French only. In short, the Parti Québécois hoped to obtain by law for French in Quebec what the "free market" and "free choice" assured English elsewhere in Canada.

The new minority status of Quebec anglophones necessitated often painful adjustments. Although the federal commissioner of official languages commented in 1978, after the adoption of Bill 101, that "Quebec's anglophones are much better off than their francophone counterparts in other provinces," many Anglo-Quebeckers, including a large proportion of young adults convinced that they could have a better future elsewhere, left the province. At the same time, a large number of corporate head offices in Montreal, complaining of the language legislation, high taxes, the dangers of separatism, and poor relations with unions, decided to move westward, mainly to Toronto.

Among the English-speakers who chose to stay in Quebec, bilingualism increased significantly; by 2001, fully 66 percent of this group were bilingual. (Bilingualism outside Quebec, among English-speakers, grew slowly but remained largely an elitist phenomenon.) At the same time, Quebec's "Frenchness" was attenuated by the fact that nearly 40 percent of the majority French-language group reported that they could also speak English; this figure was even higher for younger age groups. In addition, half of those Quebeckers whose mother tongue was neither French nor English said that they were trilingual. Commenting on the census figures of 2001, *The Globe and Mail* suggested that Trudeau's dream of a bilingual Canada might endure only in Quebec.

WHERE SOCIAL SCIENTISTS DISAGREE

The Origins and Effects of Quebec's Language Legislation

In 1969, the Quebec government began to adopt laws intended to augment the use of French in the province. These laws, the most important aspects of which have affected education, the workplace, and public signage, provoked passionate debate and intense conflict.

Many social scientists have viewed the linguistic revolution as the result of a *prise de conscience* (realization) by the French-speaking majority of its economic inferiority in Quebec. Geographer Eric Waddell pointed out that, traditionally, French-speaking Quebeckers who wished to function in the world of industry and commerce had to achieve fluency in English, even though French-speakers were a large numerical majority in the province. In this environment, most anglophones remained unilingual. "Transported to a country-wide level in which francophones were an effective *minorité*," Waddell argued, "such inequalities could only be reinforced."[1] Quebec's language laws should thus be seen as attempts to come to terms with the "asymmetrical" nature of French–English relations in Canada. The Canadian and North American context places the French language at a heavy disadvantage in regard to English. Even in Quebec, the English language enjoys a visibility that French does not possess outside Quebec. In marked contrast to Waddell's reasoning, the federal Official Languages Act places all minorities on a theoretically equal footing.

Political scientist Richard Handler also asserted that language laws were "aimed at redressing the economic balance of power within Quebec."[2] Marc V. Levine reached similar conclusions in his analysis of Quebec's efforts to promote the visibility of French.[3] In another study covering a portion of the 1980s, Levine noted the extent of the francophone reconquest of Montreal's economy by that time and concluded that Quebec's language legislation had indeed made an important contribution to this dramatic change.[4]

While agreeing with the fundamental importance of the economic roots of Quebec's linguistic upheaval, some analysts have delved more deeply into the class composition of Quebec society in search of the forces underlying the measures taken to strengthen the role of the French language. Political scientist William Coleman, for instance, stressed the class nature of language reform: university-educated Quebeckers working in the public sector, the main component of a "petite bourgeoisie," successfully "francized" schools and public signs, but their advances in the private sector were largely blocked in the 1970s by powerful anglophone and conservative francophone capital.[5]

The new and obviously less powerful status of Quebec's anglophones has been the subject of several studies. Many anglophones left Quebec in the 1970s, presumably motivated at least in part by political and linguistic fears. In a controversial study, however, Uli Locher concluded that, even after the adoption of Bill 101 in 1977, anglophones were leaving Quebec primarily because of the lure of greater prosperity in Toronto and the West.[6] Most observers judged that anglophones remaining in Quebec still enjoyed far greater rights and privileges than most francophones did elsewhere in Canada. But political scientist Garth Stevenson cautioned that Quebec's more generous treatment of its minority could not be explained solely by the goodwill of the majority. Rather, it was a logical consequence of the demographic balance in Canada and in North America as well as of the vast economic power that anglophones wielded in Quebec until recent times.[7]

Philosopher Charles Taylor attempted to define the basis for the divergent views of anglophones and francophones on the language question. He saw most anglophones, like Americans, putting forth a liberal view of society in which individual rights took precedence over collective goals. Provisions for bilingualism in federal law could be justified in terms of individual rights: francophones across Canada, at least theoretically, can obtain federal government services in French. Francophones tended to espouse a collective goal: to ensure that there would still be francophones in the next generation. Taylor believed that Quebeckers also shared liberal values but that, in order to retain their identity, they distinguished between fundamental liberties, which should never be infringed, and privileges, which are only important.[8]

The issue of language continues to be debated within Quebec, though far less heatedly than in the 1970s and 1980s. Some English-speakers decry the very existence of language legislation, while francophones will always feel culturally insecure because of the enormous pressures of the continent's English environment. Because of the emotional nature of the question, it will remain a subject of passionate discussion and an important challenge for Quebec and Canadian society.

---

1   Eric Waddell, "State, Language and Society: The Vicissitudes of French in Quebec and Canada," in Alan C. Cairns and Cynthia Williams, eds., *The Politics of Gender, Ethnicity, and Language in Canada* (Toronto: University of Toronto Press, 1986), p. 88.

2   Richard Handler, *Nationalism and the Politics of Culture in Quebec* (Madison: University of Wisconsin Press, 1988), p. 170.

3   Marc V. Levine, "Language, Policy, and Quebec's *Visage Français*: New Directions in *La Question Linguistique*," *Quebec Studies* 8 (1989): 1–16.

4   Marc V. Levine, *The Reconquest of Montreal: Language Policy and Social Change in a Bilingual City* (Philadelphia: Temple University Press, 1990).

5   William Coleman, "The Class Basis of Language Policy in Quebec, 1949–1975," *Studies in Political Economy* (Spring 1980): 93–117.

6   Uli Locher, *Les anglophones de Montréal: émigration et évolution des attitudes, 1978–1983* (Quebec: Conseil de la langue française, 1988).

7   Garth Stevenson, *Unfulfilled Union: Canadian Federalism and National Unity*, 3rd ed. (Toronto: Gage, 1989).

8   Charles Taylor, "Shared and Divergent Values," in Ronald L. Watts and Douglas M. Brown, eds., *Options for a New Canada* (Toronto: University of Toronto Press, 1991), pp. 53–76.

With considerable federal support, some anglophones in Quebec responded to Bill 101 by launching or supporting legal challenges to several of its clauses. Court rulings, as well as amendments to the law introduced by both the Parti Québécois and, after 1985, the new Quebec Liberal government under Robert Bourassa, weakened the legislation. While many anglophones judged the amendments insufficient and indeed wanted an end to all language legislation, francophones continued to worry over the fragility of the status of French.

The Referendum Debate, 1980

Of even greater interest to Canadians than the language question was Quebec's referendum on political sovereignty, which would decide Quebec's—and Canada's—future. In a shrewdly worded question, which implicitly recognized Quebeckers' divided loyalties, the Parti Québécois government asked voters for a mandate to negotiate political sovereignty within an economic association with the rest of Canada. In hopes of obtaining majority support, the government appealed both to Quebeckers' desire for change and, by asking voters to give it only the right to *negotiate*, to their more conservative instincts. No unilateral declaration of independence would follow a positive vote. The campaign debate was fierce, dividing families and friends, but it was not violent. Claude Ryan, Robert Bourassa's successor as the Quebec Liberal leader, led the *non* forces. Prime Minister Trudeau intervened late in the campaign, promising unspecified constitutional change if Quebeckers voted *non*.

On May 20, 1980, Quebeckers defeated the referendum proposal by a 60–40 margin. While almost all non-French-speaking Quebeckers voted no, the French-speaking population split

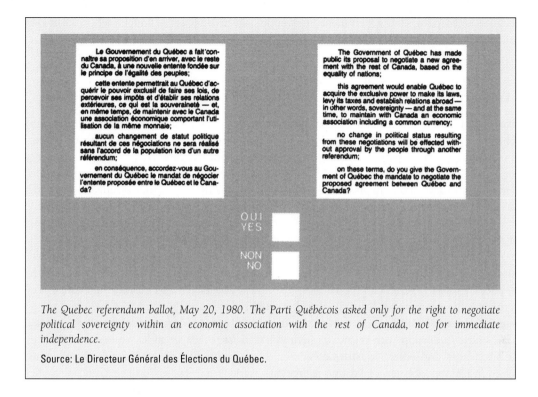

The Quebec referendum ballot, May 20, 1980. The Parti Québécois asked only for the right to negotiate political sovereignty within an economic association with the rest of Canada, not for immediate independence.

Source: Le Directeur Général des Élections du Québec.

virtually in half. Analyses of the vote showed that the older age groups, the economically disadvantaged, and those with relatively little education tended to vote *non*. Those in the younger age groups and people with more education and higher incomes more often answered *oui*.

The 1980s: The Wheel Turns

The mood of the early 1980s in Quebec was pessimistic. The 1981–82 recession dramatically cut employment in the resource and manufacturing industries. Unions suffered membership losses as well as rising unpopularity among a public weary of strikes and agitation. Universities reeled beneath the government's stringent cutbacks in financing.

Nor did the outcome of the constitutional debate cause much rejoicing in Quebec. The federal government's proposals gave Quebec none of the powers that its provincial governments had consistently claimed since 1960. Moreover, Ottawa managed to isolate Quebec by playing it off against the other nine provinces. In slightly amended form, the constitutional proposals became law despite Quebec's objections. Neither Premier René Lévesque nor opposition leader Claude Ryan attended the celebrations on April 17, 1982, when Queen Elizabeth II proclaimed the new Constitution. Quebec was legally bound by its terms, but the document lacked moral legitimacy in the province.

Perhaps Quebeckers looked for a balance when they reelected the Parti Québécois in 1981, after having said no to the government's constitutional proposition in May 1980. Regretting their victory, even some *péquistes* warned that the party needed a spell in opposition to rethink its positions and that the economic downturn did not favour its chances for the immediate future. They proved to be right. The harsh recession and a severe budget crisis forced the government to reduce services and increase taxes. Its draconian measures to recover part of the salary increases that had been granted to public service workers alienated the unions. Moreover, the era of large-scale spending and government interventionism had passed as budget deficits increased and a new conservative mood gained strength throughout the Western world, including Quebec. Individualism was celebrated as the new cult, and business leaders became its high priests.

Nationalism in Decline

Nationalist sentiment weakened after the defeat in the referendum of 1980. The now-middle-aged champions of yesterday's nationalist causes became disillusioned, and younger Quebeckers worried more about finding jobs than about championing political causes. The growing unpopularity of the PQ led some observers to predict nationalism's demise. Sensing the waning of nationalist fervour in the face of the stinging defeats of 1980 and 1982, René Lévesque decided to put aside, at least for the foreseeable future, the issue of sovereignty, a decision that provoked a dramatic revolt within the party and, in 1985, Lévesque's own resignation. In the elections held in December 1985, the party lost power to the Liberals under their resurrected leader, Robert Bourassa.

In the years following the recession of the early 1980s, Quebec's rapid economic growth made it a leader among Canada's provinces. Reassured by the new political stability and by the reduced level of government interference, investment accelerated and business flourished. The provincial government held spending in check and reduced certain taxes.

While the Bourassa government prided itself on offering competent administration, it failed to exercise leadership with regard to environmental issues. Paper mills, aluminum manufacturing plants, and other industries continued to foul water and air with chemical pollutants, often in flagrant violation of existing regulations. Agricultural wastes, fertilizers, and pesticides fouled the province's rivers. Critics worried that the huge new hydroelectric megaprojects planned for Quebec's north would go forward without adequate study of the potential threats to the environment. Several incidents involving fires deliberately set in toxic waste and tire dumps dramatized both the dangers of pollution and the government's ecological neglect. While it was no worse than that of several other provinces, Quebec's environmental record gave Quebeckers, reputed by polls to be among the most environmentally conscious of Canada's citizens, little cause for satisfaction.

The Revival of Nationalism

Those who had proclaimed nationalism's demise in the early 1980s proved poor prophets. By the end of the decade, both the language issue and Quebec's future links with Canada again became important public topics. The language issue emerged with renewed force in late 1988 over the relatively minor issue of public signs. When the Supreme Court of Canada found Quebec's sign law (which required French-only signs) to be in violation of the freedom of expression provisions of both the federal and the Quebec charters of rights, Bourassa had to act. The Supreme Court had admitted that signs solely in English could be prohibited and that the government could require "the predominant display of the French language, even its marked predominance." Bourassa's solution was to invoke the Constitution's "notwithstanding clause," which enables a province to suspend certain rights for five-year periods, and to introduce legislation requiring French-only signs outdoors, while authorizing bilingual signs within certain stores. Quebec's, and Canada's, anglophones protested vehemently, and three English-speaking ministers resigned from Bourassa's cabinet. In the 1989 election, many English-language voters abandoned the Liberals and rallied to the Equality party, a new political formation committed to anglophone rights.

Supporters of French-only signs argued that Quebec needed a French "face" in order to persuade new immigrants to integrate into the francophone community. They added that the enormous weight of English in the North American context could be counterbalanced only by legislation protecting the French majority. The debate became rancorous; even historians (reputed to be coldly analytical) entered aggressively into the fray. One historian quoted in the *Toronto Star* suggested that an army of sign painters be sent to Quebec; a counterpart in Quebec City told readers of *Le Soleil* that the painters should stop off at Cornwall, Ontario, near the Quebec border, where they would find ample work to do painting signs in French. Both obviously preached to a converted audience. Passions cooled over time and, when the five-year period ran out in 1993, the Bourassa government adopted more liberal legislation. The language issue undoubtedly contributed to the failure of the Meech Lake constitutional accord in 1990. Many Anglo-Canadians, ignoring the often unenviable fate of francophone minorities throughout Canada, said they wanted no part of a "distinct society" that would be free to "oppress" its anglophone minority. In turn, francophones within Quebec showed little enthusiasm for an agreement that might not give Quebec sufficient power to act to protect the French language.

Assessing the overall impact of Quebec's controversial language legislation since the early 1970s is a difficult task. In spite of the progressive weakening of Bill 101's clause on the language of signs, Montreal in the mid-1990s "looked" much more French than it had in 1970. By 1990, almost all immigrant children were enrolled in French schools, but, in many of these, they constituted an overwhelming majority and had little contact with Quebeckers whose mother tongue was French. Thanks in part to the exodus of many anglophones, more francophones now held upper-level positions in business. More workers earned their living in French, but language legislation did not cover small enterprises, and many employers insisted that their French-speaking personnel be able to serve anglophones in English. Adversaries of Bill 101 warned that language legislation would hurt economic development and tarnish Quebec's reputation, since English-language media gave abundant publicity to anglophone complaints. At the same time, perhaps no other solution existed to the language problem. It would have been impossible to promote the use of French energetically without undermining the important, even dominant, role of English in Quebec, particularly in the province's economy.

Meech Lake

The constitutional issue followed the linguistic debate. Meeting in Edmonton in August 1986, the provincial premiers agreed to undertake a "Quebec round" of negotiations, to bring about "Quebec's full and active participation in the Canadian federation" before moving on to other concerns. Quebec put forth five conditions, which, it stipulated, were "minimal." They included the recognition of the province as a "distinct society" and greater powers with regard to immigration.

In June 1987, Prime Minister Brian Mulroney and the ten provincial premiers met in Ottawa and, after arduous all-night negotiations, gave unanimous assent to an accord amending the Constitution. Robert Bourassa proclaimed that Quebec could now adhere to the Canadian Constitution "with dignity and honour."

In the months that followed, the federal government and eight provinces, beginning with Quebec, ratified the proposals. Then the accord began to unravel as newly elected premiers in the two remaining provinces, New Brunswick and Manitoba, arguing that they were not bound by their predecessors' signatures, demanded substantial modifications. Subsequently, a third premier, Clyde Wells of Newfoundland, had his province rescind its approval. Groups representing women, Native peoples, ethnic associations, and northerners objected that their own concerns had not been addressed. Other critics, including former prime minister Pierre Trudeau, argued that the Meech Lake Accord would seriously weaken federal authority and promote linguistic ghettos within Canada. In addition, while the agreement's opponents in English-speaking Canada feared that the accord would confer unwarranted additional powers on Quebec, a minority of Quebeckers were convinced that their province would in fact obtain too little by virtue of the agreement.

About 200 000 people marched in Montreal's St. Jean Baptiste Day parade, June 24, 1994. The lead banner proclaims, "Next Year—My Country."

Source: CP Picture Archive/Ryan Remiorz.

As the three-year period for approval of the accord drew to a close in June 1990, protracted negotiations among the premiers produced an add-on agreement that included promises to work for a revamped Senate that would represent regional interests more effectively. Then, under intense pressure, the premiers of Manitoba and Newfoundland promised to submit the accord to their respective legislative assemblies. Developments in the final moments were unexpected. With the support of Native leaders from across Canada, Elijah Harper, a Cree NDP member of the Manitoba legislature, denounced the Meech Lake Accord for ignoring the rights of Canada's Aboriginal people and signalled his intention to use the rules of parliamentary procedure to kill it. On June 23, 1990, as the deadline for approval expired, the Meech Lake Accord died.

Most Canadians outside Quebec felt relief at the failure of the accord; polls showed that a growing majority had opposed it. In Quebec, however, the failure of this new episode of constitutional reform had grave repercussions. Nationalists, including many federalists, perceived the death of the agreement as signifying English Canada's refusal to accommodate even the province's minimal concerns. Independence now seemed the only possible choice for those who could not accept the status quo. Several federal members of Parliament from Quebec quit their parties to join a new group, the Bloc Québécois, headed by former Conservative cabinet minister Lucien Bouchard. To deflect criticism of his government, Robert Bourassa set up a nonpartisan commission to study Quebec's constitutional future, and promised to hold a referendum. Political scientist Vincent Lemieux has argued that Bourassa wished to use the "threat of independence" to elicit new propositions for a reform of Canadian federalism, and thus make it possible to "avoid independence."[6]

Constitutional Impasse

After the failure of the Meech Lake Accord, the federal government decided to reopen the constitutional issue; this time, it began by holding consultations across Canada. Native peoples, among other groups, played a far more important role in the discussions. Quebec, however, refused to participate in the talks until the final round of negotiations, held in Charlottetown. Quebeckers reacted without enthusiasm to the ensuing agreement. Premier Bourassa claimed that it was the best he could do, while his political adversaries asserted that he had accepted much less than the Meech Lake Accord had offered. In a referendum held in October 1992, voters in six provinces, including Quebec, rejected the Charlottetown agreement and constitutional negotiations ceased. Sociologist Maurice Pinard pointed out that polls showed a strong majority of Quebeckers felt that the accord offered too little to Quebec; in English Canada, nearly 60 percent of voters felt it gave Quebec too much.[7] This time, however, Quebeckers did not view the failure of the agreement as a rejection by English Canada, since they themselves had voted against it.

The Referendum of 1995

The seeming impossibility of reaching any constitutional agreement with the rest of Canada favoured an increase in nationalist sentiment in Quebec. More importantly, Jean Chrétien, who became Canada's prime minister in 1993 after the Liberal electoral victory, was perceived by

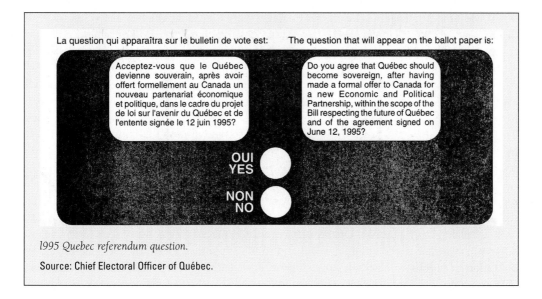

La question qui apparaîtra sur le bulletin de vote est: The question that will appear on the ballot paper is:

> Acceptez-vous que le Québec devienne souverain, après avoir offert formellement au Canada un nouveau partenariat économique et politique, dans le cadre du projet de loi sur l'avenir du Québec et de l'entente signée le 12 juin 1995?

> Do you agree that Québec should become sovereign, after having made a formal offer to Canada for a new Economic and Political Partnership, within the scope of the Bill respecting the future of Québec and of the agreement signed on June 12, 1995?

OUI
YES

NON
NO

1995 Quebec referendum question.

Source: Chief Electoral Officer of Québec.

even moderate nationalists as rigidly opposed to Quebec's claims for greater autonomy. In that same election, the nationalist Bloc Québécois proved far more popular than Chrétien's Liberals within the province. The return to power of the Parti Québécois in 1994 made a new referendum certain.

In this referendum, held on October 30, 1995, the provincial government asked electors if they wished Quebec to become "sovereign," after having formally offered Canada a new economic and political partnership. The federalist *non* won a razor-thin victory, with only 50.6 percent of the valid ballots cast, in a consultation in which more than 93 percent of eligible voters participated. Maurice Pinard felt that, had the referendum been held immediately after the failure of the Meech Lake Accord, "the 'yes' vote would have won."[8] Lucien Bouchard's prominent role in the campaign helped explain the strong showing of the *oui*, favoured by well over 60 percent of French-speaking voters. Yet Vincent Lemieux cautioned that, for many electors, a vote for "sovereignty" did not necessarily signify a vote for "independence" and a break with Canada. Anglophones, allophones, and members of First Nations communities supported the *non* option with near-unanimity; their behaviour was not surprising, since these groups shared none of the discontent or the aspirations of the francophones.

Ottawa's Strategy Toward Quebec

The "love" shown toward Quebec by large numbers of English-speaking Canadians, who invaded Montreal just before the referendum for an enthusiastic pro-Canada demonstration, evaporated rapidly after the vote. Many reacted with bitterness to the outcome of the referendum, feeling that separation was now inevitable and

Lucien Bouchard (left) and Jacques Parizeau (right) in Quebec City on October 2, 1995, shortly before the referendum. Premier Parizeau resigned after the referendum; Lucien Bouchard replaced him.

Source: CP Picture Archive/Jacques Boissinot.

that it was time to prepare to drive a hard bargain with a seceding Quebec that would deprive the province of important parts of its territory. In her examination of media reaction in English Canada, sociologist Maryse Potvin saw evidence of a "national psychosis."[9] Biographer Lawrence Martin, for example, portrayed Quebec Premier Lucien Bouchard as the "Lucifer of our Land," whose culture was "most unCanadian." A psychological portrait of Bouchard stimulated considerable interest: a Vancouver daily published the premier's photo and asked, "Is this man crazy?" Journalist Diane Francis denounced what she saw as a racially motivated separatist conspiracy. Analogies were drawn between Quebec sovereigntists and Nazis. Journalist Norman Lester responded by producing *The Black Book of English Canada*, in which he purloined "racist xenophobia" in English-speaking Canada.

In Ottawa, the Chrétien government adopted a hard line toward Quebec and sought legal means to block secession. In 1998, in an advisory opinion suffused with Solomon-like wisdom, the Supreme Court of Canada affirmed unanimously that no province enjoyed a legal right to secede unilaterally. If, however, Quebeckers repudiated the existing constitutional order unambiguously in regard to the question asked and to the support received, then all parties had an obligation to negotiate constitutional change in good faith.[10] The Court thus recognized that Quebec's constitutional future was a political question. The Chrétien government then adopted, in 1999, legislation that sought to give Ottawa the right to determine unilaterally the conditions under which it would recognize the result of any future referendum. Quebec responded by asserting the right of its citizens to determine their own political future, and judged the law unconstitutional and antidemocratic.

During these years, Ottawa invested millions of dollars in programs designed to increase Ottawa's visibility in Quebec. Lucrative contracts went to Montreal advertising agencies that were generous donors to the Liberal party. When the RCMP launched an investigation into allegations of political favouritism and mismanagement of public funds, Prime Minister Chrétien dismissed evidence of impropriety with an appeal to patriotism: maintaining Canadian unity was well worth "the theft of a few million dollars." Later, when a federal commission inquired into the so-called "sponsorship scandal," detailed revelations of money laundering and false accounting tarnished the entire Liberal party and led to a sharp decline of its support among Quebec francophones during federal elections held in 2004, after Chrétien's departure and his replacement by Paul Martin, formerly Chrétien's finance minister and, even worse, in the elections of 2006. Indeed the Liberals placed third in that election, after the first-place Bloc Québécois, which promoted sovereignty for Quebec, and Stephen Harper's resurgent Conservatives.

Yet the fervour for independence was clearly diminishing in Quebec. Analyzing opinion polls on the issue, sociologist Maurice Pinard described the sovereigntist movement as "declining for the moment, not necessarily forever."[11] Sociologists Simon Langlois and Gilles Gagné found an explanation for the apparent demobilization of the most ardent sovereigntists—middle-class francophones, 70 percent of whom had supported independence in 1995.[12] As the birth of an independent Quebec seemed to recede into a distant future, this group found little reason to continue supporting the Parti Québécois. Concern for health and social services and other issues came to the fore. Still, relations between Ottawa and Quebec remained testy, as Ottawa, now blessed with huge budget surpluses, undertook new initiatives in such fields of provincial jurisdiction as education and health. In Quebec's case particularly, Ottawa wanted to assure a more active federal presence in the province, through scholarships to students, research chairs to universities, and grants to municipalities.

Contemporary Politics

Support for the Parti Québécois weakened in the provincial election of 1998 and the governments of Lucien Bouchard and of Bernard Landry, who succeeded Bouchard after the latter's resignation in 2001, stated that no referendum would be held unless a victory for independence was certain. In spite of an improved economy voters blamed the government for failing to improve health care, for forcing the amalgamation of cities and suburbs (Montreal expanded to comprise the entire island of Montreal in 2002), and for doing little to promote the economic development of outlying regions. Some, particularly outside Montreal, disagreed with the government's decision to abolish Catholic and Protestant school boards—they were replaced by French and English school boards—and, finally, denominational schools and the teaching of religion as well. For a time electors looked with interest at a new party, a more populist conservative grouping called Action démocratique du Québec (ADQ), which declared a unilateral moratorium on the constitutional debate and promised to reduce the size of government, allow private health care, and experiment with school vouchers. In elections held in 2003, however, the more centrist and strongly federalist Liberals, led by Jean Charest, gained power, promising to improve health care, authorize the secession of suburbs from the new cities, reduce taxes, and lessen the role of the state.

By 2007, a strong majority of voters were expressing dissatsifaction ... with the Charest government. The government had failed to honour its promises to lower taxes substantially; instead, it raised fees for various services. Most Montreal suburbs did secede from the city but did not regain the autonomy they had previously enjoyed; a new layer of supra-municipal government, put in place by the Liberals to coordinate island-wide services, functioned to no one's liking. In spite of increased spending on health care, Quebeckers generally felt that services had not improved; in particular waiting times for non-urgent operations and appointments with specialists remained lengthy and hospital emergency wards were overburdened. Plans to reform and streamline the provincial civil service were abandoned after resistance by unions. When the forest sector needed help, Charest acquiesced, but government assistance could not counter the crisis faced by the industry. With the election of a Conservative government in Ottawa in 2006, however, relations with the federal government did improve; Charest, Quebec's Liberal leader, had himself once led the federal Conservative party.

Dissatisfaction with Charest did not boost the fortunes of the Parti Québécois and its new leader, André Boisclair. Most Quebeckers did not want a new referendum on independence, a major promise of the PQ, and saw immediate problems, particularly health care, as more important. More socially conservative francophones, judging that neither the Liberals nor the Parti Québécois represented them, now preferred the ADQ, with its populist anti-elite electoral platform, shorn of the more radical proposals it had espoused earlier. On constitutional issues, the ADQ took a vaguely autonomist stance, supporting neither independence nor unconditional federalism. In addition, many left-wing and environmentally sensitive voters also abandoned the Parti Québécois in favour of small political groupings. Charest did win reelection in 2007, but with only a minority of seats in the National Assembly, most of them in districts with large numbers of anglophone voters. While the ADQ formed the official opposition, and saw itself as a government in waiting, the Parti Québécois won its lowest percentage of the popular vote since 1970, and placed third. Its leader, André Boisclair, soon resigned and was replaced with Pauline Marois, who had held numerous portfolios in previous Parti Québécois governments and who now became the first woman to head a major Quebec political party.

Quebec's Economy Since 1990

Economic recession in the early 1990s provoked a substantial rise in unemployment. Many jobs in inefficient, formerly tariff-protected industries such as textiles and furniture, disappeared in the face of competition from low-wage developing nations. For a time, Montreal was afflicted with the highest jobless rate of any major Canadian city.

Then, in the mid-1990s, the provincial economy improved markedly. Free trade stimulated exports, 60 percent of which now went to the United States. Economist Gilles Soucy credited the provincial government with a role of catalyst, as it actively sought investments and worked to reinvigorate provincial institutions such as the Société générale de financement. The disastrous ice storm of January 1998, which deprived three million Quebeckers of electricity, some for lengthy periods of time, triggered a period of particularly rapid growth in the months that followed. In the fall of 2001, when the terrorist attacks in the United States seemed to pose a threat to the health of the economy, the provincial government accelerated public investments at home. After attaining a summit of more than 14 percent in 1992, the unemployment rate dropped to about 8 percent in 2002. Economist Pierre Fortin calculated that, by 2000, Quebeckers' per capita revenues reached 86 percent of Ontario levels, up from only 74 percent in 1960. According to Fortin, the increasing productivity of the Quebec work force (due to improved technology, research and development, and educational advances) explained the province's improved performance.[13]

From 2000, Montreal's economy underwent exceptional expansion, boosted by growth in such sectors as aeronautics, biotechnology, information technology, pharmaceuticals, and telecommunications. Publicly owned Hydro-Québec increased its profits, half of which it then remitted to its sole shareholder, the Quebec government. Yet there were failures. In spite of Quebec's promises of new investments, General Motors closed its huge plant in Boisbriand, north of Montreal, the only automobile plant in the province. Development lagged in many of the province's regions, which suffered substantial out-migration. Nor did greater prosperity disguise the fact that, according to the National Council of Welfare, poverty afflicted more than one-fifth of Quebeckers.

After 2005, the province's economy again encountered serious weaknesses. The rising Canadian dollar (from 62 cents in American currency in 2002 to 97 cents in 2007), stimulated by the huge American demand for western Canada's oil and gas, in combination with a slowing of the American economy, harmed exports. The forest industry, with its innumerable small local sawmills and its lack of value-added wood products, was hit especially hard. Textile and furniture manufacturers continued to close their doors. Bright spots in the economy included new hydroelectric projects in the north, government spending on public transportation, the construction of methane gas port facilities on the St. Lawrence River and, in Montreal, the creation of many new jobs in information technologies and video-games publishing.

Public Finances

Public finances, and hence government spending on health, education, and other services, depended on the state of the economy. Budget deficits burgeoned, in Quebec as in other provinces, through the early 1990s, not only because of lower tax revenues but also as a result of Ottawa's own major spending cuts; in response, Quebec increased taxes and cut services. In the universities, for example, declining provincial subsidies combined with low tuition costs to produce a severe crisis. By 1999, the province had balanced its budget, in part by sending hundreds of medical personnel into early retirement, and then even lowered taxes, earning the approval of bond rating agencies, the business establishment, and undoubtedly of taxpayers, but displeasing those who found services less accessible. Yet balanced budgets did not prevent the province's debt, already high, from increasing by several billion dollars each year; Quebec's auditor general blamed the provincial government's artful accounting for the discrepancy. Another worsening problem, faced by all provinces, was the ever increasing portion of the budget—nearly 45 percent of Quebec's spending in 2007—that had to be devoted to health care, and health costs for a rapidly ageing population were rising each year at well above the rate of inflation.

Population

Recent demographic trends raised concerns for Quebec's future. The 2006 census showed that Quebec was still growing, although at a much slower rate than Alberta and Ontario, the country's fastest growing provinces. As in other provinces, birth rates remained well below levels necessary for population replacement: Quebec women were bearing on average 1.6 children. As well, more people continued to leave Quebec than entered it, but the difference, in the years 2001–2006, was small and constituted a significant improvement over the 1990s. Quebec did put considerable effort into attracting immigrants from abroad, particularly from French-speaking countries, and in integrating them into Quebec society. Yet as a French-speaking province in English-speaking North America, Quebec suffered inevitably from a competitive disadvantage in regard to neighbouring Ontario. In the years 1996–2001, an excess of births over deaths explained only one-third of Ontario's population gain, but 80 percent of Quebec's.

In hopes of boosting the number of births, the Bourassa government established a system of baby bonuses in 1987. Birth rates did increase. While a study by the C.D. Howe Institute affirmed that the policy had had positive effects, other observers thought that the bonuses had simply encouraged couples to have children earlier. The Parti Québécois replaced the program in 1997 with tax-supported day-care services at $5 per day, with the objective of helping young couples conciliate work and family. A program of lengthy parental leaves after the birth of a baby also appeared to contribute to a slight rise in the birth rate.

Language and Culture in Quebec Today

Three decades after the adoption of Bill 101, the French language charter, a large majority of francophones still felt that the survival and development of the French language in Quebec continued to be threatened. Francophone workers complained that many companies forced workers to use English-language manuals and tended to advertise virtually all positions as necessitating the ability to communicate in English. English remained the language of work of many small businesses, exempted from the language-of-work stipulations of Bill 101. Some reports signalled a marked deterioration in the use of French in Montreal, especially among immigrants. Large numbers of newcomers whose mother tongue was neither French nor English adopted English as the language usually used at home. Although immigrant children were obliged by law to do their primary and secondary schooling in French, they tended to frequent English-language institutions of higher education. The Quebec government refused, however, to impose new restrictions in this sector. For many newcomers to the province, English remained the language of social mobility. Many francophones agreed, feeling that increased trade relations with the United States meant that it was important to learn English. In general, they supported the Liberal government's decision to introduce mandatory English language study from the first grade, in 2006. Enrolment in English-language schools increased, as francophone children of mixed marriages entered them. Studies showed that many French-speaking high school graduates had poor mastery of the language. Decidedly, the survival of the French language in Quebec would always be in question.

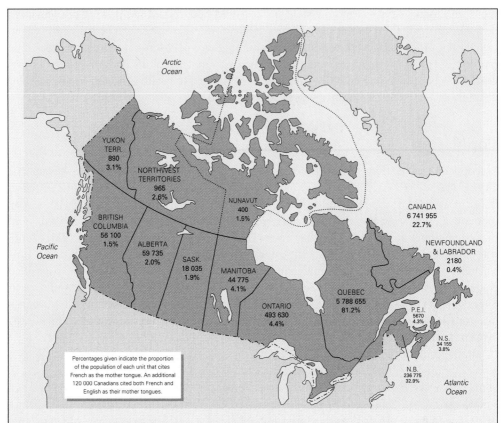

Canada's francophone population, 2001. Note the French-speaking community's strong majority position in Quebec, but minority status (less than 5 percent of the total population) in all other provinces and territories, with the exception of New Brunswick.

Source: Statistics Canada, 2001 Census, Highlight Tables, *Mother Tongue: Canada, Provinces, Territories.*

Culture in an Era of Globalization

What effects did globalization, with its disappearing borders, have on Quebec culture? Essayist Jacques Godbout wrote of Quebec artists: "Our head may often be in Paris and our heart in America, but we are not schizophrenics, that is simply our way of being." Well beyond the borders of Quebec, stage director and playwright Robert Lepage, lyricist Luc Plamondon, and especially popular singer Céline Dion (see this chapter's Historical Portrait), gained recognition. The Cirque du Soleil, a troop of acrobats and other entertainers, performed regularly in Las Vegas and across the United States; annual receipts topped $800 million in 2006 alone. Pierre Garand, better known by his stage name, Garou, whose career was launched when he played Quasimodo in Luc Plamondon's musical hit, *Notre-Dame de Paris*, released his first solo album, *Seul*, in 2000; within a month it had sold more than 250 000 copies worldwide. He then set to work on a CD in English. Kevin Parent, another popular singer, released a new recording, *Les vents ont changé*, to which an impressive panoply of internationally known musicians contributed. Singer Lynda Lemay authored four successful albums in the 1990s, then took on the French market with impressive results. Her lyrics had broad appeal and spoke of such subjects as loneliness, suicide, relationships, and children. Artist and songwriter Pierre Lapointe launched his first album in 2004, then, in 2006, a second, *La Forêt des mal-aimés*. Critics acclaimed what they termed a masterpiece. Lapointe, too, became popular in France. Although American cultural products, such as the film *Titanic*, attracted Quebeckers quite as much as they fascinated other Canadians, in Quebec the hockey film *Les Boys* ran neck-and-neck with it. For some, globalization was perhaps a threat to Quebec's distinct culture; for others, it obviously presented new opportunities.

In modern Quebec's pluralistic society, allophone novelists made important cultural contributions. Not surprisingly, they often emphasized themes linked to the pain of exile and the hopes for a better life in the new land. Marco Micone, an immigrant from Italy, told Quebeckers in a poem, *Speak What*: "We are a hundred peoples come from afar to share your dreams and your winters." The hero in one of Shanghai-born Ying Chen's novels lives in two worlds, in two societies, in two eras. Dany Laferrière and Émile Ollivier, both from Haiti, Sergio Kokis, born in Brazil, and Abla Farhoud, who grew up in Lebanon, are among the voices "from afar" who have enriched contemporary francophone literature.

A HISTORICAL PORTRAIT

Luc Plamondon, Céline Dion, and the Global Village

In the 1950s, several Quebec artists, among them poet and singer Félix Leclerc, first achieved fame abroad, particularly in Paris, before continuing their careers in Quebec. In the 1960s and the 1970s, stars such as Gilles Vigneault, Jean-Pierre Ferland, and Pauline Julien, many of them ardent nationalists, rose to fame in Quebec, although on occasion they performed abroad. Since the 1980s, however, many of Quebec's most talented artists have quite literally gone global, working in Montreal, Toronto, Los Angeles, Paris, London, and elsewhere. Luc Plamondon and Céline Dion epitomized this new tendency.

Luc Plamondon grew up in modest circumstances in a small town in Quebec's Eastern Townships. He first built a career in Quebec, then extended his activities to France, notably as a songwriter for popular singer Diane Dufresne. France offered possibilities that Quebec, with its small population, could not. As Plamondon put

it, "the Paris region contains 12 million potential spectators, twice the entire population of Quebec." And yet Plamondon built his major shows, the rock opera *Starmania* and more recently the musical production *Notre-Dame de Paris*, based on Victor Hugo's celebrated novel, largely with Quebec talent. *Starmania* began playing in Paris in 1979; by 2002, the most successful French-language musical in history had been seen by three million people on stage and had sold more than five million copies. French radio played the show's major songs, such as "Le Blues du businessman" and "Les uns contre les autres," from morning to night. The pop opera *Notre-Dame de Paris*, which opened in Paris in 1998, attracted tremendous success, with performances always sold out well in advance. Its dazzling choreography, its seductive and romantic music, and its songs, such as the enormously popular "Belle" and "Le temps des cathédrales," sung by Quebecker Bruno Pelletier, thrilled audiences. The show then took to the road to perform elsewhere in Europe and in Quebec. Plamondon, who promised himself in 1960 that he would create for the French-speaking world a musical hit that would be what *Hair* was to the English-speaking world, could boast of his contribution to a living French language, as his contemporary hits even managed to push American successes off the airwaves in France. Plamondon currently resides in Ireland, which offers artists generous fiscal treatment.

Céline Dion, another planetary superstar with unpretentious roots, first became a child star in Quebec in the 1980s. In 1984, she sang for Pope John Paul II at Olympic Stadium in Montreal. In 1988, she won first place at the annual Eurovision competition, Europe's Olympics of song contests, held in Dublin and viewed by 600 million telespectators. The year 1992 saw her win awards for her CD containing songs written by Luc Plamondon, a recording that was hugely successful in Quebec and France. Then, in 1993, she won Juno awards in Toronto, singing in recently learned English and, in the words of gushing critics, bridging the cultural gap between Canada's "two solitudes." In 1997, she performed two songs for the Academy Awards to an audience that reportedly numbered one billion people. She also picked up two Grammy Awards in New York City. In her acceptance speech, she addressed Quebeckers in French, a gesture that one *Globe and Mail* columnist thought worth more than "a trillion distinct society clauses."

By 2000, Dion, whom *Time* magazine proclaimed a "global diva," had sold more than 130 million albums, with 26 megahits, including "Falling into You" and "Let's Talk About Love." Biographer Barry Grills saw her as building cultural bridges

Source: CP Photo/AP Photo/Express-News, Kevin Geil.

from Quebec to the rest of the planet; she occupied "a huge international territory, while still maintaining a direct connection to the culture where, for her, it all began."[1] Yet Dion asserted, in an interview, "I am very much Americanized." In this regard, she seemed to voice the attraction to the American dream that many Quebeckers have felt throughout their history. In 2002, "Canada's biggest cultural export," as *The Globe and Mail* styled Dion, came out of retirement and released a new English-language CD, *A New Day Has Come*; thanks in part to lavish publicity, it immediately became a top hit. A *New York Times* critic hypothesized that Dion's success came from her never being specific: the more general and abstract her message, the more people were able to relate what was said to the particularities of their own experience. Here undoubtedly was globalization in action. Dion then

1 Barry Grills, *Falling into You: The Story of Céline Dion* (Kingston, ON: Quarry Press, 1997), pp. 9–10.

Although borders became more porous, Canada's two solitudes did not dissolve. When well-known radio host Peter Gzowski, known as "the voice of Canada," died in 2002, many English-speaking observers deplored the scanty coverage given to his career by the media in Quebec, where Gzowski was virtually unknown. When Montreal daily *La Presse* drew up a list of 25 influential figures of Quebec's arts scene, including novelist Marie Laberge, who had sold 400 000 copies of her trilogy, *Le goût du bonheur*, set in Depression-era and postwar Quebec, and television scriptwriter Fabienne Larouche, some of whose series like *Urgence* and *Scoop* drew a million viewers, a journalist commented in *The Globe and Mail* that these individuals were virtually unknown in English-speaking Canada. Cultural differences remained a fact.

The Environment

In the early 1990s, interest in the environment became less fashionable. Reflecting this decreased interest, the Quebec government created no new land-based parks during the decade. Air pollution, most of it originating from industries and coal-fired electric power stations in Ontario and the American Midwest, continued to degrade Quebec's lakes and forests, and worsened the problem of urban smog. Agricultural pollution of water remained a grave problem, but governments feared that new regulations on farm practices would alienate rural voters. Industrial pollution of the St. Lawrence River and its tributaries also continued, but polluting industries were also important employers. At hundreds of lakes in southern Quebec, cottage owners continued to artificialize shores by building retaining walls and making lawns; fertilizers, wastewater, and sediment from erosion washed into the lakes, jeopardizing their survival. South of the St. Lawrence River, farmers cut down large tracts of remaining forest to make more fields to produce more corn to feed more pigs or to obtain land for spreading manure from huge pig farms. The power of the so-called "pig barons" was portrayed in 2001 in a film, *Bacon*.

By the end of the 1990s, the pendulum began to swing back toward greater concern for environmental degradation. Environmentalists warned that the province's forests were being cut down at a rate substantially in excess of their capacity to regenerate. In 1999, well-known pop singer Richard Desjardins even produced a film, *L'Erreur boréale*, denouncing what he saw as the collusion between timber companies and the government that allowed clearcutting of huge tracts of land to go ahead with no concern for the survival of forest ecosystems. Finally, after a government-commissioned report called for a substantial reduction of logging quotas, the provincial government did impose lower limits but had to face substantial opposition from companies and workers who blamed government policy and environmentalists rather than a declining resource for their plight.

Like people elsewhere, Quebeckers discussed climate change and ways to reduce the production of greenhouse gases. The Liberal government of Jean Charest launched a plan, financed largely with federal money, whose objective was to enable Quebec to respect the objectives fixed by the 2001 international agreement on the reduction of greenhouse gases, the Kyoto Protocol (see Chapter 20). Quebec's contribution to gas emissions was already far below the Canadian average, since the province had no oil or gas industry and depended almost entirely on hydro-electricity. Although the government invested in public transport to encourage commuters to leave their cars home, it promised, at the same time, to build a new bridge across the river from Montreal to Laval as well as more expressways. Nor was it willing to risk the wrath of drivers by imposing the mandatory inspections of automobiles necessary to remove aged and highly polluting vehicles from the roads. Quebec also encouraged the establishment of wind-power farms although some citizens complained that the huge turbines might have a negative impact on the spectacular scenery that attracted so many tourists.

In the name of conserving biodiversity, the government promised to create new protected areas from which logging and mining operations would be excluded, mostly in northern forests, but it delayed acting in the face of strong opposition from industrial lobbies; in any case, its much-renewed promise to protect 5 percent of Quebec's territory was far below the Canadian average of 10 percent and the international norm of 12 percent. What it did was adopt legislation (later rescinded after heavy public pressure) to amputate one famous existing park of part of its territory so that commercial activities could proceed in the newly privatized sector. Environmentalists also urged Quebec to act to protect the province's remaining wetlands, which performed enormous services as filters and sponges for water. Nearly three-quarters of the wetlands of southern Quebec had been destroyed since 1975. Yet governments, particularly municipal, tended to heed the wishes of developers, interested in draining and building, in view of the additional tax monies that new housing, shopping centres and industrial parks would procure. Environmental organizations themselves were frequently accused of attempting to block important development projects that could create jobs and wealth.

Although Quebec will remain predominantly French-speaking for the foreseeable future, the French language will continue to be spoken by a declining minority outside the province, and by an infinitely smaller minority elsewhere in North America. Canada's commitment to bilingualism and to equal status for its francophone citizens also risks being called into question. Inevitably, the threat of assimilation will continue to weigh heavily upon francophones, and the French-speaking community will have to devote constant effort to revitalizing its language and culture.

Regardless of the province's constitutional and linguistic evolution, Quebeckers, like other Canadians, will have to create a society that affords women the same opportunities it offers men, and to find solutions to the problems posed by living in an increasingly pluralistic society. As the dramatic confrontation with the Mohawks at Oka in the summer of 1990 acutely demonstrated, Quebeckers, again like other Canadians, must continue to work for an accommodation with the Native peoples to settle longstanding grievances. Recent steps in this direction include the "Paix des Braves," a new accord signed in 2002 with the Cree of Northern Quebec designed to deal with Native dissatisfaction with the agreement of 1975, as well as the recognition as "nations" of eleven First Nations groups living within Quebec's boundaries. Much energy will have to be directed to combating such social problems as poverty, violence, and a painfully high suicide rate among young Native males. In addition, all Quebeckers, regardless of language or origin, will have to meet the challenges and pay the price of creating and preserving an environment in which human life can flourish in harmony with nature. Much work lies ahead.

NOTES

1. Susan Mann, *The Dream of Nation: A Social and Intellectual History of Quebec* (Montreal/Kingston: McGill-Queen's University Press, 2002, 1982), p. 284.

2. Guy Rocher, *Le Québec en mutation* (Montreal: Hurtubise, 1973), p. 18.

3. Marcel Rioux, *La question du Québec* (Paris: Seghers, 1969), p. 104.

4. Dale C. Thomson, *Jean Lesage and the Quiet Revolution* (Toronto: Macmillan, 1984), p. 309.

5. Susan Mann, *The Dream of Nation*, pp. 318–20.

6. Vincent Lemieux, "Les partis et l'idée de souveraineté," in Maurice Pinard, Robert Bernier, and Vincent Lemieux, *Un combat inachevé* (Ste-Foy, QC: Presses de l'Université du Québec, 1997), p. 18.

7. Maurice Pinard, "Les fluctuations du mouvement indépendantiste depuis 1980," in Maurice Pinard et al., *Un combat inachevé* (Ste-Foy, QC: Presses de l'Université du Québec, 1997), p. 97.

8. Ibid., p. 99.

9. Maryse Potvin, "Some Racist Slips About Quebec in English Canada Between 1995 and 1998," *Canadian Ethnic Studies* 32 (2000): 1–26.

10. John T. Saywell, *The Lawmakers: Judicial Power and the Shaping of Canadian Federalism* (Toronto: University of Toronto Press, 2002), p. 306.

11. Quoted by Lysiane Gagnon, "Sovereignty Is Not Dead, Just Sleeping," *The Globe and Mail*, November 11, 2002.

12. Gilles Gagné and Simon Langlois, *Les raisons fortes: nature et signification de l'appui à la souveraineté du Québec* (Montreal: Presses de l'Université de Montréal, 2002).

13. Pierre Fortin, "L'évolution de l'économie depuis 1960: le Québec a comblé la moitié de son retard sur l'Ontario," *Le Devoir*, March 27, 2000.

BEYOND THE BOOK

Weblinks

First Nations Lands History in Quebec
http://www.lsd.nrcan.gc.ca/english/fh_e.asp
A history of First Nations territorial lands in Quebec. Complete with detailed maps reflecting changes over time, and descriptions of historical changes to territory.

Quebec Elections: 1960–2007
http://archives.cbc.ca/300c.asp?IDCat=73&IDDos=651&IDLan=1&IDMenu=73
Digitized television and radio archives describe the history of elections in Quebec from 1960 to 2007.

1995 Quebec Referendum
http://archives.cbc.ca/IDD-1-73-1891/politics_economy/1995_referendum
A video retrospective of the events of the 1995 Quebec referendum.

Hydro-Québec

http://www.canadianeconomy.gc.ca/english/economy/1962HydroQuebec.html

A detailed history of Hydro-Québec, a major economic entity in the province.

Bill 101

http://www.cbc.ca/news/background/bill101

A historical backgrounder describing events leading to Bill 101, and a look back since.

Medical Services and the 1998 Ice Storm

http://www.cmaj.ca/cgi/reprint/158/4/520.pdf

An account in the Canadian Medical Association Journal of the health effects of the 1998 "ice storm of the century," and its impact on the availability of medical services to citizens.

Films & Novels

Breaking Point: Canada/Quebec—The 1995 Referendum. CBC. 2005.

René Lévesque: The Miniseries. CBC. 2006.

October 1970. CBC. 2006.

RELATED READINGS

The following articles in R. Douglas Francis and Donald B. Smith, eds., *Readings in Canadian History: Post-Confederation*, 7th ed. (Toronto: Thomson Nelson, 2006), deal with topics relevant to this chapter in greater depth: Richard Jones, "Politics and the Reinforcement of the French Language in Canada and Quebec, 1960–1986," pp. 537–51; and Alain-G. Gagnon, "Quebec-Canada's Constitutional Dossier," pp. 551–67.

BIBLIOGRAPHY

Although considerable scholarly material on Quebec exists in English, students wishing exposure to a full range of often controversial viewpoints need a reading knowledge of French. Two useful general syntheses are Susan Mann, *The Dream of Nation: A Social and Intellectual History of Quebec* (Montreal/Kingston: McGill-Queen's University Press, 2002, 1983); and John Dickinson and Brian Young, *A Short History of Quebec*, 3rd ed. (Montreal/Kingston: McGill-Queen's University Press, 2003). Recent research on modern Quebec is summarized in English translation in Paul-André Linteau et al., *Quebec Since 1930* (Toronto: James Lorimer, 1991). A dispassionate general analysis is available in Kenneth McRoberts, *Quebec: Social Change and Political Crisis*, 3rd ed. with a postscript (Toronto: Oxford University Press, 1999). Ramsay Cook presents his interpretations in *Canada, Québec, and the Uses of Nationalism*, 2nd ed. (Toronto: McClelland & Stewart, 1995); and in *Watching Quebec: Selected Essays* (Montreal/Kingston, McGill-Queen's University Press, 2005). David Chennells offers a useful synthesis in *The Politics of Nationalism in Canada: Cultural Conflict Since 1760* (Toronto: University of Toronto Press, 2001). See also Ronald Rudin's provocative analysis of Quebec historiography, *Making History in Twentieth-Century Quebec* (Toronto: University of Toronto Press, 1997).

On the Duplessis years see Conrad Black, *Render Unto Caesar: The Life and Legacy of Maurice Duplessis* (Toronto: Key Porter, 1998); Herbert F. Quinn, *The Union Nationale: Quebec Nationalism from Duplessis to Lévesque*, 2nd ed. (Toronto: University of Toronto Press, 1979); and, for a brief sketch, Richard Jones's booklet *Duplessis and the Union Nationale Administration* (Ottawa: Canadian Historical Association, 1983). Michael Behiels, *Prelude to Quebec's Quiet Revolution: Liberalism Versus Neo-Nationalism, 1945–1960* (Montreal/Kingston: McGill-Queen's University Press, 1985), examines the ideological conflicts among Duplessis's opponents. Recent research on Quebec society during the Duplessis years is available in Louise Bienvenue, *Quand la jeunesse entre en scène: l'Action catholique avant* la *Révolution tranquille* (Montreal: Boréal, 2003); Michael Gauvreau, *The Catholic Origins of Quebec's Quiet Revolution, 1931–1970* (Montreal/Kingston: McGill-Queen's University Press, 2005); Dominique Marshall, *The Social Origins of the Welfare State: Quebec Families, Compulsory Education, and Family Allowances, 1940–1955* (Waterloo, ON: Wilfrid Laurier University Press, 2006); and Alain-G. Gagnon and Michel Sarra-Bournet, *Duplessis: Entre la Grande Noirceur et la société libérale* (Montreal: Québec Amérique, 1997).

Dale C. Thomson studies the early 1960s in *Jean Lesage and the Quiet Revolution* (Toronto: Macmillan, 1984). Marcel Martel studies relations between Quebec and French-speaking minorities in *French Canada: An Account of Its Creation and Break-up, 1850–1967* (Ottawa: Canadian Historical Association, 1998). Critical views of the Quiet Revolution may be had in Gilles Paquet, *Oublier la révolution tranquille: pour une nouvelle socialité* (Montreal: Liber, 1999); and E.-Martin Meunier and Jean-Philippe Warren, *Sortir de la grande noirceur: l'horizon personnaliste de la révolution tranquille* (Quebec: Septentrion, 2002). For a journalistic account of the Bourassa years see L. Ian MacDonald, *From Bourassa to Bourassa: Wilderness to Restoration*, 2nd ed. (Montreal/Kingston: McGill-Queen's University Press, 2002). On the independentist movement in general consult William D. Coleman, *The Independence Movement in Quebec, 1945–1980* (Toronto: University of Toronto Press, 1984). Graham Fraser studies the Parti Québécois in *René Lévesque and the Parti Québécois in Power*, 2nd ed. (Montreal/Kingston: McGill-Queen's University Press, 2002). Philosopher Charles Taylor proposes an original analysis of French–English relations in Guy Laforest, ed., *Reconciling the Solitudes: Essays on Canadian Federalism and Nationalism* (Montreal/Kingston: McGill-Queen's University Press, 1993). See also Guy Laforest and Roger Gibbins, eds., *Beyond the Impasse: Toward Reconciliation* (Montreal: Institute for Research on Public Policy, 1998).

On the referendum of 1980 see Gertrude Robinson, *Constructing the Quebec Referendum: French and English Media Voices* (Toronto: University of Toronto Press, 1998). Constitutional issues are examined extensively by Edward McWhinney in two books: *Quebec and the Constitution, 1960–1978* (Toronto: University of Toronto Press, 1979); and *Canada and the Constitution, 1979–1982: Patriation and the Charter of Rights* (Toronto: University of Toronto Press, 1982). For Quebec viewpoints see Christian Dufour, *A Canadian Challenge: Le défi québécois* (Lantzville, BC: Oolichan Books, 1990); Louis Balthazar, Guy Laforest, and Vincent Lemieux, *Le Québec et la restructuration du Canada, 1980–1992: enjeux et perspectives* (Sillery, QC: Septentrion, 1991); Alain-G. Gagnon, *Québec: État et société* (Montreal: Québec Amérique, 1994); and Robert A. Young, *The Secession of Quebec and the Future of Canada*, rev. ed. (Montreal/Kingston: McGill-Queen's University Press, 1998). Alan Cairns, *Charter Versus Federalism: The Dilemmas of Constitutional Reform* (Montreal/Kingston: McGill-Queen's University Press, 1992), proposes a thoughtful essay.

Among the many publications bearing on the Meech Lake Accord see Michael D. Behiels, ed., *The Meech Lake Primer: Conflicting Views of the 1987 Constitutional Accord* (Ottawa: University of Ottawa Press, 1989); Andrew Cohen, *A Deal Undone: The Making and Breaking of the Meech Lake Accord* (Vancouver: Douglas & McIntyre, 1990); Jean-François Lisée, *The Trickster: Robert Bourassa and the Quebeckers, 1990–1992* (Toronto: James Lorimer, 1994); Guy Laforest, *Trudeau and the End of a Canadian Dream* (Montreal/Kingston: McGill-Queen's University Press, 1995); and Patrick J. Monahan, *After Meech Lake: An Insider's View* (Kingston: Institute of Intergovernmental Relations, Queen's University, 1990). A fine overview of English-Canadian reaction to Quebec nationalism is provided by Kenneth McRoberts, *Beyond Quebec: Taking Stock of Canada* (Montreal/Kingston: McGill-Queen's University Press, 1995); see also his *Misconceiving Canada: The Struggle for National Unity* (Toronto: Oxford University Press, 1997), a study highly critical of Pierre Trudeau's policies for national unity. Constitutional developments after Meech are examined in Kenneth McRoberts and Patrick Monahan, *The Charlottetown Accord: The Referendum, and the Future of Canada* (Toronto: University of Toronto Press, 1993); and in Robert A. Young, *The Struggle for Quebec: From Referendum to Referendum* (Montreal/Kingston: McGill-Queen's University Press, 1999). Brian Mulroney presents his point of view on the constitutional debate in *Memoirs 1939-1993* (Toronto: Douglas Gibson Books, 2007).

Analyses of the language question include articles by Richard Jones and William D. Coleman in Michael D. Behiels, ed., *Quebec Since 1945: Selected Readings* (Toronto: Copp Clark Pitman, 1987), pp. 223–62; Pierre Godin, *La poudrière linguistique: La revolution tranquille, 1967–1970* (Montreal: Boréal Express, 1990); and Michel Plourde, ed., *Le français au Québec: 400 ans d'histoire et de vie* (Quebec: Conseil de la langue française, 2000); and Graham Fraser, *Sorry, I Don't Speak French: Confronting the Canadian Crisis That Won't Go Away* (Toronto: McClelland & Stewart, 2006). Works on Quebec's English-speaking minority include Ronald Rudin, *The Forgotten Quebecers: A History of English-Speaking Quebec, 1759–1980* (Quebec: Institut québécois de recherche sur la culture, 1985); Josée Legault, *L'invention d'une minorité: Les Anglos-Québécois* (Montreal: Boréal Express, 1992); Martha Radice, *Feeling Comfortable? The Urban Experience of Anglo-Montrealers* (Quebec: Presses de l'Université Laval, 2000); and Garth Stevenson, *Community Besieged: The Anglophone Minority and the Politics of Quebec* (Montreal/Kingston: McGill-Queen's University Press, 1999).

Cultural development is examined in Richard Handler, *Nationalism and the Politics of Culture in Quebec* (Madison: University of Wisconsin Press, 1988). A summary of Martin Pâquet's important study of immigration is available in a brochure, *Toward a Quebec Ministry of Immigration* (Ottawa: Canadian Historical Association, 1997). Lucia Ferretti chronicles religious history in *Brève histoire de l'Église catholique au Québec* (Montreal: Boréal, 1999). Pierre Anctil, Ira Robinson et Gérard Bouchard, eds., *Juifs et Canadiens français dans la société québécoise* (Sillery, QC: Septentrion, 2000), examines relations between Jews and French Canadians. For a study of the postwar generation in Quebec, see François Ricard, *The Lyric Generation: The Life and Times of Baby Boomers* (Don Mills, ON: Stoddart, 1994). The experience of women in Quebec is covered in Micheline Dumont et al., *Quebec Women: A History* (Toronto: Women's Press, 1987). A revised version of this study is available in French only. Danielle Lacasse examines a social problem in *La prostitution féminine à Montréal, 1945–1970* (Montreal: Boréal, 1994).

Denis Monière's *Ideologies in Quebec* (Toronto: University of Toronto Press, 1981) is a useful intellectual history. On labour history, see Jacques Rouillard, *Histoire du syndicalisme au Québec* (Montreal: Boréal, 1989). Studies of Quebec society include Fernand Dumont, ed., *La société québécoise après 30 ans de changements* (Quebec: Institut québécois de recherche sur la culture, 1990); the same author's *Genèse de la société québécoise* (Montreal: Boréal, 1993); and Simon Langlois et al., *Recent Social Trends in Quebec, 1960–1990* (Montreal/Kingston: McGill-Queen's University Press, 1992).

Sylvie Vincent and Garry Bowers have edited a collection of essays on the first James Bay hydro-electric project: *Baie James et nord québécois: dix ans après/James Bay and Northern Quebec: Ten Years After* (Montreal: Recherches amérindiennes au Québec, 1988). Richard F. Salisbury's *A Homeland for the Cree: Regional Development in James Bay, 1971–1981* (Montreal/Kingston: McGill-Queen's University Press, 1986) is another analysis of the project's impact on the Cree. See also Hans M. Carlson, "A Watershed of Words: Litigating and Negotiating Nature in Eastern James Bay, 1971–75," *Canadian Historical Review* 85 (2004), pp. 63–84. Studies of Quebec-based businesses include Maurice Chartrand and René Pronovost, *Provigo: An Outstanding Entrepreneurial Success* (Scarborough, ON: Prentice-Hall, 1989); Peter Hadekel and Ann Gibbon, *Steinberg: The Breakup of a Family Empire* (Toronto: Macmillan, 1990); and Larry MacDonald, *The Bombardier Story: Planes, Trains, and Snowmobiles* (Toronto: J. Wiley Publishers, 2001).

Chapter Eighteen

IMMIGRATION AND MULTICULTURALISM

TIME LINE

1946	A first group of postwar European refugees arrives in Canada
1947	Parliament repeals the Chinese Exclusion Act adopted in 1923
1956	Thousands of Hungarian refugees, fleeing Soviet tanks sent to repress an uprising, enter Canada as immigrants
1962	Racial discrimination is officially ended in Canada's immigration regulations
1966	Department of Manpower and Immigration established
1971	Ottawa adopts a multiculturalism policy, giving official status to minority ethnic groups
1982	The Charter of Rights and Freedoms accords constitutional protection to multiculturalism
1986	The Employment Equity Act comes into effect; it favours increased representation of visible minorities in private companies
1988	The Mulroney government acts to stem illegal immigration
1993	Parliament adopts new legislation on immigration to attract more highly educated newcomers
2003	Census statistics showed that fully 18.4 percent of Canada's population were immigrants; the country's foreign-born population was second only to Australia's (22 percent)
2007	Ottawa increases its annual immigration target to between 240 000 and 265 000, the highest level in 25 years

The history of Canada's immigrants and ethnic minority groups since 1945 involves three closely intertwined elements: the Canadian government's changing immigration policy; Canadians' response to recent newcomers who have made Canada their new home; and the experience of the immigrants themselves. Discussion of the immigrants' experience gives rise to several more specific questions: Where have the immigrants come from, and why? How have they reacted and adapted to their new environment? How have immigrant communities been transformed, and what impact have they had on Canadian society?

Members of Canada's non-French, non-British ethnic minorities began to question their place in Canadian society, particularly after the mid-1960s, at a time when so many other components of Canada's population were also challenging the perceived inequalities of their own status. They naturally expressed serious reservations about the then-popular concept of two nations, or two founding peoples, which, while it ignored the existence of the Native peoples, appeared to give special treatment to Canadians of French and British origins. The federal government's multiculturalism policy, announced in 1971, accorded minority ethnic groups an official status they had not enjoyed in the past. The Canadian constitution of 1982 gave additional recognition to ethnic minorities. These acts served as recognition of how Canada, in one century, had become a multiethnic and multicultural society, one in which those of backgrounds other than English or French made up nearly one-third of the total population, a proportion that continues to increase.

Postwar European Immigration, 1945–57

In 1946, millions of destitute refugees from wartorn areas of Europe remained crowded in camps, awaiting a permanent haven. Canada felt little responsibility for them. The country had received virtually no immigration during the preceding fifteen years. Most Canadians, tired of being told to "do their part," probably agreed that the country had other, more urgent priorities to attend to. Canada had its own children, as well as its injured soldiers and veterans, to look after. Furthermore, economists worried that the war's end would bring on another depression, as it had immediately after World War I. A wave of new arrivals risked swelling the ranks of the unemployed.

European Refugees

Prime Minister William Lyon Mackenzie King sensed Canadians' hesitancy about immigration. He saw little electoral advantage to be gained by opening the country's doors to Europe's homeless. Pressure, however, continued to mount. In the House of Commons, a few, mainly CCF, MPs denounced the government's "shameful" vacillation and insisted on Canada's "moral and Christian duty" toward the unfortunates of Europe. Certain religious groups and ethnic associations also spoke in favour of the refugees. Finally, after hearings in the spring of 1946, the Senate Committee on Immigration and Labour recommended that immigration offices be opened in Europe to process as many displaced persons and refugees as the country could absorb.

The Canadian government moved cautiously. The first refugees to arrive in 1946 were some 4000 Polish veterans who had fought with British military units in the war. Hugh Keenleyside, deputy minister of mines and resources (the department that had responsibility for immigration), believed Canada must act quickly to select the best immigrants. By admitting a few thousand displaced persons immediately, he argued, Canada could obtain good candidates, improve the country's international image, and encourage other nations to follow suit. John Holmes, an external-affairs officer, claimed that Canada selected refugees "like good beef cattle, with a preference for strong young men who could do manual labour and would not be encumbered by aging relatives."[1] By the fall of 1948, 40 000 refugees had reached Canadian shores. Although the numbers then began to decrease, about 165 000 refugees had come to Canada by 1953. Many of them, after arrival, applied to bring in their close relatives.

One of these refugees was Ann Kazimirski, a Jew born in eastern Poland. After the German invasion of her region in June 1941, the Nazis murdered most of her family. In 1942 she married a local dentist and, because dentists were needed to treat German troops, the couple was allowed to live outside the Jewish ghetto. As Nazi killings of Jews increased, a friend of the Kazimirskis agreed to hide the couple in an attic. One night troops rounded up most of the town's Jewish population of 18 000, took them away in trucks to the outskirts of town, and shot them. Shortly afterwards Ann's mother was captured and murdered before her daughter's eyes. The Kazimirskis escaped through the town's sewers, and hid in the surrounding countryside. In 1949 they reached Canada. Ann later testified in Germany during the trial for war crimes of the Nazi district administrator, identified by Ann as the person in charge of the killings; he was acquitted. Kazimirski returned to Canada and founded a choir group in Montreal, convinced that, while there was much to cry about, there was even more to sing about. She also told her story in a book, *Witness to Horror*.[2]

Maria Redekop Wall was another refugee. At the age of 47, she reached Canada with her six children and her meagre belongings in September 1948. Historian Marlene Epp recounts that Wall was part of a group of 8000 Mennonites, a majority of whom were women, who immigrated to Canada in the years 1947–52.[3] Wall had lived in a Mennonite village in the Ukraine. In 1938, her husband, like numerous other Mennonite men, was arrested by Soviet police and disappeared. In 1941, Hitler's armies occupied the Ukraine. When the Germans were forced to retreat in September 1943, Wall and her co-religionists, as ethnic Germans, had no choice but to follow. After an arduous four-month trek in horse-drawn vehicles, they reached Poland, where the remaining men were conscripted into the German army. With the Soviet advance into Poland in 1944, the Mennonites were again uprooted. Most were taken prisoner by the Soviets; rape and suicides were common. Wall managed to reach a refugee camp in West Germany but spent many anxious months fearing she would be sent back to the USSR. Indeed, at the end of the war, the Red Army did forcibly repatriate thousands of eastern Europeans behind the "Iron Curtain," often condemning them to prison, persecution, and even death. After spending three years in the camp, Wall was finally chosen to go to Canada. She settled in the Fraser Valley in British Columbia where she bought a berry farm. Adaptation to the new society was not without problems, however, and even within the Mennonite community divergent lifestyles and experiences often strained relations between more conservative Canadian Mennonites and women who had long been forced by extraordinary, and often tragic, circumstances to make difficult decisions and compromises.

A number of refugees were well-educated professionals or highly skilled workers. Often they concealed their training in order to better their chances with Canadian officials, who sought manual labourers. Industries in need of unskilled labour sponsored many of the refugee immigrants, who readily accepted almost any job, salary, and working conditions. Once in Canada, they fulfilled their contractual obligations on farms, in lumber camps, in mines, and often, in the case of women, in domestic service, before moving on to more suitable occupations.

Immigrant Labour

Employers frequently exploited new immigrants. One notorious scheme involved Ludger Dionne, an MP and owner of the Dionne Spinning Mill Company at Saint-Georges-de-Beauce, south of Quebec City. In 1947, Dionne obtained government authorization to recruit 100 Polish women for his mill. *Time* reported that he paid them 20 cents an hour; after deductions of $6 a week for board, they were left with $3.60 weekly. Dionne assured parliamentarians that young women from Quebec City did not want to work in the small towns and that his working conditions were better than those in Toronto. For good measure, he also accused his detractors of being propagandists for communism.

Economically, many immigrants progressed rapidly. By 1971, Latvians and Estonians, for example, had incomes that were 25 percent higher than the Canadian average. Political scientist Karl Aun explains this evolution in part by the fact that such groups included unusually large numbers of educational, community, cultural, and political leaders.[4] Yet stories abound like the one about the poor Estonian fisherman who, after settling in southern Ontario, saved as much as possible from the earnings of all family members. Then, with the help of a loan from the Estonian Credit Union, he bought a house with several apartments, continued saving and purchased a second apartment house, moved into the best unit, and eventually sent his children to university.

Historian Franca Iacovetta has described the lives of many poor peasant farmers and rural artisans from southern Italy who settled in Toronto where they faced considerable hardship before they were able to secure a stable life for themselves and their families.[5] Jobs were often dirty, disagreeable, and risky. Iacovetta also examined the personal histories of women refugees from elsewhere in Europe.[6] Each story was unique. Eighteen-year-old Elena Krotz was recruited by Canadian officials in a displaced-persons camp in West Germany. She had fled her native Czechoslovakia when communist authorities sought to arrest her after she had participated in a student protest. After staying for a few weeks at a government hostel, Krotz was sent to the home of a farm couple in southwestern Ontario, to work as a servant. She arrived with all her worldly belongings in two tiny bags: a blanket and one change of clothes. A drive to succeed, the encouragement and mutual support of the community, and the relative youth of the newcomers combined to help these immigrants adjust to their new environment.

Postwar Federal Immigration Policy

Since most prospective immigrants to Canada, even in the early postwar years, were not refugees, the country needed a general immigration policy. In a much-discussed speech to the House of Commons on May 1, 1947, Prime Minister King attempted to satisfy both supporters and opponents of immigration. He said that Canada would benefit by boosting its population and that immigration would make the country more prosperous and more secure. At the same time he put forth the nebulous notion of Canada's "absorptive capacity," promising that the government would "ensure the careful selection and permanent settlement" of only as many immigrants as could "advantageously be absorbed in our national economy." The number admitted could vary from year to year, in an alternating open-door/closed-door approach.

King's comments also reveal Canadian racial attitudes of the era. Responding to those who denounced racial distinctions in immigration policy, the prime minister asserted Canada's right to choose its future citizens. The government did repeal the blatantly discriminatory Chinese exclusion law of July 1, 1923. Nevertheless, it continued to apply severe restrictions on Asian immigration since, in King's words, the "massive immigration of Orientals would alter the fundamental composition of the Canadian population" and "give rise to social and economic problems."

Canadian Responses to Postwar Immigration

Canadians could not agree on how many immigrants the country needed and who should be admitted. Business and financial leaders lobbied for substantial immigration. They argued that a larger population would benefit the economy and yield per capita savings in areas such as transportation and administration. Ethnic associations and several religious groups also favoured increased immigration.

Many Canadians, however, were reluctant to receive any sizable influx of immigrants. By 1954, only 45 percent of Canadians favoured increased immigration, down from 51 percent in 1947. Many Canadians of British origin feared that immigration would weaken the British element in Canada. Workers often viewed immigrants as competitors willing to work for lower wages. Unions wanted immigrants to be carefully selected and preferably to occupy unattractive jobs in remote regions that Canadians did not want. As the economy began to slow in the late 1950s, a majority of Canadians felt the country was accepting too many immigrants. Senator David Croll, who had been an enthusiastic advocate of higher immigration a decade before, now joked: "If you put pants on a penguin, it could be admitted to this country." After 1957, the new Progressive Conservative government substantially reduced immigration levels.

French-Speaking Immigrants

As late as 1947, it appeared that if the birth rate of French Canadians remained high, they might one day constitute the largest part of Canada's population. Yet large-scale immigration of non-French-speakers risked undermining the demographic situation of Canada's French-speaking minority. Even in Quebec, francophones often perceived immigrants as a threat because most joined the ranks of the English-speaking minority.

Jack Pickersgill (right), the federal minister responsible for immigration in the St. Laurent government, greets the dean of the faculty of forestry engineering at the University of Sopron, Hungary, in Montreal, 1957. Some 37 000 young and highly skilled Hungarians, including the entire faculty and student body of this faculty, arrived in Canada during and immediately after the Hungarian uprising of 1956.

Source: Champlain Marcil/Library and Archives Canada/PA-147725.

In the fall of 1948 the federal government, in hopes of satisfying French-speaking members of the Liberal caucus as well as French-Canadian public opinion, put French nationals on an equal legal footing with British subjects and American citizens for purposes of entry into Canada. Civil servants, however, immediately slowed down the new policy for "security" reasons, arguing that a large proportion of would-be French immigrants might be either communists or former Nazi collaborators.[7]

All told, Ottawa's new policy on French immigration had only a slight effect: between 1946 and 1950, fewer than 5000 French immigrants came to Canada. Although the French authorities did not encourage emigration, prospective immigrants literally besieged Canadian consular offices in Paris. While the Canadian consul in Paris made urgent requests for more staff and more office space, Hugh Keenleyside advised the deputy minister of labour to channel "all efforts in the same direction, that is to say, the encouragement of British immigration to Canada."

Clearly, during this period, the Canadian government preferred British immigrants over all others. J.W. Pickersgill, minister of citizenship and immigration, stated in 1955: "We put forth much more effort in the United Kingdom than in any other country." It was only natural, he asserted, that Canada favour British immigration since it was easier to transplant individuals into "similar soil." Although he viewed the massive influx of new arrivals in 1956–57, 40 percent of whom were British, as "too big for Canada to digest," he added candidly that any attempt to stem the tide of British immigration "would be the finish of the Liberal party in many Anglo-Saxon constituencies."

French immigration did increase in the 1950s and 1960s, before declining again. In the years 1945–80, between one-half and two-thirds of immigrants to Canada were English-speaking, whereas French-speakers numbered only about 3 percent, and bilinguals 4 percent. The remainder, speaking other languages, soon learned English. By 2000, although Canada's major sources of immigrants were no longer European, more than half of new immigrants—many of them from India—still spoke English whereas fewer than 5 percent spoke French. The census of 2001 showed that immigration was the primary factor in explaining the relative decline of Quebec's population in regard to Canada's total population. Immigration also explained, together with assimilation, why the proportion of francophones in the English-speaking provinces also continued to decline. Immigration, then, reinforced the numerical strength of English-speaking Canada linguistically, although diversifying it ethnically and culturally.

An Evaluation of Postwar Immigration Policy

This first wave of postwar immigration, which brought 1.7 million immigrants to Canada, ended in the late 1950s, when rising unemployment led the Canadian government to reconsider its policy. The year 1957, however, proved a sort of boom before the bust, with 282 000 arrivals—a figure that still paled in comparison with the 400 000 immigrants who came in 1913. Some 37 000 of these new arrivals were mainly young and often highly skilled Hungarians who fled their homeland in 1956 as Soviet armies crushed the Hungarian revolution. Among them came the entire student body and faculty of a Hungarian school of forestry. Transported across Canada on a "freedom train," they were relocated at the University of British Columbia. In general, the resettlement of the Hungarian refugees proceeded smoothly.

Such major movements of people gave rise to myths and half truths. In theory, humanitarian ideals and a sense of international responsibility guided Canadian immigration policy. Canadians believed themselves to be generously offering liberty and opportunity to victims of persecution. In practice, economics usually dictated how many and which immigrants came to Canada. Ottawa sought immigrants possessing certain skills, and initiated bulk labour schemes. Federal authorities directed many immigrants, once in Canada, to farms and to unattractive jobs in remote resource regions. Once they fulfilled their contracts, however, many immigrants soon left for the cities.

Racial bias explains why few immigrants gained entrance from outside Europe and the United States. In 1958, the director of the Immigration Branch explained why "coloured British subjects" from the Caribbean were excluded from Canada: "They do not assimilate rapidly and pretty much vegetate to a low standard of living." The introduction of tiny quotas, which remained in effect until 1967, also limited immigration from the Indian subcontinent. The location of immigration offices and the nature of government promotional

The Haim Abenhaim family, Sephardic Jewish immigrants from Morocco, arriving in Montreal, 1960. In the early 1970s, immigrants from developing countries began to come to Canada in significant numbers.

Source: Canadian Jewish Congress National Archives/PC 2/1/7 A.4.

This 1955 poster questions the colour code applied to immigrants from within the British Commonwealth.

Source: Library and Archives Canada/Marcil Ray/PA-139579.

literature ensured that the great majority of immigrants came from Britain and the European continent, as well as from the United States.

Emigration

During the economic downturn of the late 1950s and early 1960s, immigrants experienced the obverse side of immigration. Disappointed with the lack of opportunities in Canada and embittered by what they considered false promises on Canada's part, many thousands, particularly British, returned home. There they contributed to tarnishing Canada's image, if only temporarily. From the early 1950s to the early 1970s, one in every three or four immigrants to Canada either returned home or moved to the United States.

Even more worrisome to many Canadians was the movement southward of 800 000 native-born Canadians in the period 1952–71. Perhaps one-tenth of this group consisted of professionals or managers—the much-publicized "brain drain." *Maclean's* estimated in 1963 that 8000 graduates of the University of Toronto lived in the United States and that 800 of these taught in American colleges. Historian Arthur Lower conjectured that this loss of talent helped keep Canada "in that state of low water which has always been the object of the Yankee's good-natured scorn."[8] After a temporary reversal of the brain drain in the 1960s and early 1970s, at the time of the Vietnam War and race riots in the United States, the movement to the south resumed in the late 1970s and 1980s. In the mid-1980s, 50 000 Canadians departed annually, attracted largely by the buoyant American economy and, perhaps, by southern sunshine.

The problem worsened in the 1990s, when some 275 000 Canadians took up residence in the United States. In certain years, the number of nurses and physicians who emigrated represented the equivalent of about one-half of the number of graduates from Canada's nursing and medical schools. Many engineers, scientists, teachers, and managerial workers also joined the trek south, attracted to the United States by the prospect of better working conditions and higher salaries. In 2001, some 30 000 Canadians left Canada to settle in California, New York, or Florida, more than double the number who had left in 1999 and nearly six times the number of Americans who immigrated to Canada. The cost to Canada was substantial, as emigrants took with them skills they had developed in largely publicly financed postsecondary schools.

The Immigrant Experience in the 1960s and 1970s

Due to an economic slowdown, the Diefenbaker years (1957–63) witnessed a slump in immigration. Fewer agents staffed Canadian immigration offices abroad. Unions exerted pressure to decrease immigration, and most parliamentarians were at best indifferent. Even Diefenbaker, despite favourable public pronouncements in speeches aimed at ethnic groups, appeared to have little interest in the question.

Sometimes immigration made sensational headlines. The press reported numerous cases of foreign seamen who jumped ship in Canadian waters and then hurriedly married Canadian women in order to remain in Canada. Large-scale illegal Chinese immigration, promoted by a Hong Kong–based group that bought and sold false identities, also appeared to overwhelm the government. Ottawa promised to grant amnesty to most illegals who would come forth and declare themselves (many thousands did), but the program did not eliminate the illegal immigration rings.

Toward a Colour-Blind Immigration Policy

The Conservatives introduced new regulations in 1962 that ended the use of race and national origin as reasons for exclusion from Canada. The old discriminatory provisions appeared unacceptable in an era that discredited racism. In 1960, Diefenbaker had proudly presented the Canadian Bill of Rights, which rejected discrimination by reason of race, national origin, colour, religion, or sex. Economic factors also contributed to the reversal of the former policy: Canada could no longer obtain the labour it needed from the "old countries." For a time, southern Europe supplanted Britain and northern Europe as the area of origin of most immigrants to Canada. Then, immigration diminished from these countries, too, and Canada turned its attention toward Asia and the Caribbean.

A New Wave of Immigrants

Assisted by the return of economic prosperity in the early 1960s, the Pearson government (1963–68) instituted structural changes designed to increase immigration. In 1966, it established the Department of Manpower and Immigration to relate immigration to the needs of the labour market, while the Department of the Secretary of State obtained responsibility for the integration of immigrants into Canadian society.

In 1967, new immigration regulations set up a points system for selecting independent immigrants. Criteria included education and training, personal qualities, occupational demand, and age and linguistic capacity. Sponsored dependants and, particularly, non-dependent relatives now found it more difficult to gain admittance. The government also set up the independent Immigration Appeal Board, which was almost immediately overwhelmed with appeals from alleged "visitors" who had applied to stay but had been refused and ordered deported.

The gradual elimination of racial discrimination from Canada's immigration policy, the decline of European sources of immigrants, and the expansion of the network of immigration offices around the world rapidly transformed the face of Canadian immigration. In 1966, for example, 87 percent of immigrants were of European origin; only four years later, 50 percent came from other regions. The West Indies, Haiti, Guyana, India, Hong Kong, the Philippines, and the Indochinese nations all figured among the major suppliers of immigrants in the 1970s.

Immigrant Settlement

Newcomers to Canada did not spread out evenly across the country. Since 1945, more than one-half have settled in Ontario, especially southern Ontario. Good employment opportunities and the region's prosperous image attracted them, as did well-established ethnic communities with religious centres, clubs, welfare organizations, newspapers, and professional and other services. Quebec, with one-quarter of Canada's population, has usually received fewer than 15 percent

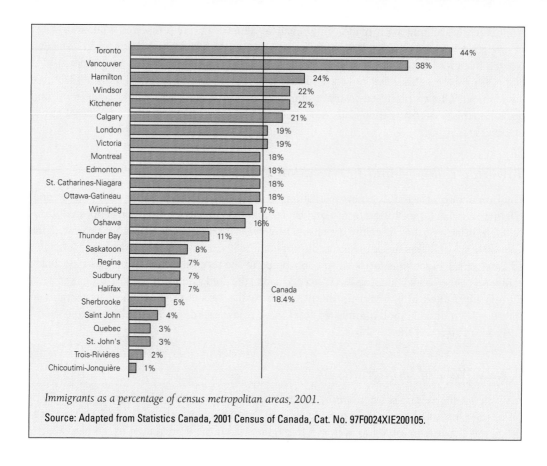

Immigrants as a percentage of census metropolitan areas, 2001.

Source: Adapted from Statistics Canada, 2001 Census of Canada, Cat. No. 97F0024XIE200105.

of new arrivals—about the same proportion as British Columbia. Alberta, especially during oil booms, also attracted many immigrants, although most newcomers arrived from other provinces. The Atlantic provinces, for their part, experienced little immigration.

In all regions, immigrants settled mainly in major metropolitan areas. As many as one-half of all immigrants to Ontario chose Toronto which, with the rise of Asian immigration during the 1990s, became North America's most ethnically diverse city and possibly the world's. Vancouver and Montreal also attracted large numbers of immigrants. Big-city Canada thus became much more cosmopolitan.

Immigration in Recent Years

The deep recession of the early 1980s again caused immigration to decline. Economic problems contributed to an anti-immigrant backlash, as many Canadians saw immigrants as competitors for scarce jobs or believed they were crowding the welfare rolls.

Most studies on the relationship between immigration and employment tend to demonstrate that immigrants do not increase unemployment among indigenous workers but rather help to create a larger, more flexible, and more adaptable labour force. Immigrants often work at jobs that Canadians cannot or will not do. For some time after arrival, they may require more social services; yet a report produced by the Economic Council of Canada in 1992 concluded that the proportion of welfare recipients among recent immigrants is not significantly different from that of the native-born. Moreover, through their need for housing, food, clothing, and other consumer goods, immigrants increase the size of the domestic market and thereby assist in boosting growth. Additional research carried out by two York University sociologists indicated that "the objective evidence does not support the view that the relation between immigration and unemployment is a major problem."[9] Other studies have shown that most immigrants have been able to obtain jobs soon after arrival, although Third World immigrants in the independent immigrant category often worked in jobs for which they were overqualified.

Regardless of the assurances of sociologists, the image of immigrants lined up outside employment offices in times of recession has probably influenced public opinion far more. Thus, in view of Canada's economic problems in the early 1980s, the government felt it necessary to revise each year's quotas downward, according to its vague predictions of what the economy could bear. Immigration declined to its lowest levels in more than two decades. After 1986, the government did, however, facilitate the entry into Canada of several thousand "business class" immigrants—wealthy entrepreneurs, especially from Hong Kong. These individuals agreed to invest their capital in Canada, set up businesses, and hopefully create jobs for Canadians. Most immigrant investors chose to settle in British Columbia, Quebec, and Ontario.

How Many Immigrants and From Where?

In the late 1980s, Ottawa gradually raised the ceiling on immigration from 100 000 to 200 000. But taking into account annual emigration of at least 50 000, the net immigration figure was substantially lower. Then, in 1990, the federal government announced further increases—a politically risky decision as the economy slowed again and as certain groups, such as the Reform party, based in western Canada, attacked immigration and multiculturalism policies. An average of nearly 220 000 immigrants were nonetheless admitted to Canada each year during the period 1992–99.

By the 1990s, Sri Lanka and Taiwan had replaced the Caribbean nations as major homelands of arriving immigrants. In the years immediately preceding Hong Kong's cession to China in 1997, the former British colony was Canada's major source of immigrants. Some 200 000 of these returned to Hong Kong after obtaining Canadian citizenship following three years of residence in Canada. From 2000, annual arrivals fluctuated between 225 000 and 250 000. More than one-quarter of newcomers to Canada now came from just two countries: China, in first place, and India. By 2007, India seemed poised to take first place. More stringent selection criteria favoured Indians, generally able to speak English. Frustration with long delays in processing files—a five-year wait for an interview is usual—and China's booming economy appeared to explain smaller numbers of Chinese immigrants. The Philippines, Pakistan, Iran, and Korea were also major source countries. Outside Asia many immigrants came from the United States and the United Kingdom (although many people from Britain were of Indian origin), as well as Colombia, France, Romania, and Russia.

Thanks to Caribbean and then to Asian immigration, so-called "visible minorities" became an important part of Canada's social fabric. While only 12 000 West Indians lived in Canada in 1961, the figure climbed to 225 000 in 1986. The number of Canadians of Chinese origin increased from 60 000 to nearly 350 000 in the same period, and then to 1 million by 2001. In 2001, such minorities made up 13 percent of the country's population and more than 35 percent of the populations of Vancouver and Toronto. It was expected that these two cities would become "majority-minority" cities by 2017—in other words, that more than one-half of their inhabitants would belong to visible minorities.

Leading Source Countries of Immigrants, Selected Years

1960	1976	1984	1991–96	2001–05
Italy	Britain	Vietnam	Hong Kong	China
Britain	United States	Hong Kong	China	India
United States	Hong Kong	United States	India	Philippines
Germany	Jamaica	India	Philippines	Pakistan
Netherlands	Lebanon	Britain	Sri Lanka	South Korea
Portugal	India	Poland	Poland	United States
Greece	Philippines	Philippines	Taiwan	Iran
France	Portugal	El Salvador	Vietnam	Romania
Poland	Italy	Jamaica	United States	United Kingdom
Austria	Guyana	China	Britain	Sri Lanka

Source: Employment and Immigration Canada, Immigration Statistics, various years.

Immigrants and Canada's Economy

In the early 1990s, fewer than 40 percent of immigrants belonged to the so-called "economic class" in which one family member, the principal applicant, was seen as a potential investor in the Canadian economy or assessed for skills deemed in demand in Canada. Fully 75 percent of immigrants had belonged to this group in 1968. By far the great majority of immigrants admitted to Canada now belonged to the other two categories of "family class" (i.e., close relatives of Canadian residents) and refugees. In response to critics who urged the government to link immigration more closely to economic needs, Ottawa adjusted its rules in 1993 to favour more highly educated newcomers, and the number of immigrants with university diplomas rose sharply.

By 2001, thanks to new selection criteria, more than 60 percent of immigrants were independent workers (including their dependants) and investors, chosen with the objective of responding to labour market requirements. About 30 percent were family relatives, and some 10 percent were refugees. Revised rules set out in 2002 favoured educated applicants with work experience and a confirmed job offer, people judged to be adaptable and to have "flexible and transferable skills" for the "knowledge economy."

Still Canada's immigration system showed signs of strain. In its search for highly educated and well-trained immigrants, Canada had to work to compete with several other countries including the United States and Australia. Construction companies begged the government to admit the skilled tradespeople they needed and to regularize the status of the thousands of undocumented immigrants it allegedly employed, often for less than the minimum wage; Ottawa, in 2006, refused an amnesty that risked encouraging more illegal immigration. Moreover, many workers selected because of their high qualifications had difficulty having their foreign credentials recognized in Canada. As one Toronto newspaper commented, "Foreign-trained engineers may make wonderful taxi drivers, but they also deserve a chance, if their credentials stand up to scrutiny, to be wonderful engineers." Ontario, which received more than half of Canada's immigrants, attempted to force self-governing professions to maintain fair, clear, and open licensing processes. At the same time, the province's economy appeared simply unable to absorb the large numbers of immigrant engineers who arrived every year, and many immigrants were not covered since they were in non-regulated professions. Unsurprisingly, a Statscan survey showed that poverty rates among immigrants, despite their high levels of education, remained high. Worse, 40 percent of economic immigrants left Canada within ten years.

Business, with its demands for more skilled workers to alleviate worrying labour shortages, was not alone in seeking high numbers of immigrants. Policy analysts including demographers warned that, because of current low fertility rates—Canadian women were expected to have on average 1.5 children—the country's population would begin to contract in the medium term, even at present levels of immigration. Some middle-aged Canadians began to worry about who would pay for their old-age pensions and future health care, and urged the government to bring in more immigrant taxpayers.

Adaptation

Most immigrants from developing countries found their new life in Canada a considerable material improvement over the past. Certainly political conditions prevented refugees from returning home, even if they so desired. Modern-day immigrants did, however, face a much greater cultural shock than did earlier British and European immigrants. Provincial governments and community associations have, to an extent, attempted to assist the new arrivals. Mutual aid and support among families have also been important, although the traditionally close interaction of the extended family, common in many cultures and providing an extensive support system, has gradually disappeared in North America, where the functional unit is now the nuclear family.

Immigrants also faced the upsetting necessity of coming to terms with Canadian customs. A study of South Asians (people from India, Pakistan, Bangladesh, and Sri Lanka) showed that "only a small proportion" of homeland cultural practices survive the settlement process.[10]

Sod-turning for Edmonton's Hindu Centre, 1976.
Source: Provincial Archives of Alberta.

Culinary habits and cultural celebrations tend to be maintained in those cities where immigrant groups are sufficiently numerous, but it is more difficult to retain religious practices: Hindu parents, for example, often find that children know far more about Christianity than they do about Hinduism.

Furthermore, the clash between contemporary Canadian values and mores and accepted values and attitudes in the country of origin has frequently caused painful problems for immigrants and raised controversial issues within Canadian society. Parental authority has also weakened in the context of Canada's much more permissive society. In South Asia, for example, parents tend to choose marriage partners for their children, and dating is a "foreign" practice. In Canada, the generation gap between immigrant parents and their children has often deepened into a gulf as children become Canadianized through the schools, television, and contacts with friends.

A HISTORICAL PORTRAIT

The Immigrant Experience

For many immigrants who have come to Canada, material betterment has been accompanied by a sense of cultural loss. Historian Hugh Johnson recorded the story of Tara Singh Bains, a Punjabi who arrived in Vancouver in 1953 and has since made many journeys back to the land of his origin. The now-elderly Bains, a man of strong religious convictions, told Johnson he deplored what he saw as the erosion of spiritual values among members of his community. Bains testified, "Materialism has created so many doorways to attract human thinking towards luxury, enjoyment, and selfishness, and in Western society ... the guidance of the family, the school and the church has fallen away."[1]

Serious generational conflicts among members of ethnic communities, as among Canadians in general, have been frequent. Sociologist Edite Noivo has studied the life histories of members of three generations of Portuguese Canadians living in Montreal. These stories reveal sharp tensions.

Noivo found, for example, that many first-generation parents objected to a son's wish to marry, because his departure represented a serious financial loss. One father reported that he told his son that "we couldn't afford it now and that he had to wait a couple of years more." Although the son at first agreed to abide by his father's will, he later, in the father's words, "got impatient and started to make a big fuss ... so I allowed him to get married." Sons saw marriage as an advantage because it would bring financial independence. One son explained, "I had been handing over my weekly pay since the age of fourteen.... By the time I was 22, I still didn't have a penny for myself.... So I figured that I had to get married.... If I got married I'd keep my paycheque."[2]

A young third-generation Portuguese Canadian adapted in a different fashion to parents' constraints in matters concerning relations with the opposite sex. He reported, "None of the Portuguese girls I know are allowed to go to parties.... I can go, but my sister and cousins never do.... I can't take them along, my parents and their parents don't trust me.... Of course, none of my girlfriends are Portuguese, but they're just for fun. Like my mother says, a girl who is not a virgin at marriage is no good; I mean, she can't be trusted.... Sure I'll want to get married ... to someone Portuguese like myself."[3]

Noivo herself had to face her respondents' disapproval of her own lifestyle. One first-generation male told her that she was only "half a woman.... One cannot be a full woman unless one is married and a mother." A second-generation female made the same comment "in a more acrid and distasteful tone."[4]

---

1 Hugh Johnson, *The Four Quarters of the Night: The Life Journey of an Emigrant Sikh* (Montreal/Kingston: McGill-Queen's University Press, 1995), p. 227.

2 Edite Noivo, *Inside Ethnic Families: Three Generations of Portuguese-Canadians* (Montreal/Kingston: McGill-Queen's University Press, 1997), pp. 67–68.

3 Ibid., p. 119.

4 Ibid., p. 39.

Discrimination

Many immigrants, especially members of visible minorities, have suffered discrimination in Canada. In the 1970s and 1980s, the media gave wide publicity to certain cases, such as one in which "white" and South Asian members of a railway crew in Daysland, Alberta clashed with bottles and axes. In numerous instances, Sikhs were attacked and had their turbans forcibly removed. Blacks were frequently harassed or physically assaulted. In Montreal, a taxi company fired its Haitian drivers, claiming that it was losing business to companies that employed only white drivers. (Haitians responded by buying the city's second-largest taxi company.) Incidents of police shootings of young African Canadians in Montreal and Toronto sparked widespread demands for inquiries into alleged racism in police forces.

Historian Stanley Barrett's research on a suburban Toronto community in the early 1990s showed the existence of widespread racism against visible minorities. He suggested that South Asians saw racism as inevitable, and sought to defend themselves by fostering strong links with their own ethnic communities. African Canadians, more in contact with the "white" community, often felt bitterness and anger in the face of what they perceived as rejection by their neighbours. Barrett also found strong negative attitudes toward French Canadians, who were seen as "intent on taking over and running the country."[11]

Most complaints about discrimination have concerned employment and housing. A study done in Toronto in 1985 found that when immigrants from South Asia or the Caribbean with the same qualifications as white applicants applied for job openings, they learned, in two cases out of five, that the opening no longer existed. In some instances, the same employer on the same day then interviewed white candidates for the same position. One survey showed that three-quarters of West Indians judged employment discrimination in Toronto to be "very serious." Surveys in eleven other Canadian cities repeated the same finding. Arabs spoke of having to confront much mistrust, particularly since the terrorist attacks of 2001. Provincial human-rights commissions did receive numerous complaints of discrimination. Yet most victims probably failed to report incidents, believing that nothing would be done or, worse, fearing retaliation. Human-rights defence groups have criticized the courts for their slowness and their leniency, and have denounced existing laws for their lack of severity.

Reactions to Immigration

"Established" Canadians have had mixed reactions to the new arrivals from the developing nations. Religious and civic groups have strongly urged the admission of refugees, such as the Indochinese "boat people" in the late 1970s and refugees from Kosovo in 1999. Yet many Canadians, at times even a majority, thought that Canada accepted too many newcomers, regardless of the number of immigrants actually admitted. Some cited the deleterious effects on the environment and on living conditions of rapid population growth, fuelled largely by immigration, particularly in congested urban areas of southern Ontario and British Columbia's Lower Mainland. Others worried that immigration favoured the emergence of new social problems, such as a violent gang culture. Crime, fuelled by drugs and guns, became a major worry for many Canadians in Toronto and in several cities in the western provinces.

The rise of international terrorism brought more debate about Canada's immigration policy. Critics accused Ottawa of not sufficiently screening new immigrants, thus permitting the entry into the country of militants who favoured the use of violence to promote the causes they espoused. As evidence, they cited several incidents, among them the bombing in 1985 of an Air India airplane, which resulted in the death of 329 people, most of them Canadian citizens of Indian origin. It was Canada's worst mass murder. Police and prosecutors blamed Sikh militants but were unable to solve the crime and obtain convictions. In 2006, the Conservative government launched a commission of inquiry to study the investigation of the bombing. In other instances, investigative journalists linked Canadian-based militants of various national origins with participation in terrorist activities abroad.

Studies have also shown that many Canadians dislike immigrants' speaking their home languages in public or wearing traditional dress. They tend to see immigrants as ignorant of Canadian cultural practices and unwilling to "act like Canadians," and they have expressed discomfort with the changes in Canadian society that have been brought about by immigration.

The arrival in Canada, particularly in Vancouver, of a relatively large number of wealthy Chinese immigrants from Hong Kong in the late 1980s provoked strong reactions. Government and business leaders appreciated the large financial investments a number of newcomers made. But some Canadian residents spoke with derision of the "yacht people," criticizing what they perceived as ostentatious displays of wealth, such as the construction of "monster homes." Reacting to a number of unpleasant incidents, Vancouver's first Chinese-Canadian city councillor complained, "The Chinese are damned if they're poor and damned if they're rich." British Columbia's lieutenant governor, Chinese-Canadian David Lam, attempted to calm tensions, recommending that newcomers become more involved in the community and that older residents turn a blind eye to pretentious houses.

The role of women in the family and in society, particularly in certain Asian cultures, has generally been defined very rigidly; male authority generally goes unchallenged, and male financial supremacy backs up that authority. Contact with Canadian mores in this regard has often provoked conflict within the immigrant family as well as increasing public controversy. Ontarians discussed whether Muslims could establish religious courts to decide issues of family law; the Ontario government decided they could not. Quebeckers debated the meaning of "reasonable accommodation" of religious differences. Canadians in general attempted to define so-called "Canadian values" that, they said, should not be compromised and included democracy, tolerance, and equality between men and women.

Refugees

Much of the criticism directed at federal immigration policy since 1980 concerned refugees. Across the world, millions of human beings became refugees, fleeing war and persecution in their own lands. Canada could not be immune to such mass movements. Humanitarian and refugee-advocacy groups as well as ethnic communities favouring more immigration from their home countries judged Canada's refugee quotas to be unreasonably low. They also denounced the government's cumbersome procedures for studying the cases of refugee-status claimants, resulting in backlogs that grew larger each year.

During this period public opinion became notably less sympathetic to the cause of refugees: surveys showed that nearly half of all Canadians thought Canada had no moral obligation to open its doors to persons fleeing persecution in other lands. Many critics were undoubtedly influenced by the large numbers of would-be immigrants who entered Canada illegally—so-called "queue jumpers"—and who claimed refugee status, but whose reasons for emigrating seemed to be primarily economic. Indeed, the "hearing" that virtually all refugee-status claimants requested—an unforeseen consequence of earlier legislation—became "a routine channel for evading the normal admission requirements and getting easy access to Canada."[12] In 1986, the dramatic arrival of a large group of Tamil immigrants from Sri Lanka on the shores of Newfoundland and, the following year, of a group of Sikhs from India on the coast of Nova Scotia, was sufficient proof for many Canadians that Ottawa had lost control over entry into the country.

Public pressure led the Mulroney government to act against illegal immigration in 1988, by which time government efforts to clear the huge backlog of refugee-status claimants had become hopelessly bogged down. In addition, immigration officials had to study the applications of new refugees who arrived at Canada's borders and airports. The number of new claimants declined, and the government declared that it had succeeded in driving off manifestly unfounded claims. New legislation in 1993 further limited the right of rejected applicants to appeal, resulting in a further drop in the number of claimants arriving in Canada. Through the 1990s, the acceptance rate of refugee claimants declined from about 75 percent to about 50 percent—admittedly a much higher rate than existed in most western countries. Refugee lawyers blamed "compassion fatigue": panel members, they said, were becoming hardened to stories of abuse and persecution. Religious and ethnic groups feared that the measures also discouraged true political refugees.

The terrorist attacks of September 11, 2001 in the United States brought new and tighter immigration rules, which took effect in 2003. In response to American accusations that Canada admitted too many refugees without proper security vetting, Canada decided to turn back claimants arriving at Canadian land borders and invited them to seek asylum in the United States, whose rules were reputedly more restrictive. Critics maintained that henceforth more refugees would seek to enter Canada illegally, in order to make their claim from inside Canada. Newspaper reports asserted that claimants still enjoyed far too many possibilities for appeal and that economic migrants were displacing genuine refugees. In 2006 Canada began a new system for processing certain refugee applications. The change provided for the acceptance en masse of large groups of displaced people including Sudanese, Somalis, and Afghans.

Multiculturalism

Canadians have often taken pride in the image of their country as a "cultural mosaic" (or a "tossed salad," in one writer's words), rather than as an American-style "melting pot." Official policy no longer favours rapid assimilation, and social scientists prefer to speak instead of integration or of acculturation. In his first speech in the Senate in 1964, Senator Paul Yuzyk, born in Manitoba of Ukrainian origin, discussed the emergence of what he termed a "third force," consisting of Canadians of neither French nor British descent. The Royal Commission on Bilingualism and Biculturalism also widened its scope to include a study of the cultural contributions of other ethnic groups.

In October 1971, Prime Minister Trudeau told the House of Commons that the government "accepts the contention of other cultural communities that they, too, are essential elements in Canada and deserve government assistance in order to contribute to regional and national life in ways that derive from their heritages." Multiculturalism—but not multilingualism—was to be encouraged. The new Canadian constitution of 1982 gave additional, though somewhat vague, protection to multiculturalism by declaring that the Canadian Charter of Rights and Freedoms "shall be interpreted in a manner consistent with the preservation and enhancement of the multicultural heritage of Canada." Still, various ethnic associations denounced what they termed the unacceptable primacy that the Charter accorded English and French in Canada. Then, in 1988, a revised Multiculturalism Act provided new funds for promoting cultures and reducing discrimination. Contrary to what many ethnic groups had sought, however, it did not take the highly symbolic step of establishing a separate ministry of multiculturalism.

Politicians understood the potential electoral benefits of recognizing the contributions of ethnic groups. Also, the Trudeau government hoped that recognition of multiculturalism would attenuate existing hostility toward bilingualism and biculturalism and that it would appeal to English-Canadian nationalists who wanted a distinct Canadian identity. These rather ambitious objectives were certainly not fulfilled. Many Canadians, including the British, the French, and the so-called "lukewarm white ethnics" from northern and western Europe, found multiculturalism meaningless. As time went on, impatience with the whole concept grew, especially when governments agreed to provide funding.

By the mid-1980s, the federal government was investing modestly in multiculturalism, funding ethnic day-care centres, heritage-language classes, cultural festivals, and conferences, and providing grants for the preparation of histories of the major Canadian ethnic groups. Money was made available to complete the revitalization of Vancouver's Chinatown and to transform this ethnic neighbourhood into a shining symbol of Canada's new multicultural nature

Hockey legend Willie O'Ree, the first African-Canadian player in the NHL, chats with children at the Harmony Brunch in East Preston, Nova Scotia, held to commemorate the International Day for the Elimination of Racial Discrimination.

Source: Nova Scotia Human Rights Commission.

and, at the same time, a valuable tourist attraction. (By 2000, however, Vancouver's Chinatown was in decline; it had also lost its exclusiveness as new Chinatowns grew up in suburbs such as Richmond.)

Several provincial governments also contributed financially to support multicultural policy. The Ontario government, for example, used its Wintario lottery funding program to create a research institute, the Multicultural History Society of Ontario. Many school boards set up courses in non-official languages. In Edmonton, for example, immersion schooling could be had in Arabic, Chinese, Hebrew, Ukrainian, and German. Such policies have practical relevance: already by the late 1980s, English was *not* the mother tongue of 50 percent of the children enrolled in Toronto public schools nor of 40 percent of those enrolled in Vancouver schools.

The federal government's support of ethnic diversity has given rise to the question of who really speaks for the ethnic communities and, thus, of which associations the government ought to support. Twenty organizations, for example, now represent Edmontonians of various Asian origins. In Vancouver, the well-established Chinese Benevolent Association has on occasion feuded with newer, more activist, organizations, such as the Chinese Cultural Centre, over various local issues, in particular a plan to build a freeway through Chinatown. In Toronto, West Indians have a multitude of often-competing organizations whose membership is determined by island of origin.

Increasingly, observers of multiculturalism have expressed fears that the official emphasis on maintaining cultural diversity has impeded the integration of newcomers. For example, they cite the rising tendency of immigrant groups, particularly South Asians and Chinese, to live in self-segregated, often middle-class, "ethnic enclaves," defined by Statistics Canada as communities with 30 percent of their population from one visible minority group. In such communities, contacts with the host society are greatly reduced. Market researcher Allan Gregg commented, "In Canada, we may live in a multicultural society, but the evidence suggests that fewer and fewer of us are living in multicultural neighbourhoods."[13] Did such ghettos explain the disturbing conclusion in a report published by Statistics Canada in 2007 that second-generation immigrants belonging to minorities felt less Canadian than children of European immigrants? Were discrimination and exclusion also major factors? Was there a risk that marginalized immigrant communities would lead to social upheavals as in several European countries? There were no sure answers to these questions.

WHERE SOCIAL SCIENTISTS DISAGREE

Evaluating Canada's Multicultural Policy

The arrival in Canada of large numbers of immigrants, first from Europe and, since the late 1960s, from the Caribbean, Latin America, Asia, and Africa, has immensely diversified Canada's population. Until the 1950s, the federal and the provincial governments espoused a policy of rapid assimilation of newcomers into the "Canadian mainstream." But many immigrants and their descendants attempted to conserve at least part of their ethnic heritage. As interest in the rights of minorities grew throughout the Western world during the 1960s, these groups sought government intervention to help them attain their goals. In response, the federal government elaborated, in 1971, a somewhat vague multicultural policy. Since then, governments and public agencies at all levels have launched programs favouring the retention of national cultures.

Official federal policy views multiculturalism as "a powerful bonding agent" that "helps unite us and identify us, while at the same time allowing every element of our society to retain its own characteristics and cultural heritage."[1] Observers have generally been somewhat suspicious of these stated intentions. In 1988, Howard Palmer described federal policy as, at least in part, an attempt to win the ethnic vote in urban Ontario and to temper western Canada's rising opposition to the policy of bilingualism.[2] Jean Burnet has criticized the "ambiguous conceptualization" of multiculturalism but believes that its basic aims are a valid response to the Canadian situation.[3]

Regardless of the inevitable political considerations underlying the policy, has multiculturalism been worth pursuing? Yes, thinks Norman Buchignani, who feels that federal policy has helped groups such as the South Asians feel "comfortable about being South Asian and Canadian at the same time."[4] He also views multicultural policy as heightening awareness among native-born Canadians of the new communities that have recently established themselves in their midst. Elliot L. Tepper agrees; in his view, multiculturalism "fosters acceptance of the reality that Canada is a nation of immigrants."[5] More critically, Lance W. Roberts and Rodney A. Clifton argue that the policy at least has symbolic value, permitting members of ethnic groups to "participate and benefit as members of a complex industrial society while retaining the sense that they belong to a smaller, more intimate community."[6]

Other observers express doubt. C. Michael Lanphier and Anthony H. Richmond argue that it is probably impossible to reconcile equality of opportunity and integration with "the maintenance of separate identities and cultural pluralism."[7] Gilles Paquet agrees. He sees multiculturalism as having heightened the belief among "other" Canadians that they do not have to adapt their mores while, at the same time, the "dominant cultures" have remained dominant. "The gap between expectations and realities has generated much ... frustration."[8] Peter S. Li and B. Singh Bolaria hold a similar opinion. For them, multiculturalism is "the failure of an illusion, not of a policy."[9] The illusion is that a cultural solution, such as multiculturalism, could solve problems such as ethnic inequality and racial discrimination, whose roots are political and economic. (Perhaps such criticisms explain why, in the 1980s, government multicultural programs broadened their involvement in race relations.)

Wenona Giles, a student of Toronto's Portuguese community, also asserts that multiculturalism, which she sees as a major component of Canadian nationalism, will not facilitate access to education and other basic resources "unless it is linked to more broadly based struggles against racism, and gender and class inequities."[10] For his part, novelist Neil Bissoondath, who refuses the role of "ethnic" which would have him labelled an "East Indian-Trinidadian-Canadian-Quebecker," argues in a controversial book that the policy of official multiculturalism, by encouraging immigrants to focus on "There," the ancestral homeland, rather than on "Here," the new homeland, actually highlights the differences that divide Canadians rather than the similarities that unite them. Such a policy, he believes, "stultifies the personality, creates stereotypes," and strips the individual of uniqueness.[11]

Regardless of the disagreements, Robert A. Harney, a student of the Italian community in particular, saw merit in simply pursuing the debate. Multiculturalism, he said, was part of Canada's eternal search to define itself. "Survival lies in traveling toward an identity, and we will all be better served if that traveling itself remains our identity."[12]

---

1   *Multiculturalism … Being Canadian* (Ottawa: Secretary of State for Multiculturalism, 1987), p. 9.

2   Jean R. Burnet with Howard Palmer, *"Coming Canadians": An Introduction to a History of Canada's Peoples* (Toronto: McClelland & Stewart, 1988), p. 176.

3   Jean Burnet, "Multiculturalism Ten Years Later," in Jean Leonard Elliott, ed., *Two Nations, Many Cultures* (Scarborough, ON: Prentice-Hall, 1983), p. 241.

4   Norman Buchignani and Doreen M. Indra with Sam Srivastiva, *Continuous Journey: A Social History of South Asians in Canada* (Toronto: McClelland & Stewart, 1985), p. 227.

5   Elliot L. Tepper, "Immigration Policy and Multiculturalism," in J.W. Berry and J.A. Laponce, eds., *Ethnicity and Culture in Canada: The Research Landscape* (Toronto: University of Toronto Press, 1994), p. 95.

6   Lance W. Roberts and Rodney Clifton, "Multiculturalism in Canada: A Sociological Perspective," in Peter S. Li, ed., *Race and Ethnic Relations in Canada* (Toronto: Oxford University Press, 1990), p. 133.

7   C. Michael Lanphier and Anthony H. Richmond, "Multiculturalism and Identity in 'Canada Outside Quebec,'" in Kenneth McRoberts, ed., *Beyond Quebec: Taking Stock of Canada* (Montreal/Kingston: McGill-Queen's University Press, 1995), p. 314.

8   Gilles Paquet, "Political Philosophy of Multiculturalism," in J.W. Berry and J.A. Laponce, eds., *Ethnicity and Culture in Canada: The Research Landscape* (Toronto: University of Toronto Press, 1994), p. 63.

9   Peter S. Li and B. Singh Bolaria, *Racial Minorities in Multicultural Canada* (Toronto: Garamond Press, 1983), introduction.

10 Wenona Giles, *Portuguese Women in Toronto: Gender, Immigration, and Nationalism* (Toronto: University of Toronto Press, 2002), p. 110.

11 Neil Bissoondath, *Selling Illusions: The Cult of Multiculturalism in Canada*, rev. ed. (Toronto: Penguin Canada, 2002), p. 222.

12 Robert A. Harney, "'So Great a Heritage as Ours': Immigration and the Survival of Canadian Policy," in *Daedelus* 117 (Fall 1988), p. 93.

Indeed, the ethnic communities themselves have questioned whether the federal and provincial governments fund the right programs, or whether they have preferred short-term, highly visible manifestations of what has been labelled "ethnic exotica." Perhaps rather than keeping immigrants "singing and dancing and talking their own language," as one journalist put it, the federal government should address "real" problems such as ethnic inequality in the Canadian labour market. Certain groups such as the Ukrainians have vigorously proposed the recognition of minority-language rights. Other students of multiculturalism doubt that English–French dualism and ethnocultural pluralism can really be reconciled, or that the vastly diverse multicultural third force has the power to assure changes in the traditional bases of Canadian society. Further attempts to foster ethnic and linguistic heterogeneity might facilitate national unity or, conversely, might make unity more difficult to attain. Agreement on such issues currently appears impossible.

A recent graduating class of Jarvis Collegiate Institute, Toronto.

Source: *Canadian Geographic*, January/February 2001, pp. 40–41. Photo courtesy of David Trattles.

Non-official Languages

Heritage-language programs emphasize retention of the mother tongue and are seen to have moral and psychological value. However, immigrants and their offspring, in order to integrate into Canadian society, have had to learn English or, in Quebec, to a lesser degree, French. And although such groups as the Portuguese, the Greeks, and the Chinese have had considerable success in retaining the language of the country of origin, assimilative trends generally become more pronounced over time and the retention of non-official languages diminishes sharply. As ethnolinguist Joshua Fishman put it, "for 95 percent of the third generation, the language of the cradle is the language of the streets."[14] Indeed, the 2001 census revealed that one Canadian in six had a mother tongue that was neither English nor French; yet about one-third of this group rarely or never spoke their mother tongue and had adopted an official language, generally English.

Barely 15 percent of Ukrainian Canadians, for example, speak Ukrainian as a home language, and intermarriage has hastened the pace of assimilation. Historian Varpu Lindstrom-Best views second- and third-generation Finns as having become an "indistinguishable part" of Canadian society, although they will still glue a Finnish flag to their bumper or, after relaxing in the sauna, "demonstrate their legendary 'sisu' (tenacity) by jumping for a refreshing dip in an icehole"![15] Dutch Canadians have also become "invisible ethnics."[16] In a study of Poles in Canada, Henry Radecki concludes that ethnic identification will have to depend on knowledge of Poland's culture and history rather than on "rapidly declining" mastery and use of the language in Canada.[17] Of Toronto's half-million-strong Italian community, historian Robert Harney estimated in 1984 that fewer than 150 000 (belonging generally to the original immigrant generation) were "active in Italian institutions."[18] In his opinion, large numbers of Italians have deliberately broken their ethnic links and taken refuge in "Anglo conformity" because of the prejudice they have faced. Studies carried out by sociologist Jeffrey Reitz suggest strongly that linguistic assimilation leads to destruction of the cohesive ethnic community.[19] While the prognosis for linguistic survival appears bleak for older ethnic communities from Europe, the number of Canadians speaking such languages as Chinese, Spanish, Punjabi, Tagalog, and Arabic is increasing rapidly as immigration rejuvenates these groups.

TOP TEN COUNTRIES OF BIRTH FOR RECENT IMMIGRANTS AND ALL IMMIGRANTS, 2001

RECENT IMMIGRANTS*	NUMBER	%
1. People's Republic of China	197 360	10.8
2. India	156 120	8.5
3. Philippines	122 010	6.7
4. Hong Kong	118 385	6.5
5. Sri Lanka	62 590	3.4
6. Pakistan	57 990	3.2
7. Taiwan	53 755	2.9
8. United States	51 440	2.8
9. Iran	47 080	2.6
10. Poland	43 370	2.4
Subtotal	910 100	49.8
All other countries†	920 580	50.3
Total	1 830 680	100.1

*Immigrants counted in 2001 and who came to Canada between 1991 and 2001.

†Major "other" countries include the former Yugoslavia, Poland, United Kingdom, South Korea, Vietnam, Romania, and Russia.

ALL IMMIGRANTS‡	NUMBER	%
1. United Kingdom	605 955	11.1
2. People's Republic of China	322 825	6.1
3. Italy	315 455	5.8
4. India	314 690	5.8
5. United States	237 920	4.4
6. Hong Kong	235 620	4.3
7. Philippines	232 670	4.3
8. Poland	180 415	3.3
9. Germany	174 070	3.2
10. Portugal	153 535	2.8
Subtotal	2 783 195	51.1
All other countries	2 665 285	48.9
Total	5 448 480	100.0

‡All people counted in 2001 not born in Canada.

Source: *Adapted from Statistics Canada, 2001 Census of Canada, Cat. No. 97F0009XCB01002 and 97F0009XCB01003.*

The Impact of Immigration

Immigrants have had an immeasurable impact on Canada's economic, political, social, and cultural life. The contributions of entrepreneurs such as the Reichmann brothers (born in Austria and Hungary), Thomas Bata and Stephen Roman (both born in the former Czechoslovakia), and David Lam (from Hong Kong), of Montreal publisher Alain Stanké (born in Lithuania), of journalists Adrienne Clarkson and Michaëlle Jean (born in Hong Kong and in Haiti, respectively, both of whom became governors general of Canada) are noteworthy. Film director Atom Egoyan was born in Cairo, Egypt of Armenian refugee parents, who settled in Victoria, British Columbia in 1963. The young Egoyan at first renounced his ethnic roots; but later, as a university student, he sought to reconnect with them, as his film *Ararat*, bearing on the Turkish massacre and deportation of as many as one million Armenians in 1915, attests.

Since the late 1970s the number of non-British, non-French writers in Canada has grown substantially, and Canadian literature has become increasing diversified. Indeed, Canada became part of the literary global village as many novels written by new Canadians featured settings that often had little to do with Canada. Austin Clarke, born in Barbados, set *The Polished Hoe*, a

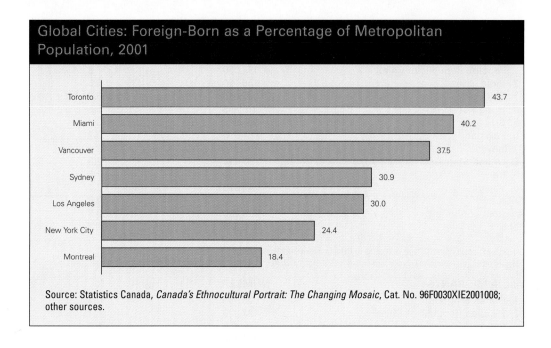

Global Cities: Foreign-Born as a Percentage of Metropolitan Population, 2001

City	Percentage
Toronto	43.7
Miami	40.2
Vancouver	37.5
Sydney	30.9
Los Angeles	30.0
New York City	24.4
Montreal	18.4

Source: Statistics Canada, *Canada's Ethnocultural Portrait: The Changing Mosaic*, Cat. No. 96F0030XIE2001008; other sources.

poignant account of injustice, on an imaginary West Indian island in the 1950s; this novel, his ninth, won him the Giller Prize in 2002. Indian-born Rohinton Mistry used India as his setting for *A Fine Balance* and *Family Matters*, while Michael Ondaatje, from Sri Lanka, set his fourth novel, *The English Patient*, in Tuscany, Italy in the closing moments of World War II. In business, in the arts, in politics, indeed in virtually all spheres of activity, the Canada of 2000 reflected the increasing presence of the Asians, Latin Americans, West Indians, Europeans, and other immigrants who had settled in the country in earlier years.

Immigrants have brought new political questions to the fore in such areas as education and social policy, and the ethnic vote has become significant in many constituencies. Immigration has also enabled urban Canada to acquire a much more diverse and vibrant cultural life. Demographically, immigration has boosted Canada's population significantly: from 1981 to 1986, net immigration represented one-fifth of the country's population growth; from 1991 to 1996, more than one-half; and from 1996 to 2006, fully two-thirds. With immigration, the importance of both the British and the French components of the population has declined; while, from a linguistic point of view, the fact that the great majority of immigrants eventually adopt English as their new language has contributed to weakening the relative position of Canada's francophone population and increasing that community's fears for survival.

Immigration brought much of the blue-collar labour that the country needed for large-scale industrial and resource development in the 1950s. By 1961, 12 percent of the country's work force, and fully one-fifth of Ontario's, was composed of postwar immigrants. Immigration also provided many of the skilled workers and professionals that the country needed. In the 1960s, for example, hundreds of American university professors entered the country, permitting the rapid expansion of the Canadian university system but also setting the stage for the nationalist outcry against American domination in the early 1970s. Bringing in educated immigrants at that time helped ease the pressure on an already overburdened educational system in Canada, a country with a much higher proportion of young people than most European nations. Ironically, for a country that has often complained of suffering a brain drain to the United States, Canada has been criticized by some developing countries for attracting the highly qualified people that those developing nations so desperately need to keep at home.

Immigration and multiculturalism will surely continue to be much-discussed issues just as they have been in the past. There is little prospect that Canadians can ever agree on how many immigrants the country needs, how many refugees it should welcome, where immigrants should come from, and what role they should play in Canadian society. The integration of immigrants will in some instances be painful, and relations between new arrivals and the host society will raise controversial issues. Nevertheless, there can be no doubt that, because of immigration, the Canada of the first years of the twenty-first century is a much more diverse land than the country that emerged from World War II, and diversity in the future is bound to increase even more.

NOTES

1. John W. Holmes, *The Shaping of Peace: Canada and the Search for World Order 1943–1957*, vol. 1 (Toronto: University of Toronto Press, 1979), p. 101.

2. This story is told by M. J. Stone in "Ann Kazimirski, Music Teacher 1922–2006," *The Globe and Mail*, November 3, 2006.

3. Marlene Epp, *Women without Men: Mennonite Refugees of the Second World War* (Toronto: University of Toronto Press, 2000).

4. Karl Aun, *The Political Refugees: A History of the Estonians in Canada* (Toronto: McClelland & Stewart, 1985).

5. Franca Iacovetta, *Such Hardworking People: Italian Immigrants in Postwar Toronto* (Montreal/Kingston: McGill-Queen's University Press, 1992).

6. Franca Iacovetta, "Remaking Their Lives," in Joy Parr, ed., *A Diversity of Women: Ontario, 1945–1980* (Toronto: University of Toronto Press, 1995), pp. 135–67.

7. The subject of postwar French immigration is examined in Richard Jones, "Spécificités de l'immigration française au Canada au lendemain de la deuxième guerre mondiale," *Revue européenne des migrations internationales* 2 (1986): 127–43.

8. Quoted in Christina McCall Newman, "The Canadian Americans," *Maclean's*, July 27, 1963, p. 10.

9. Quoted in Henry Aubin, "Do Immigrants Steal Jobs or Create New Ones?," *The Gazette* (Montreal), January 10, 1985.

10. Norman Buchignani and Doreen M. Indra with Ram Srivastiva, *Continuous Journey: A Social History of South Asians in Canada* (Toronto: McClelland & Stewart, 1985), p. 163.

11. Stanley R. Barrett, *Paradise: Class, Commuters, and Ethnicity in Rural Ontario* (Toronto: University of Toronto Press, 1994), p. 235.

12. Gerald E. Dirks, *Controversy and Complexity: Canadian Immigration Policy During the 1980s* (Montreal/Kingston: McGill-Queen's University Press, 1995), pp. 79–80.

13. Quoted in Marina Jimenez, "Do Ethnic Enclaves Impede Immigration?," *The Globe and Mail*, February 8, 2007, p. 8.

14. Quoted in Robert Harney, "'So Great a Heritage as Ours': Immigration and the Survival of the Canadian Policy," *Daedelus* 117 (Fall 1988): 83.

15. Varpu Lindstrom-Best, *The Finns in Canada* (Ottawa: Canadian Historical Association, 1985), p. 18.

16. Herman Ganzevoort, *A Bittersweet Land: The Dutch Experience in Canada, 1890–1980* (Toronto: McClelland & Stewart, 1988), p. 127.

17. Henry Radecki with Benedykt Heydenkorn, *A Member of a Distinguished Family: The Polish Group in Canada* (Toronto: McClelland & Stewart, 1976), p. 106.

18. Quoted in Margot Gibb-Clark, "'Italian Community's a Myth,' Historian Says," *The Globe and Mail*, October 20, 1984, p. 14.

19. Jeffrey G. Reitz, "Language and Ethnic Community Survival," in Jay E. Goldstein and Rita M. Bienvenue, eds., *Ethnicity and Ethnic Relations in Canada* (Toronto: Butterworths, 1980), p. 122.

BEYOND THE BOOK

Weblinks

Portraits of Canadian Women of African Descent
http://www.civilization.ca/cultur/citoyennes/citoyennese.html
Interviews and digitized mementos of immigrant Canadian women of African descent.

Seeking Sanctuary
http://archives.cbc.ca/IDD-1-71-348/conflict_war/draft_dodgers
Video and radio material detailing the challenges faced by American immigrants to Canada who left in opposition to the Vietnam War.

Auswanderer to Canadians
http://www.virtualmuseum.ca/Exhibitions/Migrations/english/avh/p1.html
Interviews with postwar German immigrants to Canada.

Healthy Living for Immigrant Women
http://www.cmaj.ca/cgi/reprint/159/4/385.pdf
Description of a community-level health education program designed for immigrant women to Canada.

Citizenship and Immigration Canada
http://www.cic.gc.ca/english/index.html
Official website of the Canadian federal ministry Citizenship and Immigration Canada. Details the process and rules of immigration to the country.

Films & Novels

Immigrant. Directed by Bojan Bodruzic. 2007.

RELATED READINGS

The following article in R. Douglas Francis and Donald B. Smith, eds., *Readings in Canadian History: Post-Confederation*, 6th ed. (Toronto: Nelson Thomson Learning, 2002), relates to a topic in this chapter: Will Kymlicka, "The Merits of Multiculturalism," pp. 480–89.

BIBLIOGRAPHY

Two comprehensive overviews of Canada's immigration policy are available: Ninette Kelley and Michael Trebilcock, *The Making of the Mosaic: A History of Canadian Immigration Policy* (Toronto: University of Toronto Press, 1998); and Donald H. Avery, *Reluctant Host: Canada's Response to Immigrant Workers, 1896–1994* (Toronto: McClelland & Stewart, 1995). The 1980s in particular are examined in Gerald E. Dirks, *Controversy and Complexity: Canadian Immigration Policy During the 1980s* (Montreal/Kingston: McGill-Queen's University Press, 1995). Questions relating to immigration are discussed in Peter S. Li, *Destination Canada: Immigration Debates and Issues* (Toronto: Oxford University Press, 2003). On refugees see the early study by Gerald E. Dirks, *Canada's Refugee Policy: Indifference or Opportunism?* (Montreal/Kingston: McGill-Queen's University Press, 1977).

Critical works on Canadian immigration policy include Daniel Stoffman, *Who Gets In: What's Wrong with Canada's Immigration Policy—And How to Fix It* (Toronto: Macfarlane Walter & Ross, 2002); Victor Malarek, *Haven's Gate: Canada's Immigration Fiasco* (Toronto: Macmillan, 1987); Reg Whitaker, *Double Standard: The Secret History of Canadian Immigration* (Toronto: Lester & Orpen Dennys, 1987); and David Matas and Ilana Simon, *Closing the Doors* (Toronto: Summerhill Press, 1989). Howard Margolian has researched a fascinating subject in *Unauthorized Entry: The Truth About Nazi War Criminals in Canada, 1946–1956* (Toronto: University of Toronto Press, 2000). Journalist Stewart Bell has penned a serious indictment of Canadian immigration and refugee policies in *Cold Terror: How Canada Nurtures and Exports Terrorism Around the World*, rev. ed. (Mississauga, ON: James Wiley & Sons, 2006). An analysis of the costs and gains of immigration is available in Don J. DeVoretz, ed., *Diminishing Returns: The Economics of Canada's Recent Immigration Policy* (Toronto: C.D. Howe Institute, 1995).

Among the many publications on ethnicity see Peter S. Li, ed., *Race and Ethnic Relations in Canada*, 2nd ed. (Toronto: Oxford University Press, 1999); Augie Fleras and Jean Leonard Elliott, *Unequal Relations: An Introduction to Race, Ethnic and Aboriginal Dynamics in Canada*, 3rd ed. (Scarborough, ON: Prentice-Hall Allyn Bacon, 1999); Leo Driedger, ed., *Multi-ethnic Canada: Identities and Inequalities* (Toronto: Oxford University Press, 1996); Raymond Breton et al., *Ethnic Identity and Equality: Varieties of Experience in a Canadian City* (Toronto: University of Toronto Press, 1990); and Raymond Breton and Jeffrey Reitz, *The Illusion of Difference: Realities of Ethnicity in Canada and the United States* (Toronto: C.D. Howe Institute, 1994).

Informative essays on all immigrant groups may be found in Paul Robert Magocsi, ed., *Encyclopedia of Canada's Peoples* (Toronto: Multicultural History Society of Ontario and University of Toronto Press, 1999). Monographs on groups of refugees include Milda Danys, *DP: Lithuanian Immigration to Canada After the Second World War* (Toronto: Multicultural History Society of Ontario, 1986); Morton Beiser, *Strangers at the Gate: The 'Boat People's' First Ten Years in Canada* (Toronto: University of Toronto Press, 1999); Marlene Epp, *Women Without Men: Mennonite Refugees of the Second World War* (Toronto: University of Toronto Press, 2000); and Lubomyr Y. Luciuk, *Searching for Place: Ukrainian Displaced Persons, Canada, and the Migration of Memory* (Toronto: University of Toronto Press, 2000). Elizabeth McLuhan, ed., *Safe Haven: The Refugee Experience of Five Families* (Toronto: Multicultural History Society of Ontario, 1995) personalizes the immigrant experience. Norman Hillmer and J.L. Granatstein have compiled an anthology of immigrant testimonies in *The Land Newly Found: Eyewitness Accounts of the Canadian Immigrant Experience* (Toronto: Thomas Allen Publishers, 2006).

Howard Palmer and Tamara Palmer, eds., *Peoples of Alberta: Portraits of Cultural Diversity* (Saskatoon: Western Producer Prairie Books, 1985) is a good study of one province's ethnocultural groups. Dutch immigration and assimilation are described in Herman Ganzevoort, *A Bittersweet Land: The Dutch Experience in Canada, 1890–1980* (Toronto: McClelland & Stewart, 1988). The very different Chinese experience is examined in Peter S. Li, *The Chinese in Canada*, 2nd ed. (Toronto: Oxford University Press, 1998). See also Wing Chung Ng, *The Chinese in Vancouver, 1945–80: The Pursuit of Identity and Power* (Vancouver: UBC Press, 1999). On Asians see Norman Buchignani et al., *Continuous Journey: A Social History of South Asians in Canada* (Toronto: McClelland & Stewart, 1985). Studies of Italian immigrants include Nicholas DeMaria Harney, *Eh Paesan!: Being Italian in Toronto* (Toronto: University of Toronto Press, 1998); Kenneth Bagnell, *Canadese: A Portrait of Italian Canadians* (Toronto: Macmillan, 1989); and Franca Iacovetta studies one important Italian community in *Such Hardworking People: Italian Immigrants in Postwar Toronto* (Montreal/Kingston: McGill-Queen's University Press, 1992). On Portuguese immigrants, see Carlos Teixeira and Victor M.P. Da Rosa, eds., *The Portuguese in Canada* (Toronto: University of Toronto Press, 2000). Scholarly works on the Jewish community include Robert J. Brym, William Shaffir, and Morton Weinfeld, eds., *The Jews in Canada* (Toronto: Oxford University Press, 1993); and Alan T. Davies, *Antisemitism in Canada: History and Interpretation* (Waterloo, ON: Wilfrid Laurier University Press, 1992). Harold Troper and Morton Weinfeld examine problems of intergroup relations in *Old Wounds: Jews, Ukrainians and the Hunt for Nazi War Criminals in Canada* (Markham, ON: Viking, 1989). The immigration of so-called "draft dodgers" is studied in John Hagan, *Northern Passage: American Vietnam War Resisters in Canada* (Cambridge: Harvard University Press, 2001).

Immigrant adjustment is studied in Shiva S. Halli and Leo Driedger, eds., *Immigrant Canada: Demographic, Economic, and Social Challenges* (Toronto: University of Toronto Press, 1999). On multiculturalism, see Andrew Cardozo and Louis Musto, eds., *The Battle over Multiculturalism* (Ottawa: Pearson-Shoyama Institute, 1997); Richard J.F. Day, *Multiculturalism and the History of Canadian Diversity* (Toronto: University of Toronto Press, 2000); and Augie Fleras and Jean Leonard Elliott,

Engaging Diversity: Multiculturalism in Canada, 2nd ed. (Toronto: Nelson Thomson Learning, 2002). Vigorous critiques of this policy may be found in Reginald Bibby, *Mosaic Madness: The Poverty and Potential of Life in Canada* (Toronto: Stoddart, 1990); Neil Bissoondath, *Selling Illusions: The Cult of Multiculturalism in Canada*, rev. ed. (Toronto: Penguin Canada, 2002); Wenona Giles, *Portuguese Women in Toronto: Gender, Immigration, and Nationalism* (Toronto, University of Toronto Press, 2002); and Keith Banting, Thomas J. Courchene, and F. Leslie Seidle, ed., *Belonging? Diversity, Recognition and Shared Citizenship in Canada* (Montreal: Institute for Research on Public Policy, 2007).

Racism and discrimination are studied in Evelyn Kallen, *Ethnicity and Human Rights in Canada*, 2nd ed. (Toronto: Oxford University Press, 1995); B. Singh Bolaria and Peter S. Li, *Racial Oppression in Canada*, 2nd ed. (Toronto: Garamond Press, 1988); Frances Henry, *The Caribbean Diaspora in Toronto: Learning to Live with Racism* (Toronto: University of Toronto Press, 1994); Eleanor Laquian et al., *The Silent Debate: Asian Immigration and Racism in Canada* (Vancouver: Institute of Asian Research, 1998); Frances Henry et al., *The Colour of Democracy: Racism in Canadian Society*, 2nd ed. (Toronto: Harcourt Brace, 2000); Leo Driedger and Shiva S. Halli, *Race and Racism: Canada's Challenge* (Montreal/Kingston: McGill-Queen's University Press, 2000); and Jeffrey G. Reitz and Rupa Banerjee, *Racial Inequality and Policy Issues in Canada* (Montreal: Institute for Research on Public Policy, 2007).

Language retention is discussed in J.G. Reitz, *The Survival of Ethnic Groups* (Toronto: McGraw-Hill Ryerson, 1980); Ronald Wardhaugh, *Language and Nationhood: The Canadian Experience* (Vancouver: New Star Books, 1983); and Edward N. Herberg, *Ethnic Groups in Canada: Adaptations and Transitions* (Scarborough, ON: Nelson, 1989). Ethnic groups in politics is the subject of a study prepared for the Royal Commission on Electoral Reform: Kathy Megyery, ed., *Ethnocultural Groups and Visible Minorities in Canadian Politics: The Question of Access* (Toronto: Dundurn Press, 1992). The political activities of the Canadian Ethnocultural Council are examined in Leslie A. Pal, *Interests of State: The Politics of Language, Multiculturalism, and Feminism in Canada* (Montreal/Kingston: McGill-Queen's University Press, 1993).

The scholarly review *Canadian Ethnic Studies* contains a wealth of material on the various facets of the immigrant experience. An ongoing series, "Canada's Ethnic Groups," published by the Canadian Historical Association with the support of the Canadian government's multiculturalism program, provides useful syntheses of immigrant experience in Canada. The brochures are available on the Internet at www.cha-shc.ca/english/publ. The "Generations: A History of Canada's Peoples," a series published by McClelland and Stewart in conjunction with the Multiculturalism Directorate, includes studies of the Portuguese, the Poles, the Japanese, the Scots, the Dutch, the Norwegians, the Greeks, the Arabs, the Hungarians, the Estonians, the Ukrainians, the Croatians, the Chinese, and the South Asians. The introductory volume to the series is Jean R. Burnet with Howard Palmer, *"Coming Canadians": An Introduction to a History of Canada's Peoples* (Toronto: McClelland & Stewart, 1988). Statistical information on immigration to Canada is available at www.statcan.ca.

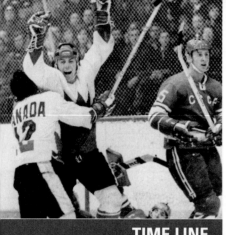

CANADA IN THE 1970s AND 1980s: CONSTITUTION AND FREE TRADE

TIME LINE	
1970	Greenpeace founded in Vancouver, an important event in the shaping of Canada's environmental movement
1971	Peter Lougheed's Conservatives defeat Social Credit, in power since 1935, and form the government in Alberta Quebec rejects the Victoria Charter, Trudeau's proposals for constitutional reform and repatriation
1972	Team Canada vanquishes the Soviet hockey team National Action Committee on the Status of Women established
1976	Montreal hosts the Twenty-First Olympic Games
1980	Trudeau launches the National Energy Program, condemned in the West
1981	Terry Fox dies of cancer after running halfway across Canada
1982	Proclamation of the new Canadian Constitution and the Charter of Rights and Freedoms The *Ocean Ranger*, an exploratory oil drilling rig, capsizes in the Atlantic Ocean off St. John's, Newfoundland, killing all 84 crew members
1984	The Progressive Conservatives led by Brian Mulroney take power in Ottawa
1985	The Liberals take power in Ontario, ending a Conservative reign of 32 years
1986	Expo 86 held in Vancouver
1988	The Free Trade Agreement signed between Canada and the United States The Winter Olympics held in Calgary
1989	14 women students slain at l'École Polytechnique in Montreal (Parliament commemorated this tragedy in 1991 by instituting the National Day of Remembrance and Action on Violence Against Women)

The 1970s and 1980s brought continued change to Canada and to the lives of Canadians in all sectors of activity. Two major political figures dominated public life: Pierre Elliott Trudeau and Brian Mulroney. Trudeau had been chosen leader of the Liberal party in 1968. Progressive Conservatives chose Mulroney to head their party in 1983. Both leaders succeeded in convincing Canadians to give them strong mandates in the House of Commons, but both soon found it difficult to maintain a workable political consensus in the face of rising discontent. Questions concerning the economy and public finances, relations between the provinces and Ottawa, trade and other links with the United States, and social issues divided Canadians. Regional imbalances within Canada compounded the difficulties. Yet each leader made changes that were to have a profound impact upon Canada's society and economy. Pierre Trudeau repatriated the Canadian constitution from Britain and in particular inserted within it a Charter of Rights and Freedoms. Brian Mulroney negotiated and finalized the Free Trade Agreement with the United States.

During this period, women, Aboriginal peoples, francophones, gays and lesbians, ethnic groups and other minorities lobbied governments in favour of further recognition of their rights. Some groups made effective use of the Charter of Rights, adopted in 1982, to bring governments to revise laws and policies in their favour. Public opinion gradually accepted these changes that were transforming Canadian society. Environmental groups gained increased visibility, showing that more Canadians were coming to appreciate the harmful effects of unregulated economic growth on their environment.

Immense technological change came to the world, and to Canada, in these years. Memory chips, microprocessors, and floppy disks made their appearance in the early 1970s, and the first hobby computers came on the market later in that decade. In 1981, IBM, a maker of high-end mainframe computers used by companies and governments to manage data, released its revolutionary personal computer, instantly known as the PC. Bundled together with an optional monochrome display, a dot-matrix printer, up to 256K of user memory, two floppy-disk drives, and appropriate software, the package could cost a consumer well over $10 000 in today's dollars. Proud owners could run database systems, do word processing, or play games. Writers found them an extraordinary improvement over typewriters. After a few short years, as new and more powerful machines appeared, the earliest models became museum pieces, or more likely headed for landfill sites.

Yet in some ways, more conservative attitudes and values asserted themselves. Economic difficulties, including a deep recession in the early 1980s, contributed to fostering more individualistic preoccupations. The transition proved painful. Increased state intervention in most aspects of life in the 1960s and 1970s had made citizens more dependent on governments and thus more demanding of them. Governments taxed more, but they also borrowed heavily to finance new social programs and address new challenges. Then, particularly after 1980, overstrained public finances dictated cuts in expenditures and rising taxes. In such circumstances there was little money for new programs. When governments promised to lower taxes to make reductions in services more acceptable, they then had to cut programs even further to finance such tax cuts.

The Trudeau Government

Although Canadians had given Trudeau a solid majority in the elections of 1968, they soon began to blame him for economic mismanagement as the country faced inflation as well as bouts of high unemployment. After 1970, rising prices became a serious and constant worry for consumers. Food and housing costs in particular went up steeply. In the space of a single year, 1973, shoppers paid 30 percent more for meat, 40 percent more for poultry, and 40 percent more for eggs. House prices that jumped upward by as much as 20 percent in cities such as Vancouver, Toronto, Calgary, and Ottawa pushed younger Canadians out of the housing market. Prices rose even higher in 1974 as the country endured double-digit inflation. Low-income families, who had to spend three-quarters of their income on food and housing, were hardest hit, because the prices of these two components of the cost of living index increased the fastest.

Politicians blamed outside forces for these substantial price increases. After all, inflation plagued most other countries, particularly the United States, where it was fed by the war in Vietnam. Moreover, world food prices moved sharply upward in response to greater demand. The Organization of Petroleum Exporting Countries (OPEC) increased oil prices substantially too, in 1973 and again in 1979. Motorists complained bitterly. But they also slowed down to conserve expensive gasoline; and, for a time, they abandoned their roomy, high-powered American automobiles in favour of smaller, more efficient, imported vehicles, mostly from Japan.

Nevertheless, domestic causes of inflation also existed. Unions were accused of making unrealistically high wage demands that forced companies to raise their prices. In turn, labour blamed rising prices on excessive corporate profits. Inflation conditioned individuals to expect more inflation and to demand bigger wage increases. This behaviour, though understandable, ensured that the problem persisted.

Trudeau's Critics

The failure to curb inflation only partially explains rising popular discontent with the government. The wave of Trudeaumania on which Pierre Elliott Trudeau had ridden to power in 1968 had, by the time of the elections held in 1972, been transformed into a swelling tide of Trudeauphobia, as the seemingly modest Trudeau of 1968, who had said that he wanted to "dialogue" with Canadians and promote a "just society," became an arrogant, remote, temperamental personality. Questions of policy influenced electors as well. Trudeau had attempted to give French Canada a larger stake in Ottawa by making it easier for francophones to use French in federal institutions and by recruiting more French-speaking politicians and civil servants. Although Quebeckers naturally approved of initiatives designed to give francophones greater equality within Canada, many anglophones did not. Indeed, a backlash against bilingualism and "French power" in English-speaking Canada cost the Liberals much support. The government's apparent inability to handle economic and social issues—not only inflation, but also unemployment, welfare, strikes, and high taxes—also galvanized voter disaffection. New Democratic Party (NDP) leader David Lewis's aggressive campaign against the "corporate welfare bums" who had, he said, unjustifiably benefited from government subsidies and tax privileges accounted for that party's relatively strong performance in 1972.

Following the election of 1972, which the Liberals nearly lost, the Trudeau government worked to win back voter approval. It greatly increased public spending on social programs and indexed income-tax brackets and exemptions to the cost of living in order to protect taxpayers from inflation—measures that soon had catastrophic effects on government finances. It liberalized unemployment insurance access rules. (This decision gave the Atlantic fishing industry a vested interest in creating a maximum number of short-term jobs that would enable everyone to claim unemployment insurance in the off-season.) To win support in populous central Canada, the government promised to keep oil prices (then increasing rapidly) at levels substantially below world levels—a policy that naturally infuriated the oil-producing provinces of western Canada. When opposition leader Robert Stanfield promised a wage and price freeze in 1974, labour hesitated, then gave its support to Trudeau, who declared his opposition to such a freeze. "Zap!

You're frozen!" he mocked in one notorious bit of repartee. Voters gave Trudeau a majority in 1974. The next year the Liberals reversed themselves and adopted a wage and price freeze. These controls, which affected the public sector and large private companies, lasted three years. The rate of increase in prices did slow, but it took more than controls and guidelines to defeat inflation.

The Rise and Fall of Economic Nationalism

By 1970, many Canadians, particularly in industrialized southern Ontario, expressed concern for the high degree of foreign (especially American) ownership of the Canadian economy. Nationalist authors published books with provocative titles: *Silent Surrender*; *The Precarious Homestead*; *Partner to Behemoth*; and *The Elephant and the Mouse*. These works portrayed Canada as a satellite of the American metropolis. Journalist Peter Newman warned that "the end of the Canadian dream" was imminent. In response, the militant socialist and nationalist Waffle faction within the NDP urged large-scale nationalization of foreign-owned businesses and resources. More moderate nationalists called for a gradual buying-back only of large enterprises. Still others believed that actual ownership mattered little if Ottawa exercised stronger control over giant foreign-owned corporations operating in the country. Canadians living in less-developed regions of the country tended to agree with Newfoundland premier Joey Smallwood, who affirmed in his typically colourful manner that he would not hesitate to deal with the devil if he had money to invest.

In an effort to appease nationalist discontent, the Trudeau government in 1971 set up the Foreign Investment Review Agency (FIRA) to screen takeovers and determine whether they were of "significant benefit" to Canada. Yet FIRA did not noticeably prevent American investment in Canada. In 1980, the American ambassador himself expressed satisfaction with the agency's 90 percent approval rate.

Change Within Western Canada

The 1970s were years of rapid political, economic, and social change in Canada's western provinces. In spite of important distinctions among the provinces themselves, the region as a whole acquired greater power within Canada and now spoke with a louder voice.

In British Columbia, disenchantment with the long-governing Social Credit government of W.A.C. Bennett favoured the election of the NDP, which promised greater economic and social equality. Under combative leader Dave Barrett, it initiated many controversial reforms—its opponents accused it of "legislating by thunderbolt"—including public automobile insurance, a new innovative labour code, and an attempt to preserve agricultural land. Barrett's reforms, high spending, and new taxes led conservative forces to unite in reaction. An economic downturn assisted this new coalition in bringing the populist Social Credit party back to power in 1975, under W.R. "Bill" Bennett, W.A.C. Bennett's son.

In neighbouring Alberta, Calgary lawyer Peter Lougheed revived the provincial Progressive Conservative party, infusing it with the promise both of change and of continuity with conservative traditions. Strongly supported by urban Alberta, the Conservatives won power in 1971 and established a new political dynasty, sweeping Social Credit, which had governed the province for 36 years, almost out of political existence. The immense amounts of oil money flowing into the Alberta treasury allowed Albertans to enjoy high-quality social services while paying the country's lowest provincial income taxes and no provincial sales tax.

Saskatchewan's booming economy in the 1970s also generated increasing revenues that enabled the province's NDP government led by Allan Blakeney to pursue an agenda of "province-building." It nationalized a large American-owned potash company, and launched a vigorous exploration and development program in uranium. It established an enterprise that served as a holding company for the province's state-owned companies such as Sask Tel, Sask Power, and Saskoil, and that also bought large blocks of shares in private companies.

Agriculture, the province's largest industry, remained subject to violent swings, depending on world wheat prices, export markets, and weather conditions. Low prices for grain and the high costs of technological innovation forced smaller and less efficient farmers to sell their land to larger operators and to migrate elsewhere in search of work. Between 1976 and 1996, Saskatchewan lost 14 000 farms. Disused grain elevators, abandoned rail lines, and closed hospitals symbolized the sad breakdown of small-town Saskatchewan.

Blakeney considered the low living standards of Aboriginal people to be the province's most serious social problem. Although his government acted to improve conditions in Aboriginal communities in the north, it failed to address the serious social problems of Natives living in the cities. Other western cities faced similar problems.

The left-wing New Democratic Party also governed Manitoba for much of the 1970s. In these years of relative prosperity, it spent heavily on public housing and adopted major tax and social reforms. It also launched a second huge hydroelectric development project in the north. As in British Columbia and Saskatchewan, critics on the right denounced increased state intervention under the NDP, warning that the province was moving toward socialism.

Prime Minister Pierre Trudeau and Alberta Premier Peter Lougheed, 1973, at the Western Economic Opportunities Conference in Calgary. Appearances can be deceiving— despite the cordiality evident in this photograph, animosity existed between the two leaders over the federal government's pricing of Alberta oil and gas.

Source: Herald Collection/Glenbow Archives, Calgary, Canada/NA-2864-23502.

Continuing Dissatisfaction

Between 1974 and 1979, the polls showed support for the federal Liberals fluctuating wildly. By 1979, with Canada again in a severe inflationary crisis, the business community in particular worried about the foundering economy and the rapidly rising federal deficit, which the government financed by borrowing heavily, even at historically high interest rates.

Regional discontent increased, too. Westerners, in particular, complained that Trudeau paid little heed to their concerns; the Liberals, they noted, depended on Ontario and Quebec for most of their votes. Alberta and Saskatchewan feuded with Ottawa over the pricing and taxing of natural resources. Frustrated wheat farmers, hurt by mounting world surpluses of wheat and sagging prices, exhorted the federal government to act, while a frustrated Trudeau asked rhetorically: "Why should I sell your wheat?" With the notable exception of Quebec, the Trudeau consensus largely broke apart, with the result that the Progressive Conservatives, under their new leader, Joe Clark, a federal MP from Alberta, won a fragile mandate in the election of May 1979.

Conservative Interlude

Joe Clark's unfavourable image as a weak and indecisive leader, though largely undeserved and based on a superficial appreciation of the individual, proved a heavy yoke for the Conservatives to bear. Journalist Jeffrey Simpson concluded that the Tories won the election of 1979 not because of Clark but in spite of him. Although Clark was not afflicted with Trudeau's arrogance, he lacked the Liberal leader's enviable international reputation.

The energy question precipitated the collapse of Clark's brief minority government and a return to power of the Liberals in elections held in February 1980. Promoting a policy of "short-term pain for long-term gain," Clark's finance minister announced a 4-cent-per-litre excise tax on gasoline designed to bring billions of dollars into the federal treasury in order to attack the rising deficit. Defeated in the House of Commons, the government resigned. During the ensuing election campaign, former-and-new leader Pierre Trudeau promised to revoke the immensely unpopular tax. After regaining power, he soon imposed new gasoline taxes.

National Energy Program

Trudeau's final mandate began with a bitter crisis in relations between the federal government and Alberta. Strongly influenced by Ontario's pressures to have oil and gas considered "national commodities, belonging to all Canadians," the Trudeau government established the National Energy Program (NEP), with a "made-in-Canada" oil price that allowed Canadian consumers to pay prices lower than the world price. The producing provinces resented federal price controls, which deprived them of billions of dollars. They argued that they deserved the best deal possible before the depletion of their reserves. Alberta's Premier Peter Lougheed, galled by the federal government's intention to appropriate a greater share of huge oil revenues for federal purposes, likened the plan to "having strangers take over the living room." Ottawa responded that too great a transfer of wealth to one province was dangerously upsetting the equilibrium of Confederation.

Reacting to the federal government's measures, the Alberta government reduced the flow of crude oil to the East, and some Alberta automobile bumpers sported stickers belligerently inviting easterners to "freeze in the dark." Western anger grew, and suddenly respectable separatist parties urged westerners "to take to the lifeboat of independence before it's too late." All of these movements denounced what they perceived as Ottawa's subservience to Quebec.

Another objective of NEP was to Canadianize the petroleum industry by reducing the role of American oil companies in Canada. The Alberta government also opposed this aspect of the Trudeau government's policy, blaming it for the decline in investment in the oil fields. Likewise western Canada's business community denounced Ottawa's intervention, while the U.S. trade representative, worried about the consequences of discrimination against American firms, threatened: "We have a quiver full of arrows and we are prepared to shoot them in self-defense if we must."

The federal government's initiative proved ill-timed. Just as it spent billions of dollars purchasing foreign oil companies and assisting exploration by Canadian companies, oil prices crashed dramatically. Canada's biggest corporate liability became Dome Petroleum, a creation of Liberal energy policies that had accumulated a debt of more than $6 billion by the mid-1980s. Ironically, it was then sold to an American oil company.

Recession struck the Canadian economy in 1981–82; throughout the country Canadians quite naturally blamed Ottawa's economic policies. The recession resulted in part from government monetary policy, particularly high interest rates, designed to dampen inflationary pressures. (Indeed, there appeared to be no solution that would enable governments to combat inflation and unemployment simultaneously.) Recession also stemmed from worldwide overproduction in the resource industries, in agriculture, and in secondary manufacturing. The daily press offered a sombre litany of factory closings, layoffs, and cutbacks. Magazine articles frequently evoked the Great Depression of the 1930s.

In the West in particular, the recession undermined the heady confidence that people had felt during the prosperous 1970s. The decline in demand for oil, followed by sharply lower oil prices in 1986, checked Alberta's growth and clearly showed the basic fragility of its resource-based economy. Construction on the huge synthetic-oil production and heavy-oil upgrading projects ceased. The province's jobless rate matched eastern Canadian levels; indeed, many unemployed workers returned home to eastern and central Canada. Real estate values fell sharply. The oil industry called upon both Edmonton and Ottawa for assistance; after having denounced Ottawa's attempts to impose a ceiling on oil prices in 1980, it now urged the federal government to apply a floor price to provide some stability to the industry. At the same time, agriculture faced serious difficulties, as drought afflicted farmers in the province's southern region and declining world prices and increased costs wiped out profit margins. Wracked by internal wrangling and splits, western separatism failed to become more than a fringe phenomenon, primarily centred in Alberta and having no real impact on electoral politics. Then the departure from political life of Pierre Trudeau in 1984 removed the principal target of western anger.

The Constitution of 1982

Trudeau had more success with his plan to "patriate" the Constitution and particularly to insert within it a Charter of Rights and Freedoms and an amending formula by which the United Kingdom's formal consent would no longer be necessary for constitutional changes. Although most Canadians outside Quebec approved of Trudeau's initiative, Quebec refused to sign the agreement, which had been negotiated in its absence during what that province's delegates termed "the night of the long knives." Thus, the province that since 1960 had been most insistent on the need for constitutional change was not a party to the reformed Constitution.

Women's groups won the inclusion in the Charter of an article affirming the equality of male and female persons. The Aboriginal peoples' associations succeeded in their efforts to entrench Aboriginal and treaty rights. The Métis also achieved constitutional recognition as an Aboriginal people. But the Charter recognized only existing rights, and left these undefined.

The signing of the Canadian Constitution by Her Majesty Queen Elizabeth II, April 1982. Prime Minister Trudeau looks on. The new Constitution ended the British Parliament's power to amend the British North America (BNA) Act, and also included a Charter of Rights and Freedoms.

Source: Bob Cooper/Library and Archives Canada/PA-140705.

Trudeau's Record

In the immediate, however, most Canadians were primarily interested in bread-and-butter issues. Finally, the constantly unfavourable polls resulting from

Canadians' dissatisfaction with the Liberals' management of the economy and the selection by the Conservatives of businessman Brian Mulroney to replace Joe Clark as party leader convinced Trudeau that he should resign.

The Trudeau years were replete with paradoxes. Trudeau championed the trusty Liberal theme of national unity at each election. Yet, during his term in office, the country faced the most serious threats to its existence that it had ever confronted, especially from Quebec, which held a referendum on its future links with Canada in 1980 (see Chapter 17) and the western provinces. Trudeau had also pushed for the inclusion of the Charter of Rights and Freedoms in the Constitution, insisting on the need to defend Canadians' political liberties. Yet, during the FLQ crisis of October 1970, his government invoked the War Measures Act and thereby effectively suspended civil liberties, enabling the police to arrest hundreds of individuals and to hold them incommunicado for several days, without ever laying charges against most of them.

Trudeau frequently denounced the dangers of nationalism, especially French-Canadian and Quebec nationalism, but his legislation controlling foreign investment, as well as his National Energy Program of 1980, convinced Americans that he was a strident nationalist. Furthermore, Trudeau had promised to battle regional imbalances. Although measures such as increased equalization payments and other transfers helped reduce disparities, they had "little effect," as economist Paul Phillips has pointed out, "on their root causes."[1]

Trudeau had long spoken of the need to build a "just society," but what role were women to play in bringing such a society about? During the first Trudeau mandate (1968–72), the House of Commons had only one female member. A *Chatelaine* article commented bitterly: "There are 56 whooping cranes in Canada, and one female federal politician." Feminists complained that parties showed no interest in working to recruit promising female candidates. Although society's changing attitudes brought a slow improvement, by 1980 only 15 women, representing three parties, had won seats in the House. A decade later, although more women were involved in the various phases of party activity, most continued, in political scientist Sylvia Bashevkin's words, to "toe the lines" and to fill "conventional maintenance roles."[2]

In foreign affairs, Trudeau rejected Canada's traditional role as a "helpful fixer" in favour of a policy based on national self-interest. Certainly the sale of arms to military dictatorships during his tenure showed the precedence commercial interests took over human rights. Nonetheless, Canada did increase its developmental assistance to Third World nations significantly. In the early 1970s Trudeau cut defence spending, thereby incurring the wrath of Canada's NATO allies. But Canada ultimately retained all of its alliance commitments, and defence spending increased thereafter.

The Charter and Bilingualism

By the time of Trudeau's death in 2000, Canadians believed the Charter of Rights and Freedoms to be his greatest legacy, a defining element of the Canadian identity. People said they trusted judges more than politicians to defend their rights. Certainly Charter decisions changed the face of Canada, by upholding minority and individual rights. Conservatives accused judges of too often acting as social engineers who usurped the power of elected legislators or who were too lenient on crime. From the early 1990s, however, the courts assumed a more deferential stance toward parliamentarians and law enforcement.

Trudeau's dream of a bilingual Canada at first enthused many Canadians, particularly French-speakers who aspired to linguistic equality. His government adopted the Official Languages Act in 1969 in an effort to make government services more widely available in French. While slow progress made French Canadians despair of ever attaining genuine equality, many English-speaking Canadians complained that they were now the victims of unfair treatment.

At Trudeau's death, French immersion programs remained popular, despite questions about their effectiveness. But while English-language study was mandatory in Quebec, second-language instruction remained optional in several English-speaking provinces. In Alberta, for example, the minister of learning expressed regrets that only 20 percent of the province's high school students completed second-language courses in 2002, a substantial decline since 1990. The federal official languages commissioner blamed the federal government for failing to show leadership in promoting bilingualism. Outside Quebec, many federal offices designated as bilingual were unable to offer service in French. Air Canada consistently flouted language laws with impunity. The census of 2001 showed that, while the number of French-speaking Quebeckers able to converse in English increased to over 40 percent, English-speaking Canadians outside Quebec became even less bilingual.

Francophone minorities outside Quebec also turned to provincial governments in their attempts to obtain recognition of linguistic rights. Some provincial governments acted to make French-language schooling more easily available. Manitoba, for example, authorized the use of French as a language of instruction in schools in 1971, thus restoring a right taken away in the nationalist frenzy of World War I. In 1968, New Brunswick adopted the Official Languages Act that gave official recognition to bilingualism. Then, through the 1970s and 1980s, the province's government cautiously proclaimed and applied the law's various clauses. In the early 1970s, Acadians confronted Moncton's mayor, Leonard Jones, an adamant opponent of bilingual municipal services. Jones's obstinacy—which students from the Université de Moncton underlined by depositing a severed pig's head on the mayor's doorstep—probably served as a catalyst for the Acadians' struggle.

In one instance in particular, the battle for rights reached epic proportions. In 1985, the Supreme Court of Canada found that Manitoba had violated the Constitution when it abolished official bilingualism nearly a century earlier. When the court ordered that thousands of public documents be translated into French, francophones proposed a compromise involving far less translation in exchange for new more useful French-language services. The government agreed, but the provincial Conservative party, then in opposition, appealed to what historian Raymond Hébert described as the "underlying virulent racism" of anti-francophone populist groups and adamantly opposed any new "concessions."[3] The NDP government retreated. After the Conservatives came to power in 1988, they bitterly attacked new Quebec legislation that restricted the use of English on commercial signs, thus helping to turn opinion against the Meech Lake Accord. Yet the crisis in Manitoba eventually helped Franco-Manitobans obtain new rights, primarily the right to administer their own schools, by forcing them to return before the courts.

New rights in the provinces as well as federal assistance to French-language minorities did not stem the decline through rapid assimilation of most French-speaking minorities outside Quebec. Census statistics in 1991 and in 2001 showed clearly that, except in Quebec and New Brunswick, the promise of a bilingual Canada seemed to flounder beneath the overwhelming weight of English.

The Progressive Conservatives in Power

Trudeau left John Turner, his successor as Liberal party leader and prime minister, to justify his failures. In 1984, Canadians reacted by voting for what appeared to be real change: they gave Brian Mulroney and his Conservative party a resounding victory, with 211 of the 282 seats in the House of Commons, including a majority of Quebec's ridings. Though women still held fewer than 10 percent of the seats in the House, they made up one-fifth of Mulroney's first cabinet.

The Canada of the mid-1980s differed greatly from that of the 1970s. As in the United States, a more conservative mood prevailed. For many Canadians, Liberal support of increased state intervention and of the federal government's strategic role in the economy now signified unacceptably high levels of government spending, rising taxes, and government interference. The Conservatives' praise for free enterprise and their vision of a more decentralized Canada, a "community of communities," appeared more appropriate.

The Rise and Fall of Corporate Giants

As a sign of the times, a new group of entrepreneurs kindled popular interest. Among them were the Bronfmans, whose corporate empire included 152 companies, with assets of $120 billion in 1988; Albert and Paul Reichmann, who built a vast real-estate and resource empire, much of which crashed down with the collapse of property values after 1990; Conrad Black of the Toronto-based Argus Corporation, whom journalist Peter Newman presented rather heroically as the new prince of the Canadian establishment—Black would soon be given a seat in the British House of Lords; developer Robert Campeau, whose purchases of American department-store chains with borrowed money brought admiration for his gall, then perhaps amazement at his almost immediate fall in what was until that point the fourth-largest bankruptcy in American history; Galen Weston, who succeeded in the 1980s and 1990s in turning around the seemingly moribund Loblaws supermarket chain and making it into the industry leader; and Pierre Péladeau, of Quebecor in Montreal, whose holdings grew from a tiny periodical, bought in 1950 with a loan of $1500, to a $450 million newspaper and printing empire. Canadians also watched in alarmed fascination as big multinational businesses became even bigger through mergers frequently worth billions of dollars.

The First Mulroney Government

Although business welcomed the new Conservative government, Mulroney's appeal was much wider. He had promised an "era of national reconciliation," notably in federal–provincial relations. Mulroney appeased the West by dismantling the National Energy Program, and he pleased Quebec by promising to negotiate that province's acceptance of the Constitution of 1982.

Mulroney also satisfied Nova Scotia and Newfoundland by yielding them control of offshore mineral resources. The discovery of gas and oil off the Atlantic coast raised hopes for an economic boom, and the premier of Nova Scotia proclaimed optimistically that exploitation of energy resources would end "going down the road" in search of jobs elsewhere. To stimulate the region's economy, Mulroney set up the Atlantic Canada Opportunities Agency, which, like earlier programs, offered grants to businesses operating in the Atlantic provinces. All told, federal grants to businesses in the region under Trudeau and Mulroney totalled more than $5 billion between 1970 and 1995, but they produced "no appreciable closing of the gap between have and have-not provinces as measured by per capita income or unemployment rates."[4] Direct money transfers from Ottawa to individuals, in the form of unemployment insurance, welfare, and other payments did help to boost household incomes.

The Conservatives had also blamed the Liberals for Canada's uneasy relations with the United States. Announcing that Canada was again "open for business," the Mulroney government defanged what it called "the FIRA tiger," transforming it into a new agency, Investment Canada, with a mandate to encourage foreign investment. In the course of Mulroney's two mandates, Canada–U.S. relations were to undergo, as historian John Herd Thompson put it, "a revolutionary shift toward ideological and political convergence and a remarkable accommodation on a wide range of divisive issues."[5]

Prime Minister Brian Mulroney greets American President Ronald Reagan on his arrival for the "Shamrock Summit" at Quebec City, 1985, during which both leaders made much of their Irish origins. Mulroney hailed the summit as the inauguration of a new positive era in Canadian–American relations.

Source: CP Picture Archive/Paul Chiasson.

Other Conservative foreign-policy initiatives gained approval from specific interest groups. Human-rights advocates praised Mulroney for his condemnation of racial discrimination in South Africa and vigorous support of sanctions against that country. French Canada approved of Mulroney's efforts to forge closer links with *la francophonie*, a loose association of the world's French-speaking states. Most Canadians took pride in Canada's commitment to international peacekeeping and to developmental assistance. Peace, women's, labour, and religious groups did, however, criticize the government's decision to commit modest Canadian forces to the Persian Gulf War against Iraq in 1991; they favoured giving sanctions more time to work.

The strong economic recovery also aided the Conservatives. Unemployment fell, although young people still found it difficult to find jobs. The decline in the inflation rate, from 12.5 percent in 1981 to only 4 percent in 1985, brought interest rates down, making it possible again for businesses and consumers to borrow. The omens appeared favourable for the construction of a new political consensus among Canadians.

The Conservative honeymoon proved brief. The Mulroney government's frequent bouts with scandal soon hurt its public image. Regionalism rose phoenix-like out of the country's flagrantly unequal economic recovery. While metropolitan Toronto and southern Ontario basked in virtually full employment, Quebec, the West, and the Atlantic provinces faced continued high jobless rates. The decline of oil and resource prices, coinciding with a severe farm crisis, hurt the economies of the western provinces.

The Federal Deficit

Mulroney also found it difficult to reduce his government's budgetary deficit. In 1985, the government had a record shortfall of more than $38 billion. A newspaper item depicted a wailing infant above the caption: "Already $8000 in debt." That was each Canadian's share of the $200-billion-and-growing national debt. A decade later, the baby owed nearly $27 000 when rising provincial and municipal indebtedness was taken into account, and Ottawa devoted about one-quarter of its revenues simply to paying the interest on its borrowings. Most economists and business leaders saw the deficit as a "time bomb, ticking away." In 1986, Brian Mulroney promised Canadians: "Our determination to reduce it or eradicate it is, and will be, unyielding and successful."

In spite of such valiant stands, the political necessity of maintaining federal expenditures hampered plans to control spending. Beleaguered farmers pleaded for cash compensation to shield them from depressed world grain prices. After two Alberta bank ventures crashed resoundingly in 1985, investors successfully sought a multibillion-dollar bailout by the federal government. When refineries closed in impoverished east-end Montreal, pressures mounted for Ottawa to intervene. In areas of high unemployment, local potentates sought an array of subsidies and low-cost loans for business to help create new jobs or save threatened ones. The defence lobby demanded money to overhaul and improve the country's defence capability.

When Ottawa reduced grants to the provinces, provincial governments accused it of pushing its deficit on them. Ordinary Canadians, especially the worried middle classes, prevailed upon the government to reaffirm its seemingly wavering faith in the universality of social programs such as old-age pensions. Indeed, when the Mulroney government expressed its intention to index old-age pensions only partially to cost-of-living increases, seniors mobilized and forced the government into a hasty retreat. After a study of unemployment insurance in 1987 recommended substantial changes to reduce costs, labour and the poorer provinces rallied to the defence of the much-maligned program. Ottawa clearly understood the political risks of effecting drastic cuts. "Rattlesnakes get warmer welcomes," said the Montreal *Gazette* of the government's own reaction to the report. Rather than cutting expenses, the government found it easier to raise income and sales taxes substantially, and to continue to borrow.

The Great Free-Trade Debate

The conclusion of a comprehensive trade agreement with the United States became the Mulroney government's most passionately debated initiative during its first mandate.

Canada has always sought wide access to foreign markets for its exports, simultaneously attempting to reduce imports to protect Canadian jobs in industries seen as unable to withstand competition from abroad. Throughout the 1970s, the government kept tariffs, especially on manufactured products, among the highest in the industrialized world. When multilateral trade negotiations in the framework of GATT discredited protective tariffs, Canada, like many other countries, erected a host of non-tariff barriers such as quotas in an effort to impede the entry of cheap imports of goods such as clothing and footwear. The downward slide of the Canadian dollar after 1976—the year it reached a high of $1.04 U.S.—helped less productive Canadian firms compete in foreign markets. It also meant that imports cost more.

Trade Relations

As trade increased with the United States, Canada insistently proclaimed its belief in diversification. It seemed risky to rely on a single country for such a large proportion of imports and exports. Rejecting both the status quo and continental integration, the Trudeau government proposed, in 1972, a "Third Option," which implied less dependence on the United States and stronger links with Europe and other countries. The new policy failed. By 1985, fully 80 percent of Canada's exports went to the United States, and 70 percent of its imports originated there. Nor did the numerous "Team Canada" trade missions to Asia, Europe, and Latin America, organized by Ottawa, have a fundamental impact on the country's trade relations.

Prime Minister Brian Mulroney now argued in favour of even closer trade relations with the Americans. He asserted that a free-trade agreement with the United States would create jobs. Increased sales of goods in that market would also diminish Canada's burgeoning balance of payments deficit in relation to the flow of investment income, tourism, services, and interest payments to foreign lenders to finance the growing mountain of federal debt.

Support for free trade came from many sources. The Royal Commission on the Economic Union and Development Prospects for Canada strongly endorsed it in 1985. Many sectors of the business community had long favoured it. Polls showed that, in the early stages of the debate, a solid majority of Canadians backed it, too. Consumers were generally convinced that free trade would bring lower prices.

In the late 1980s, economists and political scientists and even a few historians waded into the fray to debate the burning issue of free trade with the United States. Many expressed strong opposition. Economist Fred Lazar judged that the agreement "curtailed Canada's sovereignty to an unwarranted degree" and virtually gave the American government the right to determine acceptable Canadian government policies."[1] For political scientist Garth Stevenson, free trade risked undermining the central government's raison d'être since Ottawa could exercise "only minimal powers over the economy."[2]

Political scientist Daniel P. Drache expressed strong opposition as well. In his view, Canada, "with its weak industrial sector, sharp regional divisions and stark social inequalities," would now be subject to market forces alone; governments would have to give up their time-honoured right and ability to intervene to come to the aid of the disadvantaged.[3] As for economist James Laxer, free trade was a "leap of faith" into the unknown that Canada would do well to avoid.[4] Other observers judged the project more favourably. Economist John Crispo reminded his opponents that an economically more dynamic Canada could also provide more support for culture, social security, and regional development.[5]

Many critics feared, or even hoped, that Canada would ultimately be obliged to harmonize its policies with American policies. In the opinion of political scientist Peter Cumming, it would be in Canada's own best interest if it forced the country to "revamp outdated policies."[6] According to political scientist David Leyton-Brown, the real question was whether free trade would bring about a greater degree of "harmonization" than would have occurred without free trade. His modest reply: "That question is of course unanswerable."[7]

In the field of culture, negotiators contended that Canada's sovereignty was protected. For historian John Herd Thompson, however, Canada appeared to admit the American definition of culture, that cultural industries were a business like any other. Thompson saw this convergence of understandings of culture as holding "greater peril for Canada's cultural sovereignty than any threatened U.S. retaliation to specific Canadian policies of cultural protection and promotion."[8]

The Free Trade Agreement was signed in 1988. Trade policy analyst Michael Hart noted that, by the early 1990s, freer trade had become "the norm" while its critics had been "marginalized."[9] In 1994, Mexico joined Canada and the United States in launching the North American Free Trade Agreement (NAFTA). Cross-border trade and investment more than doubled in the years 1990-95. In regard to culture and values, had free trade made Canadians more like Americans? Without a doubt, answered historian Jack Granatstein, provocatively, Canadians "are American in all but name."[10] Certainly not, replied pollster Michael Adams. Americans "have become a nation of God-fearing Darwinists, we have become a collection of tolerant social democrats."[11]

1 Fred Lazar, "The Trade Agreement: A Dissenting Opinion," in Marc Gold and David Leyton-Brown, eds., *Trade-offs on Free Trade: The Canada–U.S. Free Trade Agreement* (Toronto: Carswell, 1988), p. 435.

2   Garth Stevenson, "The Agreement and Dynamics of Canadian Federalism," in ibid., p. 140.

3   Daniel P. Drache, "The Mulroney–Reagan Accord: The Economics of Continental Power," in ibid., p. 87.

4   James Laxer, *Leap of Faith: Free Trade and the Future of Canada* (Edmonton: Hurtig, 1986).

5   John Crispo, *Free Trade: The Real Story* (Toronto: Gage, 1988), p. 204.

6   Peter Cumming, "Impact of the Free Trade Agreement on Public Policy," in Lazar, op. cit., p. 433.

7   David Leyton-Brown, "The Canada–U.S. Free Trade Agreement," in Andrew B. Gollner and Daniel Salée, eds., *Canada Under Mulroney: An End-of-Term Report* (Montreal: Véhicule Press, 1988), p. 117.

8   John Herd Thompson, "Canada's Quest for Cultural Sovereignty: Protection, Promotion, and Popular Culture," in Stephen J. Randall and Herman W. Konrad, eds., *NAFTA in Transition* (Calgary: University of Calgary Press, 1995), p. 410.

9   Michael Hart, *A Trading Nation: Canadian Trade Policy from Colonialism to Globalization* (Vancouver: UBC Press, 2002), p. 396.

10   Jack Granatstein, *Yankee Go Home? Canadians and Anti-Americanism* (Toronto: HarperCollins, 1996), p. 9.

11   Michael Adams, *Sex in the Snow: Canadian Social Values at the End of the Millennium* (Toronto: Penguin Books, 1998), p. 194.

Opposition to Free Trade

As the debate heated up, public support for free trade cooled. American protectionist measures weakened Canadian enthusiasm, though at the same time they seemed to make some form of agreement even more urgent. Labour unions, farmers, the churches, the federal New Democratic and Liberal parties, and the government of Ontario (whose major export, automobiles, was already protected by the Auto Pact), warned that free trade would cost thousands of jobs. They argued that American companies might close their higher-cost branch plants in Canada and serve the Canadian market from their more cost-efficient American bases. Canada might also lose control over the pricing of resources and be forced to abandon transport subsidies. Anti–free traders further warned that a deal could endanger Canada's more generous social programs. Worst of all—here were shades of the 1911 election and the reciprocity debate—free trade could jeopardize Canada's political sovereignty.

The Canada–U.S. Free Trade Agreement

Arduous negotiations culminated in an accord in 1987. By its terms, tariffs would end gradually, and Canada would gain enhanced access to most sectors of the American market. Canada did not succeed in obtaining the much-sought-after "binding mechanism for dispute resolution"; instead the agreement created a less satisfactory bi-national review panel that would simply ensure that each country's trade agencies made decisions on the basis of existing law. (The United States would later make frequent use of this measure to block or penalize imports from Canada in such sectors as lumber and agricultural products.) In future, Canada could no longer bar most American takeovers of Canadian industries. Moreover, although Canada gained unrestricted access for energy exports to the United States, the deal also secured American access to Canadian supplies even in times of shortages. But Canada did obtain exemptions for its agricultural products sold through marketing boards and its threatened cultural enterprises. Negotiators left the delicate issue of trade-distorting subsidies, given by governments to favour agriculture and certain industries, to later discussion.

By refusing to accept the accord, the Liberal-dominated Senate forced an election in late 1988. Discussion of free trade became the major issue. During a televised debate, Liberal leader John Turner accused Prime Minister Mulroney: "I happen to believe you have sold us out…. You will reduce us … to a colony of the United States." The Conservative victory, though with a substantially reduced majority, ensured ratification of the agreement in early 1989. As plant closures brought steep job losses in 1989 and 1990, the labour movement blamed free trade. Other observers placed the responsibility on high interest rates, a rising Canadian dollar, a relative decline in productivity, increased taxes, and a deteriorating international economic situation. The Conservative government pushed on. Shortly after the election, it agreed to sign a new treaty with the United States and Mexico forming a North American free-trade zone. Canada had opted for a continentalist economy. There would be no turning back.

Demography

After 1970, Canada's population growth slowed to a rate of about 1 percent a year. High levels of immigration, not births, now explained much of the country's growth. Provinces whose population continued to expand rapidly, such as Alberta in the 1970s and Ontario in the 1980s, were those whose vigorous economies attracted newcomers both from abroad and from other Canadian provinces. Urban Canada continued to grow after 1970, though more slowly than in the 1950s and 1960s. Many rural areas and centres based on the exploitation of resources lost population

The Birth Rate

By 1970, couples no longer had enough children to replace themselves. By the mid-1980s, though babies were not yet on the endangered species list, the average Canadian family had shrunk to include a mere 1.6 children. Many women simply postponed having children. But sociologists noted an increase in "yuppie-style" marriages they called "dinks"—dual-income, no kids—as many couples found it difficult to juggle children and careers. After 1970, recourse to new birth-control methods became more frequent. For example, thousands of men and women in their thirties underwent voluntary sterilization.

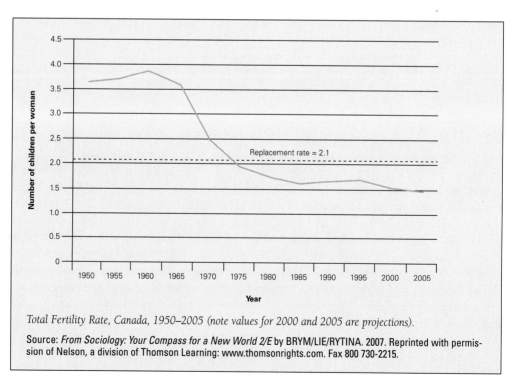

Total Fertility Rate, Canada, 1950–2005 (note values for 2000 and 2005 are projections).

Source: *From Sociology: Your Compass for a New World 2/E* by BRYM/LIE/RYTINA. 2007. Reprinted with permission of Nelson, a division of Thomson Learning: www.thomsonrights.com. Fax 800 730-2215.

The issue of abortion began to provoke passionate debate in Canada in the 1960s. Under a law adopted by Parliament in 1969, abortions remained illegal except when continued pregnancy threatened a woman's life or health. Discontented with the arbitrariness of the law, women's groups mobilized to demand the decriminalization of abortion. Finally, in 1988, the Supreme Court of Canada found the abortion law to be unconstitutional. Although the Mulroney government attempted to recriminalize abortion in a new bill in 1990, the Senate defeated the measure. The number of therapeutic abortions increased in the 1970s, then further in the 1990s, before stabilizing, after 2000, at about 30 for every 100 live births in Canada.

Changing Family Patterns

The revolution in family patterns, begun in the late 1960s, continued into the 1970s and 1980s. Divorces became even more frequent, particularly after 1985, when new legislation made "marital breakdown," evidenced by a year or more of separation or by adultery or cruelty, the only grounds for divorce. Revised laws granting each spouse half of the property accumulated during the life of the marriage also contributed to making divorce a viable financial option for the spouse who owned no property independently—most often, the wife. Common-law unions gained in popularity, especially among younger Canadians. In English-speaking Canada, such unions were often a prelude to marriage; in Quebec, where such relationships were far more widespread, marriage was less inevitable. Governments moved to adapt legislation to this trend.

Changing family patterns ensured that child care became an important issue from the 1970s. Political scientist Rianne Mahon has noted that increasing numbers of dual-earner couples and single-parent families produced a "crisis of care" that made non-parental child-care arrangements essential.[6] In Toronto, for example, a coalition of women's groups, labour unions, and urban reformers succeeded in bringing the city to make universally accessible child care available. Other Canadian cities and provinces followed.

Gays and Lesbians

Gays and lesbians increasingly worked for self-affirmation and liberation after 1970. They denounced what they viewed as police harassment and repression, and demanded better protection from "gay-bashing" and other forms of violence. They rallied to such cries as "Out of the closets and into the streets," and "Gay is just as good as straight." Gay groups pursued agendas of political and social activism. Television series began to portray homosexuals in less stereotypical terms. In 1972, when French-language Radio-Canada broadcast an episode of the popular television series *Le paradis terrestre*, in which two men were shown coming out of an elevator hand in hand, outraged spectators forced the show's cancellation. By 2000, gay roles in television series were common. In 1977, Quebec became the first province to prohibit discrimination by reason of sexual orientation.

Canada's first Gay Pride celebration was staged discreetly in Toronto, in August 1972, with activities and a picnic on Toronto Island. A quarter century later, 750 000 people attended a Gay Pride parade in Toronto, more than in any other North American city. Gay and lesbian associations were established in the workplace. Some universities, such as Ryerson Polytechnic in Toronto, introduced lesbian/gay studies into curricula. There were moving moments. After a class discussion on stereotypes relating to lesbians, one teacher commented, "We can test the stereotypes by looking at a real live lesbian. I am a lesbian ... and I don't think you would have identified me from those stereotypes." She then explained, "Coming out to my classes as a lesbian is my own personal choice. I judged that I had little to lose.... Many women cannot make that choice for fear of losing their jobs, alienating workmates, losing custody of their children."

Gay community activists in Toronto, protesting a speech by right-wing family values advocate Anita Bryant, 1978.

Source: Archives of Ontario/C193-3-0-3167, 78285-20, AO5290.

Canadians did indeed begin to show greater tolerance, but gays hastened to point out that tolerance did not mean acceptance. Many continued to fear that knowledge of their sexuality in certain heavily masculine job categories, such as professional sports, could harm their career.

The Changing Role of Women

After 1970, relations between the sexes underwent a fundamental transformation. Twenty years later, though the goal of full equality was still far from being achieved, the male-dominated society of a generation earlier had been substantially eroded. Women worked within a multitude of organizations, and promoted a variety of visions, to bring about these changes.

Institutionalized Feminism

When the government failed to act quickly on the recommendations of the Royal Commission on the Status of Women, women established, in 1972, the National Action Committee on the Status of Women, an umbrella organization now embracing 700 widely disparate associations representing more than five million members. Women formed similar groups across Canada to lobby provincial governments. Growing pressure brought Prime Minister Pierre Trudeau to appoint a minister responsible for the status of women and to establish, in 1973, the Canadian Advisory Council on the Status of Women. Most provinces appointed similar advisory councils. Quebec's Conseil du statut de la femme, equipped with funds for research, produced a detailed plan for change, *Égalité et indépendance*. Women's groups organized a multitude of conferences and workshops during 1975, the year the United Nations decreed to be International Women's Year.

The Home

In part, the home became the battleground for equality of the sexes. Change came slowly, and child care continued to be mainly women's work. Polls suggested that Canadians in general wanted men to take responsibility for a greater share of the housework; men themselves were not so sure. A federal government poster published during International Women's Year extolled the homemaker's virtues by linking "women's" jobs in the home to prestigious occupations: nurse, teacher, accountant, plumber, chef. Women criticized the publicity for failing to mention a homemaker's less-prestigious occupations: janitor, launderer, dishwasher, waitress, taxi driver, and maid.

The 1980s brought to the fore one very sombre element, hitherto seldom discussed openly: violence against women. In 1982, a House of Commons report on violence in the family showed that as many as 10 percent of wives suffered beatings and noted that the numbers appeared to be increasing. Five years later, in response to another bleak report, *Battered but Not Beaten*, Ottawa announced major funding initiatives. Local women's groups opened shelters to assist homeless and battered women. They also set up rape crisis centres, fought for laws restricting pornography, and organized assistance for Native women, immigrant and refugee women, and women on welfare.

Editorial staff of Chatelaine, 1972. *Traditionally a homemakers' magazine,* Chatelaine *switched its emphasis to women's issues in the 1970s.*

Source: Courtesy of *Chatelaine*. © Maclean Hunter Publishing Ltd.

Women in the Work Force

Unionization improved working conditions and pay in some traditional female occupations, particularly in health care, education, and government service. In the 1970s, union membership grew four times more quickly among females than it did among males, although among workers women were still less likely than men to belong to unions. Many of the unprotected majority worked in difficult-to-organize sectors such as banks, restaurants, offices, and retail stores. They often worked part-time as well. As part-time work and teleworking increased, Judy Rebick, president of the National Action Committee on the Status of Women, denounced "all the vanguard destructive forces of the right" that are "hitting women first."

Unions themselves started to pay greater heed to women's needs. In 1979, women backed by the United Steel Workers filed a complaint for discrimination with the Ontario Human Rights Commission, to force Stelco to hire women for production jobs at its plant in Hamilton. Over the preceding two decades, Stelco had received 300 000 job applications, including those of 30 000 women; it had hired 33 000 men, but no women. The commission's verdict was favourable, and Stelco began hiring women for these well-paid jobs. (Ironically, massive layoffs in the late 1980s eliminated almost all the women employed in production on the basis of seniority rules.) In Quebec, women's committees succeeded in convincing their unions to adopt policies on child care, maternity benefits, equal pay for work of equal value, job safety, sexual harassment, and discrimination. The myth of female docility evaporated rapidly as women-dominated organizations such as nurses' unions waged bitter, sometimes illegal, strikes against what they judged to be unsatisfactory working conditions. Although women remained underrepresented in union executives, particularly in international unions, they began to play a greater role, as symbolized by the election in 1975 of Grace Hartman as president of the Canadian Union of Public Employees (CUPE), Canada's largest union, and in 1986 of Shirley Carr as head of the Canadian Labour Congress. Yet Judy Darcy, elected president of CUPE in 1991, complained of the double standards that made many active women unionists feel guilty: guilty because their union work made them poor mothers, and guilty because their family responsibilities meant that they devoted less time to union duties.

By the 1970s, the principle of equal pay for men and women performing the same task had gained wide recognition. Yet, in the 1980s, the average woman's wage remained at approximately 65 percent of the average man's. Although women's lesser work experience and the generally lower educational levels of older women explained part of this difference, the continued concentration of women in low-paying occupations appeared to be the principal factor. In 1984, the federal Commission on Equality in Employment recommended mandatory employment equity programs, to be implemented through affirmative action. Ottawa responded by requiring employers under federal jurisdiction, such as banks and national transportation companies, to give women and minorities better job opportunities. It also made affirmative action plans mandatory for all firms doing business with the government.

Challenges for Labour

While the claims of women moved forward rapidly after 1970, those of labour encountered increasingly serious obstacles. The numerous strikes in the public sector during the 1970s alienated public opinion. Taxpayers quickly realized that they would have to foot the bill for what many viewed as excessive government generosity. Moreover, two of every three Canadian workers did not belong to unions. They, as well as many workers affiliated to small organizations, resented the attempts of the most powerful unions to secure a greater share of the national wealth for their members. Canada acquired a negative image for the frequency of its strike activity—only Italy had a worse record. Yet, although 11 million workdays were lost to strikes in 1975 (a particularly bad year), that figure represented barely 1.5 percent of total working time. Accidents, illness, and general absenteeism affected productivity to a far greater extent.

Union militancy, usually aimed at obtaining higher salaries and better working conditions, increased in the 1970s. In some cases, however, unions attacked the capitalist system itself, seeking to replace it with a socialist regime. In Quebec, union militants published manifestoes urging a socialist and independent Quebec. Here, indeed, was the high point of labour's confrontation with employers.

The 1980s brought new challenges. A more conservative public approved governments that moved to restrain wages and limit strikes. In Nova Scotia, for example, a Conservative government adopted anti-union legislation which, while embittering relations with labour, helped to create jobs by convincing Michelin Tire, a major employer in the province, to expand production. British Columbia's Social Credit government also adopted legislation to curb unions after a fierce confrontation with the public-sector unions.

Manufacturing industries and resource-sector companies laid off workers. Strong unions fought—sometimes quite successfully, as in the case of the autoworkers and the steelworkers—for job security and better pensions, and for wage protection against inflation and new taxes. Canadian autoworkers, favouring a less bureaucratic and more militant and democratic union, broke away from the American union in 1985 and then negotiated a made-in-Canada agreement with their employers. To reverse the decline in their numbers, unions signed up workers from outside their original jurisdictions. The steelworkers' union, for example, enrolled security workers, restaurant workers, and employees of fish-processing plants, promising that "if it moves or eats with a knife and a fork, we'll organize it." Union strength increased to levels attained in the mid-1970s, about 37 percent of the non-farm work force.

Cultural Concerns

During the 1970s, university expansion slowed. Student enrolments increased more modestly, although the proportion of women grew rapidly. By the century's end, women full-time students were far more numerous than men in university bachelor's and master's degree programs, although engineering, applied science, and mathematics faculties still represented a largely male domain. Men were still a majority in doctoral programs.

A crisis in university financing appeared during the 1980s, as deficit-ridden provinces forced universities to accept real cuts in spending. For example, historian Paul Axelrod showed how Ontario, in the face of intense public criticism of university spending, moved to get "more scholar for the dollar."[7] Significantly, not one new university opened its doors in Canada between 1980 and 1994, when the University of Northern British Columbia, at Prince George, began operations. Most provinces also imposed higher tuition fees and turned enthusiastically to corporate benefactors for additional financing. In his study of academic freedom, historian Michiel Horn worried that universities' closer relationships with business interests threatened "a fundamental university objective, one that academic freedom is meant to protect, namely, the disinterested pursuit of knowledge."[8] The late 1990s saw some public reinvestment in universities; in particular, the federal government, now laden with budget surpluses, invested heavily in research and funded large numbers of university chairs.

New religious groups in Canada. A photo taken on Ste. Catherine Street, Montreal, May 1, 1993. Religion has become both more personal and highly diversified. Sociologist Reginald Bibby claims that Canadians now want "religion 'à la carte,' preferring to pick and choose … from religious smorgasbords."

Source: Photograph by Michel Brunelle.

Contemporary Religion

Immigration from Asia diversified Canada's religious face, as sizable communities of Muslims, Buddhists, and Hindus became established. For most Canadians, however, the emphasis on individuality meant that religion became largely a personal matter. Canadians moved away from religions based on theology and denominational identification, and toward a view of religion as an inspiration for moral and ethical behaviour. The great majority said they still expected to turn to organized religion for rites such as baptisms, weddings, and funerals but, with the notable exception of members of smaller Protestant conservative and evangelical churches, they attached diminishing importance to regular attendance at worship services. The majority of Roman Catholic Quebeckers, for example, went to midnight mass at Christmas, but malls were far more crowded than churches during the rest of the year. While two Canadians in three attended weekly religious services in 1946, only one in five did so in 2001. Boomers, in a collective existential crisis, turned in the 1990s to spiritual books and seminars. Sociologist Reginald Bibby, a long-time observer of Canadian religious behaviour, judged that Canadians now wanted "religion 'à la carte,' preferring to pick and choose beliefs, practices, programs, and professional services from increasingly diversified religious smorgasbords."[9] At the same time, he viewed most churches as simply unable to "sell their product effectively."

Leisure

In the health-conscious 1970s and 1980s, many Canadians devoted long hours to exercise: they walked, they cycled, they swam, they jogged, they did aerobics, and they gardened, sometimes relentlessly. When they tired of strenuous activity, they played Trivial Pursuit, invented by two Montrealers; it became the most popular board game of the 1980s. Or they learned to cook using the microwave ovens that entered a large majority of their homes in the course of the decade. They enjoyed interactive games such as Nintendo on their home computers. And they watched more television, with more channels (for which they paid more money).They also became increasingly addicted to buying lottery tickets or to gambling in the casinos or on video-lottery terminals that cash-starved provincial governments now approved.

Sports

Spectator sports dominated popular culture. Athletes basked in glory as long as they scored goals, hit runs, or won races on the slopes in the winter and on the speedways in the summer, and as long as they avoided the steroids that proved to be widely used in certain field sports. Hockey enjoyed immense interest, but it now had to share the spotlight with football, baseball, and, increasingly, basketball. Big-league baseball came to Montreal in 1969, when the Expos began to play. Toronto had to wait until 1977 for its team, the Blue Jays, which became the most financially successful enterprise in any sport. The Ontario government invested huge sums in the building of an immense closed stadium in Toronto, the SkyDome, where the Jays entertained their local fans after its opening in 1989.

Hockey underwent an important expansion in the 1970s as the National Hockey League took in several franchises from the failed World Hockey Association. Although most players were Canadian, most new teams were American. American directors also made the important decisions, leading sports critic Bruce Kidd to decry the takeover of Canadian hockey by American business interests. Wayne Gretzky, undoubtedly the sport's brightest star of this era, attained the crowning glory of being pictured on the cover of *Time*. Shortly afterward the Edmonton Oilers relinquished their superstar to the Los Angeles Kings—an act akin to high treason in the eyes of many angry fans. As players' salaries soared, teams found survival more difficult in small Canadian markets.

The Canadian public strongly disapproved proposals for government assistance to millionaire players and owners. Some owners then sought to sell their teams. The Quebec Nordiques, for example, successful but playing in a small market, were transferred to Denver in 1995 where they promptly won the Stanley Cup.

In the late 1960s, Ottawa discovered the importance of sport as an instrument for promoting national unity and yielding political capital. It then began investing heavily in high-performance sports in order to produce more medal winners in international competitions. The Canada–Soviet hockey series in 1972 showed that the return on such investments could be considerable. Watched by the largest Canadian television audience on record until that time, Team Canada won the series in the last seconds of the dramatic final encounter. One ecstatic Canadian university president suggested that the series probably did more to create a Canadian identity than ten years of Canada Council fellowships. Politicians saw a triumph for "Canadian virtues" and for capitalist liberal democracy.

Montreal hosted the summer Olympic Games in 1976, the first time that this prestigious international gathering took place in Canada. (In 1988, Calgary was the site of the winter Olympics.) Provincial and municipal taxpayers were uneasy at the prospect of new budget deficits, but Montreal mayor Jean Drapeau assured them there was no more possibility of incurring a deficit than there was of his becoming pregnant. After the Olympic lottery, Olympic coins, Olympic stamps,

The most famous winning goal in Canadian hockey history, scored by Paul Henderson in Moscow in the final game of the 1972 Russia–Canada hockey series, with just 34 seconds of play remaining. On the 25th anniversary of the goal in 1997 Paul appeared on a postage stamp issued by Canada Post.

Source: CP Picture Archive/Frank Lennon.

and other promotional paraphernalia failed to prevent a massive deficit, delighted cartoonists drew sketches of a pregnant mayor. The games themselves provided much excitement, though Canadian prowess would be much greater at the Los Angeles Olympics in 1984.

Cultural Industries

In the nationalist climate of the 1970s, cultural development came to be inextricably linked to the affirmation of national identity. For many English-speaking Canadians, the danger to survival came increasingly from the United States, mainly because many other Canadians avidly consumed that country's cultural products.

After 1970, the Americanization of Canadian broadcasting in English continued apace, although Canadian cultural industries did enjoy some protection through regulatory barriers. These determined, for example, how much non-Canadian programming could be broadcast on Canadian television stations. Then cable television enabled almost all Canadians to gain access to the major U.S. networks. The arrival of satellite dish services in the late 1990s made protection in this area virtually impossible.

Statistics showed the extent of foreign domination of Canada's cultural industries. By 1990, for example, foreign-owned publishers had acquired 80 percent of Canada's book market. To compete with the U.S. publishing industry, Canadian publishers relied on government grants. Nearly 85 percent of recording sales were foreign, as were 80 percent of magazines sold in

Canada. When Canada moved to protect Canadian magazine publishers, the United States immediately threatened economic reprisals. In movie theatres, Canadian films had less than 5 percent of screen time, although a growing number of American producers, subsidized by the Canadian government, filmed in Toronto and Vancouver, considered a "Hollywood North." Attempts on the part of the Canadian and Quebec governments to ensure a greater distribution in movie theatres of Canadian films provoked conflict with the major American distributors, forcing a Canadian retreat. Yet some critics insisted that while Canadians consumed and borrowed American cultural products, they also reconstituted them and imprinted them with Canadian values. Sometimes they even sold them back to the Americans. One success story: Loverboy, the Vancouver high-energy rock group of the early 1980s, who sold more than three million copies of its album *Get Lucky* in the United States. In this way, cultural anthropologist Frank Manning maintained, "The beaver can, and does, bite back," although Manning was uncertain whether the bite was serious or only a playful nip.[10]

Ottawa also provided subsidies for artists in all fields and funded cultural infrastructures. The CBC continued to affirm its objective of preserving and enriching Canadianism. Yet, in the 1980s, just as new demands were made for public broadcasting to meet specific needs such as those of women, ethnic groups, Native peoples, and regions, the federal government reduced its financing. By the late 1980s, a former president of the CBC described government policy as "Americanization by importation, by privatization, and by fiscal deprivation."

The National Film Board (NFB), another important publicly supported institution, produced numerous high-quality documentaries, a field in which it excelled. Producer Claude Jutra's *Mon oncle Antoine*, a touching story of a boy's coming of age and loss of innocence, achieved the second-highest network ratings both on Radio-Canada and, in English translation, on CBC in 1973–74. Later, Bonnie Sherr Klein's documentary on pornography ran into problems with censors but proved a box-office success. The Canadian Film Development Corporation, later Telefilm Canada, gave financial backing to several critical successes, among them Peter Carter's *The Rowdyman* and Gilles Carle's *La vraie nature de Bernadette*. After the mid-1980s, it shifted its emphasis toward television production.

The late 1980s saw the production of several notable Canadian feature films. David Cronenberg's *Dead Ringers* proved a financial success, while several films by Atom Egoyan, among them *Speaking Parts*, earned him an international reputation. Canadian films in English generally played to small audiences. Most did not have the glossy production values of American successes, and modest budgets meant modest promotion and modest distribution.

Quebec films represented close to 70 percent of Canada's entire feature-film industry; they were the most successful in competing with American films. Claude Jutra's *Mon oncle Antoine*, a touching film on social life in Quebec's asbestos-mining region, illustrated the tensions between the nostalgia for bygone days and the need for change so much in evidence during the Quiet Revolution. Producer Denis Arcand portrayed decadent history teachers—surely an entirely fictional subject—in his *Decline of the American Empire*. François Girard's film *The Red Violin* captured the odyssey of a violin across four centuries and three continents.

Canadian Literature

After 1970, there were more Canadian writers and they wrote more. The growth of universities, as well as increased government funding and a larger population, help explain this significant growth. International acclaim gave many writers publicity, and established their reputations abroad as much as within Canada.

Literature mirrored Canadians' preoccupations, attitudes, and aspirations. Nationalist themes, for example, recurred frequently in novels in both English and French Canada, particularly during the 1970s. The works that secured Margaret Atwood's international reputation, including *Surfacing* and, later, *The Handmaid's Tale*, contained trenchant nationalist critiques. They were also feminist, and indeed much fiction of the contemporary period portrayed the everyday lives of women.

Many literary works explored the experience of minority groups such as Native peoples and immigrants. In his novel *The Temptations of Big Bear*, for example, Alberta writer Rudy Wiebe dwelt upon the conflict between European and First Nations cultures provoked by the arrival of European settlers. Joy Kogawa, in *Obasan*, poignantly evoked the fate of Japanese Canadians during World War II. As a child, she had been exiled with her family to an internment camp in interior British Columbia. After the war, the family were forced to move to southern Alberta to work as field labourers. Acadian author Antonine Maillet painted a new image of Acadia and its people in her works. In her play *La Sagouine*, an old Acadian woman reminisces about the material and spiritual suffering she has known. In *Pélagie-la-Charrette*, winner of the prestigious Prix Goncourt, Maillet tells the story of returning Acadian exiles. Other novels, such as those of Jane Rule and Gail Scott, and *The Wars* by Timothy Findley, which describes the growing madness of a young Canadian army officer, explore lesbian or gay themes.

Historical settings were also common. Al Purdy, the poet of a dozen styles, evoked Canada's past in such works as *In Search of Owen Roblin* and *A Splinter in the Heart*, the latter portraying a Trenton, Ontario youth in 1918, whom events turn rapidly into a man. *Les filles de Caleb*, Arlette Cousture's novel about the life of a family in the Mauricie region of Quebec a century ago, inspired a long-lasting television series that regularly attracted more than 3 million viewers.

Internationally acclaimed novelists Marie-Claire Blais and Réjean Ducharme were among those Quebec authors whose works sought to reveal the asphyxiating nature of traditional family relationships and religion. When Denise Boucher attacked the stereotypes of orthodox Roman Catholicism in *Les fées ont soif*, religious groups obtained an injunction forbidding public presentations of her play. The Supreme Court eventually decided in favour of the author.

Some writers set their works in small towns with closed societies. An example was Deptford, the scene of a powerful trilogy of novels by Robertson Davies featuring vivid central characters. Others dwelt upon the realities of urban living. Quebec playwright Michel Tremblay's works, performed around the world, have featured a wide variety of Montrealers, including elegant upper-class ladies, drag queens, country singers, and very ordinary mortals from the working-class neighbourhoods he knew as a boy. Montreal served also as the setting of Yves Beauchemin's *Le Matou*, a fast-moving thriller that sold one million copies worldwide in the mid-1980s.

Canadian literature also underlines the important role that regions have played in Canadian life. Atlantic writer David Adams Richards wrote of poverty and pride in northeastern New Brunswick in *The Coming of Winter* and *Blood Ties*, while W.O. Mitchell's *Roses Are Difficult Here* chronicled a year in the life of an Alberta foothills town called Shelby. Prairie geography inspired Robert Kroetsch's poetry. Small local publishers helped to foster a regional consciousness. One Winnipeg house, Turnstone Press, promoted poetry from all regions of the country. During the 1970s, regional theatres sprang up across the country; Theatre Calgary, for example, featured western Canadian playwrights.

New Challenges

The 1970s and 1980s defined new challenges. Canadians became more conscious of the need to take preventive measures to ensure personal good health. The warnings were unpleasant: the Canadian Cancer Society estimated that one Canadian male in four and one female in five would die of cancer. Other studies highlighted the risks and causes of heart disease. Canadians began to heed appeals to eat less salt, sugar, and fat, and to consume more vegetables, fruit, and whole grains.

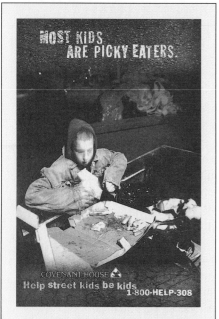

A Covenant House poster draws attention to the plight of Canadian cities' homeless youth.

Source: Courtesy of Covenant House, Toronto.

Automobile associations and victims of drunk drivers successfully lobbied governments to take measures to reduce carnage on the highways. The use of seatbelts also contributed to the steady decline in the number of Canadians killed in accidents on the roads. In addition, Canadians smoked less. Nonsmokers brought pressure to bear, legislative and otherwise, to force smokers to respect their air space. Those who did smoke paid more taxes and saw their packages covered with grisly health warnings showing black lungs, infected gums and, in an appeal to men, limp cigarettes. The rapid spread of the deadly AIDS (acquired immune deficiency syndrome) virus after 1980 finally brought health authorities to launch campaigns promoting "safe sex" or abstinence. At first the disease hit gays, because of risky sexual practices. Then it spread among drug users, hemophiliacs, blood transfusion recipients, and heterosexuals. By 2000 the disease had already killed more than 15 000 Canadians, but medical advances were helping to prolong the lives of those afflicted.

Poverty

Throughout the 1980s, poverty remained a serious problem despite what was, generally, a growing economy. Governments revamped social programs such as aid to families and pensions to seniors, taking away payments from higher-income Canadians but increasing assistance to the poorest. At the same time, spending cuts pushed Canadians on social assistance below low-income cutoff lines. The poor failed to come any closer to the rich in terms of income. Moreover, the middle class itself shrank. More workers had highly skilled, well-paid, stable jobs, but there were also additional workers in the lower-income category, often employed in part-time or temporary jobs in the traditional service sector.

Marital breakdown, together with the trend to reject the institution of marriage, resulted in large numbers of single-parent families, most of them headed by women. Their number doubled between 1971 and 1996, to one million. Many of these families had very low incomes. In the past, such women often lived on welfare. By the end of the 1990s, however, welfare rolls had shrunk but poorly educated working mothers on low salaries still remained poor. The annual report cards issued throughout the 1990s by Campaign 2000, a national antipoverty coalition, showed that poverty rates remained stable at about one child in five, slightly higher than the rates of the 1980s. One critic captured the dilemma of many poor parents in the title of a book, *Pay the Rent or Feed the Kids*.

Crime

Rising crime rates became a serious social concern in the 1970s and 1980s. Many offences were drug-related. Technological innovations such as debit cards and later the Internet offered new possibilities for fraud. Although violent crime nearly doubled in the 1980s, rates for murder and armed robbery remained far lower than in the United States. (Those least at risk from crime were teetotalling homebodies living in rural areas of eastern Canada. Those most at risk were urban males aged 18 to 29 who were members of gangs or engaged in the drug trade.) Crime rates in Canada varied from one province to another, but they tended to increase steadily from east to west. In October 1990, when one big-city newspaper swathed its front page with the headline "Our Violent City: Anyone, Anywhere, Can Be Hit," it highlighted, and undoubtedly contributed to, the fact that the fear of crime had become a more present reality than crime itself. Canadians wanted the courts to hand down more severe sentences, and many even favoured the return of capital punishment. After 1991, crime rates dropped steadily, returning to levels not seen since the 1970s as the cohort of young Canadians decreased in size.

The Environment

Environmental issues gained increasing visibility after 1970 as Canadians discovered the negative aftermath of the unbridled, almost unregulated, development of past decades. They also learned that environmental issues were global in nature: the "greenhouse effect," the depletion of the ozone layer, the pollution of air and water, and the destruction of tropical and temperate rain forests all involved worldwide responsibility, and solutions required international cooperation. During the 1980s, Canada signed several multilateral agreements on the environment, notably those concerning climate change and ozone depletion.

More importantly, many Canadians came to see themselves, and perhaps especially others, as part of the problem. An expanding and wealthier population oriented toward consumption produced large quantities of wastes. It also made unsustainable demands upon natural resources. The burning of fossil fuels to heat homes, to run automobiles, and to drive industries fouled the air; an increasing number of scientists agreed that it also favoured climate change through the so-called "greenhouse gases" it produced. As numerous lakes and streams of the Canadian Shield became lifeless and as the surrounding vegetation showed increasing evidence of damage, Canadians realized the devastating effects of acid rain. Many industries also spewed chemical effluents into both air and water.

Prime agricultural land surrounding cities disappeared beneath low-density suburbs, roads, fast-food restaurants, shopping malls, and industrial parks. Since 1931, nearly one-third of southern Ontario's rich farmland has been lost to largely unplanned suburban sprawl. Agricultural methods, such as straightening streams and small watercourses, contributed to the erosion of topsoil and, through the abundant use of pesticides, herbicides, and fertilizers, to the pollution of water. Farmers and property developers drained ecologically sensitive wetlands for agricultural or residential purposes, logging companies prepared to harvest the country's last old-growth stands of timber, and untouched wilderness receded to their northern limits.

No easy solutions existed. Concerned citizens set up associations to publicize environmental dangers or to propose solutions. Some groups had international ramifications. The World Wildlife Fund, for example, had programs in Canada and in 100 other countries. Ducks Unlimited sought to conserve wetlands and waterfowl throughout North America. Other groups were Canadian creations. Greenpeace, a well-known environmental lobby, had its origins in Vancouver in 1970. Twenty years later the organization boasted 2.5 million members in 40 countries. The Canadian Parks and Wilderness Society worked to establish new parks. Its Ontario partner, the Algonquin Wildlands League used the media and scientific research to fight for the protection of large tracts of woodland. The League won an important victory in 1973, when Quetico Park, on the north shore of Lake Superior, was reclassified as a primitive park from which all logging was banned. In the 1980s, Ontario doubled its park system, but here again debate raged on over the issue of allowing logging, mineral exploration, sport hunting, and commercial tourism in the parks.

Litigation also proved to be a useful weapon for environmentalists, Native peoples, and other concerned citizens. The Sierra Legal Defence Fund, founded in 1990, took governments to court to force them to respect their own laws and regulations concerning the environment, and to force offenders to obey environmental laws. The Nature Conservancy of Canada pursued another line of action: it sought to protect ecologically sensitive lands through outright land purchases paid for by donations.

Governments and the Environment

Public pressure brought governments to take an interest in the environment. In 1971, the federal government established the Department of the Environment, and most provinces soon followed suit. Governments established standards for clean air and clean water, and set up agencies to monitor compliance. They also provided for environmental assessments of important projects such as the construction of dams, but these proved difficult to carry out when powerful economic interests as well as provincial governments themselves supported the project, as was the case with the building of the Old Man River dam in southern Alberta.

Disposal of the millions of tonnes of wastes that Canadians produced annually proved increasingly onerous. In the early 1970s, landfill sites replaced open garbage dumps, but rural residents strenuously resisted having these sites in their "backyards." Some wastes could be incinerated, a costly process that produced dangerous gases. With the aid of provincial subsidies, municipal governments gradually instituted recycling programs for glass, metals, paper, and plastics. Tire dumps constituted a special problem, demonstrated in devastating fashion when a massive fire at a Hagersville, Ontario site raged out of control for weeks in 1990. Even worse was the problem of storing or eliminating toxic wastes. A fire at a storage site for PCBs near Montreal necessitated the evacuation of an entire suburb.

Controlling air and water pollution meant difficult and prolonged negotiations with the United States, whose industries were major polluters of Canada's water and air. In 1987, Canada and the United States signed a tougher version of the Great Lakes Water Quality Agreement of 1978. Although the Americans were reluctant to force coal-burning thermal energy plants to reduce emissions of the sulphur dioxide responsible for acidifying Canadian lakes, the U.S. Congress finally adopted, in 1990, the Clean Air Act. (A Canadian lobby group played a significant role in the bill's passage by bringing constant pressure to bear on American legislators.)

The battle for cleaner air and water involved tradeoffs. Publicly owned and heavily subsidized mines on Cape Breton Island produced high-polluting sulphurous coal, but closing them meant depriving miners of their livelihood. Pulp and paper mills polluted rivers and smelters poisoned the air, but they too provided jobs and revenues. In 1989, for example, Premier Bill Vander Zalm of British Columbia vetoed a cabinet proposal to reduce pulp and paper industry pollutants such as dioxins, declaring: "While I love the environment ... I also love those ... pulp mill workers and someone has to stand up for their jobs."

When provincial governments attempted to impose costly pollution controls, companies often resisted and threatened to shut down operations. When the Ontario government in the 1970s demanded that Inco, in Sudbury, reduce its acid rain–causing sulphur emissions (the region around Sudbury had come to resemble a lunar landscape), the company protested that jobs would be lost, production reduced, and investment postponed. Yet Inco installed new technology, reduced pollution substantially and, at the same time, became the world's lowest-cost nickel producer.

Conflicting economic and environmental preoccupations were also in evidence in regard to the problem of preserving some of what remained of Canada's wilderness. In the name of protecting biodiversity for future generations, the United Nations urged member states to set aside 12 percent of their territory, which would be off limits for industrial and commercial activities; protected areas should be representative of all natural regions in each jurisdiction. The Canadian government took one important step in this direction in 1986, when it created the huge Ellesmere Island National Park Reserve, Canada's 32nd national park, thus protecting a biologically unique ecosystem situated close to the North Pole. It remained for the provinces to act.

The 1960s have traditionally been viewed as a decade of rapid change. In many instances, however, changes begun in the 1960s continued and even accelerated during the 1970s and 1980s. The women's rights movement, for example, boasted important accomplishments in the course of these two decades. Gays and lesbians, linguistic minorities, and ethnic minorities also achieved greater equality in these years.

Political decisions brought significant change to Canadian society as well as to the country's economy. The Charter of Rights and Freedoms, part of the Canadian constitution proclaimed in 1982, enabled women and minority groups to challenge laws that, in their view, prevented them from attaining greater equality. Free trade created even closer trade relations with the United States and, in particular, signified rapidly rising exports for many Canadian producers.

As the 1980s closed, new challenges presented themselves. Regional differences and indeed rivalries became more apparent, and exercised a profound influence on federal politics. The federal government as well as most of the provinces were borrowing heavily to finance spending that greatly exceeded revenues. As the 1990s opened, Canadians would be faced with the unpleasant realities of cuts in services as governments struggled to bring budget deficits under control.

NOTES

1. Paul Phillips, *Regional Disparities* (Toronto: James Lorimer, 1982), pp. 118–19.

2. Sylvia Bashevkin, *Toeing the Lines: Women and Party Politics in English Canada*, 2nd ed. (Toronto: Oxford University Press, 1993), p. vi.

3. Raymond M. Hébert, *Manitoba's French-Language Crisis: A Cautionary Tale* (Montreal/Kingston: McGill-Queen's University Press, 2004), p. 208.

4. Robert Finbow, "Atlantic Canada: Forgotten Periphery in an Endangered Confederation?," in Kenneth McRoberts, ed., *Beyond Quebec: Taking Stock of Canada* (Montreal/Kingston: McGill-Queen's University Press, 1995), p. 67.

5. John Herd Thompson and Stephen J. Randall, *Canada and the United States: Ambivalent Allies*, 3rd ed. (Montreal/Kingston: McGill-Queen's University Press, 2002), p. 274.

6. Rianne Mahon, "Child Care as Citizenship Right? Toronto in the 1970s and 1980s," *Canadian Historical Review* 86 (2005): 285–315.

7. Paul Axelrod, *Scholars and Dollars: Politics, Economics, and the Universities of Ontario, 1945–1980* (Toronto: University of Toronto Press, 1982), pp. 141–78.

8. Michiel Horn, *Academic Freedom in Canada: A History* (Toronto: University of Toronto Press, 1999), p. 338.

9. Reginald Bibby, *Mosaic Madness: The Poverty and Potential of Life in Canada* (Toronto: Stoddart, 1990), p. 84.

10. David H. Flaherty and Frank E. Manning, eds., *The Beaver Bites Back? American Popular Culture in Canada* (Montreal/Kingston: McGill-Queen's University Press, 1993), p. 4.

BEYOND THE BOOK

Weblinks

North American Free Trade Agreement
http://www.dfait-maeci.gc.ca/nafta-alena/agree-en.asp
Full text of the North American Free Trade Agreement.

Media Coverage of the New Constitution, 1982
http://archives.cbc.ca/300c.asp?id=1-73-1092
Television archival footage of the journey to Canada's new constitution in 1982.

Brian Mulroney
http://archives.cbc.ca/IDD-1-73-1469/politics_economy/prime_ministers/brian_mulroney
A video retrospective of the political career of Brian Mulroney, Canada's prime minister for much of the 1980s.

Gay and Lesbian Rights in Canada: The 1970s
http://www.uwo.ca/pridelib/bodypolitic/gaylib/70stimeline.htm
A historical timeline of gay and lesbian rights and events in Canada over the 1970s.

Young Women in Canada in the 1970s and Today
http://www.swc-cfc.gc.ca/pubs/pubspr/0662388976/index_e.html
A comparative look at the economic characteristics and cultural behaviours of young women in the 1970s and early 21st century.

Films & Novels

Canada: A People's History—Episode 16: Brave New World. Directed by Janet Thomson. 2001.

RELATED READINGS

The following articles in R. Douglas Francis and Donald B. Smith, eds., *Readings in Canadian History: Post-Confederation*, 7th ed. (Toronto: Thomson Nelson Learning, 2006), are of relevance to this chapter: Will Kymlicka, "The Merits of Multiculturalism," pp. 502–10; and John Harles, "Multiculturalism, National Identity, and National Integration: The Canadian Case," pp. 511–31.

BIBLIOGRAPHY

Many books presented in the bibliography of Chapter 15 are also pertinent to the 1970s and 1980s. Links between demography and the economy are discussed in David K. Foot and Daniel Stoffman, *Boom, Bust and Echo: Profiting from the Demographic Shift in the 21st Century* (Toronto: Stoddart, 2000). Trade issues are discussed in Michael Hart, *A Trading Nation: Canadian Trade Policy from Colonialism to Globalization* (Vancouver: UBC Press, 2002). Stephen High studies industry closures in Ontario in *Industrial Sunset: The Making of North America's Rust Belt, 1969–1984* (Toronto: University of Toronto Press, 2003). Stephen Clarkson proposes a critical analysis of Canadian–American economic relations in *Canada and the Reagan Challenge*, 2nd ed. (Toronto: James Lorimer, 1985). Concerning the free-trade debate see Michael Hart, *Decision at Midnight: Inside the Canada–US Free-Trade Negotiations* (Vancouver: UBC Press, 1994); and Stephen J. Randall and Herman W. Konrad, eds., *NAFTA in Transition* (Calgary: University of Calgary Press, 1995). Mel Hurtig, *The Vanishing Country: Is It Too Late to Save Canada?* (Toronto: McClelland and Stewart, 2002) is a thoroughly negative appreciation. L. Ian MacDonald, *Free Trade: Risks and Rewards* (Montreal/Kingston: McGill-Queen's University Press, 2000), offers contemporary viewpoints.

Business history is presented in R.T. Naylor, *History of Canadian Business* (Montreal/Kingston: McGill-Queen's University Press, 2006). The energy question is discussed in G. Bruce Doern and Glen Toner, *The Politics of Energy* (Toronto: Methuen, 1985. On western agriculture see Grace Skogstad, *The Politics of Agricultural Policy-Making in Canada* (Toronto: University of Toronto Press, 1987); and Barry Wilson, *Farming the System: How Politicians and Producers Shape Canadian Agricultural Policy* (Saskatoon: Western Producer Prairie Books, 1990). Writings on the environment include G. Bruce and Thomas Conway, *The Greening of Canada: Federal Institutions and Decisions* (Toronto: University of Toronto Press, 1994); Chad Gaffield and Pam Gaffield, eds., *Consuming Canada: Readings in Environmental History* (Toronto: Copp Clark, 1995); Kathryn Harrison, *Passing the Buck: Federalism and Canadian Environmental Policy* (Vancouver: University of British Columbia Press, 1996; and Ken Drushka, *Canada's Forests: A History of Use and Conservation* (Montreal/Kingston: McGill-Queen's University Press, 2003).

Political issues are examined in Hugh G. Thorburn and Alain Whitehorn, eds., *Party Politics in Canada*, 8th ed. (Toronto: Prentice-Hall, 2001); and James Bickerton and Alain-G. Gagnon, *Canadian Politics*, 4th ed. (Peterborough, ON: Broadview Press, 2004). An excellent biography of Trudeau is Stephen Clarkson and Christina McCall, *Trudeau and Our Times*, vol. 1, *The Magnificent Obsession*; vol. 2, *The Heroic Delusion* (Toronto: McClelland & Stewart, 1990, 1994). On Trudeau's early years see John English, *Citizen of the World: The Life of Pierre Elliott Trudeau*, vol. I: *1919–1968* (Toronto: Knopf Canada, 2006). Guy Laforest, *Trudeau and the End of a Canadian Dream* (Montreal/Kingston: McGill-Queen's University Press, 1995), is a critical evaluation. Journalist Jeffrey Simpson has written a well-documented study of Joe Clark's brief government: *Discipline of Power: The Conservative Interlude and the Liberal Restoration* (Toronto: University of Toronto Press, 1996). Linda McQuaig offers a critical dissection of the Mulroney government in *The Quick and the Dead: Brian Mulroney, Big Business and the Seduction of Canada* (Toronto: Viking, 1991). Corruption and patronage are studied in Stevie Cameron, *On the Take: Crime, Corruption and Greed in the Mulroney Years* (Toronto: Macfarlane Walter & Ross,

1994). Mulroney tells his story in *Memoirs 1939-1993* (Toronto: Douglas Gibson Books, 2007). Works on the Canadian left include John Richards, Robert Cairns, and Larry Pratt, eds., *Social Democracy Without Illusions: Renewal of the Canadian Left* (Toronto: McClelland & Stewart, 1991); and Alan Whitehorn, *Canadian Socialism: Essays on the CCF-NDP* (Toronto: Oxford University Press, 1992). Judy Steed proves a sympathetic biographer in *Ed Broadbent: The Pursuit of Power* (Markham, ON: Viking, 1988).

Books on federal–provincial relations include David Milne, *Tug of War: Ottawa and the Provinces Under Trudeau and Mulroney* (Toronto: James Lorimer, 1986); Garth Stevenson, *Unfulfilled Union: Canadian Federalism and National Unity*, 4th ed. (Montreal/Kingston, McGill-Queen's University Press, 2004); and Richard Simeon and Ian Robinson, *State, Society, and the Development of Canadian Federalism* (Toronto: University of Toronto Press, 1990). Keith Banting and Richard Simeon, eds., *And No One Cheered: Federalism, Democracy and the Constitution Act* (Toronto: Methuen, 1983) presents a highly critical analysis of patriation. See also David Milne, *The Canadian Constitution: From Patriation to Meech Lake*, new ed. (Toronto: James Lorimer, 1989). On Ottawa–Edmonton relations in particular, see Paul Brunner, ed., *Lougheed and the War with Ottawa* (Edmonton: History Book Publications, 2003).

Robert Bothwell, *Alliance and Illusion: Canada and the World, 1945–1984* (Vancouver: UBC Press, 2007) is a recent study of Canada's foreign relations. J.L. Granatstein and Robert Bothwell, *Pirouette: Pierre Trudeau and Canadian Foreign Policy* (Toronto: University of Toronto Press, 1990), analyzes international affairs during Trudeau's tenure. On the Mulroney years see Nelson Michaud and Kim Richard Nossal, eds., *Diplomatic Departures: The Conservative Era in Canadian Foreign Policy* (Vancouver: UBC Press, 2001). Defence-related issues are examined in Ernie Regehr and Simon Rosenblum, eds., *The Road to Peace: Nuclear Weapons, Canada's Military Policies* (Toronto: James Lorimer, 1988); and Albert Legault and Michel Fortmann, *Diplomacy of Hope: Canada and Disarmament, 1945–1988* (Montreal/Kingston: McGill-Queen's University Press, 1992).

On higher education see Neil Tudiver, *Universities for Sale: Resisting Corporate Control over Canadian Higher Education* (Toronto: James Lorimer, 1999); and Paul Axelrod, *Values in Conflict: The University, the Marketplace, and the Trials of Liberal Education* (Montreal/Kingston: McGill-Queen's University Press, 2002). Studies of Canada's cultural originality include David H. Flaherty and Frank E. Manning, eds., in *The Beaver Bites Back? American Popular Culture in Canada* (Montreal/Kingston: McGill-Queen's University Press, 1993); and Ian Angus, *A Border Within: National Identity, Cultural Plurality, and Wilderness* (Montreal/Kingston: McGill-Queen's University Press, 1997). See also David M. Thomas, ed., *Canada and the United States: Differences That Count*, 2nd ed. (Peterborough, ON: Broadview Press, 2000). Daniel Francis explodes myths in his very readable *National Dreams: Myth, Memory, and Canadian History* (Vancouver: Arsenal Pulp Press, 1997). On institutions designed to favour the development of Canadian culture, see Marc Raboy, *Missed Opportunities: The Story of Canada's Broadcasting Policy* (Montreal/Kingston: McGill-Queen's University Press, 1990); and Richard Collins, *Culture, Communications, and National Identity: The Case of Canadian Television* (Toronto: University of Toronto Press, 1990). Canada's film industry is studied in George Melnyk, *One Hundred Years of Canadian Cinema* (Toronto: University of Toronto Press, 2004).

Informative studies of sports history include Donald Macintosh and David Whitson, *The Game Planners: Transforming Canada's Sport System* (Montreal/Kingston: McGill-Queen's University Press, 1990); Richard Gruneau and David Whitson, *Hockey Night in Canada: Sport, Identities, and Cultural Politics* (Toronto: Garamond, 1993); and Donald Macintosh and Michael Hawes, *Sport and Canadian Diplomacy* (Montreal/Kingston: McGill-Queen's University Press, 1994). Reginald W. Bibby proposes a provocative analysis of religion in the 1970s and 1980s in *Unknown Gods: The Ongoing Story of Religion in Canada* (Toronto: Stoddart, 1993).

On gays and lesbians see Becki L. Ross, *The House That Jill Built: A Lesbian Nation in Formation* (Toronto: University of Toronto Press, 1995); Miriam Smith, *Lesbian and Gay Rights in Canada: Social Movements and Equality-Seeking, 1971–1995* (Toronto: University of Toronto Press, 1999); and Tom Warner, *Never Going Back: A History of Queer Activism in Canada* (Toronto: University of Toronto Press, 2002). Valerie J. Korinek's research on one pioneer gay is available in "'The Most Openly Gay Person for at Least a Thousand Miles': Doug Wilson and the Politicization of a Province, 1975–83," *Canadian Historical Review* 84 (2003): 515–50.

An excellent synthesis on the history of women in Canada is Alison Prentice et al., *Canadian Women: A History*, 2nd ed. (Toronto: Harcourt Brace, 1996). The best treatment of women in unions is Julie White, *Sisters and Solidarity: Women and Unions in Canada* (Toronto: Thompson Educational Publishing, 1993). Among works on Canadian feminism see Nancy Adamson, Linda Briskin, and Margaret McPhail, *Feminist Organizing for Change: The Contemporary Women's Movement in Canada* (Toronto: Oxford University Press, 1988); Constance Backhouse and David H. Flaherty, eds., *Challenging Times: The Women's Movement in Canada and the United States* (Montreal/Kingston: McGill-Queen's University Press, 1992); Ruth Roach Pierson et al., *Canadian Women's Issues*, vol. 1, *Strong Voices*; vol. 2, *Bold Visions* (Toronto: James Lorimer, 1993, 1995); and Sylvia B. Bashevkin, *Women on the Defensive: Living Through Conservative Times* (Chicago: University of Chicago Press, 1998).

The evolution of Canada's welfare state is discussed in Raymond Blake and Jeff Keshen, eds., *Social Welfare Policy in Canada: Historical Readings* (Toronto: Copp Clark, 1995); and Raymond B. Blake, Penny E. Bryden, and J. Frank Strain, eds., *The Welfare State in Canada: Past, Present and Future* (Concord, ON: Irwin Publishing, 1997). Health-care issues are discussed in C. David Naylor, ed., *Canadian Health Care and the State: A Century of Evolution* (Montreal/Kingston: McGill-Queen's University Press, 1992); and Duane Adams, ed., *Federalism, Democracy, and Health Policy in Canada* (Montreal/Kingston: McGill-Queen's University Press, 2001). On housing, see Peter Ward, *A History of Domestic Space: Privacy and the Canadian Home* (Vancouver: UBC Press, 1999). Crime is addressed in D. Owen Carrigan, *Crime and Punishment in Canada: A History* (Toronto: McClelland & Stewart, 1991).

Chapter Twenty

CONTEMPORARY CANADA

TIME LINE

1991	Canadian troops participate in the Gulf War
1991	The NDP takes power in British Columbia and promises to support "sustainable development" policies
1992	A devastating explosion at the Westray mine in Pictou County, Nova Scotia kills 26 miners
1993	The Liberal government of Jean Chrétien takes office
1994	The North American Free Trade Agreement (NAFTA), linking Canada, the United States, and Mexico, comes into existence
1995	The Conservatives led by Mike Harris take power in Ontario and begin to implement the "Common Sense Revolution"
1997	Hibernia offshore oil platform towed into position 315 km off St. John's, Newfoundland Opening of the Confederation Bridge linking Prince Edward Island and New Brunswick
1998	British Columbia concludes treaty with Nisga'a First Nation The federal budget registers its first surplus in more than one-quarter of a century
2001	Terrorist attacks on New York City and Washington, DC
2002	Death of three important figures of Canada's cultural world: broadcaster Peter Gzowski, photographer Yousuf Karsh, and painter Jean-Paul Riopelle Canada sends combat troops to Afghanistan Canada ratifies the Kyoto Protocol (United Nations Framework Convention on Climate Change)
2003	Toronto shaken by a deadly outbreak of severe acute respiratory syndrome (SARS) virus Paul Martin replaces Jean Chrétien as Liberal party leader and prime minister
2006	The Conservative party defeats Paul Martin's Liberal minority government in elections; Stephen Harper takes office as prime minister

After the recession of the early 1990s, Canada's economy flourished, though regional imbalances were striking. Corporations improved their profits and business leaders were given handsome financial rewards. Most workers, however, saw their pay packets rise slowly, if at all, and adjustments to fierce global competition and then, after 2003, to a stronger Canadian dollar, cost many jobs, especially in manufacturing industries.

The free trade election of 1988 and the failure of the Meech Lake Accord in 1990 favoured the breakdown of political consensus. The Mulroney government's fortunes went from bad to worse. Voters showed more volatility, as old political loyalties broke down. From 1993 to 2000, a divided and regionalized opposition helped the Liberals led by Jean Chrétien to win three consecutive majorities in the House of Commons. After 1998, budgetary surpluses, the first in more than a quarter-century, made more activist government again possible. Then scandal, internal strife, and a resurgent and united Conservative opposition led by Stephen Harper, from Alberta, undermined the Liberal governments of Chrétien and his successor, Paul Martin, paving the way for a Conservative victory in federal elections held in 2006.

As the numbers of elderly Canadians increased and those of young Canadians fell, health care became a major concern, much more so than education. Expenditures on health represented a constantly increasing share of provincial budgets. Environmental issues also worried Canadians and they heatedly discussed climate change, its likely consequences, and what they could do about it.

Technological innovation continued apace after 1990. The phenomenal development of the Internet linked Canadians and the rest of the world more closely. Companies and governments could now process and move data with speeds and efficiency unimaginable scarcely a few years earlier. Individuals could send messages electronically, obtain information on any subject, pay bills, purchase goods and services, and amuse themselves. The computer age also brought new and serious challenges to citizens' rights to privacy.

In 1999, Research in Motion, a Canadian company, launched the BlackBerry, a handheld wireless device used by some businesses to provide email access to roaming employees. More and more Canadians acquired cellular phones; certainly they facilitated personal communication. Ringing cell phones were not so popular with teachers in classrooms, performers in concert halls, workers who did not want their bosses to be able to reach them 24 hours a day, and seatmates in buses and trains who preferred to read. Newer models of the phones could also be used to access the Internet, send text messages, watch movies and television, take pictures and videos, and play games. As one major service provider put it, "You'll be hooked!"

The Collapse of Consensus

The reelection of the Conservative government in 1988 soon brought about leadership changes in the two opposition parties. The NDP chose Audrey McLaughlin to succeed Ed Broadbent; she thus became the first woman to lead a federal political party. Jean Chrétien, a Quebecker who had occupied several cabinet posts under Trudeau, easily won the Liberal leadership in 1990, though his support in Quebec was weak due in part to his perceived insensitivity to Quebec's exclusion from the constitutional agreement of 1982.

After the election of 1988, the Conservatives soon plummeted to third place in the polls. Brian Mulroney joked that a small room now sufficed to bring together all his supporters. One journalist described the sour public mood: "The Mulroney government is … loathed and despised in most parts of the country." Scandals implicating cabinet ministers tarnished the government's image. Those who had fought free trade reviled Mulroney. Better-off Canadians complained when the government "clawed back" their family allowances and old-age pensions. The harsh budget of 1989, with its tax increases and, even more, the government's decision to replace the hidden manufacturers' sales tax with a fully visible goods and services tax (GST) of 7 percent, from January 1991, provoked vehement opposition. Other measures, such as cuts in subsidies to Via Rail and to the Canadian Broadcasting Corporation (CBC) as well as the privatizing of Crown corporations, also generated strong disapproval: critics accused Mulroney of dismantling national institutions. The deepening crisis in public finances limited the government's ability to respond to the demands placed on it.

High interest rates and much increased unemployment, particularly in the central provinces, only compounded the prevailing discontent. Recession descended upon Ontario in 1990 and the jobless rate rose dramatically, especially in manufacturing industries, construction, and retail sales. It would take until 1994 for that province to recover the jobs lost during the severe downturn. In 1990, after winning a stunning upset victory over the provincial Liberals, new NDP Premier Bob Rae cautioned against high expectations of radical change: "We can't just let 'er rip and hope that it'll work." Yet, when it brought down its first budget in 1991, the NDP government opted for a massive deficit of nearly $10 billion in an effort to counteract the deleterious effects of the recession on Ontario's economy. Rapidly rising welfare and interest payments on the debt contributed to successive large budget deficits. Rae raised taxes and imposed a stringent restraint program designed to control public-sector wages while protecting jobs: employees were to take unpaid holidays, baptized "Rae days." Unions condemned the measures. Popular support for the NDP collapsed, ensuring the government's defeat in 1995 not by the Liberals, as had been supposed, but by the Progressive Conservative party led by Mike Harris, who promised to implement a "Common Sense Revolution."

Ontarians also became increasingly critical of federal government policies. The provincial government had fought free trade proposals without success. It had vainly asked Ottawa to share the cost of higher welfare payments. Now Ontarians asserted that they were doing more than their share of shouldering the "burden of unity," pointing out that their taxes paid a large portion of the cost of the equalization grants, unemployment insurance, farm subsidies, and industrial-development projects that the federal government bestowed upon poorer provinces. In the words of political scientists David Cameron and Richard Simeon, Ontario was becoming a "not-so-friendly giant," with its own grievances to pursue, and its own interests to defend.[1]

For their part, western Canadians saw the Mulroney government as overly attuned to the interests of central Canada. The meteoric rise in popularity of the western-based Reform party after 1987 provided evidence of a powerful wave of dissatisfaction with the mainstream parties. Proclaiming that "the West wants in," the new party, led by Preston Manning, son of former Alberta Premier Ernest Manning, condemned the federal government's financial mismanagement, its "welfare-state approach" to meeting social needs, and its commitment to official bilingualism and multiculturalism as well as its immigration policy. It also opposed full gender equality, Aboriginal self-government, and civil rights for gays and lesbians. In the words of journalists Sydney Sharpe and Don Braid, "a hostile reaction to Quebec" contributed strongly to its rise.[2] Although the party soon toned down its West-oriented rhetoric in an effort to win support in Ontario and Atlantic Canada, Reform's major successes occurred in Alberta and British Columbia in the federal elections of 1993 and 1997.

Many Canadians outside Quebec also blamed Mulroney for the constitutional fiasco of the Meech Lake Accord, designed to bring Quebec to give its assent to the Constitution of 1982 (see Chapter 17). Within Quebec, support for sovereignty bounded upward in response to what most Quebeckers perceived as a rejection of the province's legitimate aspirations by Canadians outside Quebec. In Ottawa, several Conservative MPs from Quebec quit their party and formed a new grouping, the Bloc Québécois, committed to Quebec's independence.

The Conservatives tried again to achieve an agreement on constitutional reforms in 1991–92. This time, wide consultations took place before the federal, provincial, and territorial first ministers, and the heads of Aboriginal peoples' organizations met at Charlottetown in 1992 and agreed on proposals that attempted to respond to a host of agendas for change, including Senate reform and Aboriginal self-government. A referendum held in October 1992 saw the voters of six provinces, including Quebec, reject the agreement. A Decima poll showed that "Quebec got too much" was the most favoured reason for voting "no" outside that province; Quebeckers in turn said that they believed Quebec had obtained too little, noting in particular the gutted distinct-society clause. Constitutional change appeared dead for the foreseeable future.

Election of 1993

The federal election of 1993 underlined the importance of Canada's regional divisions. The Progressive Conservatives, now led by Kim Campbell, Canada's first woman prime minister, met with a defeat of precedent-setting proportions: only two of their candidates were elected. The Liberals won a majority, thanks in large part to Ontario. Their leader, Jean Chrétien, was the first French-speaking "old party" leader since Confederation to fail to take a majority of Quebec's seats. Quebec voters preferred to give their support to the Bloc Québécois, which became the official opposition in Parliament. Close behind came the West-based Reform party. Finally, the unpopularity of provincial NDP governments in Ontario and British Columbia contributed heavily to that party's dismal performance.

The Chrétien Government

Once in power, the Liberals accepted most of the Conservative policies it had censured while in opposition. The Chrétien government did not repeal the GST. It gave no indication that it was ready to let inflation rise, although during the campaign the Liberals had denounced the Conservative "obsession" with fighting rising prices. After vehemently criticizing free trade during the election campaign, it adopted the North American Free Trade Agreement (NAFTA) with the United States and Mexico.

In spite of a federal budget deficit that had climbed to a record $42 billion, the Liberal government did find money to launch a $6 billion infrastructure program, as it had promised during the election campaign. It sought instead to control other spending. It made very substantial cuts in grants to the provinces for health, education, and social welfare, worsening budget crises in several provinces and forcing them to make reductions in their own programs. It reduced unemployment benefits and tightened eligibility rules, provoking strong reaction among groups of workers concerned, particularly in eastern Canada. (Indeed, the federal election of 1997 saw the Atlantic region elect several NDP candidates to Parliament. It was the region's first significant experiment with third parties to convey dissatisfaction with the federal government. Prior to the election of 2000, the government retreated and eliminated rules that discouraged repeat users of employment insurance by reducing their benefits.) At the same time, it transferred into its general revenue fund most of the surplus that the employment insurance fund now accumulated because of high premiums and declining unemployment.

Government cuts to social programs signified the decline of the universal welfare state. Many Canadians regretted what they

Wilfrid Laurier took Canada into the twentieth century, and Jean Chrétien took Canada into the twenty-first.

Source: Canadian Press/Tom Hanson.

perceived as the disappearance of a widespread consensus on collective responsibility and shared risk. They blamed deficits not on excessive social spending but rather on the decreases in corporate taxation instituted by the Mulroney government and maintained by the Chrétien government. For policy critic and activist Maude Barlow, the Liberal government had become "the political agent of big business interests."

Ottawa spent less elsewhere, too. It froze civil servants' wages. It devoted less money to foreign aid. It slashed defence spending, making it necessary to cut short several peacekeeping missions for lack of soldiers and equipment. Canada's international reputation suffered.

Political Success

When Chrétien left office in late 2003, in part as a result of pressure from the more popular Paul Martin, his former finance minister and heir apparent, his political successes were evident. He had won three elections—1993, 1997, and 2000—each time with a majority of seats and about 40 percent of the votes. The opposition he faced in Parliament remained divided and regionalized. On the left, the NDP, led by Alexa McDonough from 1995 until 2003, and then by Jack Layton, searched for new credibility, as voter support dwindled. NDP activists said that the party had become irrelevant, and faulted it for having lost sight of its traditional labour and farmer constituencies and their priorities. In Quebec, after the referendum of 1995 on independence, the Bloc Québécois gradually weakened, as did sentiment for Quebec sovereignty generally.

Chrétien also benefited from disunity on the right, where two parties vied for conservative support. On the one hand, the old Progressive Conservatives attempted to regain lost popularity. On the other hand, the Reform party replaced the Bloc as the official opposition in 1997 but, even reconstituted as the Canadian Alliance in 2000 under a new leader, former Alberta government cabinet minister Stockwell Day, it failed to expand its influence beyond the West. Party strife accompanied by a precipitous decline in membership resulted in the selection of a new leader, Stephen Harper, a former Reform Party MP. While continuing to advocate fiscal conservatism, smaller government, and greater autonomy for the provinces, the Alliance also defended western positions such as opposition to federal gun registration and to environmental controls that might hurt the petroleum industry. At the same time it attempted to distance itself from the Reform Party's conservative views on abortion and gay rights. For many observers, the Alliance was simply experiencing the problems associated with any regionally based party attempting to widen its geographical base. More moderate Canadians preferred the centralist Liberals, particularly in Ontario, where the majority of Liberal seats were situated.

A lengthy list of costly administrative failures and mismanagement of public monies provoked strong criticism of the Liberal government. The auditor-general drew attention to billions of dollars of corporate taxes that went unrecovered, to questionable grants made by the Department of Human Resources, and to a firearms-registry program whose estimated costs of $100 million climbed to $1 billion. In addition, the government and even the prime minister were faulted for questionable ethics and political patronage. By the early 2000s, a strong majority of the population were telling pollsters that the Liberals were "arrogant and corrupt."

Still, voters proved ready to pardon Liberal faults. Chrétien appealed to many English-speaking Canadians for his uncompromising stand in regard to Quebec sovereignty. A prosperous economy also helped the party retain power. But the Liberal government could also boast of having finally brought order to government finances, certainly no mean feat after the failures of Trudeau and Mulroney. Thanks to spending cuts and especially to increased revenues from high taxation rates and economic growth, the federal budget finally registered a surplus in 1998. Additional surpluses enabled Ottawa to reduce income taxes, and to begin to pay down accumulated debt, which had now reached $580 billion.

Political Change

Chrétien's final months in power as well as Paul Martin's brief minority Liberal government were tarnished by the so-called "sponsorship scandal" (see Chapter 17). Daily revelations at a commission of inquiry both titillated and shocked observers. Although Martin denied knowledge of government corruption, voters, particularly in Quebec, were not inclined to pardon. Nor were conservative voters divided as they had been in previous elections. In 2003 the Progressive Conservative party agreed to merge with Stephen Harper's Canadian Alliance, to form a new Conservative party, of which Harper became leader. Harper's major challenge was to moderate Conservative rhetoric and positions. One biographer noted, Harper "has never been interested in implementing wrenching changes if it means doing lasting damage to Canadian conservatism's election chances."[3] In particular, the Conservative leader sought to appeal to voters in Ontario and even in Quebec, where the collapse of Liberal support offered new opportunity. In the campaign of 2006, Harper played to voters' anger at Liberal corruption, adopted a conciliatory stance in Quebec, and made just a few specific promises such as reducing the sales tax, providing money for child care, and adopting tougher laws against gun and gang violence in Canadian cities. He won the election and formed a minority government. For the moment, pragmatism rather than ideology seemed to govern his actions.

Hoping to obtain a majority in the next election, Harper now attempted to attract voters in populous central Canada without losing his base of support in the western provinces. He promised to redress the "fiscal imbalance" that, in the opinion of many provinces, was evidenced by huge federal surpluses and tight provincial budgets. In his government's budget in 2007, he announced substantial spending increases, with more money for the equalization grants that enable poorer provinces to provide services comparable to those offered by richer provinces. These grants pleased Quebec, a major recipient of equalization, but displeased certain other recipient provinces, such as Nova Scotia, Newfoundland and Labrador, as well as Saskatchewan, which complained that Ottawa would not allow them to keep all of their resource revenues without losing equalization. He devoted more money to health, education, and welfare, to be granted on a per capita basis, thus pleasing the wealthy and populous provinces of Ontario and Alberta, which stood to make significant gains. Ontario's Liberal government now claimed that it had won the long battle to obtain fairness in its treatment by Ottawa. Harper also announced new spending for public transit, notably in Toronto. Large budget surpluses enabled him to continue to pay down the national debt, with ensuing savings on interest payments. In addition, instead of reducing taxes for all taxpayers, he targeted in particular retirees and middle-income families in suburban Canada, groups often viewed as socially conservative. He also gave money to farmers, usually Conservative supporters. Moreover, Harper saw no urgent need to act to ensure a substantial reduction of climate-changing greenhouse gases; his reticence in this regard pleased Alberta, Canada's major producer of such gases, whose economic dynamism and wealth were so largely based on the highly polluting extraction of oil from tar sands.

The Conservatives also sought to build new strength in populous Quebec without producing a backlash in the rest of Canada. In 2006, Harper had Parliament adopt a resolution that declared that "Québécois" formed a "nation within a united Canada." The use of the word "nation" in regard to Quebec strongly displeased many English-speaking voters who said they believed in "One Canada," but it represented at least a symbolic recognition of Quebec's difference. Harper himself assured that the motion had no concrete meaning. Meanwhile the Liberals chose a new leader, Stéphane Dion, a Quebecker who had assisted Jean Chrétien during his battle against Quebec separatism and who commanded little support in Quebec. Harper's admission of the existence of a fiscal imbalance between Ottawa and the provinces, in contrast to the Liberals' refusal to do so, pleased Quebec, although Quebec wanted Ottawa to reduce tax rates, permitting the provinces to raise theirs, and to curtail federal spending in provincial areas of jurisdiction such as health, education, and social programs. Harper hoped, as Mulroney before him, to attract so-called "soft nationalists" in Quebec, those who rejected both the reputedly uncompromising Liberals and the Bloc Québécois, which sought secession. The increased equalization grants present in the budget of 2007 pleased Quebeckers, but ever-wary residents of other provinces denounced what they perceived as favoured treatment for Quebec. When Quebec's Liberal premier Jean Charest promised in the provincial election campaign that he would use some money from equalization to reduce taxes, Canadians in other provinces reacted furiously. One Toronto columnist warned that Charest's promise risked "bringing back Quebec-bashing as a national sport."

Canadian–American Relations

In the 1990s and early 2000s, Canada's trade links with the United States intensified. Exports to the United States increased substantially—86 percent of Canada's exports went there in 2000, stimulated by free trade and a depreciating Canadian dollar that, by 2002, had fallen to a mere 62 cents U.S. (As the "loonie" sank, some economists even called for Canada to adopt the American dollar as its official currency.) Huge quantities of Albertan oil and gas flowed south. Several provinces exported electricity. The automotive industry in southern Ontario sent most of its production south. Foreign ownership rose, and even business leaders expressed concern about the loss of head-office jobs to the United States.

Some sectors of Canada's economy were injured by American protectionist measures that limited imports. In 2002, for the fourth time since 1982, the United States imposed punitive anti-dumping and anti-subsidy duties on softwood lumber imports from Canada. Although Ottawa won virtually all the decisions rendered by NAFTA's dispute settlement body on the issue, Washington simply ignored the rulings. Canada then chose to negotiate. In a settlement reached in 2006, the United States agreed to return most, but not all, of the duties it had collected illegally since 2002. Canada promised to cap lumber exports and to impose export taxes in certain cases. With considerable reticence, Canada's forestry industry accepted the agreement, but the dispute, much publicized in Canada, embittered relations with the United States.

In spite of such disagreements, most Canadians supported trade liberalization. But critics contended that Canada had become dangerously dependent upon the United States and had lost control over its own resources. Indeed, when British Columbia placed a moratorium on bulk water exports in 1999, the California firm that wanted to import fresh water by tanker sued the federal government for $10 billion under NAFTA's investment provisions; the case is still pending. Trade treaties with the United States signified, according to political scientist Stephen Clarkson, that "the provincial and federal governments are handcuffed in all the policy fields of concern to U.S. corporate interests."[4] Mel Hurtig, a tireless advocate of an independent Canada, titled a new book *The Vanishing Country*.

Globalization

Some Canadians joined critics across the world in denouncing the new global economic order, propelled by technological innovation, that stripped their governments of their sovereign powers. In their view, governments were abdicating control to market forces through privatization, deregulation, and expenditure reduction. Multinational corporations now dwarfed many national governments in size. Increased global competition risked favouring reduced standards, resulting in increased poverty, diminished government services, weaker labour laws, swamped local cultures, and fewer environmental controls. Globalization, they argued, entailed more golden arches and branded clothing and footwear, while ignoring the real needs of citizens. However, globalization also had its defenders, who asserted that open trading nations tended to have higher labour and environmental standards than closed ones.

Canadian nongovernmental organizations played an important role in opposing globalization, often at international conferences where world trade and investment issues were discussed. These themes were given wide publicity in the protests and teach-ins held during the Free Trade Area of the Americas (FTAA) summit in Quebec City, in April 2001. Police cordoned off a large part of the old city with a high security steel-and-concrete fence, and used tear gas and plastic bullets to disperse demonstrators.

Terrorism

The terrorist attacks in the United States on September 11, 2001, which resulted in the deaths if some 3000 people, including 25 Canadians, had profound effects on Canada, too. When American media figures and politicians portrayed Canadian border security as lax, Ottawa felt a need to prove otherwise in order to protect jobs and investment. The government's response was far-reaching and multifaceted. It improved aviation and airport security, and invested heavily in increased border security. It announced more spending on police and intelligence agencies, and adopted an antiterrorism bill that gave new powers of investigation and detention to law-enforcement authorities. Civil libertarians decried certain of its provisions, such as preventive detention and compulsory testimony during investigative hearings. These provisions were never used and the Conservatives failed to obtain Liberal support to renew them in 2007; they then accused the Liberals of being "soft on terrorism." In a related issue, the Supreme Court held that so-called security certificates, by which immigrants suspected of being involved in terrorist activities might be imprisoned indefinitely without trial while not being informed of the case against them, were unconstitutional. Critics asserted that the country's security laws were in need of wholesale revision to ensure that Canada could face eventual terrorist threats while still protecting civil liberties.

In one highly publicized case that showed how fears of terrorism might erode citizens' basic rights, Maher Arar, a Canadian born in Syria, was detained by American authorities while changing planes in New York in 2002. Instead of then being sent to Canada (he was travelling on a Canadian passport), he was forcibly deported to Syria, where he was tortured and imprisoned in a tiny cell for almost a year. To justify their action, American authorities invoked intelligence reports, later shown to be inaccurate, received from the RCMP. Canadian diplomats in Syria relayed the substance of Arar's purported confessions to Ottawa but made no reference to the fact that torture might be occurring. After Arar's return to Canada, some police and government officials made deliberate attempts to smear Arar's reputation by leaking false information to the media. The Martin government then set up a public inquiry that absolved Arar of suspicion of any involvement in terrorist activities. The RCMP commissioner resigned in the face of contradictions in his own testimony, Arar was awarded compensation for his ordeal, and Stephen Harper issued an official apology on behalf of the Canadian government. For its part, the United States refused to admit any wrongdoing and kept Arar's name on a terrorist watch list.

Ottawa also took measures to improve infrastructure aimed at accelerating the flow of commercial traffic across the Canada–United States border. But a plan to establish a North American security perimeter and to harmonize Canadian visa requirements with those of the United States raised fears that Canada's sovereignty was in danger. The same fears were expressed when military planners evoked the possibility of integrating Canadian forces with those of the United States for North American defence. Canada, however, could do nothing to stop the United States from requiring all persons crossing the border, including returning Americans, to present a passport. It was thought that this measure would further deter Americans from travelling to Canada.

Defence

Proud Canadians had traditionally viewed peacekeeping as one of their country's core values. In 1991, Canada contributed fully 10 percent of peacekeeping troops to United Nations missions. Its armed forces possessed important expertise in peacekeeping. By the 2000s, this image had become a myth, as few Canadian peacekeepers remained. In 2006, the Conservative government announced that huge amounts of money would be spent to upgrade military equipment and increase the armed forces' capabilities. For the government, Canada's new military objective was to be able to fight terrorist insurgencies militarily and show leadership in the world community. "You can't lead from the bleachers," warned prime minister Harper.

Already, in 2002, Canada had agreed to deploy 850 combat troops to Afghanistan to serve under American control. By 2007, some 2500 of Canada's soldiers were fighting in that country, mostly in the perilous southern region of Kandahar. The hugely costly deployment was Canada's largest since the Korean War, and 70 soldiers had already lost their lives. Then, after minimal debate in Parliament, the Conservative government extended the mission to 2009. To mollify public opinion, it gave the assurances that Canadian troops also played humanitarian roles, delivering aid supplies, medical treatment, and other services, and it committed money for development projects.

The United Nations had authorized the invasion of Afghanistan after the terrorist attacks in 2001. However, when American and British troops invaded Iraq in March 2003 without UN authorization, the Chrétien

Canadian peacekeepers, part of the large Canadian force in Bosnia in 1998.

Source: Department of National Defence.

government refused to participate. Most Canadians, especially in Quebec, approved his decision. Later, the Liberal government of Paul Martin announced that Canada would not participate in the antiballistic missile defence system that the United States wished to set up. The business community feared that American anger toward Canada would hurt trade, but this proved unfounded. In any case, rising opposition to the policies of the Bush administration within the United States deflected criticism from foreign countries.

Regional Imbalances

The early 1990s were difficult years for almost all the provinces; most suffered an economic recession that had a negative impact on their budgets. Severe cuts in federal transfers only exacerbated financial problems. Balancing budgets involved painful choices and unhappy voters often reacted negatively to declining services and higher taxes. In several provinces, they turned governments out of office and elected new ones.

Canadian soldiers carry the bodies of two fellow soldiers killed in Afghanistan into a C-130 Hercules aircraft for repatriation to Canada.

Source: Department of National Defence, Combat Camera, AR2006-G017-0010.

By the mid-1990s, the economies of most regions had improved. Oil brought significant new revenues to Newfoundland and Nova Scotia. Central Canada's manufacturing firms churned out goods for the voracious American market. In the West, the exploitation and sale of natural resources brought prosperity. Then, after 2002, the rising Canadian dollar, described as a "petro-dollar" by economists because it was pushed upwards in part by higher oil prices, curtailed manufacturing exports by making them more expensive. Rising energy costs also hurt industry, offset to some degree by significant increases in manufacturing productivity. Major American automobile makers closed plants in Ontario but losses were compensated by gains from new factories opened by Toyota and other foreign manufacturers. Forestry registered significant job losses, as a result of slowing home construction in the United States. Western Canada, for its part, basked in prosperity, thanks to expensive oil.

Newfoundland and Labrador

On May 9, 1997, politicians and business people gathered at Bull Arm, northwest of St. John's, to christen the new Hibernia offshore oil production platform, which had been built with government and private money at a cost of $6 billion. The festive occasion was marred by a demonstration by hundreds of unemployed fishery workers, protesting against Ottawa's compensation program for the collapsed cod fishery. That event seemed to dramatize the contrast between the Newfoundland of yesterday, a province of low incomes and a slowly dying fishing industry, and the Newfoundland of tomorrow, richer and more developed.

Employment in the fishing industry attained a peak in 1988 of 90 000 jobs. Then, in the early 1990s, cod stocks, hitherto thought to be inexhaustible, declined precipitously as a result of overfishing, both domestic and foreign, and possibly, too, because of environmental factors. Destruction of the cod was cited in international scientific literature as a classic example of biological catastrophe. Ironically, Canada had been the first industrialized nation to ratify the United

Premier Robert Grimes and Governor General Adrienne Clarkson with the document that renames Canada's easternmost province, Newfoundland and Labrador, December 2001.

Source: CP Picture Archive/Fred Chartrand.

Nations Convention on Biological Diversity negotiated at the Earth Summit in Rio de Janeiro in 1992. From 1992 until 1998, Ottawa imposed a moratorium on catches. In 2003, as fish stocks did not recover, the federal government moved toward total closure of the fisheries. During the moratorium, Ottawa launched a five-year, $1.9 billion compensation plan to eliminate jobs. It later injected another $730 million into a program to buy back fishing licences. Layoffs reached 30 000. Shrimp and crab provided a lucrative replacement for a certain number of fishers. Others emigrated. Many in distant outports had only welfare to fall back upon.

The exploitation of natural resources represented a substantial share of Newfoundland's economy. Major hydroelectric projects were planned in Labrador. Another mega-project involved the development of huge nickel deposits at Voisey's Bay, in northern Labrador. In 2002, as nickel prices rose, agreement was finally reached between Inco and the province whereby Inco promised compensation and jobs for Native communities, and agreed to build a smelter at Argentia to process ore within the province. Production began in 2007. It was estimated that the mine and the smelter would increase the province's gross domestic product by fully 80 percent and create 2400 jobs. Such jobs were welcome, but Newfoundland needed far more to put its population to work and end out-migration. Oil and gas did not create large numbers of local jobs. Even so, resource revenues, when added to federal equalization payments, made it possible for the province to spend more per person on services than Ontario, whose wealth excluded it from equalization grants.

Maritime Provinces

High levels of unemployment also afflicted Nova Scotia, Prince Edward Island, and New Brunswick. Still, there were bright spots. In Nova Scotia, the building of the $2 billion Sable Island natural gas pipeline gave a strong boost to the construction industry, and offshore exploration continued. The Conference Board of Canada evoked bright prospects for further development, with the creation of nearly 60 000 new jobs by 2020. Prince Edward Island's economy benefited from the construction of the 13-km-long Confederation Bridge, opened in 1997. The "fixed link" across Northumberland Strait to New Brunswick stimulated tourism, a major industry on the island, and local agriculture now benefited from lower transportation costs. Job creation was also a priority for New Brunswick's Liberal government, headed by Frank McKenna. In the early 1990s, expansion in the food-processing industry, new power plants, and more service-related jobs in sectors such as telecommunications helped compensate for employment losses in the forest industry and in federal government services. In particular, the "energizer premier," as one newspaper nicknamed McKenna, proved particularly adroit at attracting telephone call centres to the province, though other provinces accused him of luring away their jobs.

Ontario and the "Common Sense Revolution"

Ontario's economy boomed after the mid-1990s, thanks to low interest rates, a dynamic U.S. economy that imported goods made in Ontario, especially automobiles, and a low Canadian dollar that favoured exports. Conservative premier Mike Harris reduced provincial income taxes substantially—the highlight of his "Common Sense Revolution." To finance lower tax rates, he imposed radical spending cuts in education, health services, and welfare as well as substantial increases in university tuition costs. These measures caused considerable protest. Then the province took control of public education funding, partly removing financing from municipally levied, residential property taxes. In return, new responsibilities were devolved upon municipalities, including welfare, child care, care for the elderly, social housing, health programs, and public transit. The government also introduced a new market-value property tax assessment system, and it ordered the merger of Metro Toronto's six municipalities. These measures provoked some of the most acrimonious debates in the province's history among prospective winners and losers.

Business praised the Harris government for restoring competitiveness by lowering taxes and for favouring globalization and increased economic integration with the United States. In economist Thomas Courchene's words, Ontario was no longer a mere province, it had become, thanks in part to Harris, "a North American region state."[5] But critics of the "Common Sense Revolution" accused the Conservative government of favouring the growth of social inequalities within the province and of dealing a harsh blow to the quality of public services.

The West

Free trade boosted Manitoba's exports to the United States in the 1990s. New markets opened for industrial products. Large construction projects also produced economic stimulus. By early 1999, Manitoba enjoyed Canada's lowest unemployment rate. Saskatchewan boasted impressive economic growth in the 1990s, assisted by strong oil and gas prices. Then, in the late 1990s, the elimination of grain subsidies in addition to low prices for grain and oil seed provoked a serious farm crisis in both Saskatchewan and Manitoba. After repeated calls for help from angry grain farmers, Ottawa finally agreed to give $400 million in assistance in 2000. Drought and competition from heavily subsidized American farmers brought further difficulties.

Alberta's abundant oil revenues gave it financial latitude that other provinces lacked. The government reduced income taxes to a flat rate of 10 percent for all workers and, one year, gave every Albertan a prosperity dividend. It eliminated the provincial debt. It increased public spending substantially, even subsidizing homes and businesses to protect them from increasing electricity and natural gas costs. It granted large wage increases to health and education personnel, thereby putting heavy pressure on neighbouring, less-favoured provinces. It earmarked billions of dollars for new schools, hospitals, bridges, and roads. By 2002, Alberta was spending more per capita on publicly financed programs than any other province. And still the province registered huge budget surpluses. It also boasted virtually full employment.

Alberta's boom did have a downside. A serious shortage of skilled labour threatened energy projects and drove up prices. Entrepreneurs in low-wage businesses found it difficult to find and retain workers. Real-estate prices made even Vancouver look affordable. Calgary's vacancy rate for rental accommodation was Canada's lowest. Growth also put tremendous pressure on infrastructure as well as on the environment.

In British Columbia, massive inflows of investment as well as large numbers of new immigrants, mainly from Asia, helped maintain an economic boom after 1990 while the rest of Canada slid into recession. Trade with Asia increased rapidly. Economic diversification continued, as new service-sector jobs, many related to tourism, more than compensated for the loss of employment in the primary sector.

The late 1990s saw British Columbia struggle with hard times. Lost markets due to Asia's faltering economy, punitive American trade policies, rising international competition, and low prices brought sawmill closures and job losses. Fortunately tourism, the film industry, business services, and high-technology industries continued to show promise. Then, after 2000, soaring trade with China, especially the sale of natural resources such as coal, minerals, and lumber, brought new prosperity to the province. The securing of the Winter Olympics of 2010 assured a booming construction industry.

Population

Continued high levels of immigration explained most of Canada's population growth after 1990. The census of 2006 showed that Canadians numbered 31.6 million, an increase of more than 10 million over 1971. Between 2001 and 2006, the country grew more rapidly than the United States, and far more rapidly than most European countries or Japan. Fully 80 percent of Canadians now lived in urban centres, and nearly one-half of them in just three areas: Toronto and the Golden Horseshoe region of southern Ontario, Montreal, and Vancouver. Many rural areas and centres based on the exploitation of resources lost population, as local sawmills and other industries closed. Alberta's population increased particularly rapidly during the 1990s and 2000s, as workers from other provinces flooded into the province in search of high-paying job opportunities. Indeed, in the space of just ten years, the province grew by 20 percent. The cost of housing climbed dramatically, and serious labour shortages developed in many occupations.

Fort McMurray, Alberta was one city that saw prodigious growth. Between 1999 and 2006 its population doubled to 80 000. Many new residents came from Newfoundland, a province whose population had been declining since 1986. The city boasted a Newfoundlanders Club with walls adorned with heartwarming photographs of Cape Spear, outports, and rocky shorelines. Median family income in Fort McMurray was $120 000, the highest in Canada. But new homes cost more than $500 000, and many newcomers had to stay in campgrounds and work camps. Municipal funds were insufficient to enable the city's overburdened infrastructure and existing services to keep pace with the population boom.

Ontario, British Columbia, and Quebec also saw substantial population gains, celebrated by boosters in the media, in government, and in business. There were few discussions of what an ideal population for Canada might be, and whether "healthy growth" in the numbers of Canadians, with their typically heavy impact on the environment and high consumption of resources, might take Canada even further away from the goal of sustainable development.

Cities and Suburbs

By 2006, Canada had become one of the most highly urbanized nations on the planet. Many people chose to live in the condominiums and highrise apartment buildings that altered the landscape of the inner suburbs or formed part of huge redevelopment projects in once-derelict port and industrial districts such as Vancouver's False Creek and Toronto's Harbourfront. But most preferred to inhabit the sprawling satellite communities that surrounded large cities. Costly infrastructures such as roads and sewer lines were necessary to serve these communities, and the use of automobiles was essential to commute to work or to find access to services. Most Canadians agreed that traffic was worsening. Vancouver's bridges and tunnels were famed for their spectacular traffic jams. By 2000, the Fraser Valley had become one of the most polluted airsheds in Canada, as toxic smog from Vancouver funnelled directly into the area.

Toronto's expressways were often congested even at off-peak times and the region had the country's longest average commute time. Dire predictions were made that by 2025, with three million new residents, drivers in the Greater Toronto Area would be facing total gridlock. Mayors across Canada appealed for more government investment in buses, streetcars, subways and light rail lines, but suburban sprawl made public transit inefficient and often prohibitively costly.

New ideas to meet these challenges were put forth. Some Vancouverites proposed redesigning their city to increase population density, ensuring fewer cars and less resource consumption, and to turn it into a model of urban sustainability. Higher density made public transit more viable. In 2006, Ontario announced its "Places to Grow" plan which aimed to reduce sprawl, protect farmland, and make better use of existing infrastructure. The plan favoured more compact living and the building of communities where people could live, work, shop and play without needing a car. Yet residents typically fought plans to bring more people into their neighbourhoods, and developers did not want governments to tell them where and what to build.

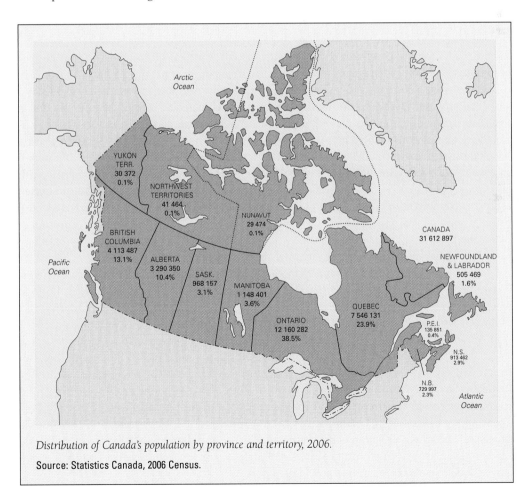

Distribution of Canada's population by province and territory, 2006.

Source: Statistics Canada, 2006 Census.

An Aging Population

While birth rates plummeted, advances in medicine and a decline in tobacco use enabled Canadians to live longer. By 2004, purportedly more robust females could expect to live to live to age 82.6. Males could anticipate reaching only 77.8, but they could at least congratulate themselves for having eliminated, over the preceding quarter-century, a large part of the gap in life expectancies that separated them from females. Canadian society began to age rapidly. By the turn of the century, the over-65s numbered 13 percent of the population—a figure well above the 8 percent criterion used by the United Nations to signify an aging population. Population changes by age group revealed Canada's greying future: while the number of preschoolers aged 0 to 4 decreased by 11 percent, seniors aged 70 to 79 increased by 27 percent, and older seniors by 41 percent.

In the 1990s, baby boomers embarked on a collective midlife crisis. In quest of their youth, some male boomers turned to Viagra and hair dye, while female boomers bought cosmetics to iron out the wrinkles. The "flower power" of the 1960s and 1970s now yielded to "grey power," forcing politicians to heed the concerns of seniors. Not surprisingly, more conservative attitudes asserted themselves. Education, emphasized so strongly in the 1960s and 1970s as the baby boomers passed school, now had to share much of the attention (and the funding) with issues of particular interest to older Canadians, among them pensions and especially health care.

Health Care

Most Canadians agreed, perhaps reluctantly, that certain entitlement programs such as old age pensions and assistance to families should be transformed in order to target benefits increasingly to specific groups of needy and vulnerable individuals, such as low-income parents. But for a large majority, universal publicly funded health care was sacred, a defining feature of Canada that distinguished it from the United States, where health care, largely in private hands, was expensive and often inefficient and coverage blatantly unequal. In the early 1980s, increasing hospital user fees and extra billing by doctors led to fears that reasonable access to public health care was threatened. Canadians applauded the Canada Health Act, adopted by Parliament with all-party support in 1984, which penalized such practices. In the 1990s, in an effort to curtail sharply expanding health costs, some provinces sought to increase the role of the private sector. Private clinics offered tests to patients who agreed to pay cash. During the election campaign of 2000, the governing Liberals surely helped their cause by assuring anxious citizens that there would be no two-tier public–private system if they were reelected.

Yet the health system was obviously in a state of crisis. In the late 1990s and early 2000s, dissatisfaction mounted as waiting lists for diagnostic tests and surgery lengthened, hospital emergency wards were overwhelmed, drug costs soared, services were disinsured, and shortages of doctors and nurses developed. The public tended to blame provincial governments, responsible for administering the system, but diminished federal grants were also a factor. In the late 1990s, improved public finances enabled governments to put more money into health care, but the crisis deepened. Asked by the federal government to report on the health-care system, Roy Romanow, a former provincial premier, urged in 2002 that the public health-care system be retained, reinforced, and expanded. Private providers of medical services were to be excluded. Ottawa agreed to inject billions of dollars to fund primary care, home care, and catastrophic drug care, but sought to hold provinces accountable for the manner in which they spent federal monies. Later the Martin government folded all its payments into a Canadian Health Transfer, and removed the requirement that provinces report.

Was Canada's health system financially sustainable in the long term? Doubts grew. New medical technologies and equipment made their appearance; while they made it possible to perform miracles, they were often very costly.

Preventive health measures became less popular during the 1990s. Rather than eat broccoli and tofu and drink fruit juices and low-fat milk, more people preferred the fare of the fast-food restaurants: triple hamburgers with cheese, large fries, and a large drink. The Canadian Institute of Child Health reported that teens, in the 1990s, consumed more soft drinks than milk. Not surprisingly, by 2000, one-half of the adult population and one-third of children were overweight. Sedentary and overweight Canadians increasingly fell victim to such chronic diseases as diabetes. By 2007, nearly one Canadian in ten, including large numbers of South Asian immigrants and Aboriginal Canadians, suffered from the illness—which could be treated, though at great cost.

An aging population also needed more care. British Columbia predicted that the number of seniors would double within 25 years. Its minister of health confessed that he went to bed each night "thanking the stars" that he was minister now and not in 25 years. Cancers occurred far more frequently among the elderly. Lung cancer in particular continued to kill large numbers of Canadians, usually a legacy of their addiction to tobacco. The Canadian Cancer Society called for a national strategy to reduce prevalence of the disease, and asserted that half of all cancer deaths were preventable. Many elderly people fell ill with the dreaded Alzheimer's disease, a degenerative disease of the brain that causes thinking and memory to become severely impaired. No cure existed, but nursing home care and medication for the half-million Canadians afflicted cost more than $5 billion each year.

Provincial health budgets increased, but chronic underfunding persisted. After a contaminated water supply made hundreds of residents sick and resulted in the deaths of seven persons in Walkerton, Ontario in the summer of 2000, a judicial inquiry laid part of the responsibility on a lack of government controls, due to spending cuts. Then, in 2003, an outbreak of severe acute respiratory syndrome (SARS) virus in Toronto resulted in 44 deaths and had serious consequences for the city's and, indeed, Canada's economy. A commission of inquiry concluded that Ontario's public health system "lacked adequate resources, was professionally impoverished and was generally incapable of fulfilling its mandate." It was necessary to spend even more on health. But would increased public health-care funding not risk crowding out spending in other important areas such as education and the environment? Could health care continue to be financed without more private-sector delivery of services?

Poverty

Poverty was another important social problem that did not lend itself to easy solutions. As unemployment grew during the recession of 1990, rising demand overwhelmed food banks in urban areas. Canadian cities also saw the emergence of a homeless class that included refugees, people with mental and physical disabilities, Native people, single mothers with children, youth, and substance abusers. In some cases, the new homeless had been evicted by developers who then renovated and upgraded dwellings before selling them to more affluent individuals. Increasingly, however, provincial spending cuts to welfare and social housing were seen as primary causes. In 1998, in a highly political move, the city of Toronto declared homelessness a national disaster and sought disaster-relief funds.

After 2000, economic growth and reduced unemployment did contribute to reducing poverty, as the proportion of Canadians defined as poor declined from nearly 16 percent in 1996 to 11 percent in 2004. Yet poverty remained very much present in Canadian cities. Vancouver's Downtown East Side, an area of decrepit boarding houses, sleazy bars, and boarded-up shops, was plagued with Canada's highest rates of poverty and drug addiction. In Calgary, the numbers of homeless increased and shelters overflowed. The Calgary Homeless Foundation and other groups brought forth a ten-year plan to build affordable lodging and to provide services to treat persons dependent on drugs or who suffered from mental illness.

Gays and Lesbians

By the 1990s, gays had obtained legal protection from discrimination. Laws changed slowly, and opposition, particularly from conservative religious groups, was substantial. The AIDS crisis of the 1980s, by attracting public attention and, finally, increased sympathy for the gay community, may have facilitated the passage of new laws. In 1999, a verdict of the Supreme Court of Canada compelled Alberta, the last province, to ban discrimination.

Gays and lesbians now turned their attention to obtaining recognition for same-sex unions. In 1995 the Supreme Court of Canada had ruled that the Charter of Rights and Freedoms prohibited discrimination against gays and lesbians. A series of court challenges established that gay couples possessed many of the rights and duties of married couples, and laws were rewritten to reflect this in such areas as spousal support, pension rights, adoption, and medical decision making. In 1997, British Columbia became the first province to amend laws to extend legal recognition to same-sex relationships. In 2002, Quebec extended full legal recognition to same-sex common-law unions, and in 2003, Ontario courts ruled that prohibiting gays and lesbians from marrying violated the equality provisions of the Charter of Rights and Freedoms. By 2005, when the federal government drafted legislation to change the definition of a marriage from a union between a man and a woman to a union between two persons, only the Alberta government remained officially opposed to gay marriage; premier Ralph Klein even suggested holding a nationwide referendum on the issue. During the election campaign of 2006, the Conservative party, most of whose candidates opposed same-sex marriage, promised to revisit the issue. When the Conservatives took power, they introduced a motion asking that the question of same-sex marriage be reopened to support the traditional definition of marriage. In a free vote, most MPs from all three opposition parties combined to defeat the motion. The new definition of marriage would stand.

Religious institutions were free to decide whether to perform marriage ceremonies for same-sex couples. The United Church of Canada authorized local congregations and clergy to choose whether to offer same-sex marriage services. Many did. The issue provoked heated debate within the Anglican church, and the worldwide Anglican communion faced a schism over the question. Some liberal Jewish congregations also agreed to welcome same-sex unions. The Roman Catholic church, Canada's largest Christian church, vigorously opposed the government's legislation; one bishop even called on the government to outlaw homosexuality.

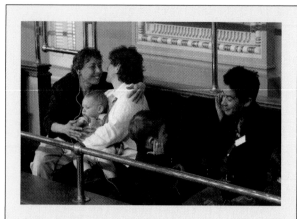

Quebec in 2002 extended full parental rights to homosexual couples. Same-sex couples also gained the same status and obligations of heterosexual married couples when they entered into a civil union. Lesbians rejoice as the Quebec National Assembly passes the law.

Source: CP Picture Archive/Tom Wells.

Women in the Work Force

As larger numbers of women took jobs outside the home, governments were called upon to make day-care facilities more affordable and available. Quebec set up a system of publicly supported centres in which parents paid just $5 a day per child; the popular system proved costly for taxpayers, and waiting lists were long, although new places were added rapidly. Across Canada, there were far more families with preschool children than there were spaces in licensed day-care centres. Women workers with small children were sometimes made to feel guilty about their choices. Newfoundland's minister of social services told lobbying women that the province needed "more conscientious mothers to sacrifice their careers and stay home to take care of their children."

Pay Equity

The notion of equal pay for work of equal value, or pay equity, became the battleground of the 1990s, as women argued that they were generally paid less than men for jobs requiring similar skills, effort, responsibility, and educational levels, and entailing similar working conditions. Ottawa and some provinces instituted pay equity laws, but the NDP government of Premier Bob Rae in Ontario went much further by forcing employers to compare the value of the work being done in their male- and female-dominated work categories and then to increase the wages of any women who, according to the results of the comparisons, were being underpaid. Reactions were predictable: the male-dominated business community expressed considerable hostility, while the one-million-member Equal Pay Coalition was disappointed that the measure did not cover casual workers and women working in small enterprises or in all-female establishments. Some provinces failed to bring in legislation to guarantee pay equity. The Supreme Court permitted the Newfoundland government to deny female public servants pay equity because of budgetary constraints.

The growing conservatism of the 1990s and early 2000s had implications for women. In Ontario, for example, the Conservative government led by Mike Harris, which took office in 1995, repealed certain elements of the pay equity legislation adopted by the previous NDP government. Women judged that government budget cuts in health, welfare, and poverty-relief programs hit them disproportionately. The armed forces' plans to recruit, train, and keep a large percentage of women in their ranks failed. In the House of Commons, only 20 percent of members elected in 2006 were women. In other sectors, there was progress. Sixty percent of university students were women, and women outnumbered men in all fields except engineering and math. (Observers now began to worry about the increasing number of male dropouts.) *Women in Canada 2000*, a report prepared by Statistics Canada, showed that the gap between higher men's pay and lower women's pay decreased substantially between 1985 and 1995. By 2000, women occupied about one-third of managerial positions, usually on lower rungs, but only 10 percent of corporate directors were women. Half of the doctors and dentists were women, and nearly half of the new lawyers and accountants. A gender-studies specialist commented, "Women have taken on men's roles, but men have not taken on to the same degree the roles of women." Not surprisingly, women experienced increased levels of stress and even depression as they attempted to hold down jobs while raising families.

Challenges for Labour

The 1990s proved difficult for unionized workers. The elimination of positions by governments at all levels, as they tried to reduce expenditures and balance budgets, led to layoffs, wage freezes, and even wage cuts. In Ontario, Premier Mike Harris acted to reduce the number of public servants, hospital workers, and teachers. These cuts and others provoked "Days of Action" protests led by organized labour against "Mean Mike" and his policies. In Alberta, Ralph Klein, a former mayor of Calgary chosen as new Conservative party leader and premier in 1992, instituted a policy of radical budget cuts to social spending and the civil service that produced a balanced budget by 1995. Real program expenditures fell by more than one-quarter.

Private-sector unions fared no better. Many high-paying manufacturing jobs disappeared as companies "rationalized" their operations, and union membership again declined. New contracts often imposed wage rollbacks, or pegged wages to profitability, or brought a reduced pay scale for new employees. The recession of the early 1990s undermined the bargaining power of unions and thus sharply reduced the number of work stoppages. Unions themselves were often torn by internal strife.

Recruitment again increased in the late 1990s, reversing a downward trend, thanks in part to an improving economy. By 2002, one-third of Canadian workers were unionized. Quebec and Newfoundland were the most unionized provinces, Alberta and Ontario the least. In Ontario, many unionized jobs disappeared in the automobile industry, as General Motors and Ford announced plant closures, while non-unionized Toyota built new factories. Private-sector unions felt themselves under attack by the forces of globalization and cutthroat competition. Moreover most of these unions were still based in the United States, and were often unresponsive to the needs of their Canadian membership. Labour attempted to reinvent itself, and to appeal to employees who now sought stress relief, schedules that did not disrupt family life, and greater control over their careers. Unions sought new members where they could find them. The United Steelworkers, for example, diversified into call centres, telemarketing, data processing, and other new-technology domains. They were even chosen to represent the University of Toronto's non-teaching staff. Still, unions often raided each other.

Spectator Sports

With the spread of the Internet in the 1990s, a new and marvellous world opened to computer users, young and even old alike. Increasingly sedentary Canadians spent long hours in front of their computer screens chatting, listening to music, and making discoveries.

Unsurprisingly, active participation in sports dropped sharply. Canadians preferred spectator sports. Huge crowds cheered the astonishing Blue Jays of Toronto on to their victories in the World Series in 1992 and 1993. From that summit, baseball in Canada went downhill. In Montreal, the Expos' hopes to reach the World Series evaporated as a strike ended the 1994 season prematurely. The team became a shadow of itself as, for financial reasons, it sold off its best players. Fans deserted, and the Expos finally moved to Washington, DC. Triple-A baseball, popular in the West, also faded away. Some observers blamed players' exorbitant salaries, which placed players in a world far remote from that of their fans. Others thought that demographic change might be a factor. Younger Canadians preferred basketball, and soccer stirred increasing interest. Football and hockey both remained popular.

The Olympic Games, summer but especially winter, created much enthusiasm and fostered pride in Canadian athletes' prowess. Canada's performance in the summer games was uneven and, at Sydney in 2000 and Athens in 2004, even disappointing. Anxious eyes then turned toward the winter Olympics held in Salt Lake City in 2002, all the more so since Canadian rankings had improved steadily in the preceding decade. When figure skaters Jamie Salé and David Pelletier failed to win first place because of a bribed judge, the resulting outcry forced Olympic officials to reconsider the result, and to award a gold medal to the Canadian couple. For their part, speed skaters Catriona Le May Doan and Marc Gagnon rose to the challenge and also secured gold medals. The Canadian women's hockey team won first place by triumphing over the American team, which had beaten them at Nagano in 1998. Then the largest audience in Canadian television history watched the men's hockey team defeat the United States and win the gold medal. Canadians felt good, and passionately Canadian. They celebrated enthusiastically in the streets, they waved flags, and they vowed, "We're not going to be pushed around by the Americans any more." Globalization had not struck down nationalism. The giant American multinational firm, General Motors, describing itself as the Canadian Olympic team's proudest sponsor, had full-page Maple Leaf flags printed in newspapers, advising readers to post them

Canadian women's hockey team, with team coach Danièle Sauvageau (in the centre), just after winning the women's gold medal at the Salt Lake City Olympics in 2002.

Source: Canadian Press/COA/Mike Redwood.

in any window "to show how proud you are of our women's and men's national hockey teams." An inspired country singer from Calgary penned new lyrics to a song: "Strong and free, led by our fearless hero, Gretzky, he should be the prime minister if you ask me. Oh, thank you, Team Canada!" A consultant in sport policy called Canadian successes an emotional high-water mark for a generation. Pelletier and Salé then went on to grace cereal boxes and, aided by Salé's winning smile, to endorse tooth-whitening products; while proudly patriotic Canadian hockey stars returned to their mostly American teams where they were paid, of course, in American dollars, flying high at the time.

In the Winter Games of 2006, Canada placed third among nations, after Germany and the United States. In hockey, however, Canadian athletes' fortunes were mixed this time: as a Vancouver daily put it, "Canada's women were pure gold, the men were just plain old." The women won the gold medal, as in 2002, while the men's team was unimpressively beaten in the preliminaries. The hero of the Games was undoubtedly speed skater Cindy Klassen, from Winnipeg, who, with five medals won in the course of the games, skated her way into Olympic history. The Hudson's Bay Company won the contract to dress the national team in its traditional colours. Ironically, before the Games ended, the Canadian business icon, founded in 1670, was sold to an American investor. In any case, Canadians preferred to shop at Wal-Mart.

Cultural Development

For George Melnyk, Canadian film remains "a secondary cultural influence" in Canada, with two distinct and complementary national cinemas.[6] Hollywood has always overshadowed Canadian filmmaking in English. One Canadian filmmaker compared the difficulty of making a movie in Canada to climbing Mount Everest without oxygen. He pointed to an indifferent public, harsh critics, tiny production budgets, promotional problems, and American-owned movie theatres.

Various federal aid programs for filmmaking have existed since the 1940s. Telefilm Canada, created in 1983, funded both feature film and independent television production. In 2004, it spent a modest $40 million to assist the production, development, distribution, and marketing of Canadian feature films. By comparison, a single production budget in the United States averaged $45 million. The president of a small Canadian feature-film company grumbled, "We don't even have the money to rent billboards." Another modest government program sought to boost audience levels and to retain talented filmmakers attracted by the lure of California.

In spite of so many obstacles, some English-language Canadian films did make waves. Film director Atom Egoyan's *The Sweet Hereafter* earned him an international reputation. It was based on a novel that depicted life in a small town in upstate New York in the wake of a terrible school-bus tragedy. Don McKellar's first feature-length film, *Last Night*, in which he mocked presumably Canadian virtues such as politeness and the welfare state, won a prize at the Cannes Festival. David Cronenberg produced several films, including *Crash*, in 1996, and *A History of Violence*, a subversive thriller, in 2005. Still, English-language films captured barely one percent of Canadian box office receipts. Most movies made in Canada were not Canadian movies at all. American majors filmed many productions in Vancouver, Toronto, and Montreal, attracted by generous federal and provincial tax credits.

French-speaking Canada boasted a far more successful movie-marketing machine and a distinctive filmmaking voice. In 2003, Canadian-made films occupied nearly 20 percent of Canada's French-language film market. *Les Boys*, *Les Boys II* and *Les Boys III*, a series of comedies featuring a group of Montreal hockey players with much typical locker-room humour, were all top-grossing films. In 2002, more than one million Quebeckers flocked to see *Séraphin: Un homme et son péché*, an adaptation of a well-known novel by Claude-Henri Grignon, and shed a tear for the long-suffering Donalda, victim of her miserly husband. The film was set in St. Adèle, a village in the Laurentians north of Montreal, in the 1890s when landless pioneers were colonizing the region's poor farmlands. *C.R.A.Z.Y.*, the story of a Quebec boy wrestling with the problems of adolescence, was the driving force behind Canadian French-language cinema in 2005. It won ten Genie awards including that for the best picture.

Some productions, like Jean-François Pouliot's *La grande séduction* and Denys Arcand's *Les invasions barbares* were also released in English and enjoyed international careers. Pouliot's film was about a small fishing village on the St. Lawrence River; Arcand's movie, which won an Oscar in 2004, was a satirical drama on capitalism, social democracy, and public health care. *Bon Cop, Bad Cop*, a police comedy replete with a multitude of typical stereotypes including "square head" and "frog," was the only Canadian-made movie in the country's top 10 box-office draws in 2006. It became the biggest blockbuster in Quebec's film history. Starring Patrick Huard, the film featured two police officers, one a Quebecker, the other an anglophone from Toronto, forced to work together to outwit a serial murderer. The period 1990–2006 represented a golden era for Quebec films. But as Telefilm Canada's budget remained frozen and production costs rose, the future looked bleaker.

Aboriginal Canada found a rare voice in the film *Atanarjuat (The Fast Runner)*, directed by Zacharias Kunuk. This first feature film in the Inuktitut language proved a fascinating cultural document and also told an exciting story. Critics wrote glowingly about the film, which won many awards.

Canadian television had notable successes, too. In 2000, the CBC produced, in English and in French, the very successful epic megaseries, *Canada: A People's History*. Using a narrative approach, it presented Canadian history as "one story" of "one people," earning praise from historians who decried a tendency among other historians to give too much emphasis to differences

Executive Producer Mark Starowicz just prior to filming the sequence on the Battle of the Plains of Abraham, in the television series Canada: A People's History.

Source: Canadian Broadcasting Corporation.

among people, be they class, gender, ethnic, linguistic, or regional. Military topics in particular received much attention. For historian Lyle Dick, the CBC's presentation represented "a more activist deployment of history in service of nation-building."[7] A book version published later was also a commercial success.

The 1990s saw the production by Radio-Canada of the series *Lance et compte*, centred on the professional and love lives of a group of hockey players; it proved an astounding success, attracting nearly half of the total French-language viewing public. The comedy series *La petite vie* also drew most Quebeckers to their television sets on Monday evenings in the late 1990s, while the miniseries *Anne* and *Road to Avonlea*, based on Lucy Maud Montgomery's perennially and internationally popular novel, *Anne of Green Gables*, enchanted more than five million nightly viewers in 1999. The "Anne industry" also attracted hundreds of thousands of foreign tourists, many of them from Japan, to Anne's supposed homestead in Prince Edward Island.

Popular Music

In music, such groups as the Philosopher Kings, the Tragically Hip, and Barenaked Ladies carried off numerous awards, while Alanis Morissette's 1995 recording *Jagged Little Pill* sold millions of copies. In 2000, pop singer Nelly Furtado burst onto the scene with her CD *Whoa! Nelly*. In the 1990s, singers Céline Dion and Shania Twain and songwriter Luc Plamondon gained international reputations (see "A Historical Portrait," Chapter 17). Gaspé native Kevin Parent's folk-tinged rock was a huge hit with Quebeckers. His "Fréquenter l'oubli" was chosen song of the year in 1998 by the Quebec public. Lac St. Jean native Pierre Lapointe's first album appeared in 2004 and brought him celebrity and a significant presence in Europe.

From 2005, sales of CD albums began to decline as music lovers could now download onto their computers the songs they preferred rather than buying entire albums. Canadian and especially Quebec musicians were slow to adapt to this new trend whose financial implications were worrying.

Canadian Literature

After 1990, an increasing number of Canadian authors wrote for international audiences. Anne Michaels's novel *Fugitive Pieces* was, for example, a huge success in Germany. Margaret Atwood's novels saw phenomenal sales abroad. *The Blind Assassin*, which won the prestigious British Booker Prize in 2000, told the story of a woman growing up in a small Ontario town before World War I. Alice Munro's books of short stories, *The Love of a Good Woman* and *The View from Castle Rock*, full of insights about human behaviour and relationships, boosted that talented writer's international reputation. In *The Friends of Meager Fortune*, David Adams Richards turned his attention to the fortunes, mostly declining, of a New Brunswick lumbering family. Victor Lam's book of short stories, *Bloodletting and Miraculous Cures*, about the inner workings of hospitals inspired by his experiences in medical school and as a physician, won him the prestigious Giller Prize in 2006. The themes chosen by some novelists had few or no links with Canada. In *Lives of the Saints*, Nino Ricci, whose parents immigrated from Italy to Leamington, Ontario, focused on a village in the Italian Apennines whose inhabitants he portrayed.

American-born Carol Shields, who had won a Pulitzer prize for a previous novel, *The Stone Diaries*, published *Unless*, in 2002, shortly before her untimely death. It portrayed a woman who had to deal with a late-flowering rebellion in her nineteen-year-old daughter. In the same year, three of the finalists for the Booker prize, Yann Martel, Carol Shields, and Rohinton Mistry, were Canadian authors; Martel was awarded the prize. In the words of one critic, foreign attention proved a wonderful reinforcement for "neurotically insecure Canadians." Here, perhaps, was the globalization of Canadian culture.

With the decline of government financing in the 1990s, cultural institutions found themselves obliged to appeal to the private sector for support. They turned to paid annual memberships and, in competition with hospitals, universities, and other institutions, they sought out wealthy philanthropists. One remarkable donor was Walter Carsen, a Toronto businessman and long-time patron of the National Ballet of Canada, the Shaw Festival, and other Canadian arts organizations. Carsen had fled Nazi Germany in 1941 and spent four years interned as an enemy alien in Britain and Canada before convincing authorities he was not a Nazi.

The Environment

Opinion research tells us that so-called bread-and-butter issues are usually citizens' primary concern. Economic issues, such as the job losses that occurred during the recession of 1990–91 or sharp increases in energy costs, as in the mid-2000s, worry people because they threaten their living standards. Health care is also a major preoccupation. Environmental issues are

Alanis Morissette.

Source: CP Picture Archives/Andrew Wallace.

generally of secondary concern, because their impact on people is less visible and less immediate. Environmental interest groups often attempt to keep such issues before the public by pointing out that they are closely linked to the health of people and that of the planet. From the late 1990s on, they succeeded in convincing many Canadians that global warming and climate change threaten Canada and the world, and that governments and people should act.

Governments are often called upon to counter threats to the environment, but action may have a negative impact on the economy that is more immediate and striking than the environmental threat itself. Moreover, when money is lacking and other priorities numerous, environmental issues are clearly less important. In the 1990s, for example, provincial governments sought first to eliminate deficits and reduce taxes. They found it politically easier to cut environmental spending than health care. Ontario, for example, reduced its spending on parks by fully 60 percent in the 1990s. Provincial governments also downloaded responsibilities on regional and municipal governments, which frequently gave priority to economic interests and ignored environmental concerns.

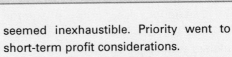

COMMUNITY PORTRAIT

The "War in the Woods" at Clayoquot Sound

On May 5, 2000 Canadian political leaders met at Clayoquot Sound, on the west coast of Vancouver Island, to unveil a plaque designating this area of great natural beauty as a United Nations biosphere reserve. Henceforth, any logging in the area was to be carried out in an environmentally friendly manner that would ensure sustainable growth. Forestry specialists described the project as the most significant ecosystem management experiment in British Columbia's history, and perhaps Canada's.

Logging had been a major industry in British Columbia for over a century. After World War II the provincial government awarded long-term licences to large companies giving them the right to harvest timber. Modernized equipment and techniques such as caterpillar tractors and automatic grapples and yarders permitted increased production with fewer labourers. Harvest rates quadrupled between 1950 and 1980. Environmental values were of little concern: forests seemed inexhaustible. Priority went to short-term profit considerations.

Then, in the early 1980s, many people began to worry about the accelerating destruction of the earth's last remaining rainforests, both tropical and temperate. Environmentalists cited biologists who argued that "rainforests"—old-growth forests, with deep, multilayered canopies, standing dead trees, and centuries of accumulated deadfall on the ground—harboured an enormous diversity of species whose survival depended on preservation of their environment. Clearcut logging, the method preferred by the forest industry, could not be reconciled with biodiversity. Indeed, many clearcuts were so degraded with erosion and compacting that they remained permanently scarred.

Coastal British Columbia boasted an important part of the world's last remaining temperate rainforests, but they were disappearing rapidly. In 1991 the federal government itself estimated that at current rates of logging all substantial ancient forest on the Pacific coast would have disappeared within 20 years.

People who were convinced that British Columbia's forestry policies made it "the Brazil of the North" joined the forestry-focused environmental groups that sprang up. Among the groups interested in wilderness conservation were Greenpeace, the Sierra Club of Canada, the Western Canada Wilderness Committee, and the Canadian Parks and Wilderness Society. In the late 1980s and early 1990s, environmentalists actively promoted preservation. The campaign to save South Moresby on the Queen Charlotte Islands attracted nationwide attention, and in 1987 Ottawa and the provincial government signed an agreement to create a national park in the region.

Clayoquot, an area of some 260 000 ha, was the last major unexploited watershed on Vancouver Island. In 1993, the provincial government, then MacMillan Bloedel's largest shareholder, gave the forestry giant permission to clearcut up to 70 percent of the area's rainforest. Angry environmentalists formed a group, "Friends of Clayoquot Sound," which, in the summer of 1993, waged a "war in the woods," a non-violent campaign of civil disobedience to protest against the government's action and attract international attention. They set up camp in the Black Hole clearcut, an area logged in the 1970s, replanted unsuccessfully four times and now badly eroded. Women were the key organizers of the protest. Fearing that concessions would encourage environmentalists to seek to protect other areas from logging, MacMillan Bloedel obtained an injunction banning demonstrations on company work sites. The government had 900 protestors arrested at the blockades, charged with criminal contempt of court

for defying the injunction, and jailed or fined. Friends of Clayoquot continued their campaign, by targeting industrial consumers of British Columbia timber in Europe and threatening boycotts of their products if they did not cease their purchases. This tactic ensured that the battle at Clayoquot achieved international notoriety.

In October 1993, the British Columbia government appointed a Scientific Panel for Sustainable Forest Practices in Clayoquot Sound. It was composed of members of the region's First Nation, the Nuu-chah-nulth, and a team of scientists and technicians. The panel recommended an ecosystem approach that emphasized the maintenance of biological diversity, watershed integrity, and the protection of cultural, scenic, and recreational values. Clearcutting as a method of harvest was to be replaced by a method called "variable-retention," an alternative silvicultural system whereby trees and patches of forest were retained to protect a variety of values and ecosystem components. In 1995, the government announced that all of the panel's recommendations would be implemented. Premier Harcourt wanted to make Clayoquot a showcase for progressive forest practices. MacMillan Bloedel, the largest company active in the area, suspended its clearcutting operations, and negotiated with First Nations and environmentalists to find a mutually acceptable approach to some continued logging.

After the Clayoquot campaign, environmentalists continued to work for preservation elsewhere. In 1994, the government set out a new Forest Practices Code that reduced the maximum size of clearcuts, mandated replanting of harvested areas, and tightened regulations and enforcement. British Columbia also moved to place 13 percent of its land base in protected areas, in recognition of its responsibilities in regard to the United Nations Convention on Biological Diversity, which Canada had signed in 1992. Environmental critics asserted, however, that protected areas were often "rock and ice" where industry had no interest, and that old-growth forests were underrepresented. Nor were there any guarantees that a future, more business-oriented government might not roll back environmental protection, or fail to monitor and enforce forest management rules. Indeed the Suzuki Foundation reported in 2003 that, on the basis of a survey of sites logged in 2001 and 2002, it was "business as usual," clearcutting being the method used.

The initiatives of the environmental movement generated substantial opposition. Plans for protecting areas of Vancouver Island led to massive demonstrations by loggers and their supporters in 1994. Compromise between preservationist and economic imperatives seemed impossible. The logging industry accused environmentalists of increasing its costs and diminishing its profits. Forestry workers argued that restrictions on logging would lead to job losses. Some rural communities feared for their very existence. At times Native peoples and environmentalists differed in their attitudes toward nature. And governments wanted the attendant tax revenues and stumpage fees that the lumber industry provided.

Yet issues were undoubtedly more complex than first appeared. Was it possible to assign a value in dollars to the maintenance of biodiversity? What would happen to jobs once all old-growth stands were cut? Was reforestation of areas already harvested not a wiser option to assure a sustainable forest industry? Could not other industries such as tourism and recreation offer new potential thanks to wilderness preservation? The environmental

A clearcut in the Temagami region in northeastern Ontario. The area was a focal point of environmental protests at the end of the 1980s. Today 95 percent of lumber harvesting in Ontario is still done by clearcut.

Source: Courtesy Canadian Parks and Wilderness Society—Wildlands League.

movement's activities brought all those interested in British Columbia's forests, and in forests elsewhere in Canada, to ask these questions, and to seek answers.

Environmentalists worked in a variety of sectors to show that the survival of humanity depended upon the health of the environment. They argued that economic growth should proceed only if environmental safeguards were sufficient to ensure its sustainability.

FURTHER READING

Benjamin Cashore, George Hoberg, Michael Howlett, Jeremy Rayner, Jeremy Wilson, *In Search of Sustainability: British Columbia Forest Policy in the 1990s* (Vancouver: UBC Press, 2001).

Michael Howlett, ed., *Canadian Forest Policy: Adapting to Change* (Toronto: University of Toronto Press, 2001).

Ron MacIsaac and Anne Champagne, eds., *Clayoquot Mass Trials: Defending the Rainforest* (Philadelphia and Gabriola Island, BC: New Society Publishers, 1994).

Richard A. Rajala, *Clearcutting the Pacific Rain Forest: Production, Science, and Regulation* (Vancouver: UBC Press, 1998).

Jeremy Wilson, *Talk and Log: Wilderness Politics in British Columbia, 1965–96* (Vancouver: UBC Press, 1998).

With lower budgets, governments often failed to apply their own environmental laws and to monitor compliance. The federal government, for example, was frequently accused of ignoring the Canadian Environmental Protection Act, which regulates toxic chemicals, and the Fisheries Act, which prohibits polluting oceans, rivers, and lakes. Although smog caused 5000 premature deaths each year, Ottawa's program for smog reduction, announced with great fanfare in 1990, remained a dead letter.

Habitat Conservation

As urbanization, agriculture, and resource exploitation occupied an ever-larger portion of the globe's surface, increasing numbers of wildlife species and plants faced the threat of extinction. Calling for immediate action, scientists warned that mankind's actions were leading to the disappearance of life forms at a rate that the world had not seen since the age of the dinosaurs. In 1992, Canada played a key at the Earth Summit at Rio de Janeiro. With other nations it signed a convention on biological diversity by which it agreed to take measures to protect threatened species and their habitats. Yet only in 2002, after a decade during which the number of species on the endangered list increased markedly, did Parliament adopt a Species at Risk Act. Four years later, wildlife conservation groups called upon NAFTA to launch an investigation into what they saw as Canada's failure to enforce endangered species laws.

Ottawa and several provinces did take action to set aside and protect habitat necessary for the survival of ecosystems. In 2002, Jean Chrétien announced the creation of ten new national parks and five marine conservation areas. Yet, at the same time, forestry, mining, agriculture, and recreational activities in areas adjacent to existing parks, as well as within them, were causing increased ecological stress on the parks themselves. Provinces also moved to create new protected areas and take better care of existing ones. In 2006, for example, Ontario adopted new legislation to protect the ecological integrity of its 600 provincial parks and conservation reserves, which covered an area the size of New Brunswick. In British Columbia, the provincial government together with environmental organizations, Native communities, and the forest industry reached an agreement in that would protect the Great Bear Rainforest, a huge area on the province's north and central coasts rich in wildlife and flora, from major logging. Yet many natural regions, particularly in heavily urbanized southern Canada, still had few or no protected areas. In partial remedy, in its budget of 2007, Ottawa attributed $225 million to the Nature Conservancy of Canada, to which it gave the responsibility for finding matching sums from private sources and then of purchasing and protecting ecologically important lands.

Air and Water Pollution

Waste disposal remained a serious issue. At one point, Torontonians were warned that they risked being buried beneath their own garbage if Michigan, northern Ontario, or Quebec refused to take it. Throughout the 1990s and the 2000s, environmental interest groups continued to point out that air and water pollution represented a grave health hazard for Canadians as well as a threat to the survival of natural ecosystems.

Industry continued to use the atmosphere for free waste disposal; it spewed into the air large quantities of contaminants, such as nitrogen oxides associated with smog, particulate matter linked to respiratory illness, and toxic cancer-causing chemicals. A Hudson Bay Mining and Smelting facility in Flin Flon, Manitoba, was Canada's largest toxic polluter, while two Inco operations in Ontario placed not far behind. Then came Syncrude and Suncor plants in Alberta, and the coal-fired electric power plants of Alberta, Saskatchewan, Ontario, and Nova Scotia. With 27 percent of emissions, Alberta occupied first place among the provinces. Much-more-populated Ontario placed second, with 21 percent. During an election campaign, the Liberals promised to close Ontario's polluting coal-burning plants to reduce pollution. Once in power and faced with the prospect of electricity shortages, they retreated. Downwind, much of Quebec's air pollution came from mid-western states and Ontario.

Acid rain, caused by the sulphur dioxide produced by the burning of coal, continued to threaten much of eastern Canada, as acidity levels exceeded the soil's absorptive capacity. Because of the rise of oil and gas production, the problem of acid rain now concerned the West, too.

Water pollution remained a very current problem. In 2005, *Maclean's* published a report on sewage entitled "From Sea to Stinking Sea" in which it exposed Canada's lack of sewage treatment standards. The city of Victoria, for example, continued to dump raw sewage into the Juan de Fuca Strait. When studies showed that the lands around sewage outfalls had high levels of toxic chemicals that made them contaminated sites, the provincial government directed Victoria to come up with a plan to upgrade its sewage treatment levels. In nearby Vancouver, environmental groups and the fishing industry prosecuted the city for discharging high levels of toxic chemicals into local waters.

Ontario and Ottawa promised to clean up and restore several of the most polluted sites on the Canadian side of the Great Lakes, sites that had been contaminated over decades by the dumping of industrial waste, poorly treated municipal sewage, and agricultural runoff. The most contaminated sites, among them the St. Lawrence River near Cornwall, Hamilton Harbour, the Niagara River, and Toronto Harbour, had been identified in the mid-1980s, but lack of money had forestalled action. In spite of huge sums spent since the 1970s by companies trying to improve water quality, industrial activities continued to pollute the Great Lakes. The largest polluter on the Canadian side was the Imperial Oil refinery at Sarnia, which discharged its effluent into the St. Clair River. In 2007, Sierra Legal, now known as Ecojustice, an environmental advocacy group, issued its *Great Lakes Sewage Report Card*; it stated that 90 billion litres of raw sewage, containing human waste, pathogens, and hundreds of toxic chemicals, were still being dumped into the Great Lakes—the drinking water supply for 24 million people—every year.

The Lakes faced other threats, too, including the arrival of invasive aquatic species from abroad, introduced through ship ballast water discharges; these species had a negative impact on lake ecosystems and caused substantial economic damage. Many lakes throughout Canada registered high levels of mercury pollution caused by the burning of coal. Strongly toxic at even small levels, it contaminated fish and posed a health threat to pregnant mothers and children who ate fish. Some of the mercury emissions came from the United States and even from faraway China. Indeed, pollution recognized no borders.

The Kyoto Protocol

During the 1990s and early 2000s, the international scientific community produced numerous studies that tended to demonstrate that the earth's climate was heating up and that human activities, principally the burning of fossil fuels—gas, oil, and coal—were the principal cause. Climate change, they said, would have disastrous consequences for the planet and its inhabitants.

Wind power is an excellent source of alternative energy. Here are generators at work on the Cowley Ridge Wind Farm project near the southern Alberta town of Cowley.

Source: CP Photo/Larry MacDougall/Photo 1825053.jpg.

Discussions of the issue in international and Canadian forums tended to pit environmental considerations against economic development. The economy needed energy and most energy came from nonrenewable fossil fuels. (Some provinces were blessed with abundant sources of hydroelectricity, and several began encouraging alternative energies such as the creation of wind farms.) Advocates for action to reduce emissions claimed that moving toward a greener economy would also create jobs, and that inaction would have, sooner or later, a disastrous impact on the world's economy and on human populations.

International agreement on the reduction of so-called greenhouse gases—carbon dioxide and methane—proved difficult and the result, the Kyoto Protocol, which Canada signed in 1997, was a modest plan indeed. Objectives, agreed upon in 2001, were limited: by 2012 industrialized countries should reduce emissions of greenhouse gases to a level 6 percent below that of 1990. Developing nations such as China and India, whose gas emissions were mounting steadily, were exempted from obligations for the moment.

As time passed, opposition to Kyoto mounted in Canada. The refusal of the United States to ratify the Protocol raised concerns about Canada's competitiveness with its major economic partner. Alberta, in particular, led the charge against Kyoto, fearful that ratification would hurt its petroleum and gas sector. Industry asserted that compliance would cost jobs and investment. The automobile industry felt particularly threatened. Supporters of Kyoto asserted that Canada had become an environmental laggard, and that gas emissions were rising quickly. Canada needed to line up with the majority of industrialized countries that had ratified the Protocol, and act.

Ottawa finally ratified the Kyoto Accord in 2002. Later testimony suggested that the Chrétien government signed the treaty without a plan that would enable the country to respect its obligations. Its hope was that simply signing the treaty would galvanize public opinion in favour of action. Neither the government nor the public was ready for the tough measures required by the Kyoto plan.

Between 2000 and 2005, the Liberal governments of Jean Chrétien and Paul Martin put forward three plans for action. The government invested $6 billion in energy conservation and other measures, while gas emissions surged. The plans set weak targets for industry, often voluntary, and lacked implementation timelines. At the same time, Ottawa accorded huge subsidies to the oil and gas industry, a legacy of times when oil prices had been much lower.

The Conservative government of Stephen Harper which took office in 2006 showed little enthusiasm for acting to reduce greenhouse gas production. Harper stated that Kyoto's targets were unreachable without shutting down Canada's economy. Instead of absolute reductions in emissions, his Clean Air Act proposed so-called "intensity targets" by which the oil industry, for example, would reduce emissions per barrel by developing new technology. Increasing production would, however, ensure that real emissions would keep rising. Moreover, it set reduction targets in the far-distant future—2050. Business groups reacted favourably. Environmentalists called intensity targets "dishonest" and called for immediate reductions that would bring down total gas emissions.

Oil Sands

Transportation, notably as manifest in truck traffic and passenger vehicles, was responsible for an important share of Canada's greenhouse gas emissions. A prosperous economy assured that there were more and more trucks on the roads. In addition, drivers came to prefer gas-guzzling sport-utility vehicles and light trucks. By 2007, as gasoline prices increased, more drivers, particularly in central and eastern Canada, turned to smaller automobiles.

Heavy industry was responsible for one-half of Canada's gas emissions. Several provinces, particularly Alberta, burned coal to make electricity, and this activity produced large quantities of carbon dioxide. But it was the oil industry, especially the procedures used to extract oil from tar sands in northern Alberta, that explained why that province produced 40 percent of the country's greenhouse gases, helping to give Canada the worst record of the Group of Eight large industrial economies. Critics such as the Pembina Institute of Calgary urged the imposition of mandatory reduction targets as well as strong financial incentives and infrastructure investments such as carbon dioxide pipelines and carbon sequestration projects that could limit emissions. In response, the Alberta government said that it wished to maintain a healthy investment climate, and gave rapid approval to many new development projects. Emissions were on track to increase exponentially.

Extracting oil from tar sands in open-pit mines necessitated huge amounts of energy, usually natural gas, as well as vast quantities of fresh water, obtainable at no cost, mostly from the Athabaska River. Open-pit mines destroyed all flora and fauna on huge expanses of land. Replanting trees afterwards could not restore ecosystems. Polluted wastewater filled gigantic quarries visible from space. Calls for a moratorium that would enable industry and governments to deal with economic, social, and environmental stresses caused by the aggressive pace of development went unheeded.

Opinion polls showed that Canadians were convinced that global warming existed, that it was having a negative impact on the earth, and that it was necessary to act. Alberta had the highest number of doubters, Quebec the fewest. Only one-third of Albertans thought

Mining trucks with loads of oil-laden sand at the Albian Sands oil sands project in Fort McMurray, Alberta, August 5, 2005.

Source: CP PHOTO/Larry MacDougal.

it necessary to promote better behaviour toward the environment. Industry executives reacted according to regional and sectoral interests. Executives from central Canada said they were concerned, intensely, about climate change. A majority of western executives, particularly in the oil and gas sector, said they were only slightly or not at all concerned. Western executives opposed any restrictions on oil sands development, and opposed a tax on carbon use that would attach a price tag to pollution and could lead to reduced emissions. The issue obviously pitted central Canada against the West, and Canada as a whole against much of the rest of the industrialized world.

Since 1867, Canada has evolved into an increasingly complex society. The nation's population diversified ethnically and culturally in the nineteenth and, more rapidly, in the twentieth century. Material progress and improved living conditions, though by no means continuous, were generally apparent; their attendant costs, both human and environmental, were at first less apparent, except to their immediate victims. After 1960, however, Canadians in general came to realize that high living standards and consumer choices often caused environmental degradation. Sustainability became a new byword. The role of the state increased greatly, especially after 1930, when governments came to play a role in virtually every aspect of human existence. Associations of all types proliferated as Canadians sought to counter the powerlessness of the individual acting alone.

Although Canada has undergone immense change, most of the basic themes of the country's early history remain operative today. In 1867, four major groups made up Canada's population—the Aboriginal peoples, French-speaking Canadians, English-speaking Canadians, and immigrants; today, the same four groups are evident, although not in the same proportion as in 1867. Canada in 1867 was a nation of regions; despite modern transportation and the communications revolution, it remains so today—indeed, to such an extent that doubts have often abounded about the survival of existing political arrangements. By the 1880s, federal–provincial affairs had become acrimonious; more than a century later, conflict often pervaded intergovernmental contacts. French–English relations were the source of bitter controversy in the nineteenth century; intercultural relations continued to generate passionate debate in the twentieth. Relations with the indigenous peoples were an important preoccupation in the nineteenth century as European settlement expanded westward; during the second half of the twentieth century and into the twenty-first, Aboriginal rights became a complex but very present public-policy question.

In 1867, British and American influences weighed heavily on the new nation; today, the impact of the United States on Canada—culturally, politically, and economically—is in many ways far more weighty. Finally, despite the coming of the welfare state, flagrant social inequalities still distinguish Canadians from one another, much as they did in the past. Constant change, but equally apparent continuity: these are the two themes that reflect the past as the inhabitants of the northern half of North America enter the twenty-first century.

NOTES

1. David Cameron and Richard Simeon, "Ontario in Confederation: The Not-So-Friendly Giant," in Graham White, *The Government and Politics of Ontario*, 5th ed. (Toronto: University of Toronto Press, 1997), p. 159.

2. Sydney Sharpe and Don Braid, *Storming Babylon: Preston Manning and the Rise of the Reform Party* (Toronto: Key Porter, 1992), p. 154.

3. Paul Wells, *Right Side Up: The Fall of Paul Martin and the Rise of Stephen Harper's New Conservatism* (Toronto: McClelland & Stewart, 2006), p. 315.

4. "Canada–U.S. Relations: No More Mr. Nice Guy," *The Globe and Mail*, November 10, 2000.

5. Thomas J. Courchene with Colin R. Telmer, *From Heartland to North American Region State: The Social, Fiscal and Federal Evolution of Ontario. An Interpretive Essay* (Toronto: Centre for Public Management, University of Toronto, 1998), pp. 268–96.

6. George Melnyk, *One Hundred Years of Canadian Cinema* (Toronto: University of Toronto Press, 2004), pp. 271–72.

7. "'A New History for the New Millennium': Canada: A People's History," *Canadian Historical Review* 85 (2004), p. 109.

BEYOND THE BOOK

Weblinks

Climate Change

http://www.seasidelive.ca/oceansliveEnglish/ngototal.htm
This site describes potential effects of climate change and other contemporary environmental issues on the ecosystems and fisheries of Nova Scotia.

Federal Electoral History

http://www.elections.ca/intro.asp?section=pas&document=index&lang=e
A database of the results of all Canadian federal elections.

Canadian Heritage: Multiculturalism

http://www.canadianheritage.gc.ca/progs/multi/index_e.cfm
The Government of Canada's web portal for information about national multiculturalism programs in Canada.

Canadian Federal Budgets: 1994–2007

http://www.fin.gc.ca/access/budinfoe.html
Official budgets of the Government of Canada for 1994–2007.

Media Concentration in Contemporary Canada

http://archives.cbc.ca/IDD-1-73-790/politics_economy/concentration_press
CBC Archives clips review the history of media concentration in Canada to the present day.

Government of Canada

http://www.gc.ca/main_e.html
Official website of the Government of Canada. Links to resources about government ministries, programs, and how the government works.

Films & Novels

Itsuka. By Joy Kogawa. 1993.

Between: Living in the Hyphen. Directed by Anne Marie Nakagawa. 2005.

RELATED READINGS

The following articles in R. Douglas Francis and Donald B. Smith, eds., *Readings in Canadian History: Post-Confederation*, 7th ed. (Toronto: Thomson Nelson Learning, 2006), are of relevance to this chapter: Alain C. Cairns, "Aboriginal Peoples in the Twenty-First Century: A Plea for Realism," pp. 573–89; Reg Whittaker, "Canadian Politics at the End of the Millennium: Old Dreams, New Nightmares," pp. 590–603; and Rob Huebert, "Climate Change and Canadian Sovereignty in the Northwest Passage," pp. 603–13.

BIBLIOGRAPHY

For a critical study of Canadian-American economic relations, see Stephen Clarkson, *Uncle Sam and Us: Globalization, Neoconservatism, and the Canadian State* (Toronto: University of Toronto Press, 2002). Economist William Watson proposes a provocative critique of Canadian identity in *Globalization and the Meaning of Canadian Life* (Toronto: University of Toronto Press, 1998). Peter C. Newman examines the influence of business magnates in *Titans: How the New Canadian Establishment Seized Power* (Toronto: Penguin Books, 1998). On one controversial business leader, see Richard Siklos, *Shades of Black: Conrad Black, His Rise and Fall* (Toronto: McClelland & Stewart, 2004). The energy question is discussed in G. Bruce Doern, ed. *Canadian Energy Policy and the Struggle for Sustainable Development* (Toronto: University of Toronto Press, 2005).

Writings on the environment include Melody Hessing and Michael Howlett, *Canadian Natural Resource and Environmental Policy: Political Economy and Public Policy* (Vancouver: University of British Columbia Press, 1997); Judith I. McKenzie, *Environmental Politics in Canada: Managing the Commons into the Twenty-First Century* (Toronto: Oxford, 2002); Mark Jaccard, John Nyboer and Bryn Sadownik, *The Cost of Climate Policy* (Vancouver: UBC Press, 2002); and Karen Bakker, ed., *Eau Canada: The Future of Canada's Water* (Vancouver: UBC Press, 2006).

Kim Campbell has written her memoirs, *Time and Chance: The Political Memoirs of Canada's First Woman Prime Minister* (Toronto: Doubleday Canada, 1996). Her disastrous election campaign in 1993 is recounted in David McLaughlin, *Poisoned Chalice: The Last Campaign of the Progressive Conservative Party?* (Toronto: Dundurn Press, 1994). Studies of Jean Chrétien include Lois Harder and Steve Patten, eds., *The Chrétien Legacy: Politics and Public Policy in Canada* (Montreal/Kingston, McGill-Queen's University Press, 2006); Jeffrey Simpson, *The Friendly Dictatorship*, rev. ed. (Toronto: McClelland and Stewart, 2002); and Lawrence Martin, *Iron Man: The Defiant Reign of Jean Chrétien*, vol. 2., rev. ed. (Toronto: Penguin Books Canada, 2003). On the Reform party see Faron Ellis, *The Limits of Participation: Members and Leaders in Canada's Reform Party* (Calgary: University of Calgary Press, 2005); and Trevor Harrison, *Of Passionate Intensity: Right-Wing Populism and the Reform Party of Canada* (Toronto: University of Toronto Press, 1995). The Bloc Québécois is discussed in Manon Cornellier, *The Bloc* (Toronto: James Lorimer, 1995). Among works on the Canadian left, consult Ian McLeod, *Under Siege: The Federal NDP in the Nineties* (Toronto: James Lorimer, 1994); and James Laxer, *In Search of a New Left: Canadian Politics after the Neoconservative Assault* (Toronto: Penguin Books, 1996). Recent journalistic accounts of Canadian politics include John Gray, *Paul Martin: In the Balance* (Toronto: Key Porter Books, 2004); Hugh Segal, *The Long Road Back: The Conservative Journey in Canada, 1993–2006* (Toronto: HarperCollins, 2006); Paul Wells, *Right Side Up: The Fall of Paul Martin and the Rise of Stephen Harper's New Conservatism* (Toronto: McClelland & Stewart, 2006); Bob Plamondon, *Full Circle: Death and Resurrection in Canadian Conservative Politics* (Toronto: Key Porter, 2006); William Johnson, *Steven Harper and the Future of Canada*, rev ed. (Toronto: McClelland & Stewart, 2006); and Chantal Hébert, *French Kiss: Stephen Harper's Blind Date with Quebec* (Toronto: Knopf Canada, 2007).

Different strands composing Canada's foreign relations are examined in Roy Rempel, *Dreamland: How Canada's Pretend Foreign Policy Has Undermined Sovereignty* (Montreal/Kingston: McGill-Queen's University Press, 2006); Rosalind Irwin, ed., *Ethics and Security in Canadian Foreign Policy* (Vancouver: UBC Press, 2001); and Thomas F. Keating, *Canada in World Order: The Multilateralist Tradition in Canadian Foreign Policy*, 2nd ed. (Toronto: Oxford University Press, 2001). Canada's role in the Gulf War of 1990 is examined in Richard Gimblett and Jean Morin, *Operation Friction: Canadian Forces in the Gulf War* (Toronto: Dundurn Press, 1996). On aspects of peacekeeping, see Nicolas Gammer, *From Peacekeeping to Peacemaking: Canada's Response to the Yugoslav Crisis* (Montreal/Kingston: McGill-Queen's University Press, 2001); and Sean M. Maloney, *Canada and UN Peacekeeping: Cold War by Other Means* (St. Catharines, ON: Vanwell, 2002).

Effects on Canada of the terrorist attacks of September 2001 are discussed in Ronald J. Daniels, Patricia Macklem, and Kent Roach, *The Security of Freedom: Essays on Canada's Anti-Terrorism Bill* (Toronto: University of Toronto Press, 2001); and in Kent Roach, *September 11: Consequences for Canada* (Montreal/Kingston: McGill-Queen's University Press, 2003). Recent articles on relations between Canada and the United States include Andrew Richter, "From Trusted Ally to Suspicious Neighbour: Canada–U.S. Relations in a Changing Global Environment," *American Review of Canadian Studies* 35 (2005): 471–502; and John Herd Thompson, "Playing by the New Washington Rules: The U.S.–Canada Relationship, 1994–2003," *American Review of Canadian Studies* 33 (2003): 5–26. See also J.L. Granatstein's (strongly opinionated) essay, *Whose War Is It? How Canada Can Survive in the Post-9/11 World* (Toronto: HarperCollins, 2007).

Relations between Ottawa and the provinces are discussed in Richard Simeon, *Federal–Provincial Diplomacy: The Making of Recent Policy in Canada* (Toronto: University of Toronto Press, 2006). On the failed Charlottetown Accord, see Richard Johnston et al., *The Challenge of Direct Democracy: The 1992 Canadian Referendum* (Montreal/Kingston: McGill-Queen's University Press, 1996). David R. Cameron and Janice Gross Stein, eds., *Street Protests and Fantasy Parks: Globalization, Culture and the State* (Vancouver: UBC Press, 2002), focuses on the cultural and social realities of globalization. For a panorama of Canadian writing, W.H. New, ed., *Encyclopedia of Literature in Canada* (Toronto: University of Toronto Press, 2002) is the standard authority. Contemporary architecture is presented in Harold Kalman, *A Concise History of Canadian Architecture* (Toronto: Oxford University Press, 2000).

On sports history consult Colin Howell, *Blood, Sweat, and Cheers: Sport and the Making of Modern Canada* (Toronto: University of Toronto Press, 2001); and M. Ann Hall, *The Girl and the Game: A History of Women's Sport in Canada* (Peterborough, ON: Broadview Press, 2002). Pollster Michael Adams looks at the differences between Canadians and Americans in *Fire and Ice: The United States, Canada and the Myth of Converging Values* (Toronto: Penguin Canada, 2003). Reginald W. Bibby examines contemporary religion in *Restless Gods: The Renaissance of Religion in Canada* (Toronto: Stoddart, 2002). Populist Christianity is discussed in Sam Reimer, *Evangelicals and the Continental Divide: The Conservative Protestant Subculture in Canada and the United States* (Montreal/Kingston, McGill-Queen's University Press, 2003); and in G.A. Rawlyk, *Is Jesus Your Personal Saviour? In Search of Canadian Evangelicalism in the 1990s* (Montreal/Kingston: McGill-Queen's University Press, 1996). Sylvain Larocque, *Gay Marriage: The Story of a Canadian Social Revolution* (Toronto: James Lorimer, 2006), deals with a major gay rights issue.

Critical studies of government welfare policies are Maude Barlow and Bruce Campbell, *Straight Through the Heart: How the Liberals Abandoned the Just Society* (Toronto: HarperCollins, 1995); and Gary Teeple, *Globalization and the Decline of Social Reform: Into the Twenty-First Century* (Toronto: Garamond, 2000). On poverty see Jean Swanson, *Poor-Bashing: The Politics of Exclusion* (Toronto: Between the Lines Press, 2001). Health-care issues are discussed in Colleen Fuller, *Caring for Profit: How Corporations Are Taking Over Canada's Health Care System* (Vancouver: New Star, 1998). Child care is examined in Gordon Cleveland and Michael Krashinsky, eds., *Our Children's Future: Child Care Policy in Canada* (Toronto: University of Toronto Press, 2001).

Appendix

CANADIAN PRIME MINISTERS SINCE CONFEDERATION

Sir John Alexander Macdonald
Conservative
1867–73, 1878–91

Alexander Mackenzie
Liberal
1873–78

Sir John Joseph Caldwell Abbott
Conservative
1891–92

Sir John Sparrow David Thompson
Conservative
1892–94

Sir Mackenzie Bowell
Conservative
1894–96

Sir Charles Tupper
Conservative
1896

Sir Wilfrid Laurier
Liberal
1896–1911

Sir Robert Laird Borden
Conservative and Unionist
1911–20

Arthur Meighen
Conservative and Unionist
1920–21, 1926

William Lyon Mackenzie King
Liberal
1921–26, 1926–30,
1935–48

Richard Bedford Bennett
Conservative
1930–35

Louis Stephen St. Laurent
Liberal
1948–57

John George Diefenbaker
Progressive Conservative
1957–63

Lester Bowles Pearson
Liberal
1963–68

Pierre Elliott Trudeau
Liberal
1968–79, 1980–84

Charles Joseph Clark
Progressive Conservative
1979–80

John Napier Turner
Liberal
1984

Martin Brian Mulroney
Progressive Conservative
1984–93

Kim Campbell
Progressive Conservative
1993

Jean Chrétien
Liberal
1993–2003

Paul Edgar Philippe Martin
Liberal
2003–06

Stephen Joseph Harper
Conservative
2006–

Index